not invented here

UPGRADE PATH

and Jeff Zugale

OVERDUE
MEDIA
Seattle

Foreword

I worked in the world of software development for 18 years. When it comes to *Not Invented Here* I don't have to read it, Dottie, I *lived* it.

It's all true: Scrum. The dynamic between a program manager and a developer. The marketing folk. The bosses. Bugs. Interview training. CTO's. Reorgs. Bearded sages of code. HR. IT. Startup environments. Venture capitalists. Synergy. **SYNERGY**.

When I cry myself to sleep at night it's not because of what I've done, it's because of what I've seen. The world of the corporate/startup technology worker is strange and bizarre. Not evil per se, it's simply a world unlike, I think, the one a lot of people deal with. I've been told I need to "influence without authority" or "increase my face time with key stakeholders" in order to make the thing I am paid to do actually be effective in a system that actively works to marginalize teamwork and collaboration while demanding maximum success. I've sat around a conference table surrounded by smart people who all agreed on the right thing to do for customers having an immediate problem, and decided not to do it because another team somewhere else was going to do it. In eighteen months. I've worked at a firm with six people, three of whom were Vice Presidents.

So when I tell you *Not Invented Here* rings true, it's not some painful and cynical point I'm trying to make. It's the opposite in fact. Like all good comics, the subject matter here is accurately portrayed in such a way as to give you a glimpse into absurdity. It leaves you saying to yourself, "Ha ha that's funny! It can't possibly be that broken!"

Oh, but it is.

Not *horribly* so. Not such that it prevents good technology from being produced. But I kid you not, the world of mainstream software development is strange and quirky and fun and also not fun but mostly fun. And, by reading this book, you will get a safe glimpse into it. If you're already within the various realms and spheres described herein, you'll nod and chuckle at events that may have happened to you this very day.

Somewhere along the way there was a natural pivot in the comic to include geek culture. I can confirm this too is accurate in both its humor, observation, and critique. For instance, Steampunk. What, exactly, is so alluring about brass or narrow vision goggles that can't possibly be pulled over the wide brim of a ridiculous top hat?

It's all here. So when I was asked to write the foreword to *Upgrade Path* I happily agreed. And look at the wonderful stories you get! The "Ownd" startup adventure! The origin story of Desmond and Owen's friendship! Jeff's magnificent rendering of Desmond in a hospital gown! The appearance of the IT Crime Scene tape!

What Bill and Jeff have made here is fun stuff that rings true. That's what good comics do. So strap in, set phasers to slap fight, and enjoy.

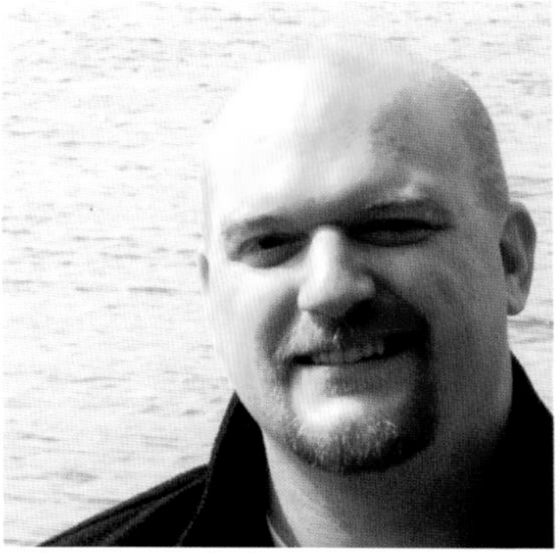

*Part former Xbox banhammer, part writer, and 100% UNSC Prime Grade A geek, Stephen "**Stepto**" Toulouse is known to bring the funk, hates steampunk, hides bodies in his trunk, invented the assisted slam dunk, once insulted a fan of Thelonius Monk, and wow this is a silly sentence, welcome to the end of it.* **www.stepto.com**

Bill Barnes spent two decades in the software business, working a variety of jobs from coding to *Slate* technology journalist to executive speechwriter, before becoming a professional cartoonist. He writes *Not Invented Here*, draws and co-writes *Unshelved,* and enjoys playing the ukulele at his family.

The original artist of *Not Invented Here* has been creating webcomics since 1999. He has adopted a secret identity to protect his family and/or loved ones.

Jeff Zugale works a day job drawing spaceships for video games, has a wife and two small children, and draws *Not Invented Here* in his copious spare time. He is tired. So very, very tired.

http://notinventedhe.re

@nihcomic

facebook.com/nihcomic

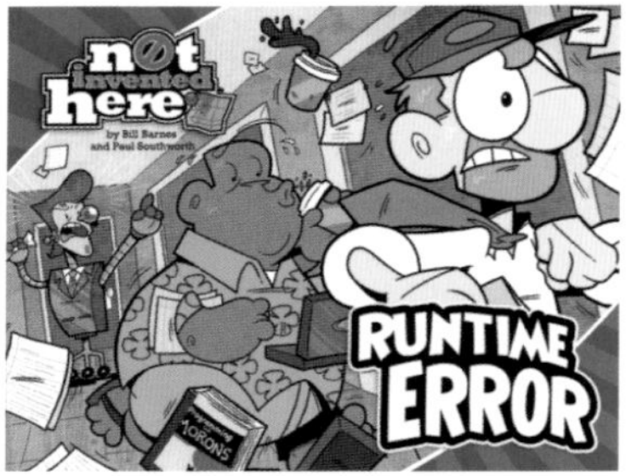
not invented here
by Bill Barnes and Paul Southworth
RUNTIME ERROR

Don't miss the first *Not Invented Here* collection, ***Runtime Error***!

Reprints *Not Invented Here* comic strips originally published on the *Not Invented Here* website from April 25, 2011 to June 20, 2013, plus new material. "Genius Barred" (pg 203) originally published on www.hijinksensue.com © 2012 Joel Watson.

ISBN-13: 978-1-937914-05-9

First printing: December 2013

Printed in China.

Prologue

INTERLUDE: RICHMOND, VIRGINIA
A CATASTROPHIC FAILURE?! BUT *HOW?!*
COOTER FELL ASLEEP ON HIS WATCH AND A RACCOON POOPED IN THE POWER SUPPLY.
AMAZON DATA CENTEЯ AND TAXIDEЯMY
DON'T WE HAVE *FAILSAFES* AGAINST THIS KIND OF THING?
COOTER'S OLD SNIFF HOUND FELL ASLEEP TOO.
TRUCKZ
WHAT WE NEED IS SOME KIND OF *ADVANCE WARNING.*
NO SUCH SOFTWARE EXISTS, SIR.
PORNO
WELL UNTIL IT DOES, PROP COOTER'S FAT ASS UP WITH A BROOM HANDLE OR SOMETHIN'.
I'LL ALERT R&D.
HATZ
XXX

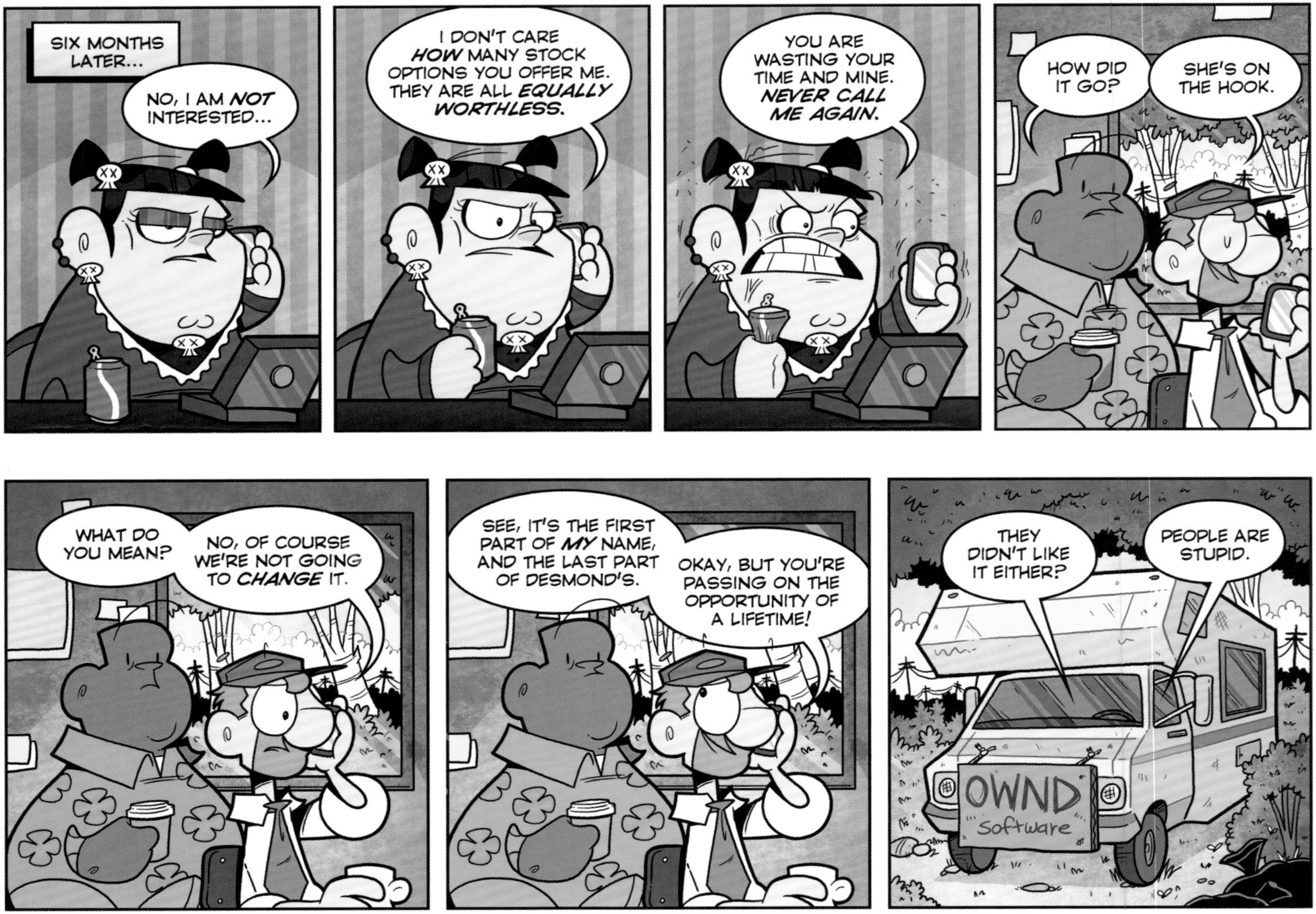
SIX MONTHS LATER...
NO, I AM NOT INTERESTED...
I DON'T CARE HOW MANY STOCK OPTIONS YOU OFFER ME. THEY ARE ALL EQUALLY WORTHLESS.
YOU ARE WASTING YOUR TIME AND MINE. NEVER CALL ME AGAIN.
HOW DID IT GO?
SHE'S ON THE HOOK.
WHAT DO YOU MEAN?
NO, OF COURSE WE'RE NOT GOING TO CHANGE IT.
SEE, IT'S THE FIRST PART OF MY NAME, AND THE LAST PART OF DESMOND'S.
OKAY, BUT YOU'RE PASSING ON THE OPPORTUNITY OF A LIFETIME!
THEY DIDN'T LIKE IT EITHER?
PEOPLE ARE STUPID.
OWND
Software

UPGRADE PATH

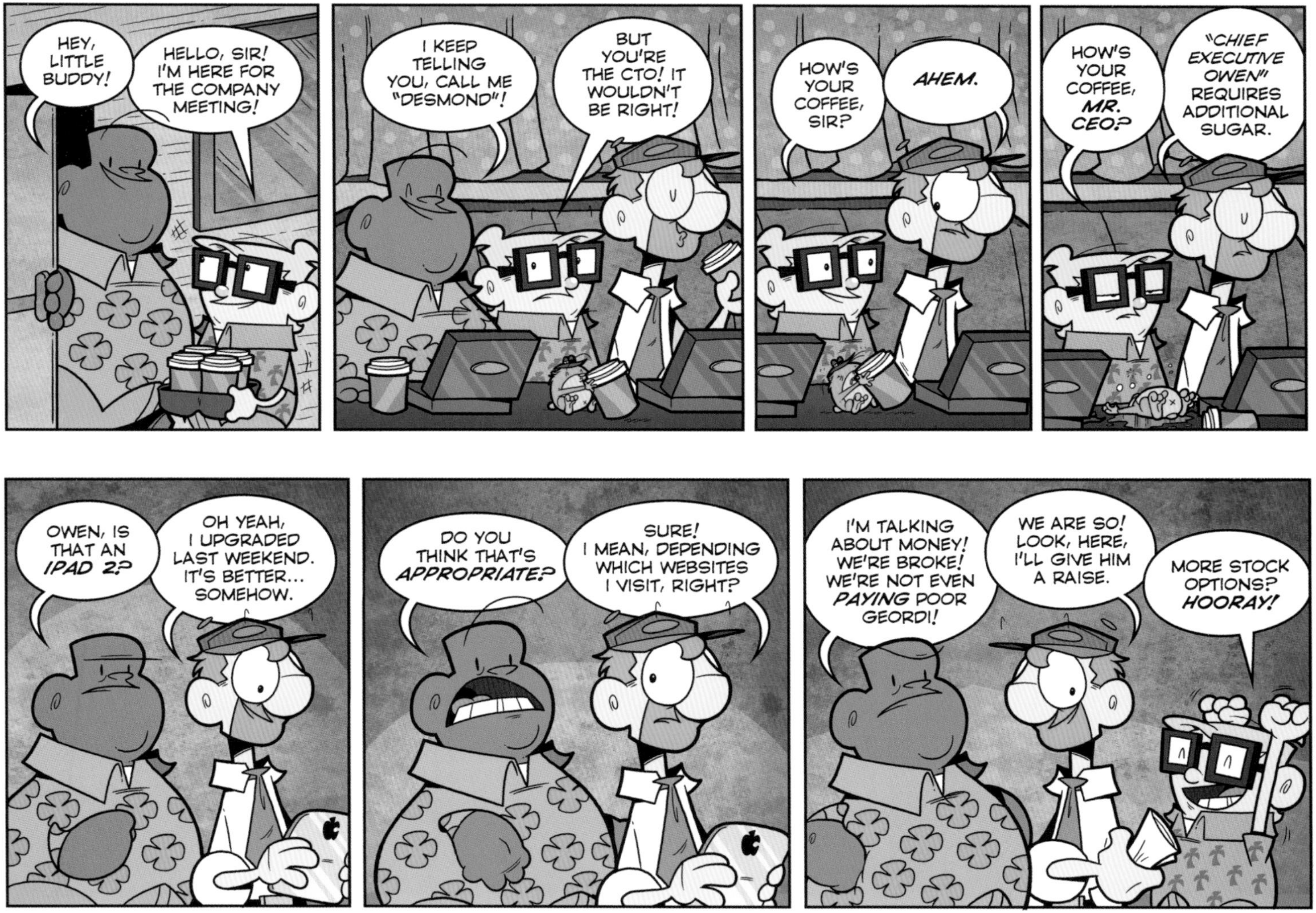
HEY, LITTLE BUDDY!
HELLO, SIR! I'M HERE FOR THE COMPANY MEETING!
I KEEP TELLING YOU, CALL ME "DESMOND"!
BUT YOU'RE THE CTO! IT WOULDN'T BE RIGHT!
HOW'S YOUR COFFEE, SIR?
AHEM.
HOW'S YOUR COFFEE, MR. CEO?
"CHIEF EXECUTIVE OWEN" REQUIRES ADDITIONAL SUGAR.
OWEN, IS THAT AN IPAD 2?
OH YEAH, I UPGRADED LAST WEEKEND. IT'S BETTER... SOMEHOW.
DO YOU THINK THAT'S APPROPRIATE?
SURE! I MEAN, DEPENDING WHICH WEBSITES I VISIT, RIGHT?
I'M TALKING ABOUT MONEY! WE'RE BROKE! WE'RE NOT EVEN PAYING POOR GEORDI!
WE ARE SO! LOOK, HERE, I'LL GIVE HIM A RAISE.
MORE STOCK OPTIONS? HOORAY!

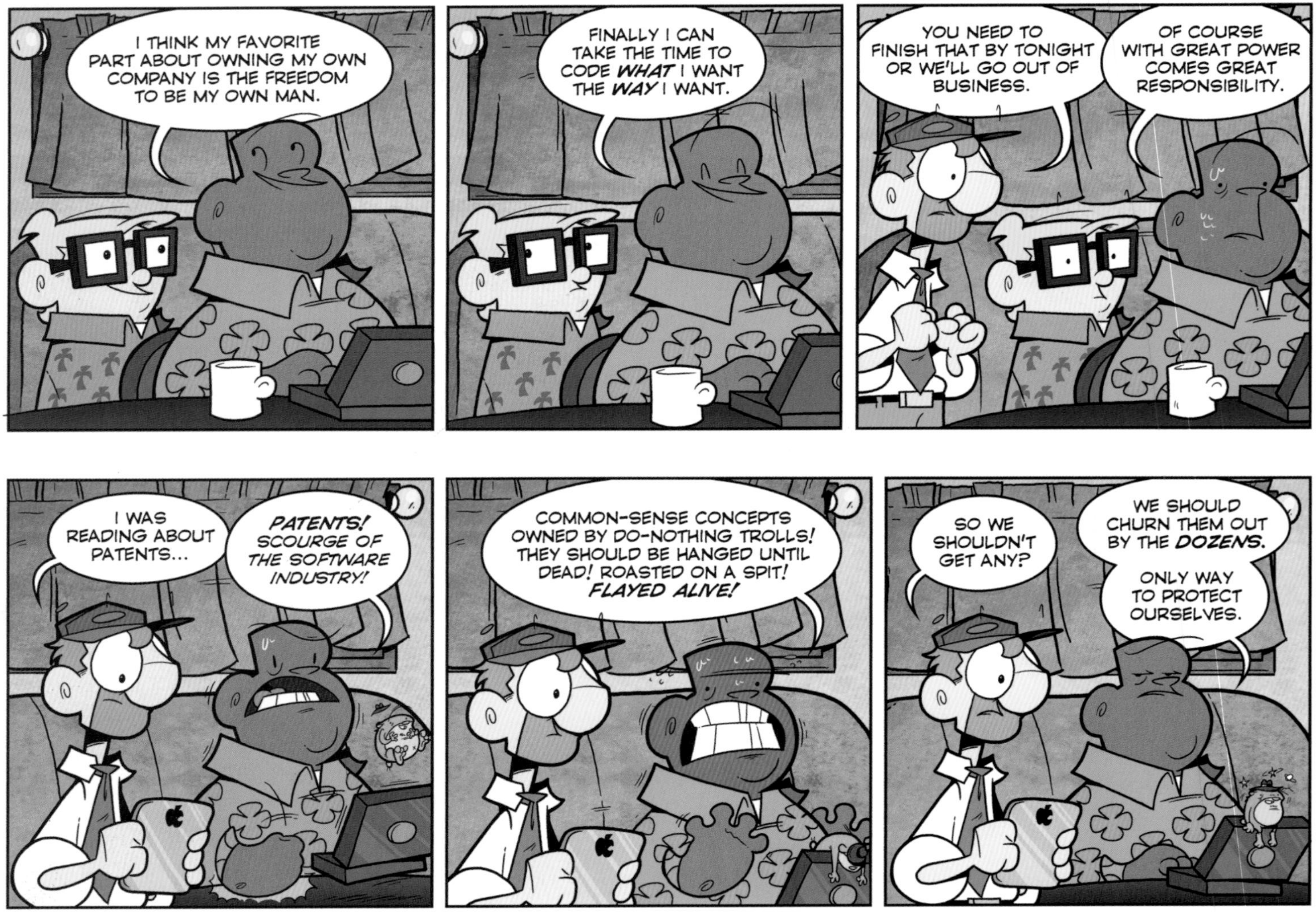
I THINK MY FAVORITE PART ABOUT OWNING MY OWN COMPANY IS THE FREEDOM TO BE MY OWN MAN.
FINALLY I CAN TAKE THE TIME TO CODE *WHAT* I WANT THE *WAY* I WANT.
YOU NEED TO FINISH THAT BY TONIGHT OR WE'LL GO OUT OF BUSINESS.
OF COURSE WITH GREAT POWER COMES GREAT RESPONSIBILITY.
I WAS READING ABOUT PATENTS...
PATENTS! SCOURGE OF THE SOFTWARE INDUSTRY!
COMMON-SENSE CONCEPTS OWNED BY DO-NOTHING TROLLS! THEY SHOULD BE HANGED UNTIL DEAD! ROASTED ON A SPIT! ***FLAYED ALIVE!***
SO WE SHOULDN'T GET ANY?
WE SHOULD CHURN THEM OUT BY THE ***DOZENS.***
ONLY WAY TO PROTECT OURSELVES.

UPGRADE PATH

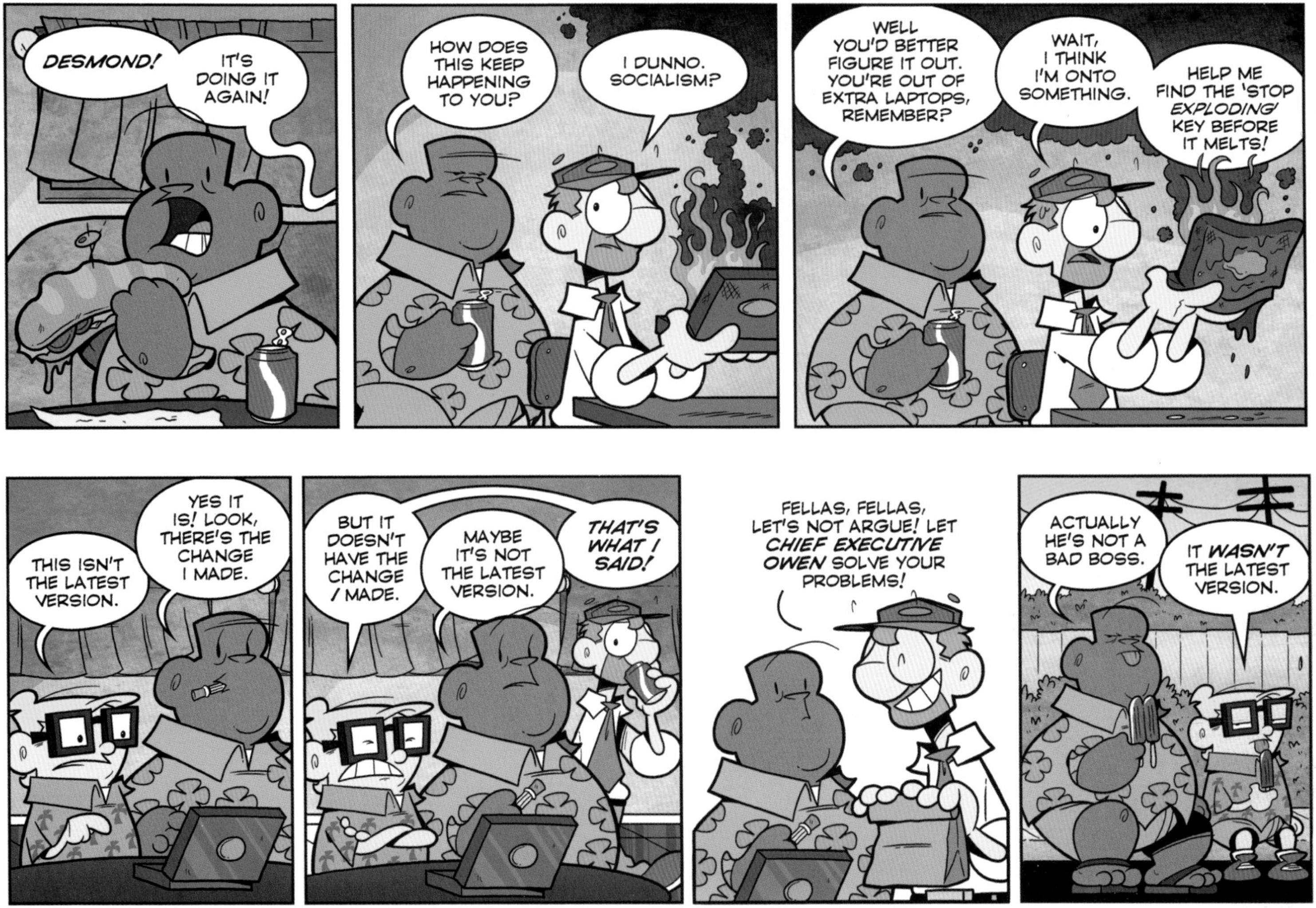
DESMOND!
IT'S DOING IT AGAIN!
HOW DOES THIS KEEP HAPPENING TO YOU?
I DUNNO. SOCIALISM?
WELL YOU'D BETTER FIGURE IT OUT. YOU'RE OUT OF EXTRA LAPTOPS, REMEMBER?
WAIT, I THINK I'M ONTO SOMETHING.
HELP ME FIND THE 'STOP *EXPLODING*' KEY BEFORE IT MELTS!
THIS ISN'T THE LATEST VERSION.
YES IT IS! LOOK, THERE'S THE CHANGE I MADE.
BUT IT DOESN'T HAVE THE CHANGE *I* MADE.
MAYBE IT'S NOT THE LATEST VERSION.
THAT'S WHAT I SAID!
FELLAS, FELLAS, LET'S NOT ARGUE! LET ***CHIEF EXECUTIVE OWEN*** SOLVE YOUR PROBLEMS!
ACTUALLY HE'S NOT A BAD BOSS.
IT ***WASN'T*** THE LATEST VERSION.

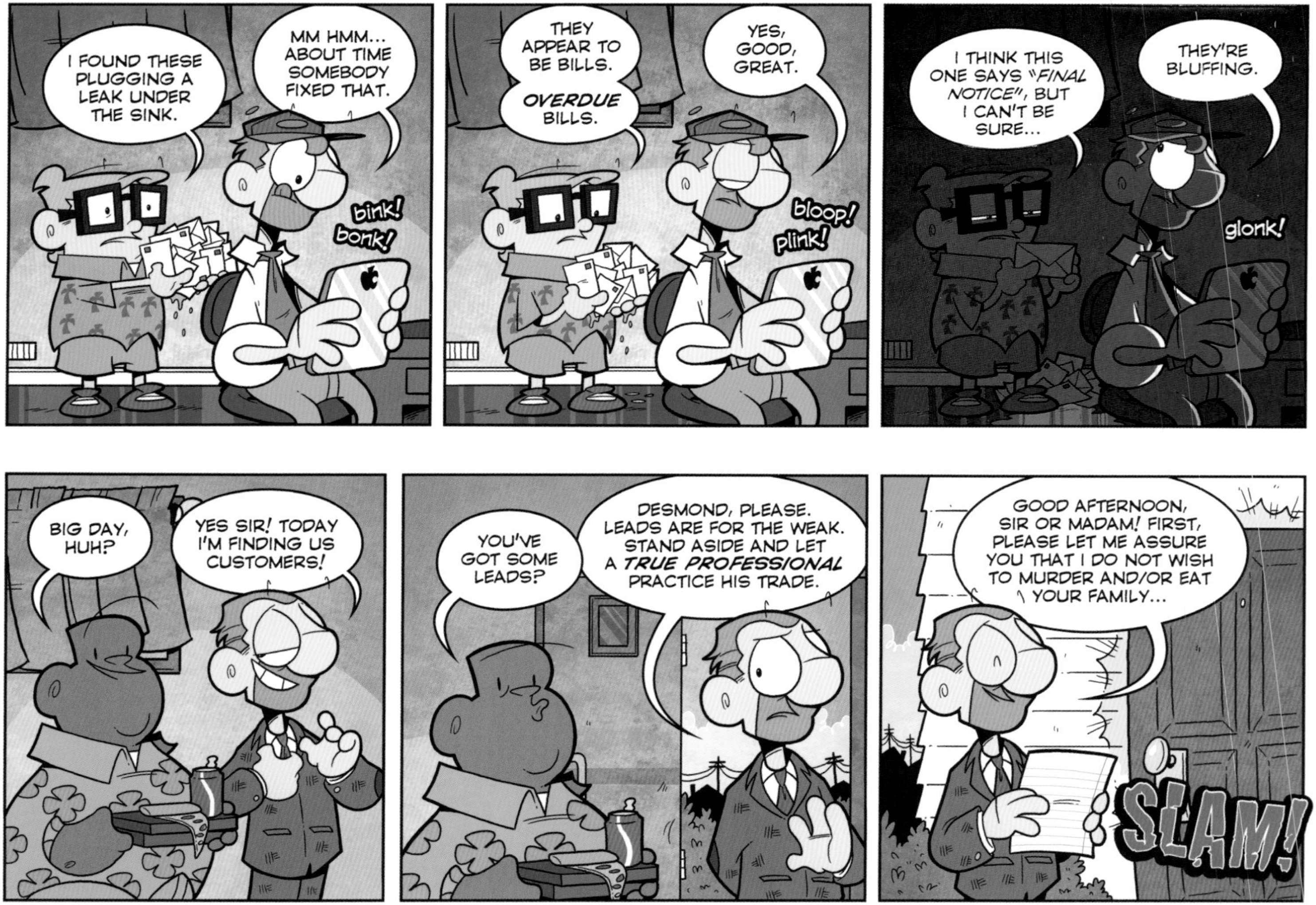
I FOUND THESE PLUGGING A LEAK UNDER THE SINK.
MM HMM... ABOUT TIME SOMEBODY FIXED THAT.
bink!
bonk!
THEY APPEAR TO BE BILLS.
OVERDUE BILLS.
YES, GOOD, GREAT.
bloop!
plink!
I THINK THIS ONE SAYS "FINAL NOTICE", BUT I CAN'T BE SURE...
THEY'RE BLUFFING.
glonk!
BIG DAY, HUH?
YES SIR! TODAY I'M FINDING US CUSTOMERS!
YOU'VE GOT SOME LEADS?
DESMOND, PLEASE. LEADS ARE FOR THE WEAK. STAND ASIDE AND LET A TRUE PROFESSIONAL PRACTICE HIS TRADE.
GOOD AFTERNOON, SIR OR MADAM! FIRST, PLEASE LET ME ASSURE YOU THAT I DO NOT WISH TO MURDER AND/OR EAT YOUR FAMILY...
SLAM!

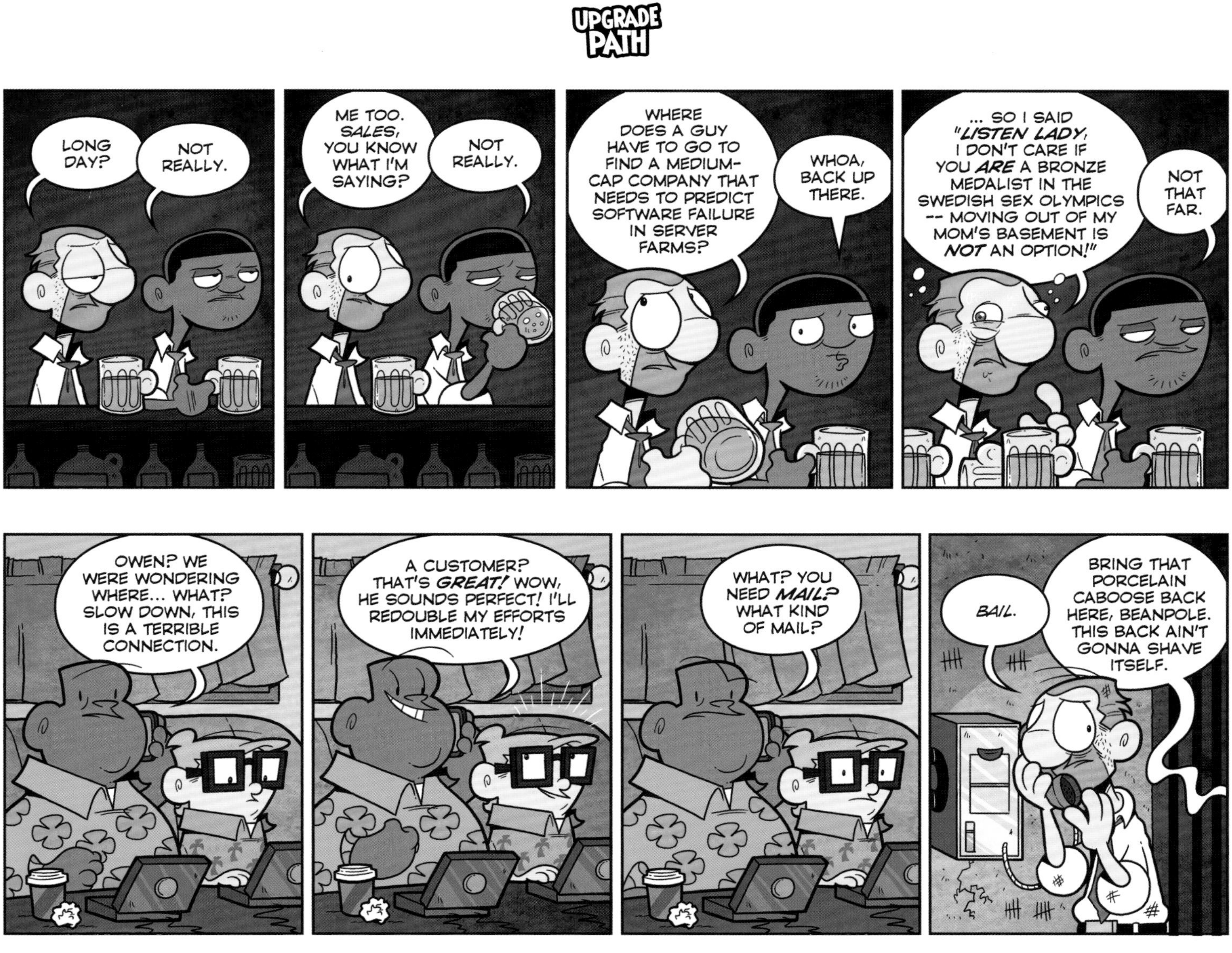
UPGRADE PATH
LONG DAY?
NOT REALLY.
ME TOO. SALES, YOU KNOW WHAT I'M SAYING?
NOT REALLY.
WHERE DOES A GUY HAVE TO GO TO FIND A MEDIUM-CAP COMPANY THAT NEEDS TO PREDICT SOFTWARE FAILURE IN SERVER FARMS?
WHOA, BACK UP THERE.
... SO I SAID "LISTEN LADY, I DON'T CARE IF YOU ARE A BRONZE MEDALIST IN THE SWEDISH SEX OLYMPICS -- MOVING OUT OF MY MOM'S BASEMENT IS NOT AN OPTION!"
NOT THAT FAR.
OWEN? WE WERE WONDERING WHERE... WHAT? SLOW DOWN, THIS IS A TERRIBLE CONNECTION.
A CUSTOMER? THAT'S GREAT! WOW, HE SOUNDS PERFECT! I'LL REDOUBLE MY EFFORTS IMMEDIATELY!
WHAT? YOU NEED MAIL? WHAT KIND OF MAIL?
BAIL.
BRING THAT PORCELAIN CABOOSE BACK HERE, BEANPOLE. THIS BACK AIN'T GONNA SHAVE ITSELF.

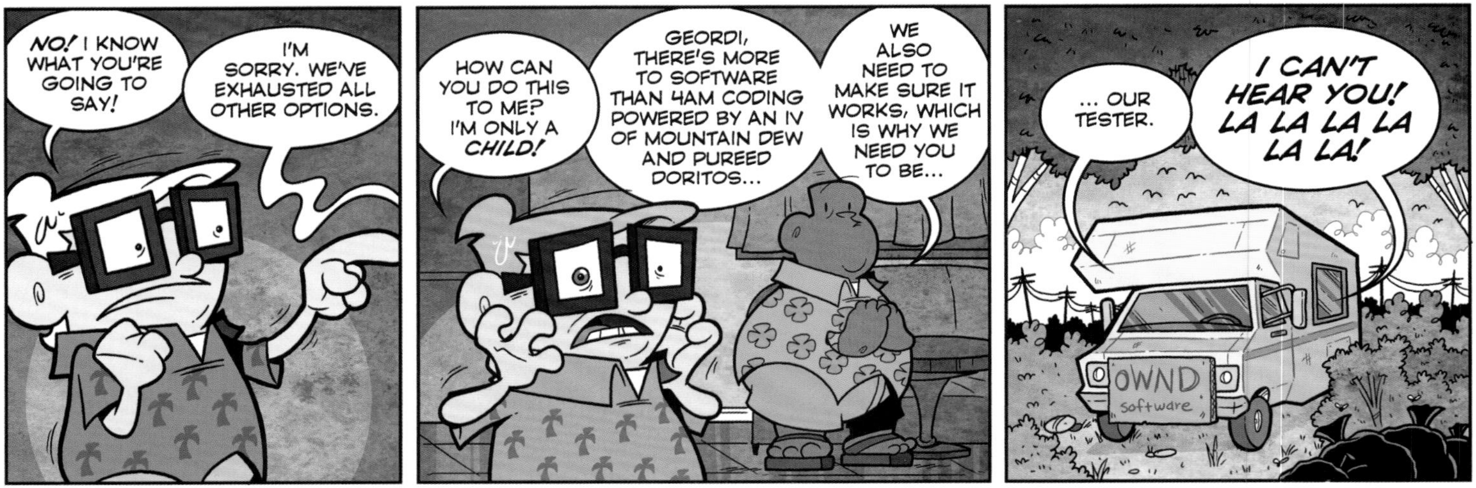
NO! I KNOW WHAT YOU'RE GOING TO SAY!
I'M SORRY. WE'VE EXHAUSTED ALL OTHER OPTIONS.
HOW CAN YOU DO THIS TO ME? I'M ONLY A CHILD!
GEORDI, THERE'S MORE TO SOFTWARE THAN 4AM CODING POWERED BY AN IV OF MOUNTAIN DEW AND PUREED DORITOS...
WE ALSO NEED TO MAKE SURE IT WORKS, WHICH IS WHY WE NEED YOU TO BE...
... OUR TESTER.
I CAN'T HEAR YOU! LA LA LA LA LA LA!
OWND software

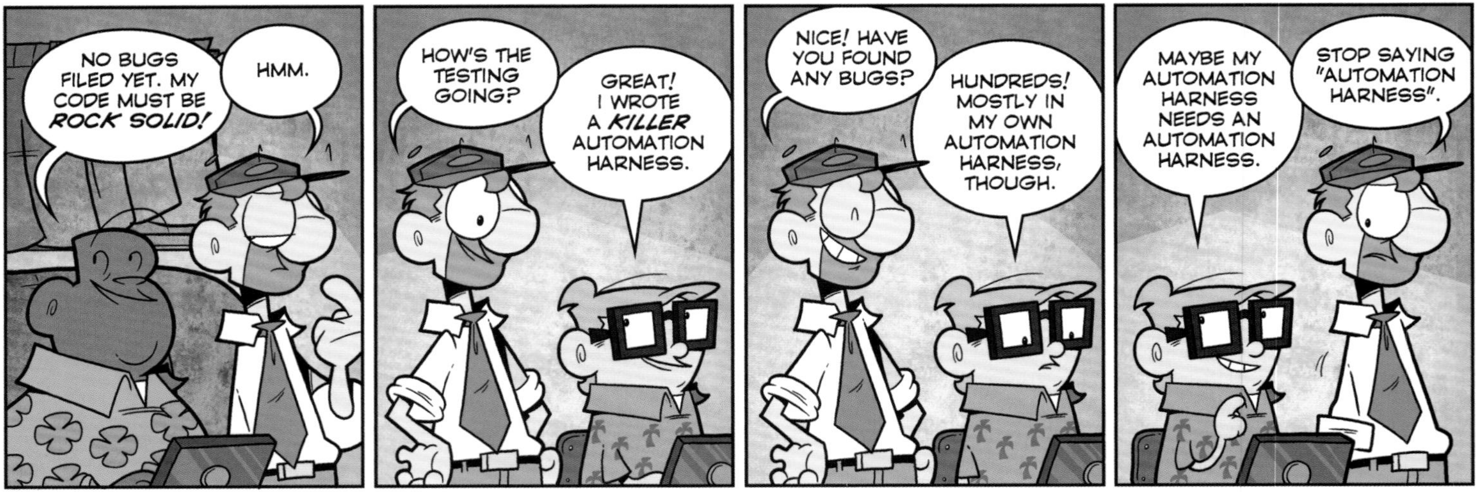
NO BUGS FILED YET. MY CODE MUST BE ROCK SOLID!
HMM.
HOW'S THE TESTING GOING?
GREAT! I WROTE A KILLER AUTOMATION HARNESS.
NICE! HAVE YOU FOUND ANY BUGS?
HUNDREDS! MOSTLY IN MY OWN AUTOMATION HARNESS, THOUGH.
MAYBE MY AUTOMATION HARNESS NEEDS AN AUTOMATION HARNESS.
STOP SAYING "AUTOMATION HARNESS".

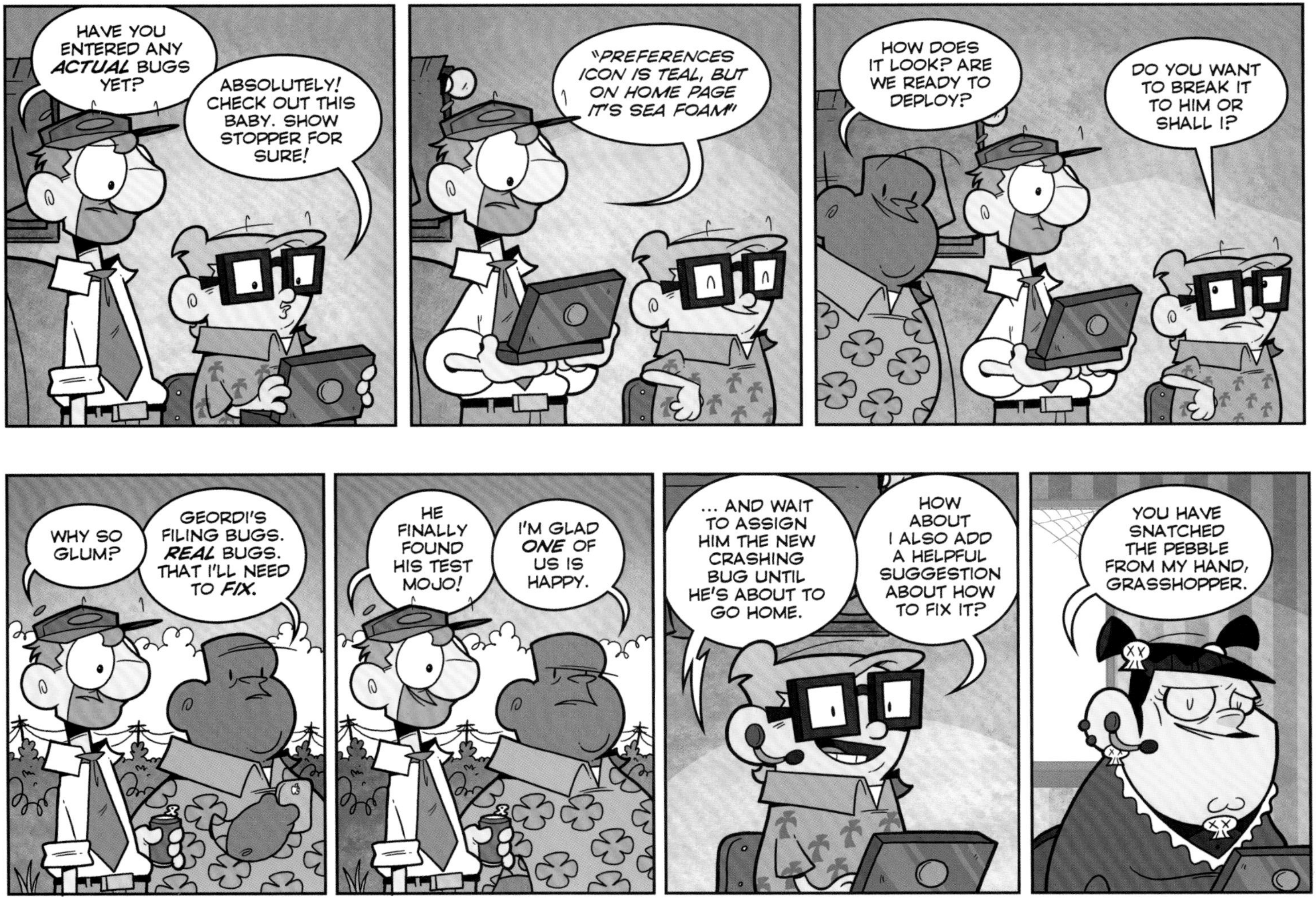
HAVE YOU ENTERED ANY ACTUAL BUGS YET?
ABSOLUTELY! CHECK OUT THIS BABY. SHOW STOPPER FOR SURE!
"PREFERENCES ICON IS TEAL, BUT ON HOME PAGE IT'S SEA FOAM"
HOW DOES IT LOOK? ARE WE READY TO DEPLOY?
DO YOU WANT TO BREAK IT TO HIM OR SHALL I?
WHY SO GLUM?
GEORDI'S FILING BUGS. REAL BUGS. THAT I'LL NEED TO FIX.
HE FINALLY FOUND HIS TEST MOJO!
I'M GLAD ONE OF US IS HAPPY.
... AND WAIT TO ASSIGN HIM THE NEW CRASHING BUG UNTIL HE'S ABOUT TO GO HOME.
HOW ABOUT I ALSO ADD A HELPFUL SUGGESTION ABOUT HOW TO FIX IT?
YOU HAVE SNATCHED THE PEBBLE FROM MY HAND, GRASSHOPPER.

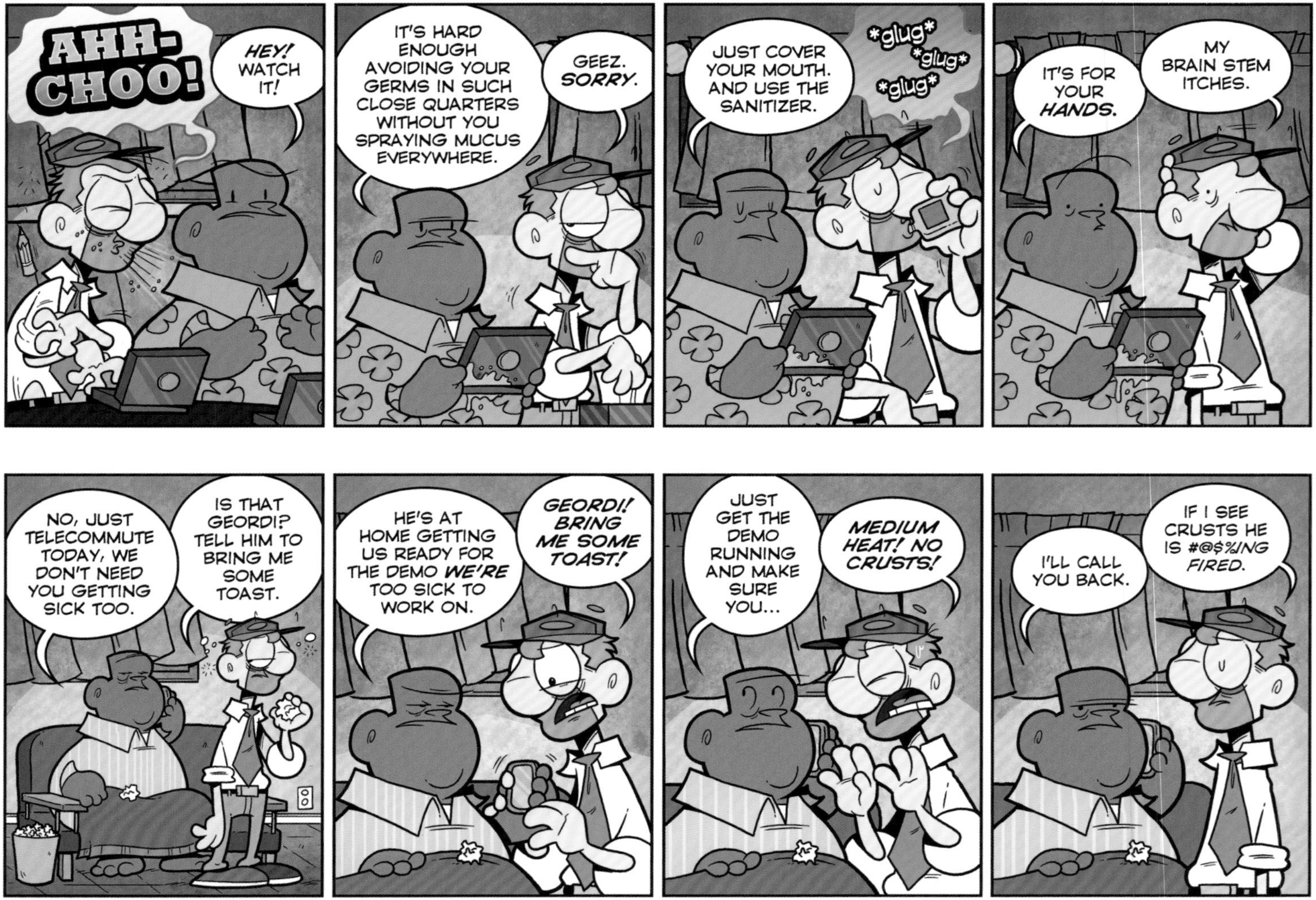
AHH-CHOO!
HEY! WATCH IT!
IT'S HARD ENOUGH AVOIDING YOUR GERMS IN SUCH CLOSE QUARTERS WITHOUT YOU SPRAYING MUCUS EVERYWHERE.
GEEZ. SORRY.
JUST COVER YOUR MOUTH. AND USE THE SANITIZER.
glug *glug* *glug*
IT'S FOR YOUR HANDS.
MY BRAIN STEM ITCHES.
NO, JUST TELECOMMUTE TODAY, WE DON'T NEED YOU GETTING SICK TOO.
IS THAT GEORDI? TELL HIM TO BRING ME SOME TOAST.
HE'S AT HOME GETTING US READY FOR THE DEMO WE'RE TOO SICK TO WORK ON.
GEORDI! BRING ME SOME TOAST!
JUST GET THE DEMO RUNNING AND MAKE SURE YOU...
MEDIUM HEAT! NO CRUSTS!
I'LL CALL YOU BACK.
IF I SEE CRUSTS HE IS #@$%ING FIRED.

UPGRADE PATH

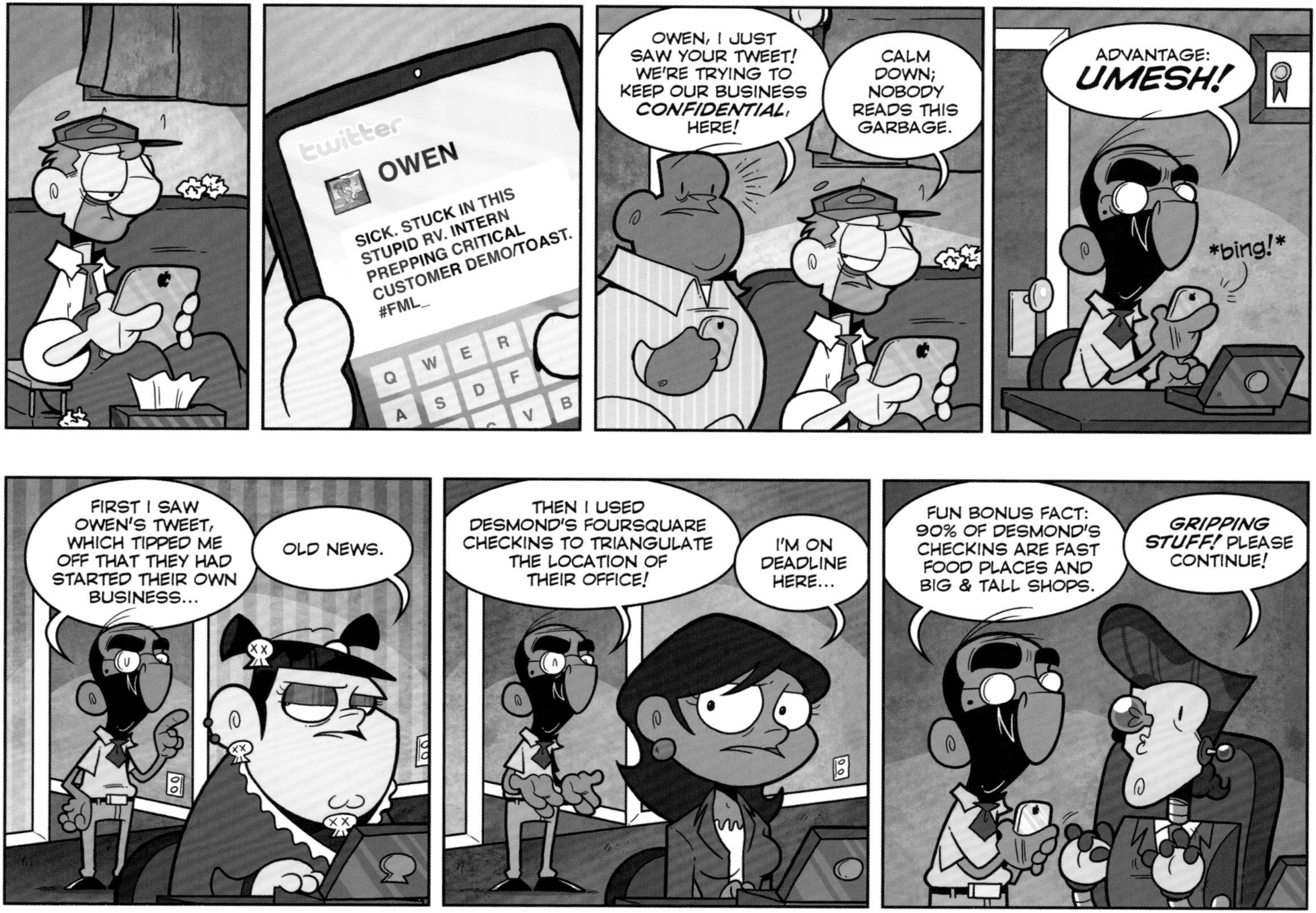
twitter
OWEN
SICK. STUCK IN THIS STUPID RV. INTERN PREPPING CRITICAL CUSTOMER DEMO/TOAST. #FML_
OWEN, I JUST SAW YOUR TWEET! WE'RE TRYING TO KEEP OUR BUSINESS CONFIDENTIAL, HERE!
CALM DOWN; NOBODY READS THIS GARBAGE.
ADVANTAGE: UMESH!
bing!
FIRST I SAW OWEN'S TWEET, WHICH TIPPED ME OFF THAT THEY HAD STARTED THEIR OWN BUSINESS...
OLD NEWS.
THEN I USED DESMOND'S FOURSQUARE CHECKINS TO TRIANGULATE THE LOCATION OF THEIR OFFICE!
I'M ON DEADLINE HERE...
FUN BONUS FACT: 90% OF DESMOND'S CHECKINS ARE FAST FOOD PLACES AND BIG & TALL SHOPS.
GRIPPING STUFF! PLEASE CONTINUE!

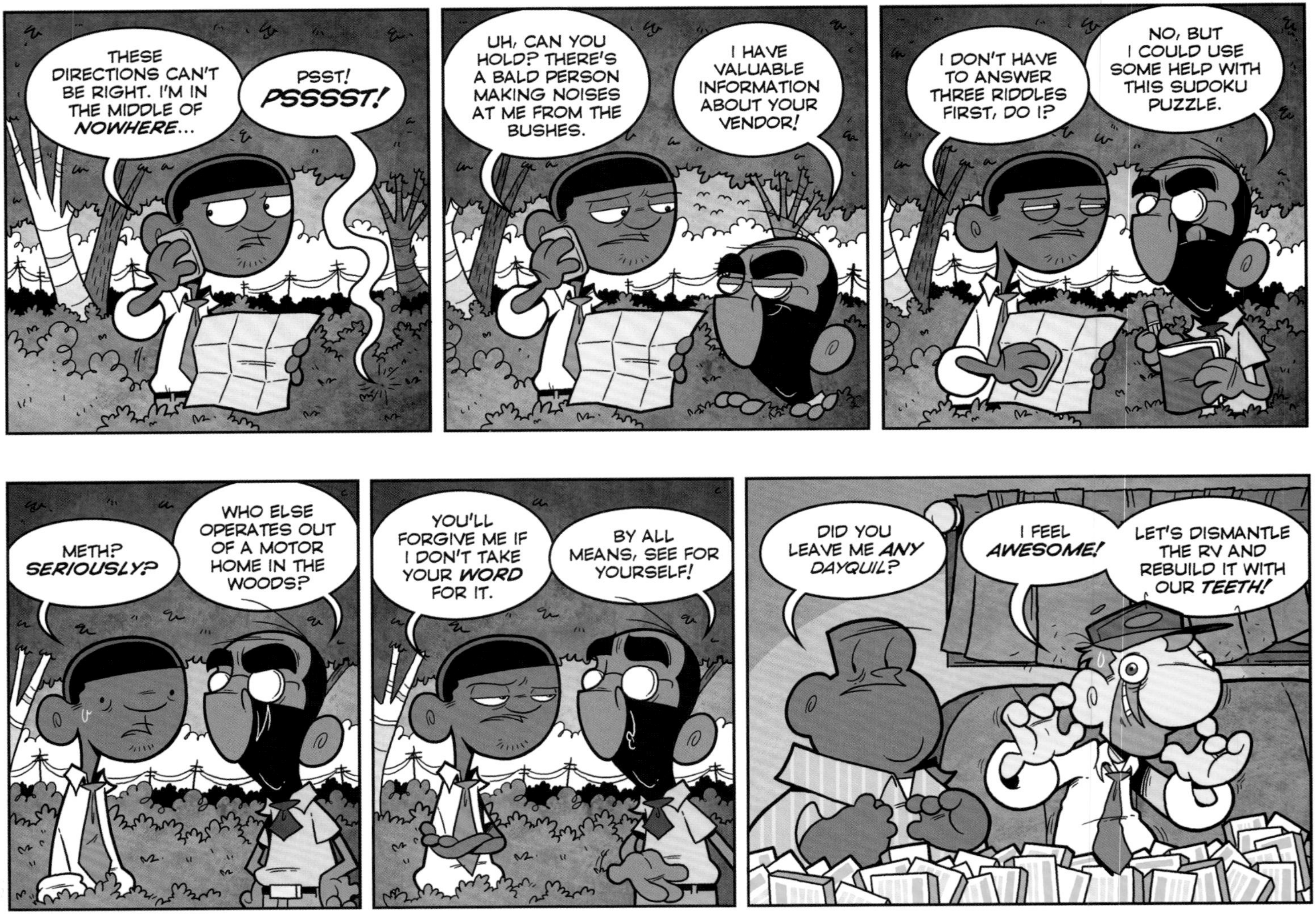
THESE DIRECTIONS CAN'T BE RIGHT. I'M IN THE MIDDLE OF *NOWHERE*...
PSST! *PSSSST!*
UH, CAN YOU HOLD? THERE'S A BALD PERSON MAKING NOISES AT ME FROM THE BUSHES.
I HAVE VALUABLE INFORMATION ABOUT YOUR VENDOR!
I DON'T HAVE TO ANSWER THREE RIDDLES FIRST, DO I?
NO, BUT I COULD USE SOME HELP WITH THIS SUDOKU PUZZLE.
METH? *SERIOUSLY?*
WHO ELSE OPERATES OUT OF A MOTOR HOME IN THE WOODS?
YOU'LL FORGIVE ME IF I DON'T TAKE YOUR *WORD* FOR IT.
BY ALL MEANS, SEE FOR YOURSELF!
DID YOU LEAVE ME *ANY DAYQUIL?*
I FEEL *AWESOME!*
LET'S DISMANTLE THE RV AND REBUILD IT WITH OUR *TEETH!*

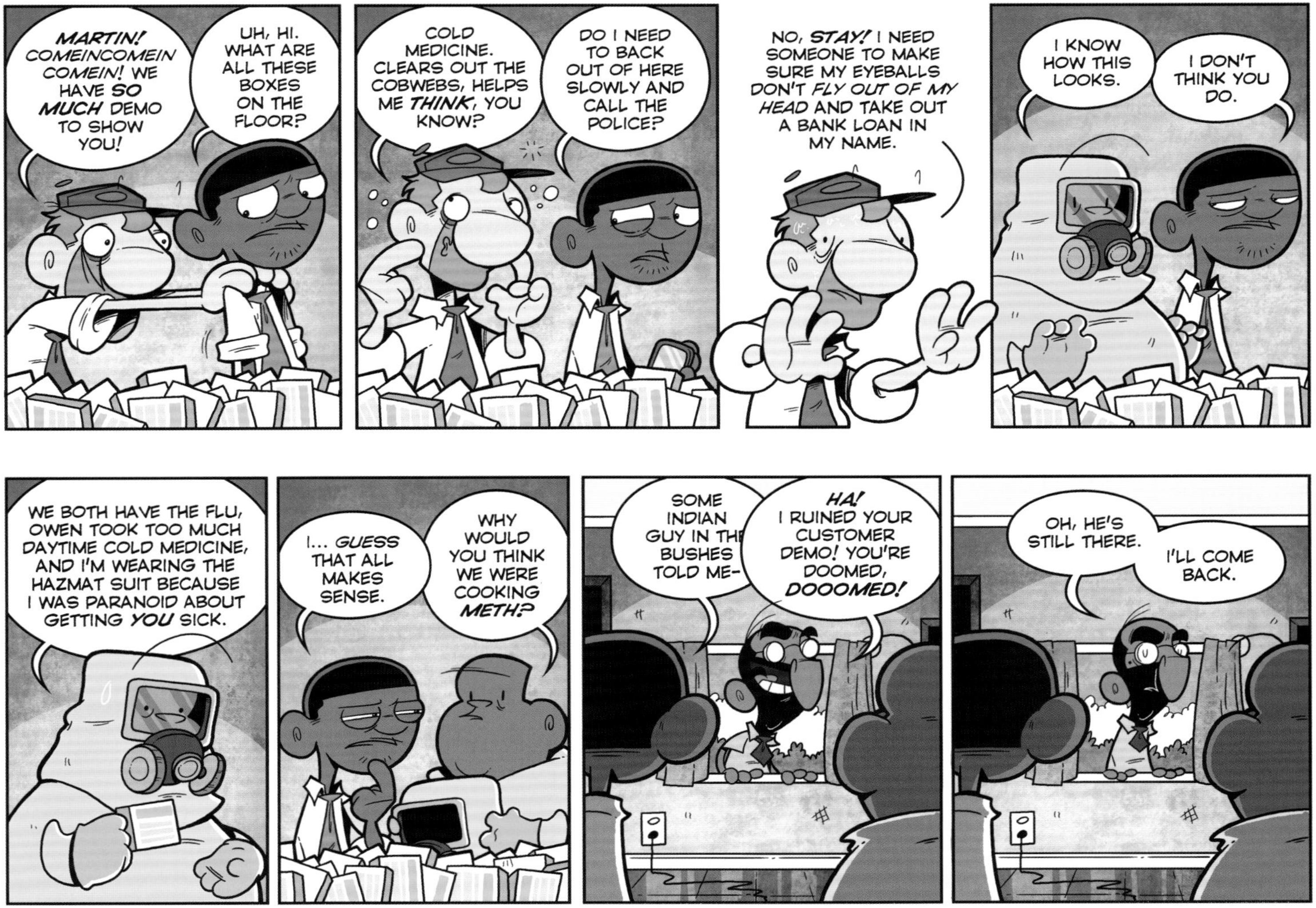
MARTIN! COMEINCOMEIN COMEIN! WE HAVE SO MUCH DEMO TO SHOW YOU!
UH, HI. WHAT ARE ALL THESE BOXES ON THE FLOOR?
COLD MEDICINE. CLEARS OUT THE COBWEBS, HELPS ME THINK, YOU KNOW?
DO I NEED TO BACK OUT OF HERE SLOWLY AND CALL THE POLICE?
NO, STAY! I NEED SOMEONE TO MAKE SURE MY EYEBALLS DON'T FLY OUT OF MY HEAD AND TAKE OUT A BANK LOAN IN MY NAME.
I KNOW HOW THIS LOOKS.
I DON'T THINK YOU DO.
WE BOTH HAVE THE FLU, OWEN TOOK TOO MUCH DAYTIME COLD MEDICINE, AND I'M WEARING THE HAZMAT SUIT BECAUSE I WAS PARANOID ABOUT GETTING YOU SICK.
I... GUESS THAT ALL MAKES SENSE.
WHY WOULD YOU THINK WE WERE COOKING METH?
SOME INDIAN GUY IN THE BUSHES TOLD ME-
HA! I RUINED YOUR CUSTOMER DEMO! YOU'RE DOOMED, DOOOMED!
OH, HE'S STILL THERE.
I'LL COME BACK.

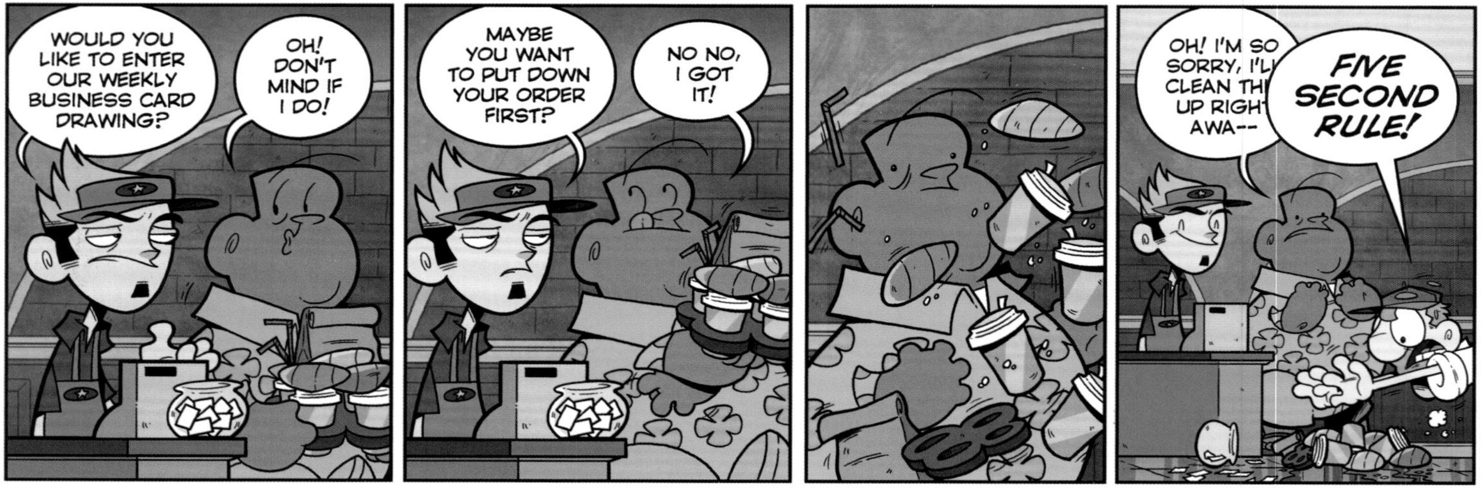
WOULD YOU LIKE TO ENTER OUR WEEKLY BUSINESS CARD DRAWING?
OH! DON'T MIND IF I DO!
MAYBE YOU WANT TO PUT DOWN YOUR ORDER FIRST?
NO NO, I GOT IT!
OH! I'M SO SORRY, I'L CLEAN THI UP RIGHT AWA--
FIVE SECOND RULE!

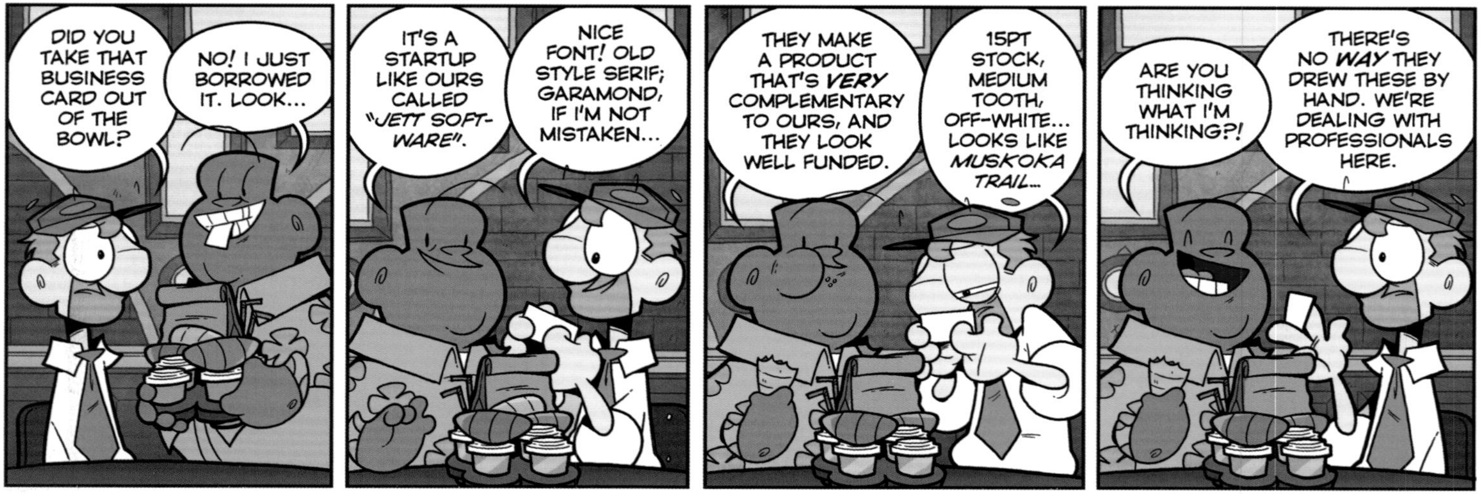
DID YOU TAKE THAT BUSINESS CARD OUT OF THE BOWL?
NO! I JUST BORROWED IT. LOOK...
IT'S A STARTUP LIKE OURS CALLED "JETT SOFTWARE".
NICE FONT! OLD STYLE SERIF; GARAMOND, IF I'M NOT MISTAKEN...
THEY MAKE A PRODUCT THAT'S VERY COMPLEMENTARY TO OURS, AND THEY LOOK WELL FUNDED.
15PT STOCK, MEDIUM TOOTH, OFF-WHITE... LOOKS LIKE MUSKOKA TRAIL...
ARE YOU THINKING WHAT I'M THINKING?!
THERE'S NO WAY THEY DREW THESE BY HAND. WE'RE DEALING WITH PROFESSIONALS HERE.

UPGRADE PATH

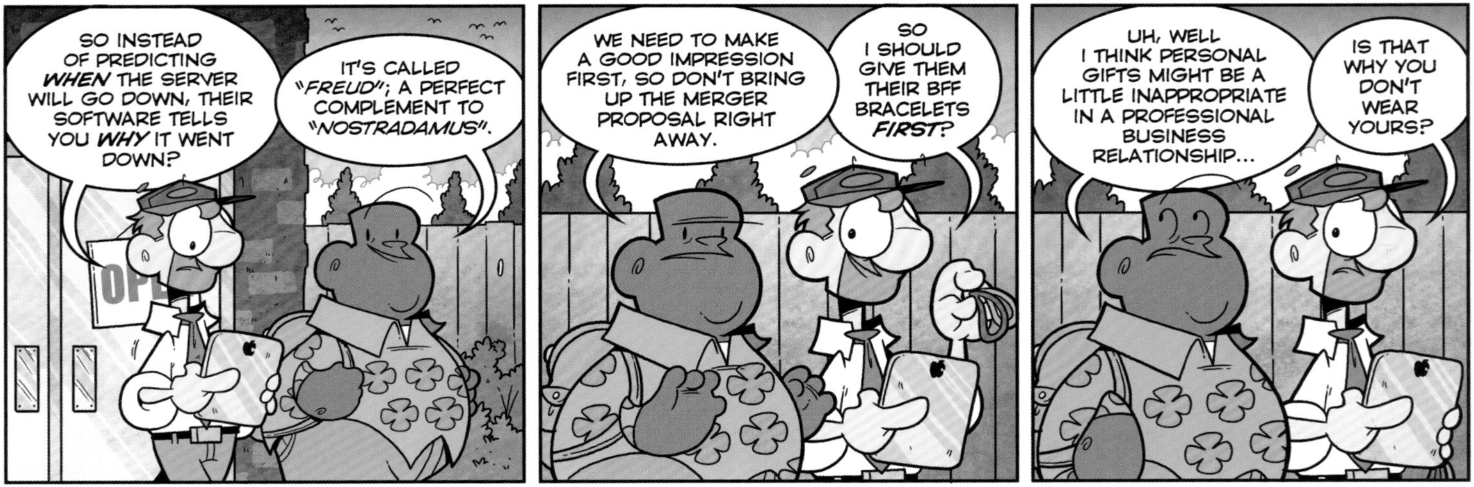
SO INSTEAD OF PREDICTING *WHEN* THE SERVER WILL GO DOWN, THEIR SOFTWARE TELLS YOU *WHY* IT WENT DOWN?
IT'S CALLED "*FREUD*"; A PERFECT COMPLEMENT TO "*NOSTRADAMUS*".
OPE
WE NEED TO MAKE A GOOD IMPRESSION FIRST, SO DON'T BRING UP THE MERGER PROPOSAL RIGHT AWAY.
SO I SHOULD GIVE THEM THEIR BFF BRACELETS *FIRST*?
UH, WELL I THINK PERSONAL GIFTS MIGHT BE A LITTLE INAPPROPRIATE IN A PROFESSIONAL BUSINESS RELATIONSHIP...
IS THAT WHY YOU DON'T WEAR YOURS?

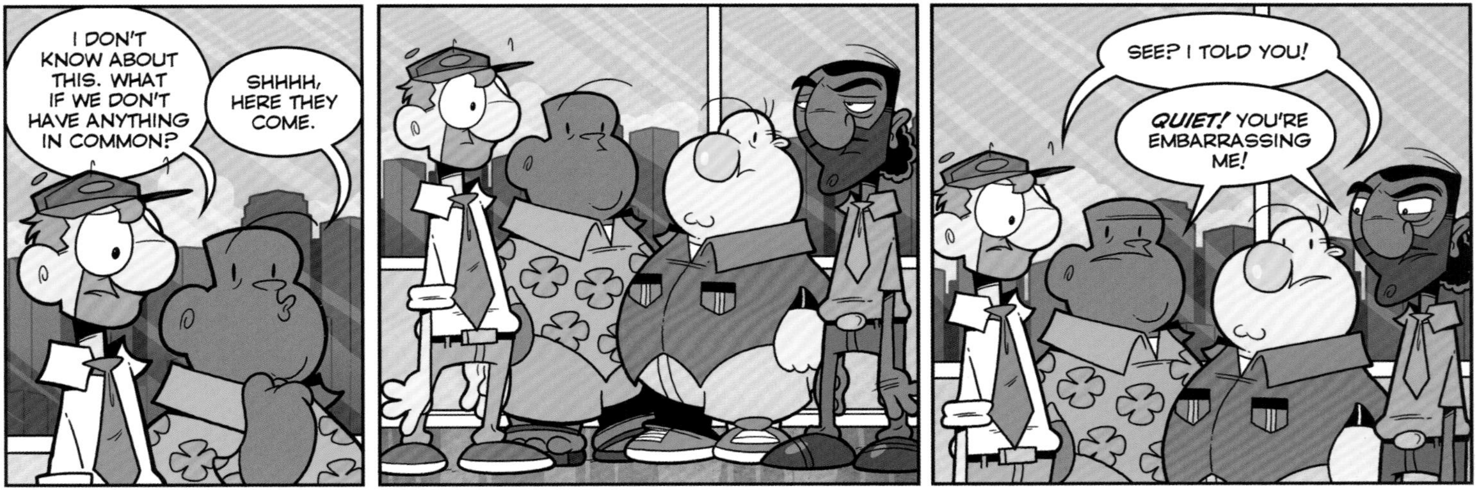
I DON'T KNOW ABOUT THIS. WHAT IF WE DON'T HAVE ANYTHING IN COMMON?
SHHHH, HERE THEY COME.
SEE? I TOLD YOU!
QUIET! YOU'RE EMBARRASSING ME!

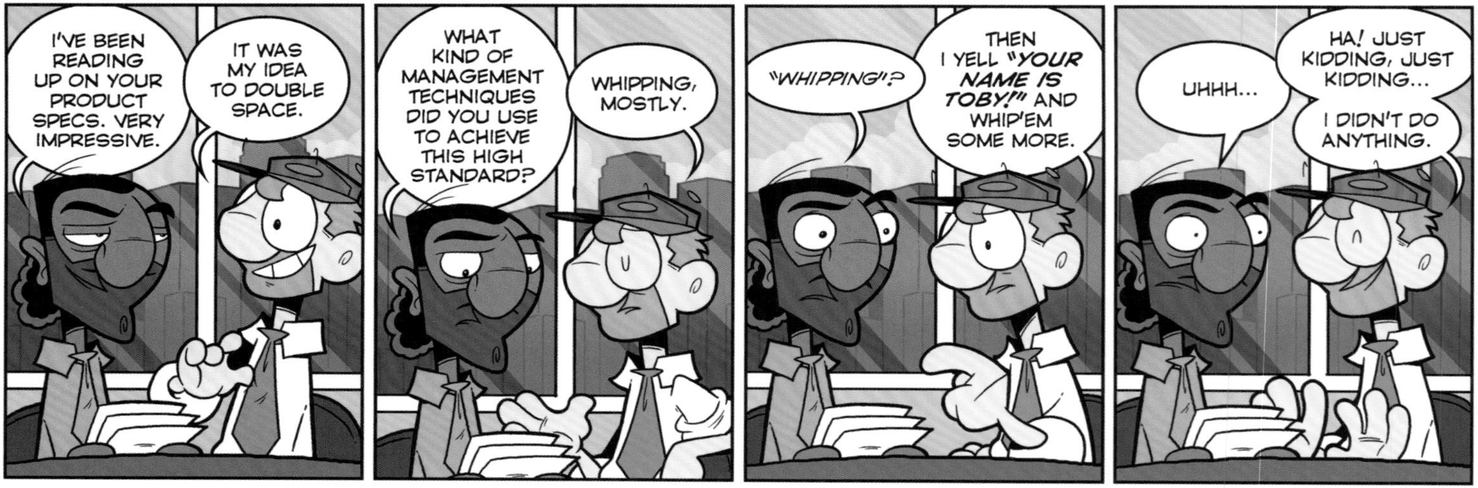
I'VE BEEN READING UP ON YOUR PRODUCT SPECS. VERY IMPRESSIVE.
IT WAS MY IDEA TO DOUBLE SPACE.
WHAT KIND OF MANAGEMENT TECHNIQUES DID YOU USE TO ACHIEVE THIS HIGH STANDARD?
WHIPPING, MOSTLY.
"WHIPPING"?
THEN I YELL "YOUR NAME IS TOBY!" AND WHIP'EM SOME MORE.
UHHH...
HA! JUST KIDDING, JUST KIDDING...
I DIDN'T DO ANYTHING.

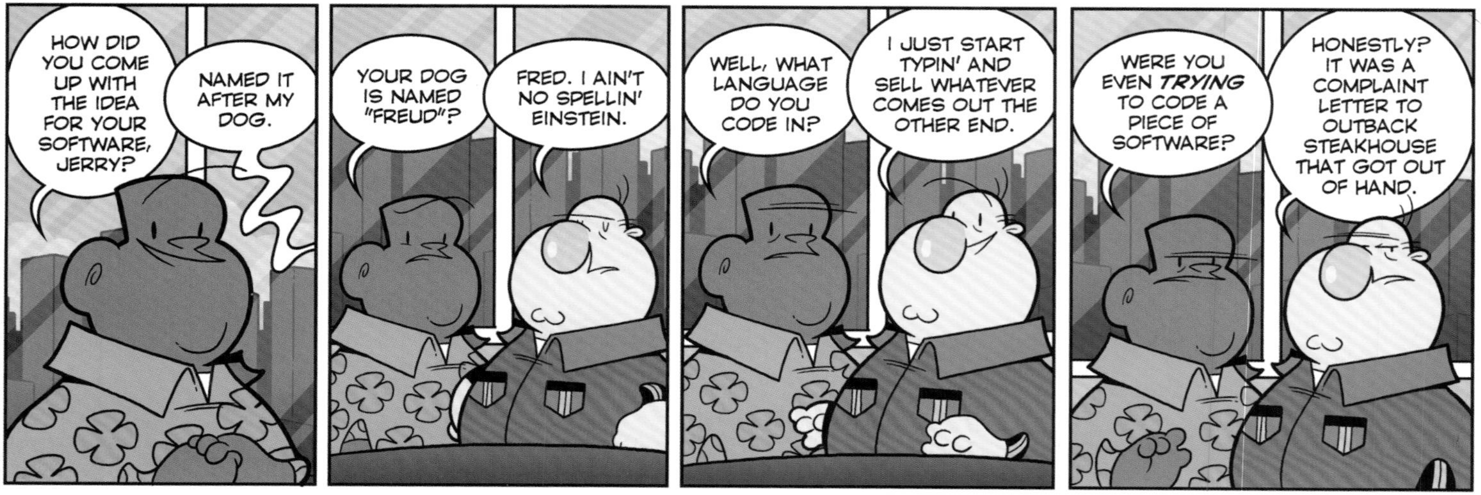
HOW DID YOU COME UP WITH THE IDEA FOR YOUR SOFTWARE, JERRY?
NAMED IT AFTER MY DOG.
YOUR DOG IS NAMED "FREUD"?
FRED. I AIN'T NO SPELLIN' EINSTEIN.
WELL, WHAT LANGUAGE DO YOU CODE IN?
I JUST START TYPIN' AND SELL WHATEVER COMES OUT THE OTHER END.
WERE YOU EVEN TRYING TO CODE A PIECE OF SOFTWARE?
HONESTLY? IT WAS A COMPLAINT LETTER TO OUTBACK STEAKHOUSE THAT GOT OUT OF HAND.

UPGRADE PATH

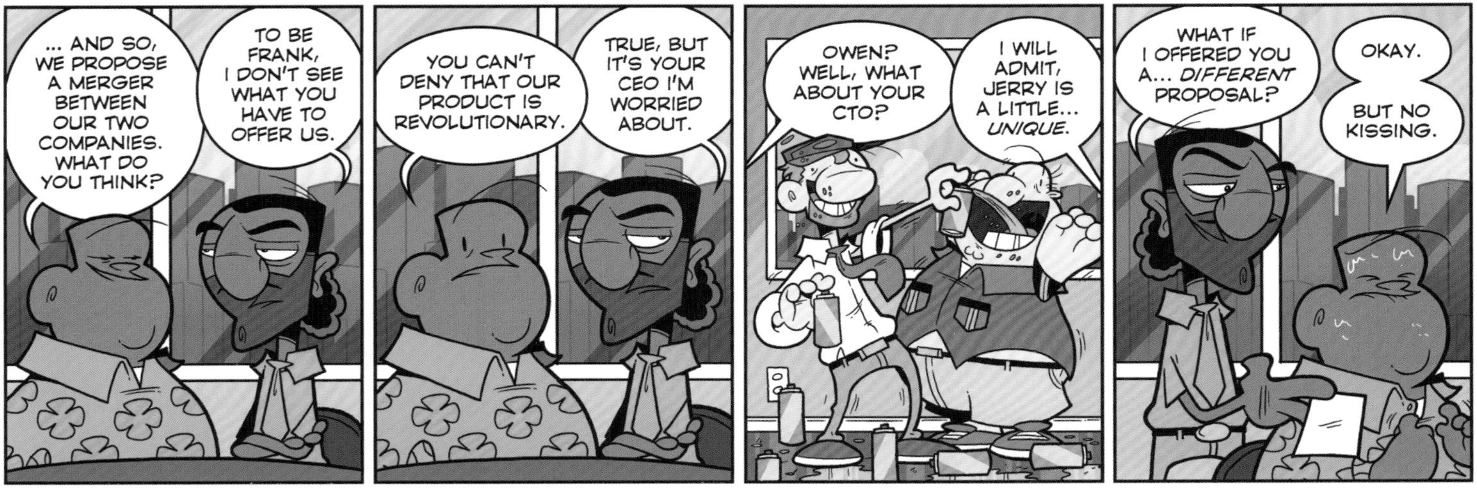

... AND SO, WE PROPOSE A MERGER BETWEEN OUR TWO COMPANIES. WHAT DO YOU THINK?
TO BE FRANK, I DON'T SEE WHAT YOU HAVE TO OFFER US.
YOU CAN'T DENY THAT OUR PRODUCT IS REVOLUTIONARY.
TRUE, BUT IT'S YOUR CEO I'M WORRIED ABOUT.
OWEN? WELL, WHAT ABOUT YOUR CTO?
I WILL ADMIT, JERRY IS A LITTLE... *UNIQUE*.
WHAT IF I OFFERED YOU A... *DIFFERENT* PROPOSAL?
OKAY.
BUT NO KISSING.

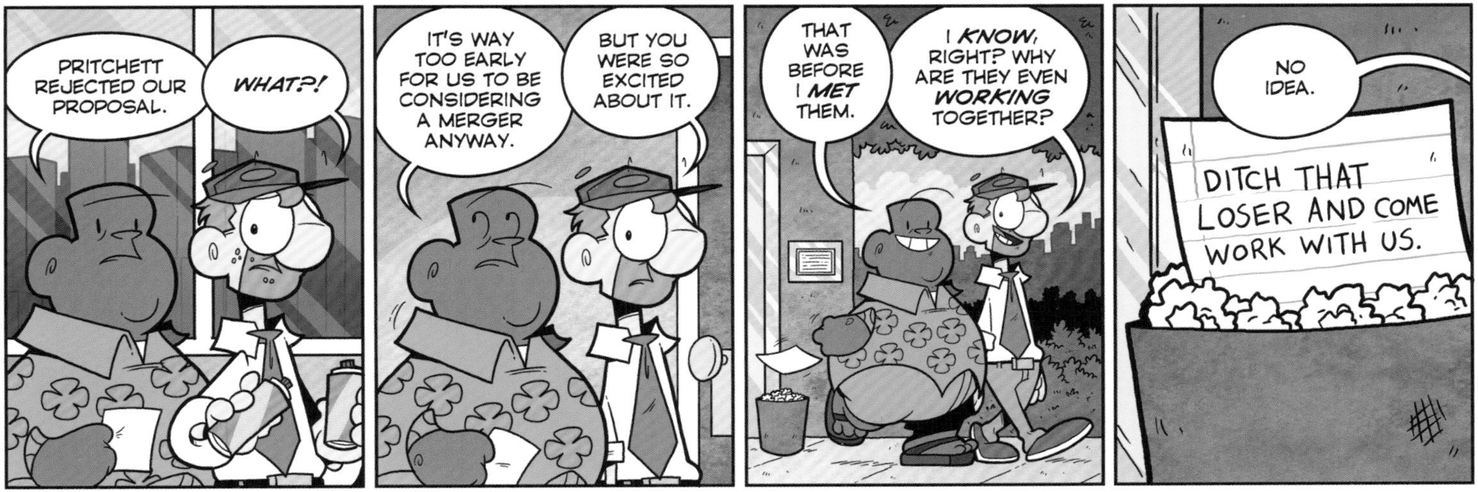

PRITCHETT REJECTED OUR PROPOSAL.
WHAT?!
IT'S WAY TOO EARLY FOR US TO BE CONSIDERING A MERGER ANYWAY.
BUT YOU WERE SO EXCITED ABOUT IT.
THAT WAS BEFORE I *MET* THEM.
I *KNOW*, RIGHT? WHY ARE THEY EVEN ***WORKING*** TOGETHER?
NO IDEA.
DITCH THAT LOSER AND COME WORK WITH US.

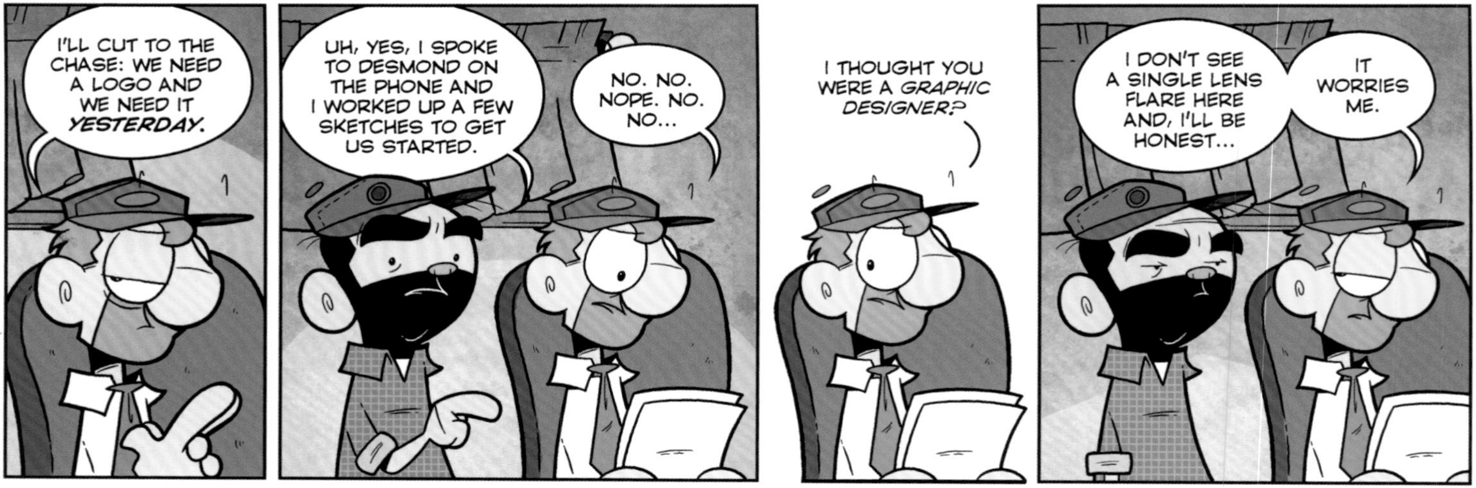
I'LL CUT TO THE CHASE: WE NEED A LOGO AND WE NEED IT *YESTERDAY.*
UH, YES, I SPOKE TO DESMOND ON THE PHONE AND I WORKED UP A FEW SKETCHES TO GET US STARTED.
NO. NO. NOPE. NO. NO...
I THOUGHT YOU WERE A *GRAPHIC DESIGNER?*
I DON'T SEE A SINGLE LENS FLARE HERE AND, I'LL BE HONEST...
IT WORRIES ME.

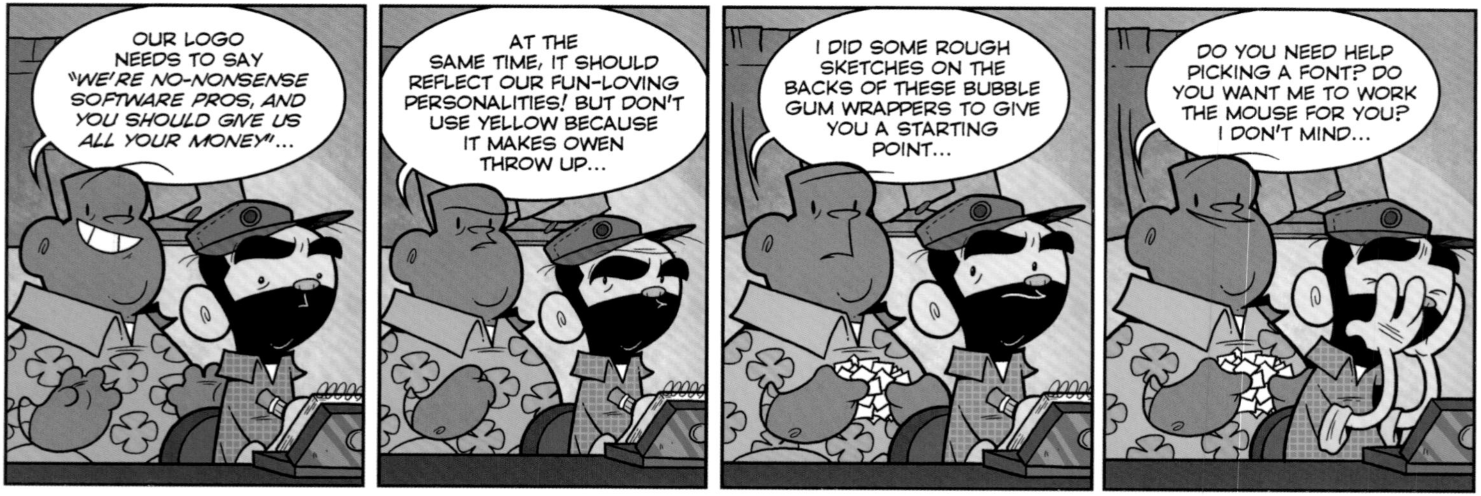
OUR LOGO NEEDS TO SAY *"WE'RE NO-NONSENSE SOFTWARE PROS, AND YOU SHOULD GIVE US ALL YOUR MONEY"*...
AT THE SAME TIME, IT SHOULD REFLECT OUR FUN-LOVING PERSONALITIES! BUT DON'T USE YELLOW BECAUSE IT MAKES OWEN THROW UP...
I DID SOME ROUGH SKETCHES ON THE BACKS OF THESE BUBBLE GUM WRAPPERS TO GIVE YOU A STARTING POINT...
DO YOU NEED HELP PICKING A FONT? DO YOU WANT ME TO WORK THE MOUSE FOR YOU? I DON'T MIND...

UPGRADE PATH

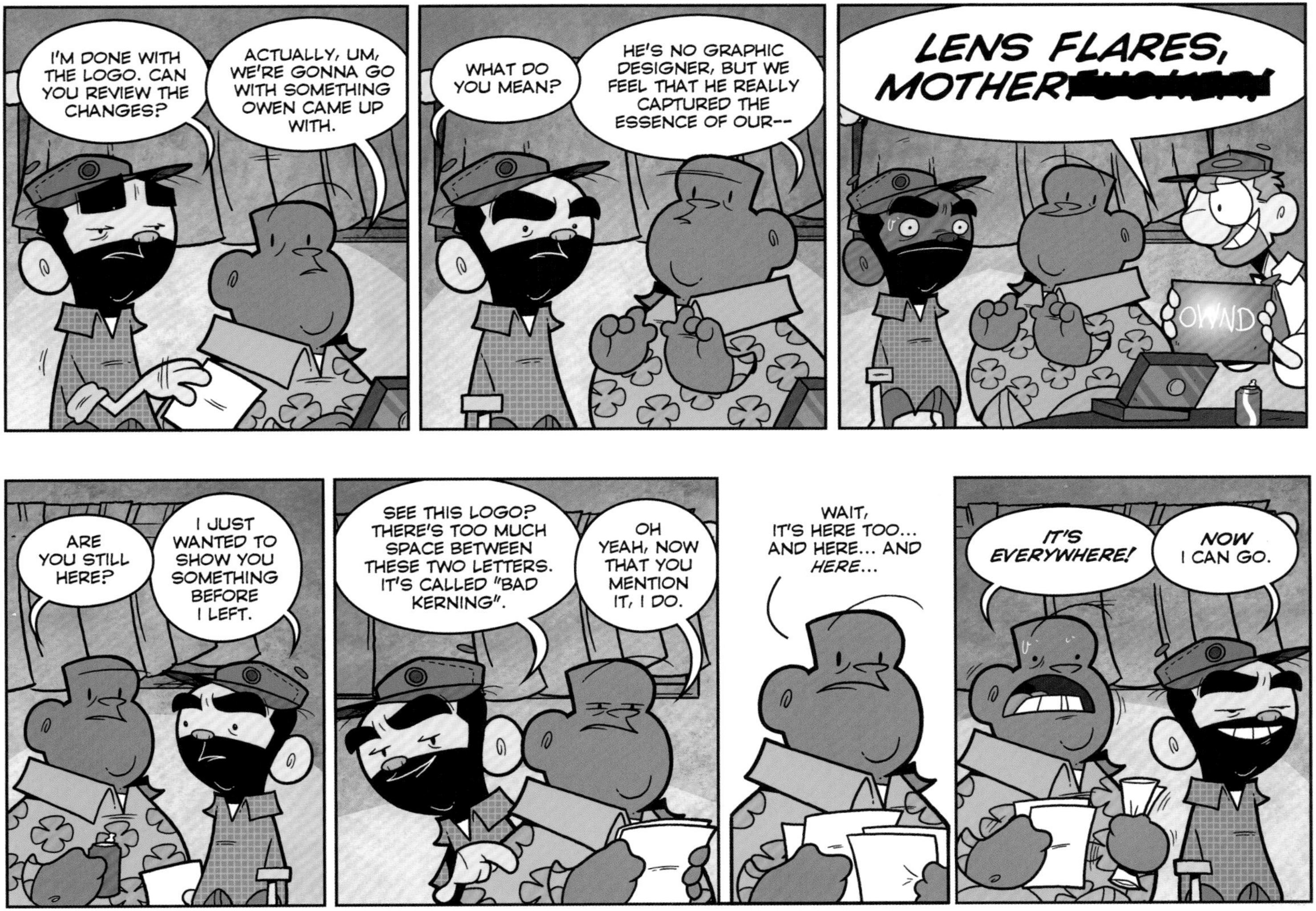

I'M DONE WITH THE LOGO. CAN YOU REVIEW THE CHANGES?
ACTUALLY, UM, WE'RE GONNA GO WITH SOMETHING OWEN CAME UP WITH.
WHAT DO YOU MEAN?
HE'S NO GRAPHIC DESIGNER, BUT WE FEEL THAT HE REALLY CAPTURED THE ESSENCE OF OUR--
LENS FLARES, MOTHER[redacted]
OWND
ARE YOU STILL HERE?
I JUST WANTED TO SHOW YOU SOMETHING BEFORE I LEFT.
SEE THIS LOGO? THERE'S TOO MUCH SPACE BETWEEN THESE TWO LETTERS. IT'S CALLED "BAD KERNING".
OH YEAH, NOW THAT YOU MENTION IT, I DO.
WAIT, IT'S HERE TOO... AND HERE... AND *HERE*...
IT'S EVERYWHERE!
NOW I CAN GO.

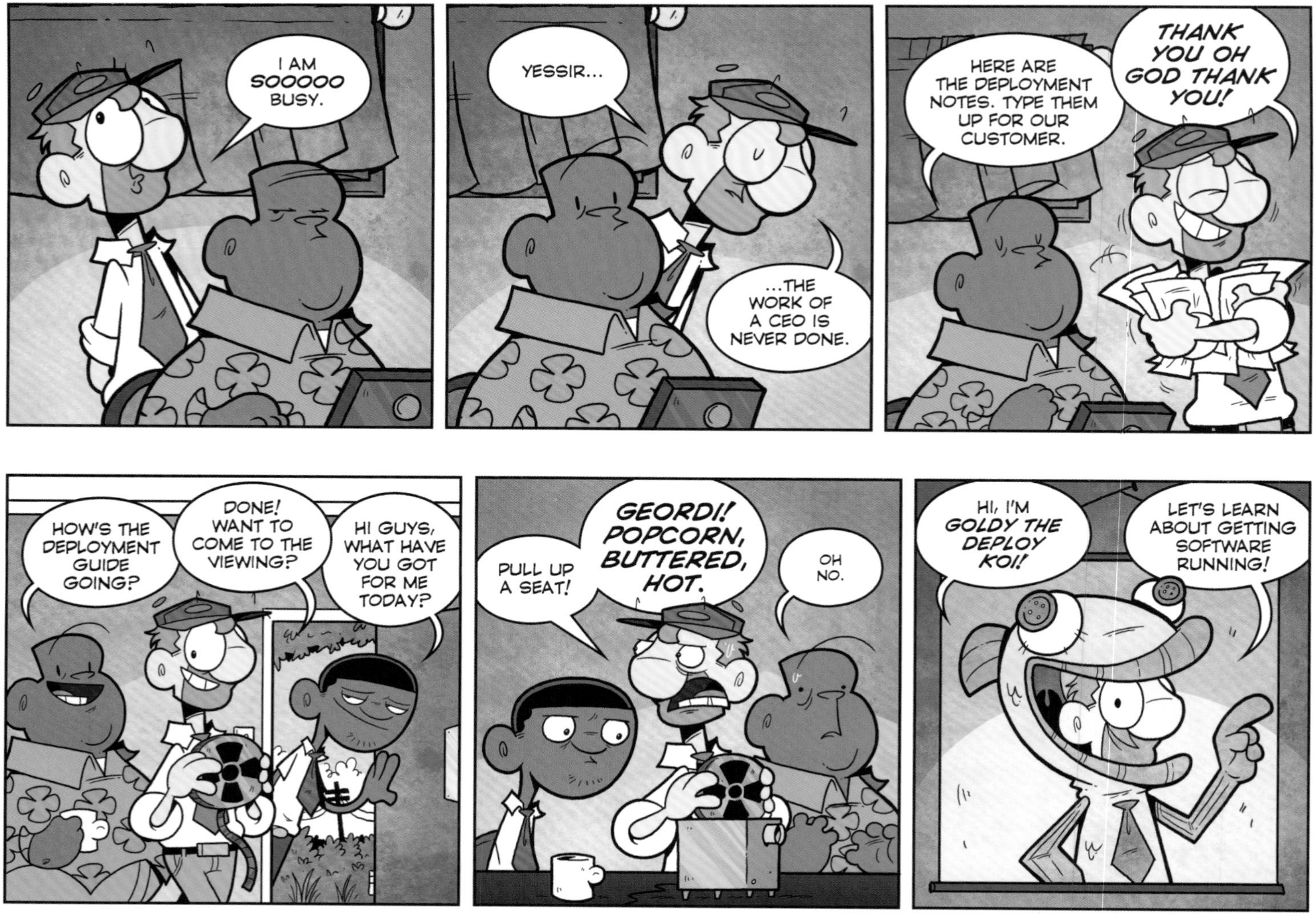
I AM SOOOOO BUSY.
YESSIR...
...THE WORK OF A CEO IS NEVER DONE.
HERE ARE THE DEPLOYMENT NOTES. TYPE THEM UP FOR OUR CUSTOMER.
THANK YOU OH GOD THANK YOU!
HOW'S THE DEPLOYMENT GUIDE GOING?
DONE! WANT TO COME TO THE VIEWING?
HI GUYS, WHAT HAVE YOU GOT FOR ME TODAY?
PULL UP A SEAT!
GEORDI! POPCORN, BUTTERED, HOT.
OH NO.
HI, I'M GOLDY THE DEPLOY KOI!
LET'S LEARN ABOUT GETTING SOFTWARE RUNNING!

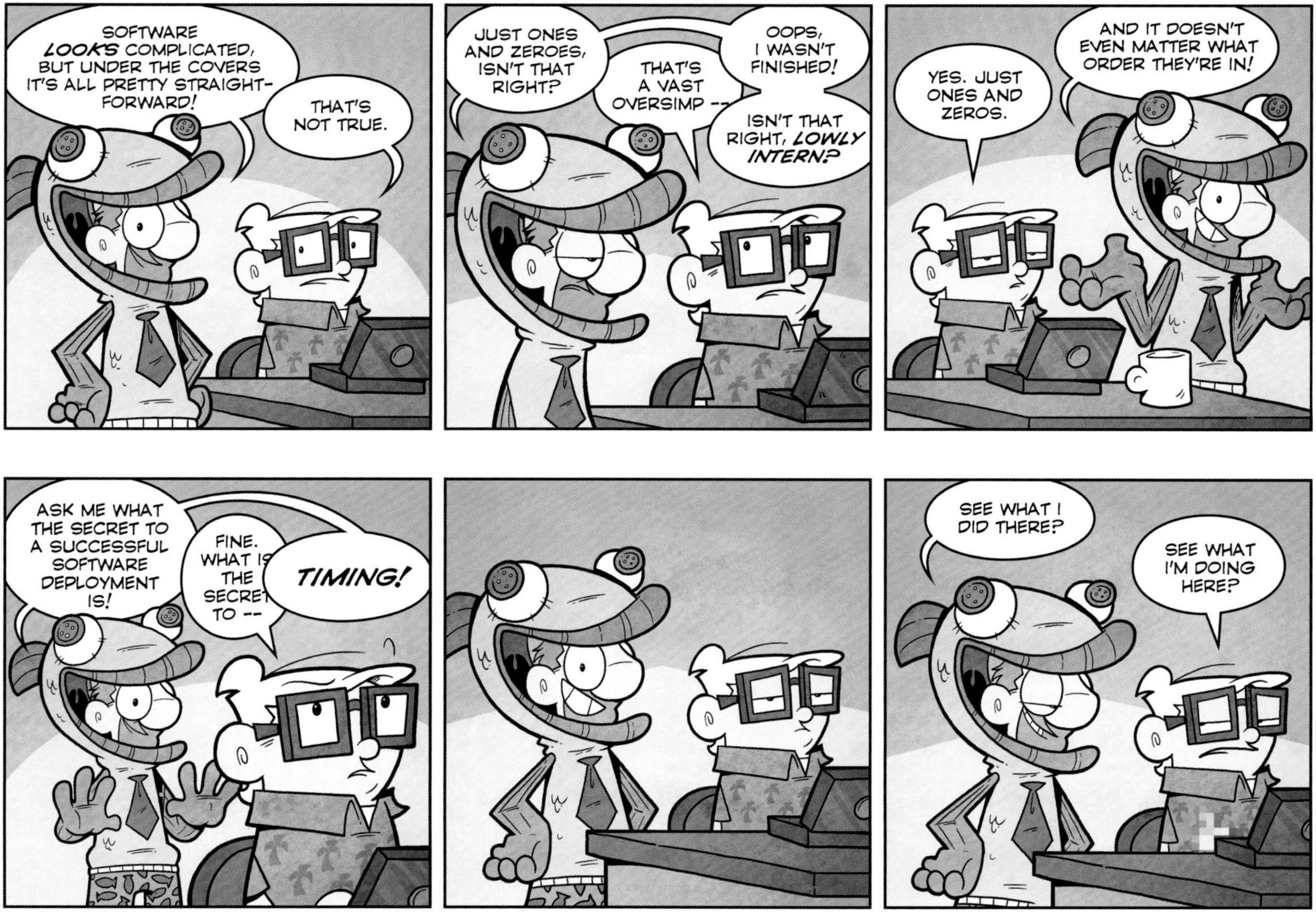
SOFTWARE *LOOKS* COMPLICATED, BUT UNDER THE COVERS IT'S ALL PRETTY STRAIGHT-FORWARD!
THAT'S NOT TRUE.
JUST ONES AND ZEROES, ISN'T THAT RIGHT?
THAT'S A VAST OVERSIMP --
OOPS, I WASN'T FINISHED!
ISN'T THAT RIGHT, *LOWLY INTERN?*
YES. JUST ONES AND ZEROS.
AND IT DOESN'T EVEN MATTER WHAT ORDER THEY'RE IN!
ASK ME WHAT THE SECRET TO A SUCCESSFUL SOFTWARE DEPLOYMENT IS!
FINE. WHAT IS THE SECRET TO --
TIMING!
SEE WHAT I DID THERE?
SEE WHAT I'M DOING HERE?

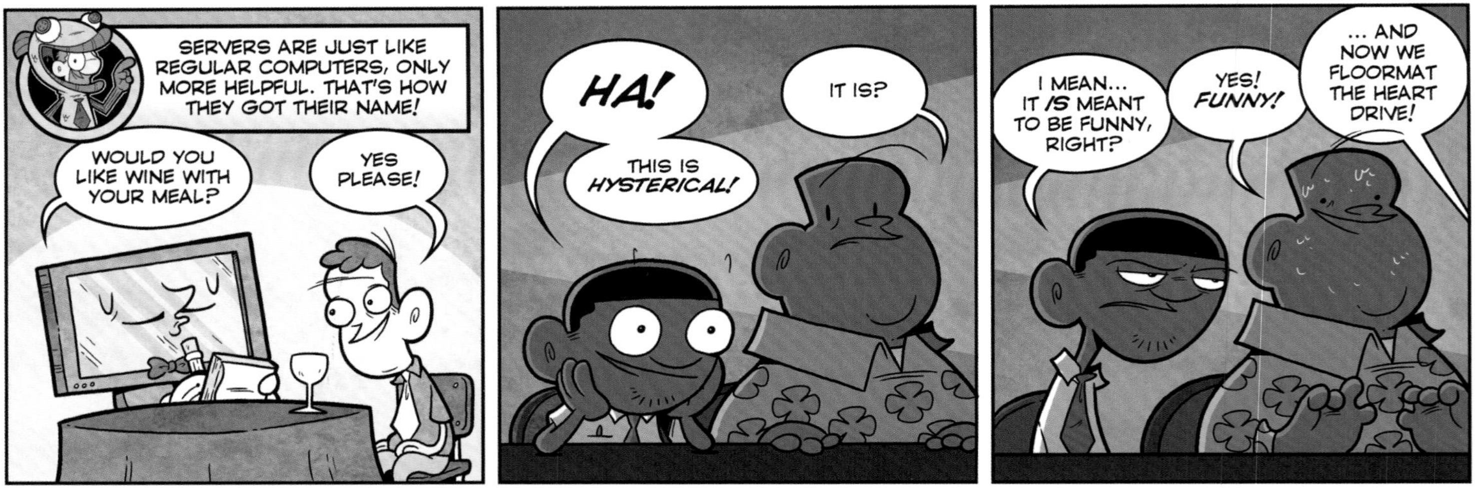
SERVERS ARE JUST LIKE REGULAR COMPUTERS, ONLY MORE HELPFUL. THAT'S HOW THEY GOT THEIR NAME!
WOULD YOU LIKE WINE WITH YOUR MEAL?
YES PLEASE!
HA!
THIS IS HYSTERICAL!
IT IS?
I MEAN... IT IS MEANT TO BE FUNNY, RIGHT?
YES! FUNNY!
... AND NOW WE FLOORMAT THE HEART DRIVE!

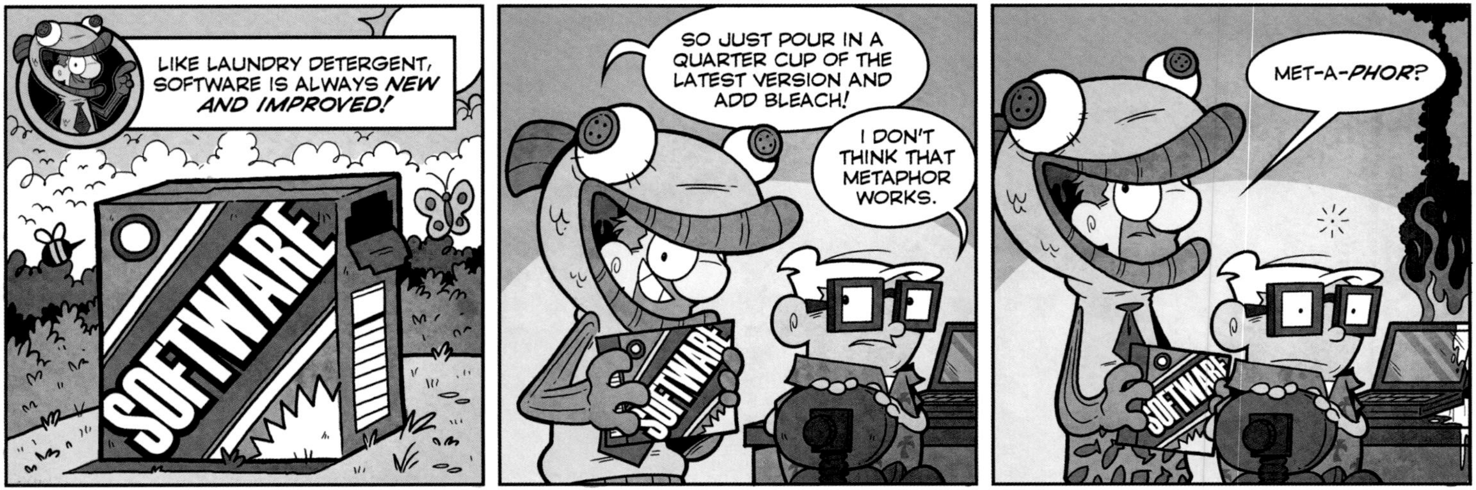
LIKE LAUNDRY DETERGENT, SOFTWARE IS ALWAYS NEW AND IMPROVED!
SOFTWARE
SO JUST POUR IN A QUARTER CUP OF THE LATEST VERSION AND ADD BLEACH!
I DON'T THINK THAT METAPHOR WORKS.
SOFTWARE
MET-A-PHOR?
SOFTWARE

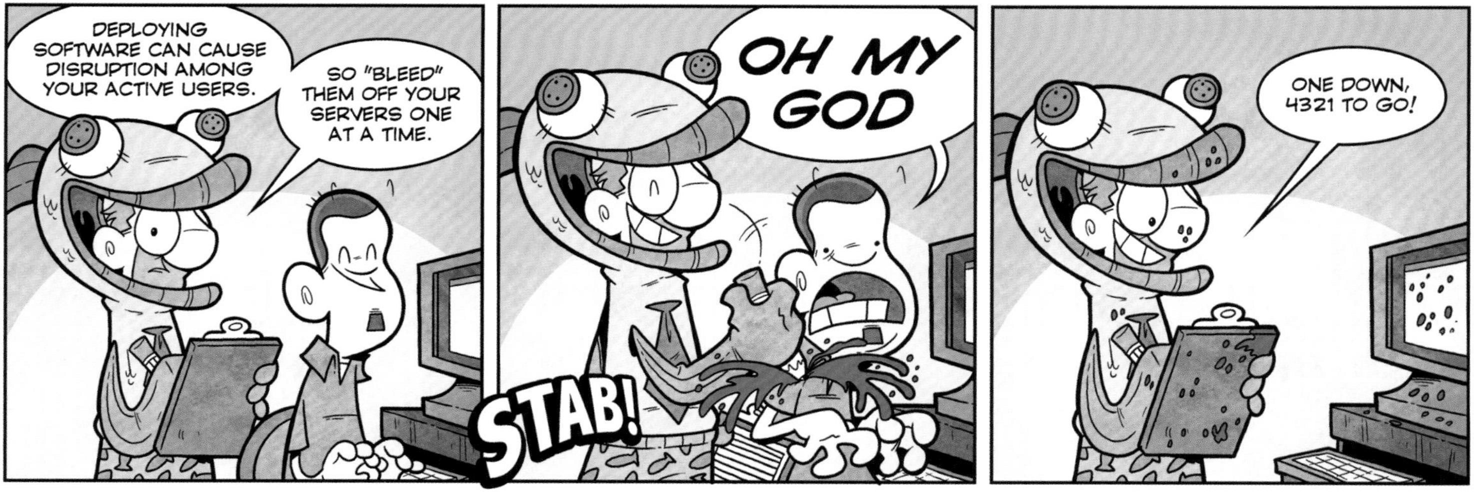
DEPLOYING SOFTWARE CAN CAUSE DISRUPTION AMONG YOUR ACTIVE USERS.
SO "BLEED" THEM OFF YOUR SERVERS ONE AT A TIME.
OH MY GOD
STAB!
ONE DOWN, 4321 TO GO!

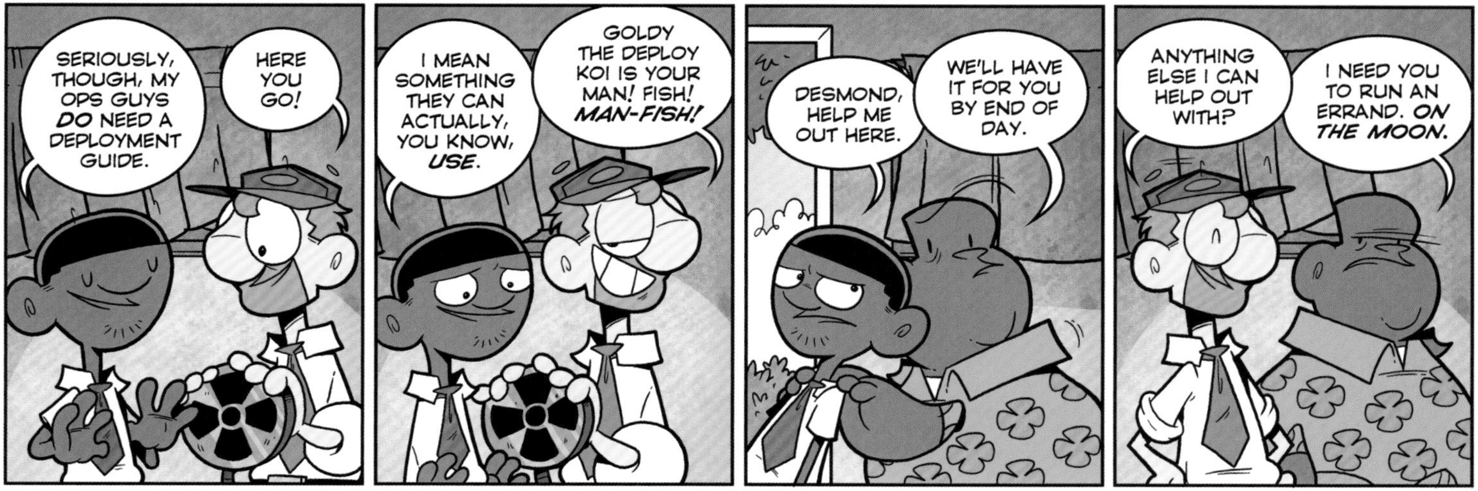
SERIOUSLY, THOUGH, MY OPS GUYS DO NEED A DEPLOYMENT GUIDE.
HERE YOU GO!
I MEAN SOMETHING THEY CAN ACTUALLY, YOU KNOW, USE.
GOLDY THE DEPLOY KOI IS YOUR MAN! FISH! MAN-FISH!
DESMOND, HELP ME OUT HERE.
WE'LL HAVE IT FOR YOU BY END OF DAY.
ANYTHING ELSE I CAN HELP OUT WITH?
I NEED YOU TO RUN AN ERRAND. ON THE MOON.

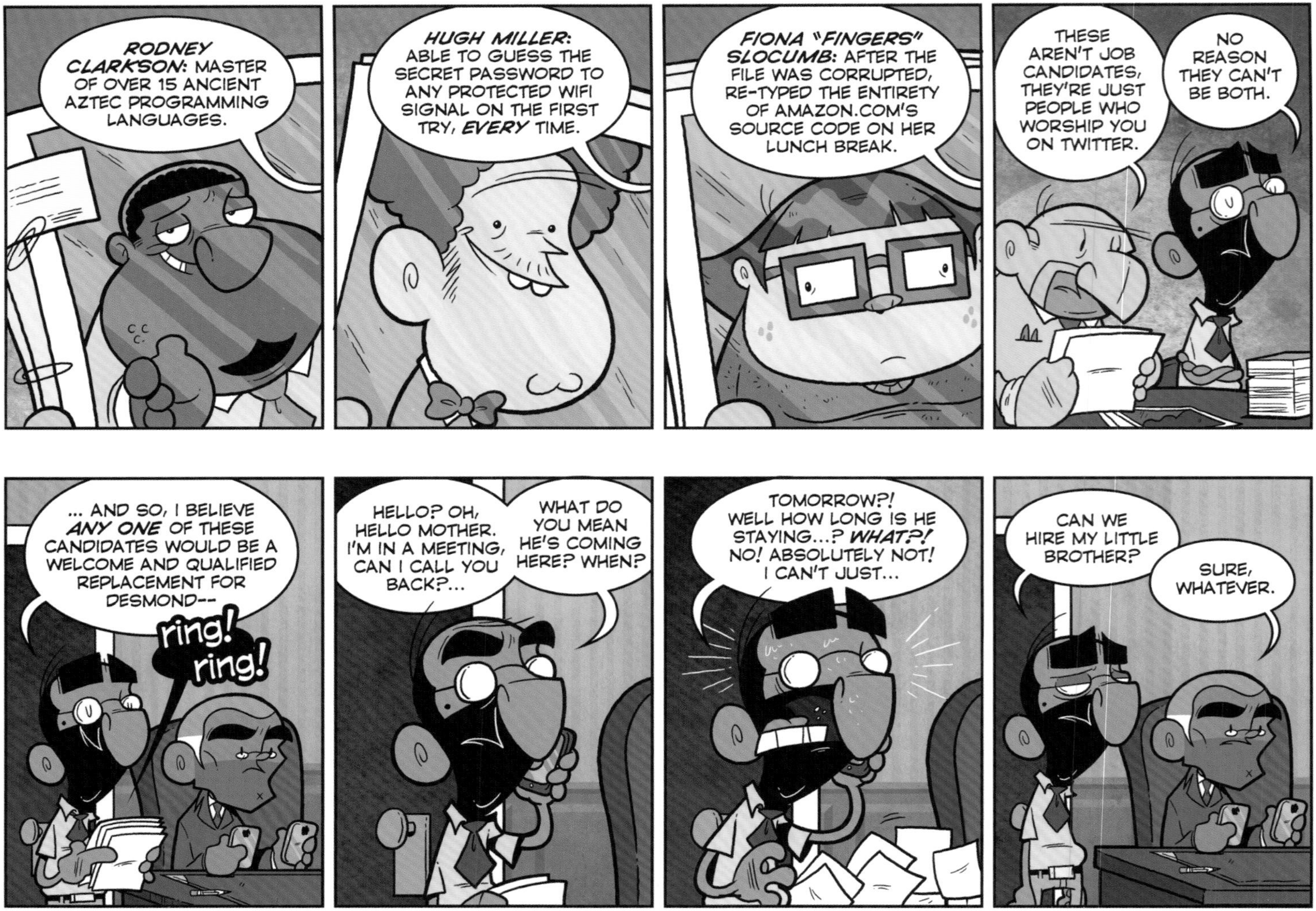
RODNEY CLARKSON: MASTER OF OVER 15 ANCIENT AZTEC PROGRAMMING LANGUAGES.
HUGH MILLER: ABLE TO GUESS THE SECRET PASSWORD TO ANY PROTECTED WIFI SIGNAL ON THE FIRST TRY, EVERY TIME.
FIONA "FINGERS" SLOCUMB: AFTER THE FILE WAS CORRUPTED, RE-TYPED THE ENTIRETY OF AMAZON.COM'S SOURCE CODE ON HER LUNCH BREAK.
THESE AREN'T JOB CANDIDATES, THEY'RE JUST PEOPLE WHO WORSHIP YOU ON TWITTER.
NO REASON THEY CAN'T BE BOTH.
... AND SO, I BELIEVE ANY ONE OF THESE CANDIDATES WOULD BE A WELCOME AND QUALIFIED REPLACEMENT FOR DESMOND--
ring! ring!
HELLO? OH, HELLO MOTHER. I'M IN A MEETING, CAN I CALL YOU BACK?...
WHAT DO YOU MEAN HE'S COMING HERE? WHEN?
TOMORROW?! WELL HOW LONG IS HE STAYING...? WHAT?! NO! ABSOLUTELY NOT! I CAN'T JUST...
CAN WE HIRE MY LITTLE BROTHER?
SURE, WHATEVER.

UPGRADE PATH

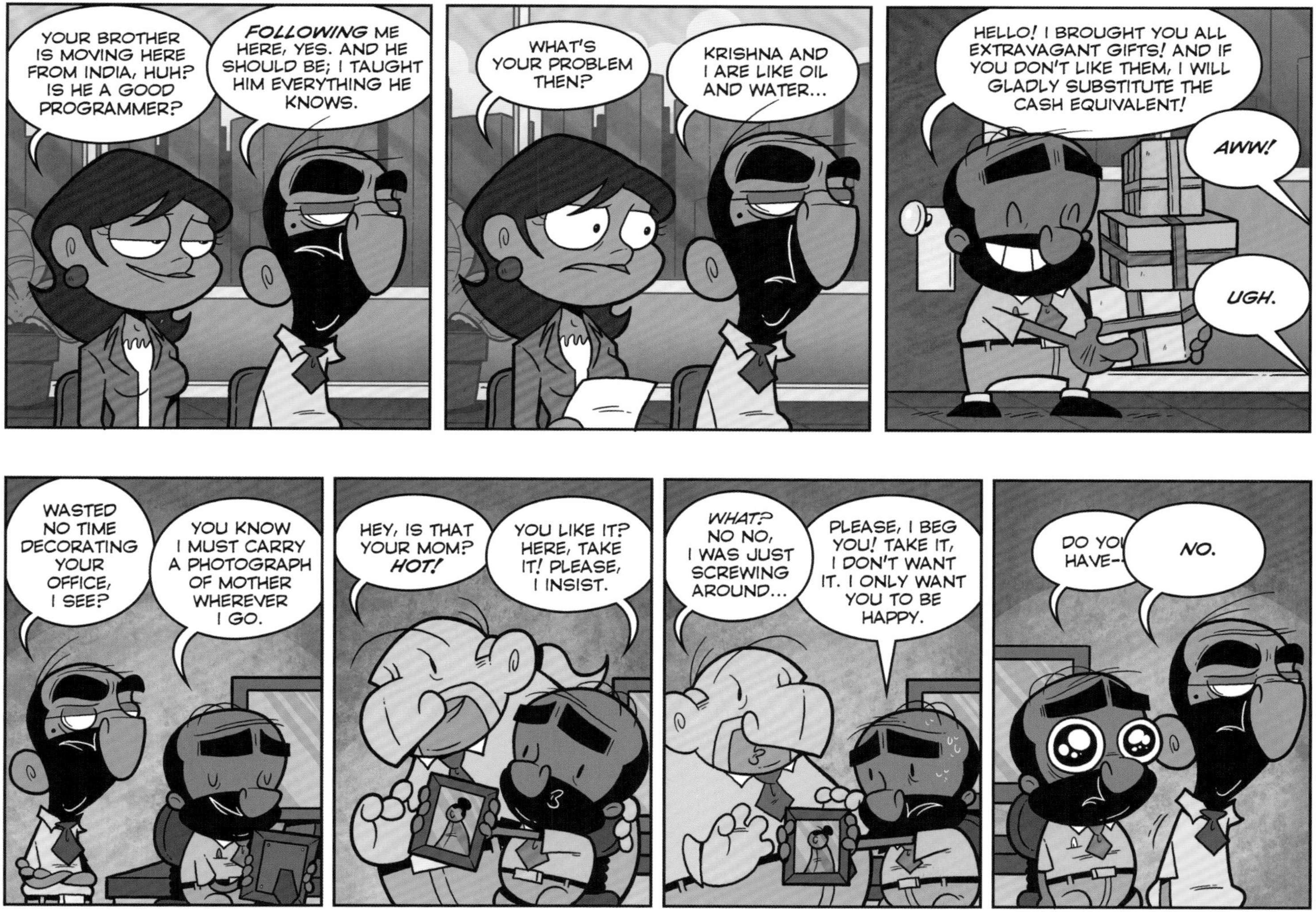
YOUR BROTHER IS MOVING HERE FROM INDIA, HUH? IS HE A GOOD PROGRAMMER?
FOLLOWING ME HERE, YES. AND HE SHOULD BE; I TAUGHT HIM EVERYTHING HE KNOWS.
WHAT'S YOUR PROBLEM THEN?
KRISHNA AND I ARE LIKE OIL AND WATER...
HELLO! I BROUGHT YOU ALL EXTRAVAGANT GIFTS! AND IF YOU DON'T LIKE THEM, I WILL GLADLY SUBSTITUTE THE CASH EQUIVALENT!
AWW!
UGH.
WASTED NO TIME DECORATING YOUR OFFICE, I SEE?
YOU KNOW I MUST CARRY A PHOTOGRAPH OF MOTHER WHEREVER I GO.
HEY, IS THAT YOUR MOM? *HOT!*
YOU LIKE IT? HERE, TAKE IT! PLEASE, I INSIST.
WHAT? NO NO, I WAS JUST SCREWING AROUND...
PLEASE, I BEG YOU! TAKE IT, I DON'T WANT IT. I ONLY WANT YOU TO BE HAPPY.
DO YO HAVE--
NO.

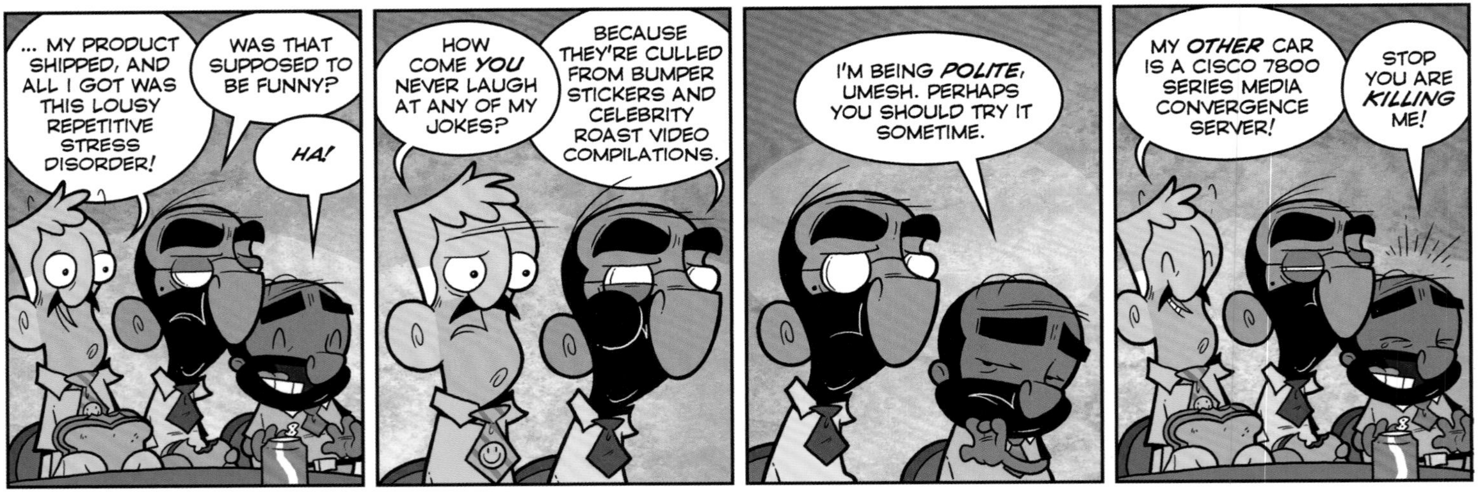
... MY PRODUCT SHIPPED, AND ALL I GOT WAS THIS LOUSY REPETITIVE STRESS DISORDER!
WAS THAT SUPPOSED TO BE FUNNY?
HA!
HOW COME YOU NEVER LAUGH AT ANY OF MY JOKES?
BECAUSE THEY'RE CULLED FROM BUMPER STICKERS AND CELEBRITY ROAST VIDEO COMPILATIONS.
I'M BEING POLITE, UMESH. PERHAPS YOU SHOULD TRY IT SOMETIME.
MY OTHER CAR IS A CISCO 7800 SERIES MEDIA CONVERGENCE SERVER!
STOP YOU ARE KILLING ME!

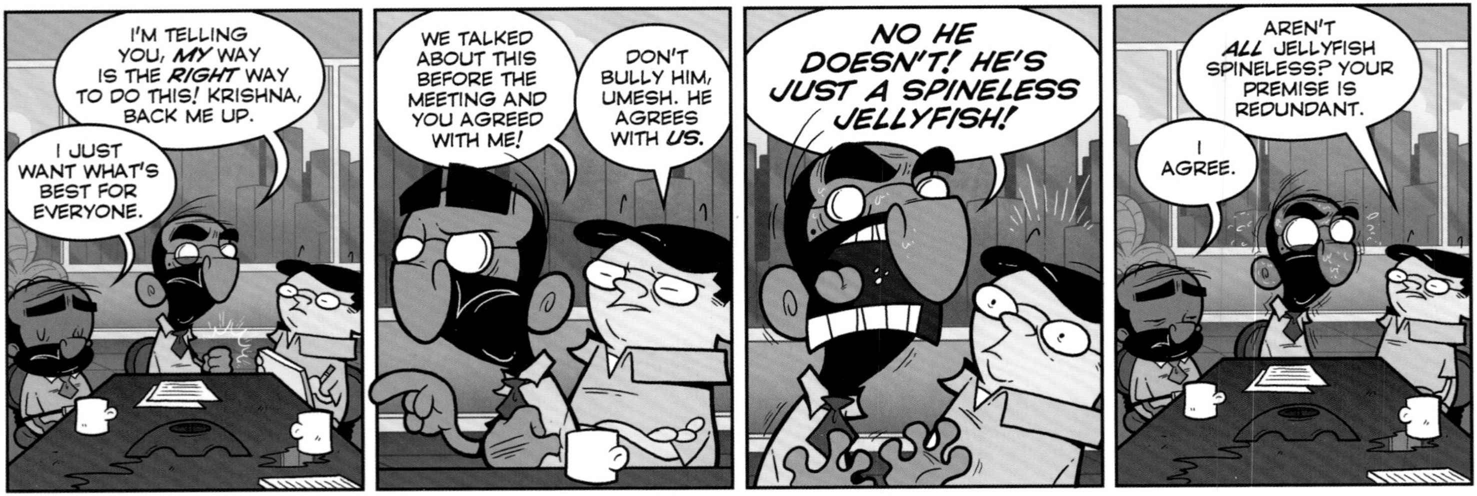
I'M TELLING YOU, MY WAY IS THE RIGHT WAY TO DO THIS! KRISHNA, BACK ME UP.
I JUST WANT WHAT'S BEST FOR EVERYONE.
WE TALKED ABOUT THIS BEFORE THE MEETING AND YOU AGREED WITH ME!
DON'T BULLY HIM, UMESH. HE AGREES WITH US.
NO HE DOESN'T! HE'S JUST A SPINELESS JELLYFISH!
AREN'T ALL JELLYFISH SPINELESS? YOUR PREMISE IS REDUNDANT.
I AGREE.

UPGRADE PATH

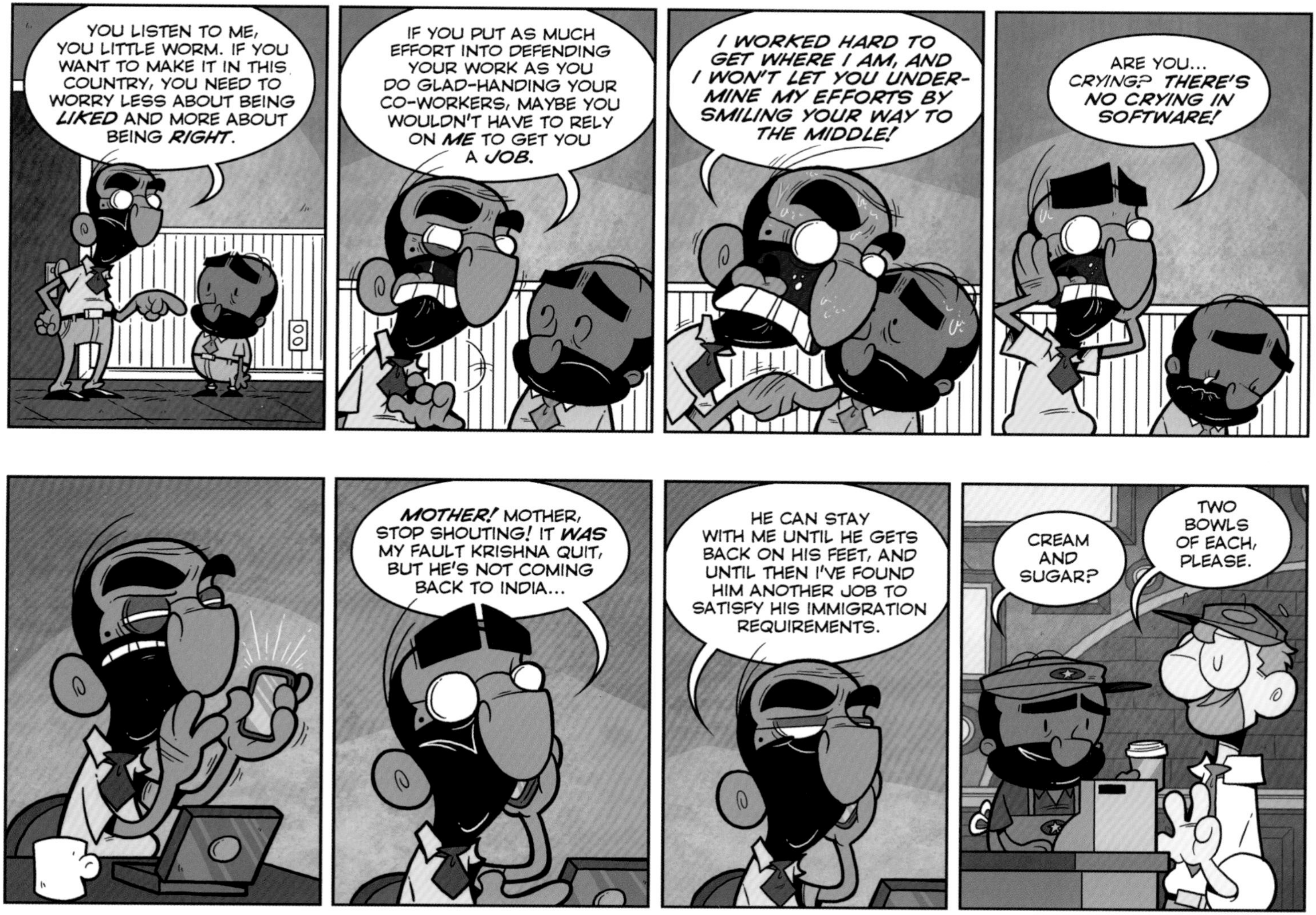
YOU LISTEN TO ME, YOU LITTLE WORM. IF YOU WANT TO MAKE IT IN THIS COUNTRY, YOU NEED TO WORRY LESS ABOUT BEING *LIKED* AND MORE ABOUT BEING *RIGHT*.
IF YOU PUT AS MUCH EFFORT INTO DEFENDING YOUR WORK AS YOU DO GLAD-HANDING YOUR CO-WORKERS, MAYBE YOU WOULDN'T HAVE TO RELY ON *ME* TO GET YOU A *JOB*.
I WORKED HARD TO GET WHERE I AM, AND I WON'T LET YOU UNDER-MINE MY EFFORTS BY SMILING YOUR WAY TO THE MIDDLE!
ARE YOU... CRYING? *THERE'S NO CRYING IN SOFTWARE!*
MOTHER! MOTHER, STOP SHOUTING! IT *WAS* MY FAULT KRISHNA QUIT, BUT HE'S NOT COMING BACK TO INDIA...
HE CAN STAY WITH ME UNTIL HE GETS BACK ON HIS FEET, AND UNTIL THEN I'VE FOUND HIM ANOTHER JOB TO SATISFY HIS IMMIGRATION REQUIREMENTS.
CREAM AND SUGAR?
TWO BOWLS OF EACH, PLEASE.

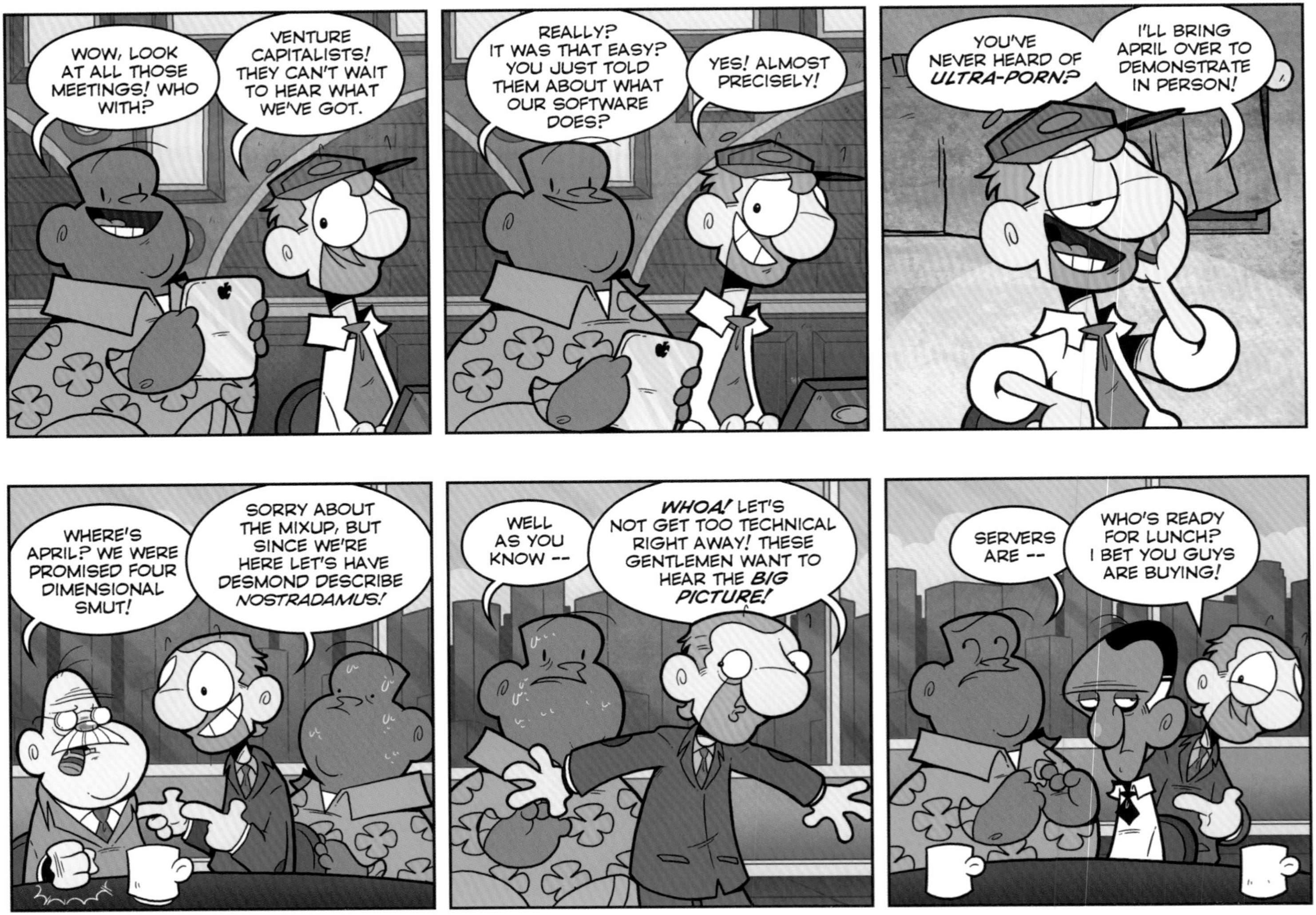
WOW, LOOK AT ALL THOSE MEETINGS! WHO WITH?
VENTURE CAPITALISTS! THEY CAN'T WAIT TO HEAR WHAT WE'VE GOT.
REALLY? IT WAS THAT EASY? YOU JUST TOLD THEM ABOUT WHAT OUR SOFTWARE DOES?
YES! ALMOST PRECISELY!
YOU'VE NEVER HEARD OF *ULTRA-PORN?*
I'LL BRING APRIL OVER TO DEMONSTRATE IN PERSON!
WHERE'S APRIL? WE WERE PROMISED FOUR DIMENSIONAL SMUT!
SORRY ABOUT THE MIXUP, BUT SINCE WE'RE HERE LET'S HAVE DESMOND DESCRIBE *NOSTRADAMUS!*
WELL AS YOU KNOW --
WHOA! LET'S NOT GET TOO TECHNICAL RIGHT AWAY! THESE GENTLEMEN WANT TO HEAR THE *BIG PICTURE!*
SERVERS ARE --
WHO'S READY FOR LUNCH? I BET YOU GUYS ARE BUYING!

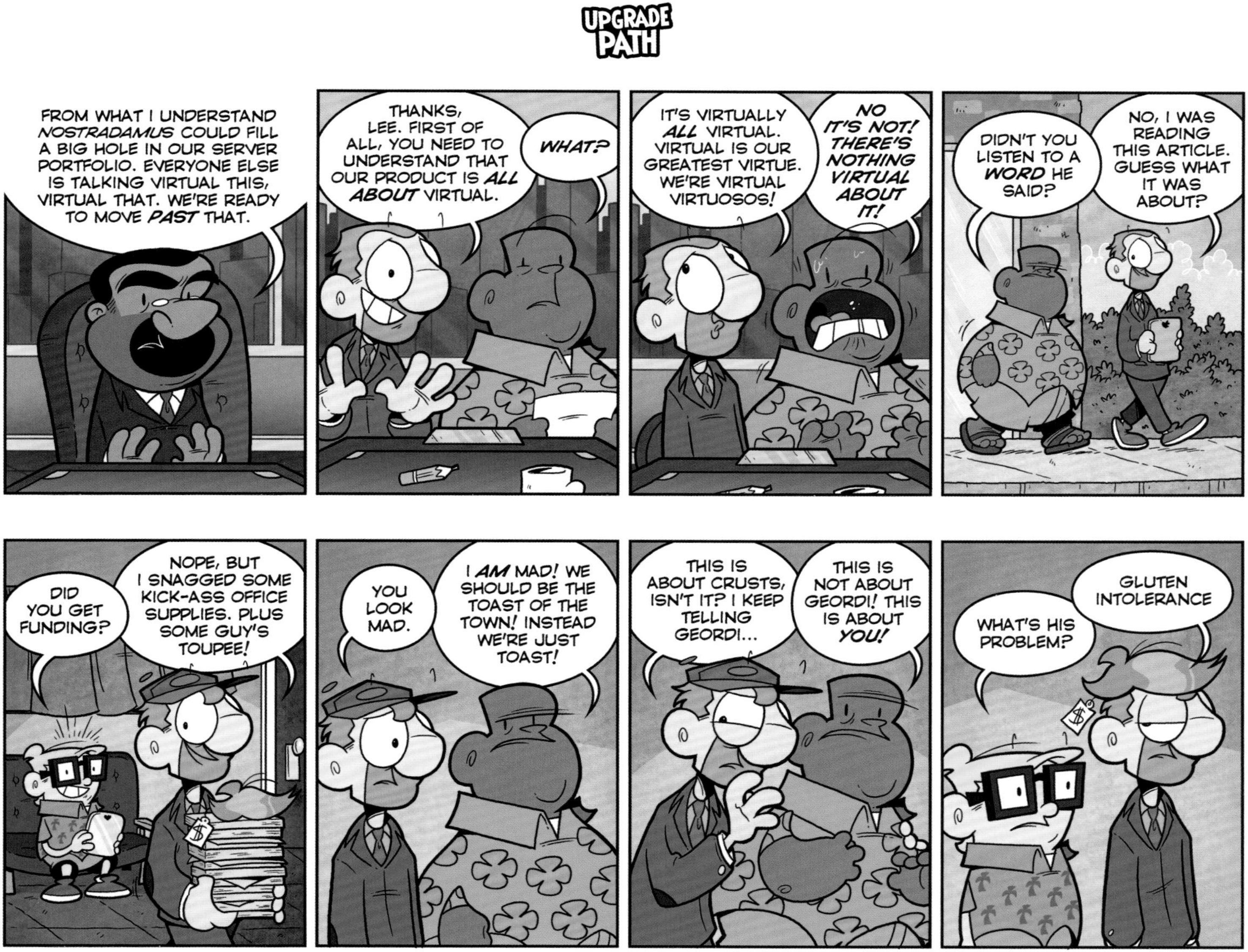
UPGRADE PATH
FROM WHAT I UNDERSTAND NOSTRADAMUS COULD FILL A BIG HOLE IN OUR SERVER PORTFOLIO. EVERYONE ELSE IS TALKING VIRTUAL THIS, VIRTUAL THAT. WE'RE READY TO MOVE PAST THAT.
THANKS, LEE. FIRST OF ALL, YOU NEED TO UNDERSTAND THAT OUR PRODUCT IS ALL ABOUT VIRTUAL.
WHAT?
IT'S VIRTUALLY ALL VIRTUAL. VIRTUAL IS OUR GREATEST VIRTUE. WE'RE VIRTUAL VIRTUOSOS!
NO IT'S NOT! THERE'S NOTHING VIRTUAL ABOUT IT!
DIDN'T YOU LISTEN TO A WORD HE SAID?
NO, I WAS READING THIS ARTICLE. GUESS WHAT IT WAS ABOUT?
DID YOU GET FUNDING?
NOPE, BUT I SNAGGED SOME KICK-ASS OFFICE SUPPLIES. PLUS SOME GUY'S TOUPEE!
YOU LOOK MAD.
I AM MAD! WE SHOULD BE THE TOAST OF THE TOWN! INSTEAD WE'RE JUST TOAST!
THIS IS ABOUT CRUSTS, ISN'T IT? I KEEP TELLING GEORDI...
THIS IS NOT ABOUT GEORDI! THIS IS ABOUT YOU!
WHAT'S HIS PROBLEM?
GLUTEN INTOLERANCE

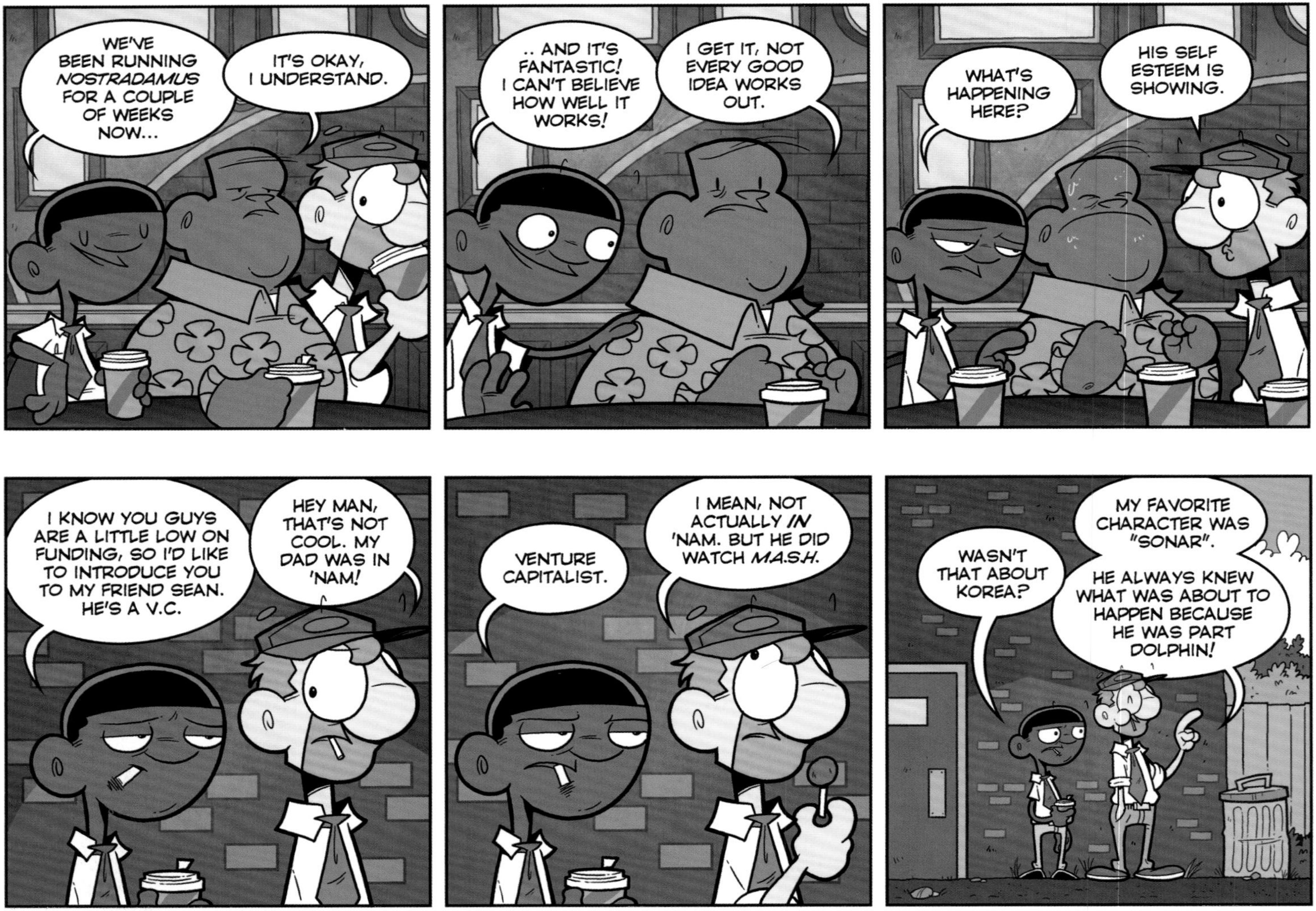
WE'VE BEEN RUNNING *NOSTRADAMUS* FOR A COUPLE OF WEEKS NOW...
IT'S OKAY, I UNDERSTAND.
.. AND IT'S FANTASTIC! I CAN'T BELIEVE HOW WELL IT WORKS!
I GET IT, NOT EVERY GOOD IDEA WORKS OUT.
WHAT'S HAPPENING HERE?
HIS SELF ESTEEM IS SHOWING.
I KNOW YOU GUYS ARE A LITTLE LOW ON FUNDING, SO I'D LIKE TO INTRODUCE YOU TO MY FRIEND SEAN. HE'S A V.C.
HEY MAN, THAT'S NOT COOL. MY DAD WAS IN 'NAM!
VENTURE CAPITALIST.
I MEAN, NOT ACTUALLY *IN* 'NAM. BUT HE DID WATCH *M.A.S.H.*
WASN'T THAT ABOUT KOREA?
MY FAVORITE CHARACTER WAS "SONAR".
HE ALWAYS KNEW WHAT WAS ABOUT TO HAPPEN BECAUSE HE WAS PART DOLPHIN!

UPGRADE PATH

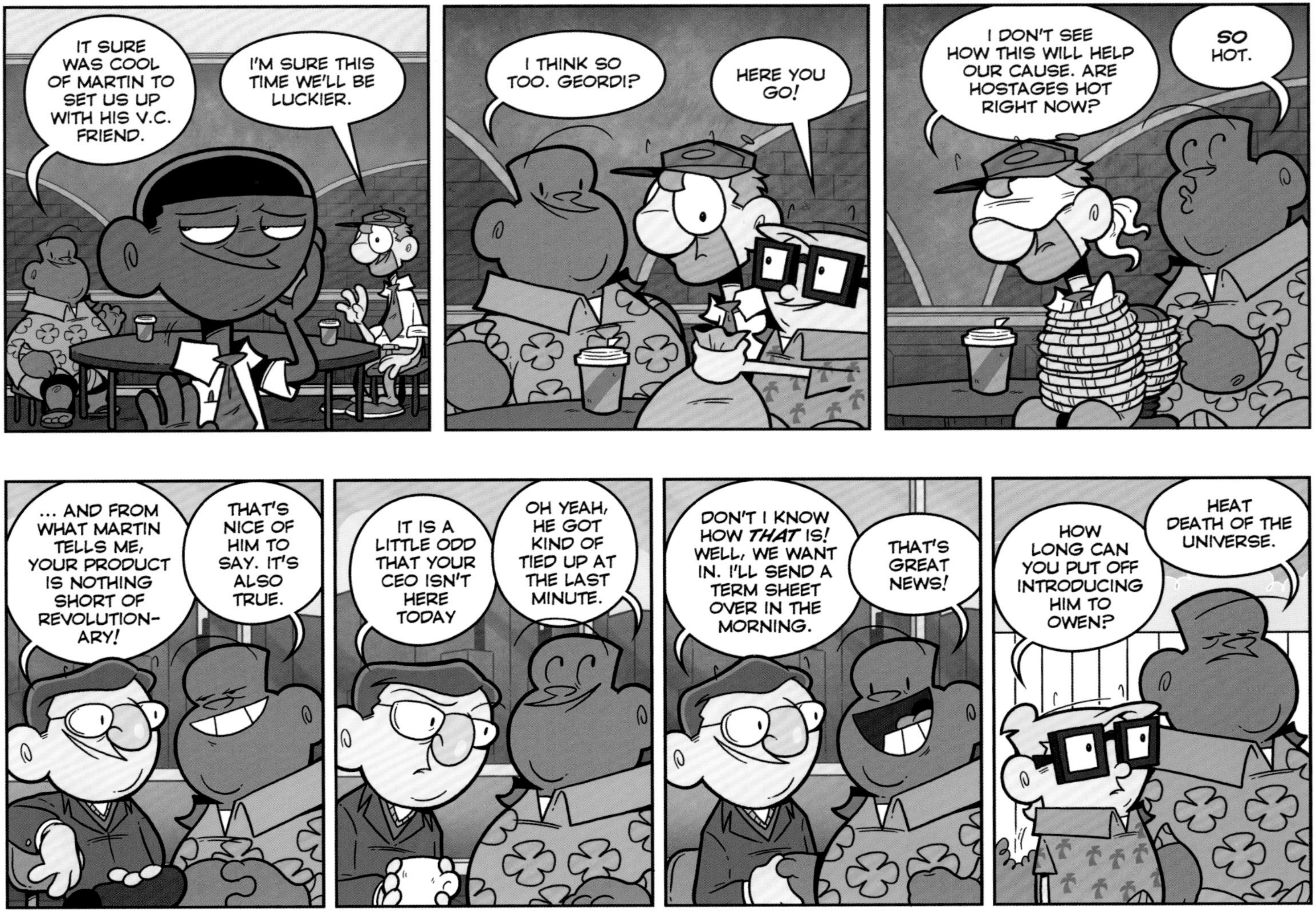
IT SURE WAS COOL OF MARTIN TO SET US UP WITH HIS V.C. FRIEND.
I'M SURE THIS TIME WE'LL BE LUCKIER.
I THINK SO TOO. GEORDI?
HERE YOU GO!
I DON'T SEE HOW THIS WILL HELP OUR CAUSE. ARE HOSTAGES HOT RIGHT NOW?
SO HOT.
... AND FROM WHAT MARTIN TELLS ME, YOUR PRODUCT IS NOTHING SHORT OF REVOLUTION-ARY!
THAT'S NICE OF HIM TO SAY. IT'S ALSO TRUE.
IT IS A LITTLE ODD THAT YOUR CEO ISN'T HERE TODAY
OH YEAH, HE GOT KIND OF TIED UP AT THE LAST MINUTE.
DON'T I KNOW HOW THAT IS! WELL, WE WANT IN. I'LL SEND A TERM SHEET OVER IN THE MORNING.
THAT'S GREAT NEWS!
HOW LONG CAN YOU PUT OFF INTRODUCING HIM TO OWEN?
HEAT DEATH OF THE UNIVERSE.

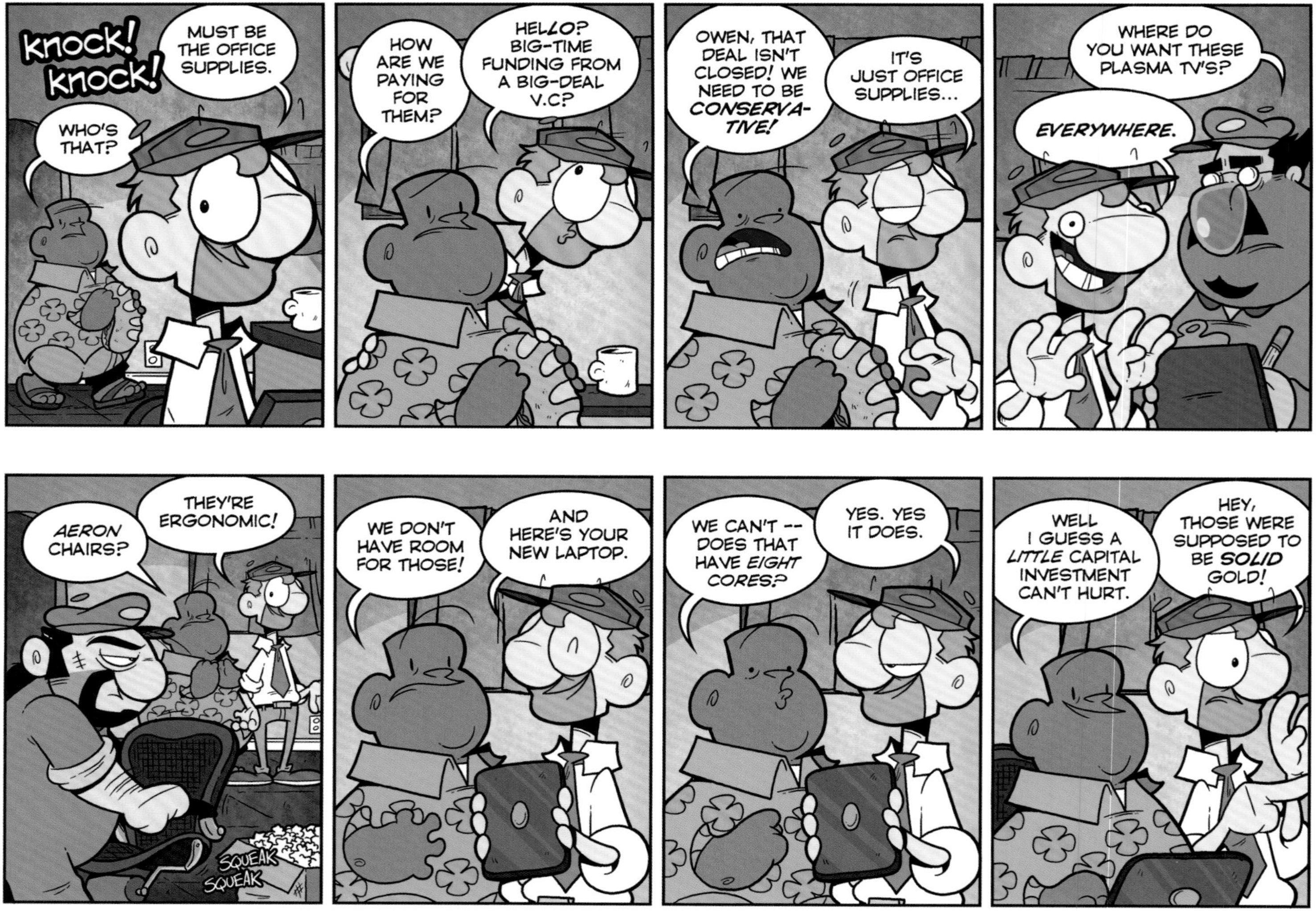
knock! knock!
MUST BE THE OFFICE SUPPLIES.
WHO'S THAT?
HOW ARE WE PAYING FOR THEM?
HELLO? BIG-TIME FUNDING FROM A BIG-DEAL V.C?
OWEN, THAT DEAL ISN'T CLOSED! WE NEED TO BE CONSERVA-TIVE!
IT'S JUST OFFICE SUPPLIES...
WHERE DO YOU WANT THESE PLASMA TV'S?
EVERYWHERE.
AERON CHAIRS?
THEY'RE ERGONOMIC!
SQUEAK SQUEAK
WE DON'T HAVE ROOM FOR THOSE!
AND HERE'S YOUR NEW LAPTOP.
WE CAN'T -- DOES THAT HAVE EIGHT CORES?
YES. YES IT DOES.
WELL I GUESS A LITTLE CAPITAL INVESTMENT CAN'T HURT.
HEY, THOSE WERE SUPPOSED TO BE SOLID GOLD!

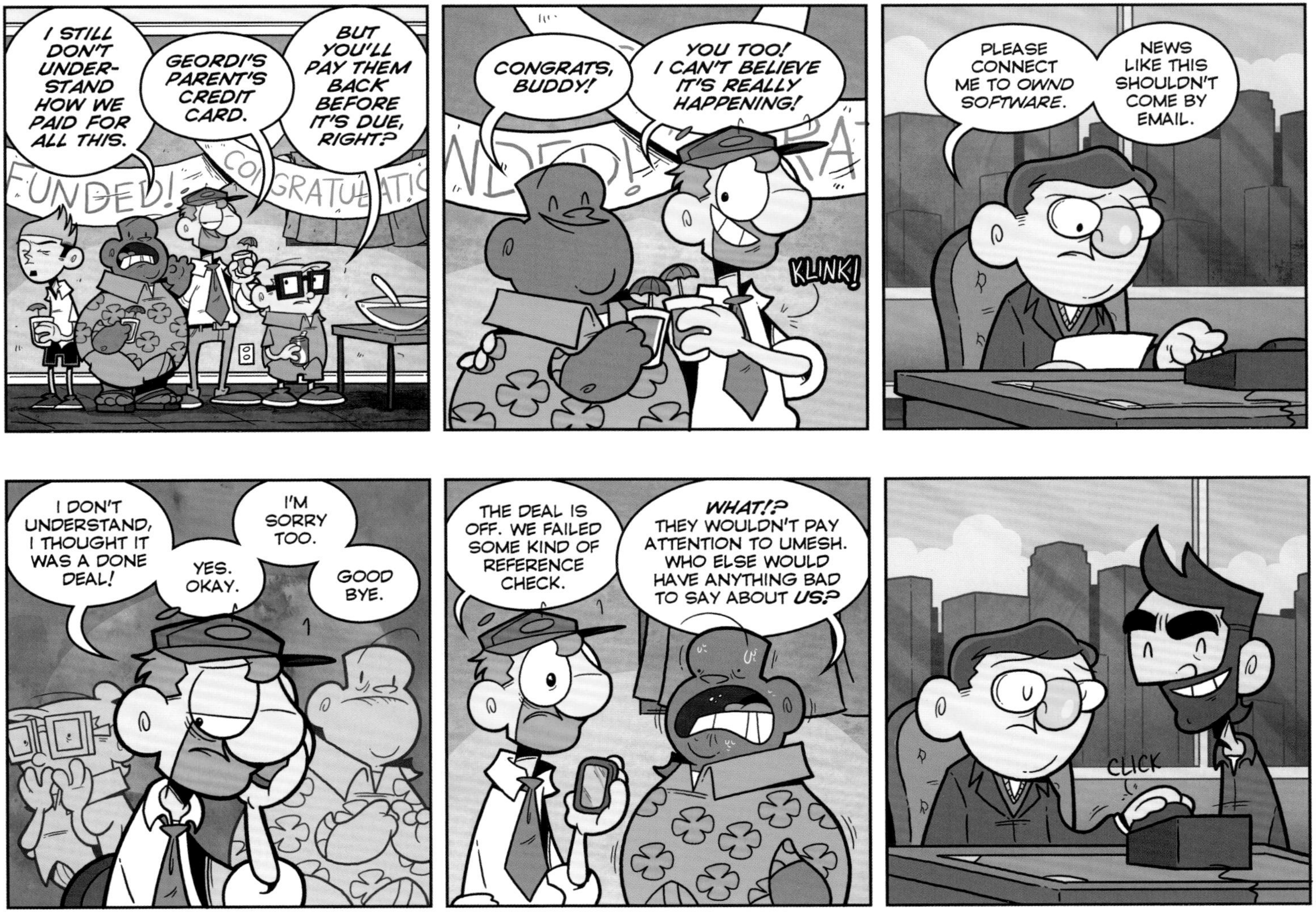
I STILL DON'T UNDERSTAND HOW WE PAID FOR ALL THIS.
GEORDI'S PARENT'S CREDIT CARD.
BUT YOU'LL PAY THEM BACK BEFORE IT'S DUE, RIGHT?
FUNDED!
CONGRATULATIO
CONGRATS, BUDDY!
YOU TOO! I CAN'T BELIEVE IT'S REALLY HAPPENING!
KLINK!
PLEASE CONNECT ME TO OWND SOFTWARE.
NEWS LIKE THIS SHOULDN'T COME BY EMAIL.
I DON'T UNDERSTAND, I THOUGHT IT WAS A DONE DEAL!
YES. OKAY.
I'M SORRY TOO.
GOOD BYE.
THE DEAL IS OFF. WE FAILED SOME KIND OF REFERENCE CHECK.
WHAT!? THEY WOULDN'T PAY ATTENTION TO UMESH. WHO ELSE WOULD HAVE ANYTHING BAD TO SAY ABOUT US?
CLICK

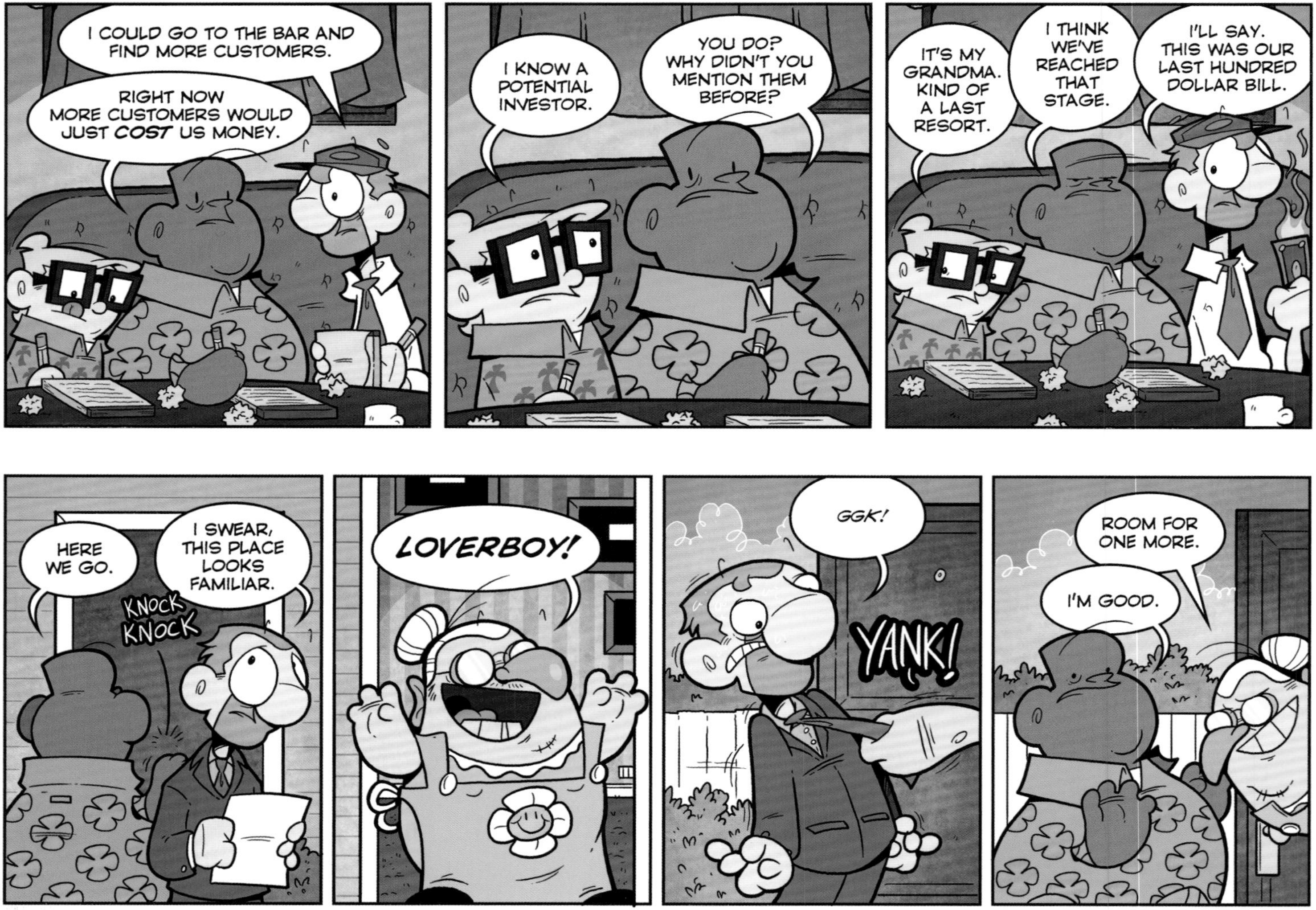
I COULD GO TO THE BAR AND FIND MORE CUSTOMERS.
RIGHT NOW MORE CUSTOMERS WOULD JUST *COST* US MONEY.
I KNOW A POTENTIAL INVESTOR.
YOU DO? WHY DIDN'T YOU MENTION THEM BEFORE?
IT'S MY GRANDMA. KIND OF A LAST RESORT.
I THINK WE'VE REACHED THAT STAGE.
I'LL SAY. THIS WAS OUR LAST HUNDRED DOLLAR BILL.
HERE WE GO.
I SWEAR, THIS PLACE LOOKS FAMILIAR.
KNOCK KNOCK
LOVERBOY!
GGK!
YANK!
ROOM FOR ONE MORE.
I'M GOOD.

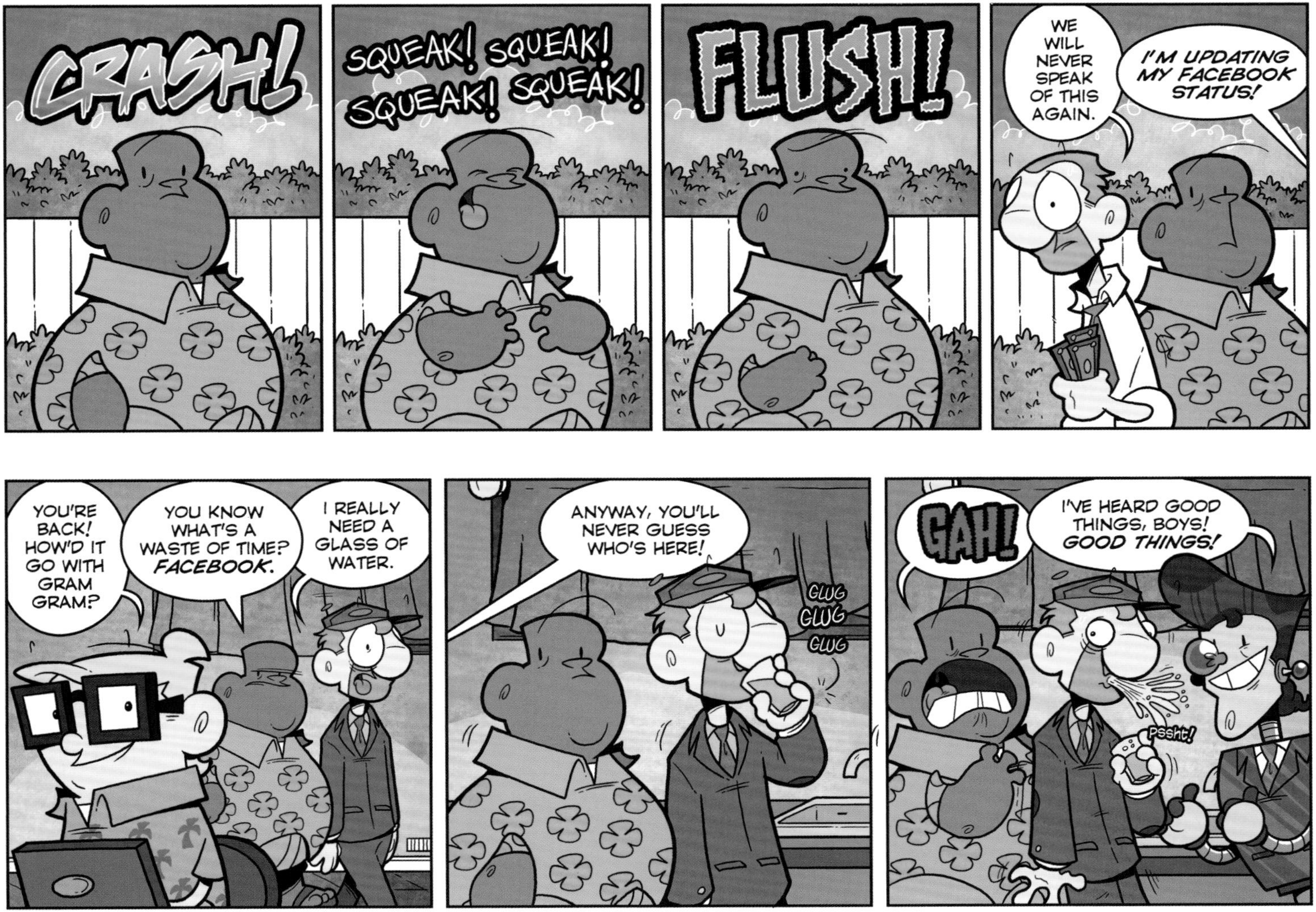
CRASH!
SQUEAK! SQUEAK! SQUEAK! SQUEAK!
FLUSH!
WE WILL NEVER SPEAK OF THIS AGAIN.
I'M UPDATING MY FACEBOOK STATUS!
YOU'RE BACK! HOW'D IT GO WITH GRAM GRAM?
YOU KNOW WHAT'S A WASTE OF TIME? FACEBOOK.
I REALLY NEED A GLASS OF WATER.
ANYWAY, YOU'LL NEVER GUESS WHO'S HERE!
GLUG GLUG GLUG
GAH!
I'VE HEARD GOOD THINGS, BOYS! GOOD THINGS!
PSSHT!

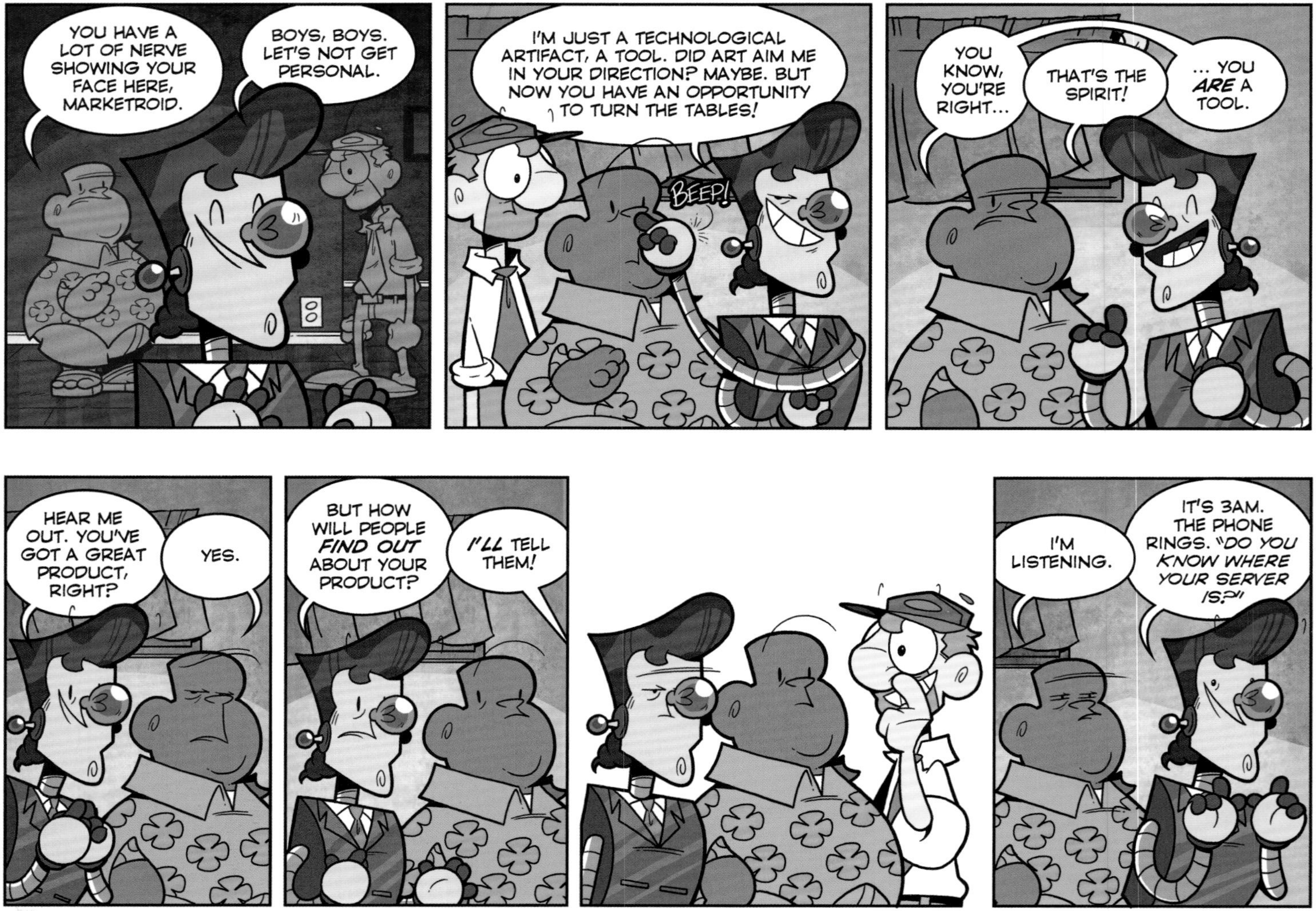
YOU HAVE A LOT OF NERVE SHOWING YOUR FACE HERE, MARKETROID.
BOYS, BOYS. LET'S NOT GET PERSONAL.
I'M JUST A TECHNOLOGICAL ARTIFACT, A TOOL. DID ART AIM ME IN YOUR DIRECTION? MAYBE. BUT NOW YOU HAVE AN OPPORTUNITY TO TURN THE TABLES!
BEEP!
YOU KNOW, YOU'RE RIGHT...
THAT'S THE SPIRIT!
... YOU ARE A TOOL.
HEAR ME OUT. YOU'VE GOT A GREAT PRODUCT, RIGHT?
YES.
BUT HOW WILL PEOPLE FIND OUT ABOUT YOUR PRODUCT?
I'LL TELL THEM!
I'M LISTENING.
IT'S 3AM. THE PHONE RINGS. "DO YOU KNOW WHERE YOUR SERVER IS?"

UPGRADE PATH

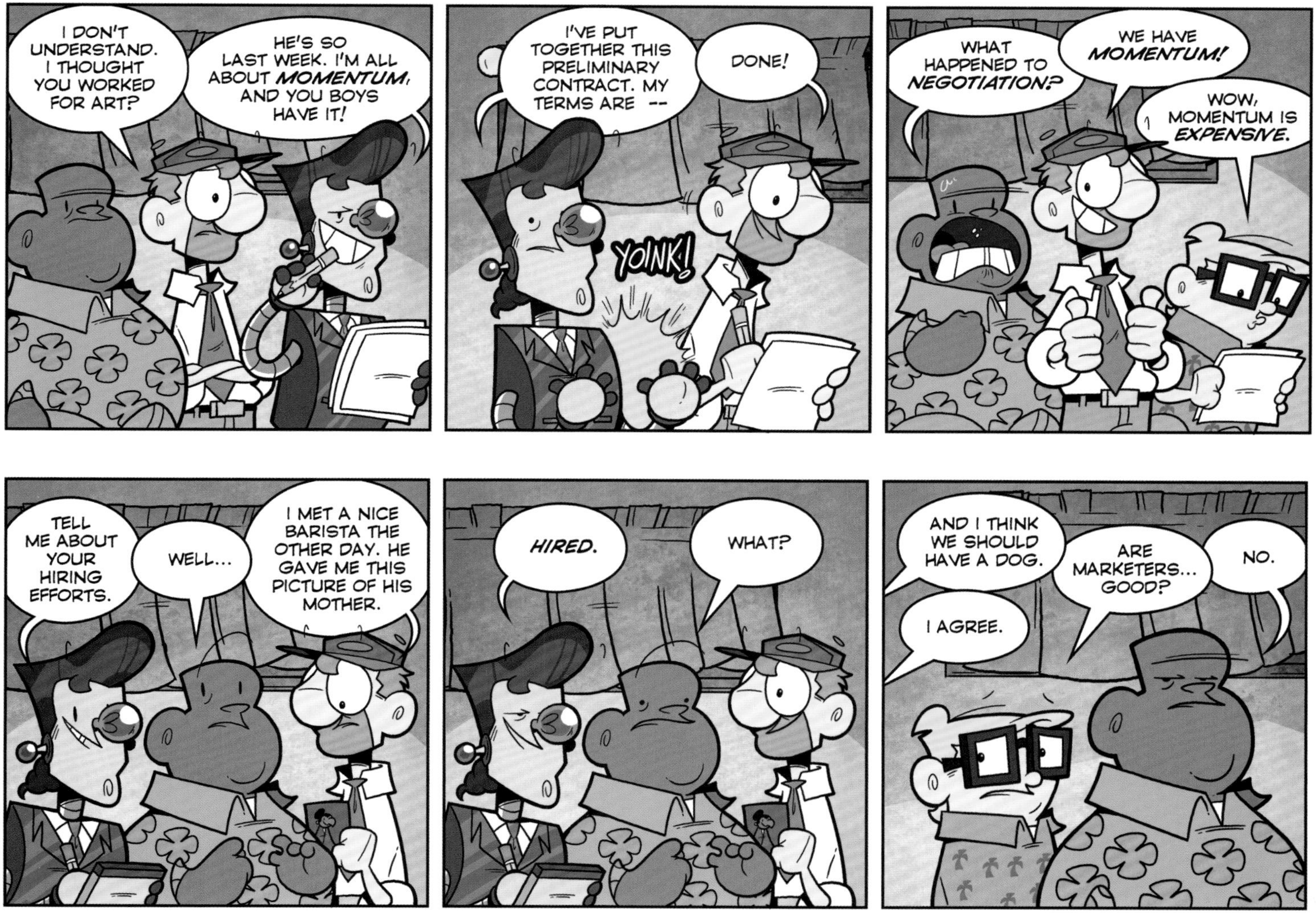
I DON'T UNDERSTAND. I THOUGHT YOU WORKED FOR ART?
HE'S SO LAST WEEK. I'M ALL ABOUT *MOMENTUM*, AND YOU BOYS HAVE IT!
I'VE PUT TOGETHER THIS PRELIMINARY CONTRACT. MY TERMS ARE --
DONE!
YOINK!
WHAT HAPPENED TO *NEGOTIATION?*
WE HAVE *MOMENTUM!*
WOW, MOMENTUM IS *EXPENSIVE*.
TELL ME ABOUT YOUR HIRING EFFORTS.
WELL...
I MET A NICE BARISTA THE OTHER DAY. HE GAVE ME THIS PICTURE OF HIS MOTHER.
HIRED.
WHAT?
AND I THINK WE SHOULD HAVE A DOG.
I AGREE.
ARE MARKETERS... GOOD?
NO.

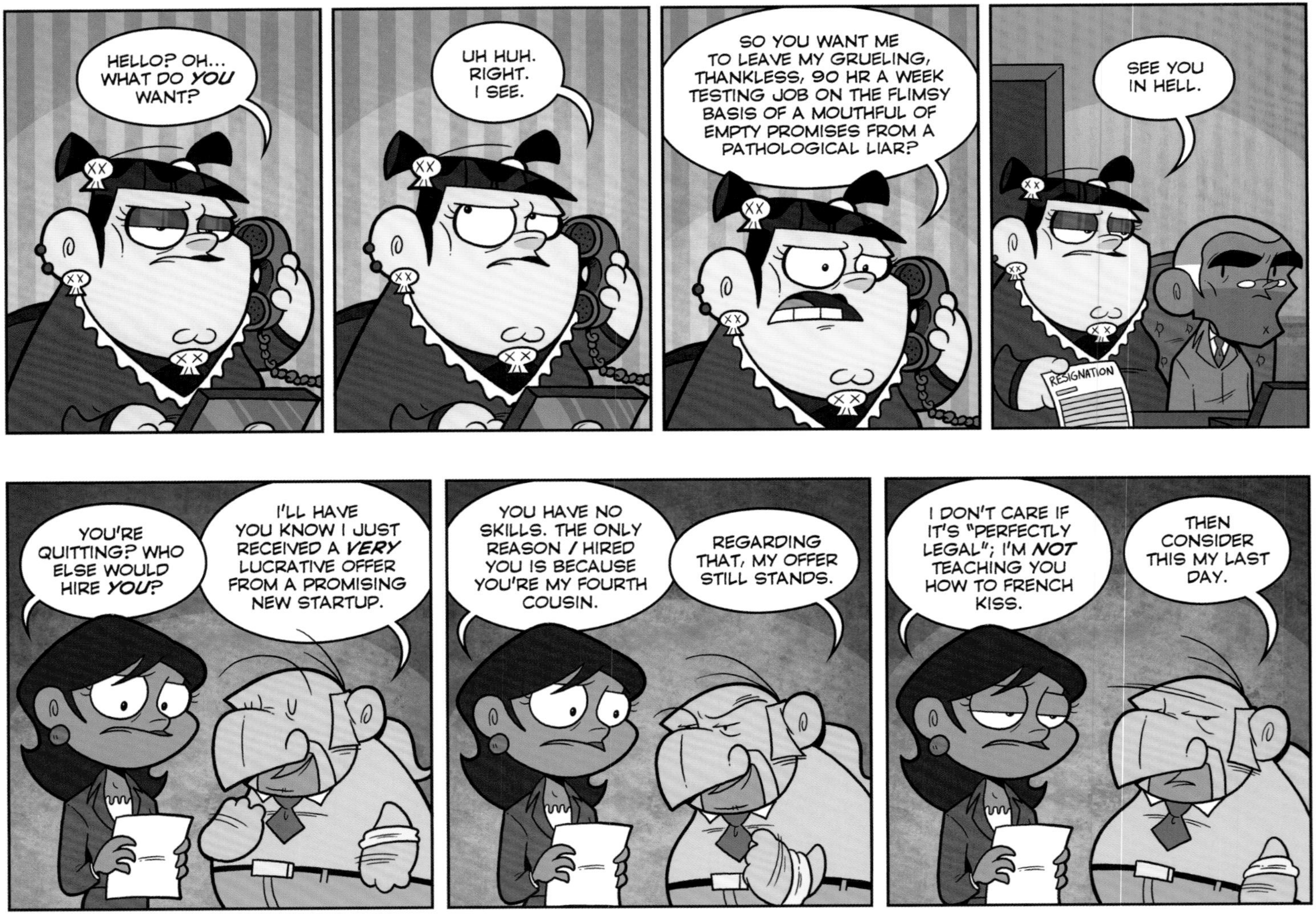
HELLO? OH... WHAT DO *YOU* WANT?
UH HUH. RIGHT. I SEE.
SO YOU WANT ME TO LEAVE MY GRUELING, THANKLESS, 90 HR A WEEK TESTING JOB ON THE FLIMSY BASIS OF A MOUTHFUL OF EMPTY PROMISES FROM A PATHOLOGICAL LIAR?
SEE YOU IN HELL.
RESIGNATION
YOU'RE QUITTING? WHO ELSE WOULD HIRE *YOU*?
I'LL HAVE YOU KNOW I JUST RECEIVED A *VERY* LUCRATIVE OFFER FROM A PROMISING NEW STARTUP.
YOU HAVE NO SKILLS. THE ONLY REASON *I* HIRED YOU IS BECAUSE YOU'RE MY FOURTH COUSIN.
REGARDING THAT, MY OFFER STILL STANDS.
I DON'T CARE IF IT'S "PERFECTLY LEGAL"; I'M *NOT* TEACHING YOU HOW TO FRENCH KISS.
THEN CONSIDER THIS MY LAST DAY.

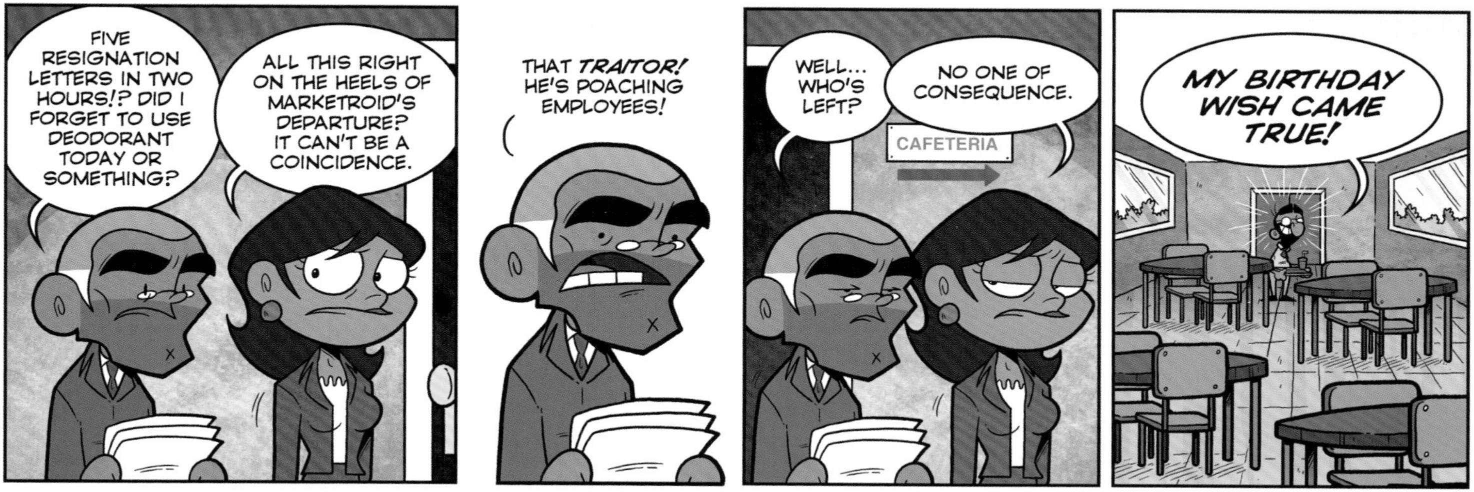
FIVE RESIGNATION LETTERS IN TWO HOURS!? DID I FORGET TO USE DEODORANT TODAY OR SOMETHING?
ALL THIS RIGHT ON THE HEELS OF MARKETROID'S DEPARTURE? IT CAN'T BE A COINCIDENCE.
THAT *TRAITOR!* HE'S POACHING EMPLOYEES!
WELL... WHO'S LEFT?
NO ONE OF CONSEQUENCE.
CAFETERIA
MY BIRTHDAY WISH CAME TRUE!

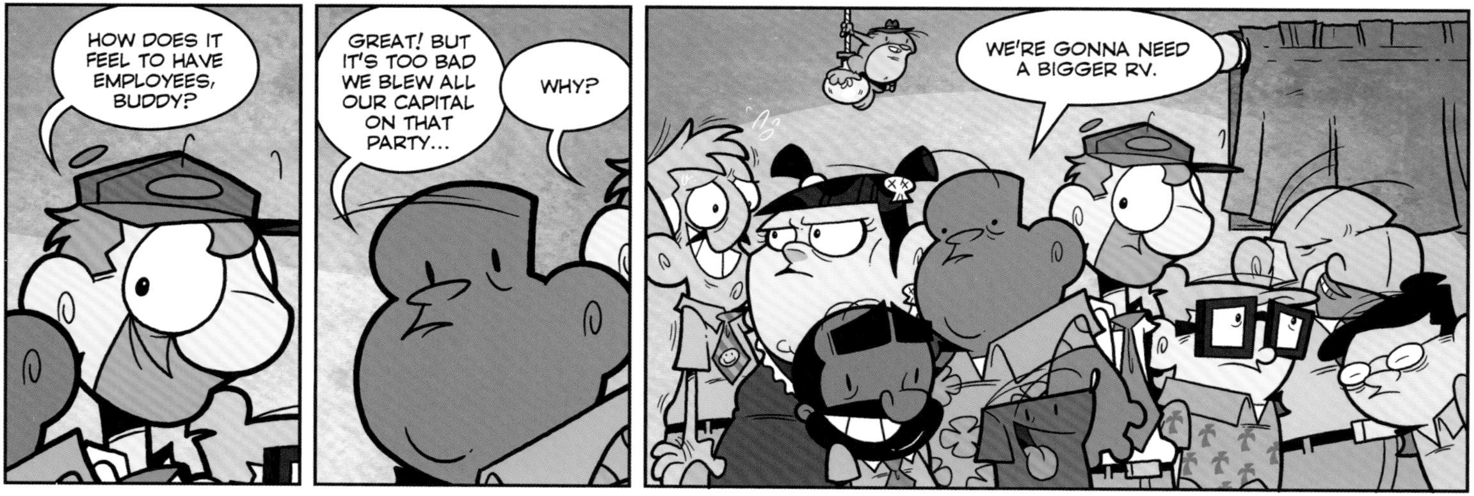
HOW DOES IT FEEL TO HAVE EMPLOYEES, BUDDY?
GREAT! BUT IT'S TOO BAD WE BLEW ALL OUR CAPITAL ON THAT PARTY...
WHY?
WE'RE GONNA NEED A BIGGER RV.

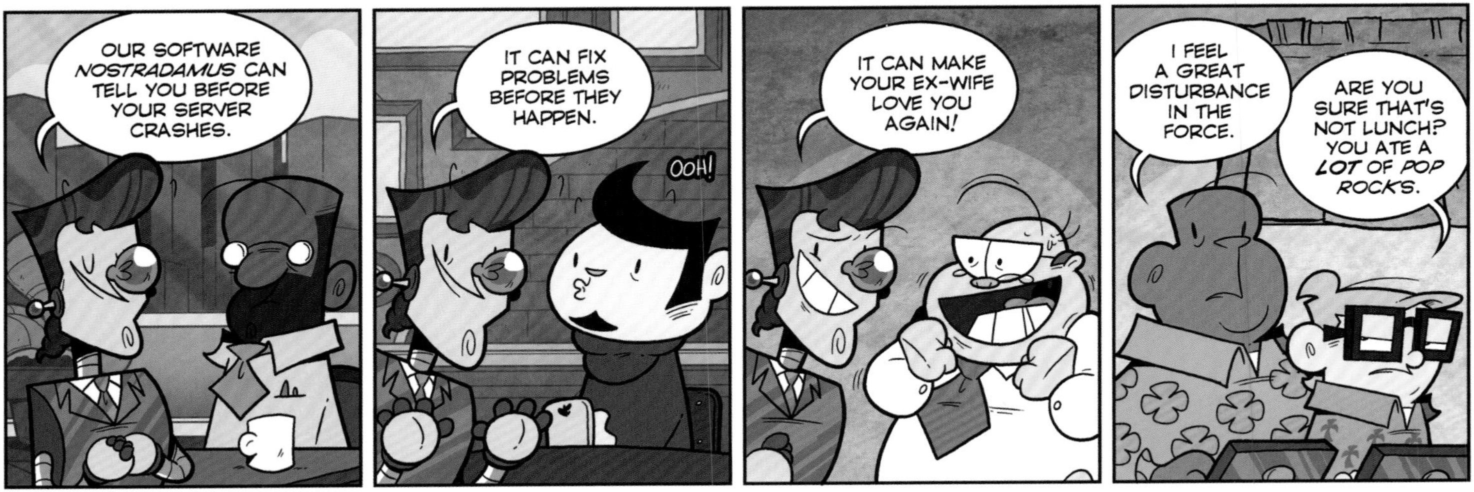
OUR SOFTWARE NOSTRADAMUS CAN TELL YOU BEFORE YOUR SERVER CRASHES.
IT CAN FIX PROBLEMS BEFORE THEY HAPPEN.
OOH!
IT CAN MAKE YOUR EX-WIFE LOVE YOU AGAIN!
I FEEL A GREAT DISTURBANCE IN THE FORCE.
ARE YOU SURE THAT'S NOT LUNCH? YOU ATE A LOT OF POP ROCKS.

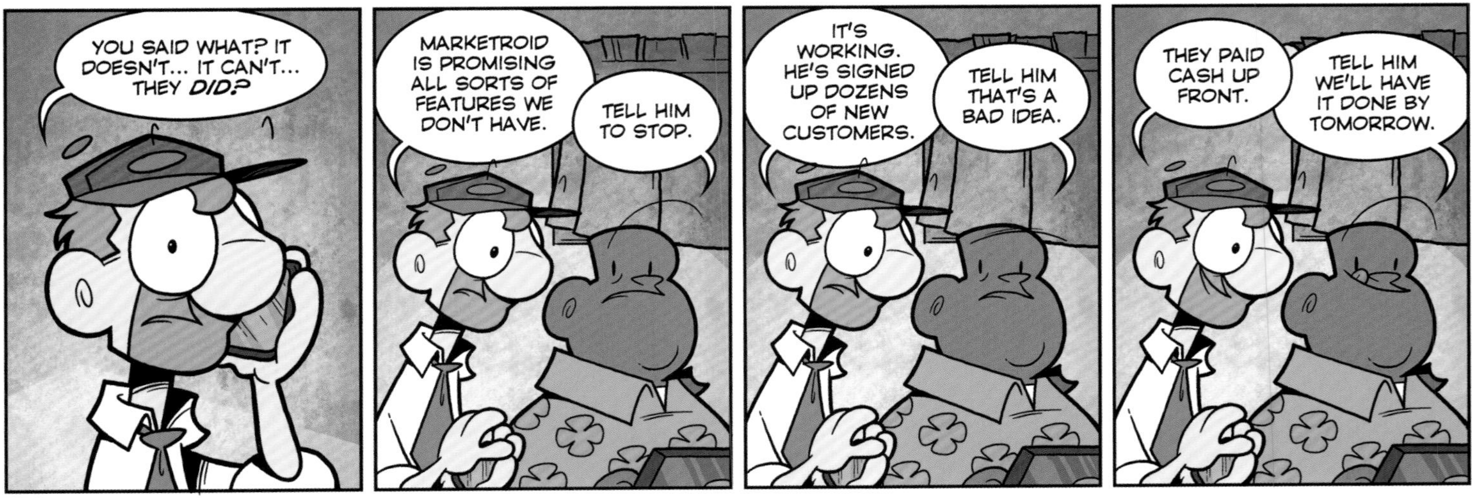
YOU SAID WHAT? IT DOESN'T... IT CAN'T... THEY DID?
MARKETROID IS PROMISING ALL SORTS OF FEATURES WE DON'T HAVE.
TELL HIM TO STOP.
IT'S WORKING. HE'S SIGNED UP DOZENS OF NEW CUSTOMERS.
TELL HIM THAT'S A BAD IDEA.
THEY PAID CASH UP FRONT.
TELL HIM WE'LL HAVE IT DONE BY TOMORROW.

UPGRADE PATH

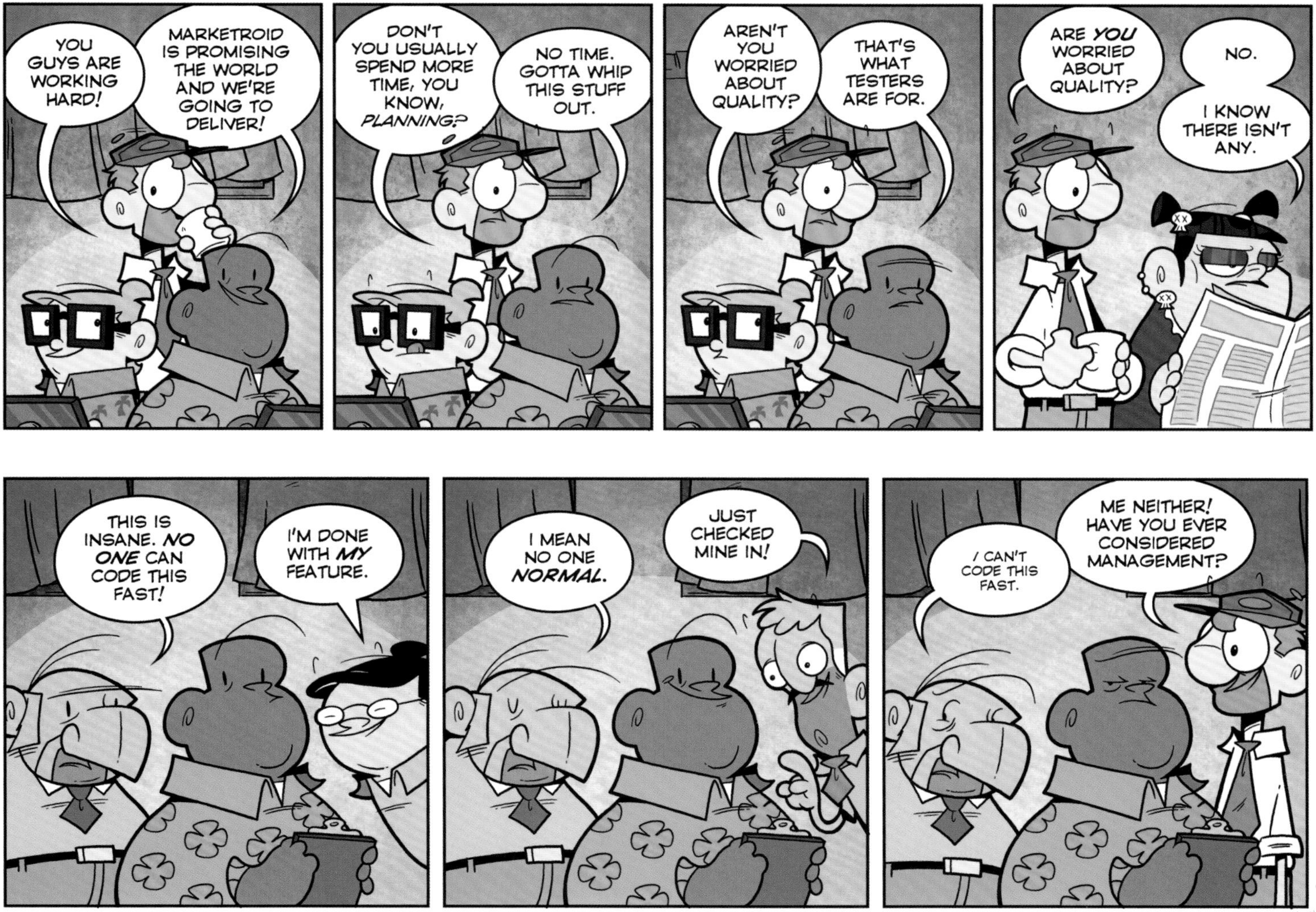
YOU GUYS ARE WORKING HARD!
MARKETROID IS PROMISING THE WORLD AND WE'RE GOING TO DELIVER!
DON'T YOU USUALLY SPEND MORE TIME, YOU KNOW, PLANNING?
NO TIME. GOTTA WHIP THIS STUFF OUT.
AREN'T YOU WORRIED ABOUT QUALITY?
THAT'S WHAT TESTERS ARE FOR.
ARE YOU WORRIED ABOUT QUALITY?
NO.
I KNOW THERE ISN'T ANY.
THIS IS INSANE. NO ONE CAN CODE THIS FAST!
I'M DONE WITH MY FEATURE.
I MEAN NO ONE NORMAL.
JUST CHECKED MINE IN!
I CAN'T CODE THIS FAST.
ME NEITHER! HAVE YOU EVER CONSIDERED MANAGEMENT?

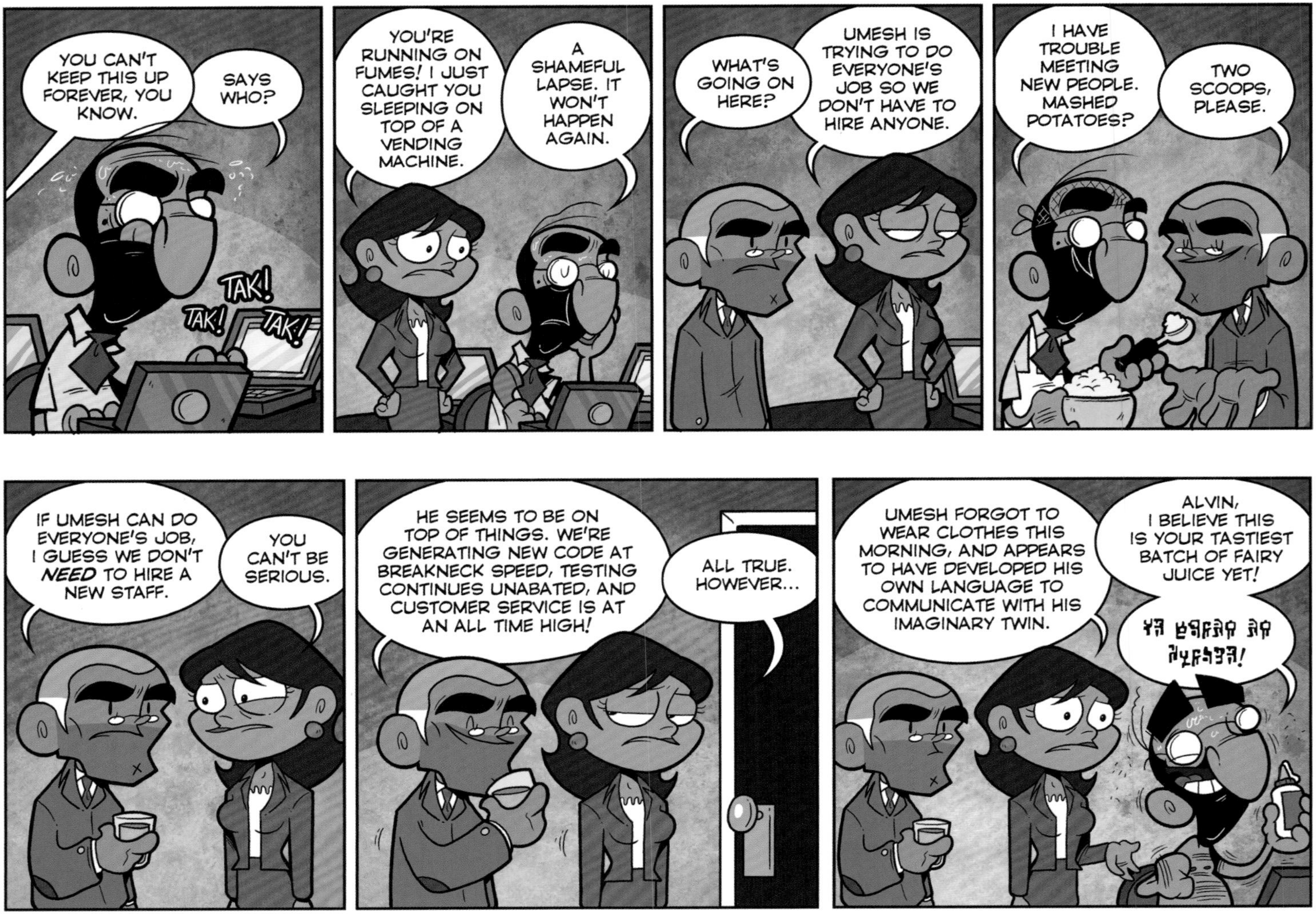
YOU CAN'T KEEP THIS UP FOREVER, YOU KNOW.
SAYS WHO?
TAK! TAK! TAK!
YOU'RE RUNNING ON FUMES! I JUST CAUGHT YOU SLEEPING ON TOP OF A VENDING MACHINE.
A SHAMEFUL LAPSE. IT WON'T HAPPEN AGAIN.
WHAT'S GOING ON HERE?
UMESH IS TRYING TO DO EVERYONE'S JOB SO WE DON'T HAVE TO HIRE ANYONE.
I HAVE TROUBLE MEETING NEW PEOPLE. MASHED POTATOES?
TWO SCOOPS, PLEASE.
IF UMESH CAN DO EVERYONE'S JOB, I GUESS WE DON'T ***NEED*** TO HIRE A NEW STAFF.
YOU CAN'T BE SERIOUS.
HE SEEMS TO BE ON TOP OF THINGS. WE'RE GENERATING NEW CODE AT BREAKNECK SPEED, TESTING CONTINUES UNABATED, AND CUSTOMER SERVICE IS AT AN ALL TIME HIGH!
ALL TRUE. HOWEVER...
UMESH FORGOT TO WEAR CLOTHES THIS MORNING, AND APPEARS TO HAVE DEVELOPED HIS OWN LANGUAGE TO COMMUNICATE WITH HIS IMAGINARY TWIN.
ALVIN, I BELIEVE THIS IS YOUR TASTIEST BATCH OF FAIRY JUICE YET!

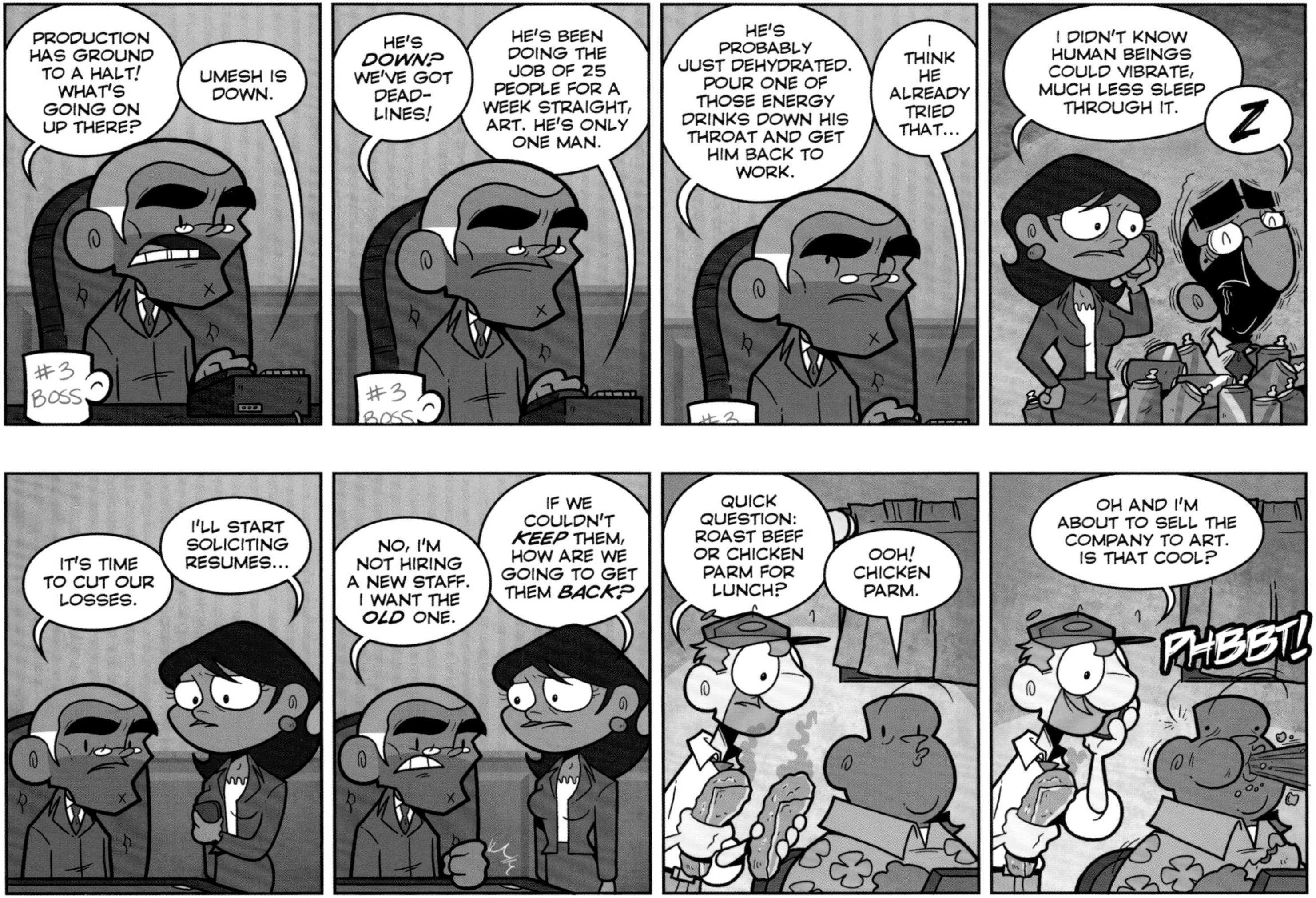
PRODUCTION HAS GROUND TO A HALT! WHAT'S GOING ON UP THERE?
UMESH IS DOWN.
#3 BOSS
HE'S DOWN? WE'VE GOT DEAD-LINES!
HE'S BEEN DOING THE JOB OF 25 PEOPLE FOR A WEEK STRAIGHT, ART. HE'S ONLY ONE MAN.
HE'S PROBABLY JUST DEHYDRATED. POUR ONE OF THOSE ENERGY DRINKS DOWN HIS THROAT AND GET HIM BACK TO WORK.
I THINK HE ALREADY TRIED THAT...
I DIDN'T KNOW HUMAN BEINGS COULD VIBRATE, MUCH LESS SLEEP THROUGH IT.
Z
IT'S TIME TO CUT OUR LOSSES.
I'LL START SOLICITING RESUMES...
NO, I'M NOT HIRING A NEW STAFF. I WANT THE OLD ONE.
IF WE COULDN'T KEEP THEM, HOW ARE WE GOING TO GET THEM BACK?
QUICK QUESTION: ROAST BEEF OR CHICKEN PARM FOR LUNCH?
OOH! CHICKEN PARM.
OH AND I'M ABOUT TO SELL THE COMPANY TO ART. IS THAT COOL?
PHBBT!

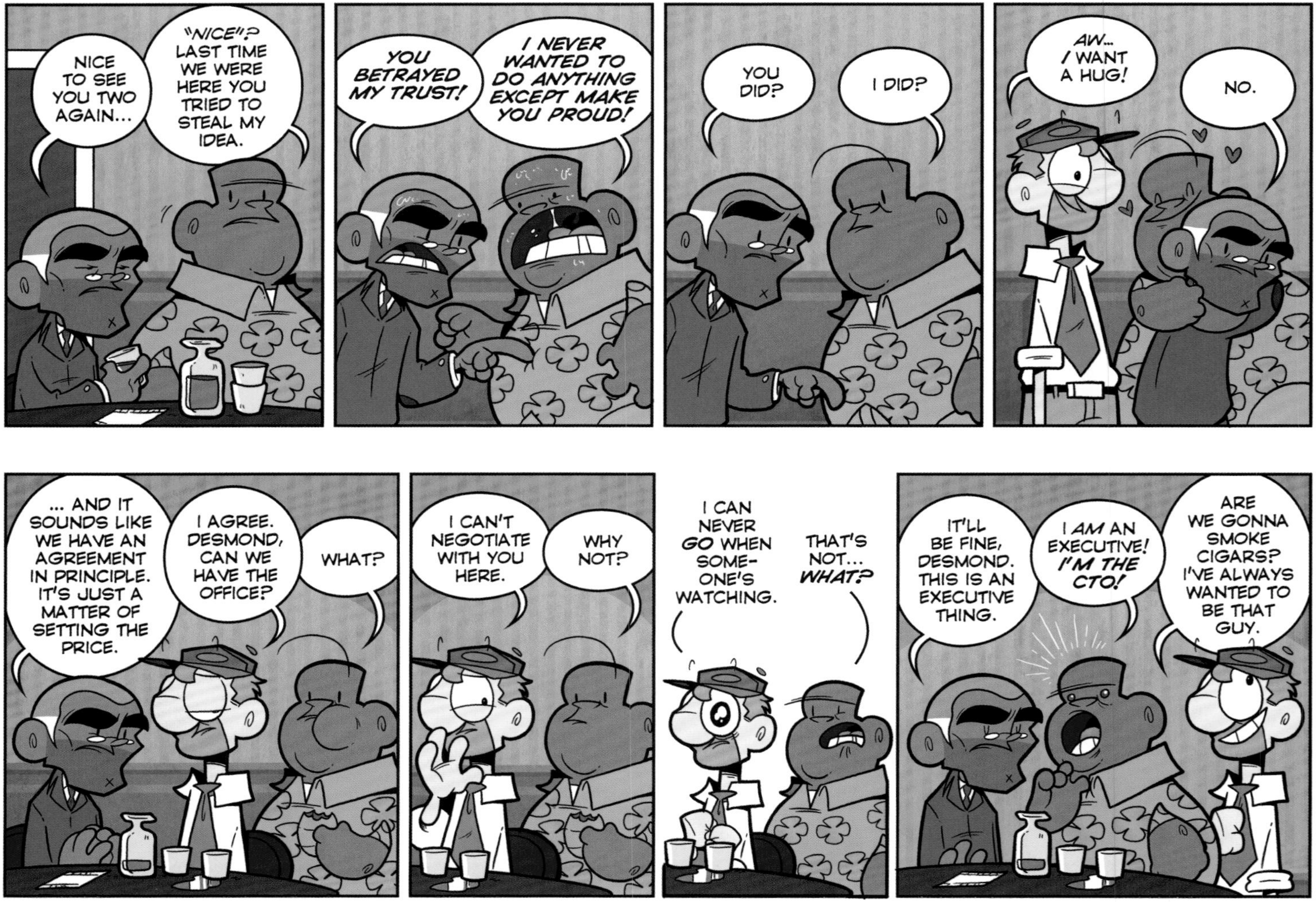
NICE TO SEE YOU TWO AGAIN...
"NICE"? LAST TIME WE WERE HERE YOU TRIED TO STEAL MY IDEA.
YOU BETRAYED MY TRUST!
I NEVER WANTED TO DO ANYTHING EXCEPT MAKE YOU PROUD!
YOU DID?
I DID?
AW... I WANT A HUG!
NO.
... AND IT SOUNDS LIKE WE HAVE AN AGREEMENT IN PRINCIPLE. IT'S JUST A MATTER OF SETTING THE PRICE.
I AGREE. DESMOND, CAN WE HAVE THE OFFICE?
WHAT?
I CAN'T NEGOTIATE WITH YOU HERE.
WHY NOT?
I CAN NEVER GO WHEN SOME-ONE'S WATCHING.
THAT'S NOT... WHAT?
IT'LL BE FINE, DESMOND. THIS IS AN EXECUTIVE THING.
I AM AN EXECUTIVE! I'M THE CTO!
ARE WE GONNA SMOKE CIGARS? I'VE ALWAYS WANTED TO BE THAT GUY.

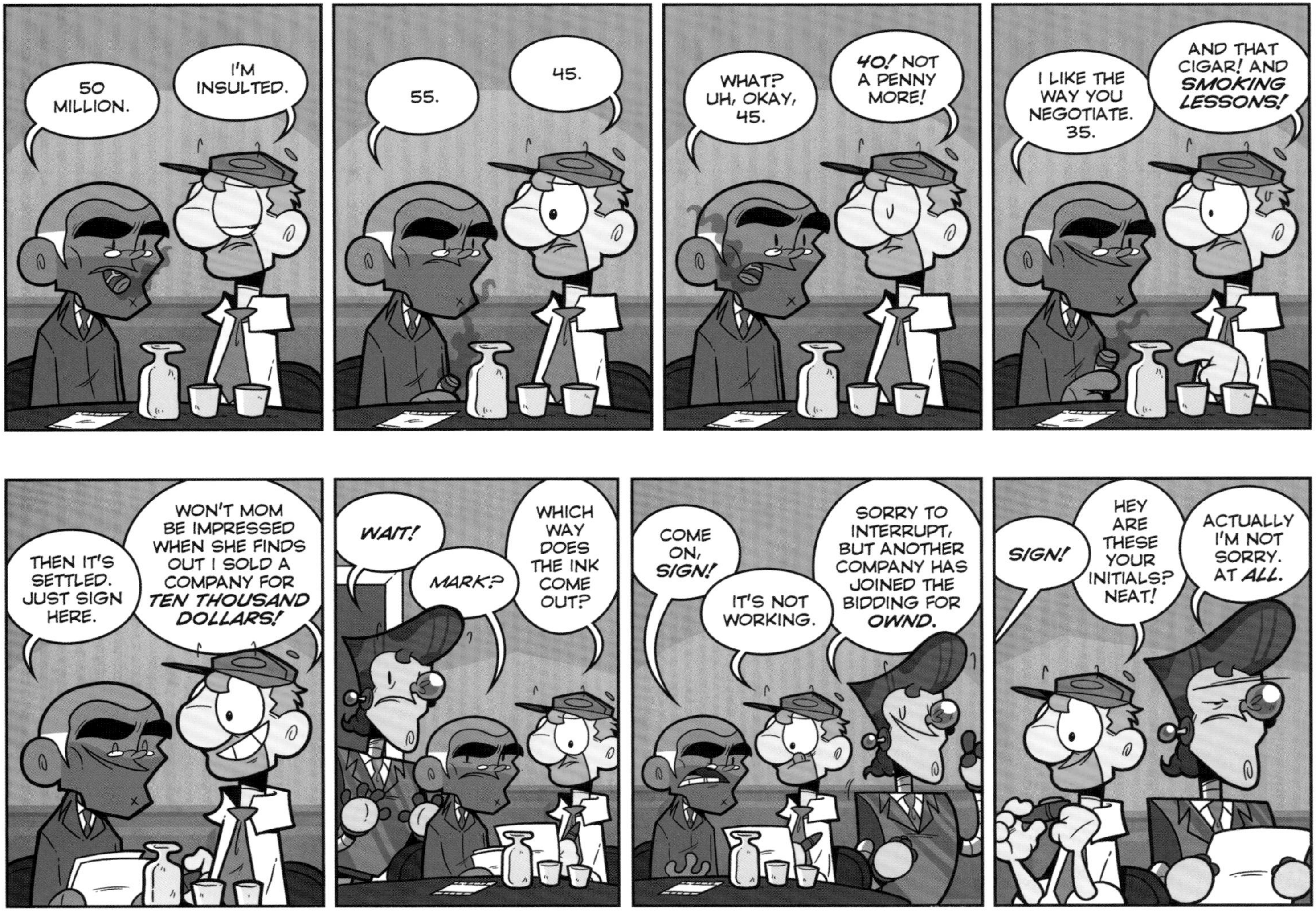
50 MILLION.
I'M INSULTED.
55.
45.
WHAT? UH, OKAY, 45.
40! NOT A PENNY MORE!
I LIKE THE WAY YOU NEGOTIATE. 35.
AND THAT CIGAR! AND SMOKING LESSONS!
THEN IT'S SETTLED. JUST SIGN HERE.
WON'T MOM BE IMPRESSED WHEN SHE FINDS OUT I SOLD A COMPANY FOR TEN THOUSAND DOLLARS!
WAIT!
MARK?
WHICH WAY DOES THE INK COME OUT?
COME ON, SIGN!
IT'S NOT WORKING.
SORRY TO INTERRUPT, BUT ANOTHER COMPANY HAS JOINED THE BIDDING FOR OWND.
SIGN!
HEY ARE THESE YOUR INITIALS? NEAT!
ACTUALLY I'M NOT SORRY. AT ALL.

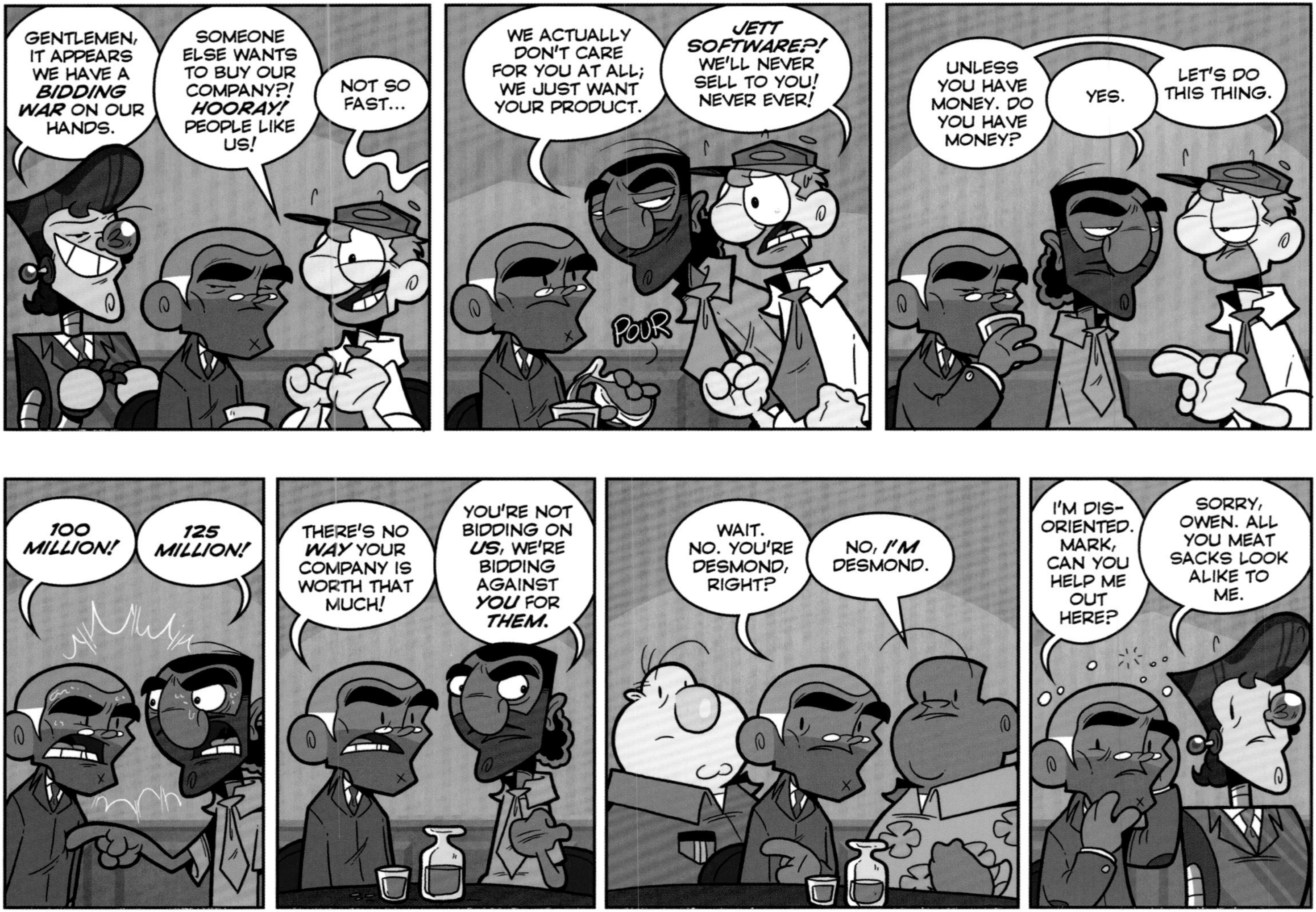
GENTLEMEN, IT APPEARS WE HAVE A BIDDING WAR ON OUR HANDS.
SOMEONE ELSE WANTS TO BUY OUR COMPANY?! HOORAY! PEOPLE LIKE US!
NOT SO FAST...
WE ACTUALLY DON'T CARE FOR YOU AT ALL; WE JUST WANT YOUR PRODUCT.
JETT SOFTWARE?! WE'LL NEVER SELL TO YOU! NEVER EVER!
POUR
UNLESS YOU HAVE MONEY. DO YOU HAVE MONEY?
YES.
LET'S DO THIS THING.
100 MILLION!
125 MILLION!
THERE'S NO WAY YOUR COMPANY IS WORTH THAT MUCH!
YOU'RE NOT BIDDING ON US, WE'RE BIDDING AGAINST YOU FOR THEM.
WAIT. NO. YOU'RE DESMOND, RIGHT?
NO, I'M DESMOND.
I'M DIS-ORIENTED. MARK, CAN YOU HELP ME OUT HERE?
SORRY, OWEN. ALL YOU MEAT SACKS LOOK ALIKE TO ME.

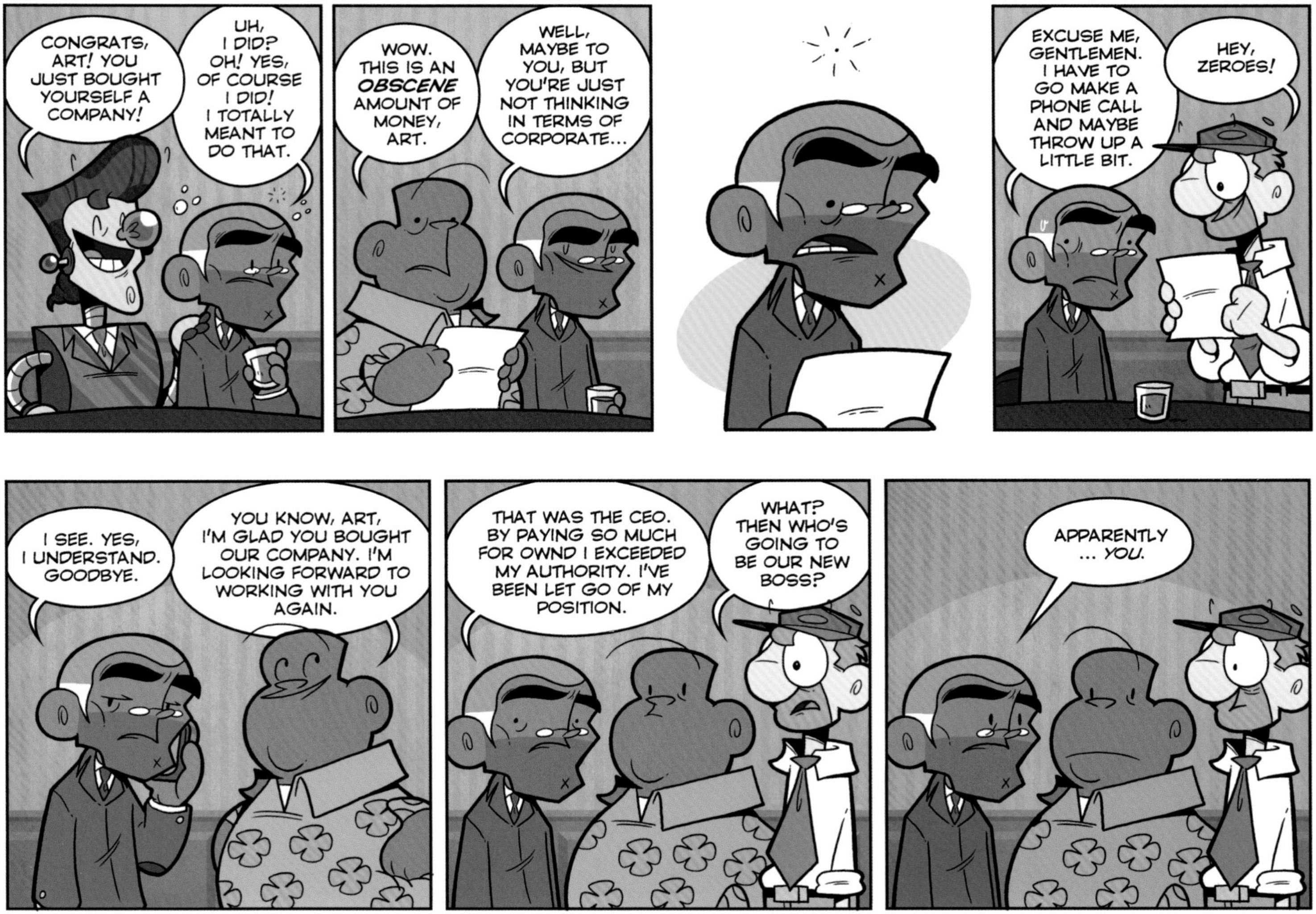
CONGRATS, ART! YOU JUST BOUGHT YOURSELF A COMPANY!
UH, I DID? OH! YES, OF COURSE I DID! I TOTALLY MEANT TO DO THAT.
WOW. THIS IS AN OBSCENE AMOUNT OF MONEY, ART.
WELL, MAYBE TO YOU, BUT YOU'RE JUST NOT THINKING IN TERMS OF CORPORATE...
EXCUSE ME, GENTLEMEN. I HAVE TO GO MAKE A PHONE CALL AND MAYBE THROW UP A LITTLE BIT.
HEY, ZEROES!
I SEE. YES, I UNDERSTAND. GOODBYE.
YOU KNOW, ART, I'M GLAD YOU BOUGHT OUR COMPANY. I'M LOOKING FORWARD TO WORKING WITH YOU AGAIN.
THAT WAS THE CEO. BY PAYING SO MUCH FOR OWND I EXCEEDED MY AUTHORITY. I'VE BEEN LET GO OF MY POSITION.
WHAT? THEN WHO'S GOING TO BE OUR NEW BOSS?
APPARENTLY ... YOU.

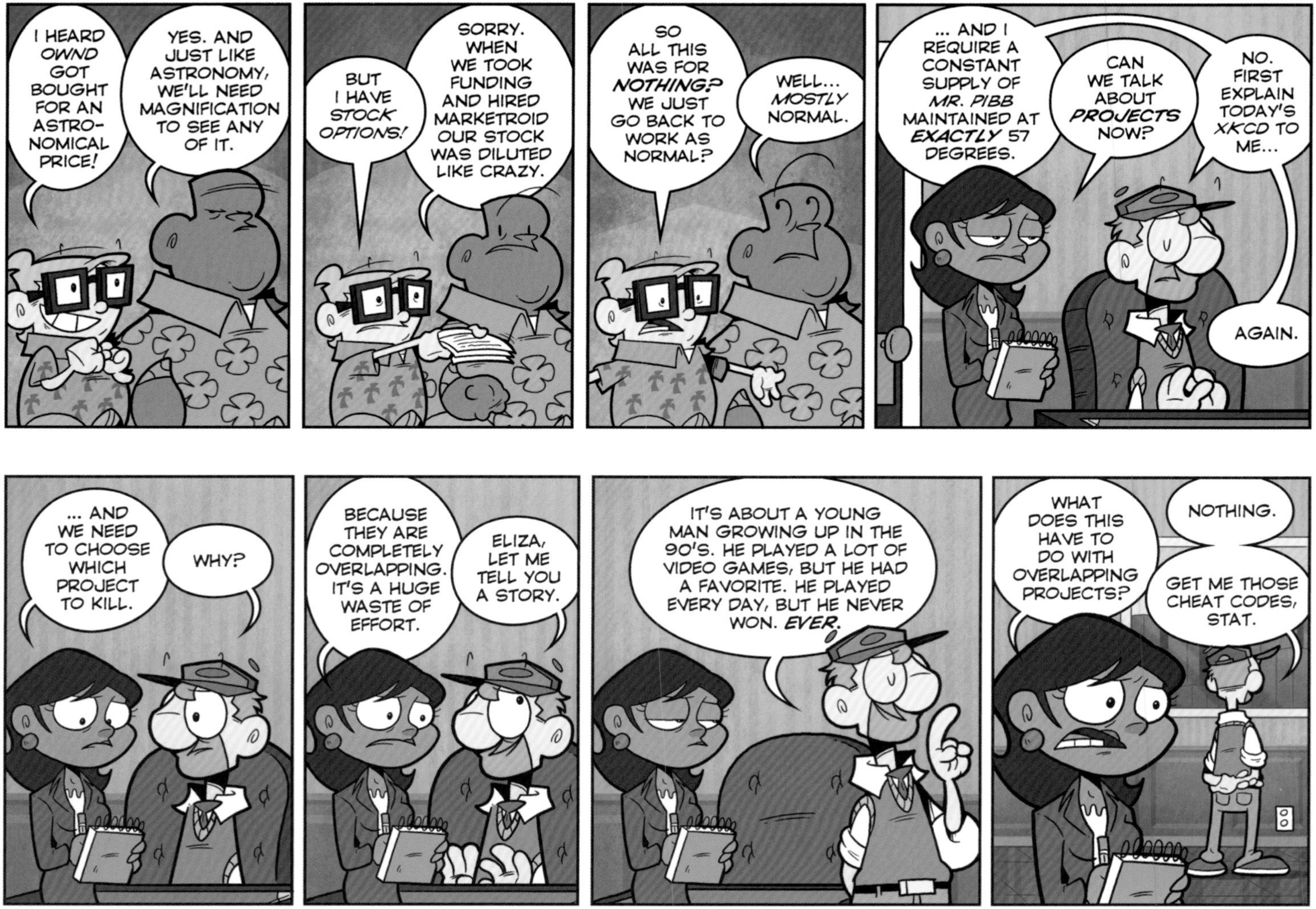
I HEARD *OWND* GOT BOUGHT FOR AN ASTRONOMICAL PRICE!
YES. AND JUST LIKE ASTRONOMY, WE'LL NEED MAGNIFICATION TO SEE ANY OF IT.
BUT I HAVE *STOCK OPTIONS!*
SORRY. WHEN WE TOOK FUNDING AND HIRED MARKETROID OUR STOCK WAS DILUTED LIKE CRAZY.
SO ALL THIS WAS FOR ***NOTHING?*** WE JUST GO BACK TO WORK AS NORMAL?
WELL... *MOSTLY* NORMAL.
... AND I REQUIRE A CONSTANT SUPPLY OF *MR. PIBB* MAINTAINED AT ***EXACTLY*** 57 DEGREES.
CAN WE TALK ABOUT ***PROJECTS*** NOW?
NO. FIRST EXPLAIN TODAY'S *XKCD* TO ME...
AGAIN.
... AND WE NEED TO CHOOSE WHICH PROJECT TO KILL.
WHY?
BECAUSE THEY ARE COMPLETELY OVERLAPPING. IT'S A HUGE WASTE OF EFFORT.
ELIZA, LET ME TELL YOU A STORY.
IT'S ABOUT A YOUNG MAN GROWING UP IN THE 90'S. HE PLAYED A LOT OF VIDEO GAMES, BUT HE HAD A FAVORITE. HE PLAYED EVERY DAY, BUT HE NEVER WON. ***EVER.***
WHAT DOES THIS HAVE TO DO WITH OVERLAPPING PROJECTS?
NOTHING.
GET ME THOSE CHEAT CODES, STAT.

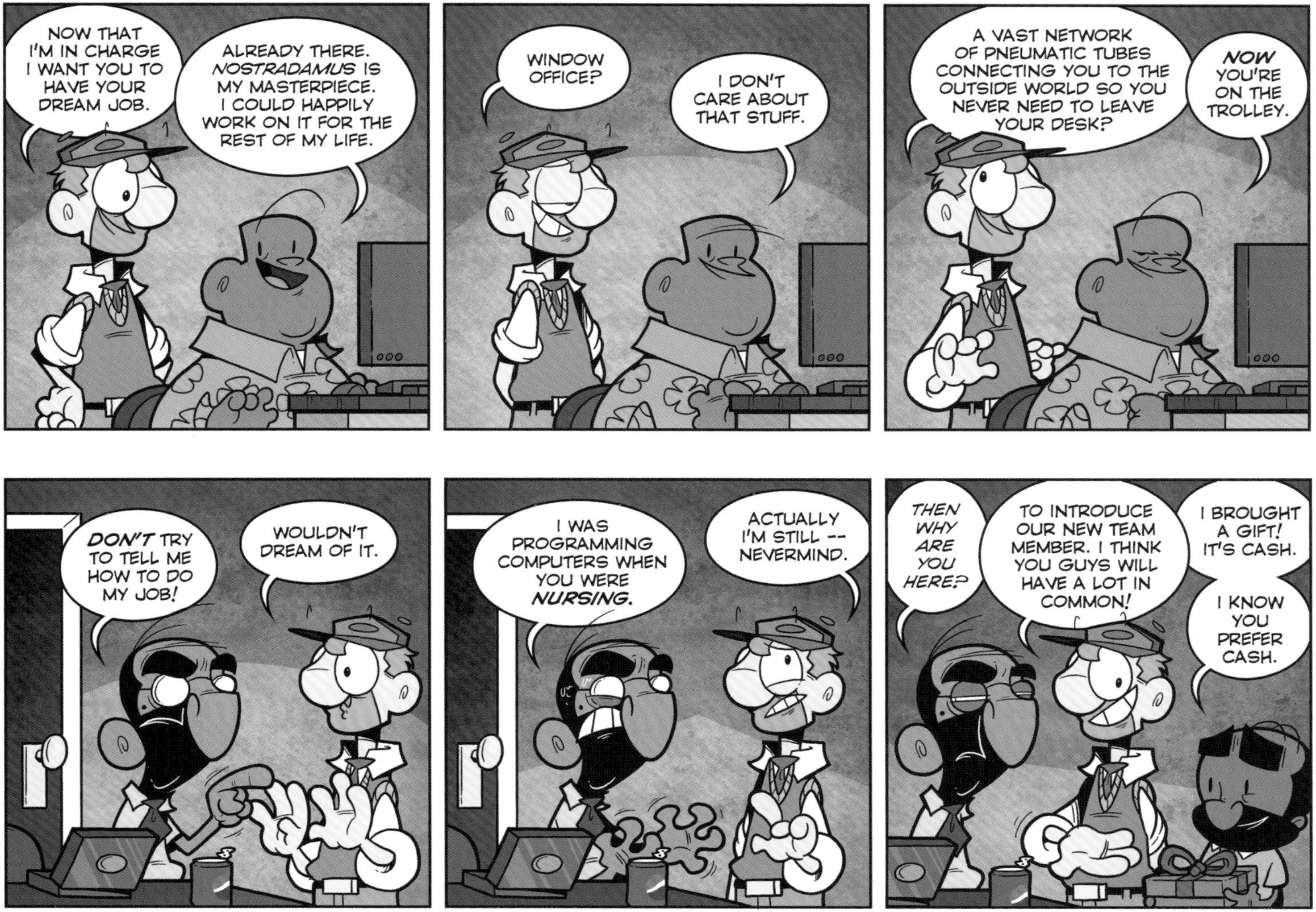
NOW THAT I'M IN CHARGE I WANT YOU TO HAVE YOUR DREAM JOB.
ALREADY THERE. NOSTRADAMUS IS MY MASTERPIECE. I COULD HAPPILY WORK ON IT FOR THE REST OF MY LIFE.
WINDOW OFFICE?
I DON'T CARE ABOUT THAT STUFF.
A VAST NETWORK OF PNEUMATIC TUBES CONNECTING YOU TO THE OUTSIDE WORLD SO YOU NEVER NEED TO LEAVE YOUR DESK?
NOW YOU'RE ON THE TROLLEY.
DON'T TRY TO TELL ME HOW TO DO MY JOB!
WOULDN'T DREAM OF IT.
I WAS PROGRAMMING COMPUTERS WHEN YOU WERE NURSING.
ACTUALLY I'M STILL -- NEVERMIND.
THEN WHY ARE YOU HERE?
TO INTRODUCE OUR NEW TEAM MEMBER. I THINK YOU GUYS WILL HAVE A LOT IN COMMON!
I BROUGHT A GIFT! IT'S CASH.
I KNOW YOU PREFER CASH.

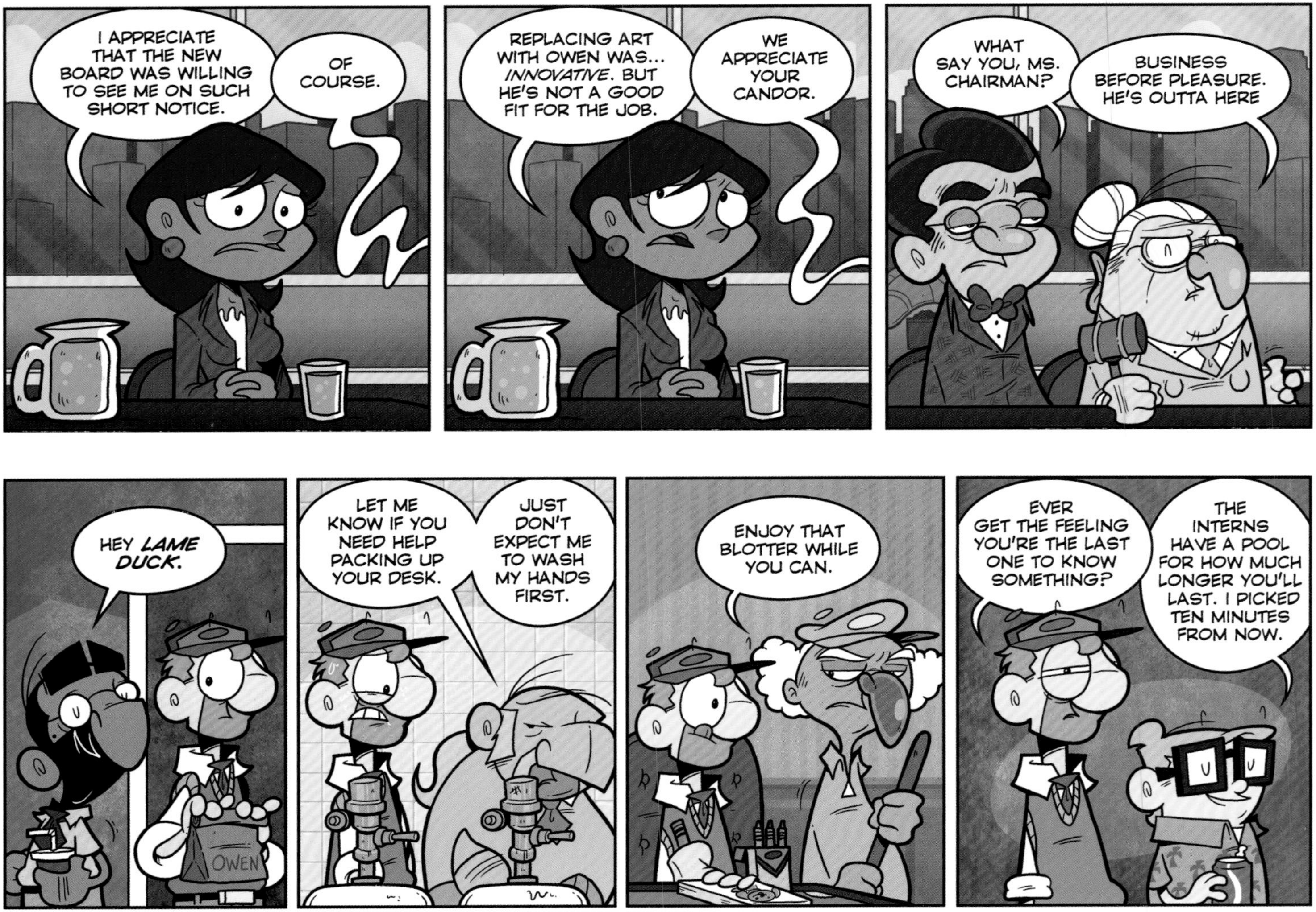
I APPRECIATE THAT THE NEW BOARD WAS WILLING TO SEE ME ON SUCH SHORT NOTICE.
OF COURSE.
REPLACING ART WITH OWEN WAS... *INNOVATIVE*. BUT HE'S NOT A GOOD FIT FOR THE JOB.
WE APPRECIATE YOUR CANDOR.
WHAT SAY YOU, MS. CHAIRMAN?
BUSINESS BEFORE PLEASURE. HE'S OUTTA HERE
HEY *LAME DUCK*.
OWEN
LET ME KNOW IF YOU NEED HELP PACKING UP YOUR DESK.
JUST DON'T EXPECT ME TO WASH MY HANDS FIRST.
ENJOY THAT BLOTTER WHILE YOU CAN.
EVER GET THE FEELING YOU'RE THE LAST ONE TO KNOW SOMETHING?
THE INTERNS HAVE A POOL FOR HOW MUCH LONGER YOU'LL LAST. I PICKED TEN MINUTES FROM NOW.

UPGRADE PATH

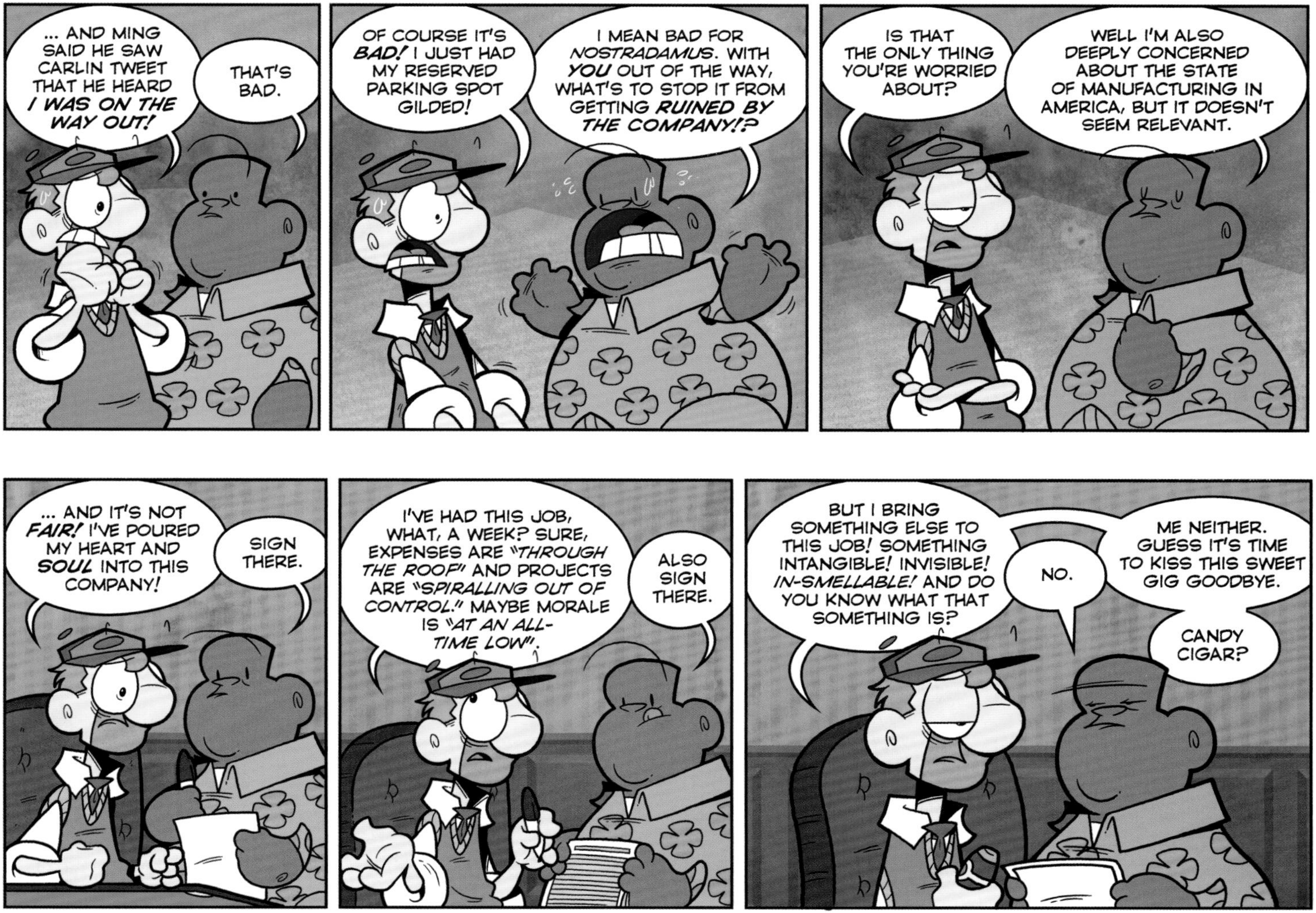
... AND MING SAID HE SAW CARLIN TWEET THAT HE HEARD *I WAS ON THE WAY OUT!*
THAT'S BAD.
OF COURSE IT'S *BAD!* I JUST HAD MY RESERVED PARKING SPOT GILDED!
I MEAN BAD FOR *NOSTRADAMUS*. WITH *YOU* OUT OF THE WAY, WHAT'S TO STOP IT FROM GETTING *RUINED BY THE COMPANY!?*
IS THAT THE ONLY THING YOU'RE WORRIED ABOUT?
WELL I'M ALSO DEEPLY CONCERNED ABOUT THE STATE OF MANUFACTURING IN AMERICA, BUT IT DOESN'T SEEM RELEVANT.
... AND IT'S NOT *FAIR!* I'VE POURED MY HEART AND *SOUL* INTO THIS COMPANY!
SIGN THERE.
I'VE HAD THIS JOB, WHAT, A WEEK? SURE, EXPENSES ARE *"THROUGH THE ROOF"* AND PROJECTS ARE *"SPIRALLING OUT OF CONTROL."* MAYBE MORALE IS *"AT AN ALL-TIME LOW"*.
ALSO SIGN THERE.
BUT I BRING SOMETHING ELSE TO THIS JOB! SOMETHING INTANGIBLE! INVISIBLE! *IN-SMELLABLE!* AND DO YOU KNOW WHAT THAT SOMETHING IS?
NO.
ME NEITHER. GUESS IT'S TIME TO KISS THIS SWEET GIG GOODBYE.
CANDY CIGAR?

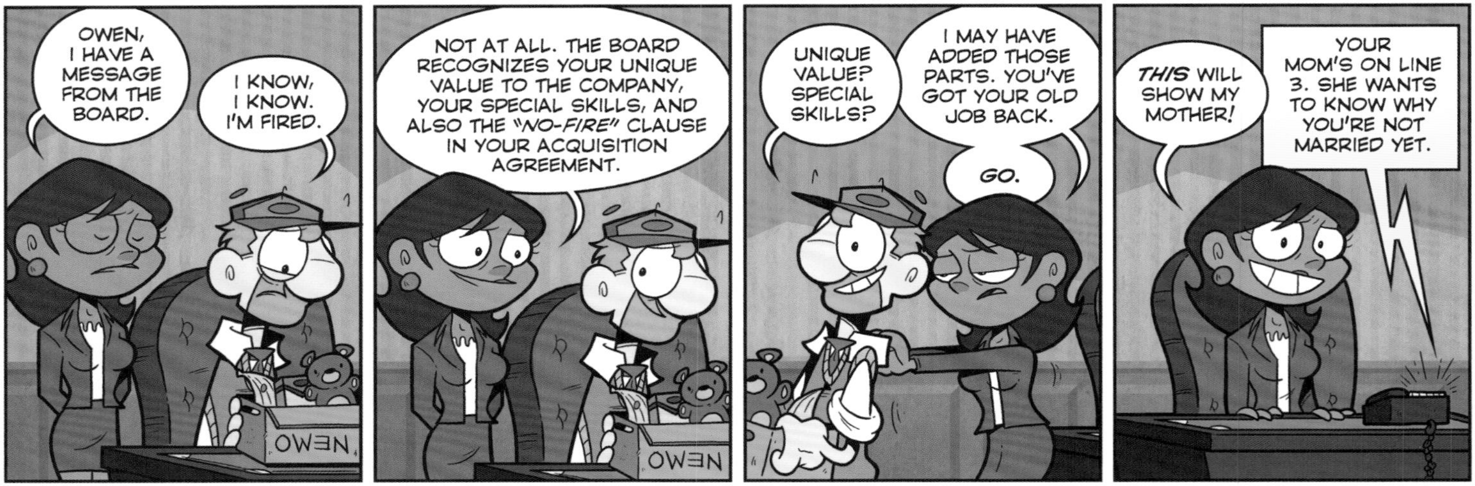
OWEN, I HAVE A MESSAGE FROM THE BOARD.
I KNOW, I KNOW. I'M FIRED.
OWEN
NOT AT ALL. THE BOARD RECOGNIZES YOUR UNIQUE VALUE TO THE COMPANY, YOUR SPECIAL SKILLS, AND ALSO THE "NO-FIRE" CLAUSE IN YOUR ACQUISITION AGREEMENT.
OWEN
UNIQUE VALUE? SPECIAL SKILLS?
I MAY HAVE ADDED THOSE PARTS. YOU'VE GOT YOUR OLD JOB BACK.
GO.
THIS WILL SHOW MY MOTHER!
YOUR MOM'S ON LINE 3. SHE WANTS TO KNOW WHY YOU'RE NOT MARRIED YET.

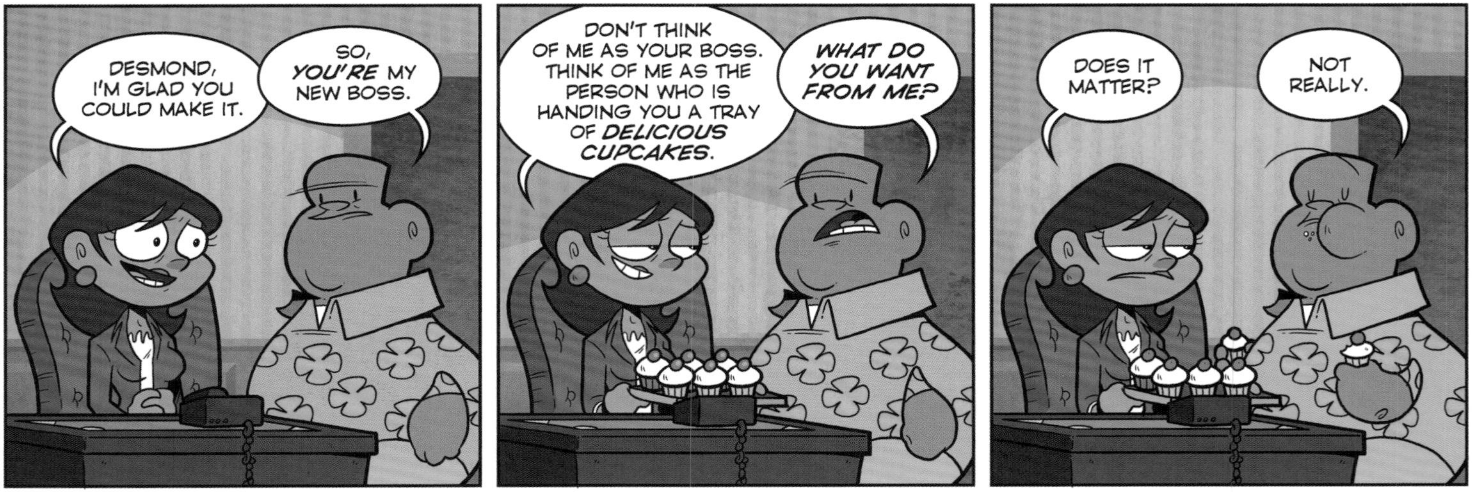
DESMOND, I'M GLAD YOU COULD MAKE IT.
SO, *YOU'RE* MY NEW BOSS.
DON'T THINK OF ME AS YOUR BOSS. THINK OF ME AS THE PERSON WHO IS HANDING YOU A TRAY OF *DELICIOUS CUPCAKES*.
WHAT DO YOU WANT FROM ME?
DOES IT MATTER?
NOT REALLY.

UPGRADE PATH

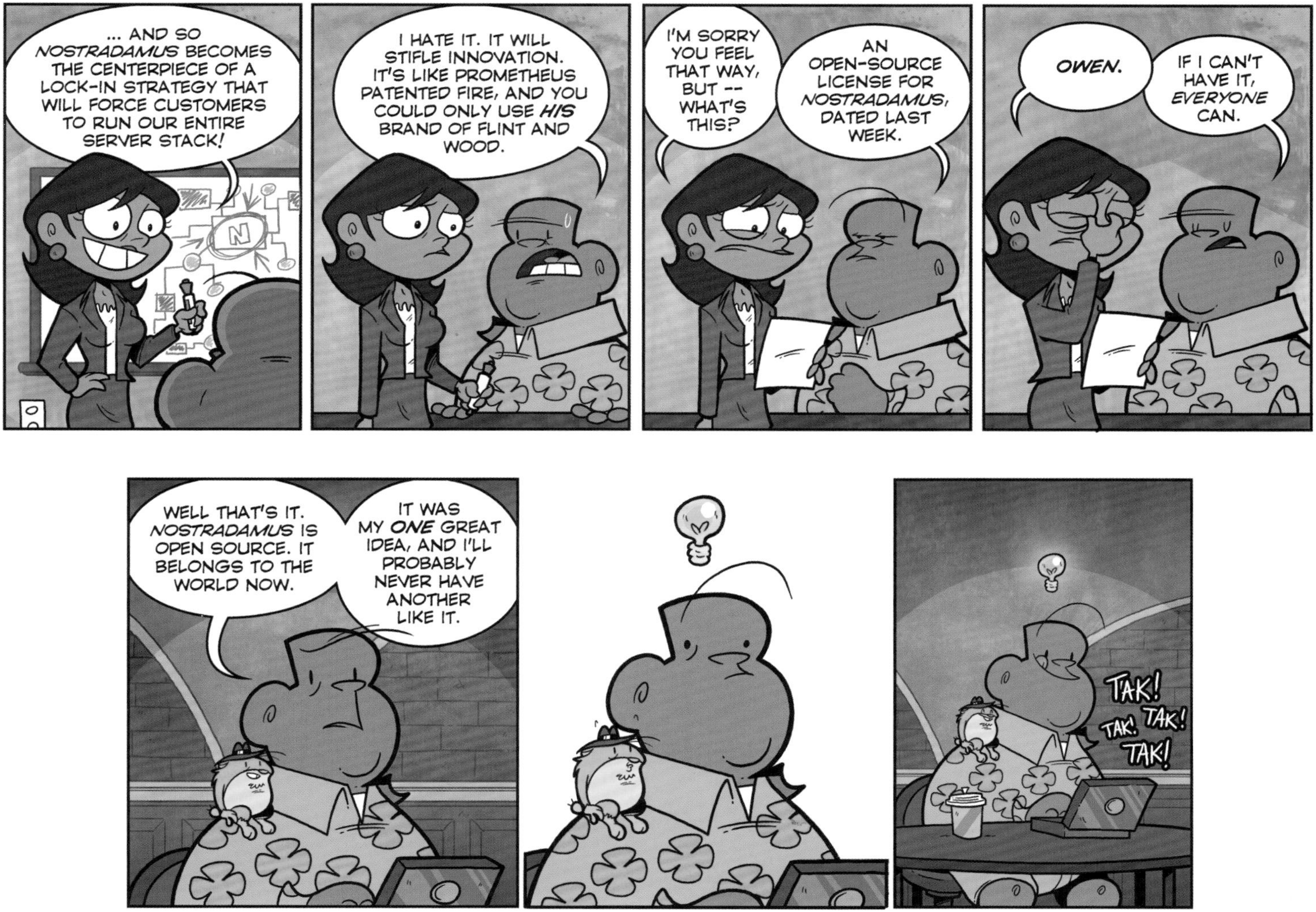

... AND SO *NOSTRADAMUS* BECOMES THE CENTERPIECE OF A LOCK-IN STRATEGY THAT WILL FORCE CUSTOMERS TO RUN OUR ENTIRE SERVER STACK!
I HATE IT. IT WILL STIFLE INNOVATION. IT'S LIKE PROMETHEUS PATENTED FIRE, AND YOU COULD ONLY USE *HIS* BRAND OF FLINT AND WOOD.
I'M SORRY YOU FEEL THAT WAY, BUT -- WHAT'S THIS?
AN OPEN-SOURCE LICENSE FOR *NOSTRADAMUS*, DATED LAST WEEK.
OWEN.
IF I CAN'T HAVE IT, *EVERYONE* CAN.
WELL THAT'S IT. *NOSTRADAMUS* IS OPEN SOURCE. IT BELONGS TO THE WORLD NOW.
IT WAS MY *ONE* GREAT IDEA, AND I'LL PROBABLY NEVER HAVE ANOTHER LIKE IT.
TAK! TAK! TAK! TAK!

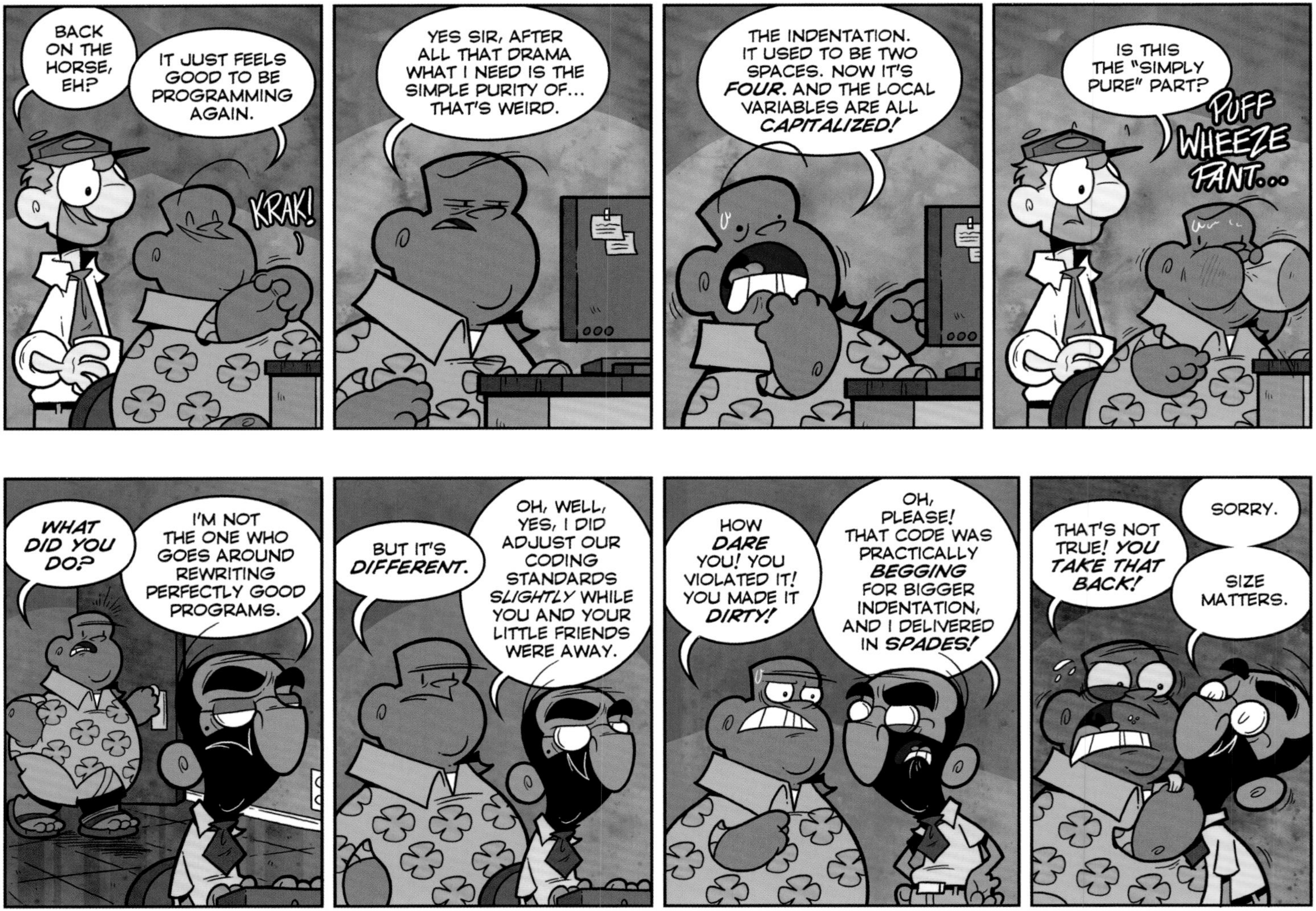
BACK ON THE HORSE, EH?
IT JUST FEELS GOOD TO BE PROGRAMMING AGAIN.
KRAK!
YES SIR, AFTER ALL THAT DRAMA WHAT I NEED IS THE SIMPLE PURITY OF... THAT'S WEIRD.
THE INDENTATION. IT USED TO BE TWO SPACES. NOW IT'S *FOUR.* AND THE LOCAL VARIABLES ARE ALL *CAPITALIZED!*
IS THIS THE "SIMPLY PURE" PART?
PUFF WHEEZE PANT...
WHAT DID YOU DO?
I'M NOT THE ONE WHO GOES AROUND REWRITING PERFECTLY GOOD PROGRAMS.
BUT IT'S *DIFFERENT.*
OH, WELL, YES, I DID ADJUST OUR CODING STANDARDS *SLIGHTLY* WHILE YOU AND YOUR LITTLE FRIENDS WERE AWAY.
HOW *DARE* YOU! YOU VIOLATED IT! YOU MADE IT *DIRTY!*
OH, PLEASE! THAT CODE WAS PRACTICALLY *BEGGING* FOR BIGGER INDENTATION, AND I DELIVERED IN *SPADES!*
THAT'S NOT TRUE! *YOU TAKE THAT BACK!*
SORRY.
SIZE MATTERS.

UPGRADE PATH

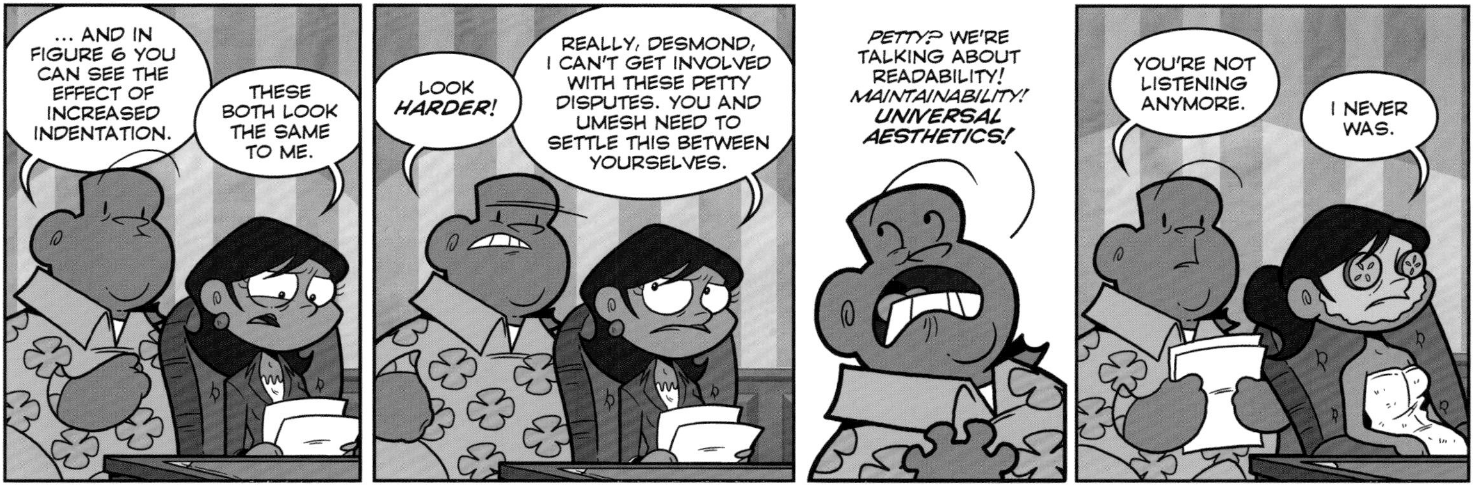
... AND IN FIGURE 6 YOU CAN SEE THE EFFECT OF INCREASED INDENTATION.
THESE BOTH LOOK THE SAME TO ME.
LOOK *HARDER!*
REALLY, DESMOND, I CAN'T GET INVOLVED WITH THESE PETTY DISPUTES. YOU AND UMESH NEED TO SETTLE THIS BETWEEN YOURSELVES.
PETTY? WE'RE TALKING ABOUT READABILITY! *MAINTAINABILITY!* ***UNIVERSAL AESTHETICS!***
YOU'RE NOT LISTENING ANYMORE.
I NEVER WAS.

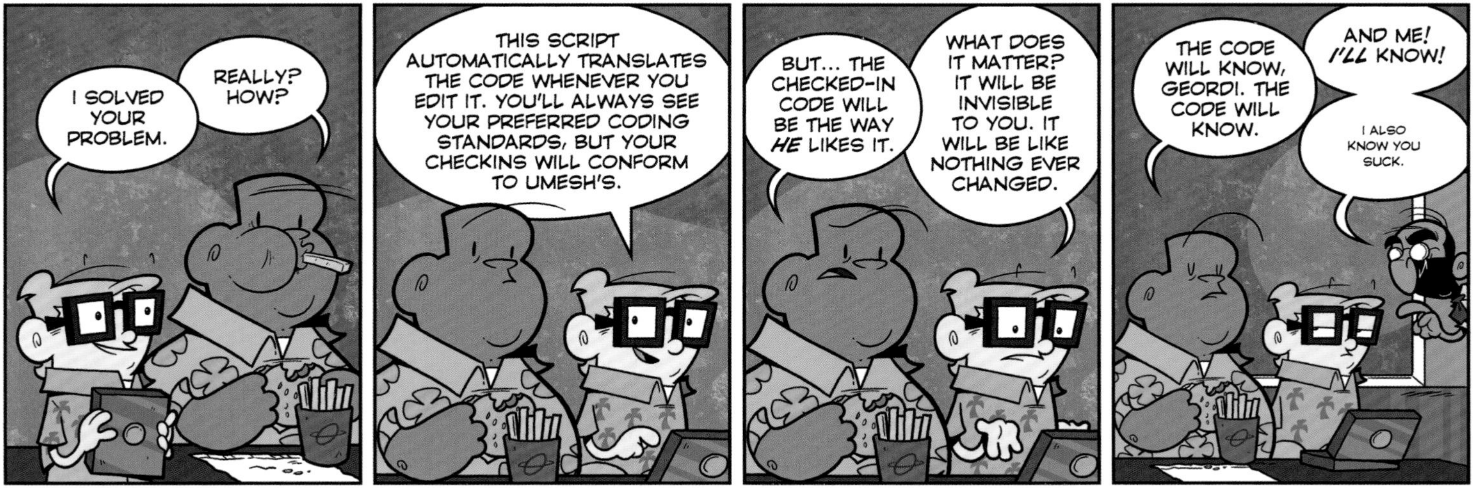
I SOLVED YOUR PROBLEM.
REALLY? HOW?
THIS SCRIPT AUTOMATICALLY TRANSLATES THE CODE WHENEVER YOU EDIT IT. YOU'LL ALWAYS SEE YOUR PREFERRED CODING STANDARDS, BUT YOUR CHECKINS WILL CONFORM TO UMESH'S.
BUT... THE CHECKED-IN CODE WILL BE THE WAY ***HE*** LIKES IT.
WHAT DOES IT MATTER? IT WILL BE INVISIBLE TO YOU. IT WILL BE LIKE NOTHING EVER CHANGED.
THE CODE WILL KNOW, GEORDI. THE CODE WILL KNOW.
AND ME! ***I'LL*** KNOW!
I ALSO KNOW YOU SUCK.

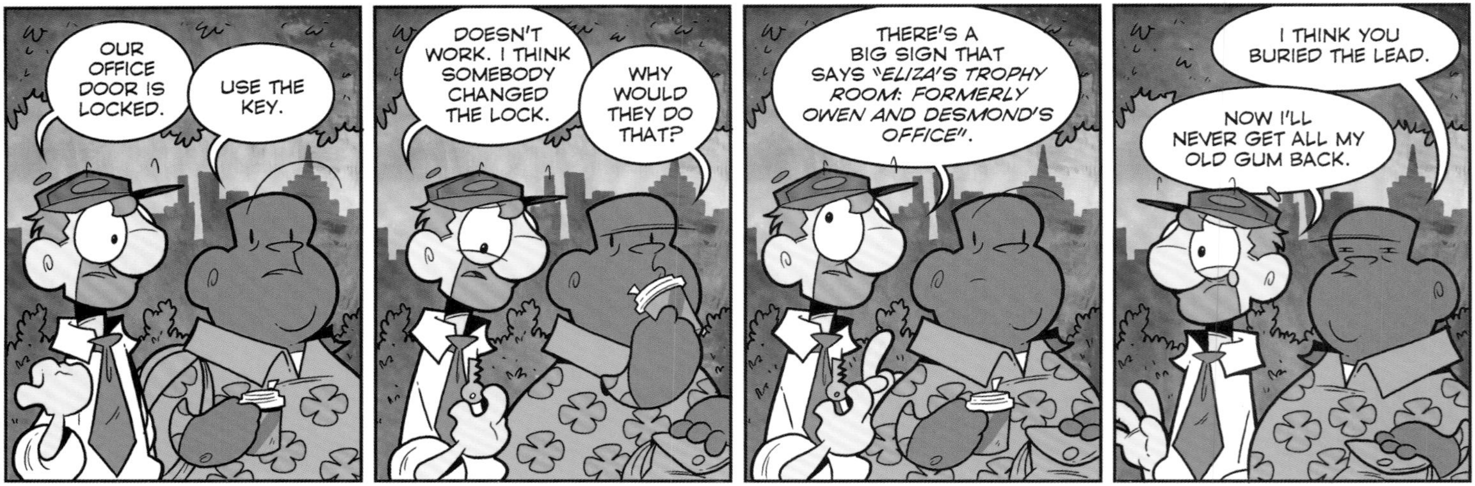
OUR OFFICE DOOR IS LOCKED.
USE THE KEY.
DOESN'T WORK. I THINK SOMEBODY CHANGED THE LOCK.
WHY WOULD THEY DO THAT?
THERE'S A BIG SIGN THAT SAYS "ELIZA'S TROPHY ROOM: FORMERLY OWEN AND DESMOND'S OFFICE".
NOW I'LL NEVER GET ALL MY OLD GUM BACK.
I THINK YOU BURIED THE LEAD.

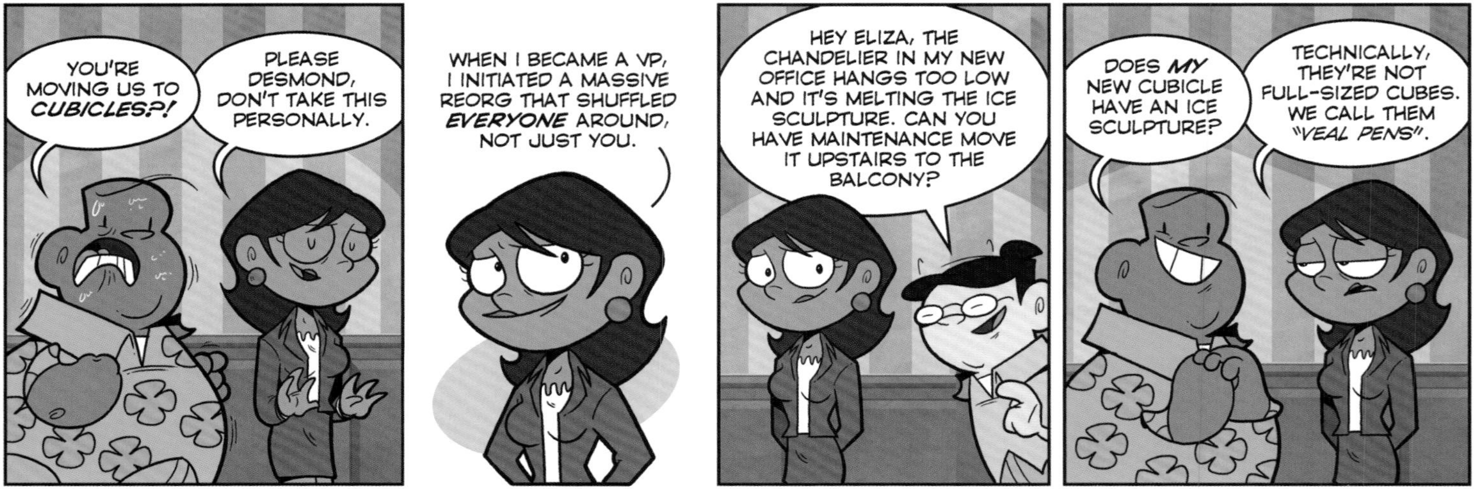
YOU'RE MOVING US TO CUBICLES?!
PLEASE DESMOND, DON'T TAKE THIS PERSONALLY.
WHEN I BECAME A VP, I INITIATED A MASSIVE REORG THAT SHUFFLED EVERYONE AROUND, NOT JUST YOU.
HEY ELIZA, THE CHANDELIER IN MY NEW OFFICE HANGS TOO LOW AND IT'S MELTING THE ICE SCULPTURE. CAN YOU HAVE MAINTENANCE MOVE IT UPSTAIRS TO THE BALCONY?
DOES MY NEW CUBICLE HAVE AN ICE SCULPTURE?
TECHNICALLY, THEY'RE NOT FULL-SIZED CUBES. WE CALL THEM "VEAL PENS".

UPGRADE PATH

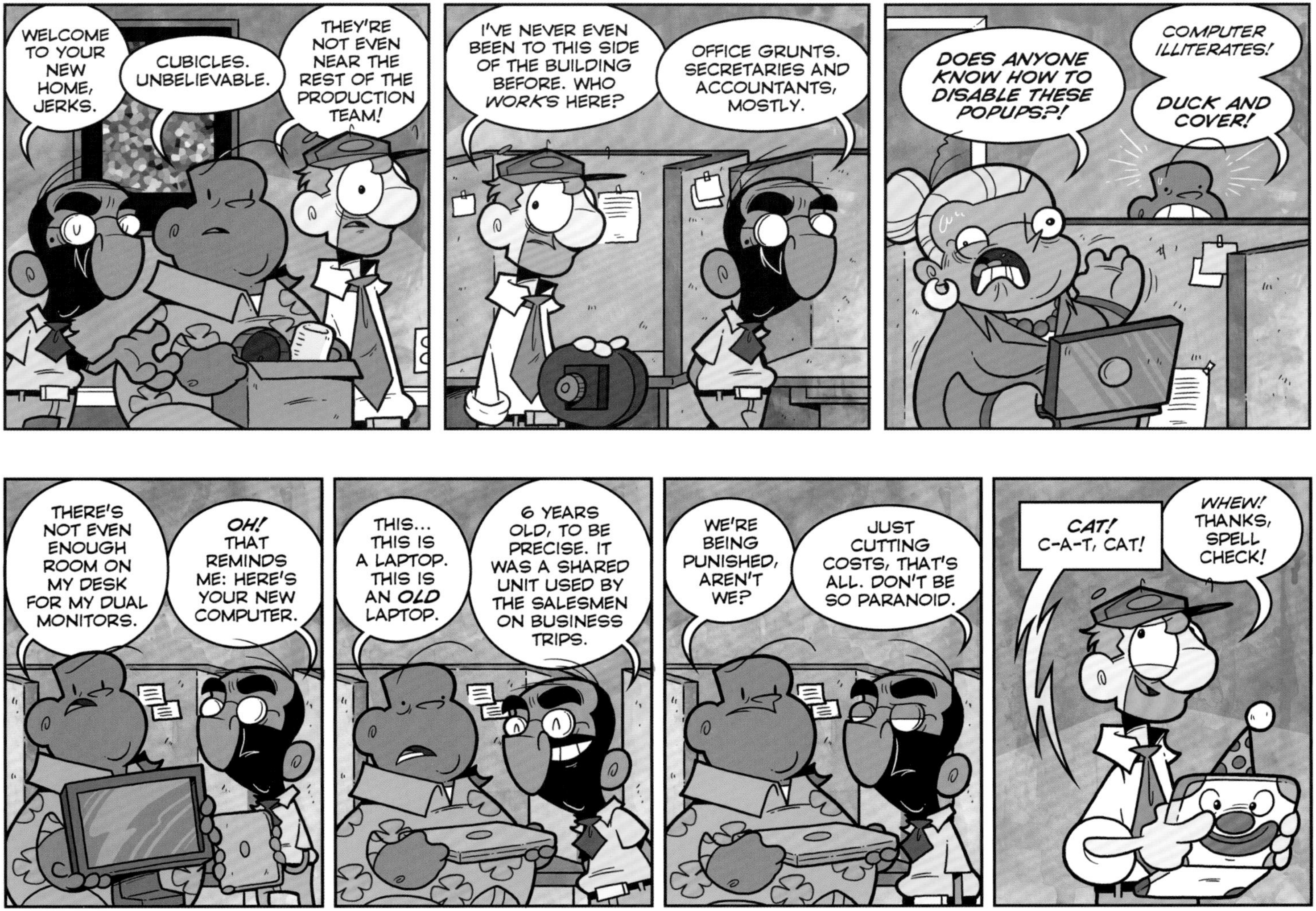
WELCOME TO YOUR NEW HOME, JERKS.
CUBICLES. UNBELIEVABLE.
THEY'RE NOT EVEN NEAR THE REST OF THE PRODUCTION TEAM!
I'VE NEVER EVEN BEEN TO THIS SIDE OF THE BUILDING BEFORE. WHO WORKS HERE?
OFFICE GRUNTS. SECRETARIES AND ACCOUNTANTS, MOSTLY.
DOES ANYONE KNOW HOW TO DISABLE THESE POPUPS?!
COMPUTER ILLITERATES!
DUCK AND COVER!
THERE'S NOT EVEN ENOUGH ROOM ON MY DESK FOR MY DUAL MONITORS.
OH! THAT REMINDS ME: HERE'S YOUR NEW COMPUTER.
THIS... THIS IS A LAPTOP. THIS IS AN OLD LAPTOP.
6 YEARS OLD, TO BE PRECISE. IT WAS A SHARED UNIT USED BY THE SALESMEN ON BUSINESS TRIPS.
WE'RE BEING PUNISHED, AREN'T WE?
JUST CUTTING COSTS, THAT'S ALL. DON'T BE SO PARANOID.
CAT! C-A-T, CAT!
WHEW! THANKS, SPELL CHECK!

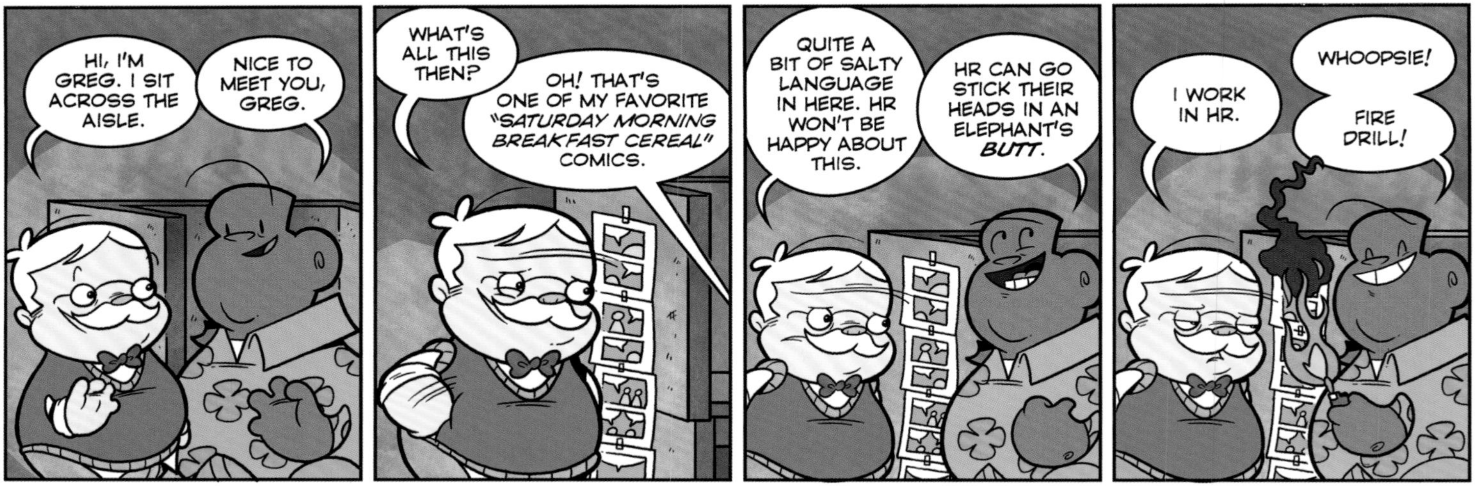
HI, I'M GREG. I SIT ACROSS THE AISLE.
NICE TO MEET YOU, GREG.
WHAT'S ALL THIS THEN?
OH! THAT'S ONE OF MY FAVORITE *"SATURDAY MORNING BREAKFAST CEREAL"* COMICS.
QUITE A BIT OF SALTY LANGUAGE IN HERE. HR WON'T BE HAPPY ABOUT THIS.
HR CAN GO STICK THEIR HEADS IN AN ELEPHANT'S ***BUTT***.
I WORK IN HR.
WHOOPSIE!
FIRE DRILL!

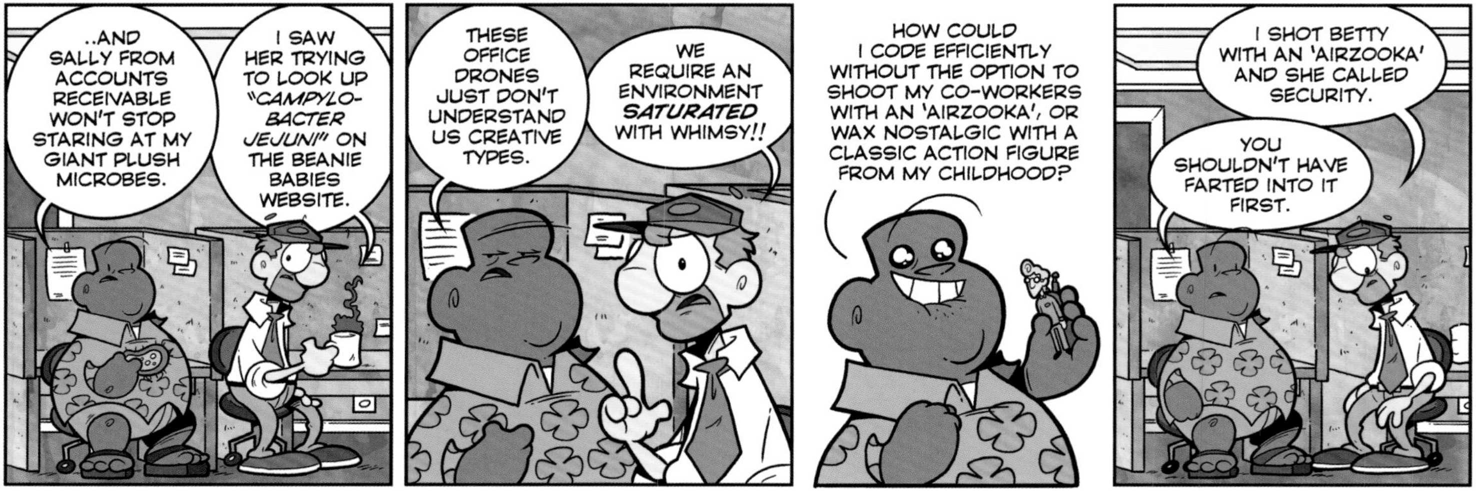
..AND SALLY FROM ACCOUNTS RECEIVABLE WON'T STOP STARING AT MY GIANT PLUSH MICROBES.
I SAW HER TRYING TO LOOK UP *"CAMPYLOBACTER JEJUNI"* ON THE BEANIE BABIES WEBSITE.
THESE OFFICE DRONES JUST DON'T UNDERSTAND US CREATIVE TYPES.
WE REQUIRE AN ENVIRONMENT ***SATURATED*** WITH WHIMSY!!
HOW COULD I CODE EFFICIENTLY WITHOUT THE OPTION TO SHOOT MY CO-WORKERS WITH AN 'AIRZOOKA', OR WAX NOSTALGIC WITH A CLASSIC ACTION FIGURE FROM MY CHILDHOOD?
I SHOT BETTY WITH AN 'AIRZOOKA' AND SHE CALLED SECURITY.
YOU SHOULDN'T HAVE FARTED INTO IT FIRST.

UPGRADE PATH

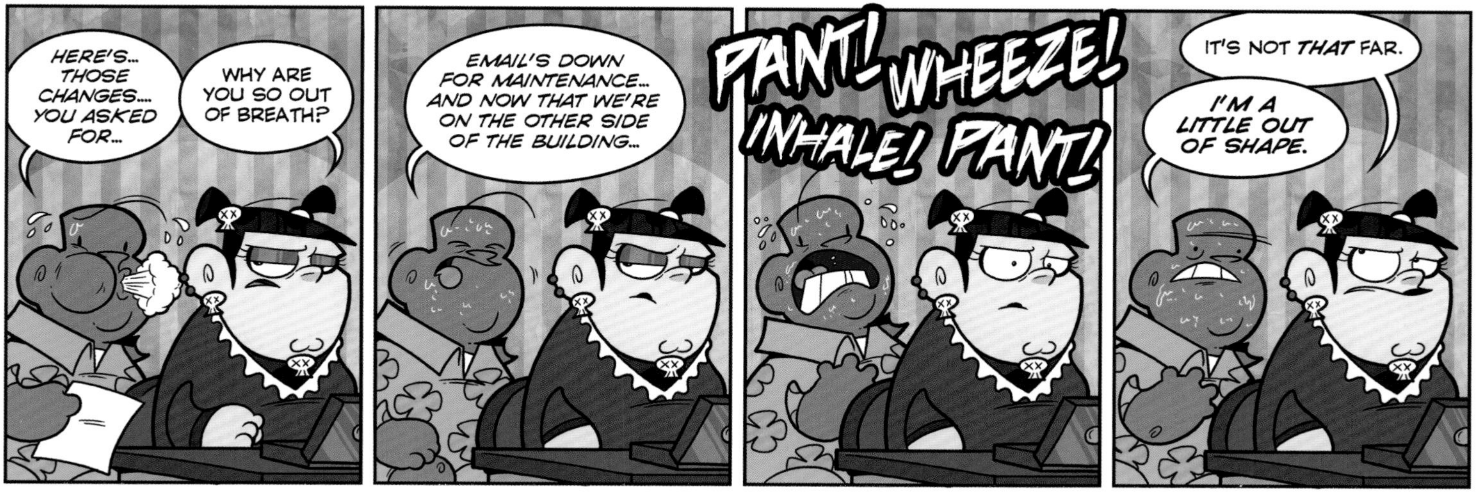
HERE'S... THOSE CHANGES.... YOU ASKED FOR...
WHY ARE YOU SO OUT OF BREATH?
EMAIL'S DOWN FOR MAINTENANCE... AND NOW THAT WE'RE ON THE OTHER SIDE OF THE BUILDING...
PANT! WHEEZE! INHALE! PANT!
IT'S NOT THAT FAR.
I'M A LITTLE OUT OF SHAPE.

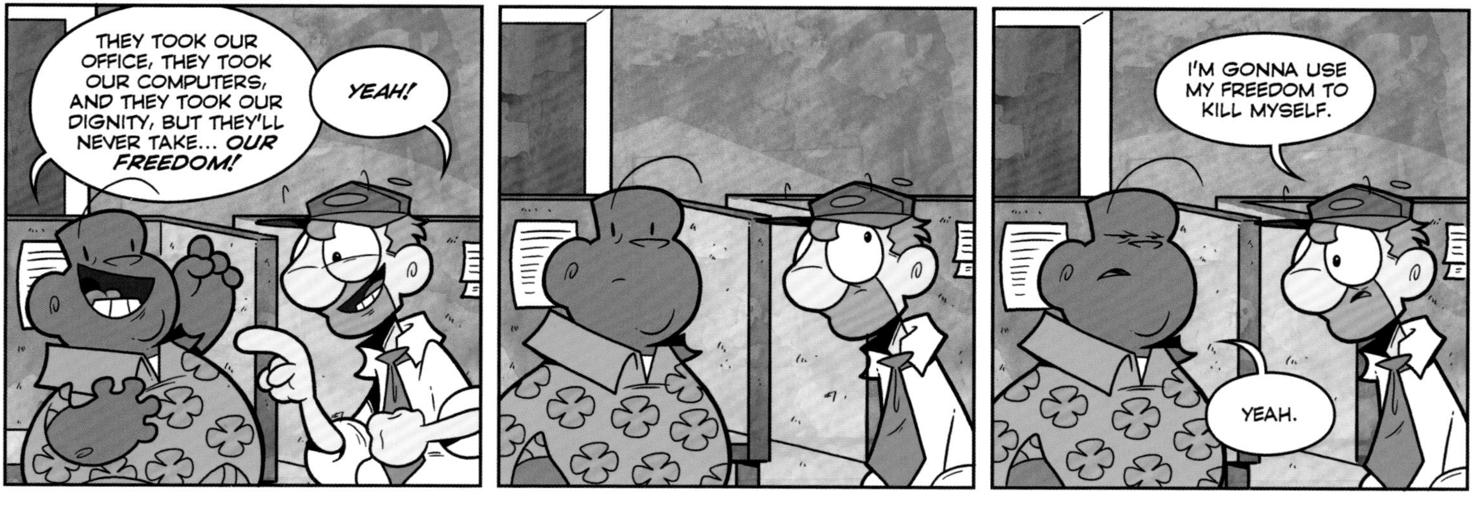
THEY TOOK OUR OFFICE, THEY TOOK OUR COMPUTERS, AND THEY TOOK OUR DIGNITY, BUT THEY'LL NEVER TAKE... OUR FREEDOM!
YEAH!
I'M GONNA USE MY FREEDOM TO KILL MYSELF.
YEAH.

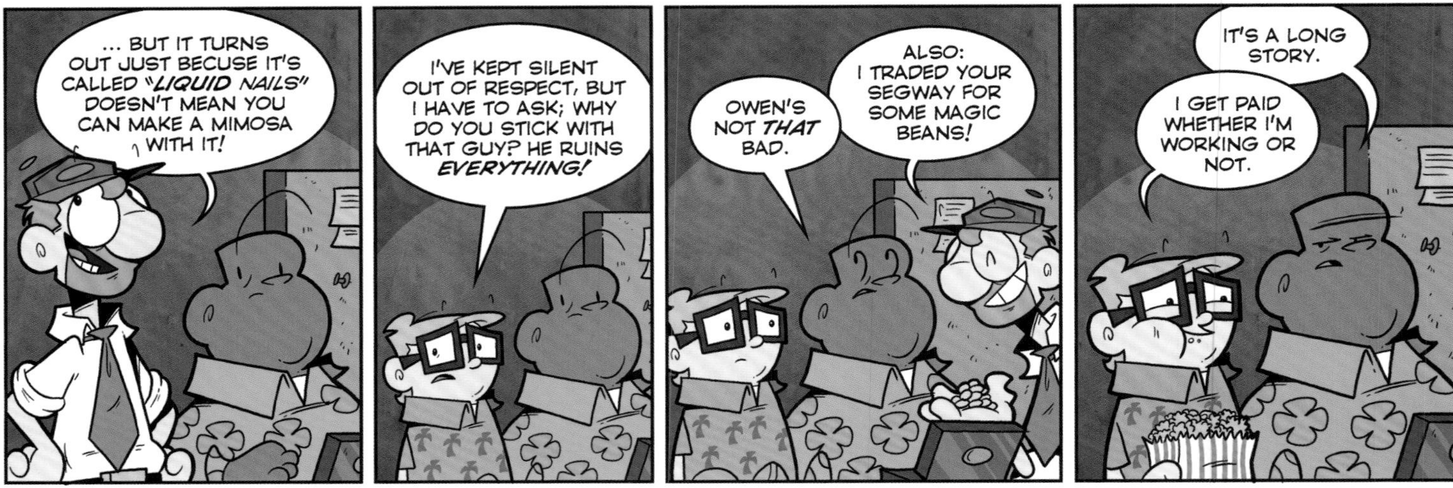
... BUT IT TURNS OUT JUST BECUSE IT'S CALLED "LIQUID NAILS" DOESN'T MEAN YOU CAN MAKE A MIMOSA WITH IT!
I'VE KEPT SILENT OUT OF RESPECT, BUT I HAVE TO ASK; WHY DO YOU STICK WITH THAT GUY? HE RUINS EVERYTHING!
OWEN'S NOT THAT BAD.
ALSO: I TRADED YOUR SEGWAY FOR SOME MAGIC BEANS!
IT'S A LONG STORY.
I GET PAID WHETHER I'M WORKING OR NOT.

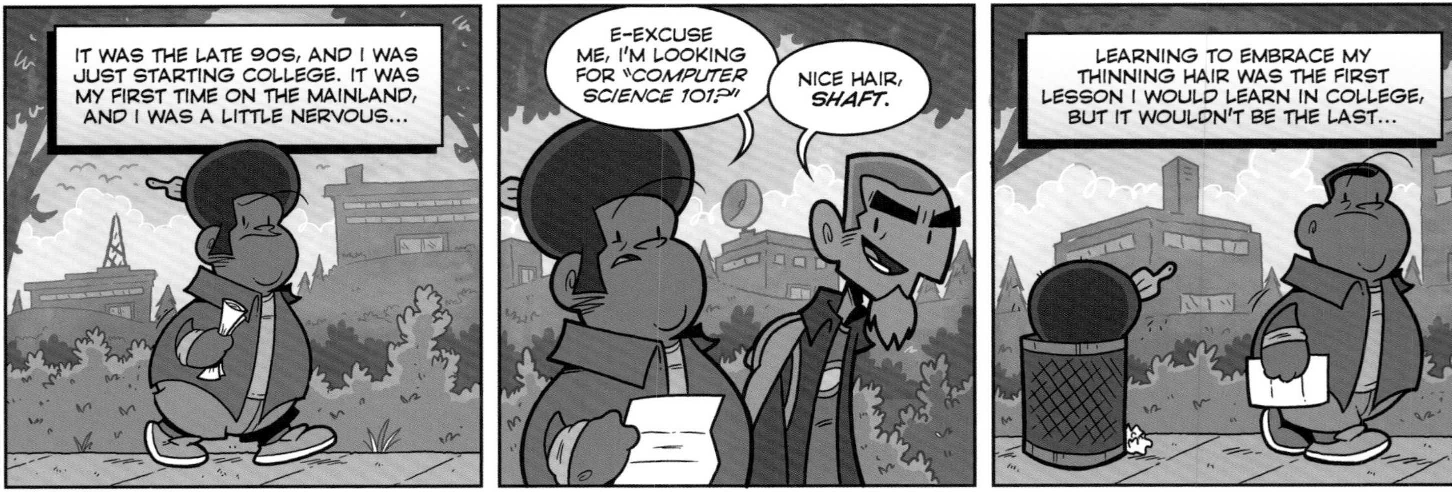
IT WAS THE LATE 90S, AND I WAS JUST STARTING COLLEGE. IT WAS MY FIRST TIME ON THE MAINLAND, AND I WAS A LITTLE NERVOUS...
E-EXCUSE ME, I'M LOOKING FOR "COMPUTER SCIENCE 101?"
NICE HAIR, SHAFT.
LEARNING TO EMBRACE MY THINNING HAIR WAS THE FIRST LESSON I WOULD LEARN IN COLLEGE, BUT IT WOULDN'T BE THE LAST...

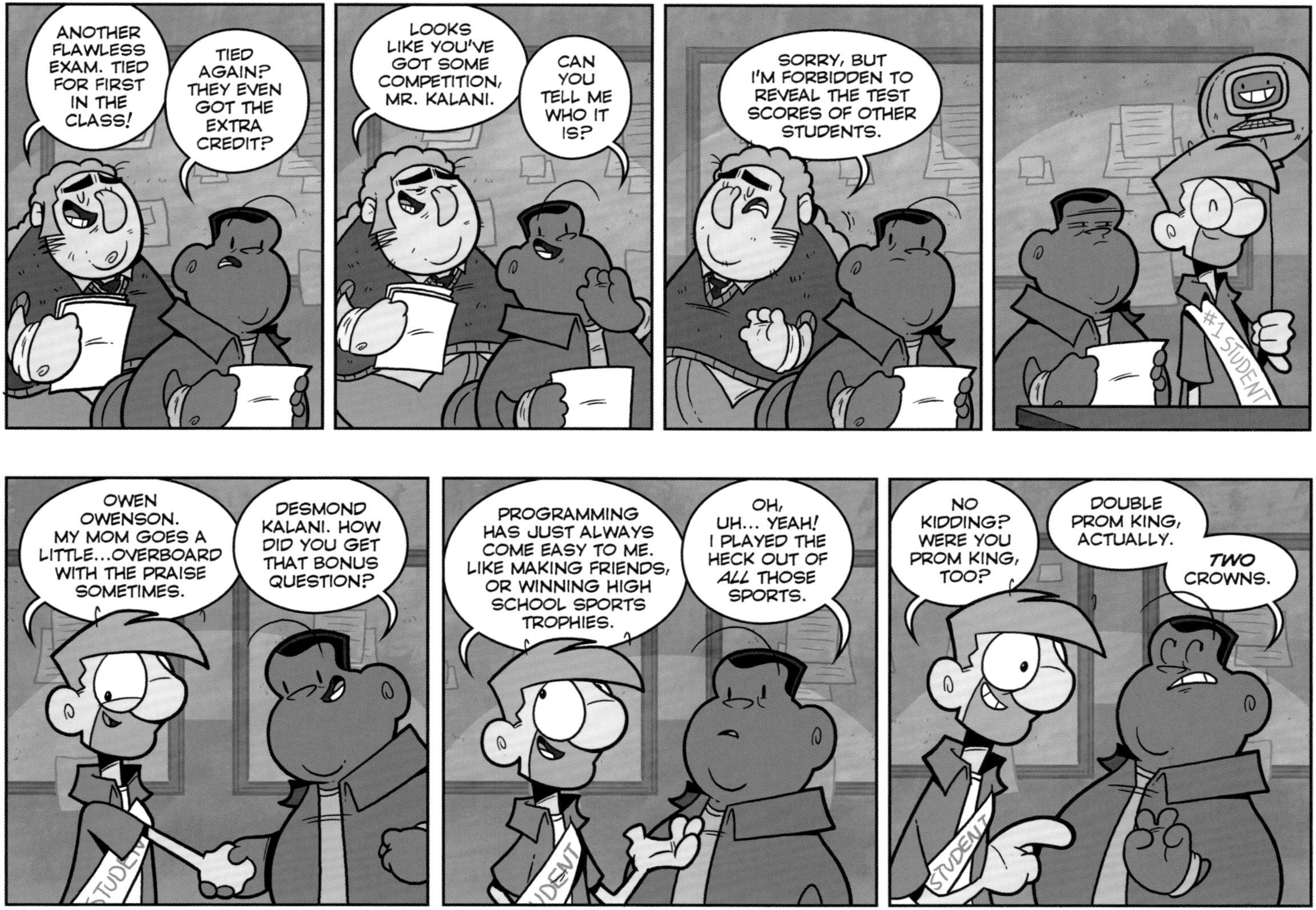
ANOTHER FLAWLESS EXAM. TIED FOR FIRST IN THE CLASS!
TIED AGAIN? THEY EVEN GOT THE EXTRA CREDIT?
LOOKS LIKE YOU'VE GOT SOME COMPETITION, MR. KALANI.
CAN YOU TELL ME WHO IT IS?
SORRY, BUT I'M FORBIDDEN TO REVEAL THE TEST SCORES OF OTHER STUDENTS.
#1 STUDENT
OWEN OWENSON. MY MOM GOES A LITTLE...OVERBOARD WITH THE PRAISE SOMETIMES.
DESMOND KALANI. HOW DID YOU GET THAT BONUS QUESTION?
PROGRAMMING HAS JUST ALWAYS COME EASY TO ME. LIKE MAKING FRIENDS, OR WINNING HIGH SCHOOL SPORTS TROPHIES.
OH, UH... YEAH! I PLAYED THE HECK OUT OF *ALL* THOSE SPORTS.
NO KIDDING? WERE YOU PROM KING, TOO?
DOUBLE PROM KING, ACTUALLY.
TWO CROWNS.

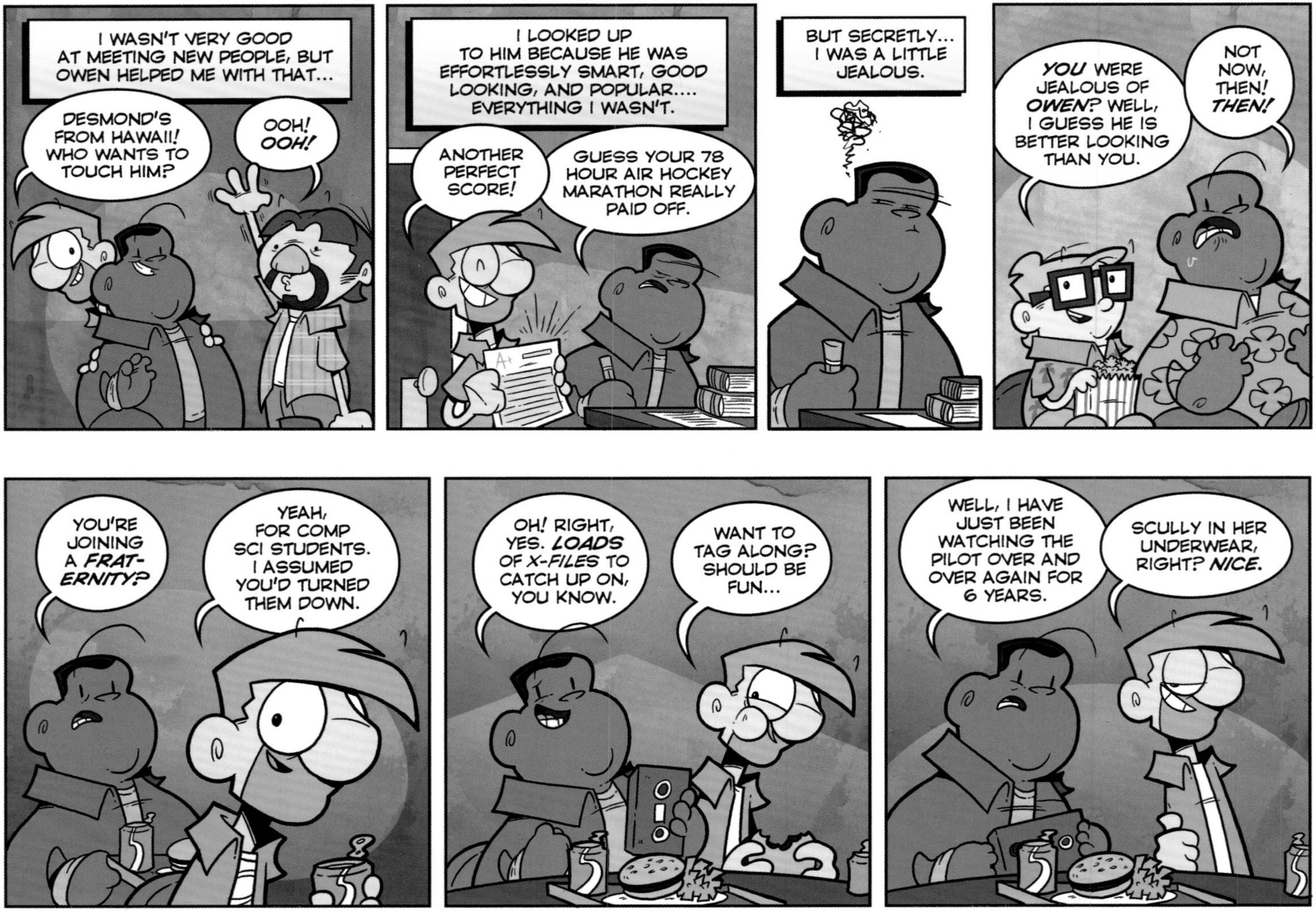
I WASN'T VERY GOOD AT MEETING NEW PEOPLE, BUT OWEN HELPED ME WITH THAT...
DESMOND'S FROM HAWAII! WHO WANTS TO TOUCH HIM?
OOH! OOH!
I LOOKED UP TO HIM BECAUSE HE WAS EFFORTLESSLY SMART, GOOD LOOKING, AND POPULAR.... EVERYTHING I WASN'T.
ANOTHER PERFECT SCORE!
GUESS YOUR 78 HOUR AIR HOCKEY MARATHON REALLY PAID OFF.
BUT SECRETLY... I WAS A LITTLE JEALOUS.
YOU WERE JEALOUS OF OWEN? WELL, I GUESS HE IS BETTER LOOKING THAN YOU.
NOT NOW, THEN! THEN!
YOU'RE JOINING A FRATERNITY?
YEAH, FOR COMP SCI STUDENTS. I ASSUMED YOU'D TURNED THEM DOWN.
OH! RIGHT, YES. LOADS OF X-FILES TO CATCH UP ON, YOU KNOW.
WANT TO TAG ALONG? SHOULD BE FUN...
WELL, I HAVE JUST BEEN WATCHING THE PILOT OVER AND OVER AGAIN FOR 6 YEARS.
SCULLY IN HER UNDERWEAR, RIGHT? NICE.

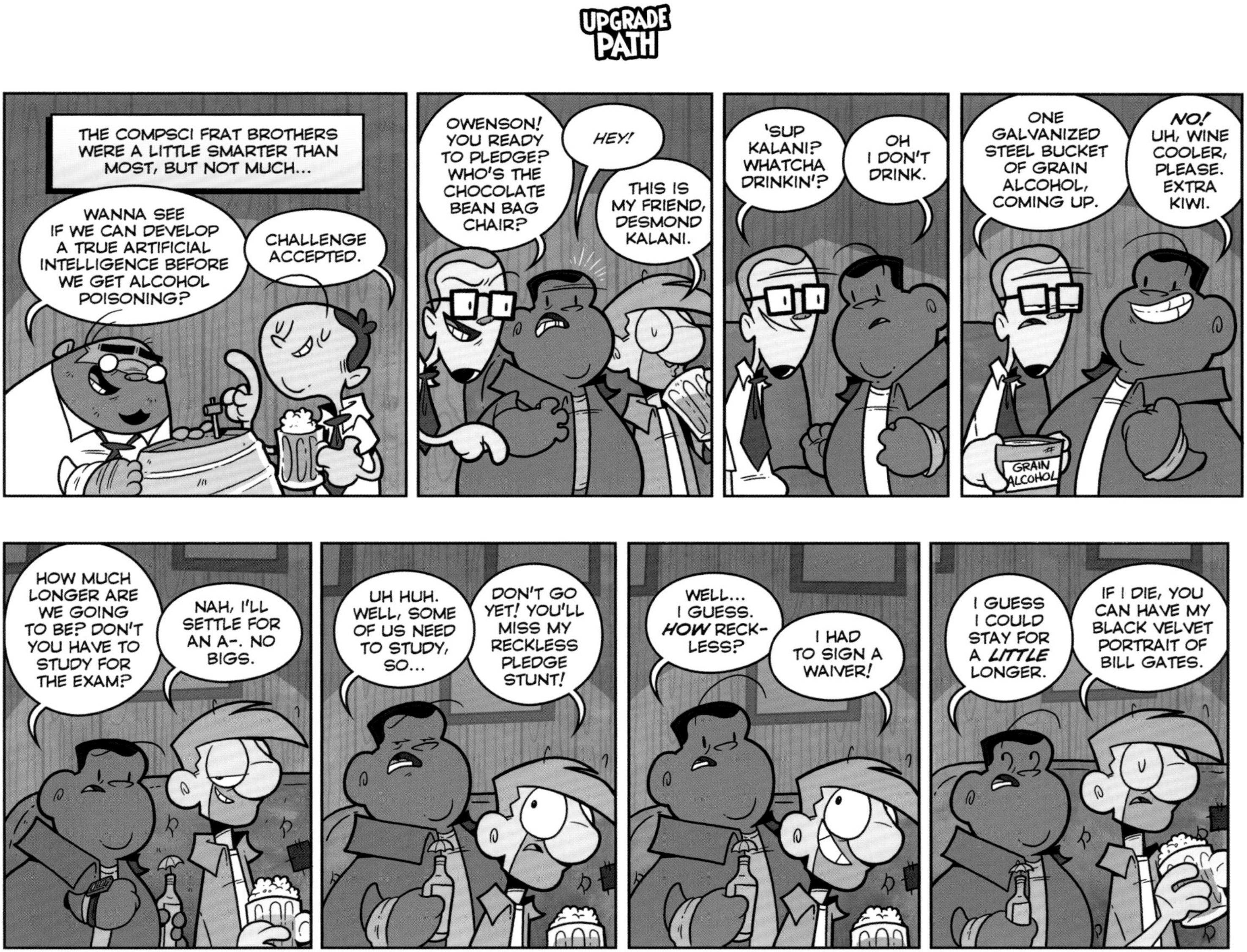
UPGRADE PATH
THE COMPSCI FRAT BROTHERS WERE A LITTLE SMARTER THAN MOST, BUT NOT MUCH...
WANNA SEE IF WE CAN DEVELOP A TRUE ARTIFICIAL INTELLIGENCE BEFORE WE GET ALCOHOL POISONING?
CHALLENGE ACCEPTED.
OWENSON! YOU READY TO PLEDGE? WHO'S THE CHOCOLATE BEAN BAG CHAIR?
HEY!
THIS IS MY FRIEND, DESMOND KALANI.
'SUP KALANI? WHATCHA DRINKIN'?
OH I DON'T DRINK.
ONE GALVANIZED STEEL BUCKET OF GRAIN ALCOHOL, COMING UP.
GRAIN ALCOHOL
NO! UH, WINE COOLER, PLEASE. EXTRA KIWI.
HOW MUCH LONGER ARE WE GOING TO BE? DON'T YOU HAVE TO STUDY FOR THE EXAM?
NAH, I'LL SETTLE FOR AN A-. NO BIGS.
UH HUH. WELL, SOME OF US NEED TO STUDY, SO...
DON'T GO YET! YOU'LL MISS MY RECKLESS PLEDGE STUNT!
WELL... I GUESS. HOW RECK-LESS?
I HAD TO SIGN A WAIVER!
I GUESS I COULD STAY FOR A LITTLE LONGER.
IF I DIE, YOU CAN HAVE MY BLACK VELVET PORTRAIT OF BILL GATES.

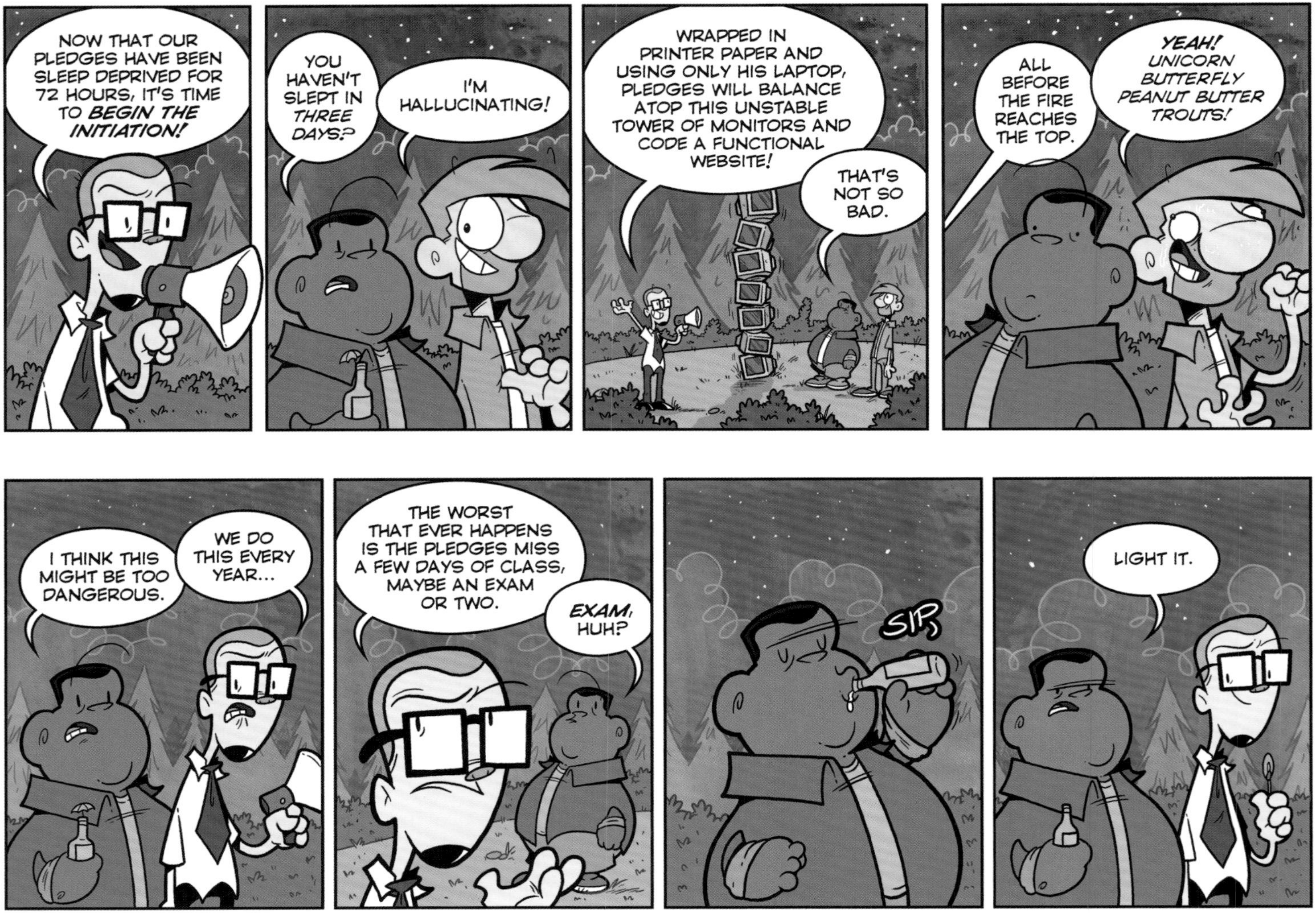
NOW THAT OUR PLEDGES HAVE BEEN SLEEP DEPRIVED FOR 72 HOURS, IT'S TIME TO BEGIN THE INITIATION!
YOU HAVEN'T SLEPT IN THREE DAYS?
I'M HALLUCINATING!
WRAPPED IN PRINTER PAPER AND USING ONLY HIS LAPTOP, PLEDGES WILL BALANCE ATOP THIS UNSTABLE TOWER OF MONITORS AND CODE A FUNCTIONAL WEBSITE!
THAT'S NOT SO BAD.
ALL BEFORE THE FIRE REACHES THE TOP.
YEAH! UNICORN BUTTERFLY PEANUT BUTTER TROUTS!
I THINK THIS MIGHT BE TOO DANGEROUS.
WE DO THIS EVERY YEAR...
THE WORST THAT EVER HAPPENS IS THE PLEDGES MISS A FEW DAYS OF CLASS, MAYBE AN EXAM OR TWO.
EXAM, HUH?
SIP,
LIGHT IT.

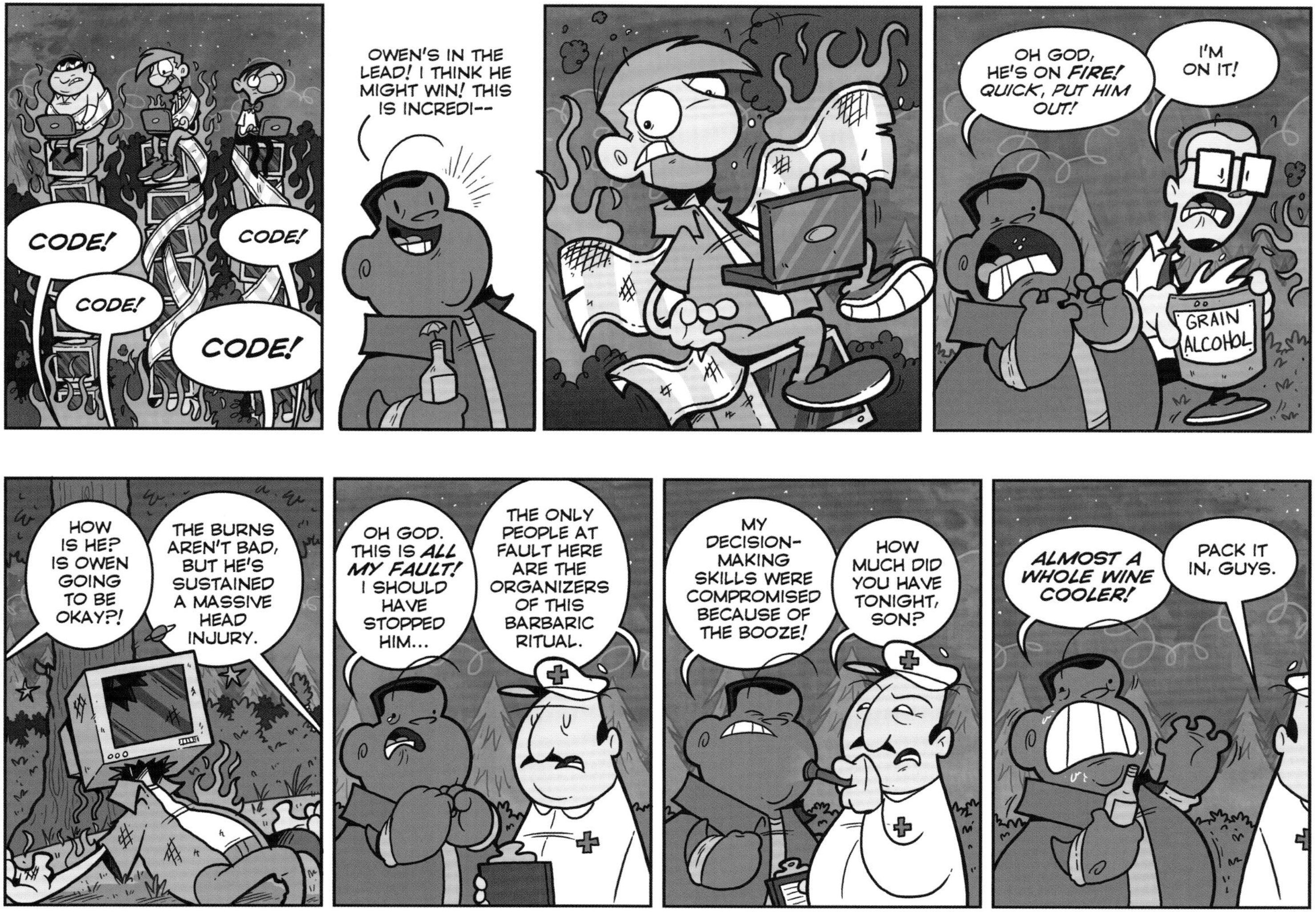
CODE!
CODE!
CODE!
CODE!
OWEN'S IN THE LEAD! I THINK HE MIGHT WIN! THIS IS INCREDI--
OH GOD, HE'S ON FIRE! QUICK, PUT HIM OUT!
I'M ON IT!
GRAIN ALCOHOL
HOW IS HE? IS OWEN GOING TO BE OKAY?!
THE BURNS AREN'T BAD, BUT HE'S SUSTAINED A MASSIVE HEAD INJURY.
OH GOD. THIS IS ALL MY FAULT! I SHOULD HAVE STOPPED HIM...
THE ONLY PEOPLE AT FAULT HERE ARE THE ORGANIZERS OF THIS BARBARIC RITUAL.
MY DECISION-MAKING SKILLS WERE COMPROMISED BECAUSE OF THE BOOZE!
HOW MUCH DID YOU HAVE TONIGHT, SON?
ALMOST A WHOLE WINE COOLER!
PACK IT IN, GUYS.

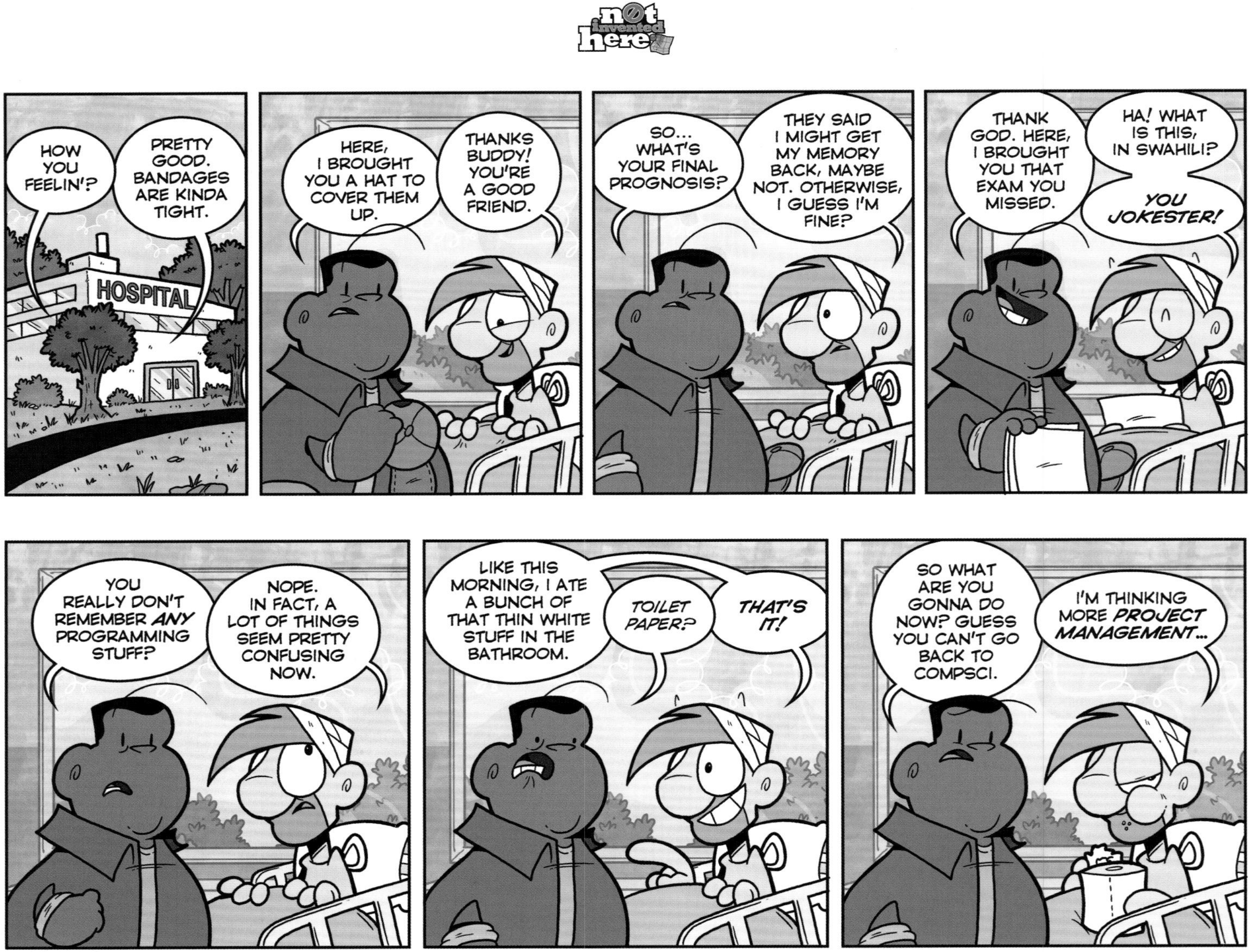
not invented here
HOW YOU FEELIN'?
PRETTY GOOD. BANDAGES ARE KINDA TIGHT.
HOSPITAL
HERE, I BROUGHT YOU A HAT TO COVER THEM UP.
THANKS BUDDY! YOU'RE A GOOD FRIEND.
SO... WHAT'S YOUR FINAL PROGNOSIS?
THEY SAID I MIGHT GET MY MEMORY BACK, MAYBE NOT. OTHERWISE, I GUESS I'M FINE?
THANK GOD. HERE, I BROUGHT YOU THAT EXAM YOU MISSED.
HA! WHAT IS THIS, IN SWAHILI?
YOU JOKESTER!
YOU REALLY DON'T REMEMBER ANY PROGRAMMING STUFF?
NOPE. IN FACT, A LOT OF THINGS SEEM PRETTY CONFUSING NOW.
LIKE THIS MORNING, I ATE A BUNCH OF THAT THIN WHITE STUFF IN THE BATHROOM.
TOILET PAPER?
THAT'S IT!
SO WHAT ARE YOU GONNA DO NOW? GUESS YOU CAN'T GO BACK TO COMPSCI.
I'M THINKING MORE PROJECT MANAGEMENT...

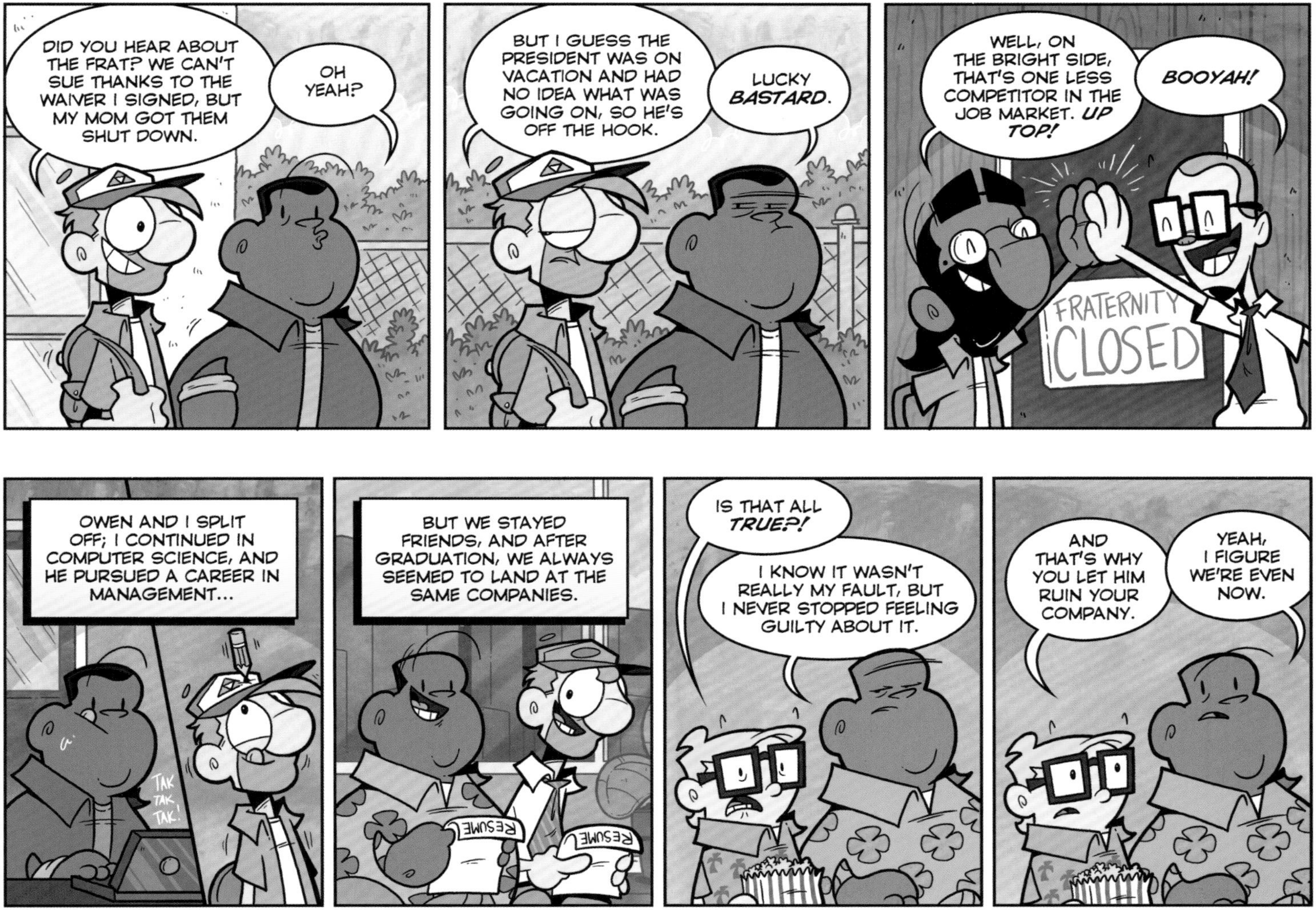
DID YOU HEAR ABOUT THE FRAT? WE CAN'T SUE THANKS TO THE WAIVER I SIGNED, BUT MY MOM GOT THEM SHUT DOWN.
OH YEAH?
BUT I GUESS THE PRESIDENT WAS ON VACATION AND HAD NO IDEA WHAT WAS GOING ON, SO HE'S OFF THE HOOK.
LUCKY BASTARD.
WELL, ON THE BRIGHT SIDE, THAT'S ONE LESS COMPETITOR IN THE JOB MARKET. UP TOP!
BOOYAH!
FRATERNITY CLOSED
OWEN AND I SPLIT OFF; I CONTINUED IN COMPUTER SCIENCE, AND HE PURSUED A CAREER IN MANAGEMENT...
TAK TAK TAK!
BUT WE STAYED FRIENDS, AND AFTER GRADUATION, WE ALWAYS SEEMED TO LAND AT THE SAME COMPANIES.
RESUME
RESUME
IS THAT ALL TRUE?!
I KNOW IT WASN'T REALLY MY FAULT, BUT I NEVER STOPPED FEELING GUILTY ABOUT IT.
AND THAT'S WHY YOU LET HIM RUIN YOUR COMPANY.
YEAH, I FIGURE WE'RE EVEN NOW.

The New Guy

After over two years of drawing *Not Invented Here*, our original artist moved on to a new project, adopting a pseudonym for reasons of national security. It was a friendly breakup, and he still helps write *NIH* and contributes the occasional guest strip (see pages 214-217). He also had the difficult task of helping choose his successor.

We knew this was going to be hard on our readers. For two years Owen, Desmond, et al., had looked a *certain way*. With a new artist would they even be recognizable as the same people?

Then we got these sketches from our friend Jeff Zugale (**www.jeffzugale.com**), a storyboard artist/video game illustrator/cartoonist/hair band musician who had made a reputation on the Internet with a series of paintings and comics commissioned by author John Scalzi. Jeff's style was undeniably a change of pace, but we both immediately found our characters looking out at us from behind these new faces. We loved that Jeff hadn't tried to slavishly emulate the old look, but instead interpreted each personality with his own style. He got the job.

And since then, as you will see, Jeff's style has continually evolved, becoming increasingly fluid and three-dimensional, which in turn has allowed us to shift our writing towards a more cinematic approach, including some truly wild perspective shots, all the while remaining quintessentially *Not Invented Here*.

Plus ça change, plus c'est la même chose!

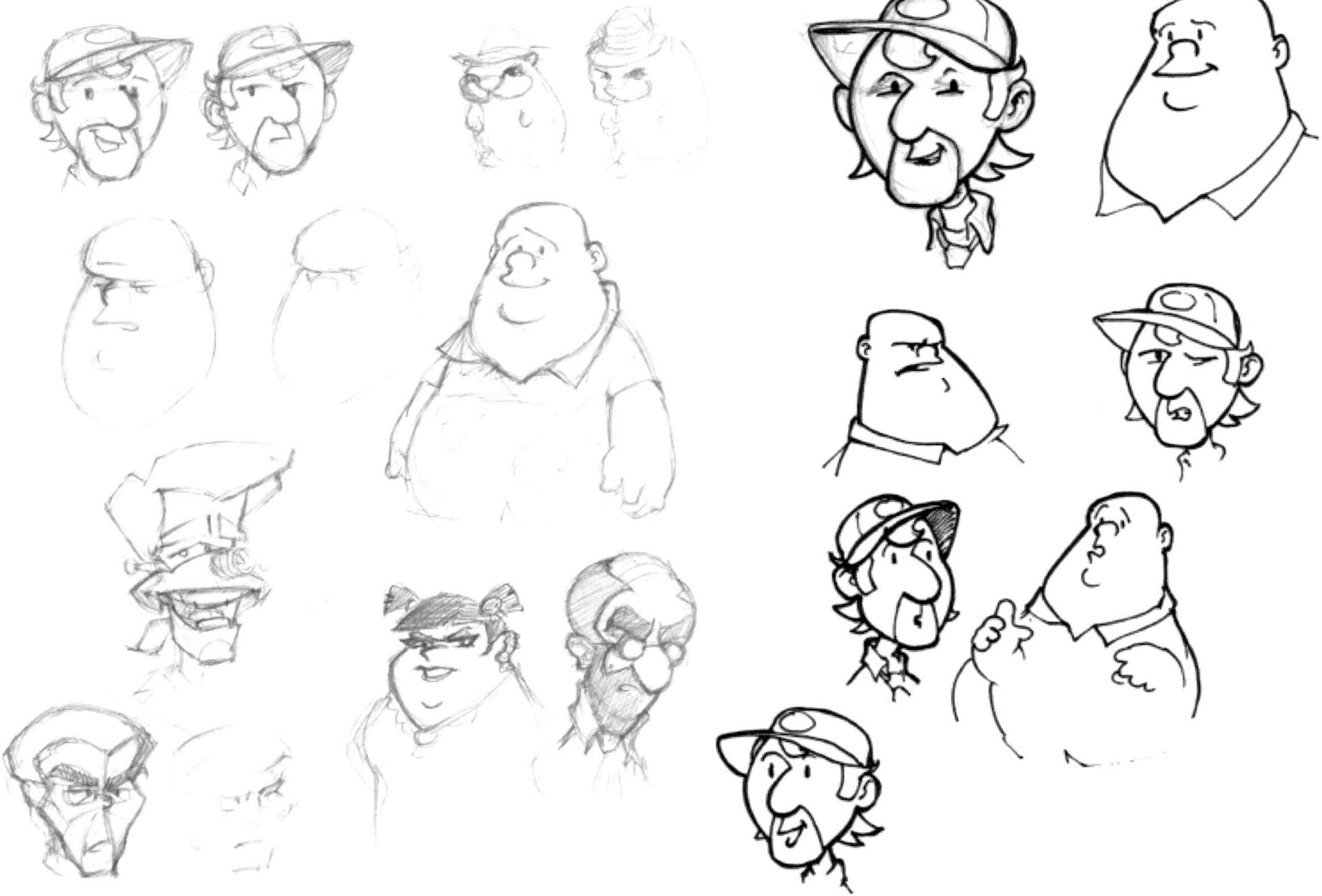

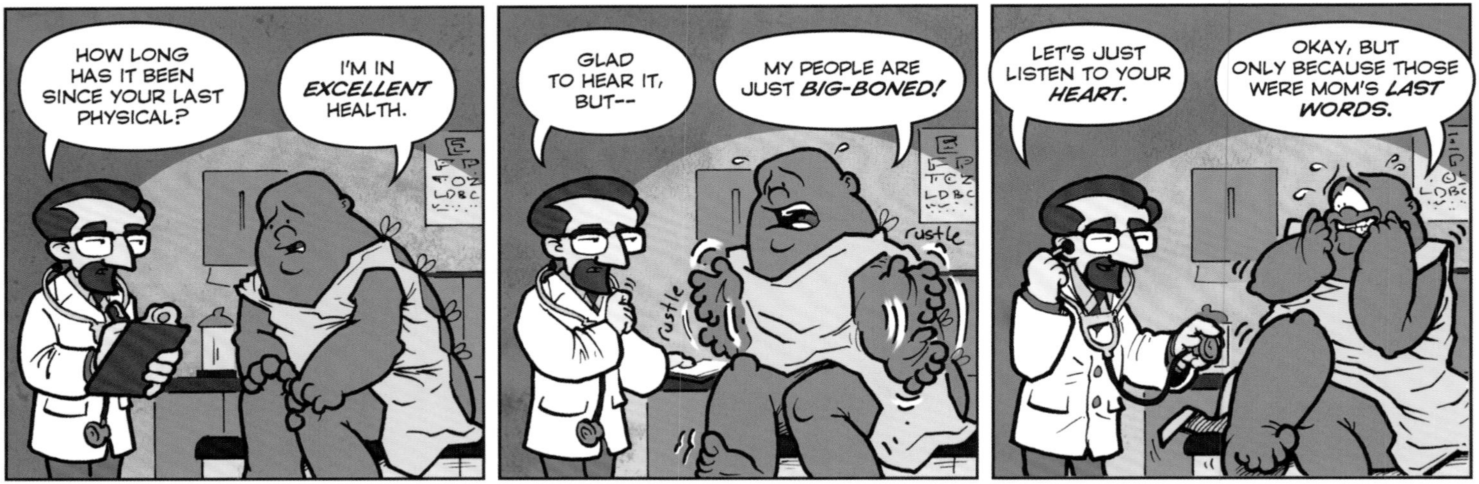
HOW LONG HAS IT BEEN SINCE YOUR LAST PHYSICAL?
I'M IN *EXCELLENT* HEALTH.
GLAD TO HEAR IT, BUT--
MY PEOPLE ARE JUST *BIG-BONED!*
rustle
rustle
LET'S JUST LISTEN TO YOUR *HEART*.
OKAY, BUT ONLY BECAUSE THOSE WERE MOM'S *LAST WORDS*.

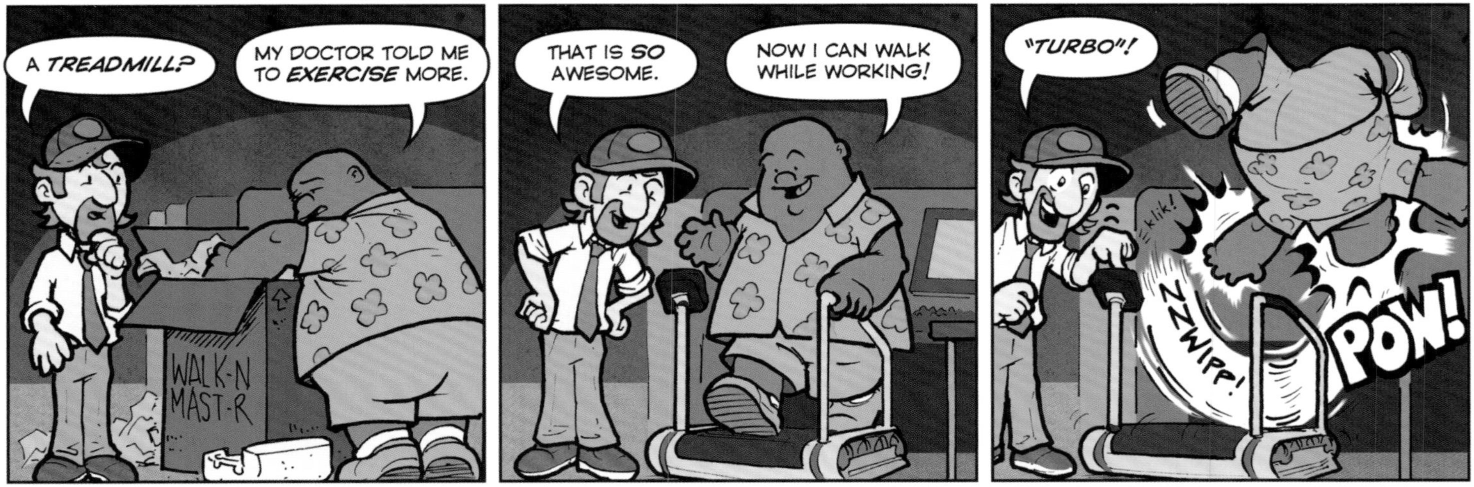
A *TREADMILL?*
MY DOCTOR TOLD ME TO *EXERCISE* MORE.
WALK-N MAST-R
THAT IS *SO* AWESOME.
NOW I CAN WALK WHILE WORKING!
"TURBO"!
klik!
ZZWIPP!
POW!

UPGRADE PATH

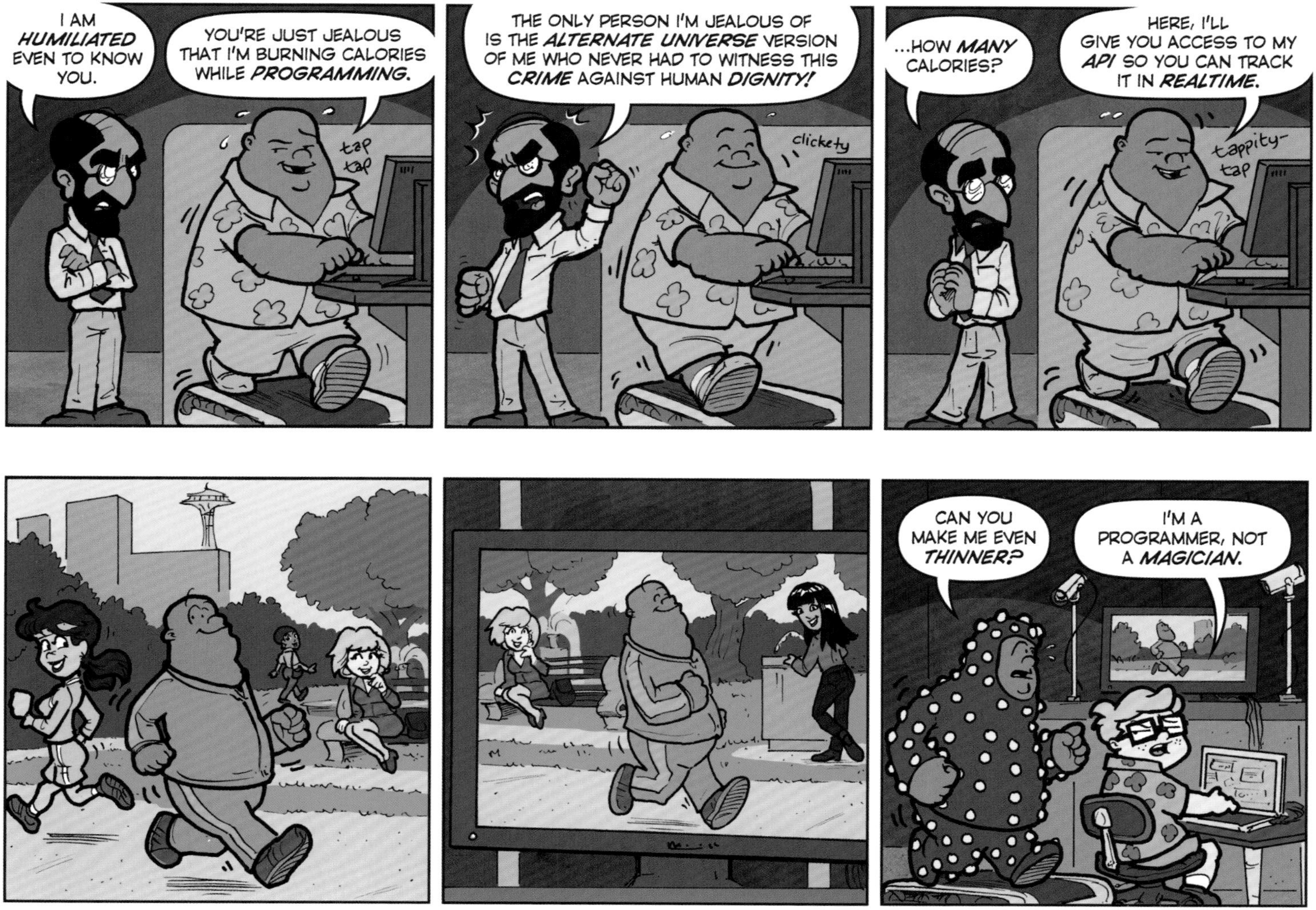
I AM HUMILIATED EVEN TO KNOW YOU.
YOU'RE JUST JEALOUS THAT I'M BURNING CALORIES WHILE PROGRAMMING.
tap tap
THE ONLY PERSON I'M JEALOUS OF IS THE ALTERNATE UNIVERSE VERSION OF ME WHO NEVER HAD TO WITNESS THIS CRIME AGAINST HUMAN DIGNITY!
clickety
...HOW MANY CALORIES?
HERE, I'LL GIVE YOU ACCESS TO MY API SO YOU CAN TRACK IT IN REALTIME.
tappity-tap
CAN YOU MAKE ME EVEN THINNER?
I'M A PROGRAMMER, NOT A MAGICIAN.

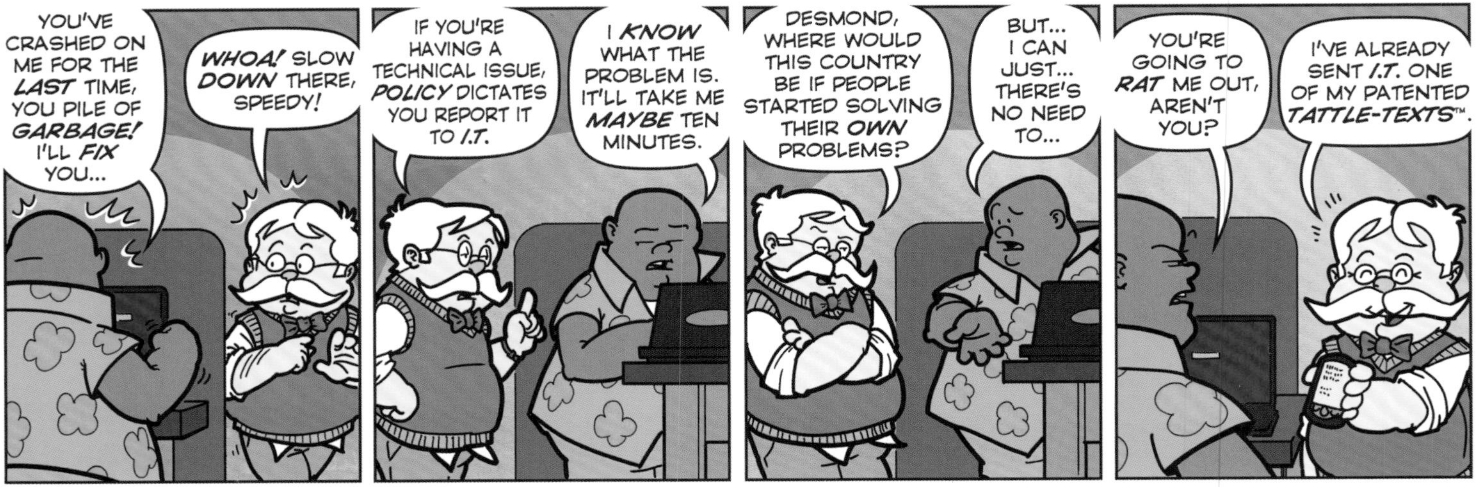
YOU'VE CRASHED ON ME FOR THE LAST TIME, YOU PILE OF GARBAGE! I'LL FIX YOU...
WHOA! SLOW DOWN THERE, SPEEDY!
IF YOU'RE HAVING A TECHNICAL ISSUE, POLICY DICTATES YOU REPORT IT TO I.T.
I KNOW WHAT THE PROBLEM IS. IT'LL TAKE ME MAYBE TEN MINUTES.
DESMOND, WHERE WOULD THIS COUNTRY BE IF PEOPLE STARTED SOLVING THEIR OWN PROBLEMS?
BUT... I CAN JUST... THERE'S NO NEED TO...
YOU'RE GOING TO RAT ME OUT, AREN'T YOU?
I'VE ALREADY SENT I.T. ONE OF MY PATENTED TATTLE-TEXTS™.

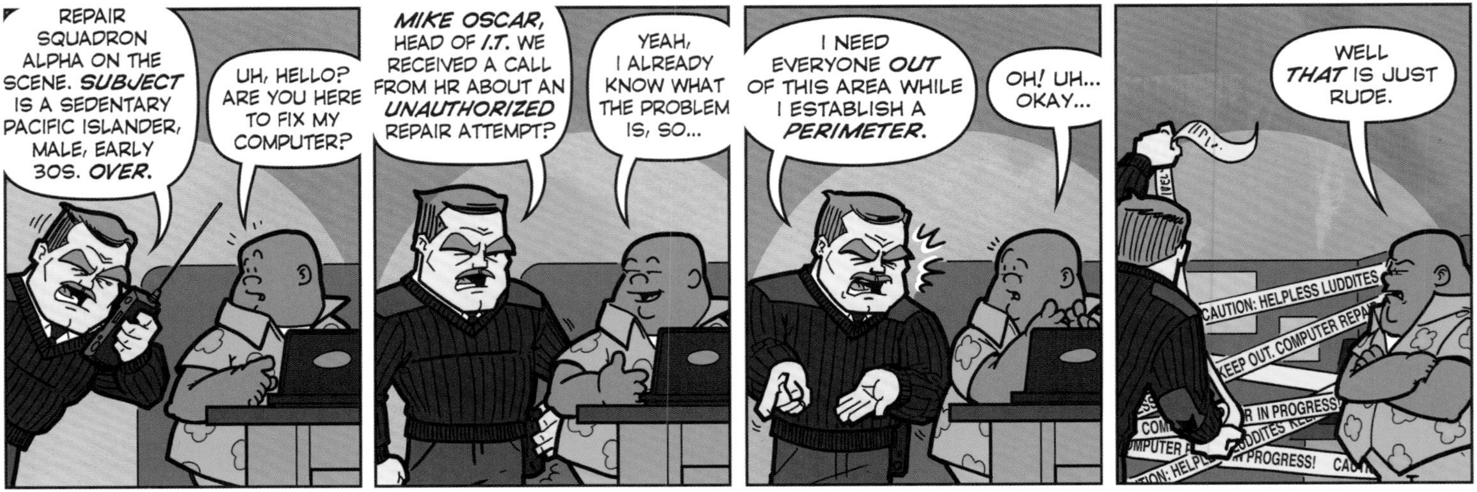
REPAIR SQUADRON ALPHA ON THE SCENE. SUBJECT IS A SEDENTARY PACIFIC ISLANDER, MALE, EARLY 30S. OVER.
UH, HELLO? ARE YOU HERE TO FIX MY COMPUTER?
MIKE OSCAR, HEAD OF I.T. WE RECEIVED A CALL FROM HR ABOUT AN UNAUTHORIZED REPAIR ATTEMPT?
YEAH, I ALREADY KNOW WHAT THE PROBLEM IS, SO...
I NEED EVERYONE OUT OF THIS AREA WHILE I ESTABLISH A PERIMETER.
OH! UH... OKAY...
WELL THAT IS JUST RUDE.
CAUTION: HELPLESS LUDDITES

UPGRADE PATH

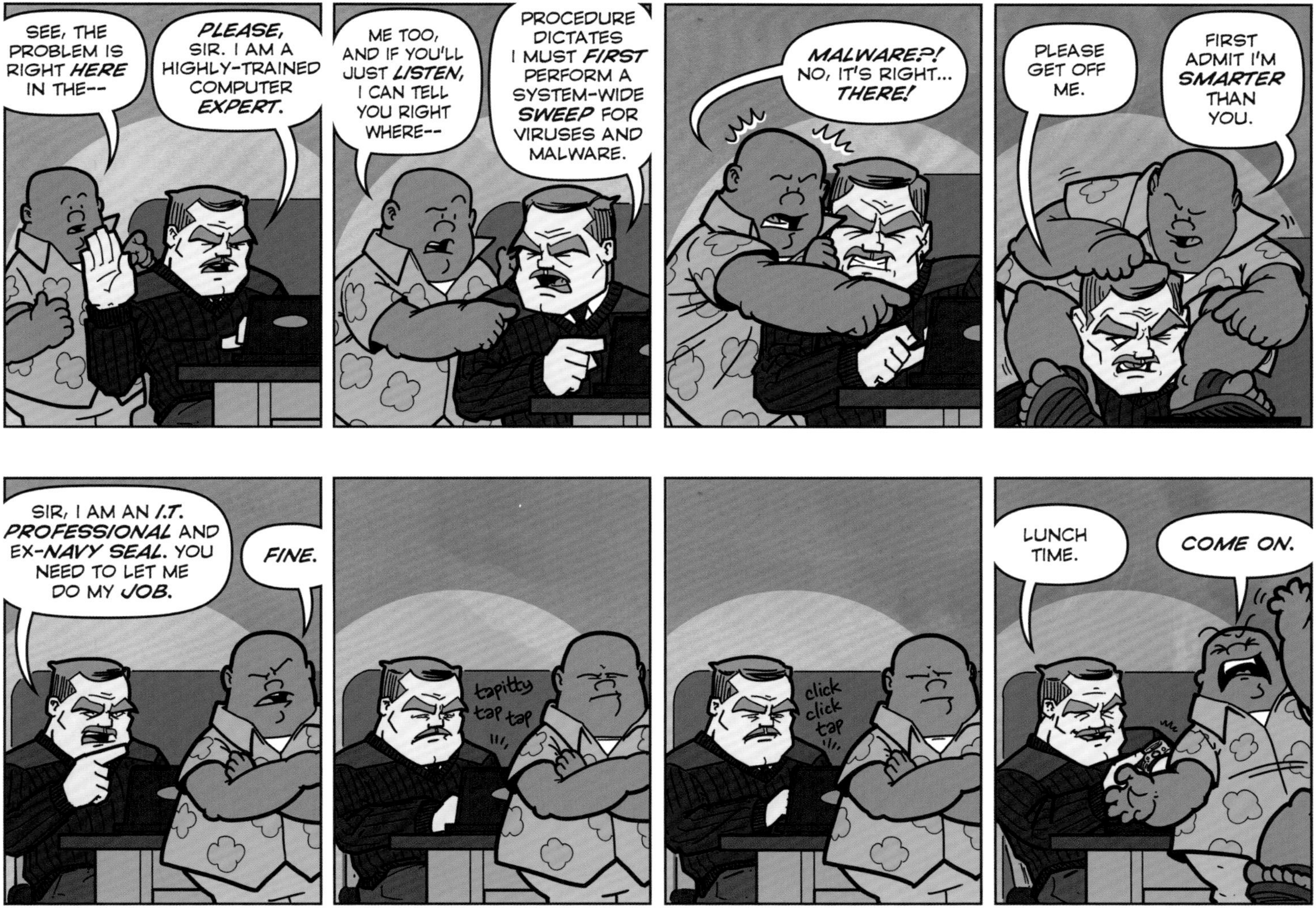
SEE, THE PROBLEM IS RIGHT *HERE* IN THE--
PLEASE, SIR. I AM A HIGHLY-TRAINED COMPUTER *EXPERT*.
ME TOO, AND IF YOU'LL JUST *LISTEN,* I CAN TELL YOU RIGHT WHERE--
PROCEDURE DICTATES I MUST *FIRST* PERFORM A SYSTEM-WIDE *SWEEP* FOR VIRUSES AND MALWARE.
MALWARE?! NO, IT'S RIGHT... *THERE!*
PLEASE GET OFF ME.
FIRST ADMIT I'M *SMARTER* THAN YOU.
SIR, I AM AN *I.T. PROFESSIONAL* AND EX-*NAVY SEAL*. YOU NEED TO LET ME DO MY *JOB*.
FINE.
tapitty tap tap
click click tap
LUNCH TIME.
COME ON.

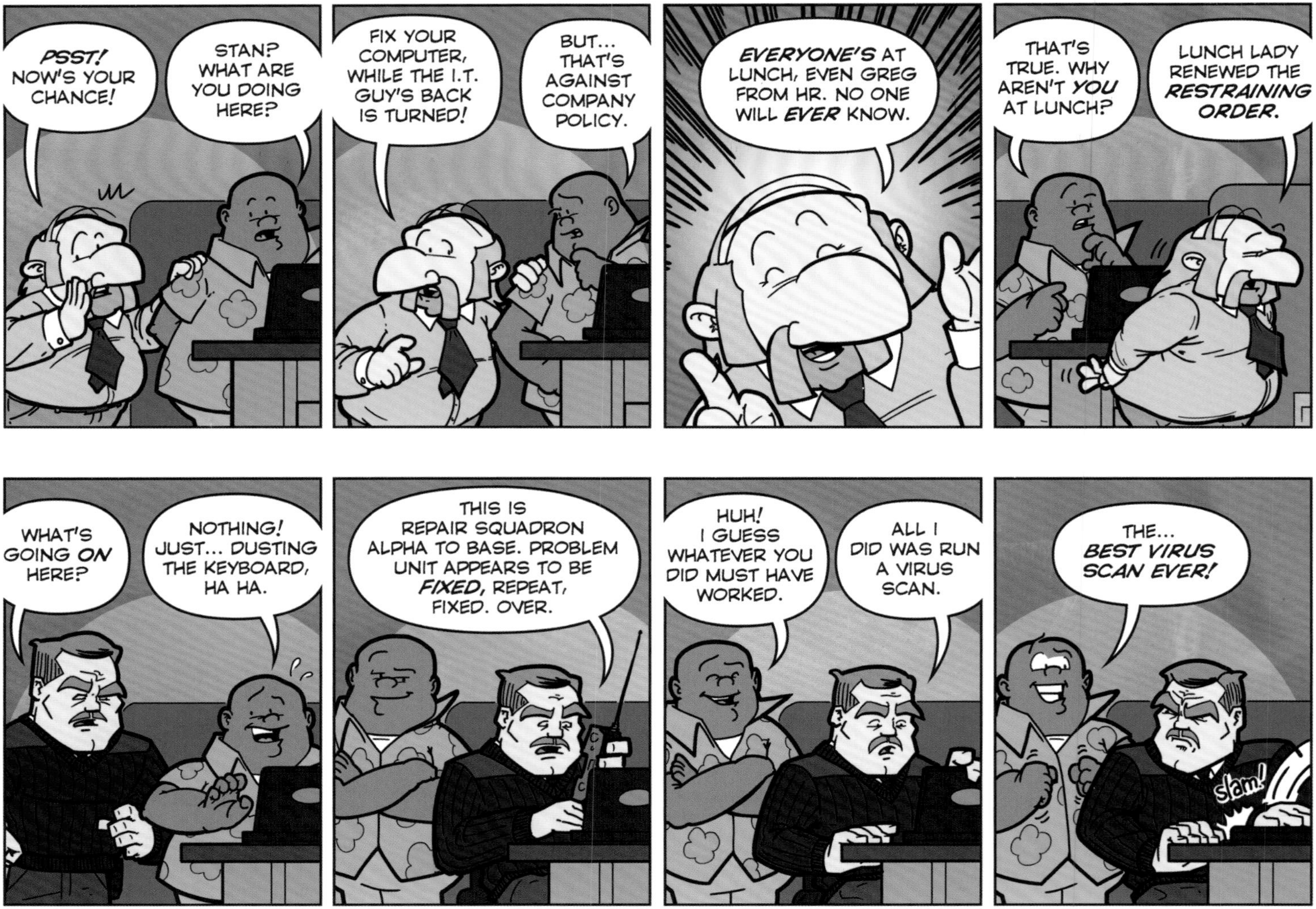
PSST! NOW'S YOUR CHANCE!
STAN? WHAT ARE YOU DOING HERE?
FIX YOUR COMPUTER, WHILE THE I.T. GUY'S BACK IS TURNED!
BUT... THAT'S AGAINST COMPANY POLICY.
EVERYONE'S AT LUNCH, EVEN GREG FROM HR. NO ONE WILL EVER KNOW.
THAT'S TRUE. WHY AREN'T YOU AT LUNCH?
LUNCH LADY RENEWED THE RESTRAINING ORDER.
WHAT'S GOING ON HERE?
NOTHING! JUST... DUSTING THE KEYBOARD, HA HA.
THIS IS REPAIR SQUADRON ALPHA TO BASE. PROBLEM UNIT APPEARS TO BE FIXED, REPEAT, FIXED. OVER.
HUH! I GUESS WHATEVER YOU DID MUST HAVE WORKED.
ALL I DID WAS RUN A VIRUS SCAN.
THE... BEST VIRUS SCAN EVER!
slam!

UPGRADE PATH

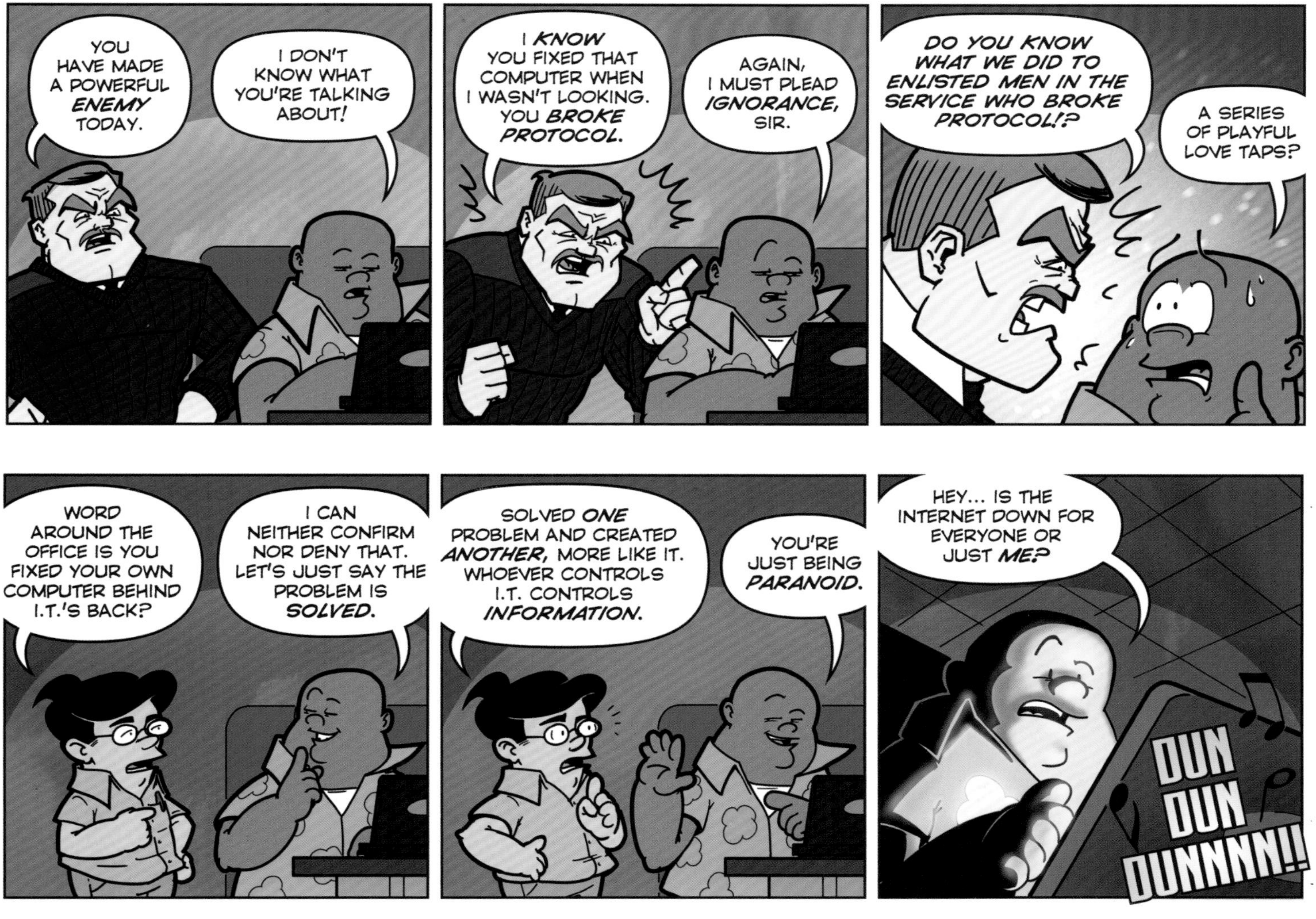
YOU HAVE MADE A POWERFUL *ENEMY* TODAY.
I DON'T KNOW WHAT YOU'RE TALKING ABOUT!
I *KNOW* YOU FIXED THAT COMPUTER WHEN I WASN'T LOOKING. YOU *BROKE PROTOCOL.*
AGAIN, I MUST PLEAD *IGNORANCE,* SIR.
DO YOU KNOW WHAT WE DID TO ENLISTED MEN IN THE SERVICE WHO BROKE PROTOCOL!?
A SERIES OF PLAYFUL LOVE TAPS?
WORD AROUND THE OFFICE IS YOU FIXED YOUR OWN COMPUTER BEHIND I.T.'S BACK?
I CAN NEITHER CONFIRM NOR DENY THAT. LET'S JUST SAY THE PROBLEM IS *SOLVED.*
SOLVED *ONE* PROBLEM AND CREATED *ANOTHER,* MORE LIKE IT. WHOEVER CONTROLS I.T. CONTROLS *INFORMATION.*
YOU'RE JUST BEING *PARANOID.*
HEY... IS THE INTERNET DOWN FOR EVERYONE OR JUST *ME?*
DUN DUN DUNNNN!!

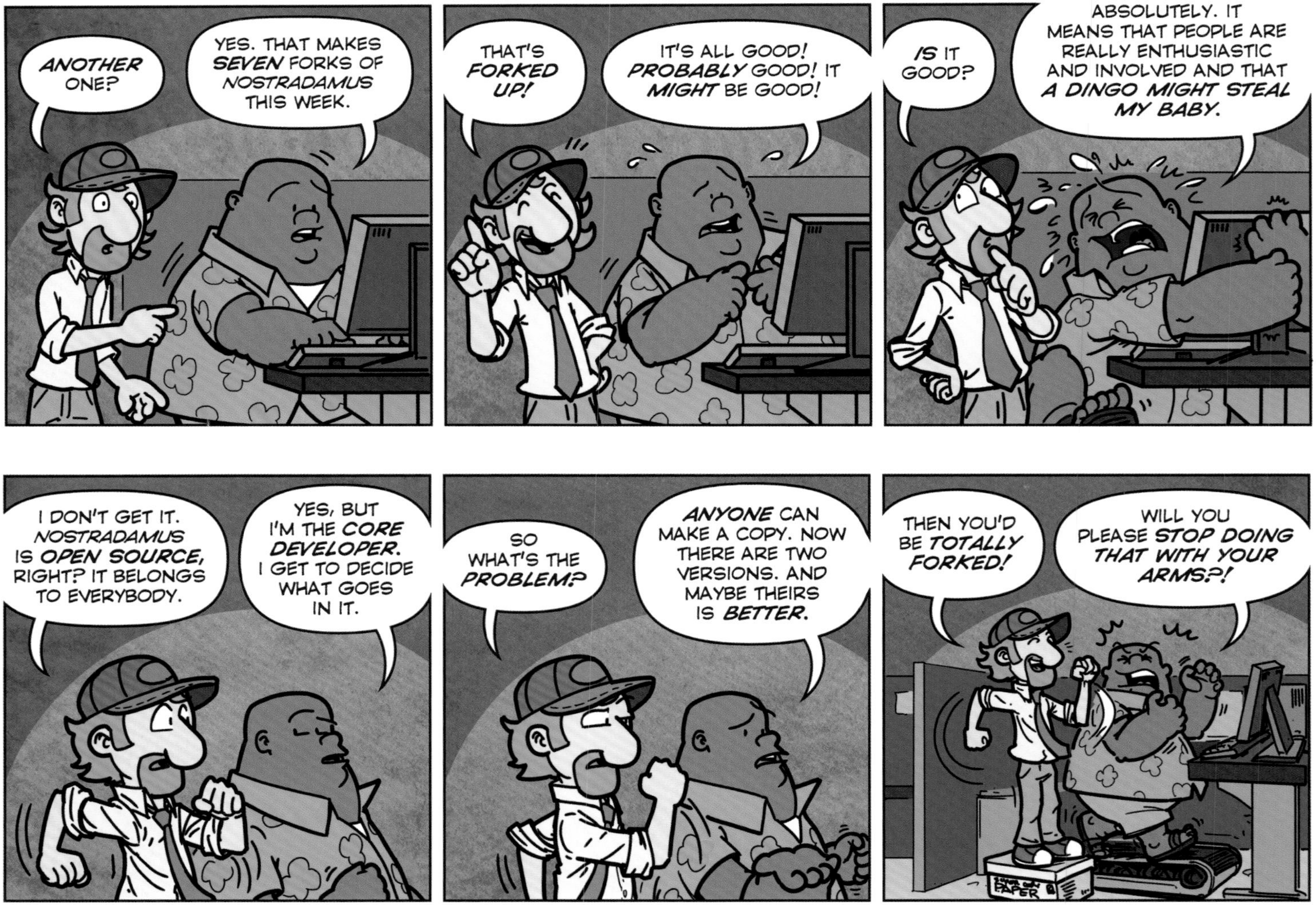
ANOTHER ONE?
YES. THAT MAKES SEVEN FORKS OF NOSTRADAMUS THIS WEEK.
THAT'S FORKED UP!
IT'S ALL GOOD! PROBABLY GOOD! IT MIGHT BE GOOD!
IS IT GOOD?
ABSOLUTELY. IT MEANS THAT PEOPLE ARE REALLY ENTHUSIASTIC AND INVOLVED AND THAT A DINGO MIGHT STEAL MY BABY.
I DON'T GET IT. NOSTRADAMUS IS OPEN SOURCE, RIGHT? IT BELONGS TO EVERYBODY.
YES, BUT I'M THE CORE DEVELOPER. I GET TO DECIDE WHAT GOES IN IT.
SO WHAT'S THE PROBLEM?
ANYONE CAN MAKE A COPY. NOW THERE ARE TWO VERSIONS. AND MAYBE THEIRS IS BETTER.
THEN YOU'D BE TOTALLY FORKED!
WILL YOU PLEASE STOP DOING THAT WITH YOUR ARMS?!

YOU KNOW, YOU GUYS ARE RIGHT. I WAS WORRYING OVER *NOTHING*.

SO *WHAT* IF PEOPLE FORK MY PROJECT? IT JUST MEANS IT'S *POPULAR*, RIGHT? *RIGHT?*

LOOK!

"PROGNOSTICATOR, A NOSTRADAMUS FORK: BECAUSE DESMOND SUCKS"

MOTHER*FORKER!*

WHY ARE YOU DOING THIS?

WHAT, WRITING CODE? THAT'S WHAT THEY PAY ME FOR.

SLAM!

DON'T PLAY DUMB WITH ME. *SOMEONE* FORKED MY PROJECT IN THE BIGGEST WAY, AND IT HAS *YOUR* FINGERPRINTS ALL OVER IT.

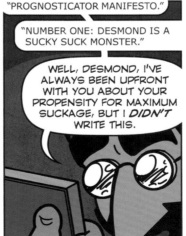

"PROGNOSTICATOR MANIFESTO."

"NUMBER ONE: DESMOND IS A SUCKY SUCK MONSTER."

WELL, DESMOND, I'VE ALWAYS BEEN UPFRONT WITH YOU ABOUT YOUR PROPENSITY FOR MAXIMUM SUCKAGE, BUT I *DIDN'T* WRITE THIS.

THEN WHO --?

"NUMBER TWO: DESMOND IS FAT."

OH I *LIKE* HIM!

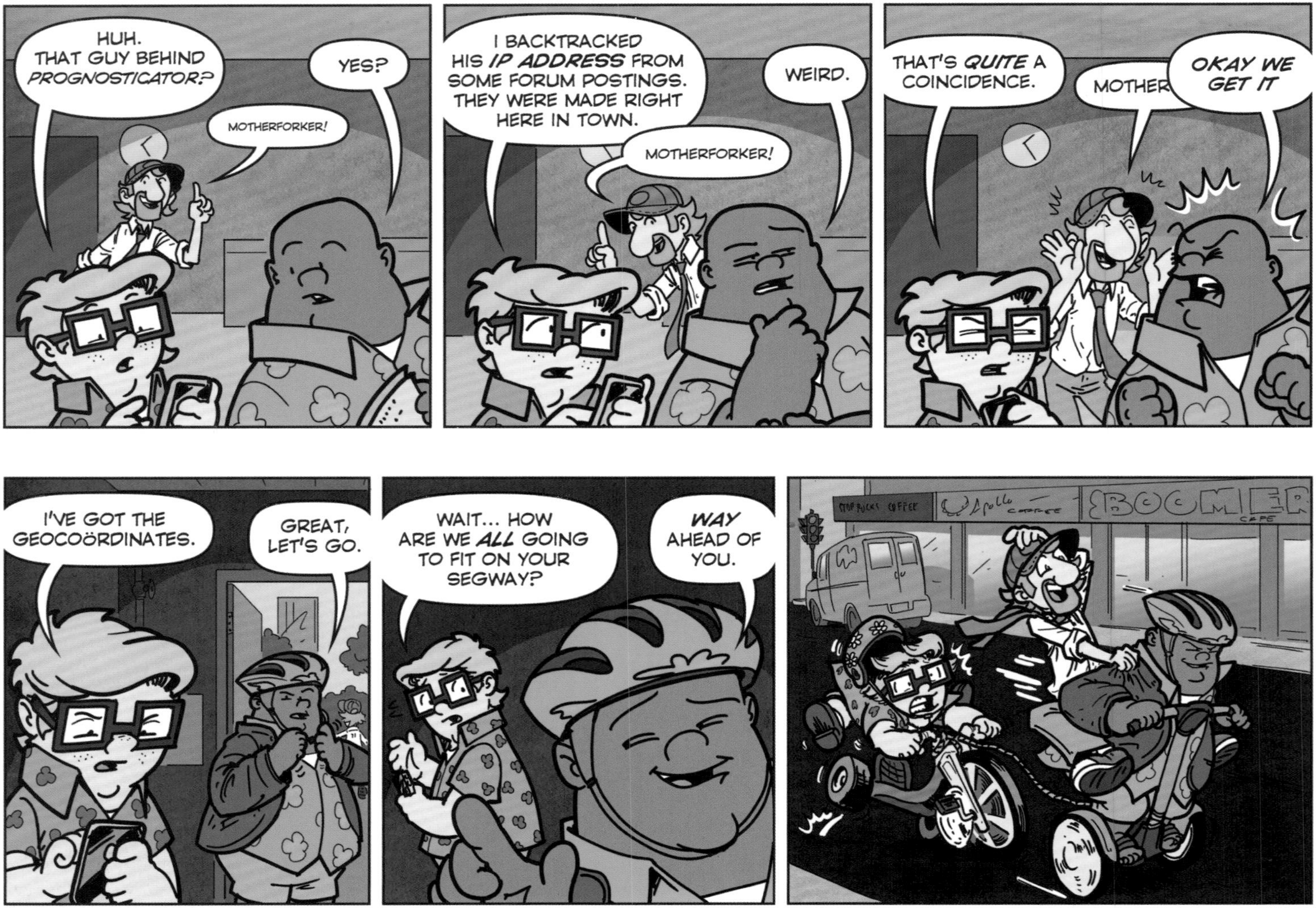
HUH.
THAT GUY BEHIND *PROGNOSTICATOR?*
MOTHERFORKER!
YES?
I BACKTRACKED HIS ***IP ADDRESS*** FROM SOME FORUM POSTINGS. THEY WERE MADE RIGHT HERE IN TOWN.
MOTHERFORKER!
WEIRD.
THAT'S ***QUITE*** A COINCIDENCE.
MOTHER
OKAY WE GET IT
I'VE GOT THE GEOCOÖRDINATES.
GREAT, LET'S GO.
WAIT... HOW ARE WE ***ALL*** GOING TO FIT ON YOUR SEGWAY?
WAY AHEAD OF YOU.
BOOMER

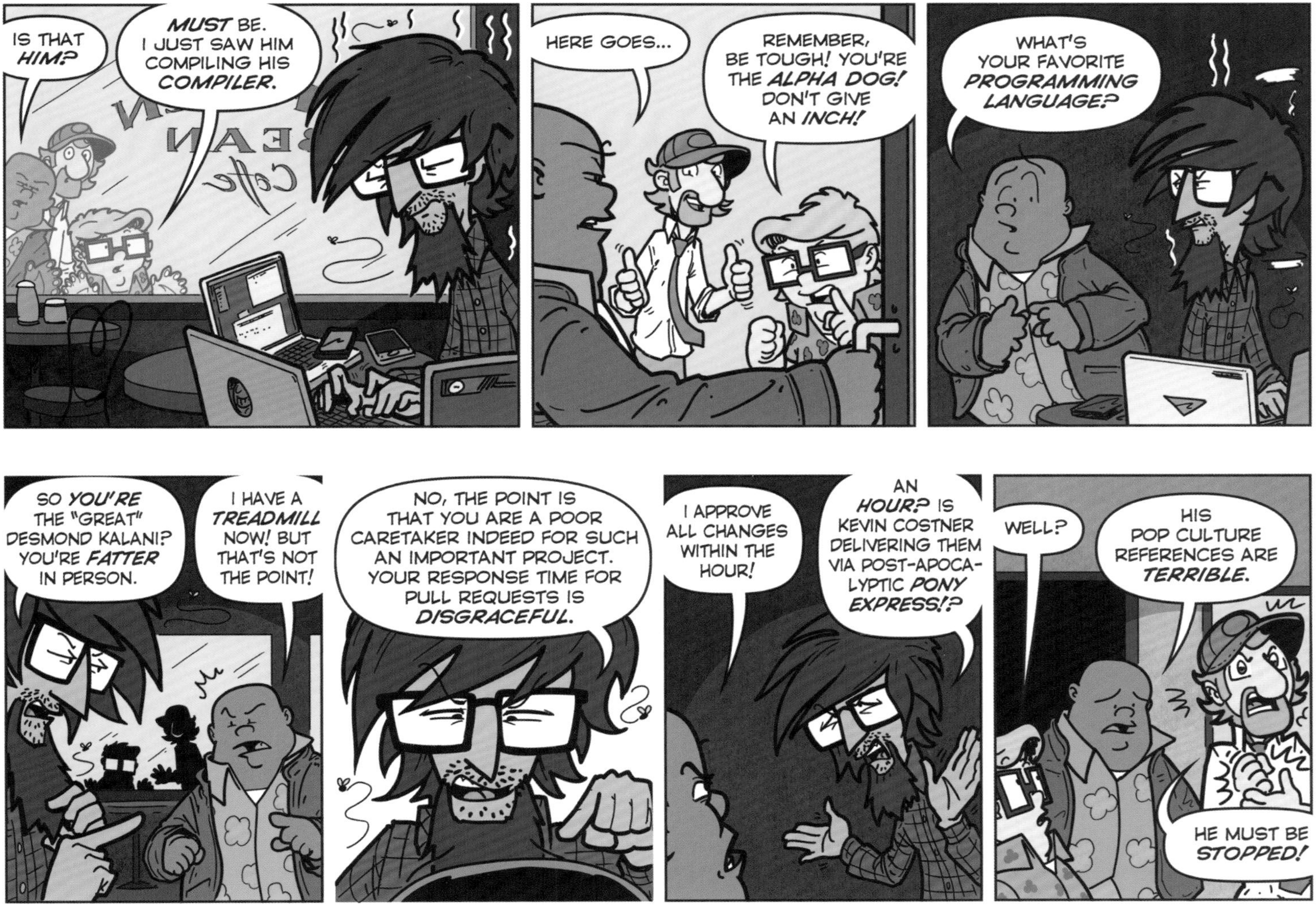
IS THAT *HIM?*
MUST BE. I JUST SAW HIM COMPILING HIS *COMPILER.*
HERE GOES...
REMEMBER, BE TOUGH! YOU'RE THE *ALPHA DOG!* DON'T GIVE AN *INCH!*
WHAT'S YOUR FAVORITE *PROGRAMMING LANGUAGE?*
SO *YOU'RE* THE "GREAT" DESMOND KALANI? YOU'RE *FATTER* IN PERSON.
I HAVE A *TREADMILL* NOW! BUT THAT'S NOT THE POINT!
NO, THE POINT IS THAT YOU ARE A POOR CARETAKER INDEED FOR SUCH AN IMPORTANT PROJECT. YOUR RESPONSE TIME FOR PULL REQUESTS IS *DISGRACEFUL.*
I APPROVE ALL CHANGES WITHIN THE HOUR!
AN *HOUR?* IS KEVIN COSTNER DELIVERING THEM VIA POST-APOCALYPTIC *PONY EXPRESS!?*
WELL?
HIS POP CULTURE REFERENCES ARE *TERRIBLE.*
HE MUST BE *STOPPED!*

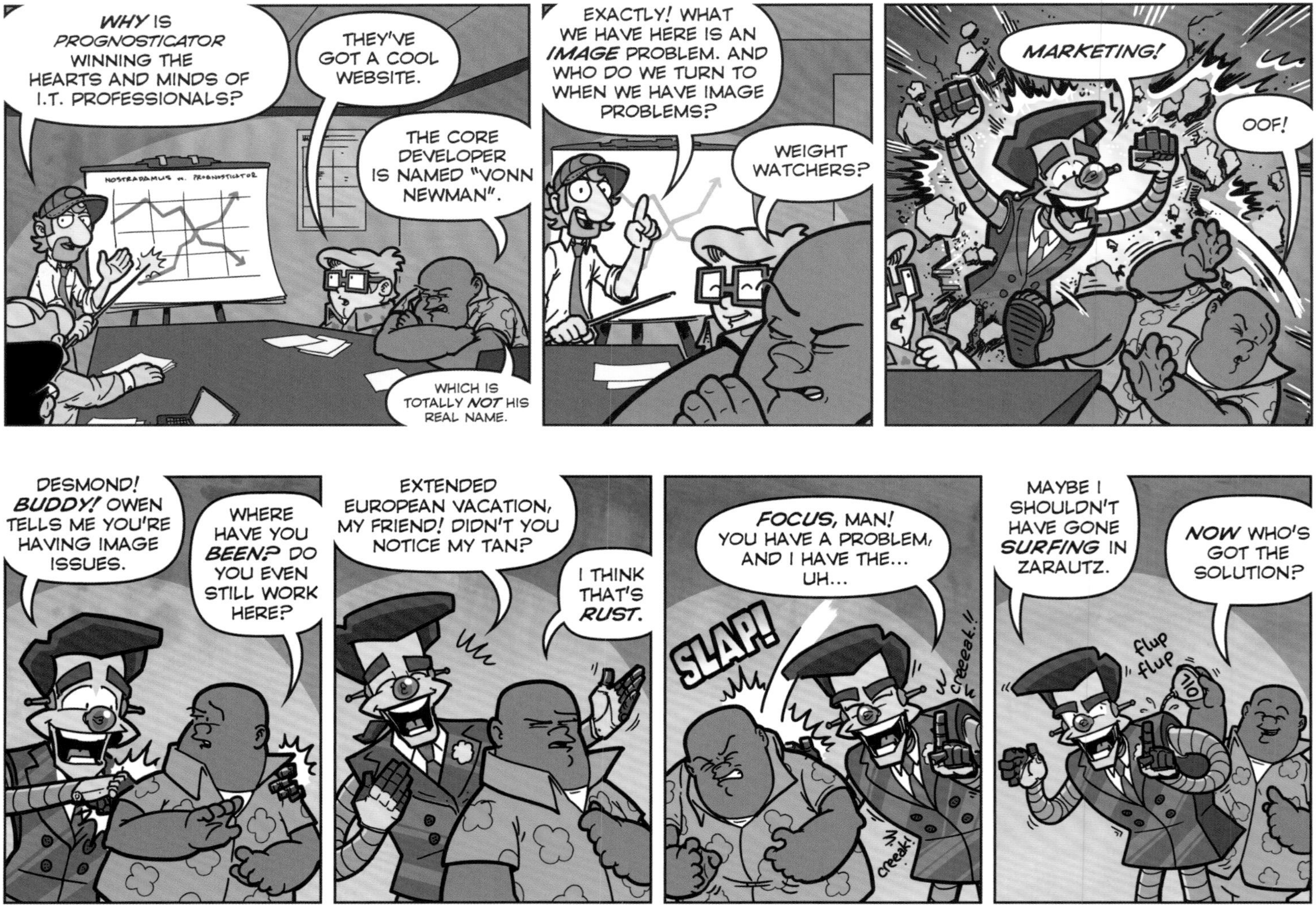
WHY IS PROGNOSTICATOR WINNING THE HEARTS AND MINDS OF I.T. PROFESSIONALS?
NOSTRADAMUS vs. PROGNOSTICATOR
THEY'VE GOT A COOL WEBSITE.
THE CORE DEVELOPER IS NAMED "VONN NEWMAN".
WHICH IS TOTALLY NOT HIS REAL NAME.
EXACTLY! WHAT WE HAVE HERE IS AN IMAGE PROBLEM. AND WHO DO WE TURN TO WHEN WE HAVE IMAGE PROBLEMS?
WEIGHT WATCHERS?
MARKETING!
OOF!
DESMOND! BUDDY! OWEN TELLS ME YOU'RE HAVING IMAGE ISSUES.
WHERE HAVE YOU BEEN? DO YOU EVEN STILL WORK HERE?
EXTENDED EUROPEAN VACATION, MY FRIEND! DIDN'T YOU NOTICE MY TAN?
I THINK THAT'S RUST.
FOCUS, MAN! YOU HAVE A PROBLEM, AND I HAVE THE... UH...
SLAP!
creeeak!!
creeak!
MAYBE I SHOULDN'T HAVE GONE SURFING IN ZARAUTZ.
NOW WHO'S GOT THE SOLUTION?
flup flup

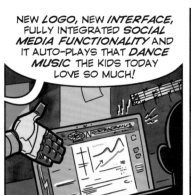

NEW *LOGO*, NEW *INTERFACE*, FULLY INTEGRATED *SOCIAL MEDIA FUNCTIONALITY* AND IT AUTO-PLAYS THAT *DANCE MUSIC* THE KIDS TODAY LOVE SO MUCH!

HOW DID YOU DO THIS SO *FAST?*

THAT'S *NOTHING!* CHECK OUT YOUR *BIO.*

"*DJ KALANI* IS A TOTALLY *SWAG* SOFTWARE DESIGNER FROM THE *JERSEY SHORE.* WHEN HE'S NOT CRUNCHING CODE, YOU CAN FIND HIM CRUNCHING HIS *SWEET ABS* IN THE GYM."

"*DJ*"?

IF ANYONE ASKS, YOUR MIDDLE NAME IS "JEFF."

MAN... SINCE WE LAUNCHED THE NEW WEBSITE, CONTRIBUTIONS TO *PROGNOSTICATOR* HAVE TAKEN A REAL NOSEDIVE.

SEE? IT'S *ALL* ABOUT THE MESSAGING.

I REFUSE TO BELIEVE THAT'S ALL IT TOOK. THERE MUST BE *ANOTHER* FACTOR.

MAYBE YOUR USERS FINALLY REALIZED THAT YOU MAY BE SLOW, BUT YOU'RE *RELIABLE.*

YUP. THAT MUST BE IT ALL RIGHT.

KALAN!!!!

MARKET DISRUPTION!!!

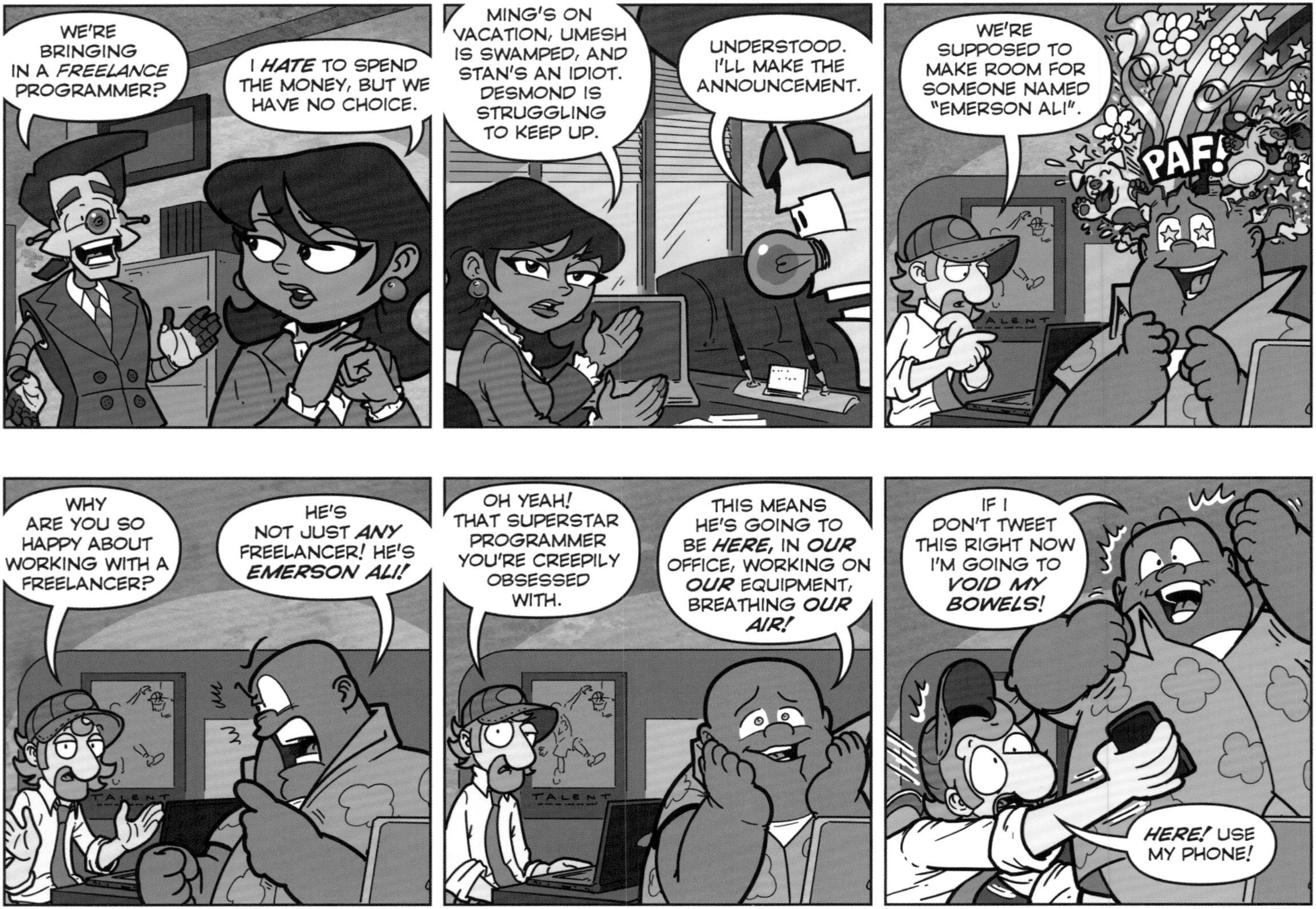
WE'RE BRINGING IN A *FREELANCE* PROGRAMMER?
I ***HATE*** TO SPEND THE MONEY, BUT WE HAVE NO CHOICE.
MING'S ON VACATION, UMESH IS SWAMPED, AND STAN'S AN IDIOT. DESMOND IS STRUGGLING TO KEEP UP.
UNDERSTOOD. I'LL MAKE THE ANNOUNCEMENT.
WE'RE SUPPOSED TO MAKE ROOM FOR SOMEONE NAMED "EMERSON ALI".
PAF!
WHY ARE YOU SO HAPPY ABOUT WORKING WITH A FREELANCER?
HE'S NOT JUST ***ANY*** FREELANCER! HE'S ***EMERSON ALI!***
OH YEAH! THAT SUPERSTAR PROGRAMMER YOU'RE CREEPILY OBSESSED WITH.
THIS MEANS HE'S GOING TO BE ***HERE,*** IN ***OUR*** OFFICE, WORKING ON ***OUR*** EQUIPMENT, BREATHING ***OUR AIR!***
IF I DON'T TWEET THIS RIGHT NOW I'M GOING TO ***VOID MY BOWELS!***
HERE! USE MY PHONE!

UPGRADE PATH

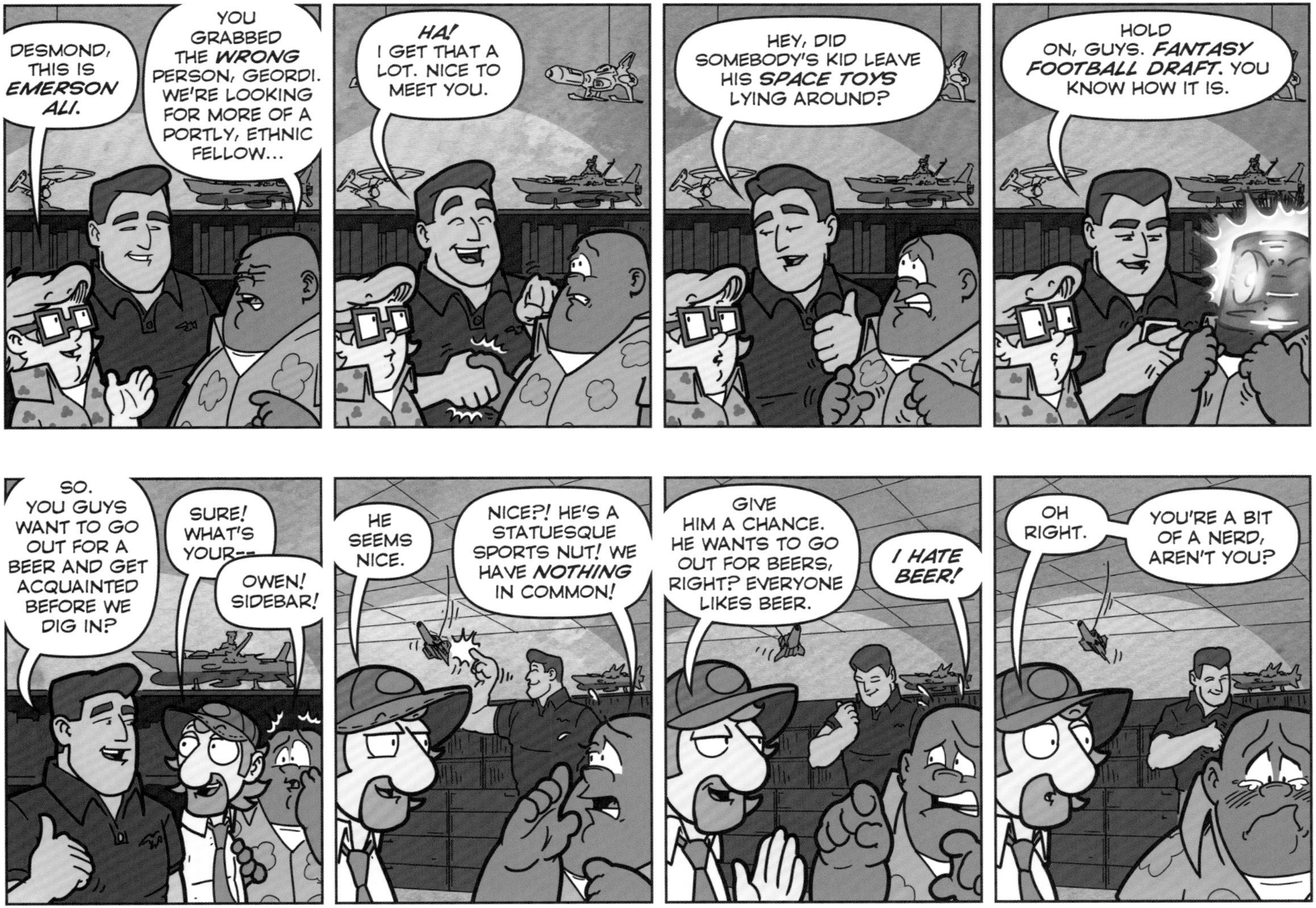
DESMOND, THIS IS *EMERSON ALI*.
YOU GRABBED THE *WRONG* PERSON, GEORDI. WE'RE LOOKING FOR MORE OF A PORTLY, ETHNIC FELLOW...
HA! I GET THAT A LOT. NICE TO MEET YOU.
HEY, DID SOMEBODY'S KID LEAVE HIS *SPACE TOYS* LYING AROUND?
HOLD ON, GUYS. *FANTASY FOOTBALL DRAFT*. YOU KNOW HOW IT IS.
SO. YOU GUYS WANT TO GO OUT FOR A BEER AND GET ACQUAINTED BEFORE WE DIG IN?
SURE! WHAT'S YOUR--
OWEN! SIDEBAR!
HE SEEMS NICE.
NICE?! HE'S A STATUESQUE SPORTS NUT! WE HAVE *NOTHING* IN COMMON!
GIVE HIM A CHANCE. HE WANTS TO GO OUT FOR BEERS, RIGHT? EVERYONE LIKES BEER.
I HATE BEER!
OH RIGHT.
YOU'RE A BIT OF A NERD, AREN'T YOU?

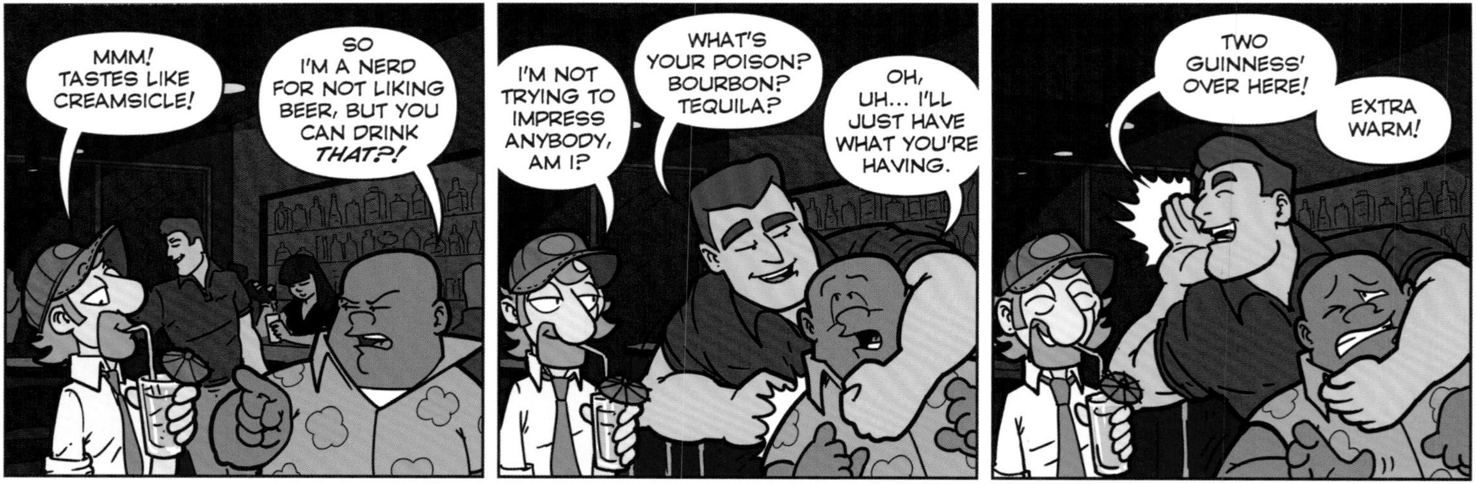
MMM! TASTES LIKE CREAMSICLE!
SO I'M A NERD FOR NOT LIKING BEER, BUT YOU CAN DRINK *THAT?!*
I'M NOT TRYING TO IMPRESS ANYBODY, AM I?
WHAT'S YOUR POISON? BOURBON? TEQUILA?
OH, UH... I'LL JUST HAVE WHAT YOU'RE HAVING.
TWO GUINNESS' OVER HERE!
EXTRA WARM!

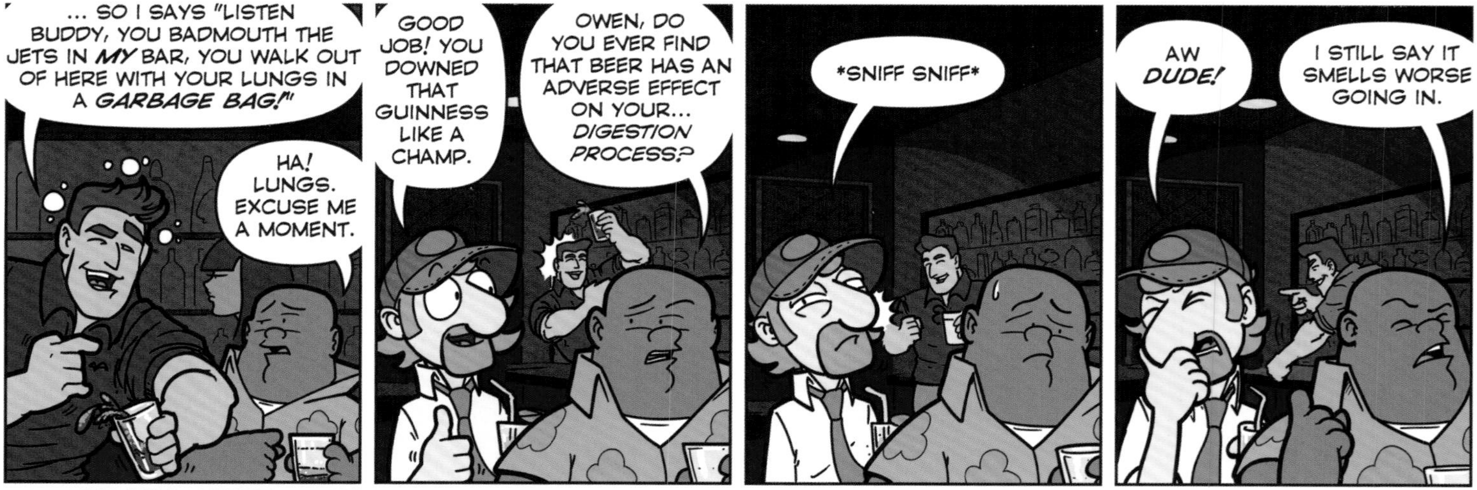
... SO I SAYS "LISTEN BUDDY, YOU BADMOUTH THE JETS IN *MY* BAR, YOU WALK OUT OF HERE WITH YOUR LUNGS IN A *GARBAGE BAG!*"
HA! LUNGS. EXCUSE ME A MOMENT.
GOOD JOB! YOU DOWNED THAT GUINNESS LIKE A CHAMP.
OWEN, DO YOU EVER FIND THAT BEER HAS AN ADVERSE EFFECT ON YOUR... *DIGESTION PROCESS?*
SNIFF SNIFF
AW *DUDE!*
I STILL SAY IT SMELLS WORSE GOING IN.

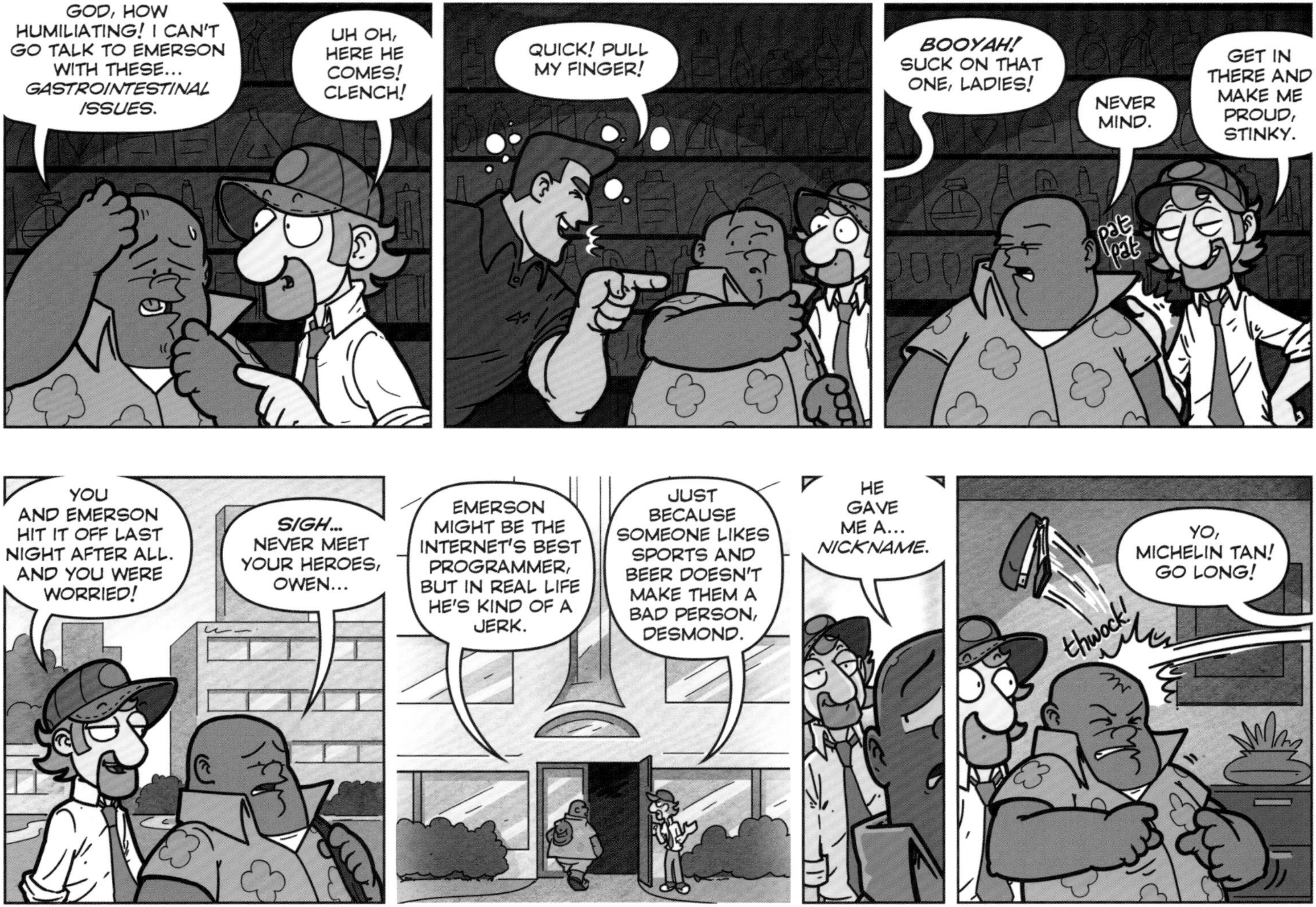
GOD, HOW HUMILIATING! I CAN'T GO TALK TO EMERSON WITH THESE... *GASTROINTESTINAL ISSUES.*
UH OH, HERE HE COMES! CLENCH!
QUICK! PULL MY FINGER!
BOOYAH! SUCK ON THAT ONE, LADIES!
NEVER MIND.
GET IN THERE AND MAKE ME PROUD, STINKY.
pat pat
YOU AND EMERSON HIT IT OFF LAST NIGHT AFTER ALL. AND YOU WERE WORRIED!
SIGH... NEVER MEET YOUR HEROES, OWEN...
EMERSON MIGHT BE THE INTERNET'S BEST PROGRAMMER, BUT IN REAL LIFE HE'S KIND OF A JERK.
JUST BECAUSE SOMEONE LIKES SPORTS AND BEER DOESN'T MAKE THEM A BAD PERSON, DESMOND.
HE GAVE ME A... *NICKNAME.*
YO, MICHELIN TAN! GO LONG!
thwock!

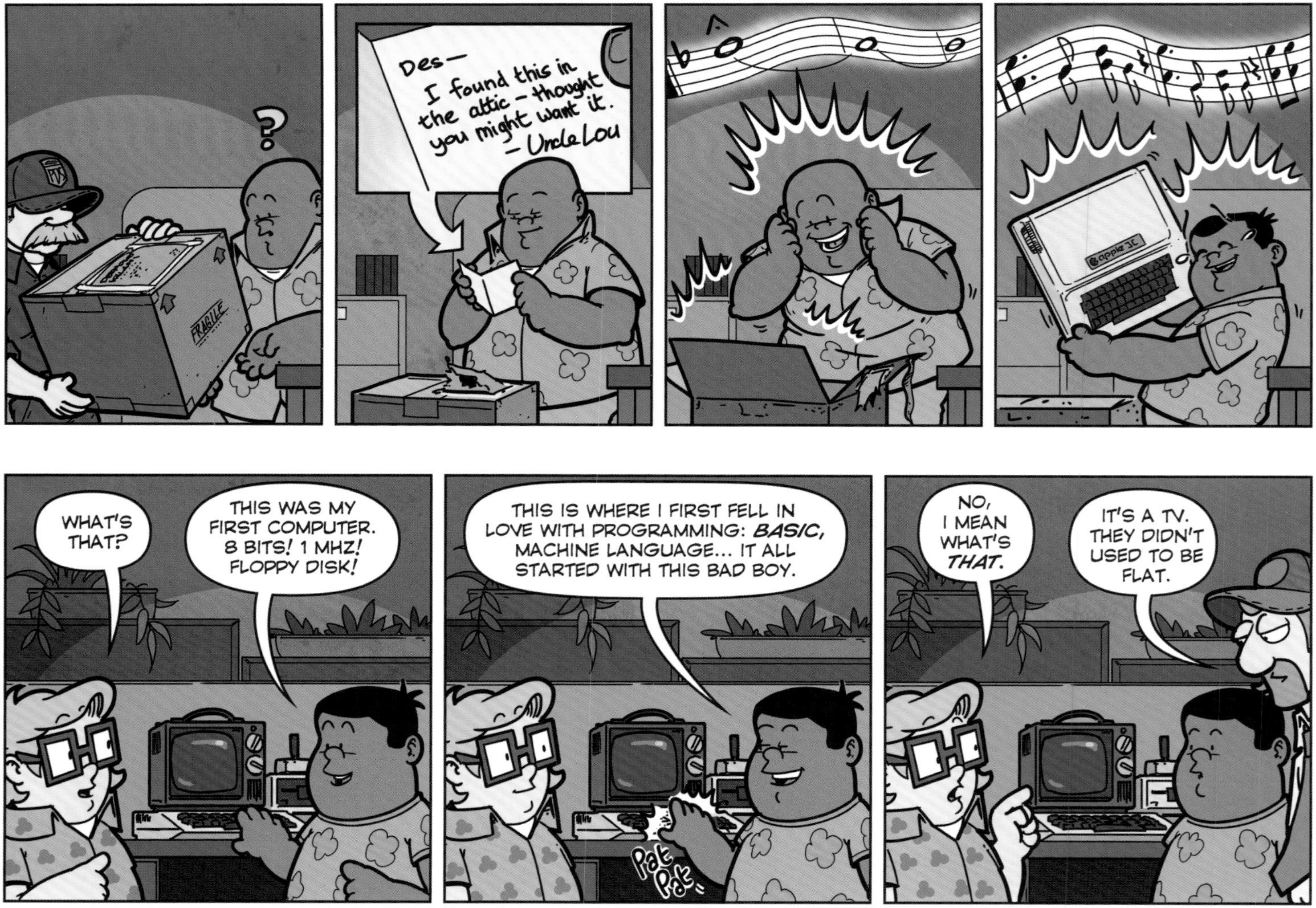
?
FRAGILE
Des—
I found this in the attic - thought you might want it.
- Uncle Lou
WHAT'S THAT?
THIS WAS MY FIRST COMPUTER. 8 BITS! 1 MHZ! FLOPPY DISK!
THIS IS WHERE I FIRST FELL IN LOVE WITH PROGRAMMING: *BASIC*, MACHINE LANGUAGE... IT ALL STARTED WITH THIS BAD BOY.
Pat Pat
NO, I MEAN WHAT'S *THAT*.
IT'S A TV. THEY DIDN'T USED TO BE FLAT.

UPGRADE PATH

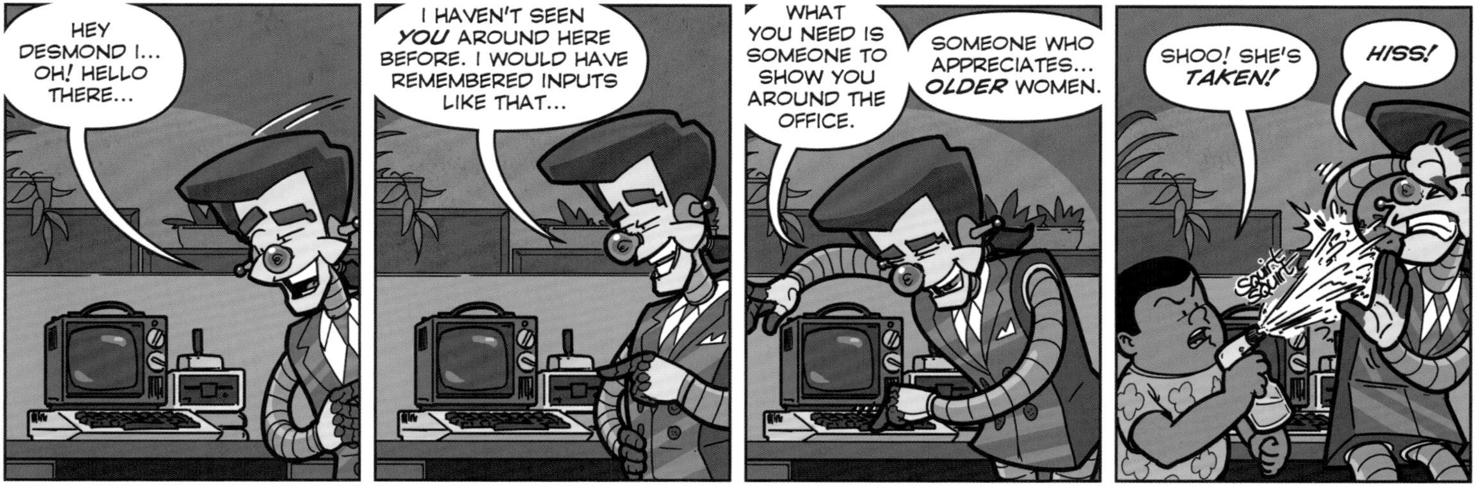

HEY DESMOND I... OH! HELLO THERE...
I HAVEN'T SEEN *YOU* AROUND HERE BEFORE. I WOULD HAVE REMEMBERED INPUTS LIKE THAT...
WHAT YOU NEED IS SOMEONE TO SHOW YOU AROUND THE OFFICE.
SOMEONE WHO APPRECIATES... *OLDER* WOMEN.
SHOO! SHE'S *TAKEN!*
Squirt Squirt
HISS!

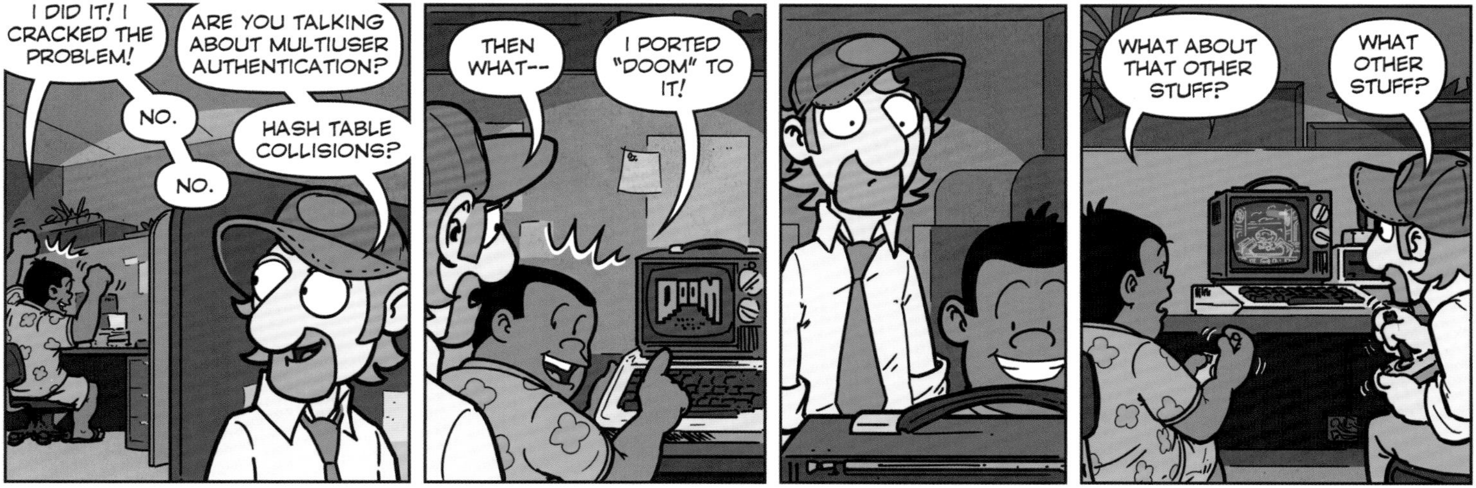

I DID IT! I CRACKED THE PROBLEM!
ARE YOU TALKING ABOUT MULTIUSER AUTHENTICATION?
NO.
HASH TABLE COLLISIONS?
NO.
THEN WHAT--
I PORTED "DOOM" TO IT!
DOOM
WHAT ABOUT THAT OTHER STUFF?
WHAT OTHER STUFF?

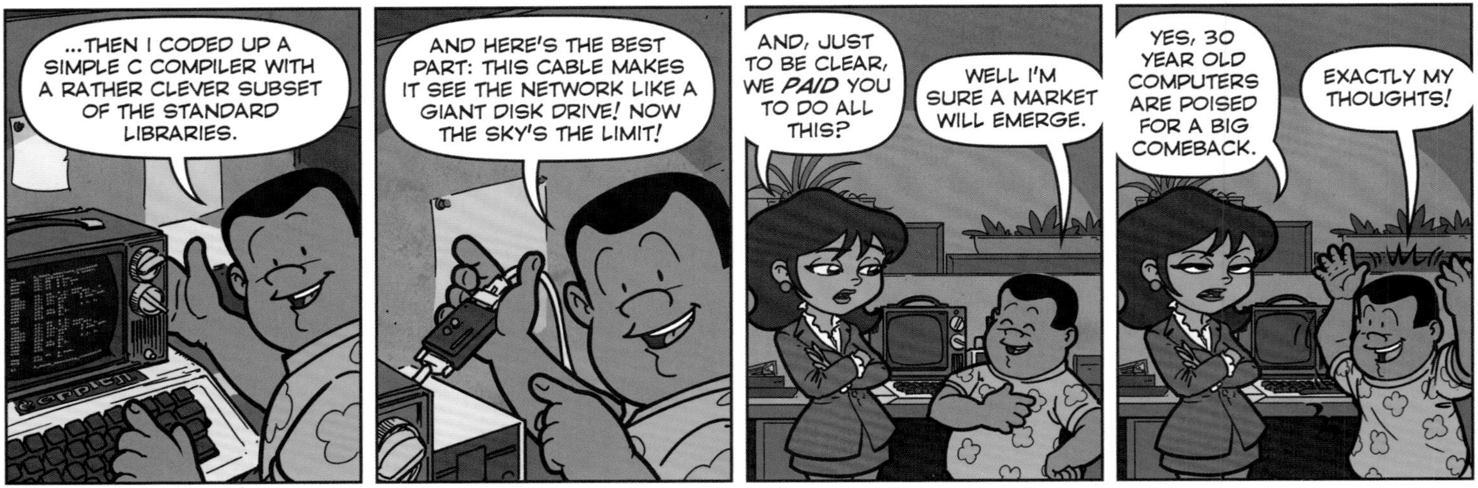
...THEN I CODED UP A SIMPLE C COMPILER WITH A RATHER CLEVER SUBSET OF THE STANDARD LIBRARIES.
AND HERE'S THE BEST PART: THIS CABLE MAKES IT SEE THE NETWORK LIKE A GIANT DISK DRIVE! NOW THE SKY'S THE LIMIT!
AND, JUST TO BE CLEAR, WE *PAID* YOU TO DO ALL THIS?
WELL I'M SURE A MARKET WILL EMERGE.
YES, 30 YEAR OLD COMPUTERS ARE POISED FOR A BIG COMEBACK.
EXACTLY MY THOUGHTS!

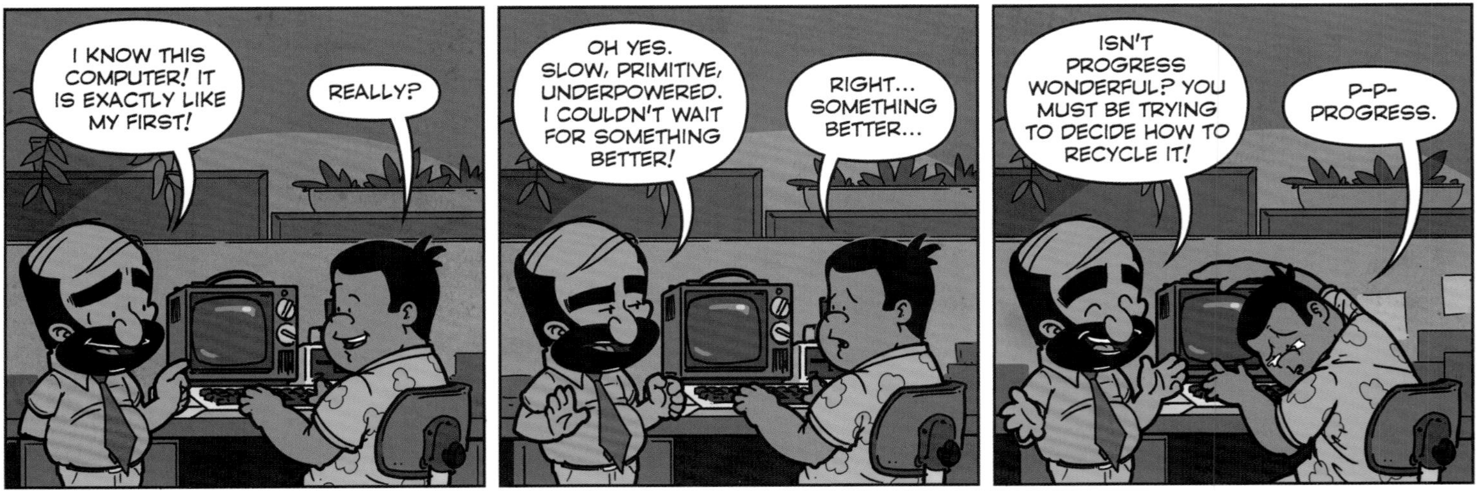
I KNOW THIS COMPUTER! IT IS EXACTLY LIKE MY FIRST!
REALLY?
OH YES. SLOW, PRIMITIVE, UNDERPOWERED. I COULDN'T WAIT FOR SOMETHING BETTER!
RIGHT... SOMETHING BETTER...
ISN'T PROGRESS WONDERFUL? YOU MUST BE TRYING TO DECIDE HOW TO RECYCLE IT!
P-P-PROGRESS.

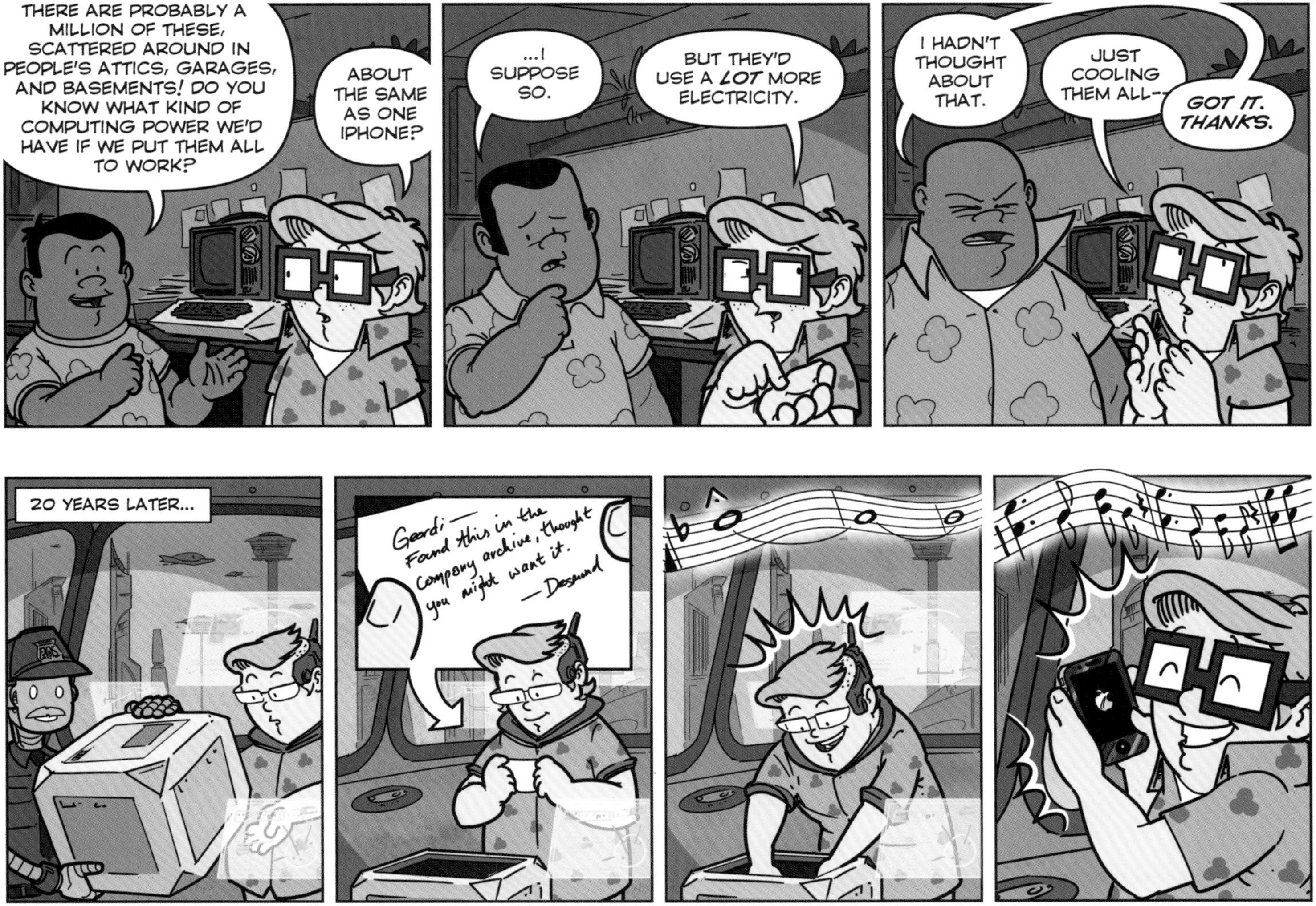
THERE ARE PROBABLY A MILLION OF THESE, SCATTERED AROUND IN PEOPLE'S ATTICS, GARAGES, AND BASEMENTS! DO YOU KNOW WHAT KIND OF COMPUTING POWER WE'D HAVE IF WE PUT THEM ALL TO WORK?
ABOUT THE SAME AS ONE IPHONE?
...I SUPPOSE SO.
BUT THEY'D USE A *LOT* MORE ELECTRICITY.
I HADN'T THOUGHT ABOUT THAT.
JUST COOLING THEM ALL--
GOT IT. THANKS.
20 YEARS LATER...
Geordi — Found this in the company archive, thought you might want it. — Desmond

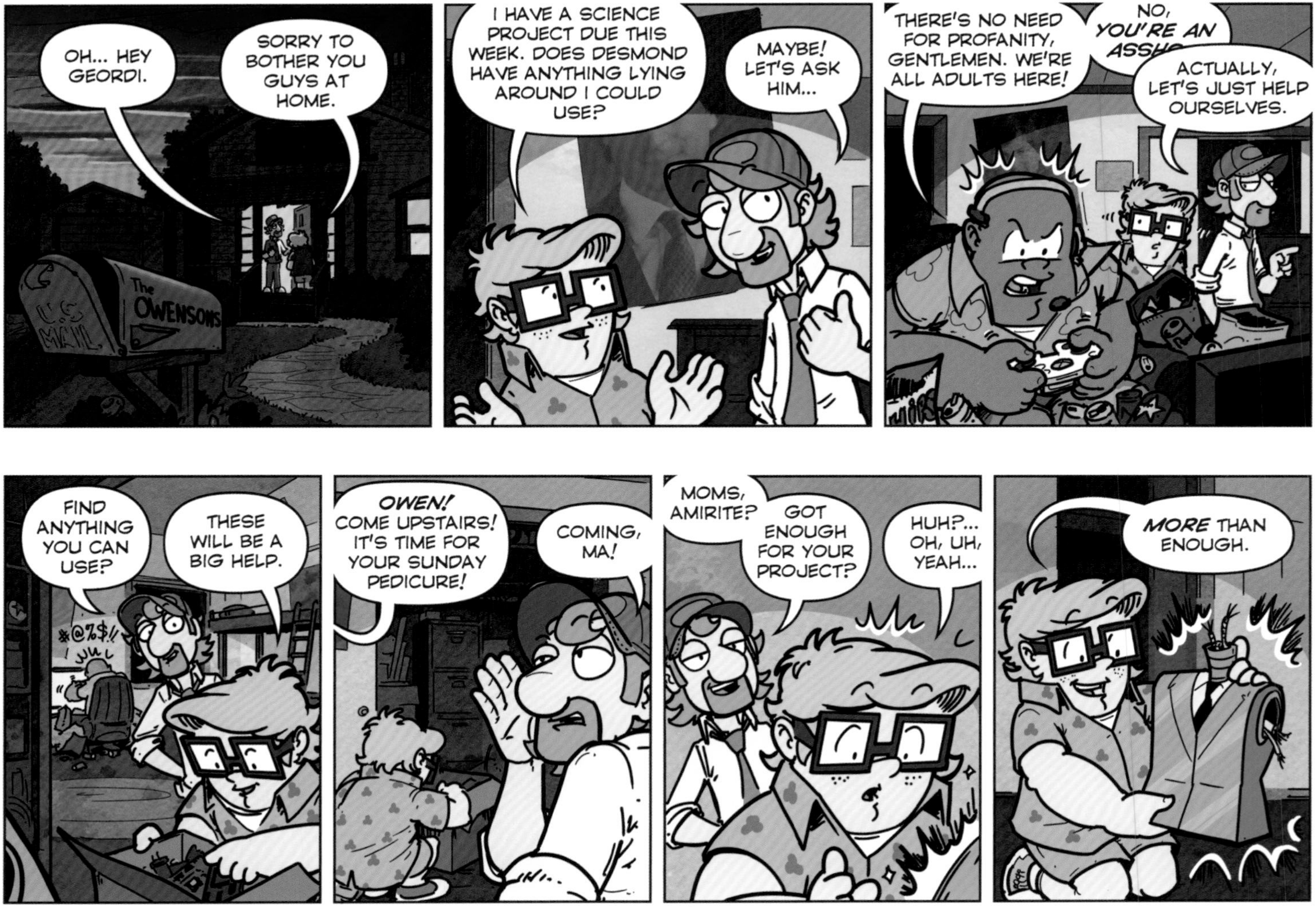
OH... HEY GEORDI.
SORRY TO BOTHER YOU GUYS AT HOME.
The OWENSONS
U.S. MAIL
I HAVE A SCIENCE PROJECT DUE THIS WEEK. DOES DESMOND HAVE ANYTHING LYING AROUND I COULD USE?
MAYBE! LET'S ASK HIM...
THERE'S NO NEED FOR PROFANITY, GENTLEMEN. WE'RE ALL ADULTS HERE!
NO, YOU'RE AN ASSH
ACTUALLY, LET'S JUST HELP OURSELVES.
FIND ANYTHING YOU CAN USE?
THESE WILL BE A BIG HELP.
OWEN! COME UPSTAIRS! IT'S TIME FOR YOUR SUNDAY PEDICURE!
COMING, MA!
MOMS, AMIRITE?
GOT ENOUGH FOR YOUR PROJECT?
HUH?... OH, UH, YEAH...
MORE THAN ENOUGH.

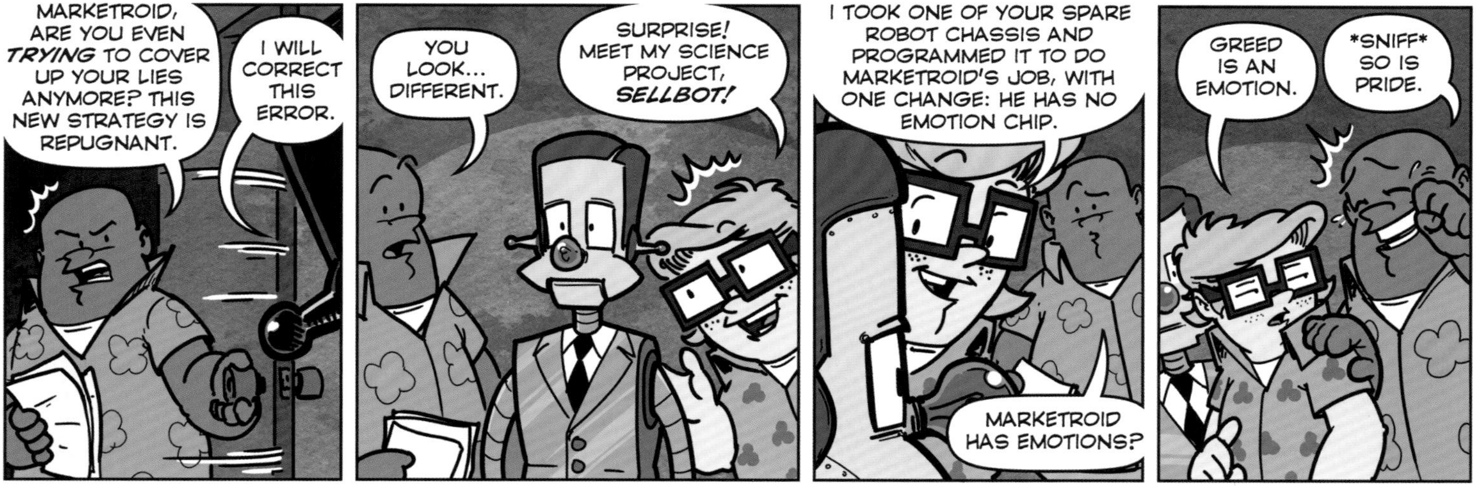
MARKETROID, ARE YOU EVEN *TRYING* TO COVER UP YOUR LIES ANYMORE? THIS NEW STRATEGY IS REPUGNANT.
I WILL CORRECT THIS ERROR.
YOU LOOK... DIFFERENT.
SURPRISE! MEET MY SCIENCE PROJECT, *SELLBOT!*
I TOOK ONE OF YOUR SPARE ROBOT CHASSIS AND PROGRAMMED IT TO DO MARKETROID'S JOB, WITH ONE CHANGE: HE HAS NO EMOTION CHIP.
MARKETROID HAS EMOTIONS?
GREED IS AN EMOTION.
SNIFF SO IS PRIDE.

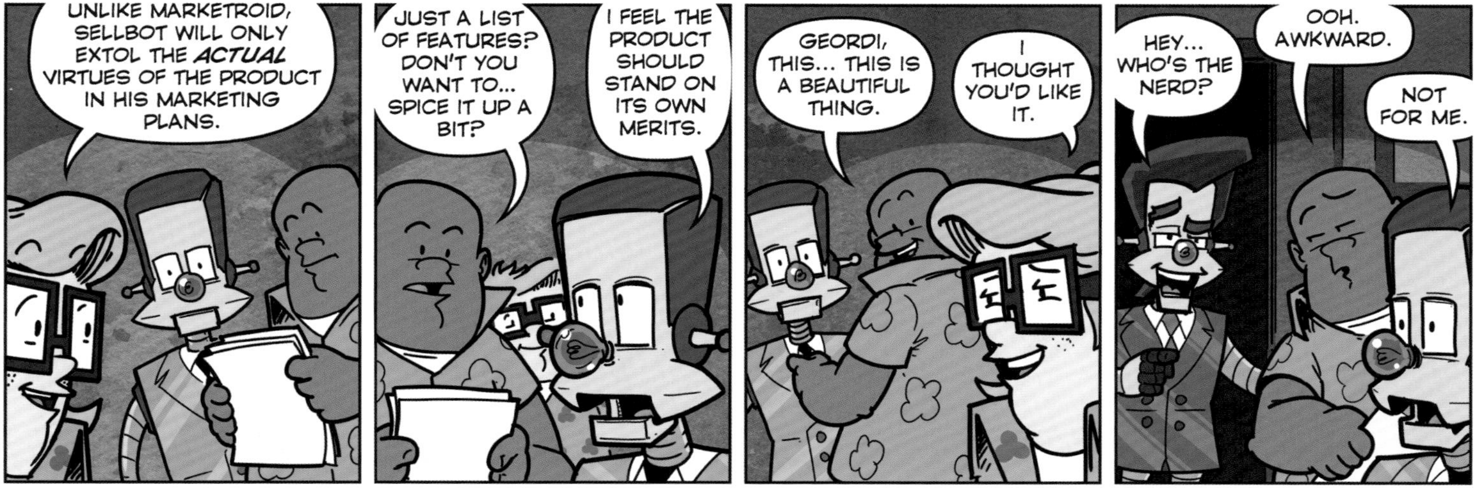
UNLIKE MARKETROID, SELLBOT WILL ONLY EXTOL THE *ACTUAL* VIRTUES OF THE PRODUCT IN HIS MARKETING PLANS.
JUST A LIST OF FEATURES? DON'T YOU WANT TO... SPICE IT UP A BIT?
I FEEL THE PRODUCT SHOULD STAND ON ITS OWN MERITS.
GEORDI, THIS... THIS IS A BEAUTIFUL THING.
I THOUGHT YOU'D LIKE IT.
HEY... WHO'S THE NERD?
OOH. AWKWARD.
NOT FOR ME.

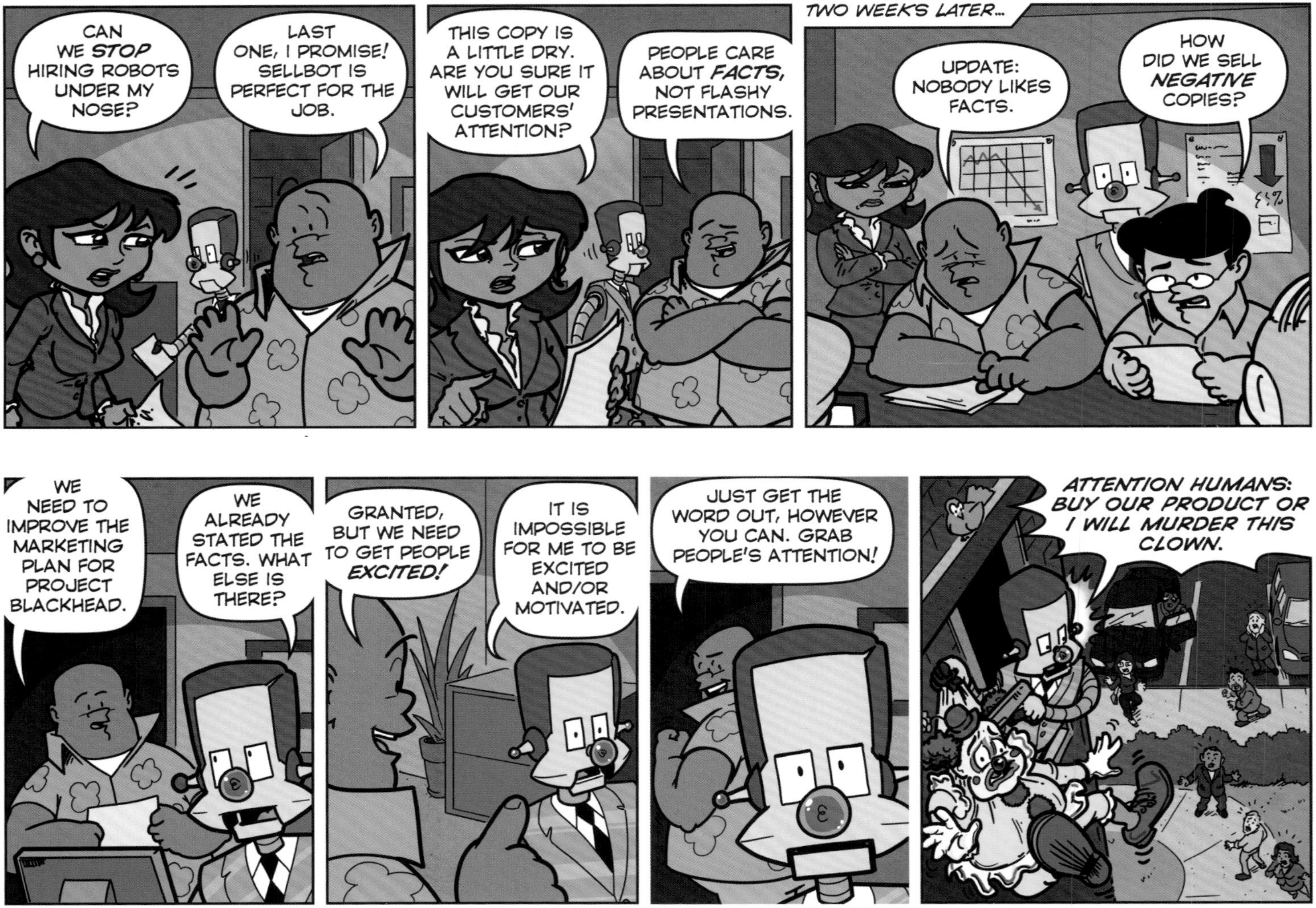
CAN WE STOP HIRING ROBOTS UNDER MY NOSE?
LAST ONE, I PROMISE! SELLBOT IS PERFECT FOR THE JOB.
THIS COPY IS A LITTLE DRY. ARE YOU SURE IT WILL GET OUR CUSTOMERS' ATTENTION?
PEOPLE CARE ABOUT FACTS, NOT FLASHY PRESENTATIONS.
TWO WEEKS LATER...
UPDATE: NOBODY LIKES FACTS.
HOW DID WE SELL NEGATIVE COPIES?
WE NEED TO IMPROVE THE MARKETING PLAN FOR PROJECT BLACKHEAD.
WE ALREADY STATED THE FACTS. WHAT ELSE IS THERE?
GRANTED, BUT WE NEED TO GET PEOPLE EXCITED!
IT IS IMPOSSIBLE FOR ME TO BE EXCITED AND/OR MOTIVATED.
JUST GET THE WORD OUT, HOWEVER YOU CAN. GRAB PEOPLE'S ATTENTION!
ATTENTION HUMANS: BUY OUR PRODUCT OR I WILL MURDER THIS CLOWN.

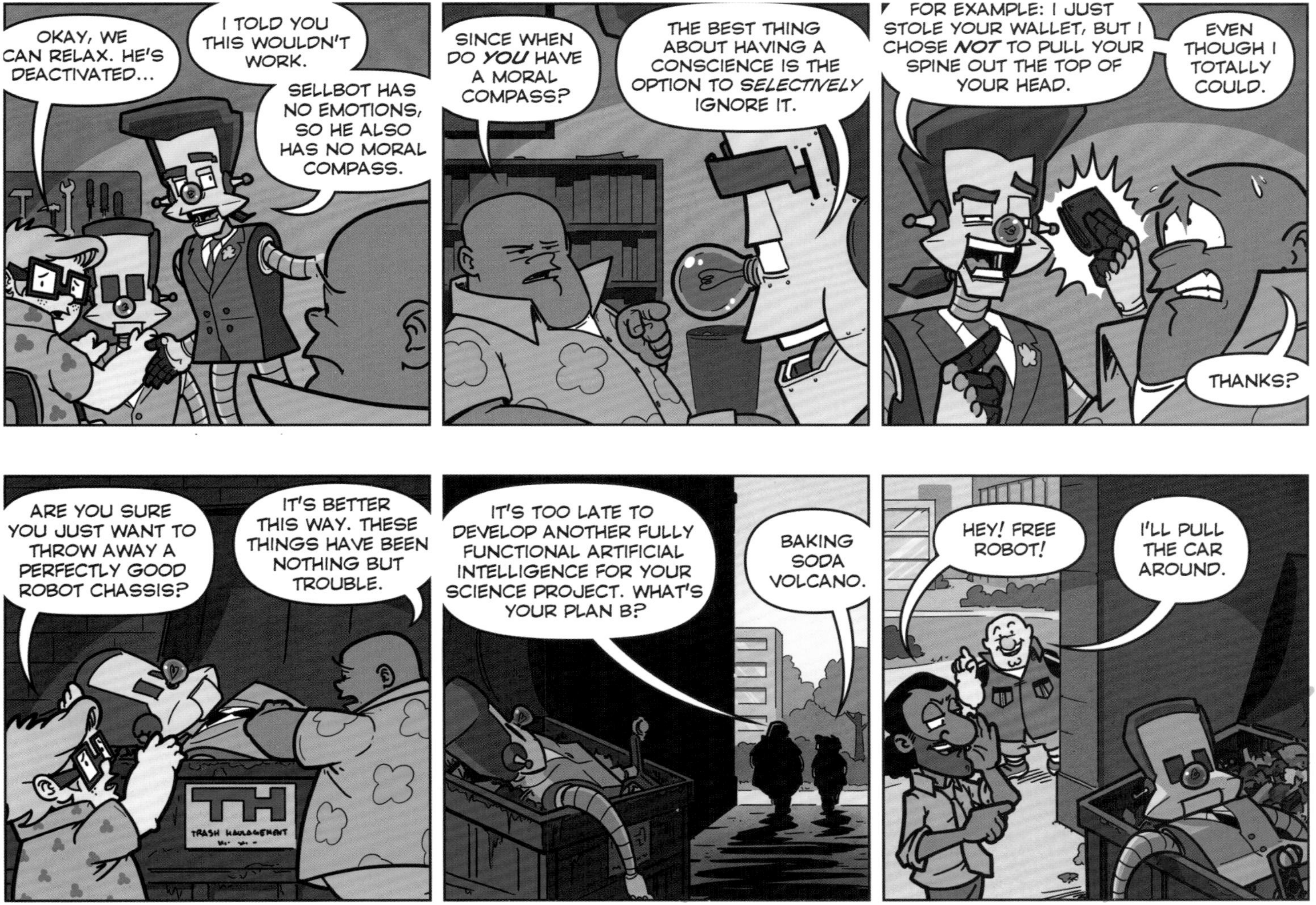
OKAY, WE CAN RELAX. HE'S DEACTIVATED...
I TOLD YOU THIS WOULDN'T WORK.
SELLBOT HAS NO EMOTIONS, SO HE ALSO HAS NO MORAL COMPASS.
SINCE WHEN DO *YOU* HAVE A MORAL COMPASS?
THE BEST THING ABOUT HAVING A CONSCIENCE IS THE OPTION TO *SELECTIVELY* IGNORE IT.
FOR EXAMPLE: I JUST STOLE YOUR WALLET, BUT I CHOSE *NOT* TO PULL YOUR SPINE OUT THE TOP OF YOUR HEAD.
EVEN THOUGH I TOTALLY COULD.
THANKS?
ARE YOU SURE YOU JUST WANT TO THROW AWAY A PERFECTLY GOOD ROBOT CHASSIS?
IT'S BETTER THIS WAY. THESE THINGS HAVE BEEN NOTHING BUT TROUBLE.
TH
IT'S TOO LATE TO DEVELOP ANOTHER FULLY FUNCTIONAL ARTIFICIAL INTELLIGENCE FOR YOUR SCIENCE PROJECT. WHAT'S YOUR PLAN B?
BAKING SODA VOLCANO.
HEY! FREE ROBOT!
I'LL PULL THE CAR AROUND.

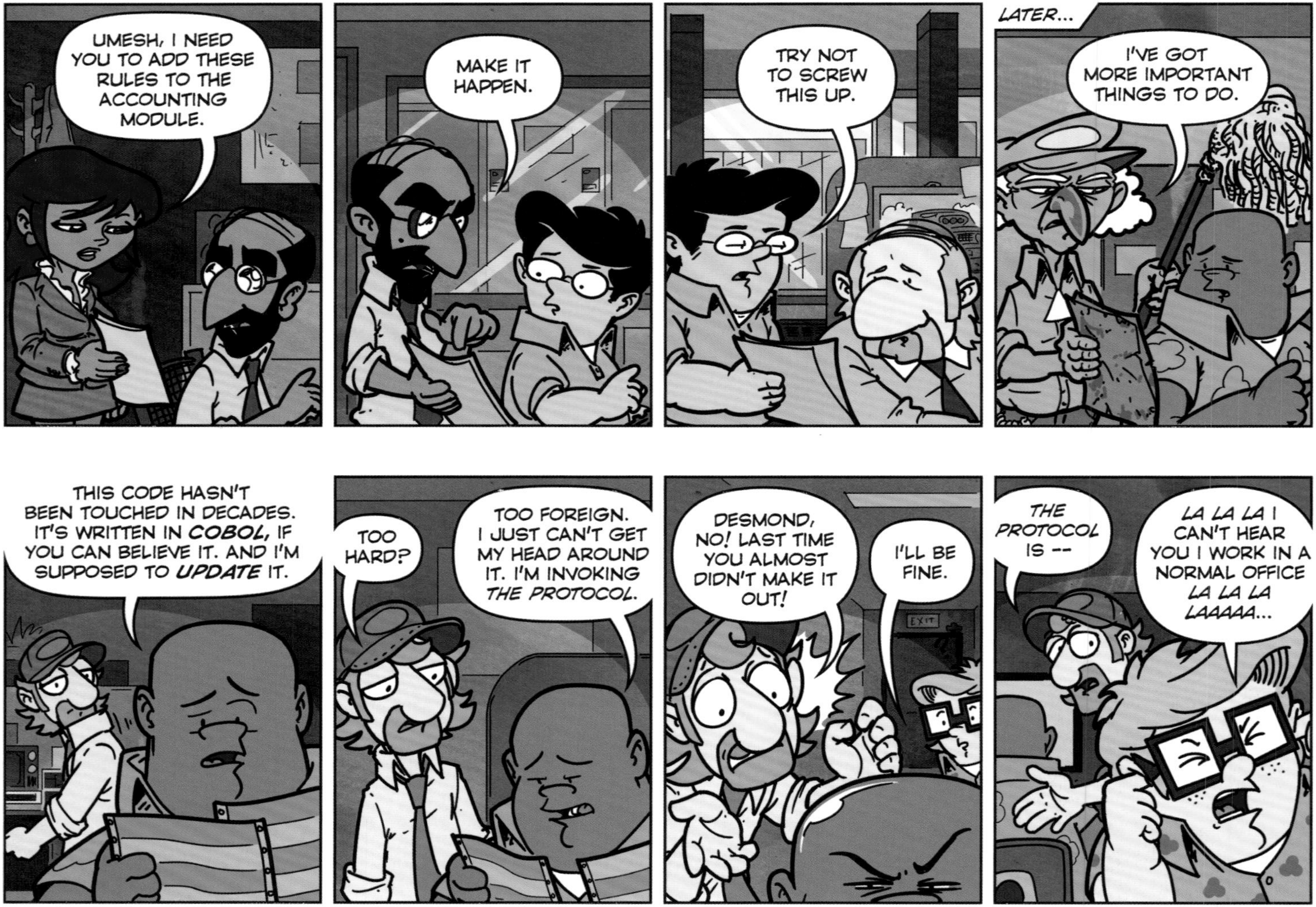
UMESH, I NEED YOU TO ADD THESE RULES TO THE ACCOUNTING MODULE.
MAKE IT HAPPEN.
TRY NOT TO SCREW THIS UP.
LATER...
I'VE GOT MORE IMPORTANT THINGS TO DO.
THIS CODE HASN'T BEEN TOUCHED IN DECADES. IT'S WRITTEN IN *COBOL,* IF YOU CAN BELIEVE IT. AND I'M SUPPOSED TO ***UPDATE*** IT.
TOO HARD?
TOO FOREIGN. I JUST CAN'T GET MY HEAD AROUND IT. I'M INVOKING *THE PROTOCOL*.
DESMOND, NO*!* LAST TIME YOU ALMOST DIDN'T MAKE IT OUT*!*
I'LL BE FINE.
EXIT
THE PROTOCOL IS --
LA LA LA I CAN'T HEAR YOU I WORK IN A NORMAL OFFICE *LA LA LA LAAAAA...*

UPGRADE PATH

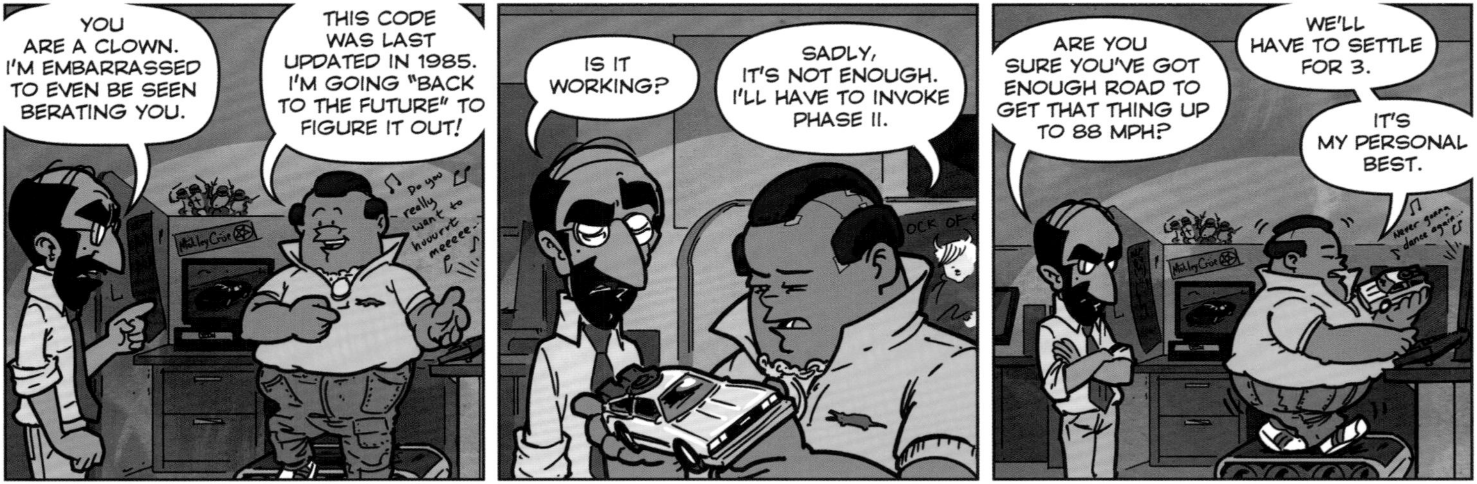
YOU ARE A CLOWN. I'M EMBARRASSED TO EVEN BE SEEN BERATING YOU.
THIS CODE WAS LAST UPDATED IN 1985. I'M GOING "BACK TO THE FUTURE" TO FIGURE IT OUT!
IS IT WORKING?
SADLY, IT'S NOT ENOUGH. I'LL HAVE TO INVOKE PHASE II.
ARE YOU SURE YOU'VE GOT ENOUGH ROAD TO GET THAT THING UP TO 88 MPH?
WE'LL HAVE TO SETTLE FOR 3.
IT'S MY PERSONAL BEST.

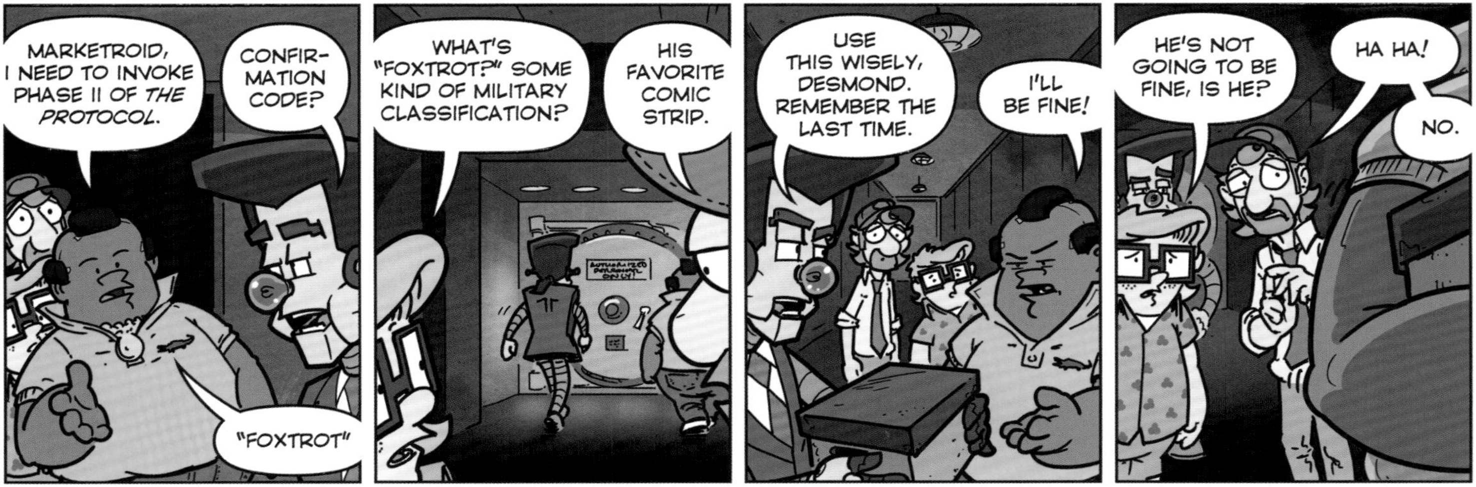
MARKETROID, I NEED TO INVOKE PHASE II OF *THE PROTOCOL*.
CONFIR-MATION CODE?
"FOXTROT"
WHAT'S "FOXTROT?" SOME KIND OF MILITARY CLASSIFICATION?
HIS FAVORITE COMIC STRIP.
USE THIS WISELY, DESMOND. REMEMBER THE LAST TIME.
I'LL BE FINE!
HE'S NOT GOING TO BE FINE, IS HE?
HA HA!
NO.

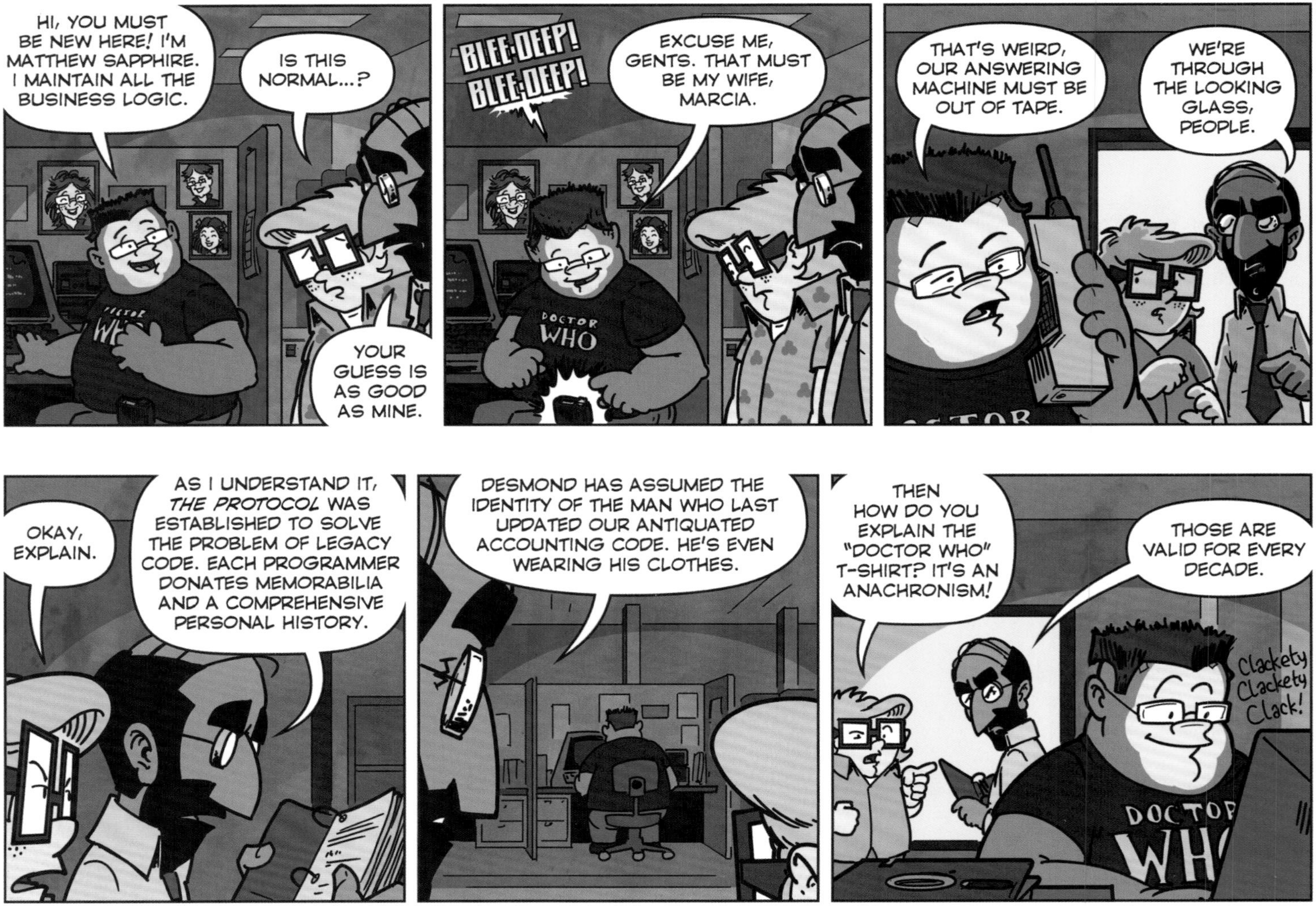
HI, YOU MUST BE NEW HERE! I'M MATTHEW SAPPHIRE. I MAINTAIN ALL THE BUSINESS LOGIC.
IS THIS NORMAL...?
YOUR GUESS IS AS GOOD AS MINE.
DOCTOR WHO
BLEE-DEEP! BLEE-DEEP!
EXCUSE ME, GENTS. THAT MUST BE MY WIFE, MARCIA.
DOCTOR WHO
THAT'S WEIRD, OUR ANSWERING MACHINE MUST BE OUT OF TAPE.
WE'RE THROUGH THE LOOKING GLASS, PEOPLE.
OKAY, EXPLAIN.
AS I UNDERSTAND IT, *THE PROTOCOL* WAS ESTABLISHED TO SOLVE THE PROBLEM OF LEGACY CODE. EACH PROGRAMMER DONATES MEMORABILIA AND A COMPREHENSIVE PERSONAL HISTORY.
DESMOND HAS ASSUMED THE IDENTITY OF THE MAN WHO LAST UPDATED OUR ANTIQUATED ACCOUNTING CODE. HE'S EVEN WEARING HIS CLOTHES.
THEN HOW DO YOU EXPLAIN THE "DOCTOR WHO" T-SHIRT? IT'S AN ANACHRONISM!
THOSE ARE VALID FOR EVERY DECADE.
Clackety Clackety Clack!

UPGRADE PATH

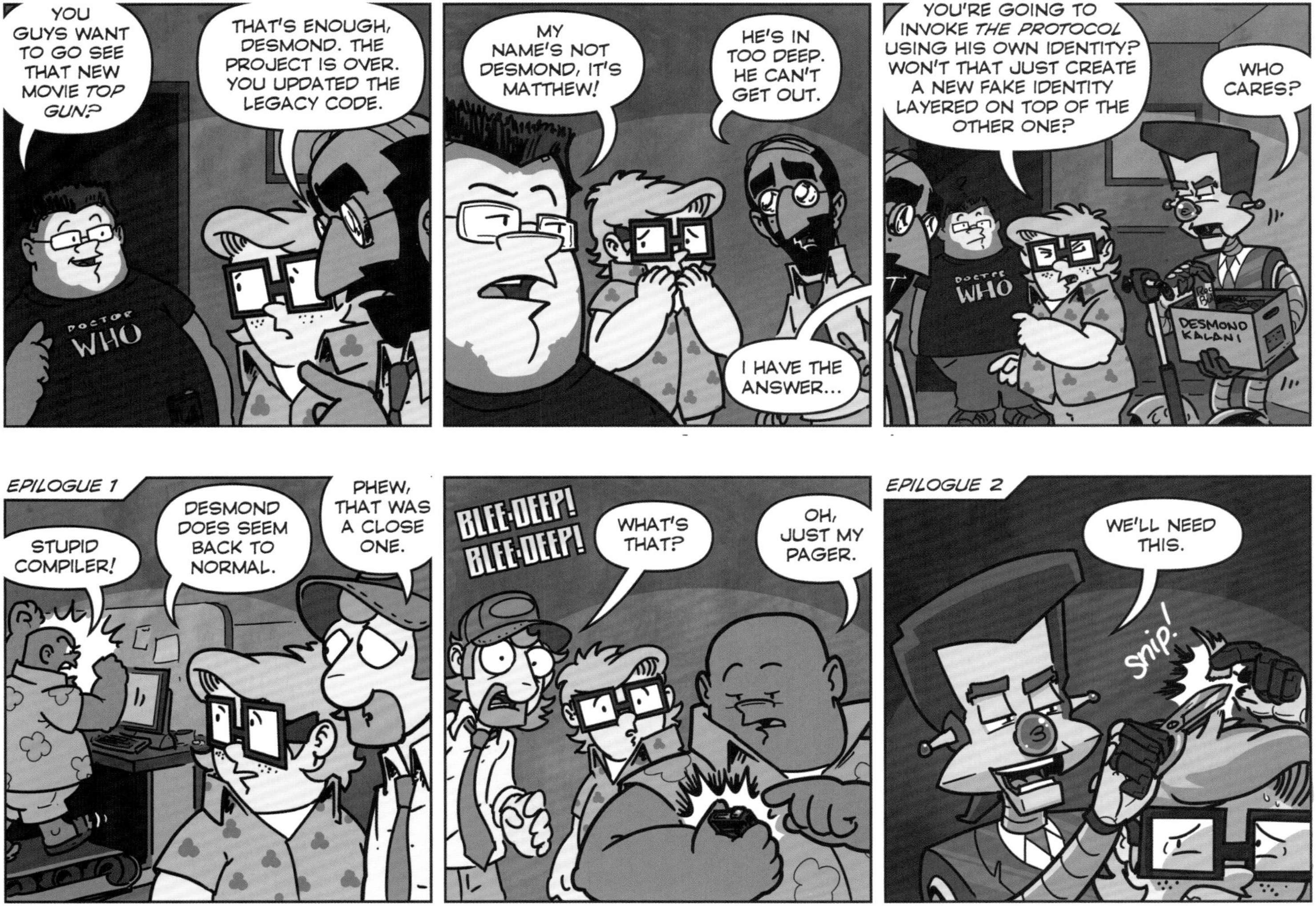
YOU GUYS WANT TO GO SEE THAT NEW MOVIE *TOP GUN?*
THAT'S ENOUGH, DESMOND. THE PROJECT IS OVER. YOU UPDATED THE LEGACY CODE.
DOCTOR WHO
MY NAME'S NOT DESMOND, IT'S MATTHEW!
HE'S IN TOO DEEP. HE CAN'T GET OUT.
I HAVE THE ANSWER...
DOCTOR WHO
YOU'RE GOING TO INVOKE *THE PROTOCOL* USING HIS OWN IDENTITY? WON'T THAT JUST CREATE A NEW FAKE IDENTITY LAYERED ON TOP OF THE OTHER ONE?
WHO CARES?
DESMOND KALANI
EPILOGUE 1
STUPID COMPILER!
DESMOND DOES SEEM BACK TO NORMAL.
PHEW, THAT WAS A CLOSE ONE.
BLEE-DEEP! BLEE-DEEP!
WHAT'S THAT?
OH, JUST MY PAGER.
EPILOGUE 2
WE'LL NEED THIS.
snip!

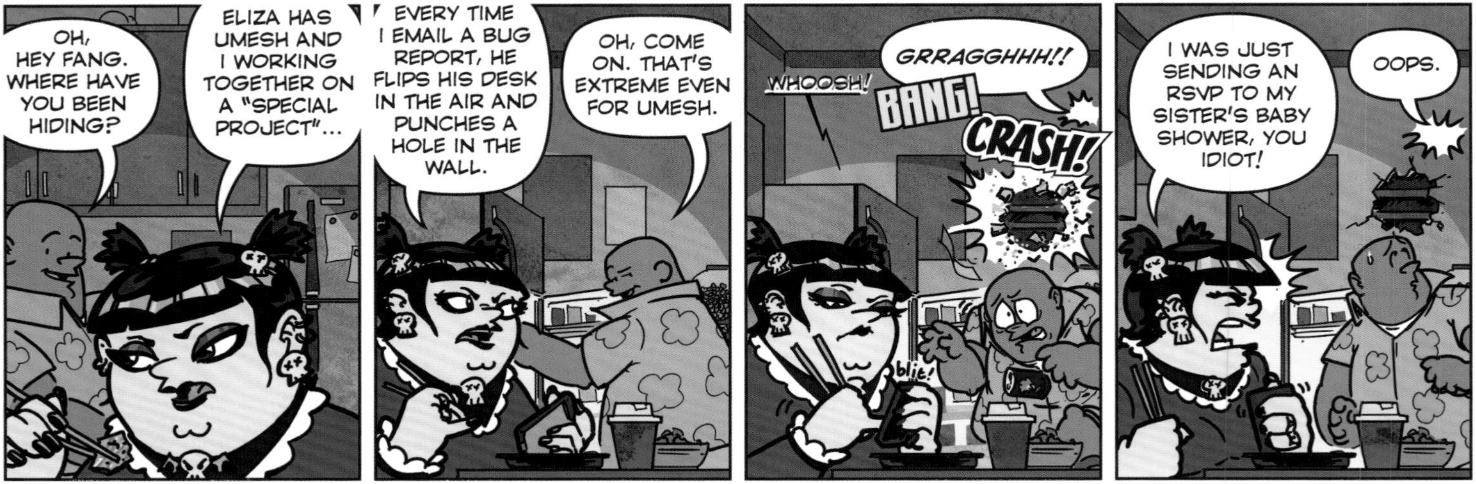
OH, HEY FANG. WHERE HAVE YOU BEEN HIDING?
ELIZA HAS UMESH AND I WORKING TOGETHER ON A "SPECIAL PROJECT"...
EVERY TIME I EMAIL A BUG REPORT, HE FLIPS HIS DESK IN THE AIR AND PUNCHES A HOLE IN THE WALL.
OH, COME ON. THAT'S EXTREME EVEN FOR UMESH.
WHOOSH!
BANG!
GRRAGGHHH!!
CRASH!
blit!
I WAS JUST SENDING AN RSVP TO MY SISTER'S BABY SHOWER, YOU IDIOT!
OOPS.

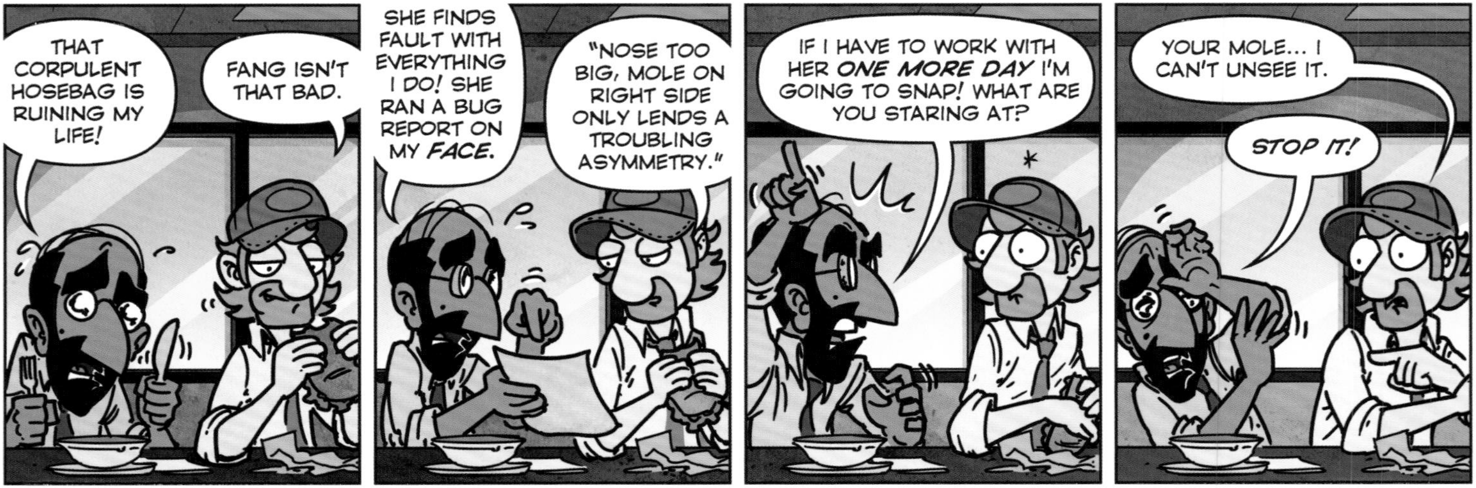
THAT CORPULENT HOSEBAG IS RUINING MY LIFE!
FANG ISN'T THAT BAD.
SHE FINDS FAULT WITH EVERYTHING I DO! SHE RAN A BUG REPORT ON MY *FACE*.
"NOSE TOO BIG, MOLE ON RIGHT SIDE ONLY LENDS A TROUBLING ASYMMETRY."
IF I HAVE TO WORK WITH HER *ONE MORE DAY* I'M GOING TO SNAP! WHAT ARE YOU STARING AT?
YOUR MOLE... I CAN'T UNSEE IT.
STOP IT!

UPGRADE PATH

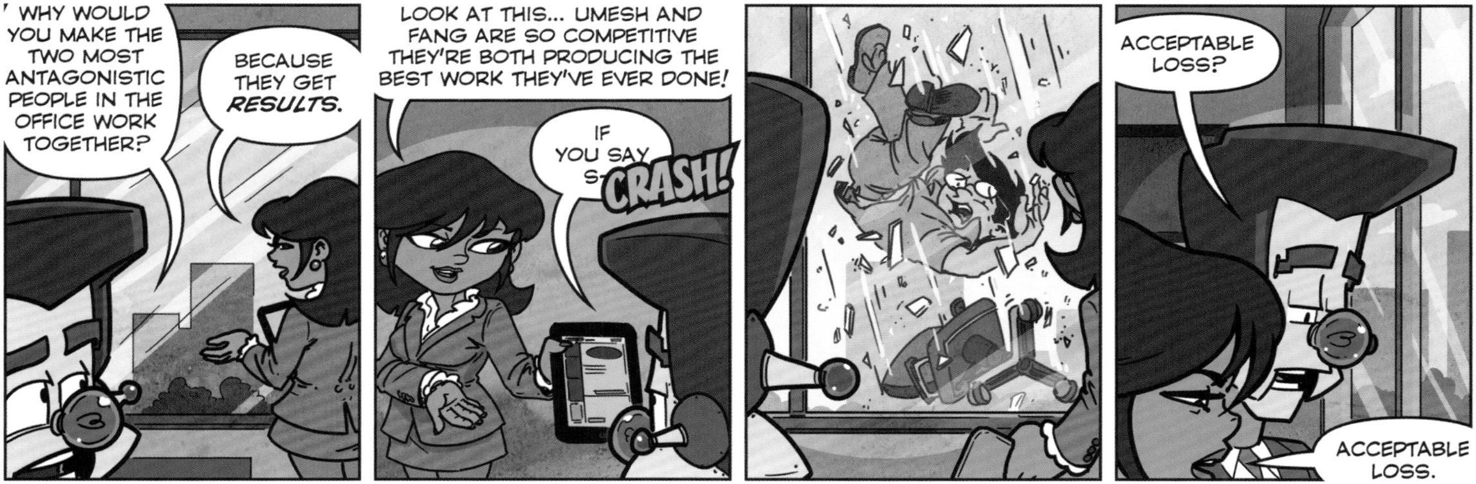
WHY WOULD YOU MAKE THE TWO MOST ANTAGONISTIC PEOPLE IN THE OFFICE WORK TOGETHER?
BECAUSE THEY GET *RESULTS*.
LOOK AT THIS... UMESH AND FANG ARE SO COMPETITIVE THEY'RE BOTH PRODUCING THE BEST WORK THEY'VE EVER DONE!
IF YOU SAY S—
CRASH!
ACCEPTABLE LOSS?
ACCEPTABLE LOSS.

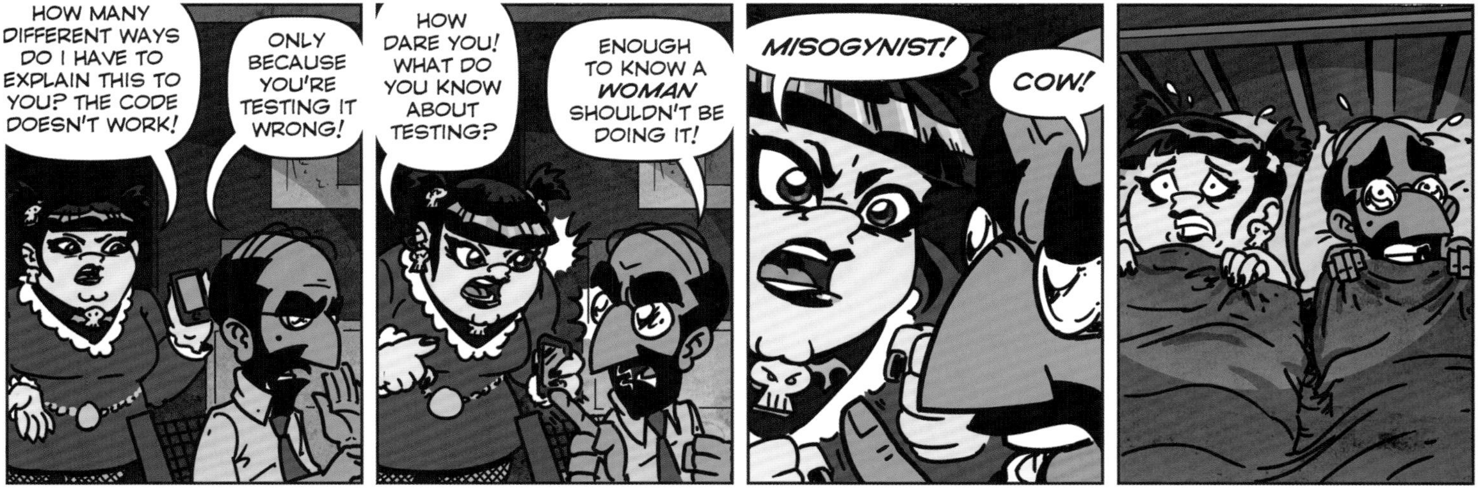
HOW MANY DIFFERENT WAYS DO I HAVE TO EXPLAIN THIS TO YOU? THE CODE DOESN'T WORK!
ONLY BECAUSE YOU'RE TESTING IT WRONG!
HOW DARE YOU! WHAT DO YOU KNOW ABOUT TESTING?
ENOUGH TO KNOW A *WOMAN* SHOULDN'T BE DOING IT!
MISOGYNIST!
COW!

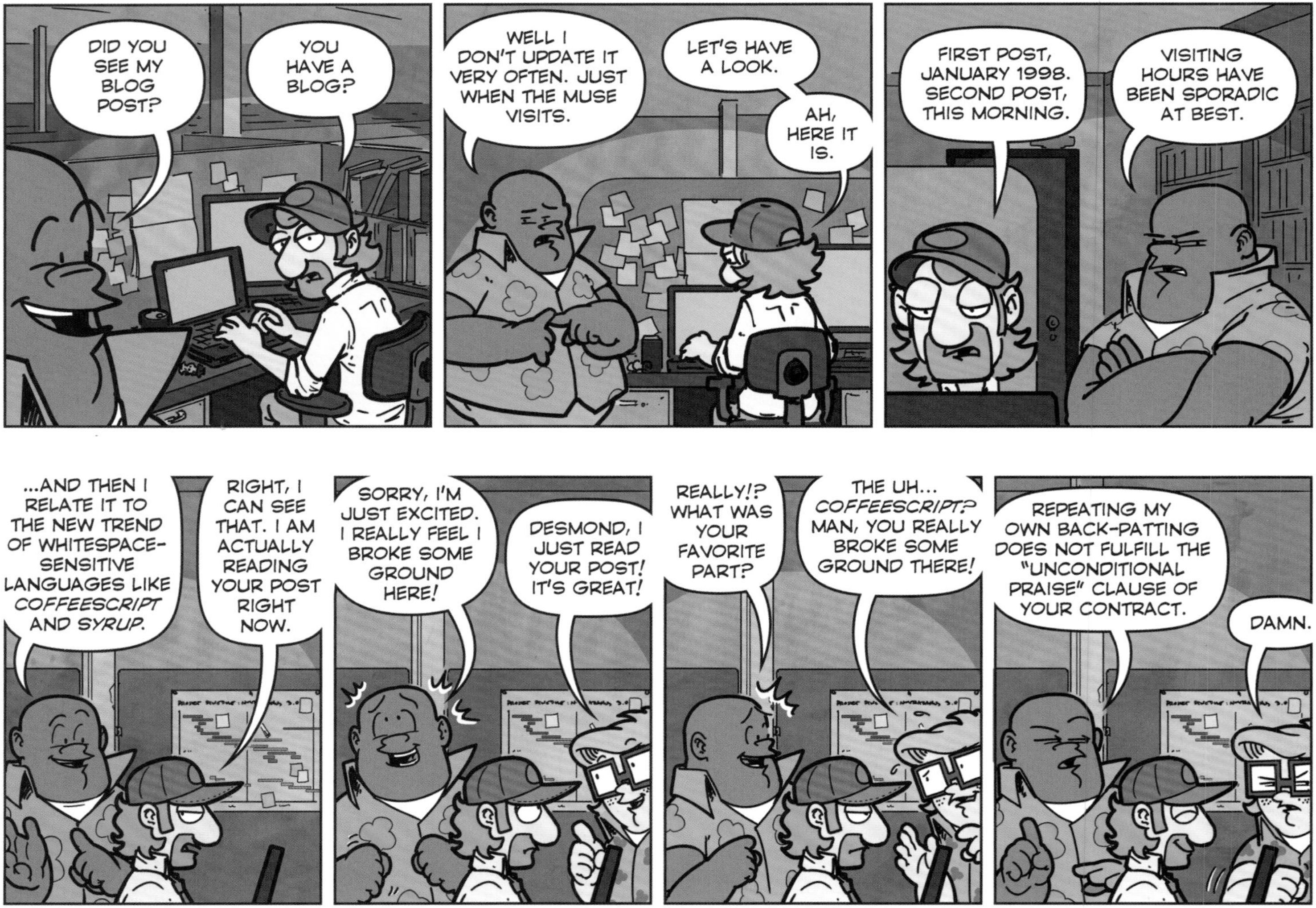
DID YOU SEE MY BLOG POST?
YOU HAVE A BLOG?
WELL I DON'T UPDATE IT VERY OFTEN. JUST WHEN THE MUSE VISITS.
LET'S HAVE A LOOK.
AH, HERE IT IS.
FIRST POST, JANUARY 1998. SECOND POST, THIS MORNING.
VISITING HOURS HAVE BEEN SPORADIC AT BEST.
...AND THEN I RELATE IT TO THE NEW TREND OF WHITESPACE-SENSITIVE LANGUAGES LIKE *COFFEESCRIPT* AND *SYRUP*.
RIGHT, I CAN SEE THAT. I AM ACTUALLY READING YOUR POST RIGHT NOW.
SORRY, I'M JUST EXCITED. I REALLY FEEL I BROKE SOME GROUND HERE!
DESMOND, I JUST READ YOUR POST! IT'S GREAT!
REALLY!? WHAT WAS YOUR FAVORITE PART?
THE UH... *COFFEESCRIPT?* MAN, YOU REALLY BROKE SOME GROUND THERE!
REPEATING MY OWN BACK-PATTING DOES NOT FULFILL THE "UNCONDITIONAL PRAISE" CLAUSE OF YOUR CONTRACT.
DAMN.

UPGRADE PATH

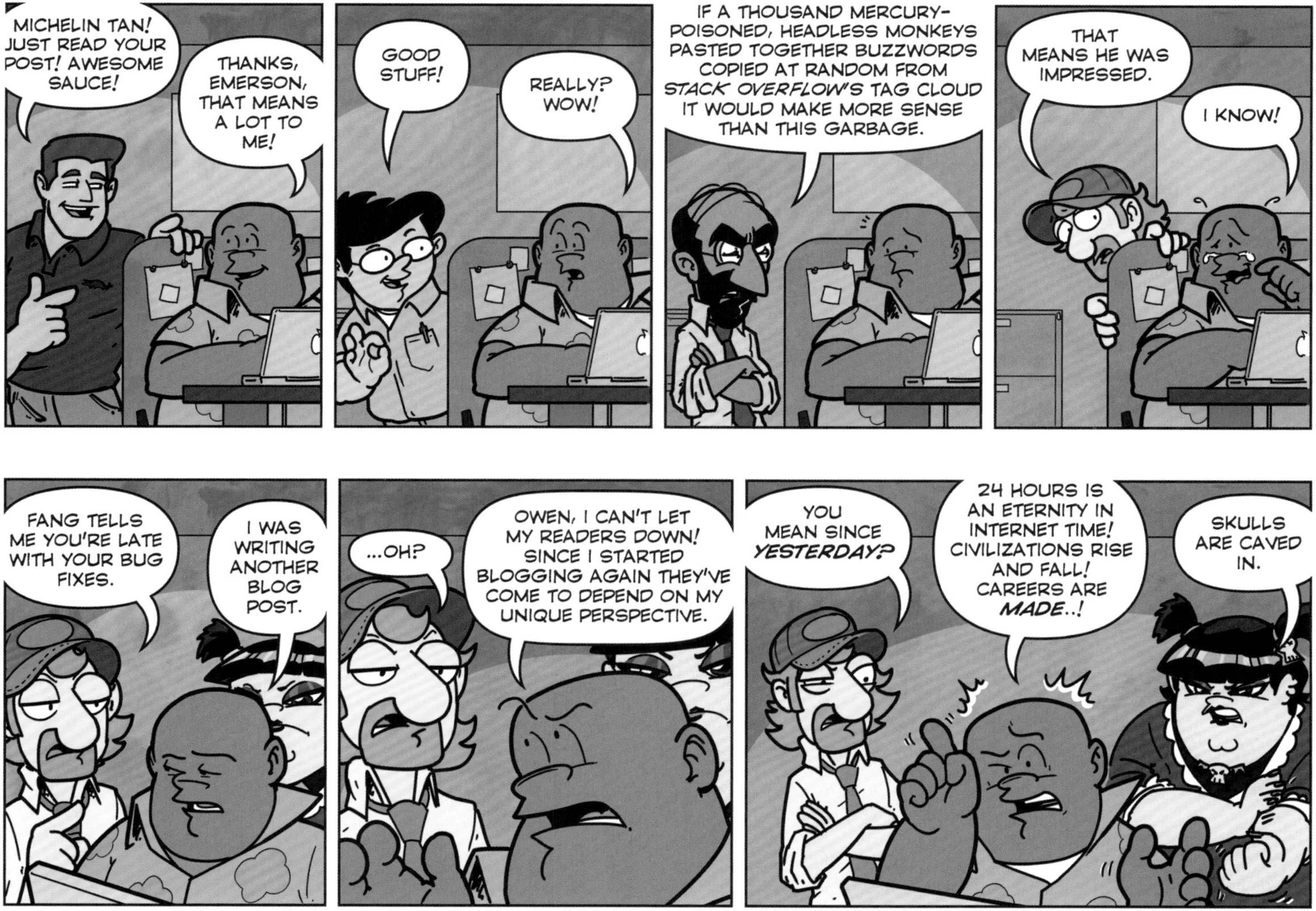
MICHELIN TAN! JUST READ YOUR POST! AWESOME SAUCE!
THANKS, EMERSON, THAT MEANS A LOT TO ME!
GOOD STUFF!
REALLY? WOW!
IF A THOUSAND MERCURY-POISONED, HEADLESS MONKEYS PASTED TOGETHER BUZZWORDS COPIED AT RANDOM FROM *STACK OVERFLOW'S* TAG CLOUD IT WOULD MAKE MORE SENSE THAN THIS GARBAGE.
THAT MEANS HE WAS IMPRESSED.
I KNOW!
FANG TELLS ME YOU'RE LATE WITH YOUR BUG FIXES.
I WAS WRITING ANOTHER BLOG POST.
...OH?
OWEN, I CAN'T LET MY READERS DOWN! SINCE I STARTED BLOGGING AGAIN THEY'VE COME TO DEPEND ON MY UNIQUE PERSPECTIVE.
YOU MEAN SINCE ***YESTERDAY?***
24 HOURS IS AN ETERNITY IN INTERNET TIME! CIVILIZATIONS RISE AND FALL! CAREERS ARE ***MADE***..!
SKULLS ARE CAVED IN.

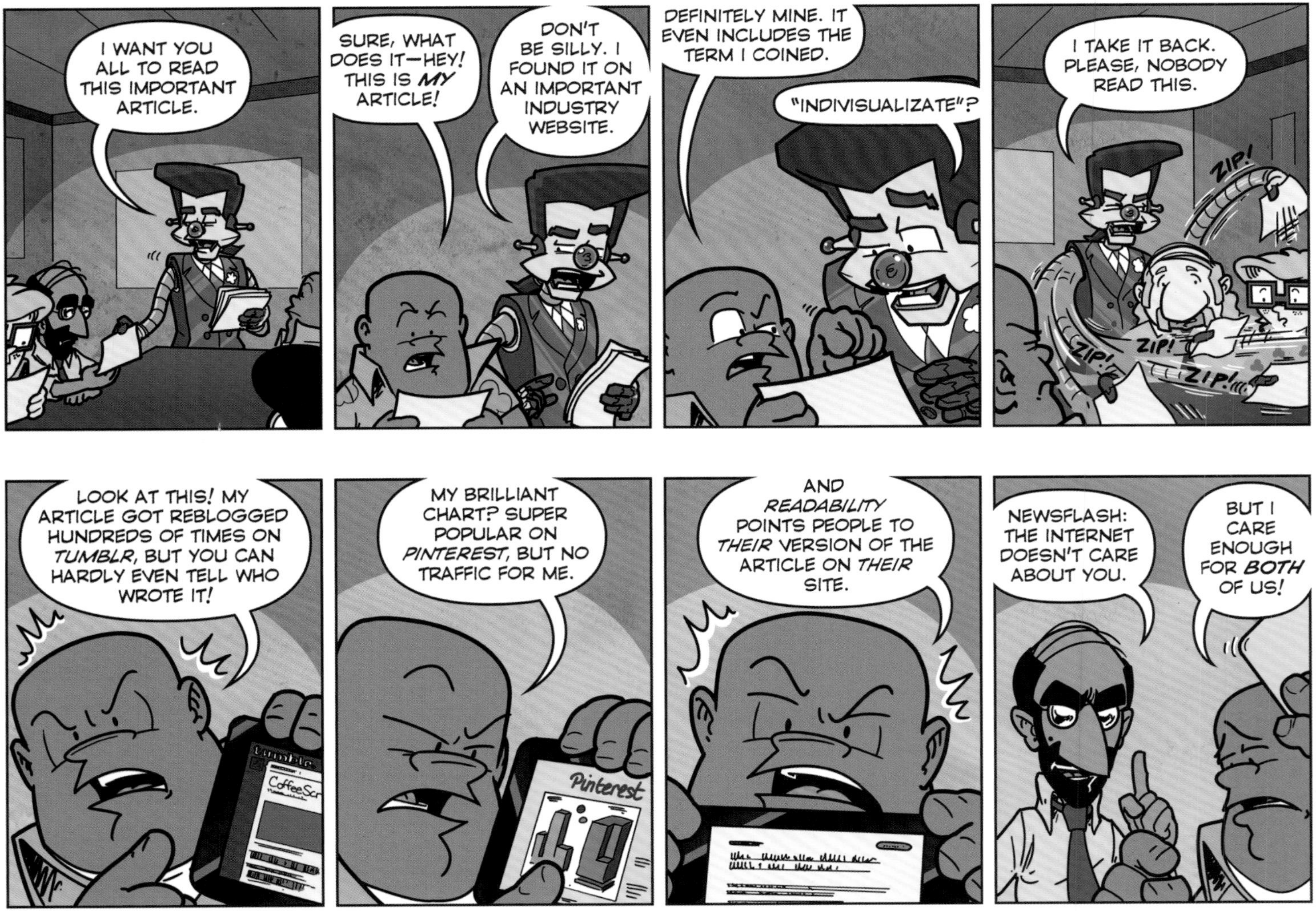
I WANT YOU ALL TO READ THIS IMPORTANT ARTICLE.
SURE, WHAT DOES IT—HEY! THIS IS *MY* ARTICLE!
DON'T BE SILLY. I FOUND IT ON AN IMPORTANT INDUSTRY WEBSITE.
DEFINITELY MINE. IT EVEN INCLUDES THE TERM I COINED.
"INDIVISUALIZATE"?
I TAKE IT BACK. PLEASE, NOBODY READ THIS.
ZIP!
ZIP!
ZIP!
ZIP!
LOOK AT THIS! MY ARTICLE GOT REBLOGGED HUNDREDS OF TIMES ON *TUMBLR*, BUT YOU CAN HARDLY EVEN TELL WHO WROTE IT!
MY BRILLIANT CHART? SUPER POPULAR ON *PINTEREST*, BUT NO TRAFFIC FOR ME.
Pinterest
AND *READABILITY* POINTS PEOPLE TO *THEIR* VERSION OF THE ARTICLE ON *THEIR* SITE.
NEWSFLASH: THE INTERNET DOESN'T CARE ABOUT YOU.
BUT I CARE ENOUGH FOR *BOTH* OF US!

UPGRADE PATH

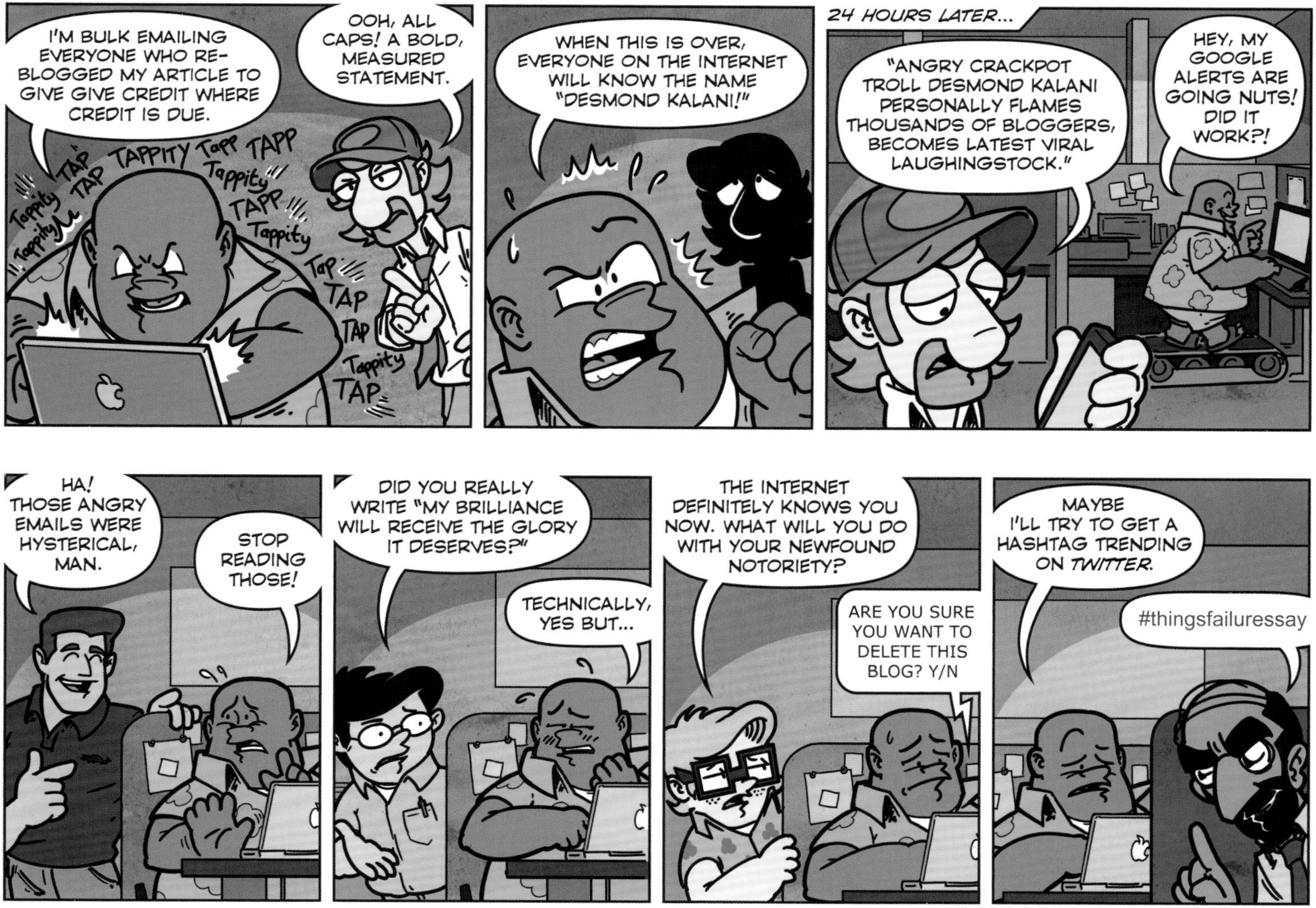

I'M BULK EMAILING EVERYONE WHO RE-BLOGGED MY ARTICLE TO GIVE GIVE CREDIT WHERE CREDIT IS DUE.
TAP TAP TAPPITY Tapp TAPP Tappity TAPP Tappity Tappity Tappity Tap TAP TAP Tappity TAP
OOH, ALL CAPS! A BOLD, MEASURED STATEMENT.
WHEN THIS IS OVER, EVERYONE ON THE INTERNET WILL KNOW THE NAME "DESMOND KALANI!"
24 HOURS LATER...
"ANGRY CRACKPOT TROLL DESMOND KALANI PERSONALLY FLAMES THOUSANDS OF BLOGGERS, BECOMES LATEST VIRAL LAUGHINGSTOCK."
HEY, MY GOOGLE ALERTS ARE GOING NUTS! DID IT WORK?!
HA! THOSE ANGRY EMAILS WERE HYSTERICAL, MAN.
STOP READING THOSE!
DID YOU REALLY WRITE "MY BRILLIANCE WILL RECEIVE THE GLORY IT DESERVES?"
TECHNICALLY, YES BUT...
THE INTERNET DEFINITELY KNOWS YOU NOW. WHAT WILL YOU DO WITH YOUR NEWFOUND NOTORIETY?
ARE YOU SURE YOU WANT TO DELETE THIS BLOG? Y/N
MAYBE I'LL TRY TO GET A HASHTAG TRENDING ON *TWITTER*.
#thingsfailuressay

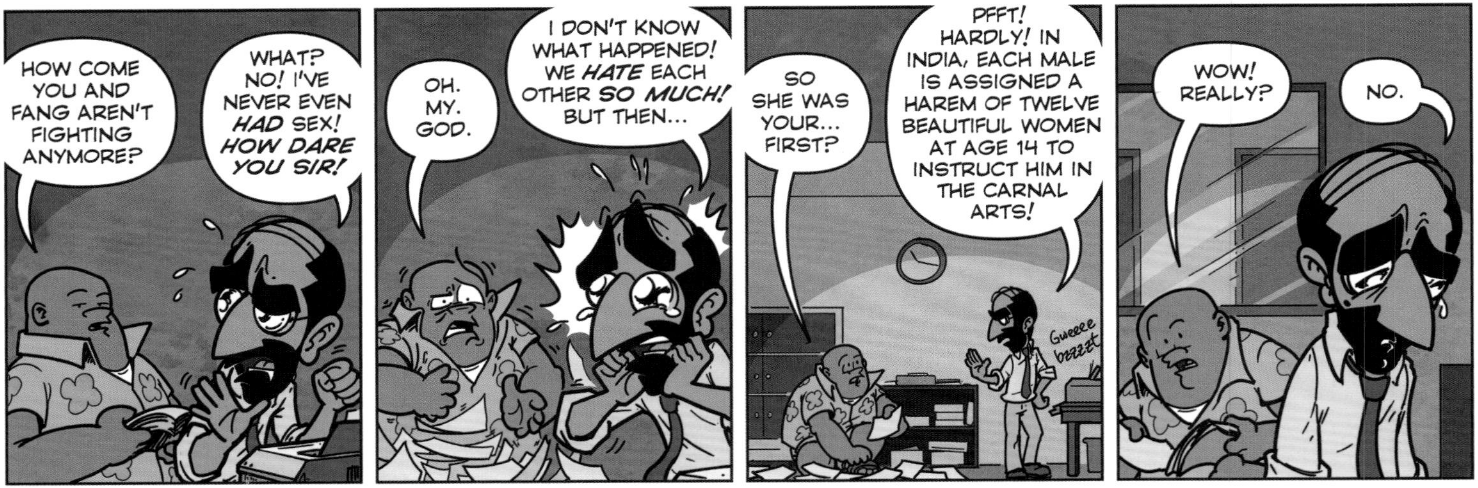
HOW COME YOU AND FANG AREN'T FIGHTING ANYMORE?
WHAT? NO! I'VE NEVER EVEN HAD SEX! HOW DARE YOU SIR!
OH. MY. GOD.
I DON'T KNOW WHAT HAPPENED! WE HATE EACH OTHER SO MUCH! BUT THEN...
SO SHE WAS YOUR... FIRST?
PFFT! HARDLY! IN INDIA, EACH MALE IS ASSIGNED A HAREM OF TWELVE BEAUTIFUL WOMEN AT AGE 14 TO INSTRUCT HIM IN THE CARNAL ARTS!
WOW! REALLY?
NO.

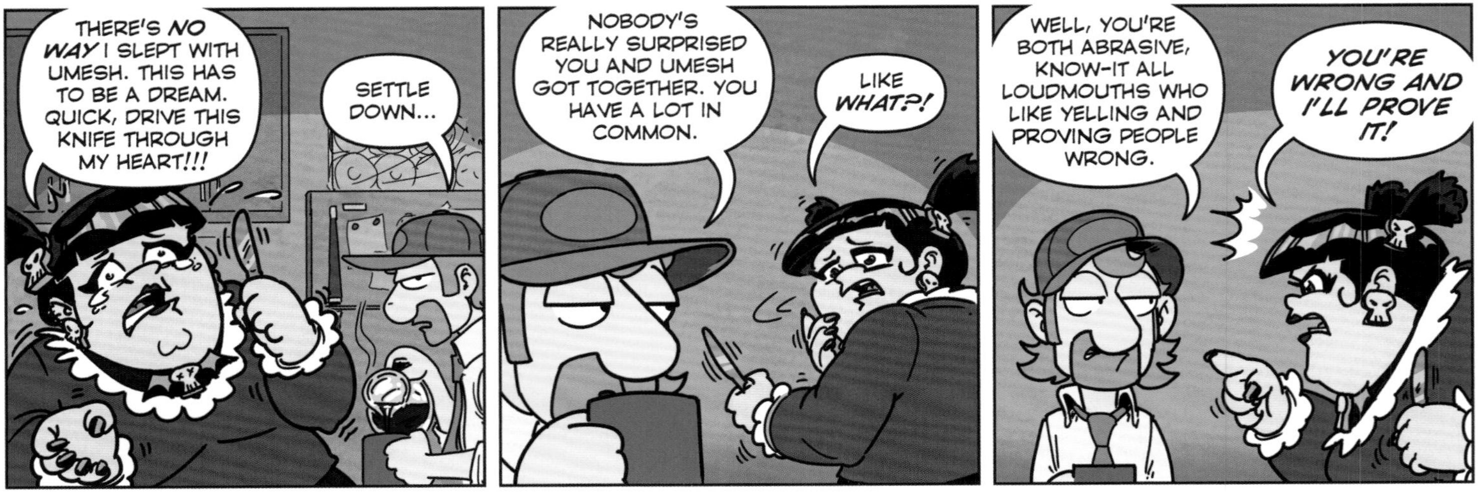
THERE'S NO WAY I SLEPT WITH UMESH. THIS HAS TO BE A DREAM. QUICK, DRIVE THIS KNIFE THROUGH MY HEART!!!
SETTLE DOWN...
NOBODY'S REALLY SURPRISED YOU AND UMESH GOT TOGETHER. YOU HAVE A LOT IN COMMON.
LIKE WHAT?!
WELL, YOU'RE BOTH ABRASIVE, KNOW-IT ALL LOUDMOUTHS WHO LIKE YELLING AND PROVING PEOPLE WRONG.
YOU'RE WRONG AND I'LL PROVE IT!

UPGRADE PATH

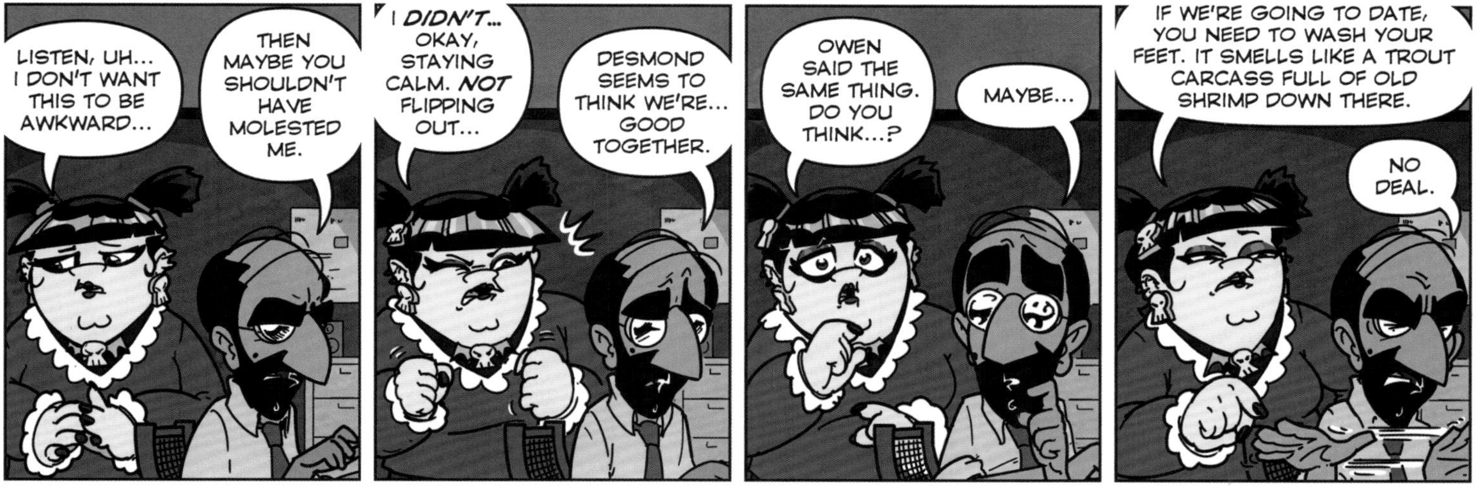
LISTEN, UH... I DON'T WANT THIS TO BE AWKWARD...
THEN MAYBE YOU SHOULDN'T HAVE MOLESTED ME.
I *DIDN'T*... OKAY, STAYING CALM. *NOT* FLIPPING OUT...
DESMOND SEEMS TO THINK WE'RE... GOOD TOGETHER.
OWEN SAID THE SAME THING. DO YOU THINK...?
MAYBE...
IF WE'RE GOING TO DATE, YOU NEED TO WASH YOUR FEET. IT SMELLS LIKE A TROUT CARCASS FULL OF OLD SHRIMP DOWN THERE.
NO DEAL.

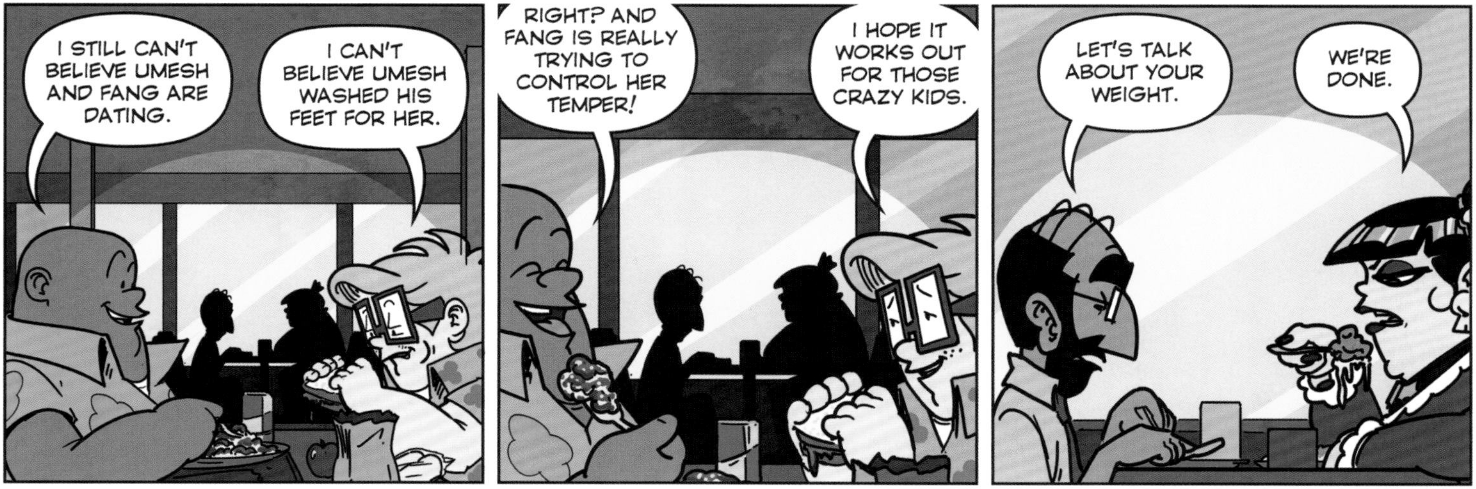
I STILL CAN'T BELIEVE UMESH AND FANG ARE DATING.
I CAN'T BELIEVE UMESH WASHED HIS FEET FOR HER.
RIGHT? AND FANG IS REALLY TRYING TO CONTROL HER TEMPER!
I HOPE IT WORKS OUT FOR THOSE CRAZY KIDS.
LET'S TALK ABOUT YOUR WEIGHT.
WE'RE DONE.

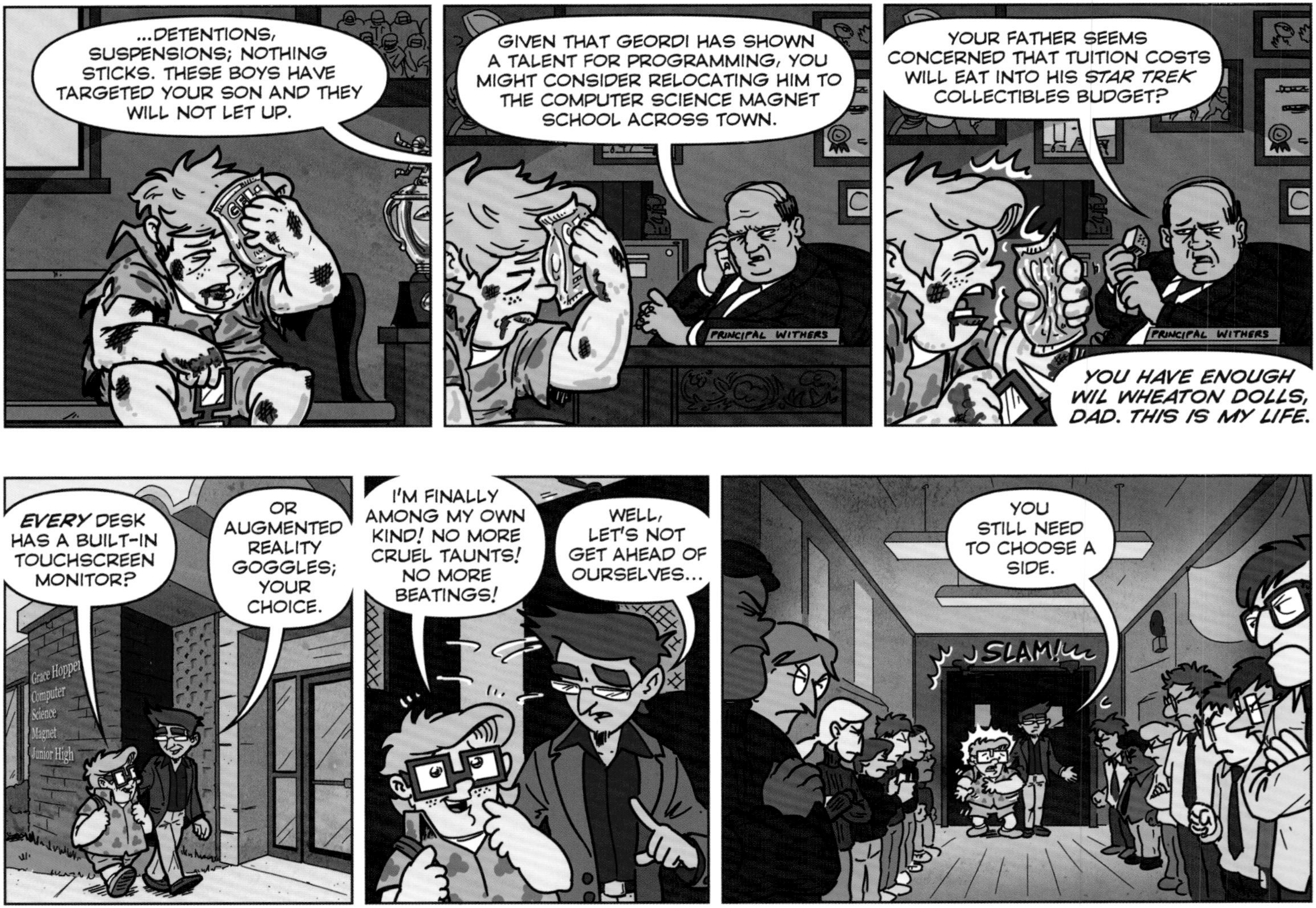
...DETENTIONS, SUSPENSIONS; NOTHING STICKS. THESE BOYS HAVE TARGETED YOUR SON AND THEY WILL NOT LET UP.
GIVEN THAT GEORDI HAS SHOWN A TALENT FOR PROGRAMMING, YOU MIGHT CONSIDER RELOCATING HIM TO THE COMPUTER SCIENCE MAGNET SCHOOL ACROSS TOWN.
PRINCIPAL WITHERS
YOUR FATHER SEEMS CONCERNED THAT TUITION COSTS WILL EAT INTO HIS STAR TREK COLLECTIBLES BUDGET?
PRINCIPAL WITHERS
YOU HAVE ENOUGH WIL WHEATON DOLLS, DAD. THIS IS MY LIFE.
Grace Hopper Computer Science Magnet Junior High
EVERY DESK HAS A BUILT-IN TOUCHSCREEN MONITOR?
OR AUGMENTED REALITY GOGGLES; YOUR CHOICE.
I'M FINALLY AMONG MY OWN KIND! NO MORE CRUEL TAUNTS! NO MORE BEATINGS!
WELL, LET'S NOT GET AHEAD OF OURSELVES...
SLAM!
YOU STILL NEED TO CHOOSE A SIDE.

UPGRADE PATH

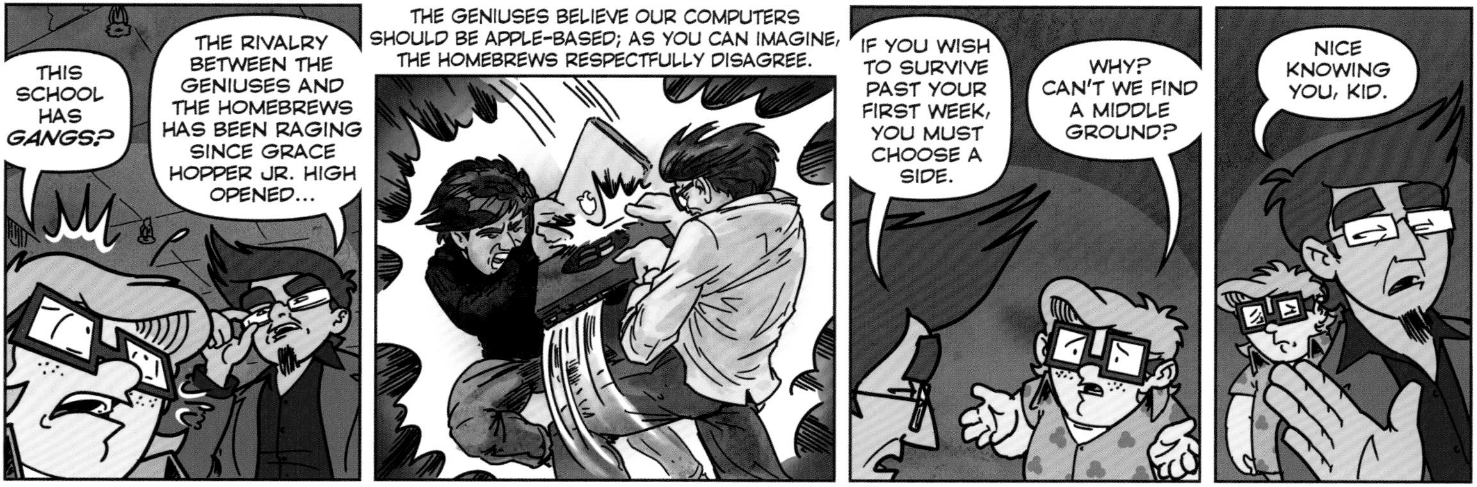
THIS SCHOOL HAS *GANGS?*
THE RIVALRY BETWEEN THE GENIUSES AND THE HOMEBREWS HAS BEEN RAGING SINCE GRACE HOPPER JR. HIGH OPENED...
THE GENIUSES BELIEVE OUR COMPUTERS SHOULD BE APPLE-BASED; AS YOU CAN IMAGINE, THE HOMEBREWS RESPECTFULLY DISAGREE.
IF YOU WISH TO SURVIVE PAST YOUR FIRST WEEK, YOU MUST CHOOSE A SIDE.
WHY? CAN'T WE FIND A MIDDLE GROUND?
NICE KNOWING YOU, KID.

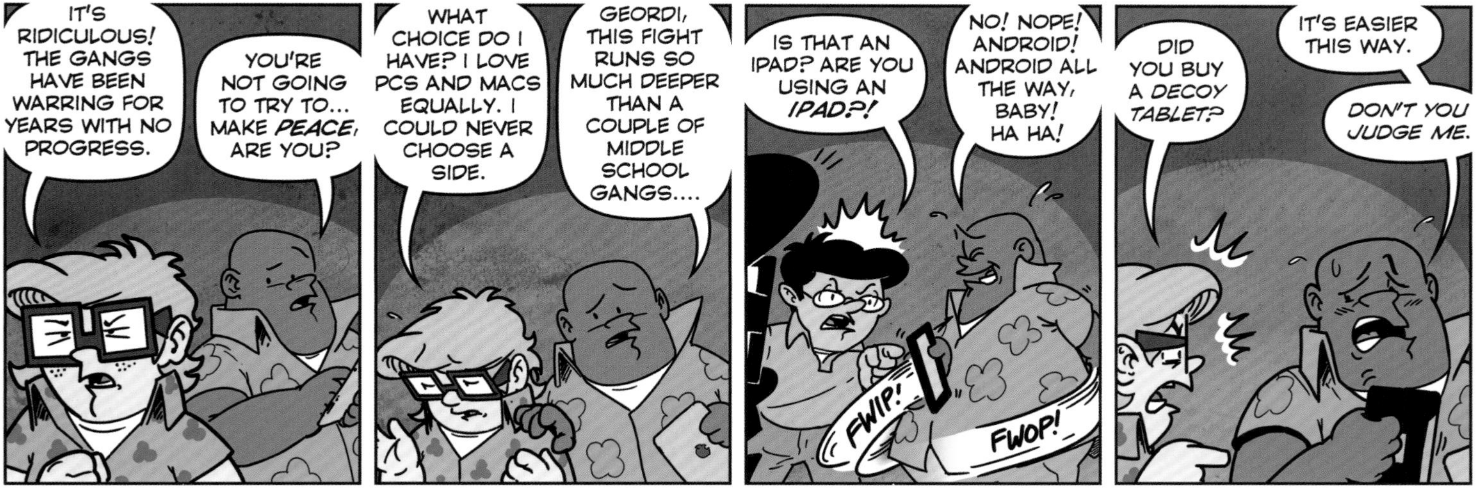
IT'S RIDICULOUS! THE GANGS HAVE BEEN WARRING FOR YEARS WITH NO PROGRESS.
YOU'RE NOT GOING TO TRY TO... MAKE *PEACE*, ARE YOU?
WHAT CHOICE DO I HAVE? I LOVE PCS AND MACS EQUALLY. I COULD NEVER CHOOSE A SIDE.
GEORDI, THIS FIGHT RUNS SO MUCH DEEPER THAN A COUPLE OF MIDDLE SCHOOL GANGS....
IS THAT AN IPAD? ARE YOU USING AN *IPAD?!*
NO! NOPE! ANDROID! ANDROID ALL THE WAY, BABY! HA HA!
FWIP!
FWOP!
DID YOU BUY A *DECOY TABLET?*
IT'S EASIER THIS WAY.
DON'T YOU JUDGE ME.

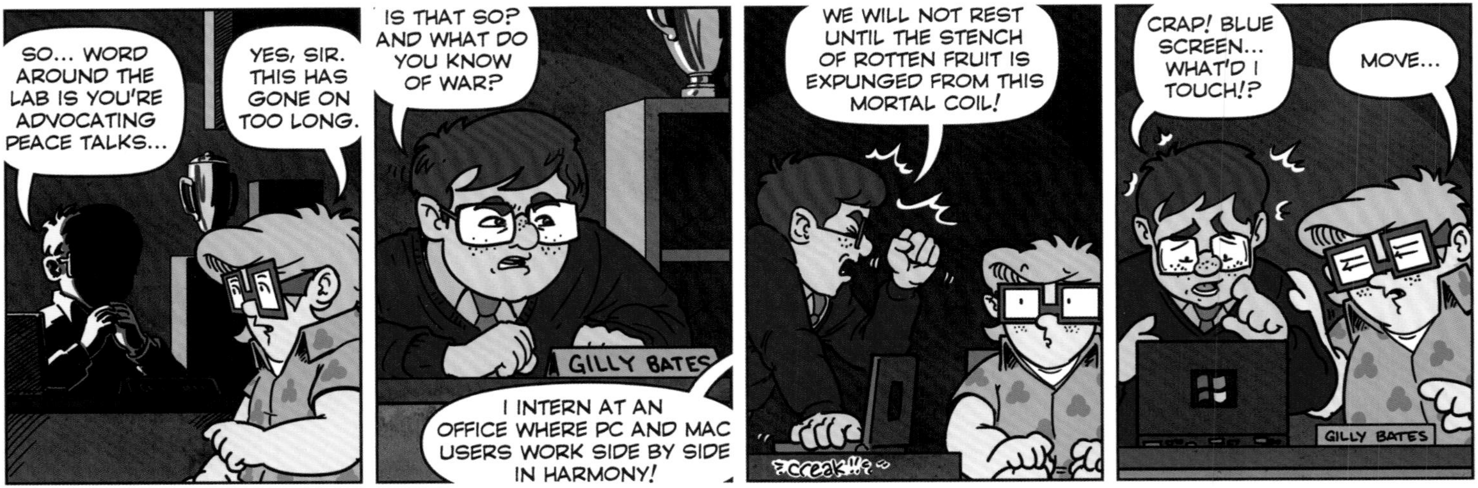
SO... WORD AROUND THE LAB IS YOU'RE ADVOCATING PEACE TALKS...
YES, SIR. THIS HAS GONE ON TOO LONG.
IS THAT SO? AND WHAT DO YOU KNOW OF WAR?
GILLY BATES
I INTERN AT AN OFFICE WHERE PC AND MAC USERS WORK SIDE BY SIDE IN HARMONY!
WE WILL NOT REST UNTIL THE STENCH OF ROTTEN FRUIT IS EXPUNGED FROM THIS MORTAL COIL!
CREAK!!
CRAP! BLUE SCREEN... WHAT'D I TOUCH!?
MOVE...
GILLY BATES

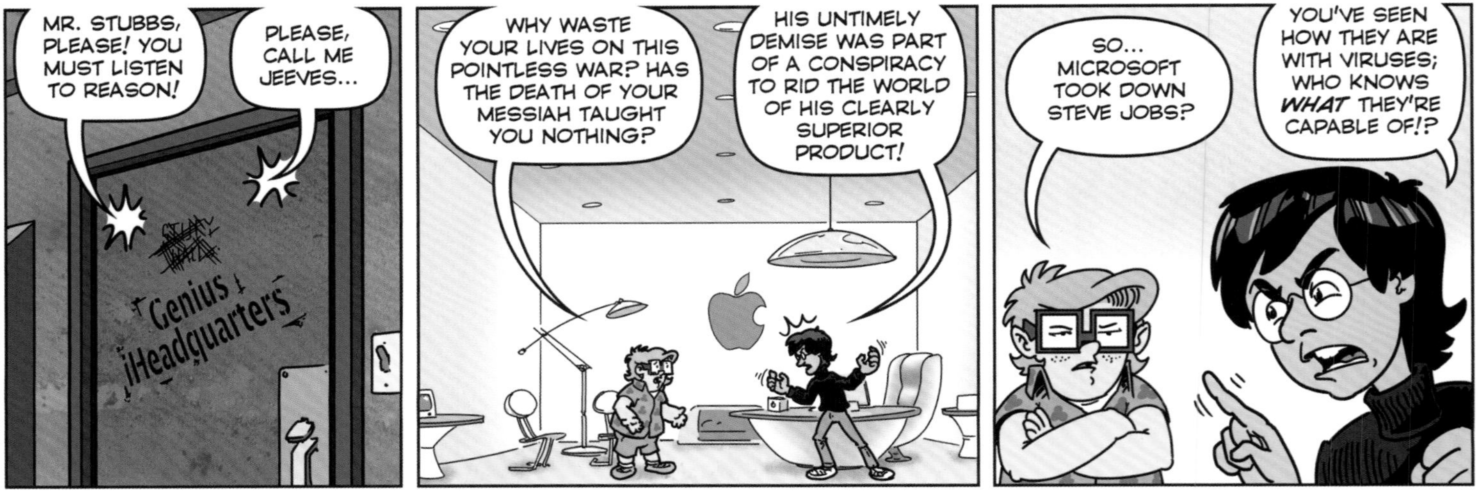
MR. STUBBS, PLEASE! YOU MUST LISTEN TO REASON!
PLEASE, CALL ME JEEVES...
Genius iHeadquarters
WHY WASTE YOUR LIVES ON THIS POINTLESS WAR? HAS THE DEATH OF YOUR MESSIAH TAUGHT YOU NOTHING?
HIS UNTIMELY DEMISE WAS PART OF A CONSPIRACY TO RID THE WORLD OF HIS CLEARLY SUPERIOR PRODUCT!
SO... MICROSOFT TOOK DOWN STEVE JOBS?
YOU'VE SEEN HOW THEY ARE WITH VIRUSES; WHO KNOWS *WHAT* THEY'RE CAPABLE OF!?

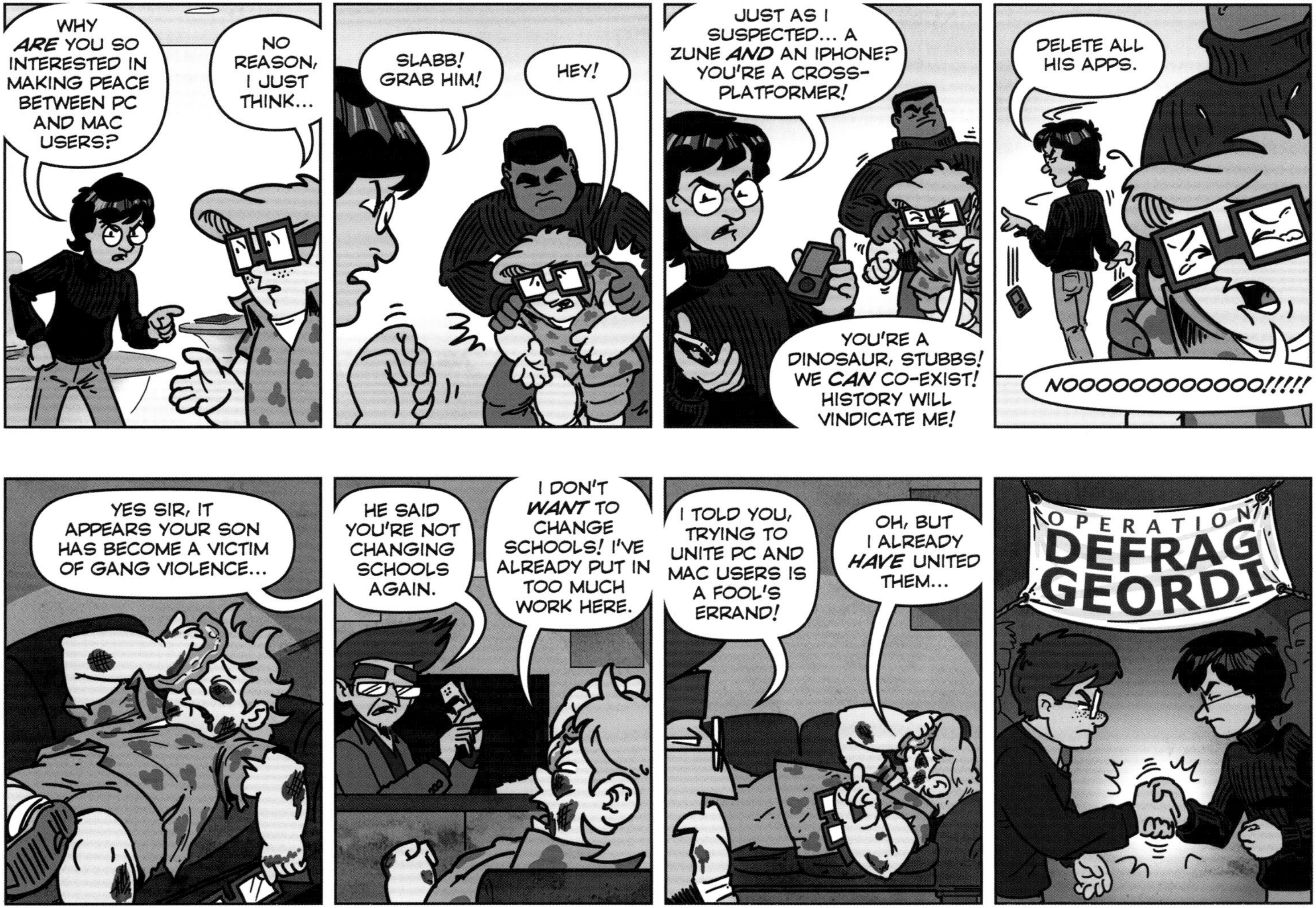
WHY ARE YOU SO INTERESTED IN MAKING PEACE BETWEEN PC AND MAC USERS?
NO REASON, I JUST THINK...
SLABB! GRAB HIM!
HEY!
JUST AS I SUSPECTED... A ZUNE AND AN IPHONE? YOU'RE A CROSS-PLATFORMER!
YOU'RE A DINOSAUR, STUBBS! WE CAN CO-EXIST! HISTORY WILL VINDICATE ME!
DELETE ALL HIS APPS.
NOOOOOOOOOOOO!!!!!
YES SIR, IT APPEARS YOUR SON HAS BECOME A VICTIM OF GANG VIOLENCE...
HE SAID YOU'RE NOT CHANGING SCHOOLS AGAIN.
I DON'T WANT TO CHANGE SCHOOLS! I'VE ALREADY PUT IN TOO MUCH WORK HERE.
I TOLD YOU, TRYING TO UNITE PC AND MAC USERS IS A FOOL'S ERRAND!
OH, BUT I ALREADY HAVE UNITED THEM...
OPERATION DEFRAG GEORDI

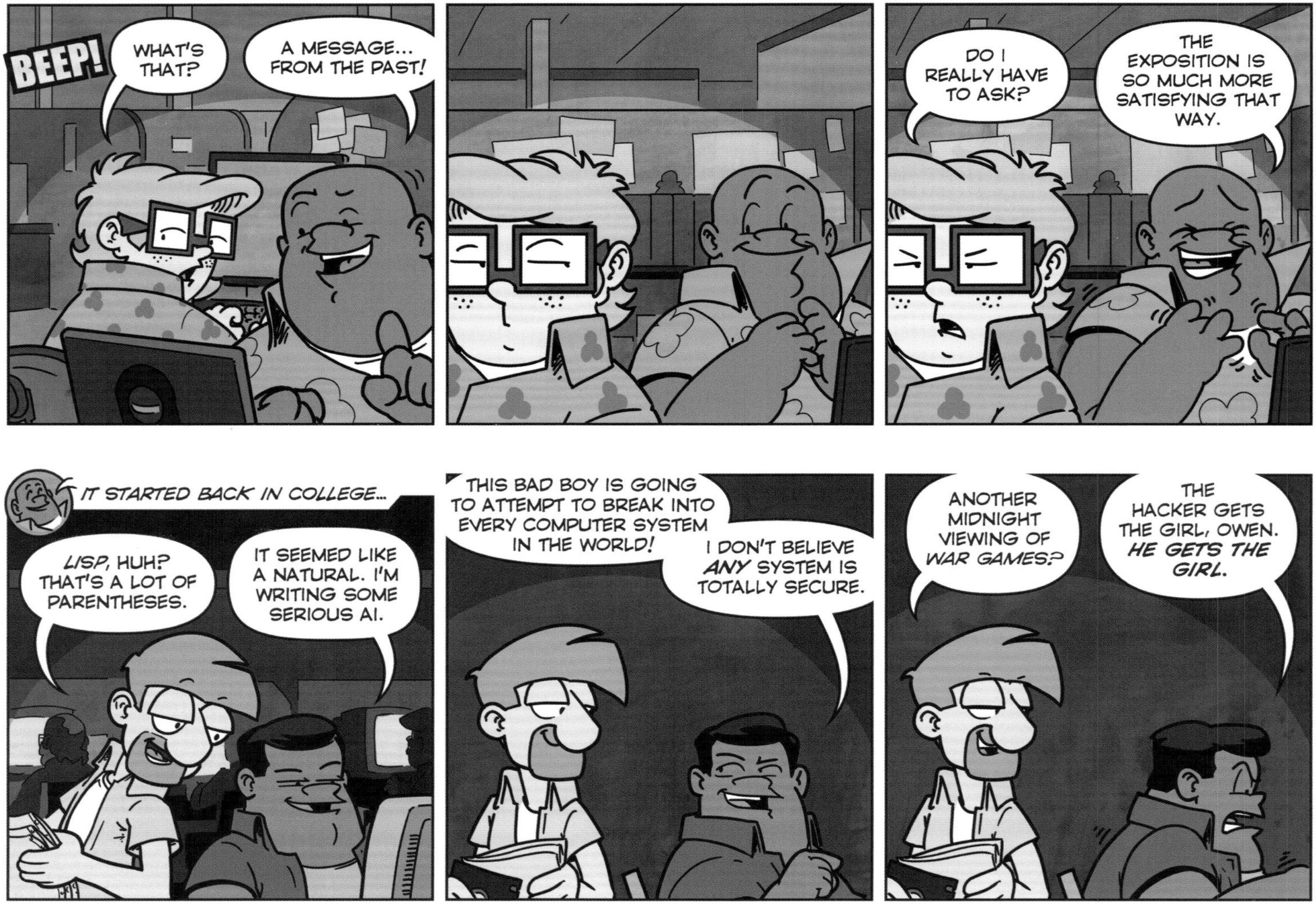
BEEP!
WHAT'S THAT?
A MESSAGE... FROM THE PAST!
DO I REALLY HAVE TO ASK?
THE EXPOSITION IS SO MUCH MORE SATISFYING THAT WAY.
IT STARTED BACK IN COLLEGE...
LISP, HUH? THAT'S A LOT OF PARENTHESES.
IT SEEMED LIKE A NATURAL. I'M WRITING SOME SERIOUS AI.
THIS BAD BOY IS GOING TO ATTEMPT TO BREAK INTO EVERY COMPUTER SYSTEM IN THE WORLD!
I DON'T BELIEVE ANY SYSTEM IS TOTALLY SECURE.
ANOTHER MIDNIGHT VIEWING OF WAR GAMES?
THE HACKER GETS THE GIRL, OWEN. HE GETS THE GIRL.

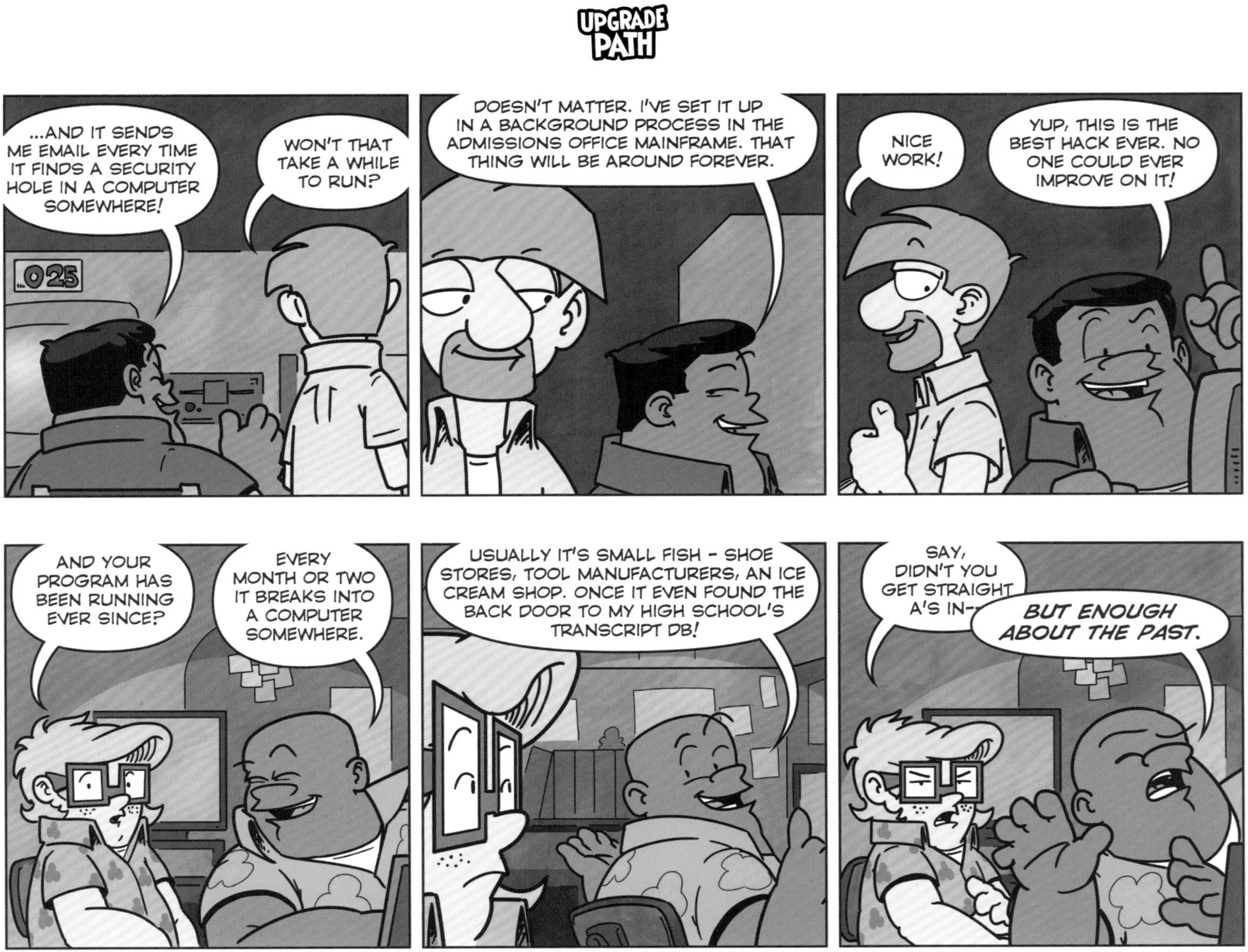
...AND IT SENDS ME EMAIL EVERY TIME IT FINDS A SECURITY HOLE IN A COMPUTER SOMEWHERE!
WON'T THAT TAKE A WHILE TO RUN?
DOESN'T MATTER. I'VE SET IT UP IN A BACKGROUND PROCESS IN THE ADMISSIONS OFFICE MAINFRAME. THAT THING WILL BE AROUND FOREVER.
NICE WORK!
YUP, THIS IS THE BEST HACK EVER. NO ONE COULD EVER IMPROVE ON IT!
AND YOUR PROGRAM HAS BEEN RUNNING EVER SINCE?
EVERY MONTH OR TWO IT BREAKS INTO A COMPUTER SOMEWHERE.
USUALLY IT'S SMALL FISH - SHOE STORES, TOOL MANUFACTURERS, AN ICE CREAM SHOP. ONCE IT EVEN FOUND THE BACK DOOR TO MY HIGH SCHOOL'S TRANSCRIPT DB!
SAY, DIDN'T YOU GET STRAIGHT A'S IN--
BUT ENOUGH ABOUT THE PAST.

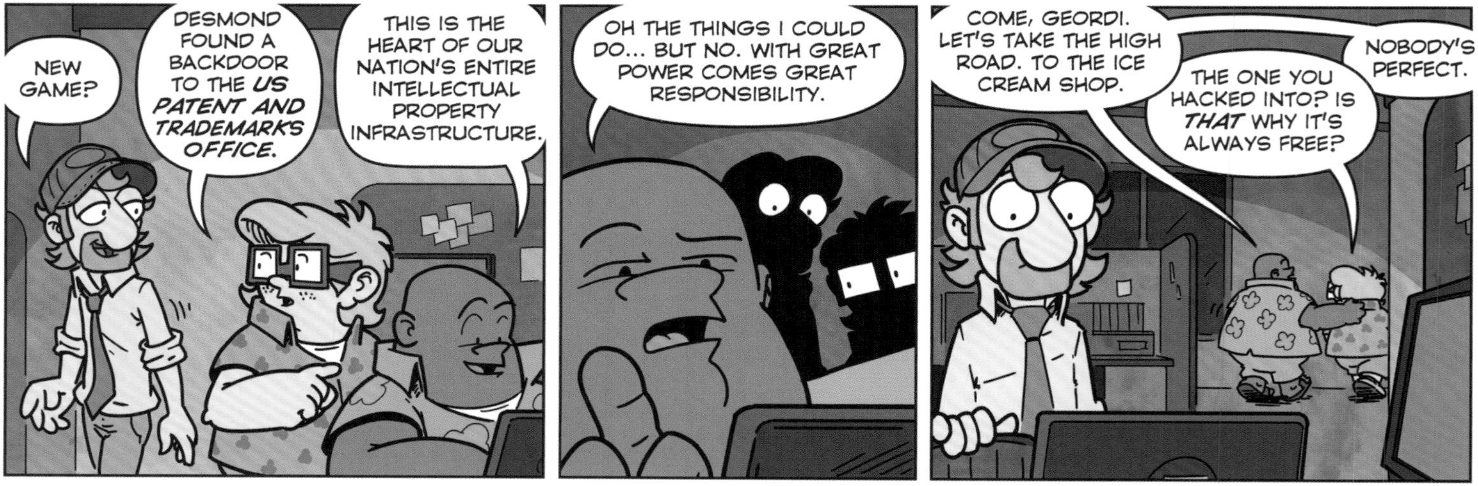
NEW GAME?
DESMOND FOUND A BACKDOOR TO THE *US PATENT AND TRADEMARKS OFFICE.*
THIS IS THE HEART OF OUR NATION'S ENTIRE INTELLECTUAL PROPERTY INFRASTRUCTURE.
OH THE THINGS I COULD DO... BUT NO. WITH GREAT POWER COMES GREAT RESPONSIBILITY.
COME, GEORDI. LET'S TAKE THE HIGH ROAD. TO THE ICE CREAM SHOP.
THE ONE YOU HACKED INTO? IS *THAT* WHY IT'S ALWAYS FREE?
NOBODY'S PERFECT.

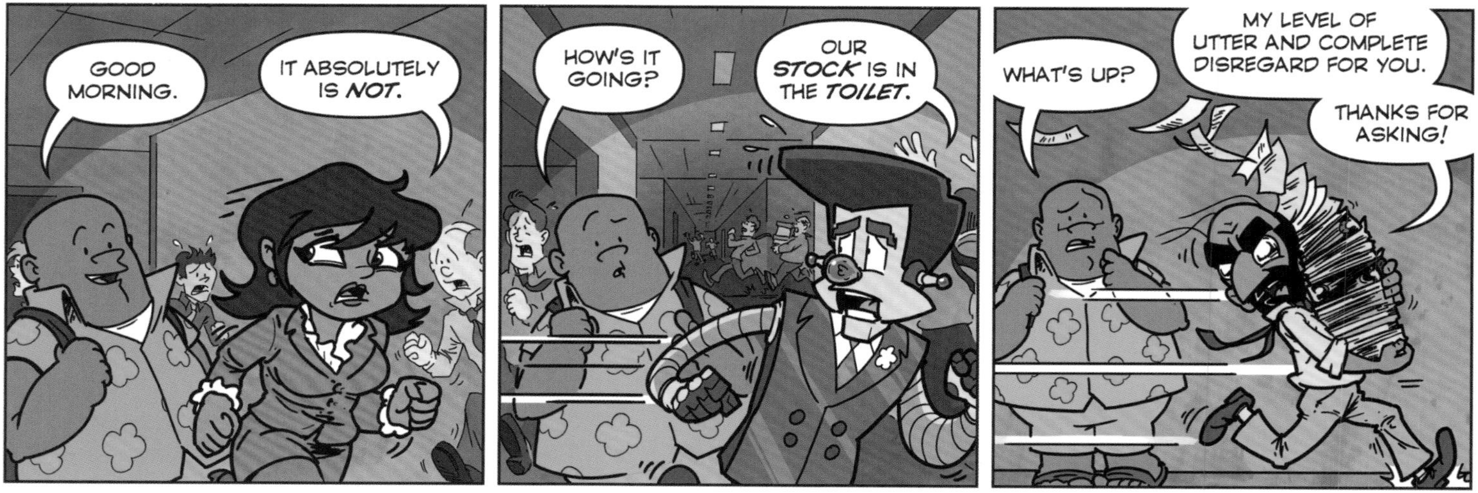
GOOD MORNING.
IT ABSOLUTELY IS *NOT.*
HOW'S IT GOING?
OUR *STOCK* IS IN THE *TOILET.*
WHAT'S UP?
MY LEVEL OF UTTER AND COMPLETE DISREGARD FOR YOU.
THANKS FOR ASKING!

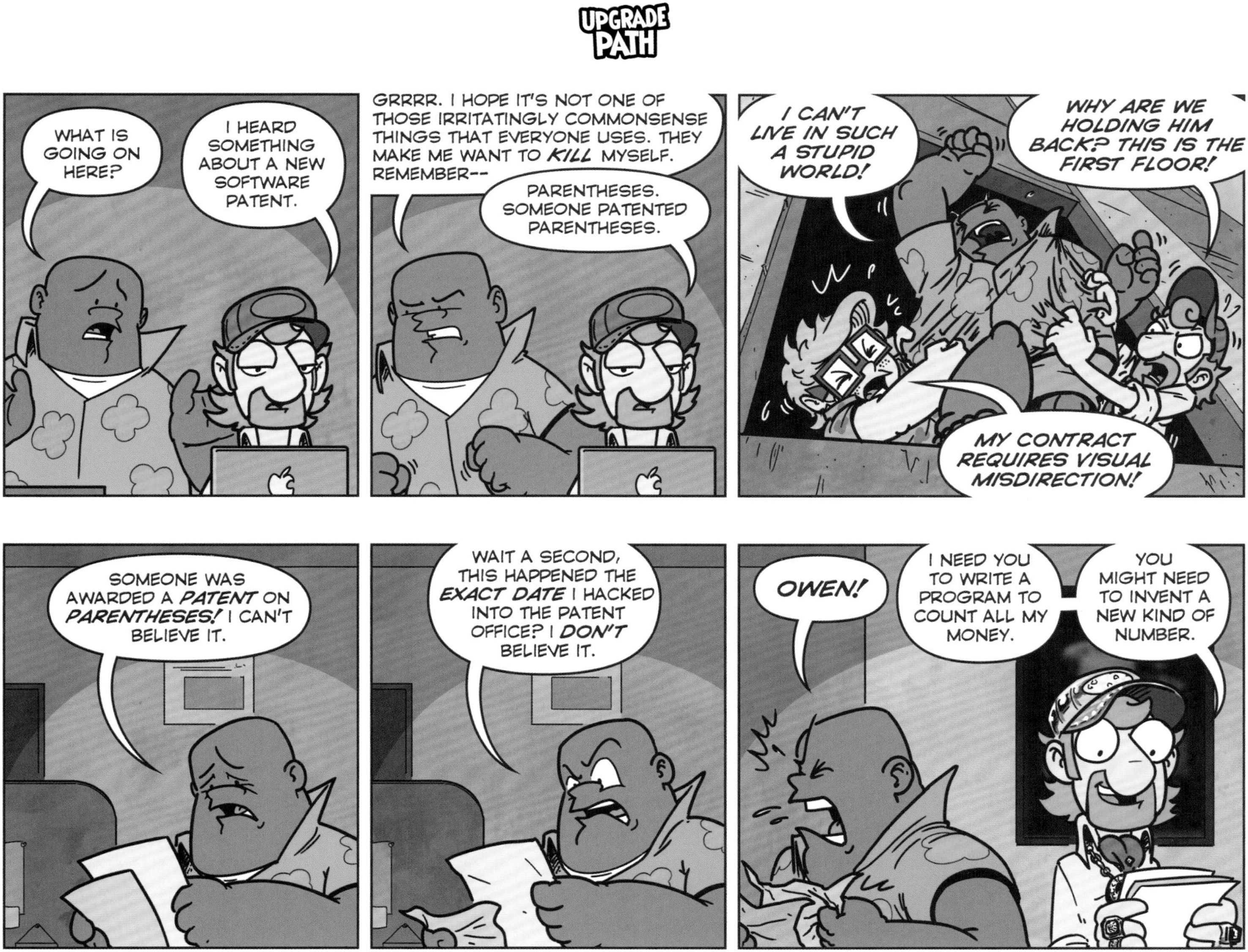
UPGRADE PATH
WHAT IS GOING ON HERE?
I HEARD SOMETHING ABOUT A NEW SOFTWARE PATENT.
GRRRR. I HOPE IT'S NOT ONE OF THOSE IRRITATINGLY COMMONSENSE THINGS THAT EVERYONE USES. THEY MAKE ME WANT TO KILL MYSELF. REMEMBER--
PARENTHESES. SOMEONE PATENTED PARENTHESES.
I CAN'T LIVE IN SUCH A STUPID WORLD!
WHY ARE WE HOLDING HIM BACK? THIS IS THE FIRST FLOOR!
MY CONTRACT REQUIRES VISUAL MISDIRECTION!
SOMEONE WAS AWARDED A PATENT ON PARENTHESES! I CAN'T BELIEVE IT.
WAIT A SECOND, THIS HAPPENED THE EXACT DATE I HACKED INTO THE PATENT OFFICE? I DON'T BELIEVE IT.
OWEN!
I NEED YOU TO WRITE A PROGRAM TO COUNT ALL MY MONEY.
YOU MIGHT NEED TO INVENT A NEW KIND OF NUMBER.

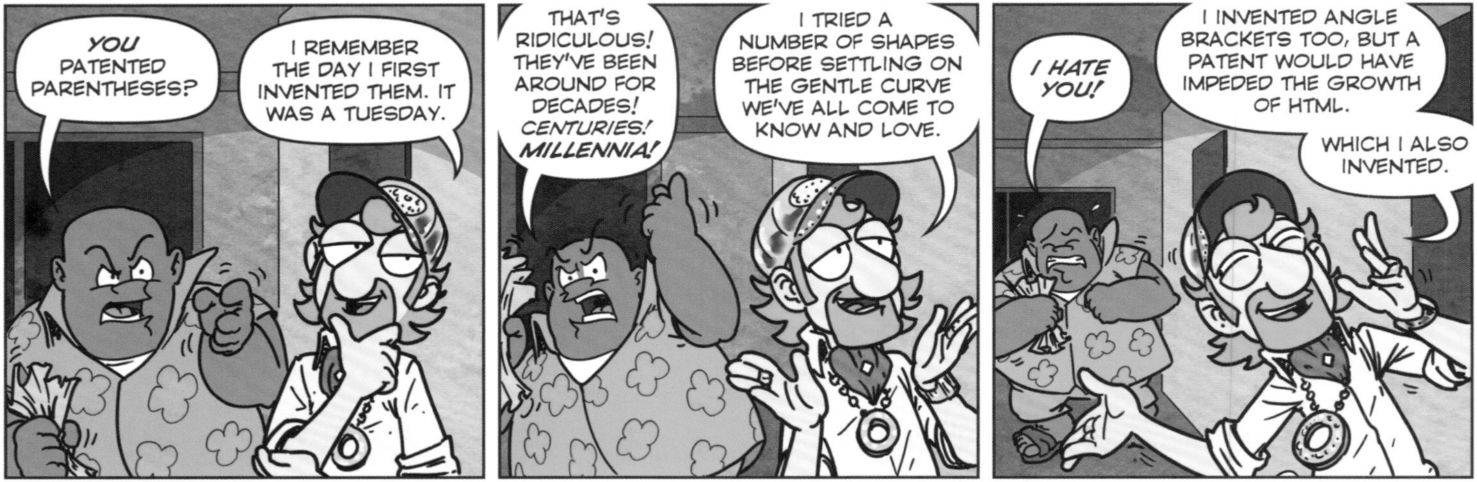
YOU PATENTED PARENTHESES?
I REMEMBER THE DAY I FIRST INVENTED THEM. IT WAS A TUESDAY.
THAT'S RIDICULOUS! THEY'VE BEEN AROUND FOR DECADES! CENTURIES! MILLENNIA!
I TRIED A NUMBER OF SHAPES BEFORE SETTLING ON THE GENTLE CURVE WE'VE ALL COME TO KNOW AND LOVE.
I HATE YOU!
I INVENTED ANGLE BRACKETS TOO, BUT A PATENT WOULD HAVE IMPEDED THE GROWTH OF HTML.
WHICH I ALSO INVENTED.

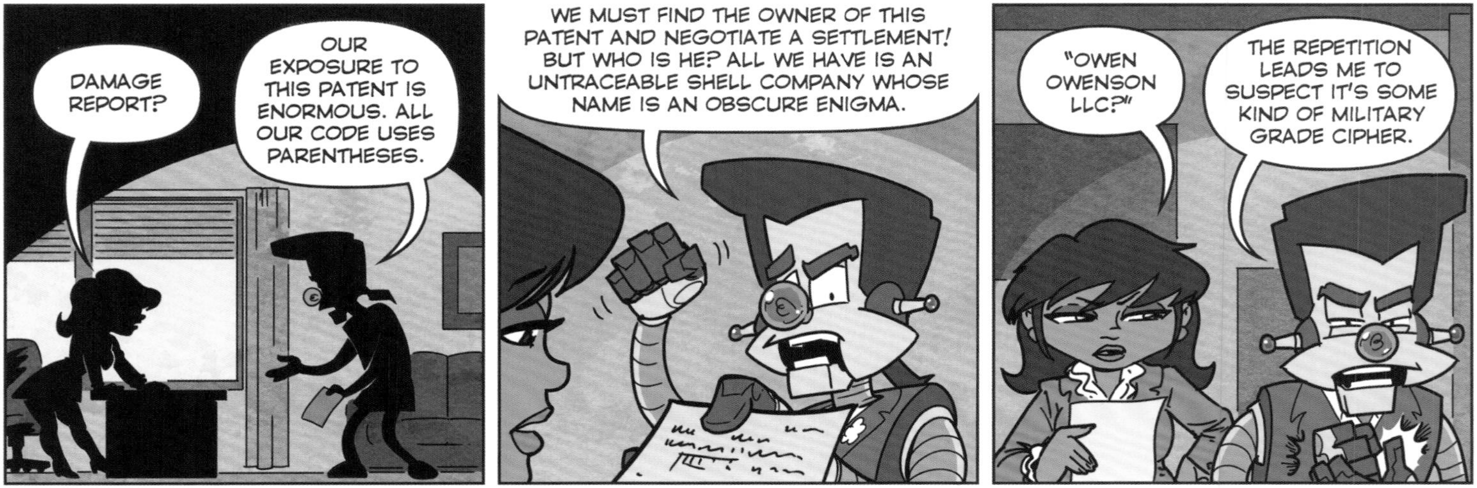
DAMAGE REPORT?
OUR EXPOSURE TO THIS PATENT IS ENORMOUS. ALL OUR CODE USES PARENTHESES.
WE MUST FIND THE OWNER OF THIS PATENT AND NEGOTIATE A SETTLEMENT! BUT WHO IS HE? ALL WE HAVE IS AN UNTRACEABLE SHELL COMPANY WHOSE NAME IS AN OBSCURE ENIGMA.
"OWEN OWENSON LLC?"
THE REPETITION LEADS ME TO SUSPECT IT'S SOME KIND OF MILITARY GRADE CIPHER.

UPGRADE PATH

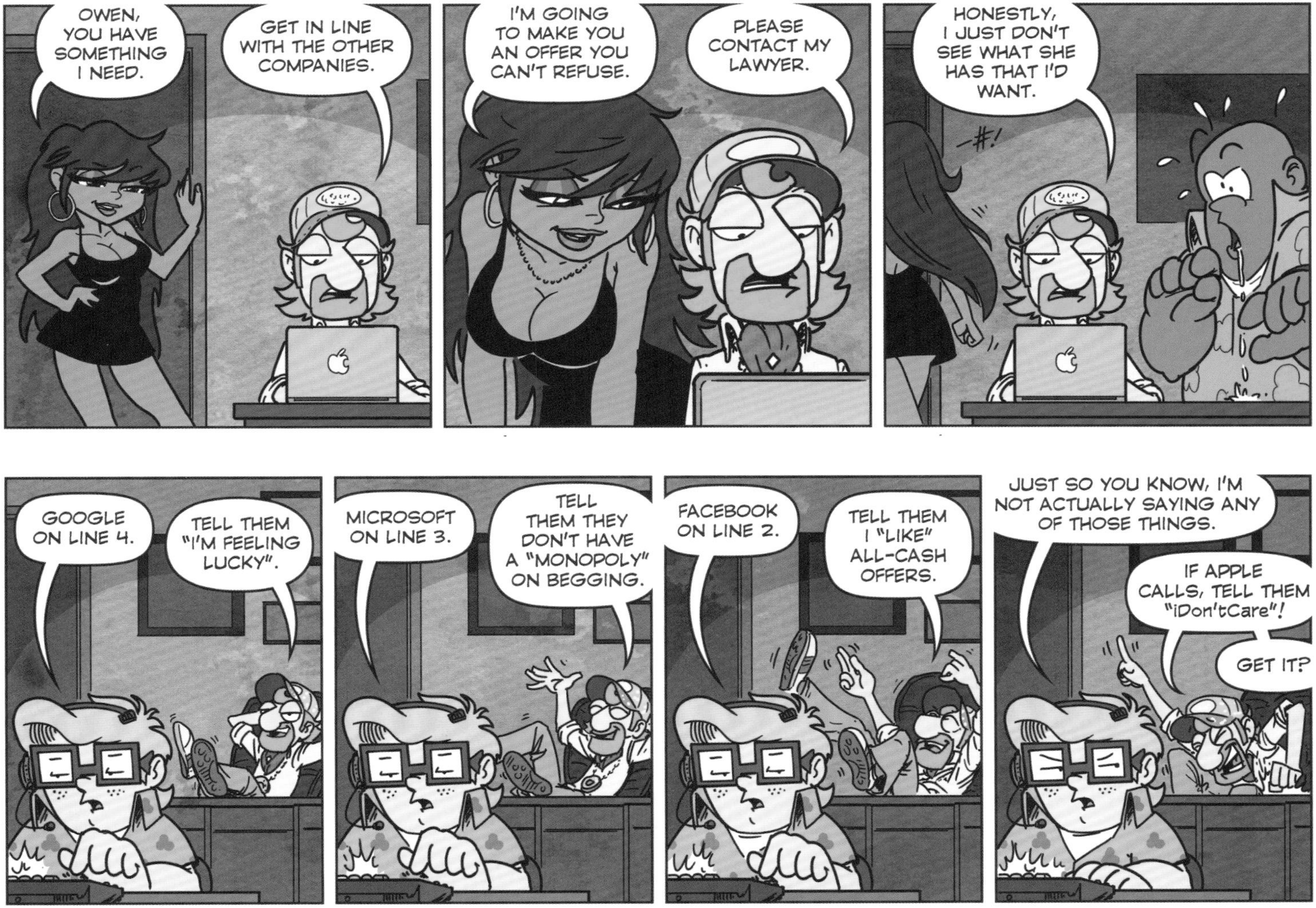
OWEN, YOU HAVE SOMETHING I NEED.
GET IN LINE WITH THE OTHER COMPANIES.
I'M GOING TO MAKE YOU AN OFFER YOU CAN'T REFUSE.
PLEASE CONTACT MY LAWYER.
HONESTLY, I JUST DON'T SEE WHAT SHE HAS THAT I'D WANT.
-#!
GOOGLE ON LINE 4.
TELL THEM "I'M FEELING LUCKY".
MICROSOFT ON LINE 3.
TELL THEM THEY DON'T HAVE A "MONOPOLY" ON BEGGING.
FACEBOOK ON LINE 2.
TELL THEM I "LIKE" ALL-CASH OFFERS.
JUST SO YOU KNOW, I'M NOT ACTUALLY SAYING ANY OF THOSE THINGS.
IF APPLE CALLS, TELL THEM "iDon'tCare"!
GET IT?

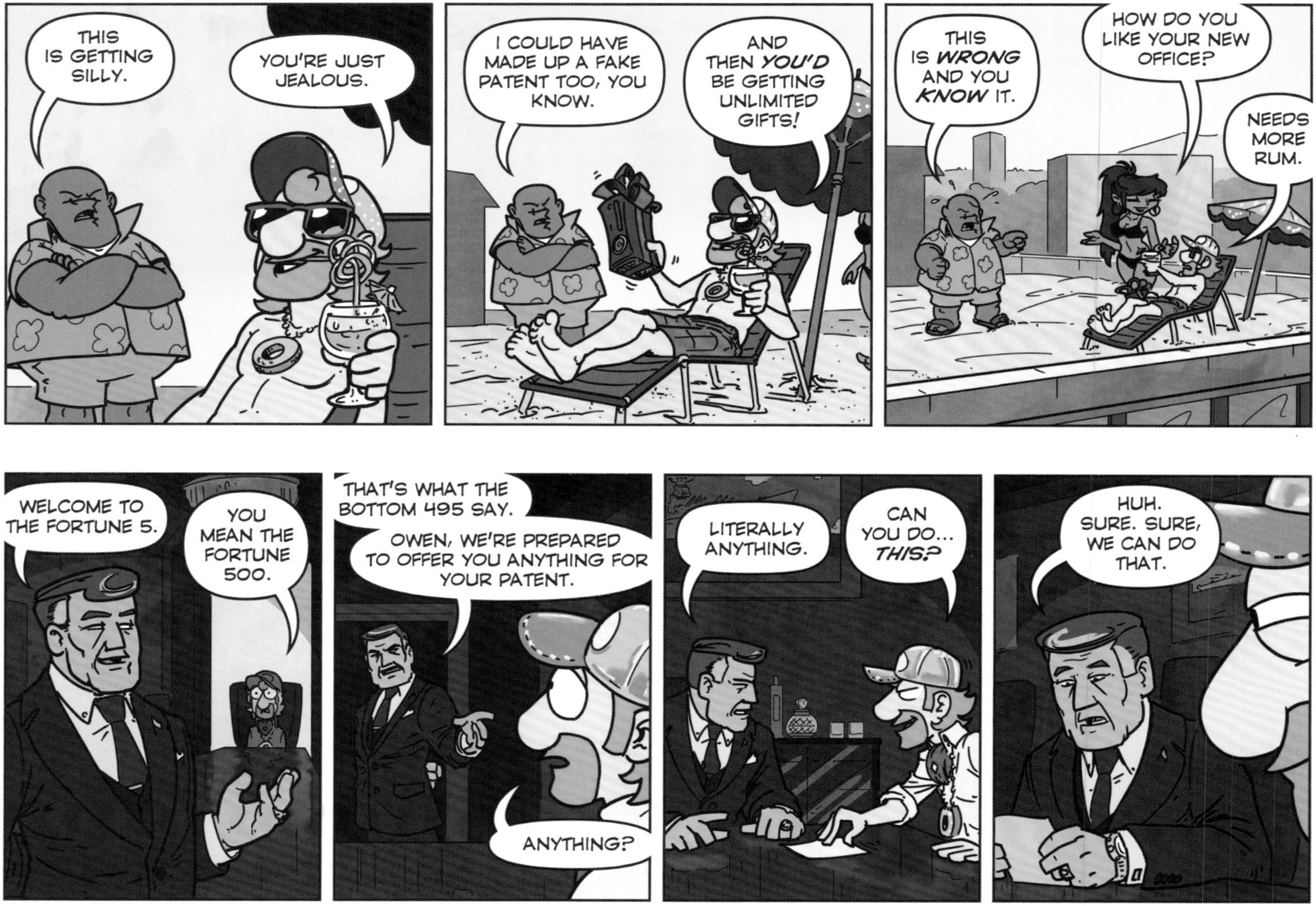
THIS IS GETTING SILLY.
YOU'RE JUST JEALOUS.
I COULD HAVE MADE UP A FAKE PATENT TOO, YOU KNOW.
AND THEN *YOU'D* BE GETTING UNLIMITED GIFTS!
THIS IS *WRONG* AND YOU *KNOW* IT.
HOW DO YOU LIKE YOUR NEW OFFICE?
NEEDS MORE RUM.
WELCOME TO THE FORTUNE 5.
YOU MEAN THE FORTUNE 500.
THAT'S WHAT THE BOTTOM 495 SAY.
OWEN, WE'RE PREPARED TO OFFER YOU ANYTHING FOR YOUR PATENT.
ANYTHING?
LITERALLY ANYTHING.
CAN YOU DO... *THIS?*
HUH. SURE. SURE, WE CAN DO THAT.

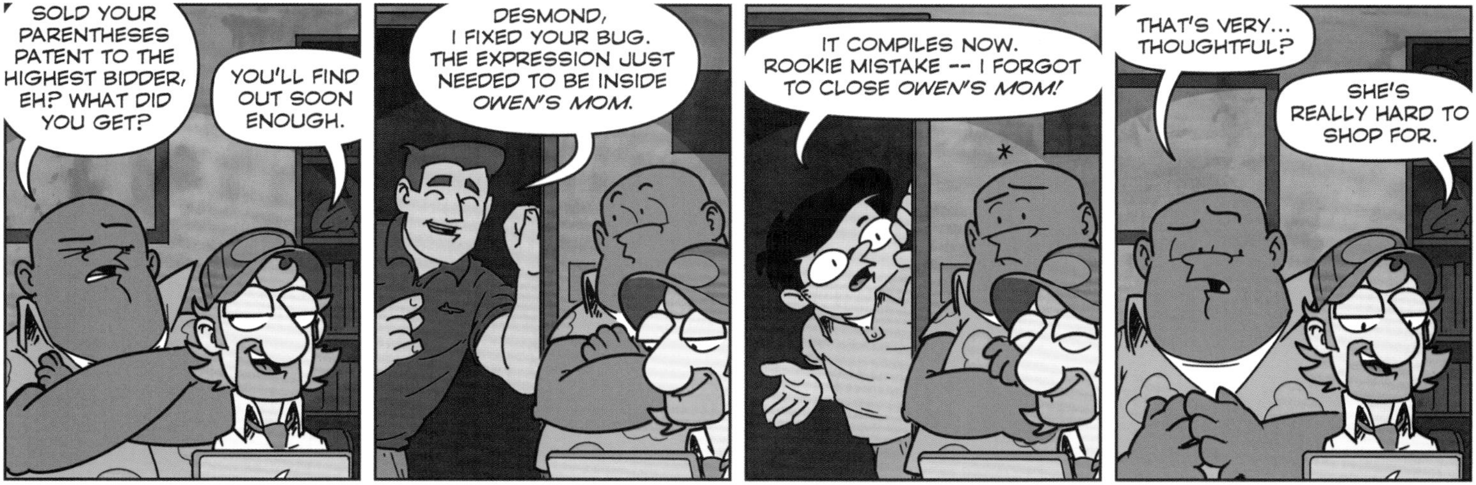
SOLD YOUR PARENTHESES PATENT TO THE HIGHEST BIDDER, EH? WHAT DID YOU GET?
YOU'LL FIND OUT SOON ENOUGH.
DESMOND, I FIXED YOUR BUG. THE EXPRESSION JUST NEEDED TO BE INSIDE *OWEN'S MOM.*
IT COMPILES NOW. ROOKIE MISTAKE -- I FORGOT TO CLOSE *OWEN'S MOM!*
THAT'S VERY... THOUGHTFUL?
SHE'S REALLY HARD TO SHOP FOR.

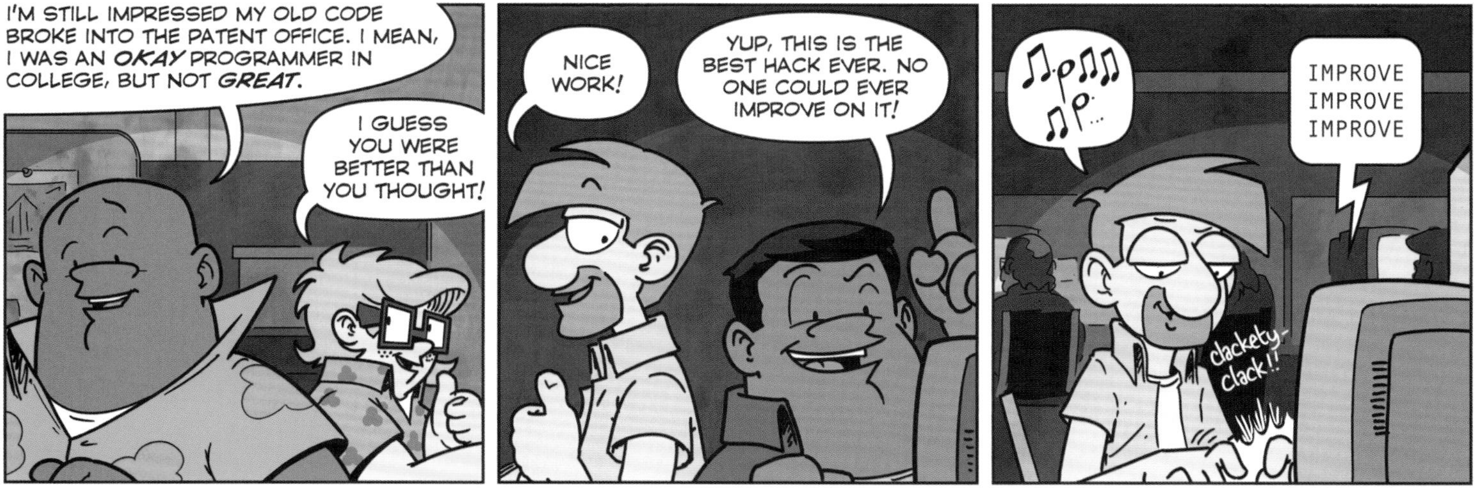
I'M STILL IMPRESSED MY OLD CODE BROKE INTO THE PATENT OFFICE. I MEAN, I WAS AN *OKAY* PROGRAMMER IN COLLEGE, BUT NOT *GREAT*.
I GUESS YOU WERE BETTER THAN YOU THOUGHT!
NICE WORK!
YUP, THIS IS THE BEST HACK EVER. NO ONE COULD EVER IMPROVE ON IT!
IMPROVE IMPROVE IMPROVE
clackety-clack!!

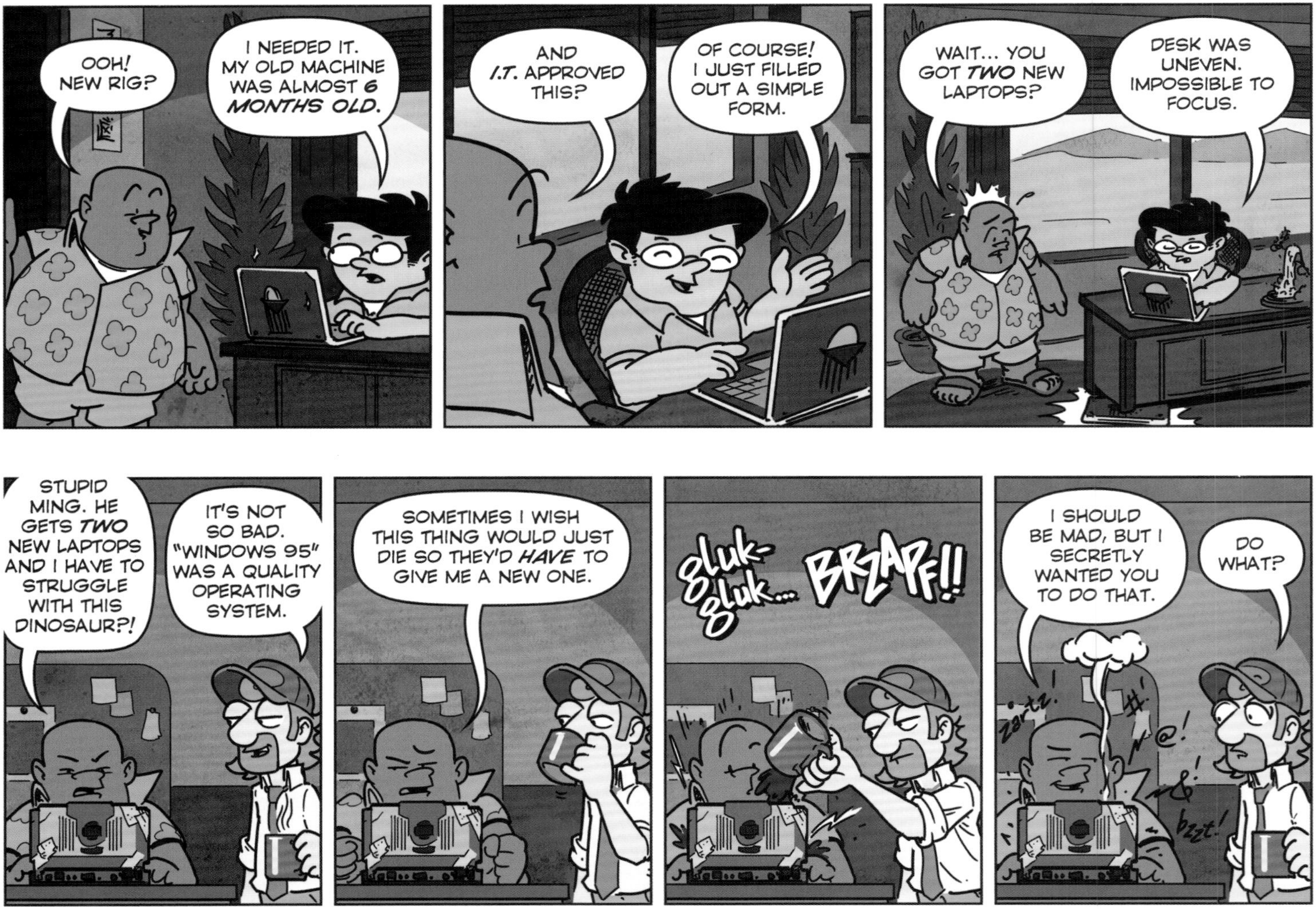

OOH! NEW RIG?
I NEEDED IT. MY OLD MACHINE WAS ALMOST 6 MONTHS OLD.
AND I.T. APPROVED THIS?
OF COURSE! I JUST FILLED OUT A SIMPLE FORM.
WAIT... YOU GOT TWO NEW LAPTOPS?
DESK WAS UNEVEN. IMPOSSIBLE TO FOCUS.
STUPID MING. HE GETS TWO NEW LAPTOPS AND I HAVE TO STRUGGLE WITH THIS DINOSAUR?!
IT'S NOT SO BAD. "WINDOWS 95" WAS A QUALITY OPERATING SYSTEM.
SOMETIMES I WISH THIS THING WOULD JUST DIE SO THEY'D HAVE TO GIVE ME A NEW ONE.
gluk-gluk...
BRZAPFF!!
I SHOULD BE MAD, BUT I SECRETLY WANTED YOU TO DO THAT.
DO WHAT?

UPGRADE PATH

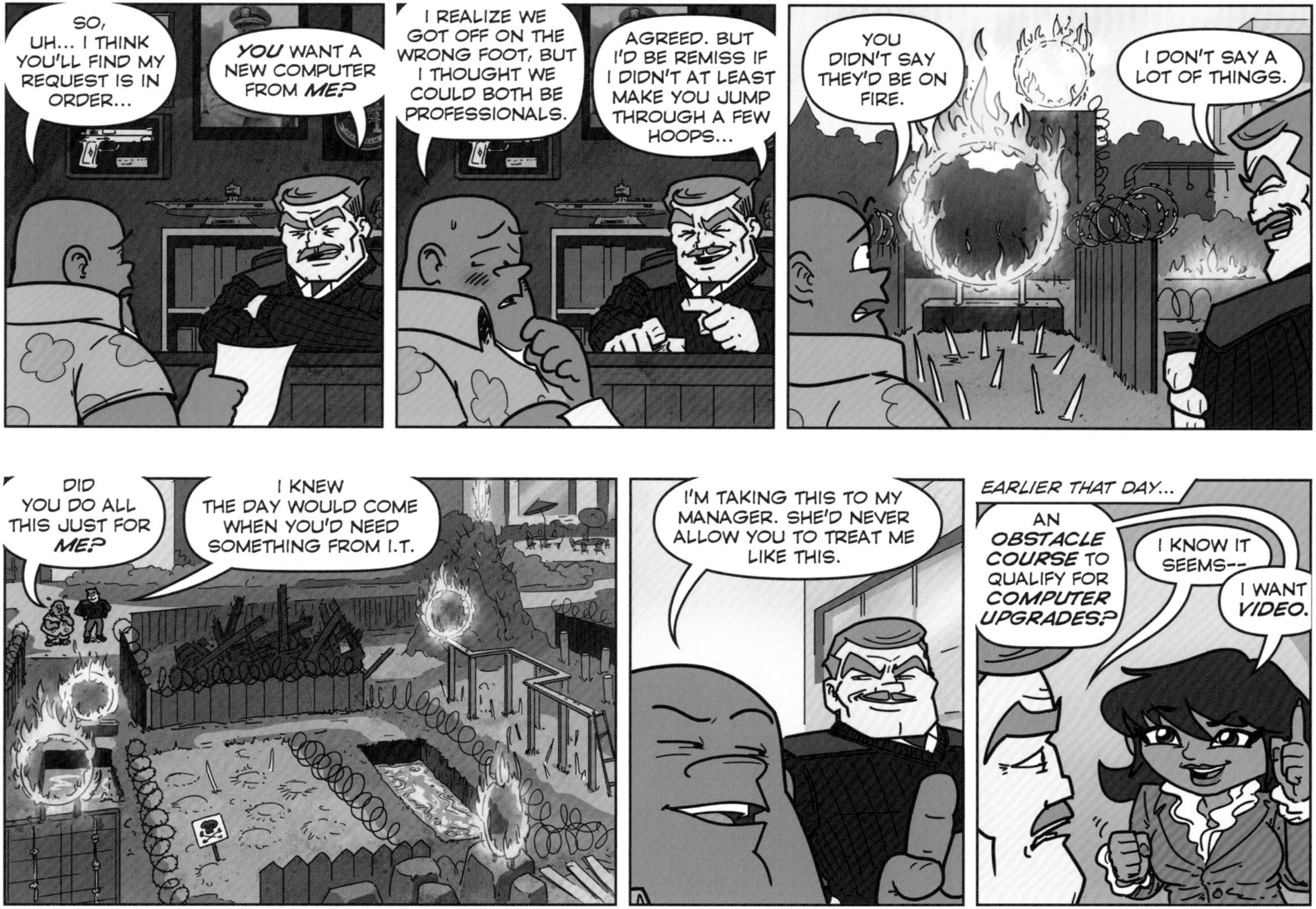

SO, UH... I THINK YOU'LL FIND MY REQUEST IS IN ORDER...
YOU WANT A NEW COMPUTER FROM *ME?*
I REALIZE WE GOT OFF ON THE WRONG FOOT, BUT I THOUGHT WE COULD BOTH BE PROFESSIONALS.
AGREED. BUT I'D BE REMISS IF I DIDN'T AT LEAST MAKE YOU JUMP THROUGH A FEW HOOPS...
YOU DIDN'T SAY THEY'D BE ON FIRE.
I DON'T SAY A LOT OF THINGS.
DID YOU DO ALL THIS JUST FOR *ME?*
I KNEW THE DAY WOULD COME WHEN YOU'D NEED SOMETHING FROM I.T.
I'M TAKING THIS TO MY MANAGER. SHE'D NEVER ALLOW YOU TO TREAT ME LIKE THIS.
EARLIER THAT DAY...
AN *OBSTACLE COURSE* TO QUALIFY FOR *COMPUTER UPGRADES?*
I KNOW IT SEEMS--
I WANT *VIDEO.*

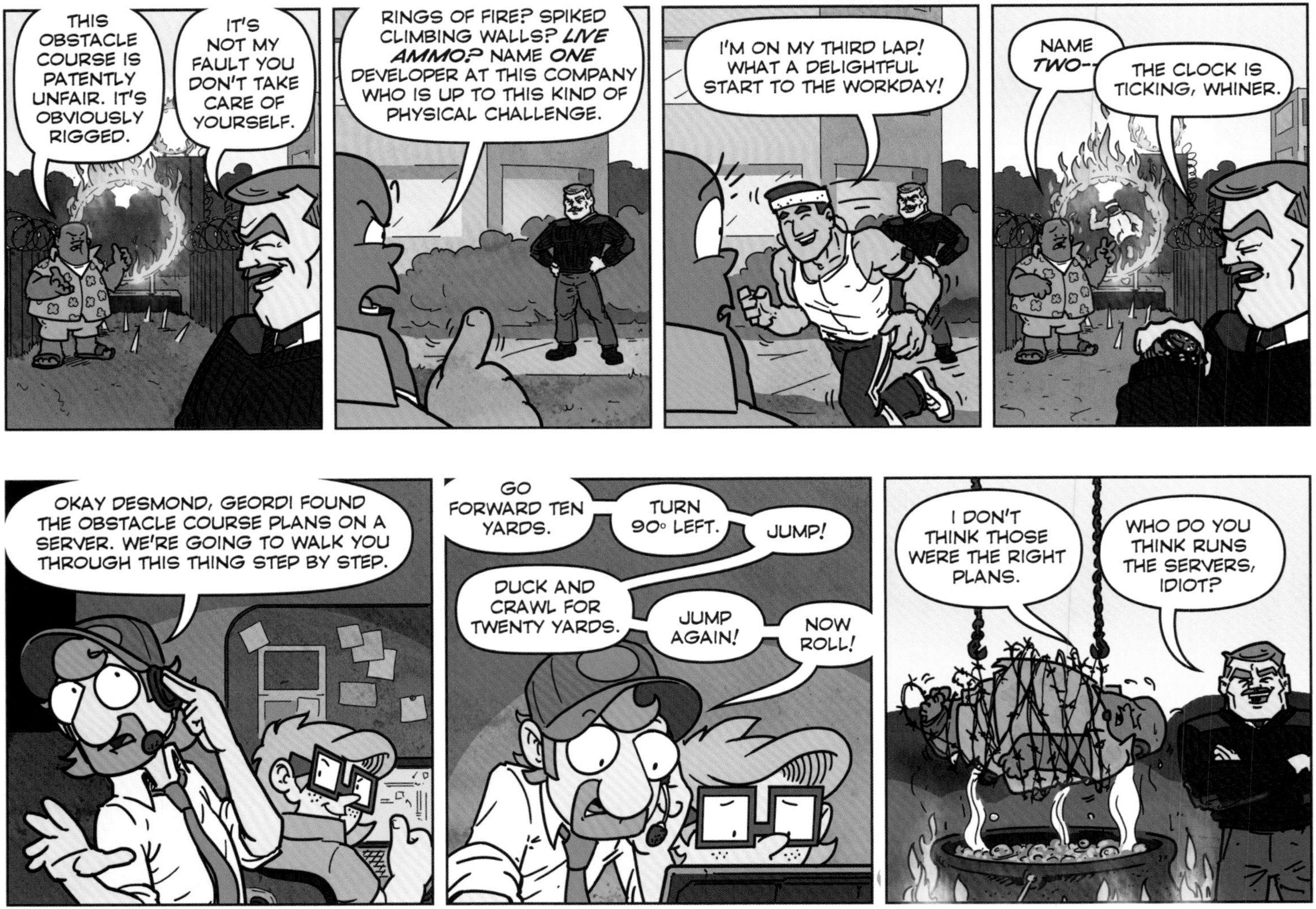
THIS OBSTACLE COURSE IS PATENTLY UNFAIR. IT'S OBVIOUSLY RIGGED.
IT'S NOT MY FAULT YOU DON'T TAKE CARE OF YOURSELF.
RINGS OF FIRE? SPIKED CLIMBING WALLS? *LIVE AMMO?* NAME *ONE* DEVELOPER AT THIS COMPANY WHO IS UP TO THIS KIND OF PHYSICAL CHALLENGE.
I'M ON MY THIRD LAP! WHAT A DELIGHTFUL START TO THE WORKDAY!
NAME *TWO*--
THE CLOCK IS TICKING, WHINER.
OKAY DESMOND, GEORDI FOUND THE OBSTACLE COURSE PLANS ON A SERVER. WE'RE GOING TO WALK YOU THROUGH THIS THING STEP BY STEP.
GO FORWARD TEN YARDS.
TURN 90° LEFT.
JUMP!
DUCK AND CRAWL FOR TWENTY YARDS.
JUMP AGAIN!
NOW ROLL!
I DON'T THINK THOSE WERE THE RIGHT PLANS.
WHO DO YOU THINK RUNS THE SERVERS, IDIOT?

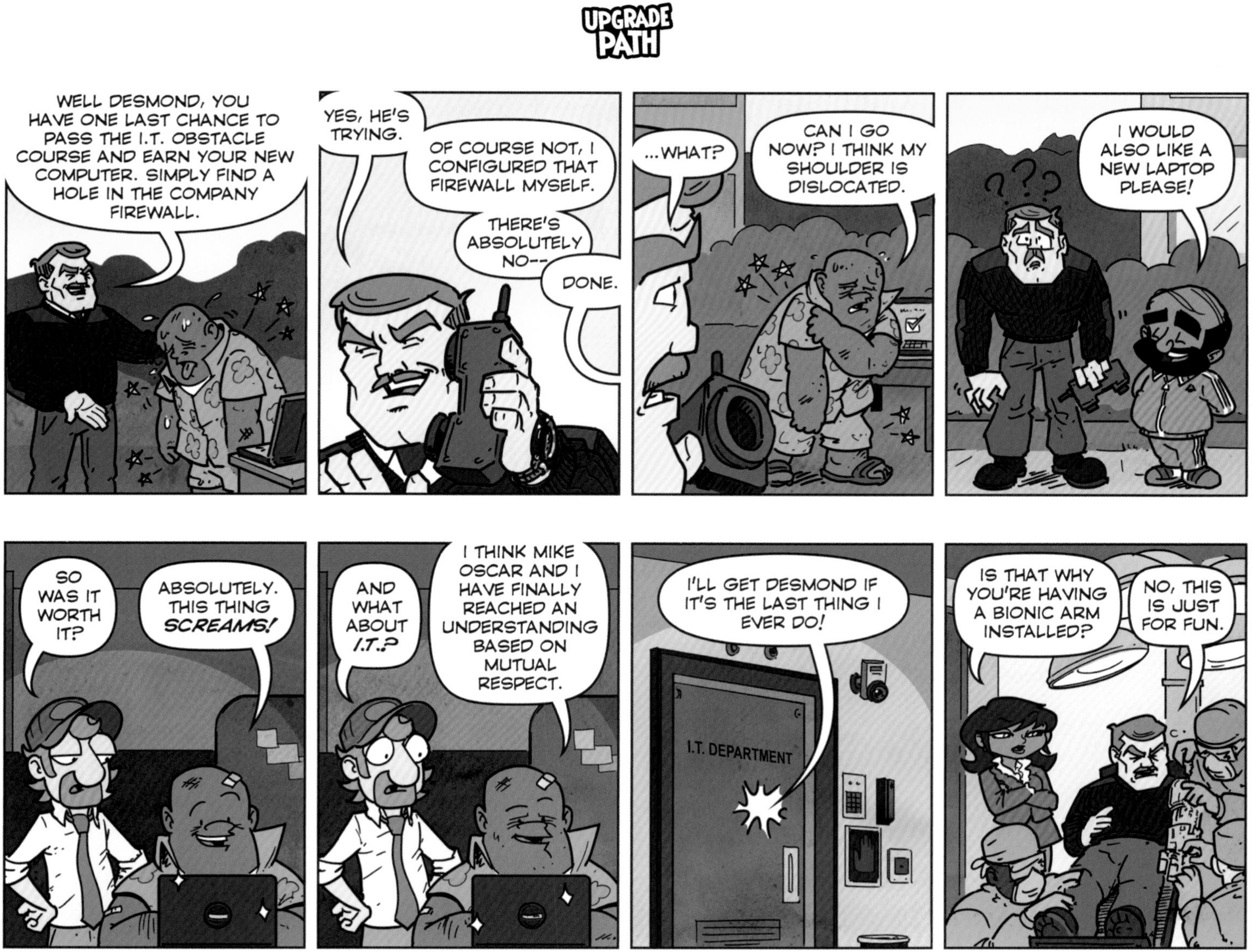
UPGRADE PATH
WELL DESMOND, YOU HAVE ONE LAST CHANCE TO PASS THE I.T. OBSTACLE COURSE AND EARN YOUR NEW COMPUTER. SIMPLY FIND A HOLE IN THE COMPANY FIREWALL.
YES, HE'S TRYING.
OF COURSE NOT, I CONFIGURED THAT FIREWALL MYSELF.
THERE'S ABSOLUTELY NO--
DONE.
...WHAT?
CAN I GO NOW? I THINK MY SHOULDER IS DISLOCATED.
???
I WOULD ALSO LIKE A NEW LAPTOP PLEASE!
SO WAS IT WORTH IT?
ABSOLUTELY. THIS THING *SCREAMS!*
AND WHAT ABOUT *I.T.?*
I THINK MIKE OSCAR AND I HAVE FINALLY REACHED AN UNDERSTANDING BASED ON MUTUAL RESPECT.
I'LL GET DESMOND IF IT'S THE LAST THING I EVER DO!
I.T. DEPARTMENT
IS THAT WHY YOU'RE HAVING A BIONIC ARM INSTALLED?
NO, THIS IS JUST FOR FUN.

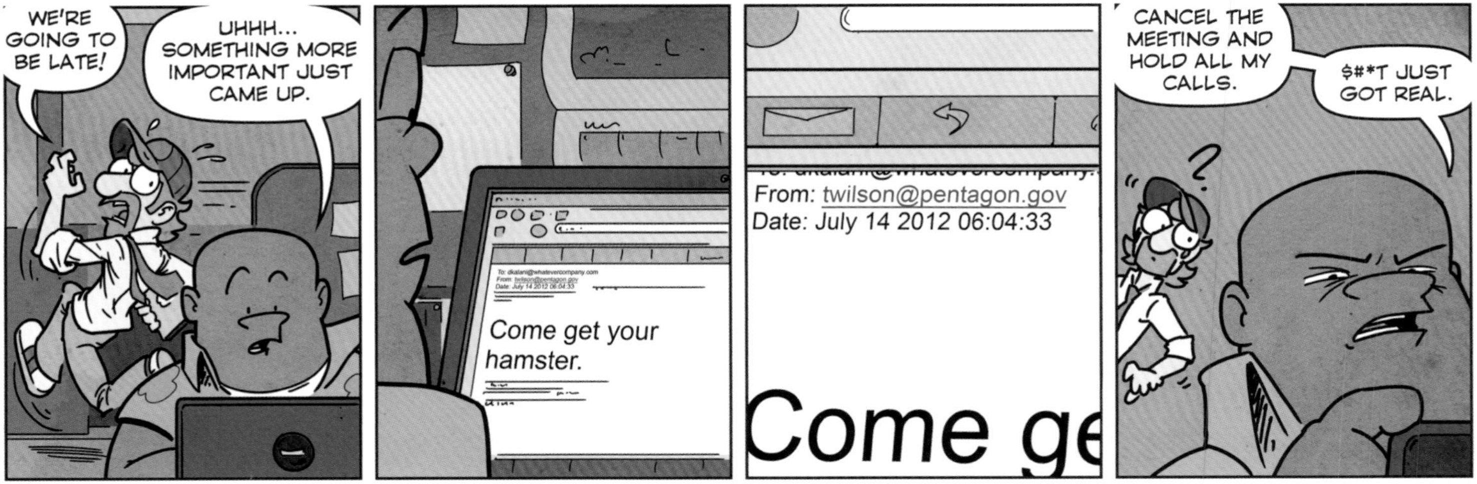
WE'RE GOING TO BE LATE!
UHHH... SOMETHING MORE IMPORTANT JUST CAME UP.
Come get your hamster.
From: twilson@pentagon.gov
Date: July 14 2012 06:04:33
Come ge
CANCEL THE MEETING AND HOLD ALL MY CALLS.
$#*T JUST GOT REAL.

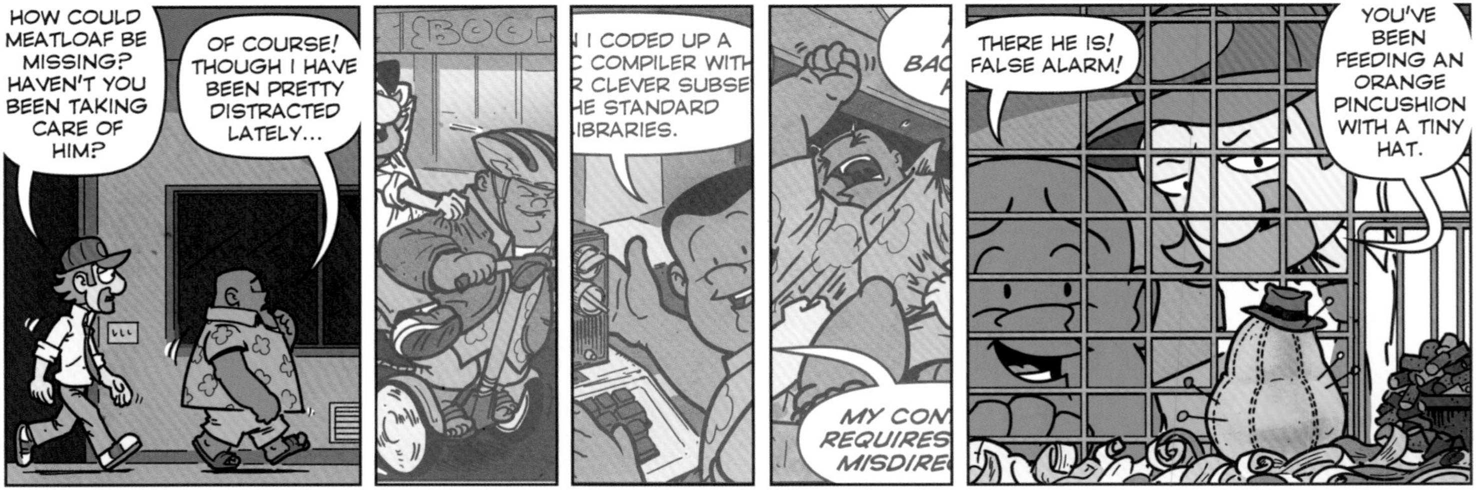
HOW COULD MEATLOAF BE MISSING? HAVEN'T YOU BEEN TAKING CARE OF HIM?
OF COURSE! THOUGH I HAVE BEEN PRETTY DISTRACTED LATELY...
N I CODED UP A C COMPILER WITH R CLEVER SUBSE HE STANDARD IBRARIES.
MY CON REQUIRES MISDIRE
THERE HE IS! FALSE ALARM!
YOU'VE BEEN FEEDING AN ORANGE PINCUSHION WITH A TINY HAT.

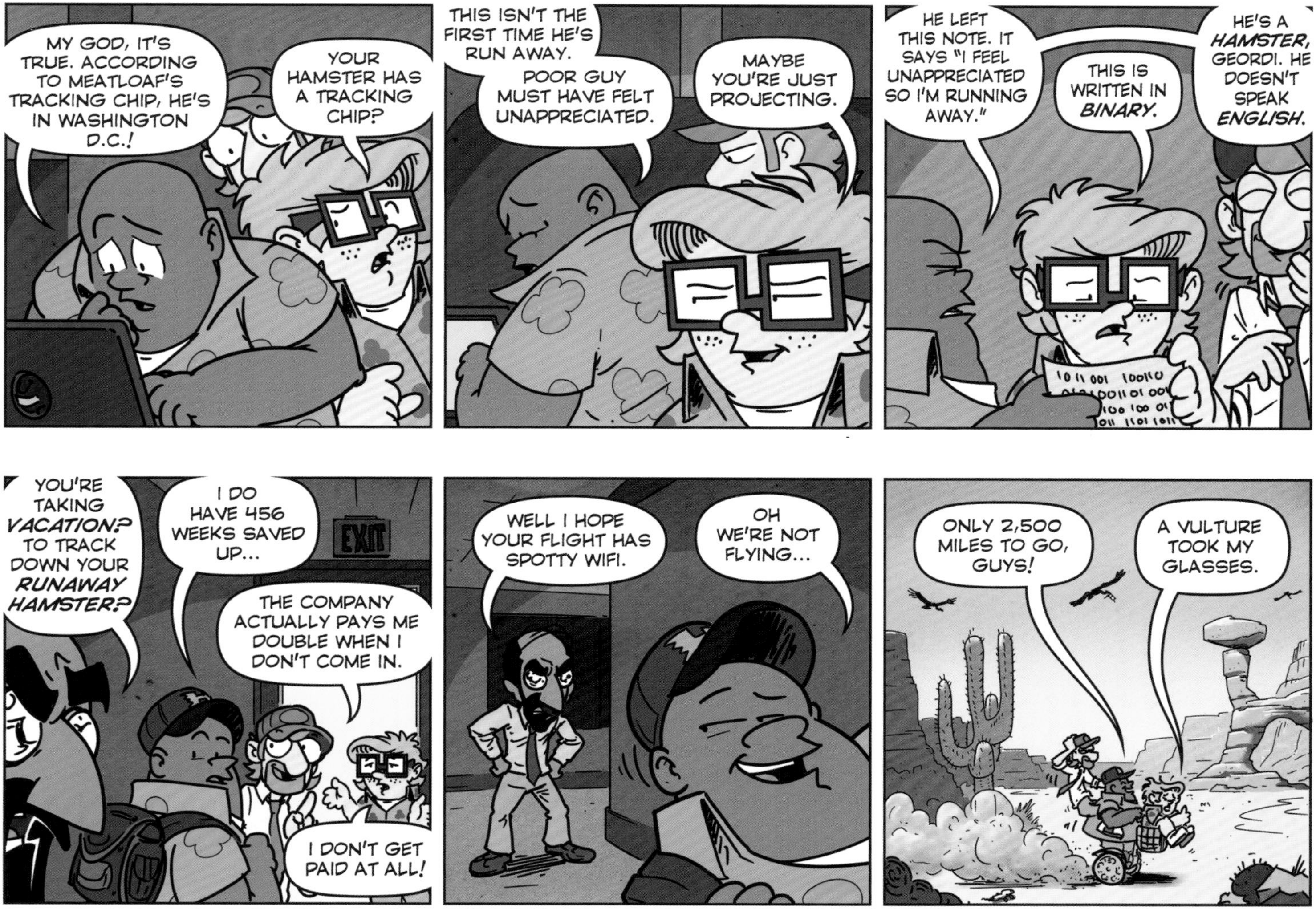
MY GOD, IT'S TRUE. ACCORDING TO MEATLOAF'S TRACKING CHIP, HE'S IN WASHINGTON D.C.!
YOUR HAMSTER HAS A TRACKING CHIP?
THIS ISN'T THE FIRST TIME HE'S RUN AWAY.
POOR GUY MUST HAVE FELT UNAPPRECIATED.
MAYBE YOU'RE JUST PROJECTING.
HE LEFT THIS NOTE. IT SAYS "I FEEL UNAPPRECIATED SO I'M RUNNING AWAY."
THIS IS WRITTEN IN *BINARY*.
HE'S A *HAMSTER*, GEORDI. HE DOESN'T SPEAK *ENGLISH*.
YOU'RE TAKING *VACATION?* TO TRACK DOWN YOUR *RUNAWAY HAMSTER?*
I DO HAVE 456 WEEKS SAVED UP...
EXIT
THE COMPANY ACTUALLY PAYS ME DOUBLE WHEN I DON'T COME IN.
I DON'T GET PAID AT ALL!
WELL I HOPE YOUR FLIGHT HAS SPOTTY WIFI.
OH WE'RE NOT FLYING...
ONLY 2,500 MILES TO GO, GUYS!
A VULTURE TOOK MY GLASSES.

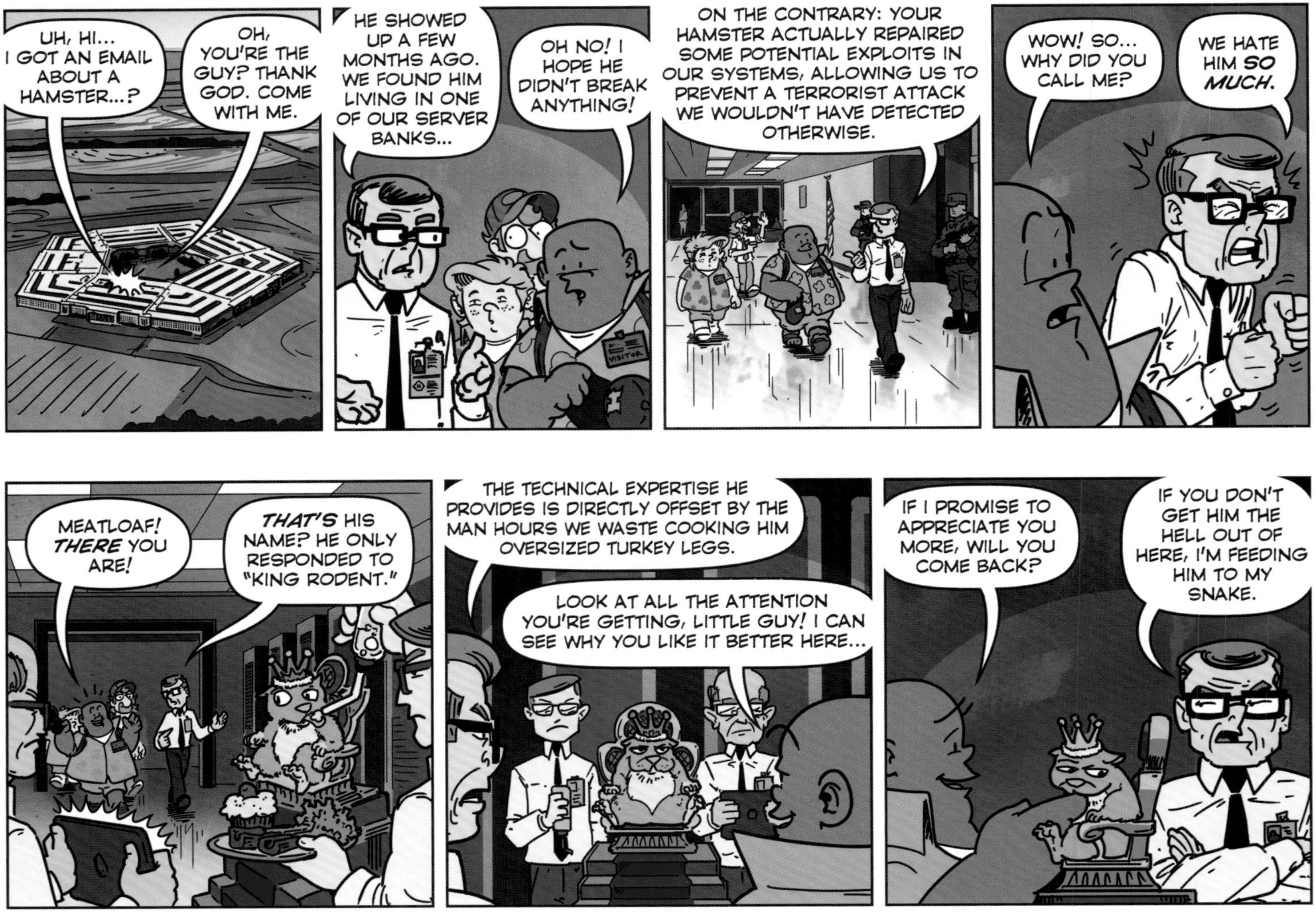
UH, HI... I GOT AN EMAIL ABOUT A HAMSTER...?
OH, YOU'RE THE GUY? THANK GOD. COME WITH ME.
HE SHOWED UP A FEW MONTHS AGO. WE FOUND HIM LIVING IN ONE OF OUR SERVER BANKS...
OH NO! I HOPE HE DIDN'T BREAK ANYTHING!
VISITOR
ON THE CONTRARY: YOUR HAMSTER ACTUALLY REPAIRED SOME POTENTIAL EXPLOITS IN OUR SYSTEMS, ALLOWING US TO PREVENT A TERRORIST ATTACK WE WOULDN'T HAVE DETECTED OTHERWISE.
WOW! SO... WHY DID YOU CALL ME?
WE HATE HIM SO MUCH.
MEATLOAF! THERE YOU ARE!
THAT'S HIS NAME? HE ONLY RESPONDED TO "KING RODENT."
THE TECHNICAL EXPERTISE HE PROVIDES IS DIRECTLY OFFSET BY THE MAN HOURS WE WASTE COOKING HIM OVERSIZED TURKEY LEGS.
LOOK AT ALL THE ATTENTION YOU'RE GETTING, LITTLE GUY! I CAN SEE WHY YOU LIKE IT BETTER HERE...
IF I PROMISE TO APPRECIATE YOU MORE, WILL YOU COME BACK?
IF YOU DON'T GET HIM THE HELL OUT OF HERE, I'M FEEDING HIM TO MY SNAKE.

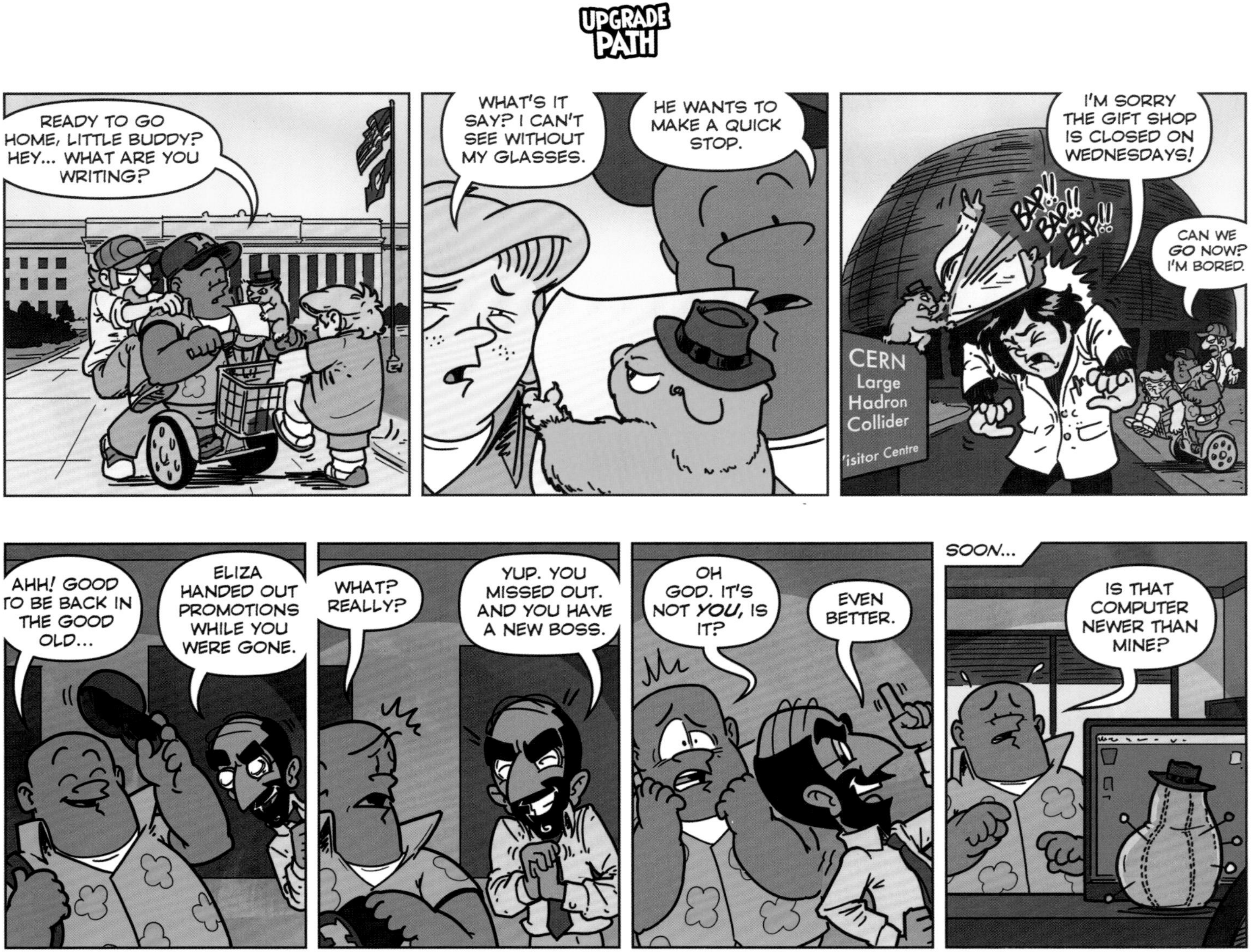
UPGRADE PATH
READY TO GO HOME, LITTLE BUDDY? HEY... WHAT ARE YOU WRITING?
WHAT'S IT SAY? I CAN'T SEE WITHOUT MY GLASSES.
HE WANTS TO MAKE A QUICK STOP.
I'M SORRY THE GIFT SHOP IS CLOSED ON WEDNESDAYS!
BAP!! BAP!! BAP!!
CERN Large Hadron Collider Visitor Centre
CAN WE GO NOW? I'M BORED.
AHH! GOOD TO BE BACK IN THE GOOD OLD...
ELIZA HANDED OUT PROMOTIONS WHILE YOU WERE GONE.
WHAT? REALLY?
YUP. YOU MISSED OUT. AND YOU HAVE A NEW BOSS.
OH GOD. IT'S NOT *YOU*, IS IT?
EVEN BETTER.
SOON...
IS THAT COMPUTER NEWER THAN MINE?

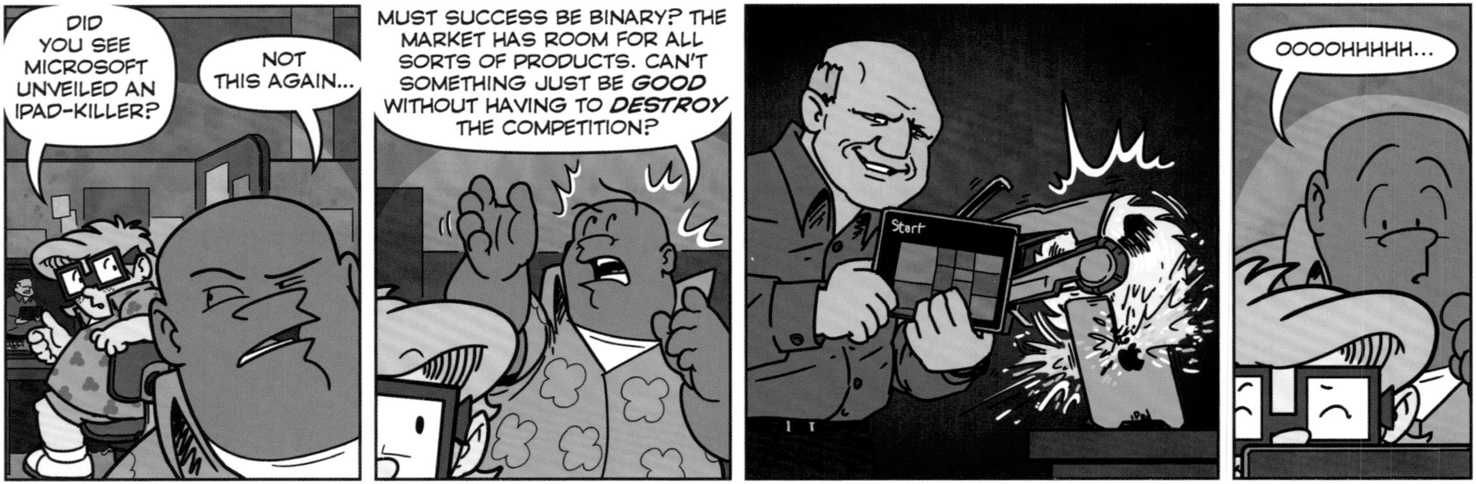
DID YOU SEE MICROSOFT UNVEILED AN IPAD-KILLER?
NOT THIS AGAIN...
MUST SUCCESS BE BINARY? THE MARKET HAS ROOM FOR ALL SORTS OF PRODUCTS. CAN'T SOMETHING JUST BE *GOOD* WITHOUT HAVING TO *DESTROY* THE COMPETITION?
Start
OOOOHHHHH...

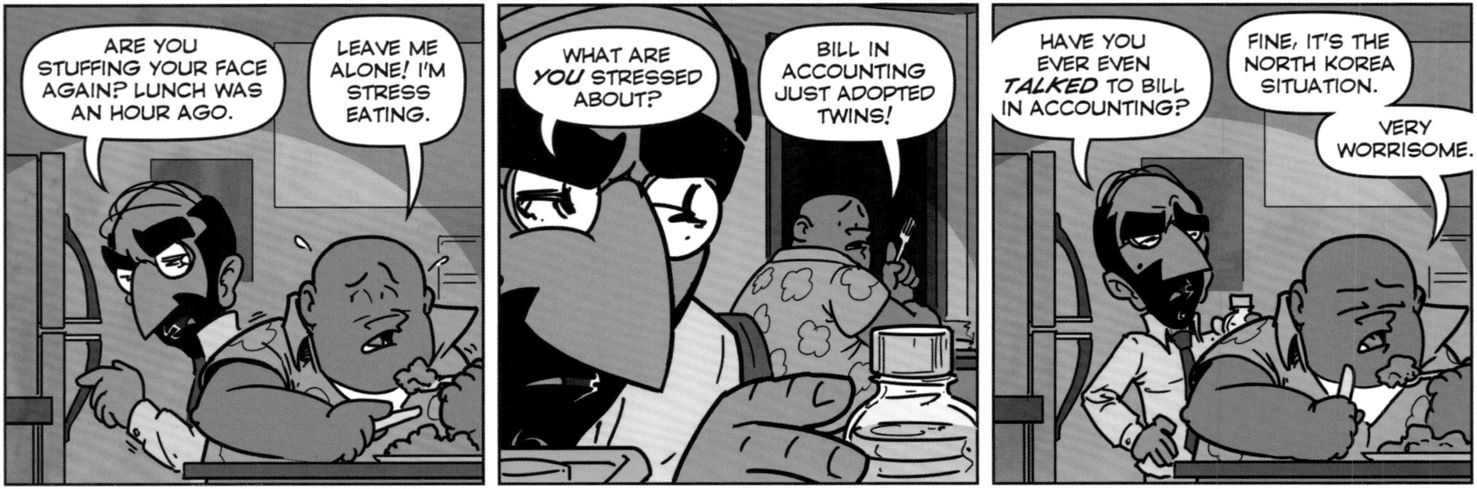
ARE YOU STUFFING YOUR FACE AGAIN? LUNCH WAS AN HOUR AGO.
LEAVE ME ALONE! I'M STRESS EATING.
WHAT ARE *YOU* STRESSED ABOUT?
BILL IN ACCOUNTING JUST ADOPTED TWINS!
HAVE YOU EVER EVEN *TALKED* TO BILL IN ACCOUNTING?
FINE, IT'S THE NORTH KOREA SITUATION.
VERY WORRISOME.

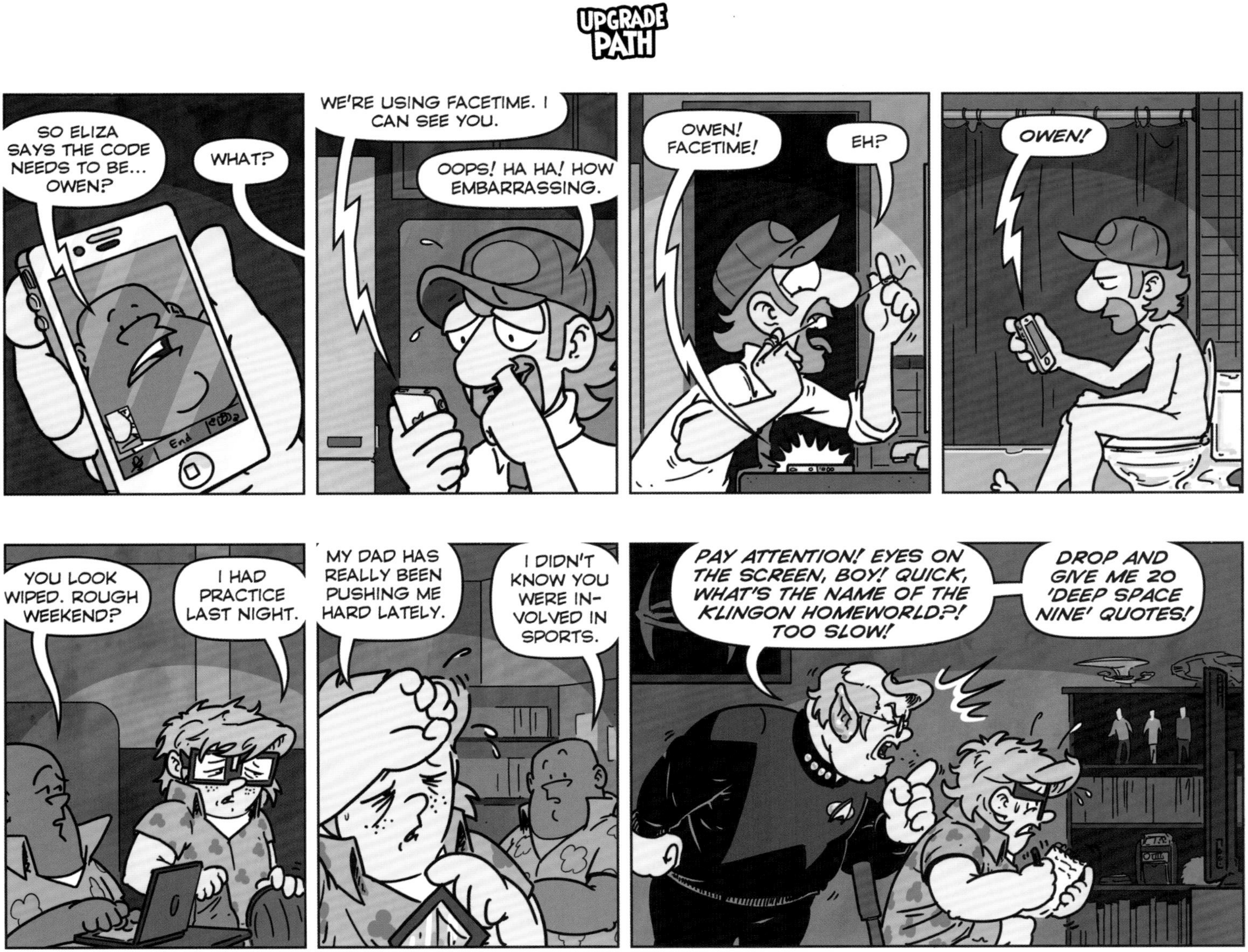
UPGRADE PATH
SO ELIZA SAYS THE CODE NEEDS TO BE... OWEN?
WHAT?
End
WE'RE USING FACETIME. I CAN SEE YOU.
OOPS! HA HA! HOW EMBARRASSING.
OWEN! FACETIME!
EH?
OWEN!
YOU LOOK WIPED. ROUGH WEEKEND?
I HAD PRACTICE LAST NIGHT.
MY DAD HAS REALLY BEEN PUSHING ME HARD LATELY.
I DIDN'T KNOW YOU WERE INVOLVED IN SPORTS.
PAY ATTENTION! EYES ON THE SCREEN, BOY! QUICK, WHAT'S THE NAME OF THE KLINGON HOMEWORLD?! TOO SLOW!
DROP AND GIVE ME 20 'DEEP SPACE NINE' QUOTES!

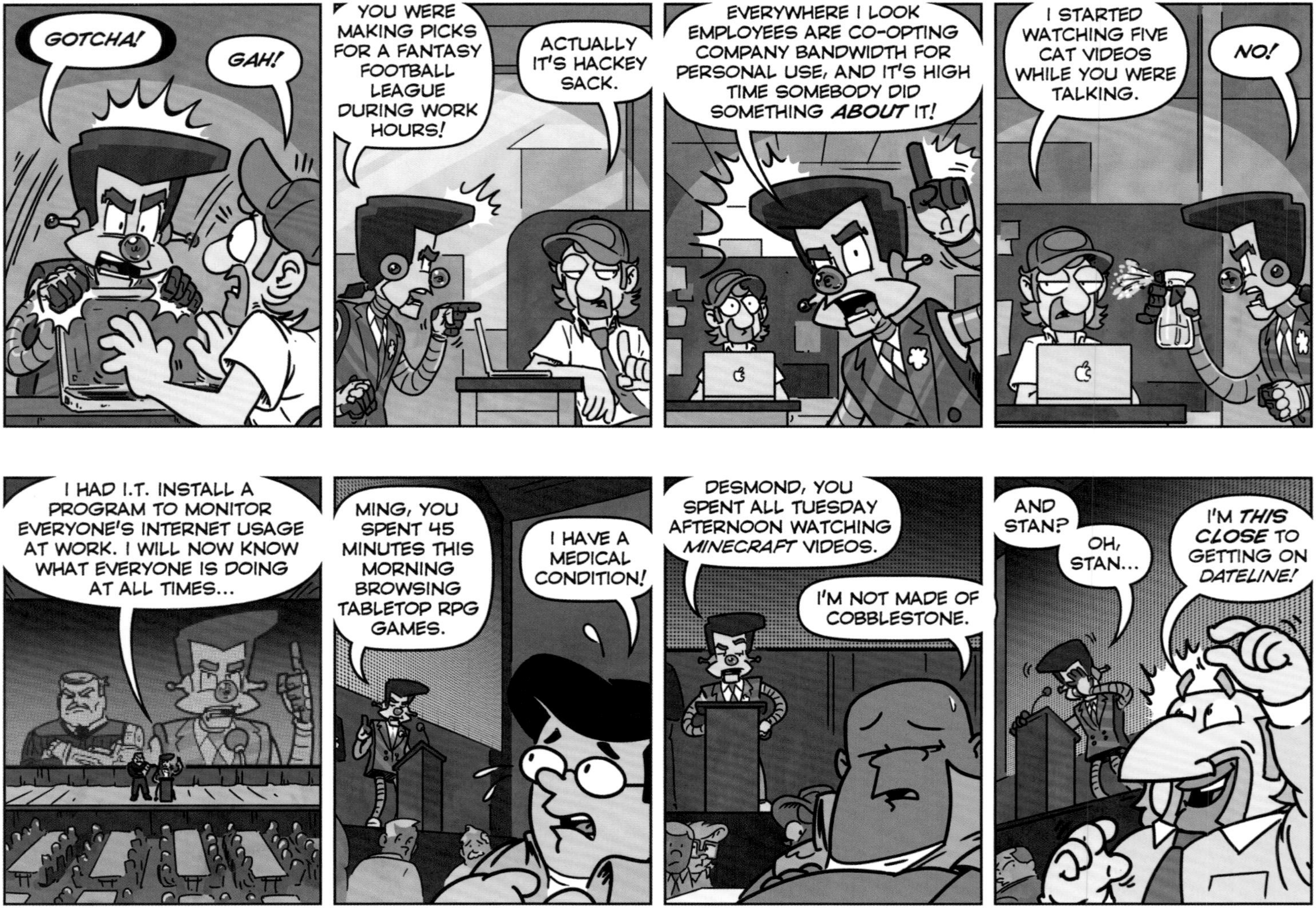
GOTCHA!
GAH!
YOU WERE MAKING PICKS FOR A FANTASY FOOTBALL LEAGUE DURING WORK HOURS!
ACTUALLY IT'S HACKEY SACK.
EVERYWHERE I LOOK EMPLOYEES ARE CO-OPTING COMPANY BANDWIDTH FOR PERSONAL USE, AND IT'S HIGH TIME SOMEBODY DID SOMETHING *ABOUT* IT!
I STARTED WATCHING FIVE CAT VIDEOS WHILE YOU WERE TALKING.
NO!
I HAD I.T. INSTALL A PROGRAM TO MONITOR EVERYONE'S INTERNET USAGE AT WORK. I WILL NOW KNOW WHAT EVERYONE IS DOING AT ALL TIMES...
MING, YOU SPENT 45 MINUTES THIS MORNING BROWSING TABLETOP RPG GAMES.
I HAVE A MEDICAL CONDITION!
DESMOND, YOU SPENT ALL TUESDAY AFTERNOON WATCHING *MINECRAFT* VIDEOS.
I'M NOT MADE OF COBBLESTONE.
AND STAN?
OH, STAN...
I'M *THIS CLOSE* TO GETTING ON *DATELINE!*

UPGRADE PATH

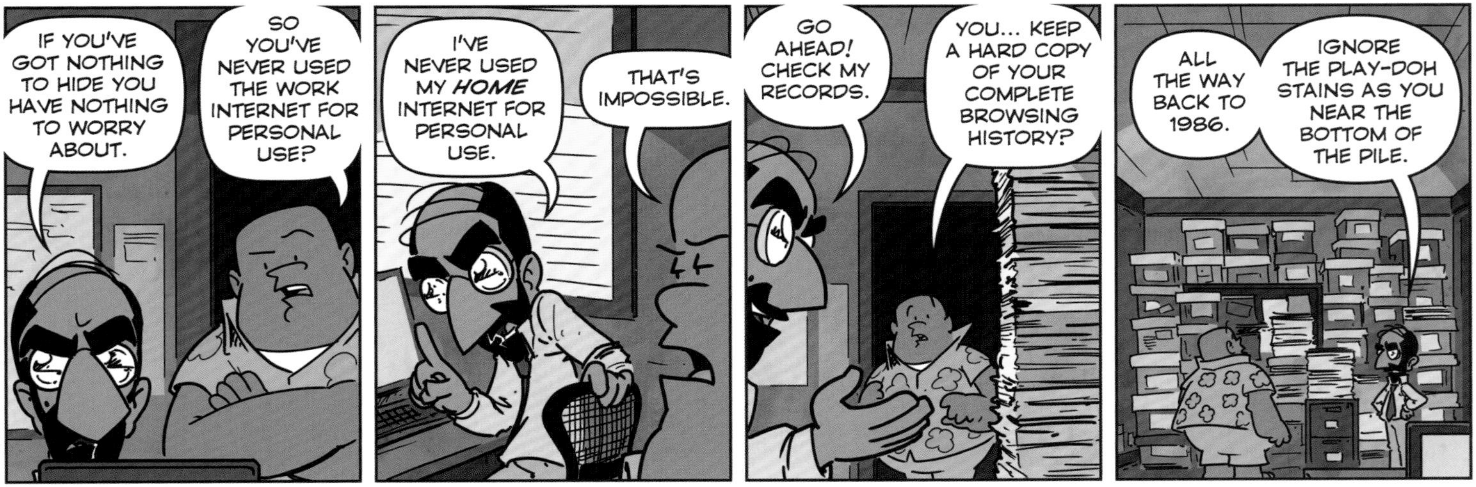
IF YOU'VE GOT NOTHING TO HIDE YOU HAVE NOTHING TO WORRY ABOUT.
SO YOU'VE NEVER USED THE WORK INTERNET FOR PERSONAL USE?
I'VE NEVER USED MY *HOME* INTERNET FOR PERSONAL USE.
THAT'S IMPOSSIBLE.
GO AHEAD! CHECK MY RECORDS.
YOU... KEEP A HARD COPY OF YOUR COMPLETE BROWSING HISTORY?
ALL THE WAY BACK TO 1986.
IGNORE THE PLAY-DOH STAINS AS YOU NEAR THE BOTTOM OF THE PILE.

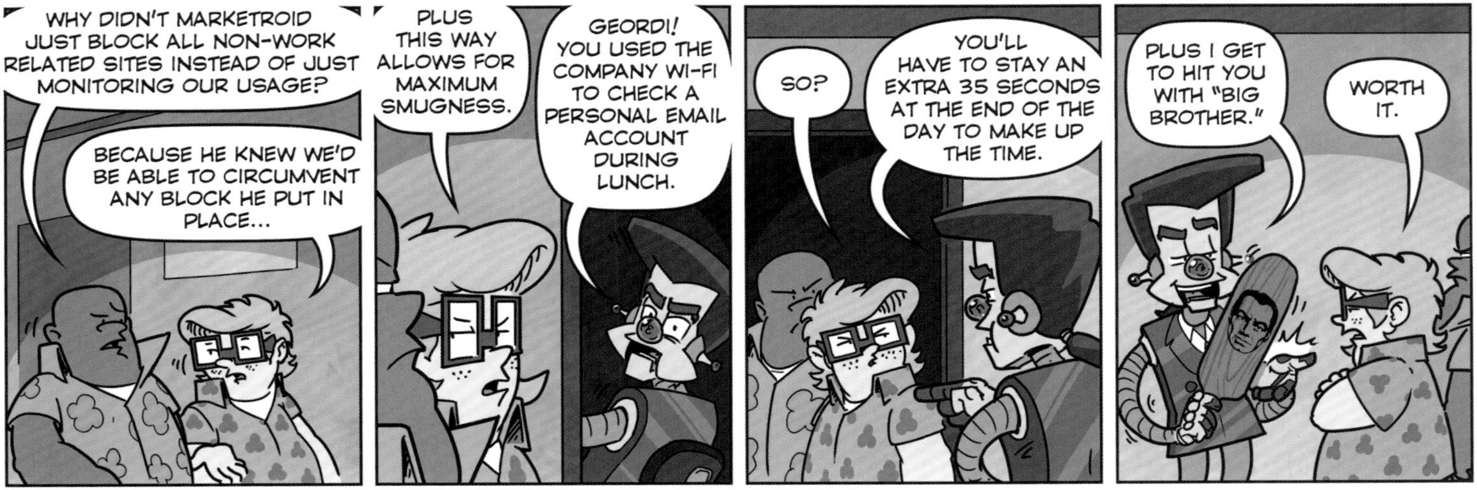
WHY DIDN'T MARKETROID JUST BLOCK ALL NON-WORK RELATED SITES INSTEAD OF JUST MONITORING OUR USAGE?
BECAUSE HE KNEW WE'D BE ABLE TO CIRCUMVENT ANY BLOCK HE PUT IN PLACE...
PLUS THIS WAY ALLOWS FOR MAXIMUM SMUGNESS.
GEORDI! YOU USED THE COMPANY WI-FI TO CHECK A PERSONAL EMAIL ACCOUNT DURING LUNCH.
SO?
YOU'LL HAVE TO STAY AN EXTRA 35 SECONDS AT THE END OF THE DAY TO MAKE UP THE TIME.
PLUS I GET TO HIT YOU WITH "BIG BROTHER."
WORTH IT.

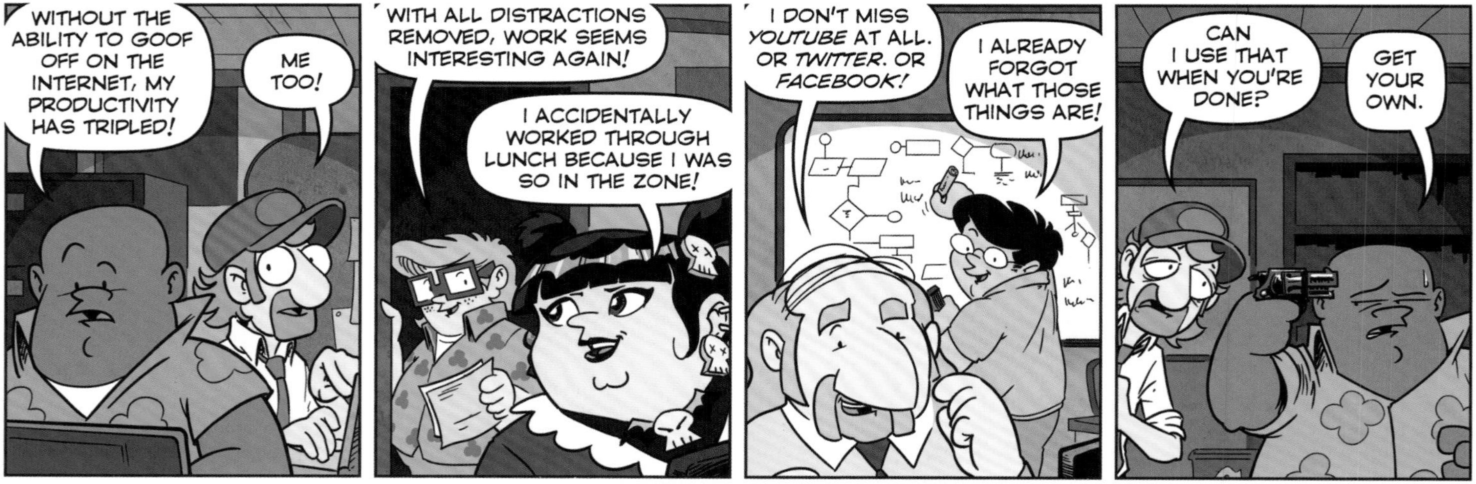
WITHOUT THE ABILITY TO GOOF OFF ON THE INTERNET, MY PRODUCTIVITY HAS TRIPLED!
ME TOO!
WITH ALL DISTRACTIONS REMOVED, WORK SEEMS INTERESTING AGAIN!
I ACCIDENTALLY WORKED THROUGH LUNCH BECAUSE I WAS SO IN THE ZONE!
I DON'T MISS *YOUTUBE* AT ALL. OR *TWITTER*. OR *FACEBOOK*!
I ALREADY FORGOT WHAT THOSE THINGS ARE!
CAN I USE THAT WHEN YOU'RE DONE?
GET YOUR OWN.

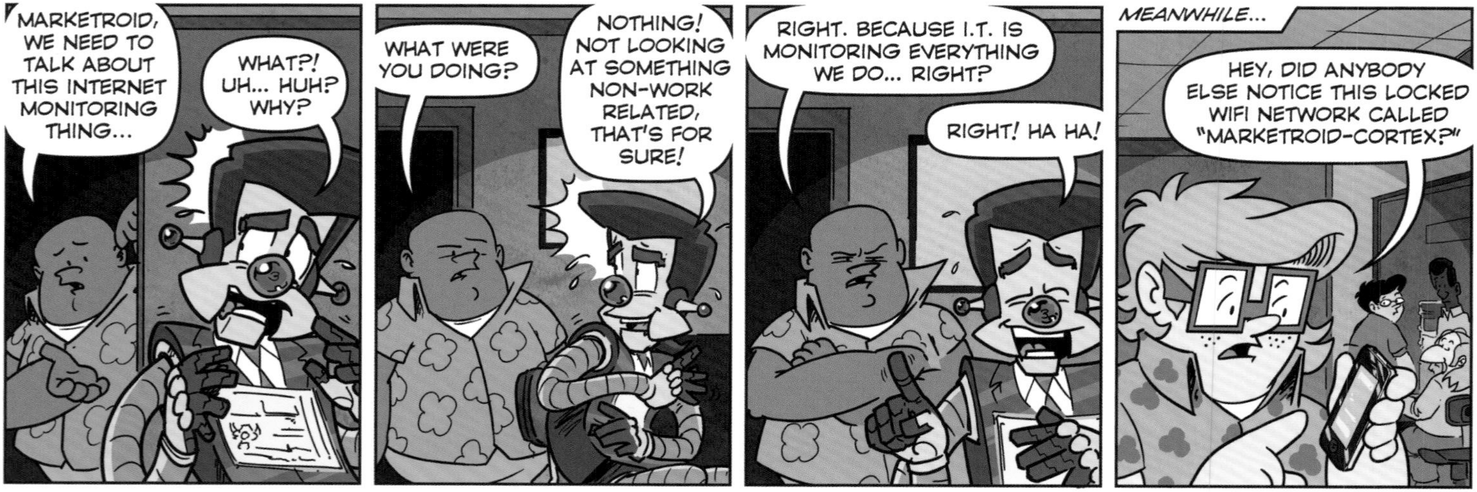
MARKETROID, WE NEED TO TALK ABOUT THIS INTERNET MONITORING THING...
WHAT?! UH... HUH? WHY?
WHAT WERE YOU DOING?
NOTHING! NOT LOOKING AT SOMETHING NON-WORK RELATED, THAT'S FOR SURE!
RIGHT. BECAUSE I.T. IS MONITORING EVERYTHING WE DO... RIGHT?
RIGHT! HA HA!
MEANWHILE...
HEY, DID ANYBODY ELSE NOTICE THIS LOCKED WIFI NETWORK CALLED "MARKETROID-CORTEX?"

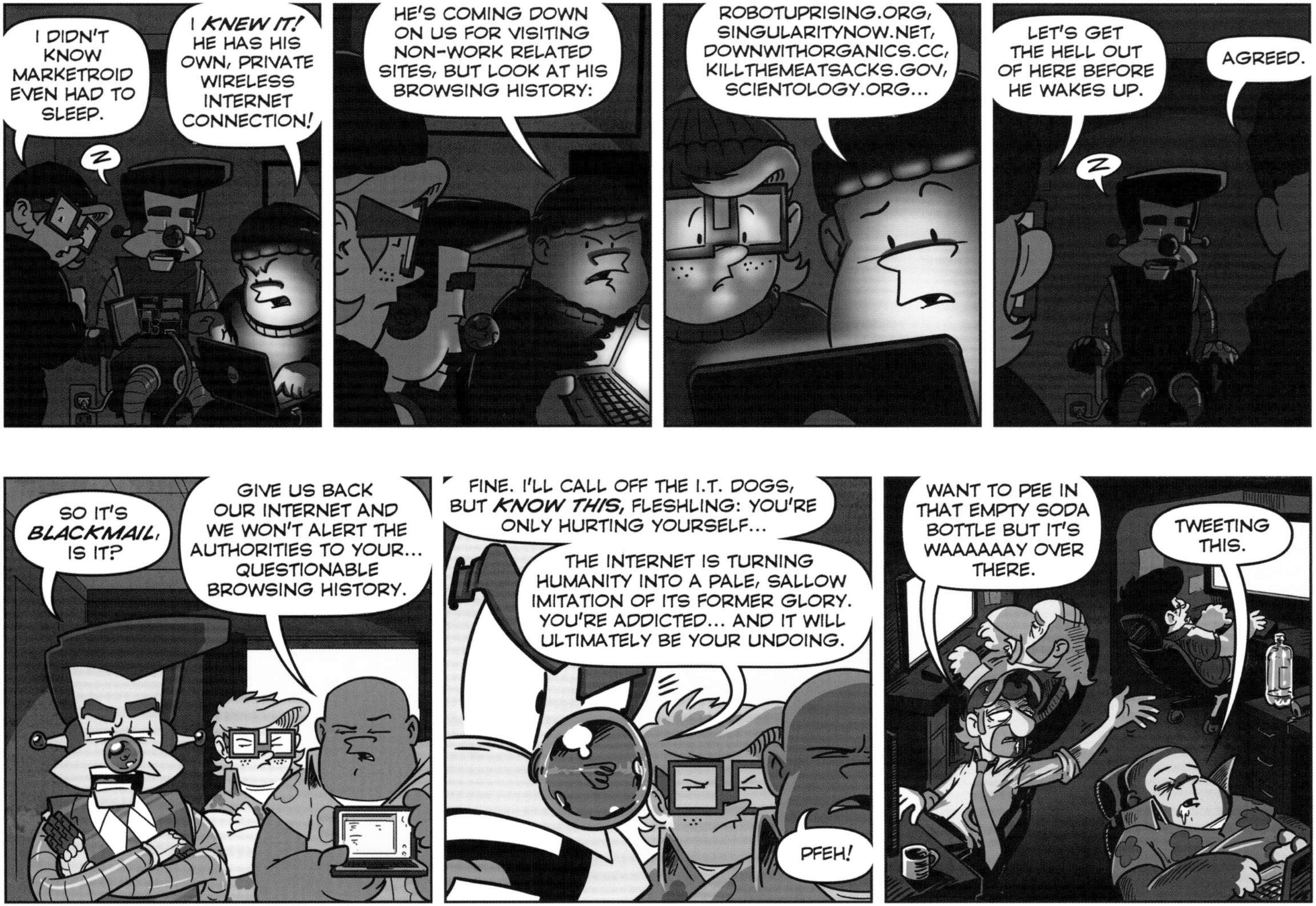
I DIDN'T KNOW MARKETROID EVEN HAD TO SLEEP.
Z
I *KNEW IT!* HE HAS HIS OWN, PRIVATE WIRELESS INTERNET CONNECTION!
HE'S COMING DOWN ON US FOR VISITING NON-WORK RELATED SITES, BUT LOOK AT HIS BROWSING HISTORY:
ROBOTUPRISING.ORG, SINGULARITYNOW.NET, DOWNWITHORGANICS.CC, KILLTHEMEATSACKS.GOV, SCIENTOLOGY.ORG...
LET'S GET THE HELL OUT OF HERE BEFORE HE WAKES UP.
Z
AGREED.
SO IT'S *BLACKMAIL*, IS IT?
GIVE US BACK OUR INTERNET AND WE WON'T ALERT THE AUTHORITIES TO YOUR... QUESTIONABLE BROWSING HISTORY.
FINE. I'LL CALL OFF THE I.T. DOGS, BUT *KNOW THIS,* FLESHLING: YOU'RE ONLY HURTING YOURSELF...
THE INTERNET IS TURNING HUMANITY INTO A PALE, SALLOW IMITATION OF ITS FORMER GLORY. YOU'RE ADDICTED... AND IT WILL ULTIMATELY BE YOUR UNDOING.
PFEH!
WANT TO PEE IN THAT EMPTY SODA BOTTLE BUT IT'S WAAAAAAY OVER THERE.
TWEETING THIS.

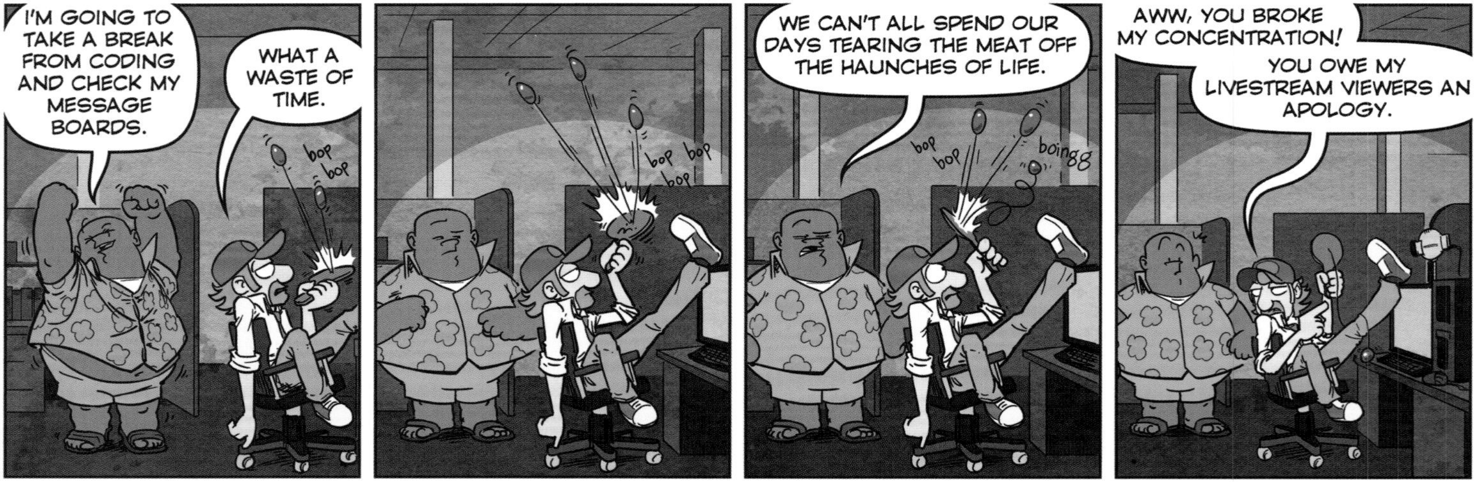
I'M GOING TO TAKE A BREAK FROM CODING AND CHECK MY MESSAGE BOARDS.
WHAT A WASTE OF TIME.
bop
bop
bop bop
bop
WE CAN'T ALL SPEND OUR DAYS TEARING THE MEAT OFF THE HAUNCHES OF LIFE.
bop
bop
boingg
AWW, YOU BROKE MY CONCENTRATION!
YOU OWE MY LIVESTREAM VIEWERS AN APOLOGY.

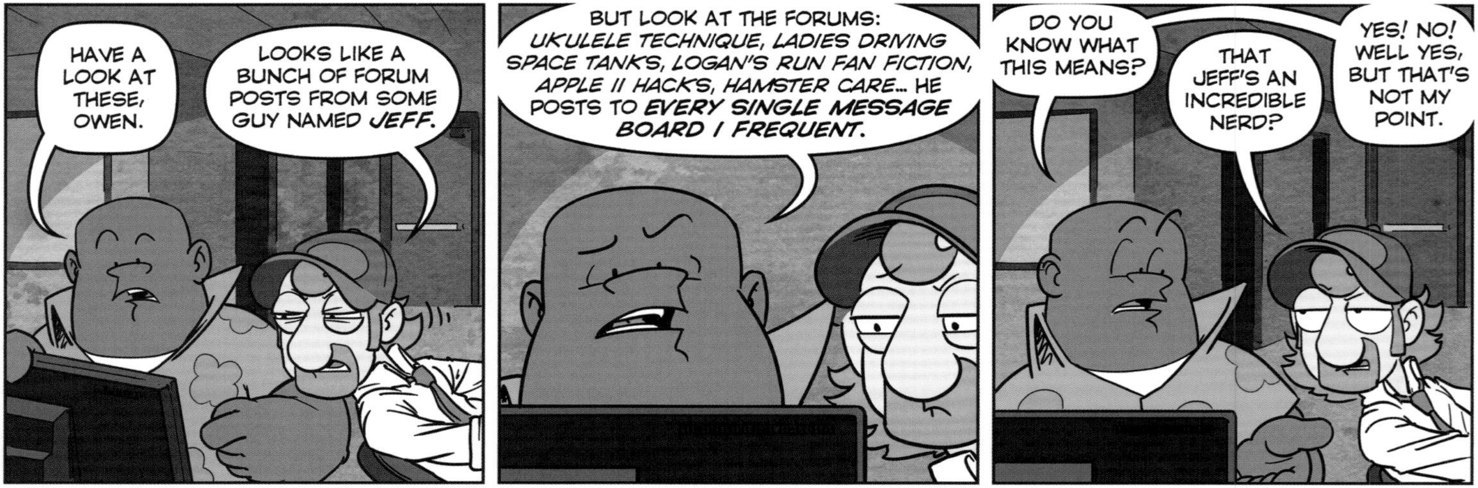
HAVE A LOOK AT THESE, OWEN.
LOOKS LIKE A BUNCH OF FORUM POSTS FROM SOME GUY NAMED JEFF.
BUT LOOK AT THE FORUMS: UKULELE TECHNIQUE, LADIES DRIVING SPACE TANKS, LOGAN'S RUN FAN FICTION, APPLE II HACKS, HAMSTER CARE... HE POSTS TO EVERY SINGLE MESSAGE BOARD I FREQUENT.
DO YOU KNOW WHAT THIS MEANS?
THAT JEFF'S AN INCREDIBLE NERD?
YES! NO! WELL YES, BUT THAT'S NOT MY POINT.

UPGRADE PATH

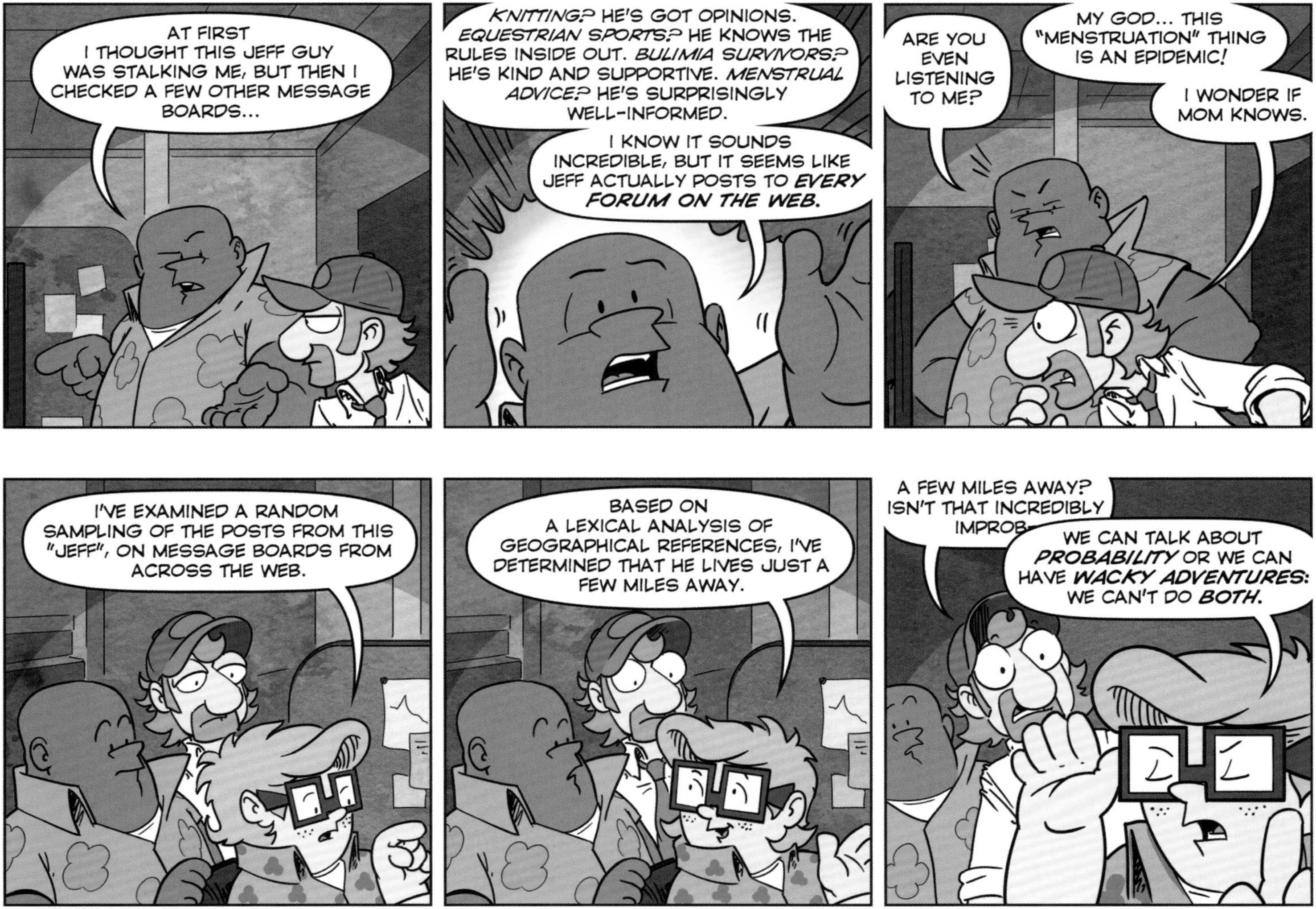
AT FIRST I THOUGHT THIS JEFF GUY WAS STALKING ME, BUT THEN I CHECKED A FEW OTHER MESSAGE BOARDS...
KNITTING? HE'S GOT OPINIONS. *EQUESTRIAN SPORTS?* HE KNOWS THE RULES INSIDE OUT. *BULIMIA SURVIVORS?* HE'S KIND AND SUPPORTIVE. *MENSTRUAL ADVICE?* HE'S SURPRISINGLY WELL-INFORMED.
I KNOW IT SOUNDS INCREDIBLE, BUT IT SEEMS LIKE JEFF ACTUALLY POSTS TO ***EVERY FORUM ON THE WEB.***
ARE YOU EVEN LISTENING TO ME?
MY GOD... THIS "MENSTRUATION" THING IS AN EPIDEMIC!
I WONDER IF MOM KNOWS.
I'VE EXAMINED A RANDOM SAMPLING OF THE POSTS FROM THIS "JEFF", ON MESSAGE BOARDS FROM ACROSS THE WEB.
BASED ON A LEXICAL ANALYSIS OF GEOGRAPHICAL REFERENCES, I'VE DETERMINED THAT HE LIVES JUST A FEW MILES AWAY.
A FEW MILES AWAY? ISN'T THAT INCREDIBLY IMPROB–
WE CAN TALK ABOUT ***PROBABILITY*** OR WE CAN HAVE ***WACKY ADVENTURES:*** WE CAN'T DO ***BOTH.***

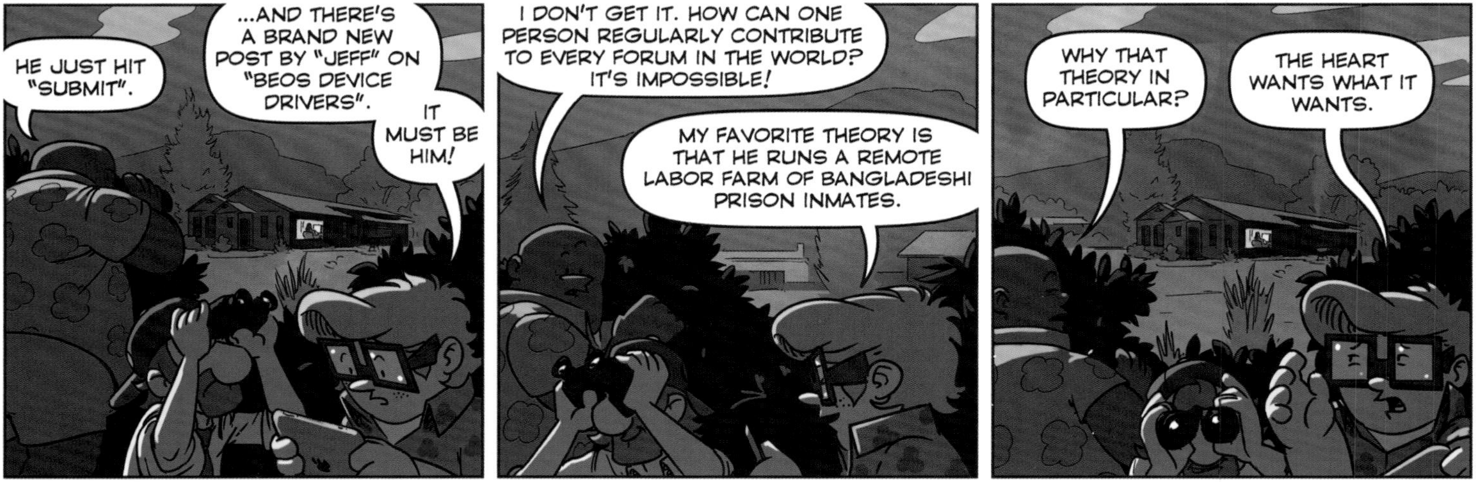
HE JUST HIT "SUBMIT".
...AND THERE'S A BRAND NEW POST BY "JEFF" ON "BEOS DEVICE DRIVERS".
IT MUST BE HIM!
I DON'T GET IT. HOW CAN ONE PERSON REGULARLY CONTRIBUTE TO EVERY FORUM IN THE WORLD? IT'S IMPOSSIBLE!
MY FAVORITE THEORY IS THAT HE RUNS A REMOTE LABOR FARM OF BANGLADESHI PRISON INMATES.
WHY THAT THEORY IN PARTICULAR?
THE HEART WANTS WHAT IT WANTS.

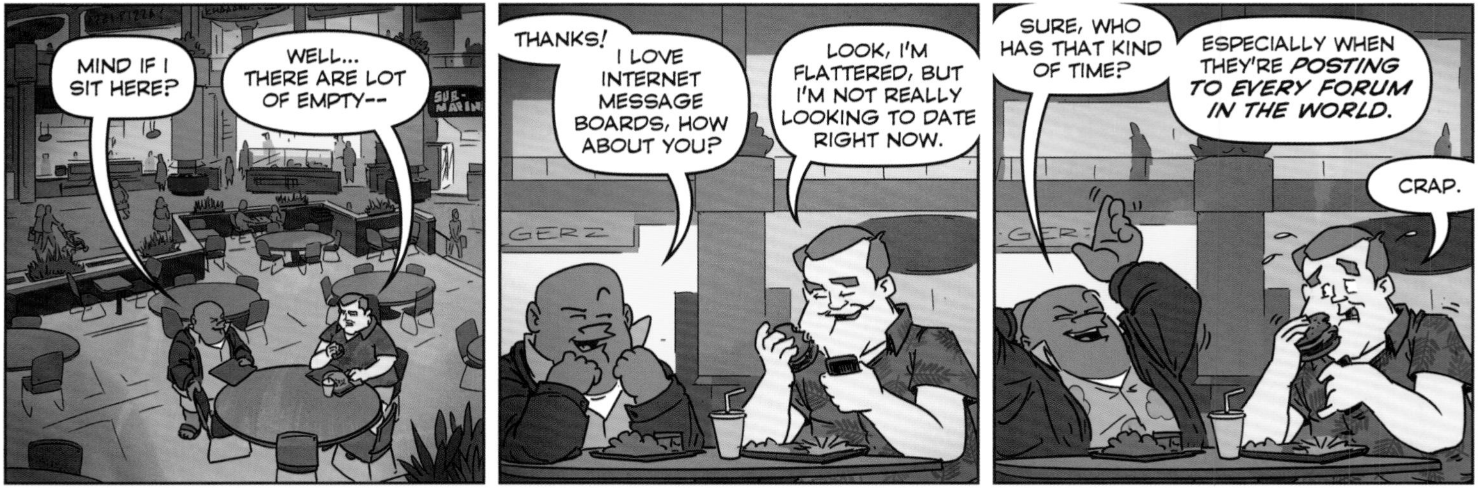
MIND IF I SIT HERE?
WELL... THERE ARE LOT OF EMPTY--
THANKS!
I LOVE INTERNET MESSAGE BOARDS, HOW ABOUT YOU?
LOOK, I'M FLATTERED, BUT I'M NOT REALLY LOOKING TO DATE RIGHT NOW.
SURE, WHO HAS THAT KIND OF TIME?
ESPECIALLY WHEN THEY'RE *POSTING TO EVERY FORUM IN THE WORLD*.
CRAP.

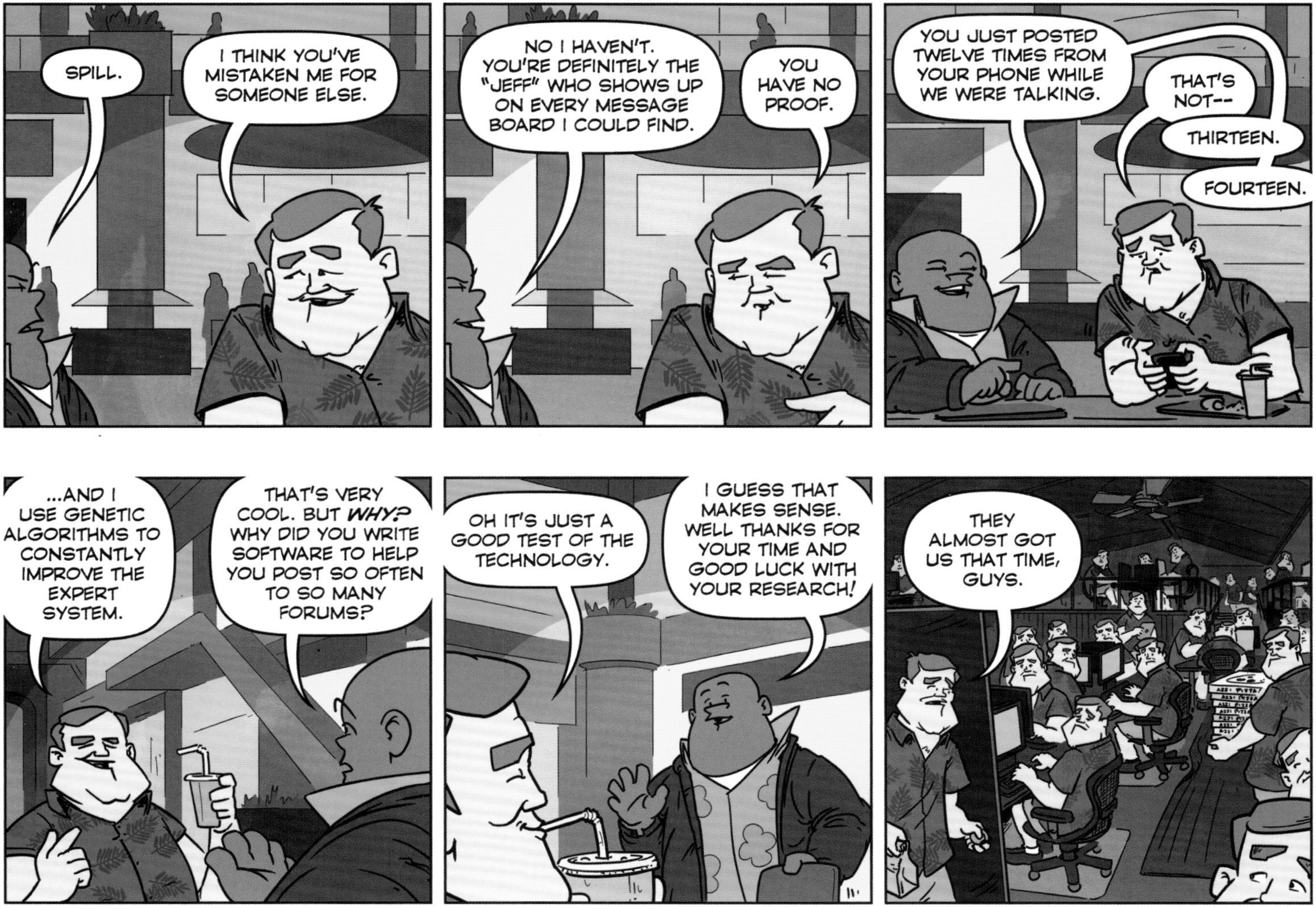
SPILL.
I THINK YOU'VE MISTAKEN ME FOR SOMEONE ELSE.
NO I HAVEN'T. YOU'RE DEFINITELY THE "JEFF" WHO SHOWS UP ON EVERY MESSAGE BOARD I COULD FIND.
YOU HAVE NO PROOF.
YOU JUST POSTED TWELVE TIMES FROM YOUR PHONE WHILE WE WERE TALKING.
THAT'S NOT--
THIRTEEN.
FOURTEEN.
...AND I USE GENETIC ALGORITHMS TO CONSTANTLY IMPROVE THE EXPERT SYSTEM.
THAT'S VERY COOL. BUT *WHY?* WHY DID YOU WRITE SOFTWARE TO HELP YOU POST SO OFTEN TO SO MANY FORUMS?
OH IT'S JUST A GOOD TEST OF THE TECHNOLOGY.
I GUESS THAT MAKES SENSE. WELL THANKS FOR YOUR TIME AND GOOD LUCK WITH YOUR RESEARCH!
THEY ALMOST GOT US THAT TIME, GUYS.

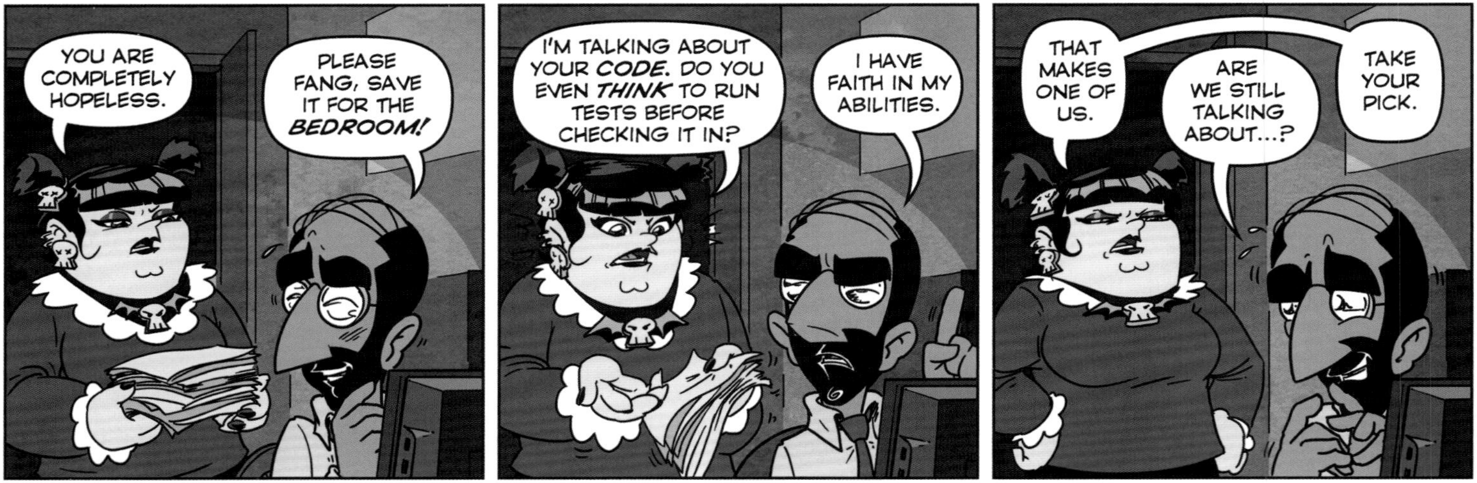
YOU ARE COMPLETELY HOPELESS.
PLEASE FANG, SAVE IT FOR THE *BEDROOM!*
I'M TALKING ABOUT YOUR *CODE.* DO YOU EVEN *THINK* TO RUN TESTS BEFORE CHECKING IT IN?
I HAVE FAITH IN MY ABILITIES.
THAT MAKES ONE OF US.
ARE WE STILL TALKING ABOUT...?
TAKE YOUR PICK.

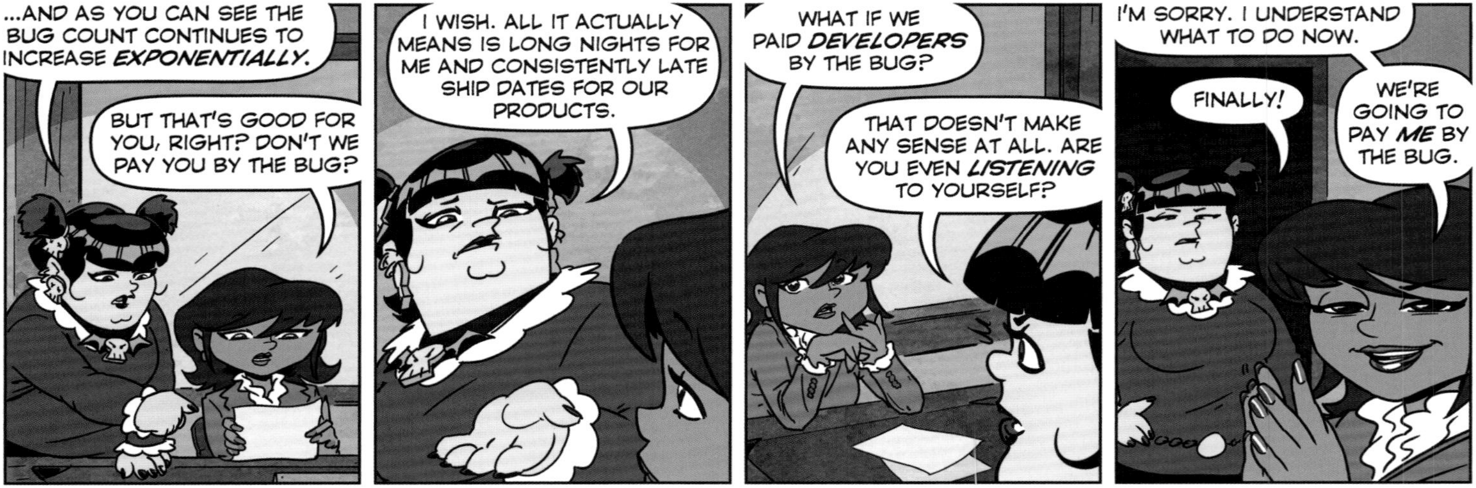
...AND AS YOU CAN SEE THE BUG COUNT CONTINUES TO INCREASE *EXPONENTIALLY.*
BUT THAT'S GOOD FOR YOU, RIGHT? DON'T WE PAY YOU BY THE BUG?
I WISH. ALL IT ACTUALLY MEANS IS LONG NIGHTS FOR ME AND CONSISTENTLY LATE SHIP DATES FOR OUR PRODUCTS.
WHAT IF WE PAID *DEVELOPERS* BY THE BUG?
THAT DOESN'T MAKE ANY SENSE AT ALL. ARE YOU EVEN *LISTENING* TO YOURSELF?
I'M SORRY. I UNDERSTAND WHAT TO DO NOW.
FINALLY!
WE'RE GOING TO PAY *ME* BY THE BUG.

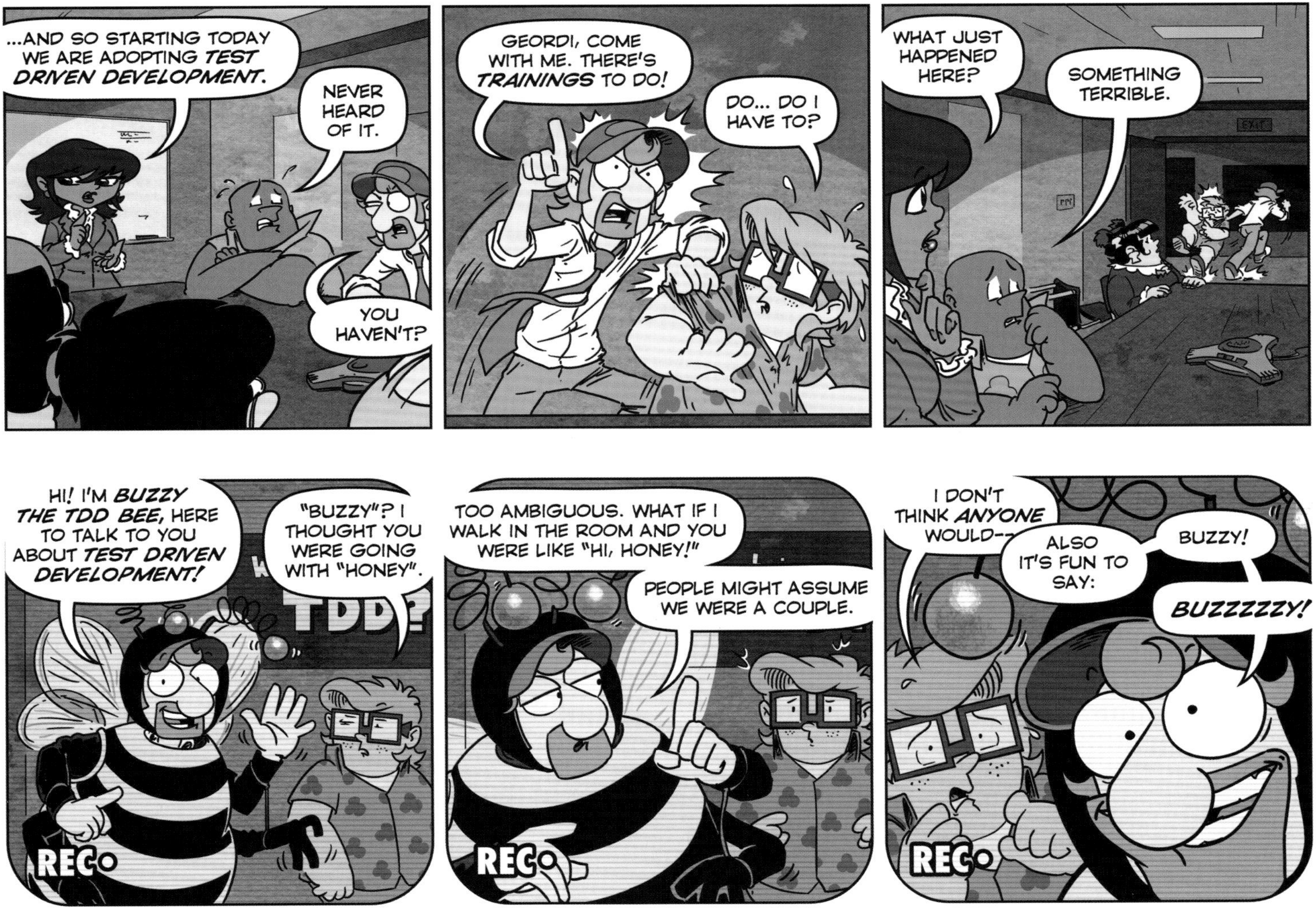
...AND SO STARTING TODAY WE ARE ADOPTING TEST DRIVEN DEVELOPMENT.
NEVER HEARD OF IT.
YOU HAVEN'T?
GEORDI, COME WITH ME. THERE'S TRAININGS TO DO!
DO... DO I HAVE TO?
WHAT JUST HAPPENED HERE?
SOMETHING TERRIBLE.
EXIT
HI! I'M BUZZY THE TDD BEE, HERE TO TALK TO YOU ABOUT TEST DRIVEN DEVELOPMENT!
"BUZZY"? I THOUGHT YOU WERE GOING WITH "HONEY".
TDD?
REC
TOO AMBIGUOUS. WHAT IF I WALK IN THE ROOM AND YOU WERE LIKE "HI, HONEY!"
PEOPLE MIGHT ASSUME WE WERE A COUPLE.
REC
I DON'T THINK ANYONE WOULD--
ALSO IT'S FUN TO SAY:
BUZZY!
BUZZZZZY!
REC

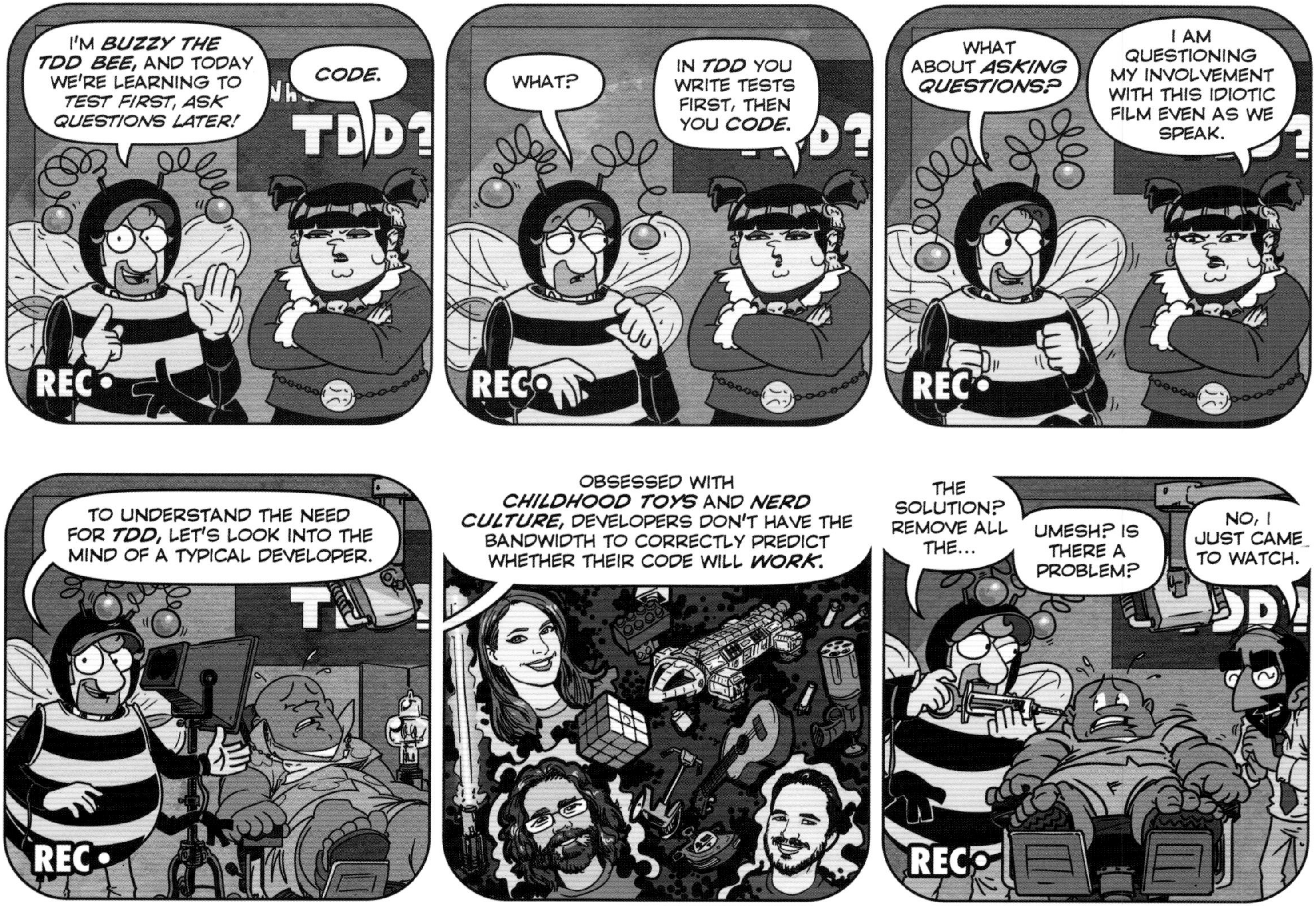
I'M BUZZY THE TDD BEE, AND TODAY WE'RE LEARNING TO TEST FIRST, ASK QUESTIONS LATER!
CODE.
TDD?
REC
WHAT?
IN TDD YOU WRITE TESTS FIRST, THEN YOU CODE.
REC
WHAT ABOUT ASKING QUESTIONS?
I AM QUESTIONING MY INVOLVEMENT WITH THIS IDIOTIC FILM EVEN AS WE SPEAK.
REC
TO UNDERSTAND THE NEED FOR TDD, LET'S LOOK INTO THE MIND OF A TYPICAL DEVELOPER.
REC
OBSESSED WITH CHILDHOOD TOYS AND NERD CULTURE, DEVELOPERS DON'T HAVE THE BANDWIDTH TO CORRECTLY PREDICT WHETHER THEIR CODE WILL WORK.
THE SOLUTION? REMOVE ALL THE...
UMESH? IS THERE A PROBLEM?
NO, I JUST CAME TO WATCH.
REC

TO PUT TDD INTO ACTION, THINK *POSITIVE!* IDENTIFY ALL THE THINGS YOUR CODE IS SUPPOSED TO *DO!*

STAVE OFF MY INEVITABLE DISMISSAL AND THE RESULTANT DESCENT INTO HOMELESSNESS?

REC

HMMM. CAN YOU THINK OF ANY OTHERS?

PAY MY CHILD SUPPORT.

FINANCE MY PRESCRIPTION DRUG HABIT.

GIVE MY SAD, LONELY LIFE THE TINIEST GLIMMER OF MEANING.

REC

GREAT! NOW JUST TURN THOSE INTO TEST CASES!

I DON'T ACTUALLY KNOW HOW TO PROGRAM.

REC

...THEN TESTERS PHYSICALLY PLACE THE CODE IN A LIMOUSINE AND DRIVE IT TO THE SERVER FARM, THUS GIVING TDD ITS NAME!

AMAZING.

YOU LIKE?

ART TOLD ME, BUT IT'S SO MUCH MORE SURREAL IN PERSON.

a film by
OWEN OWENSON

ritten & directed by
OWEN OWENSON

I HOPE THIS DOESN'T AFFECT YOUR DECISION.

ONLY MY DECISION TO QUIT DRINKING AT WORK.

IF YOU SIT THROUGH THE CREDITS THERE'S A BONUS SCENE!

SORRY, THERE WASN'T ENOUGH BUDGET FOR COSTUMES.

OR CLOTHING OF ANY KIND.

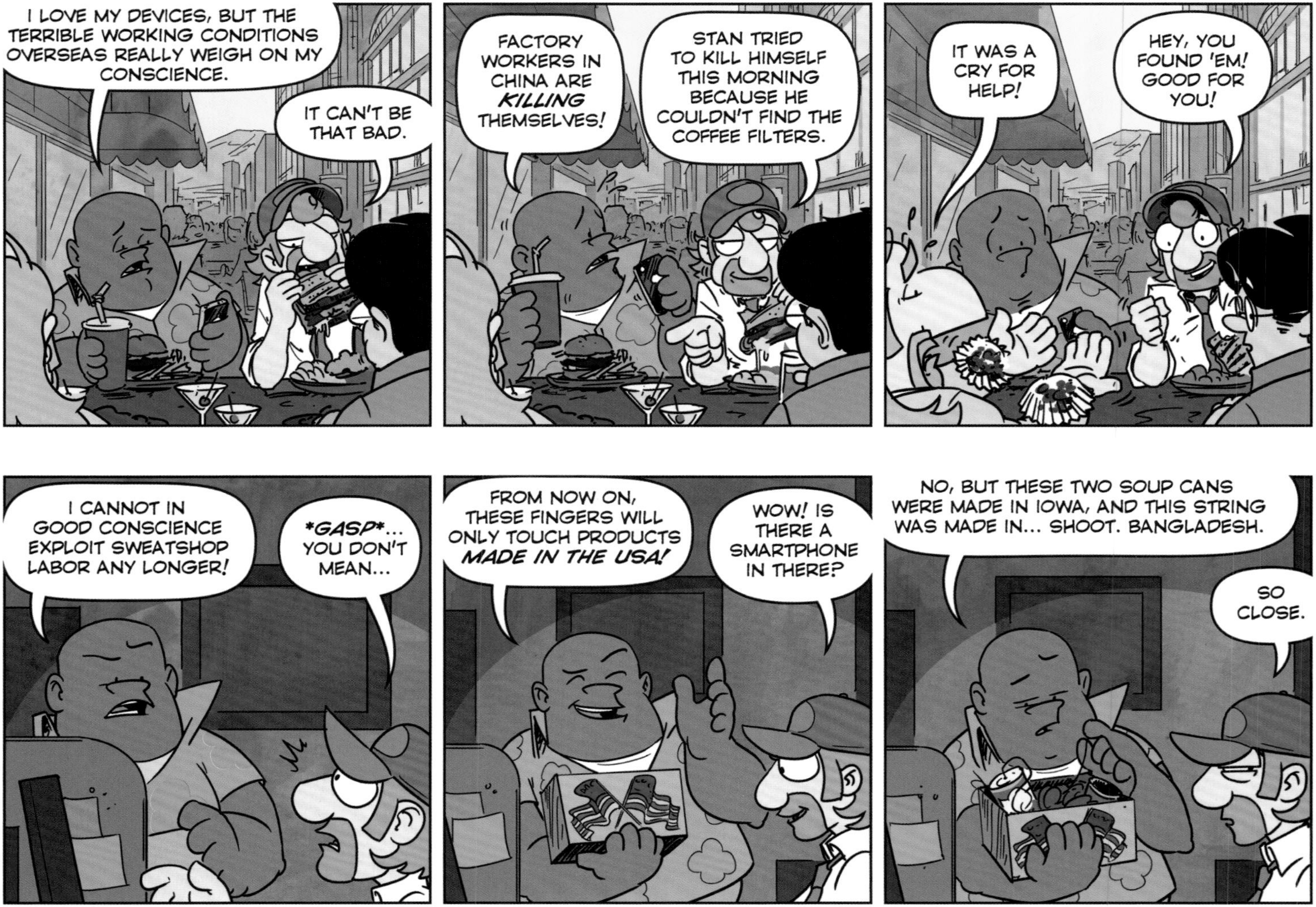
I LOVE MY DEVICES, BUT THE TERRIBLE WORKING CONDITIONS OVERSEAS REALLY WEIGH ON MY CONSCIENCE.
IT CAN'T BE THAT BAD.
FACTORY WORKERS IN CHINA ARE *KILLING* THEMSELVES!
STAN TRIED TO KILL HIMSELF THIS MORNING BECAUSE HE COULDN'T FIND THE COFFEE FILTERS.
IT WAS A CRY FOR HELP!
HEY, YOU FOUND 'EM! GOOD FOR YOU!
I CANNOT IN GOOD CONSCIENCE EXPLOIT SWEATSHOP LABOR ANY LONGER!
GASP... YOU DON'T MEAN...
FROM NOW ON, THESE FINGERS WILL ONLY TOUCH PRODUCTS *MADE IN THE USA!*
WOW! IS THERE A SMARTPHONE IN THERE?
NO, BUT THESE TWO SOUP CANS WERE MADE IN IOWA, AND THIS STRING WAS MADE IN... SHOOT. BANGLADESH.
SO CLOSE.

UPGRADE PATH

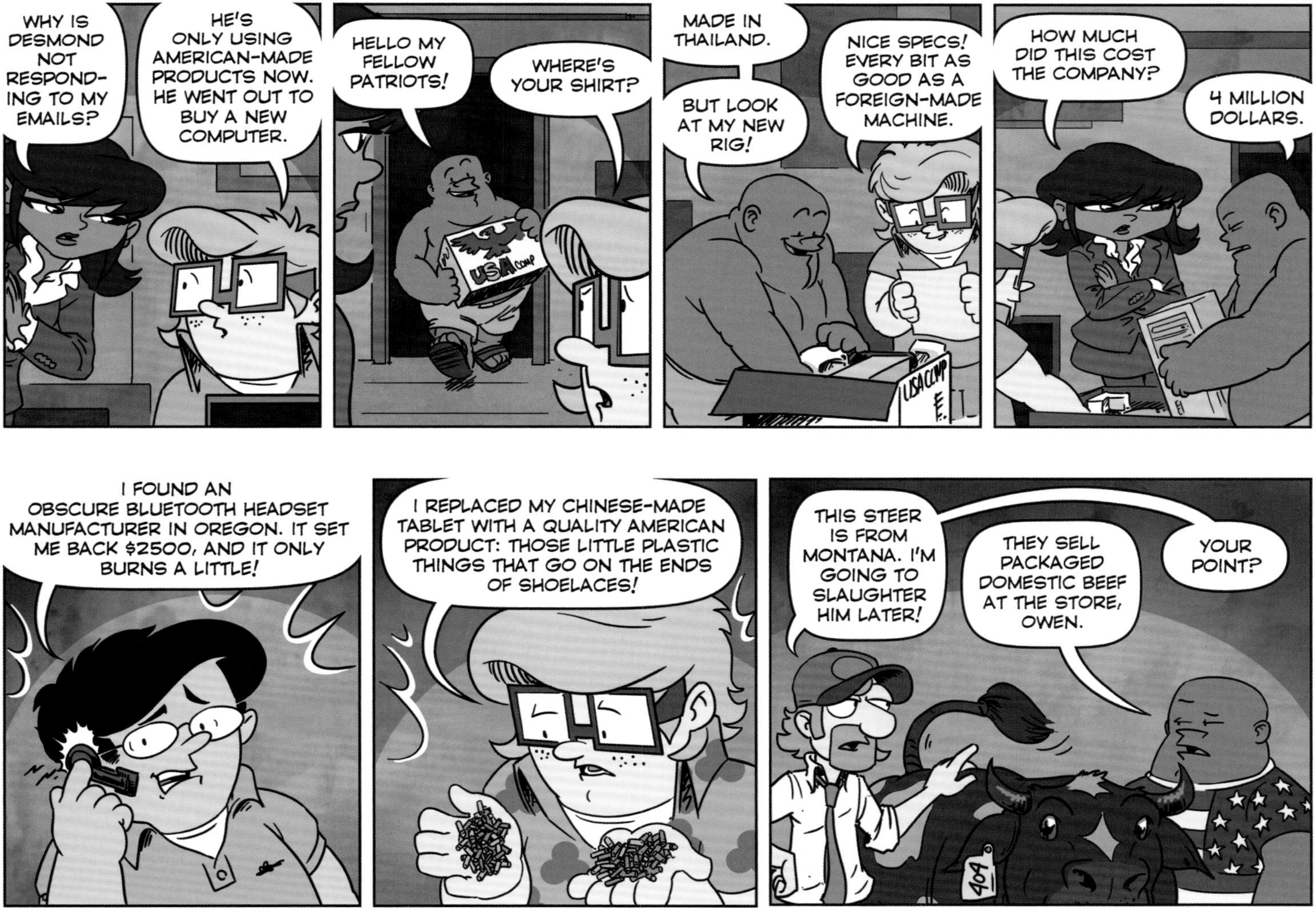
WHY IS DESMOND NOT RESPONDING TO MY EMAILS?
HE'S ONLY USING AMERICAN-MADE PRODUCTS NOW. HE WENT OUT TO BUY A NEW COMPUTER.
HELLO MY FELLOW PATRIOTS!
USA COMP
WHERE'S YOUR SHIRT?
MADE IN THAILAND.
BUT LOOK AT MY NEW RIG!
NICE SPECS! EVERY BIT AS GOOD AS A FOREIGN-MADE MACHINE.
USA COMP
HOW MUCH DID THIS COST THE COMPANY?
4 MILLION DOLLARS.
I FOUND AN OBSCURE BLUETOOTH HEADSET MANUFACTURER IN OREGON. IT SET ME BACK $2500, AND IT ONLY BURNS A LITTLE!
I REPLACED MY CHINESE-MADE TABLET WITH A QUALITY AMERICAN PRODUCT: THOSE LITTLE PLASTIC THINGS THAT GO ON THE ENDS OF SHOELACES!
THIS STEER IS FROM MONTANA. I'M GOING TO SLAUGHTER HIM LATER!
THEY SELL PACKAGED DOMESTIC BEEF AT THE STORE, OWEN.
YOUR POINT?
404

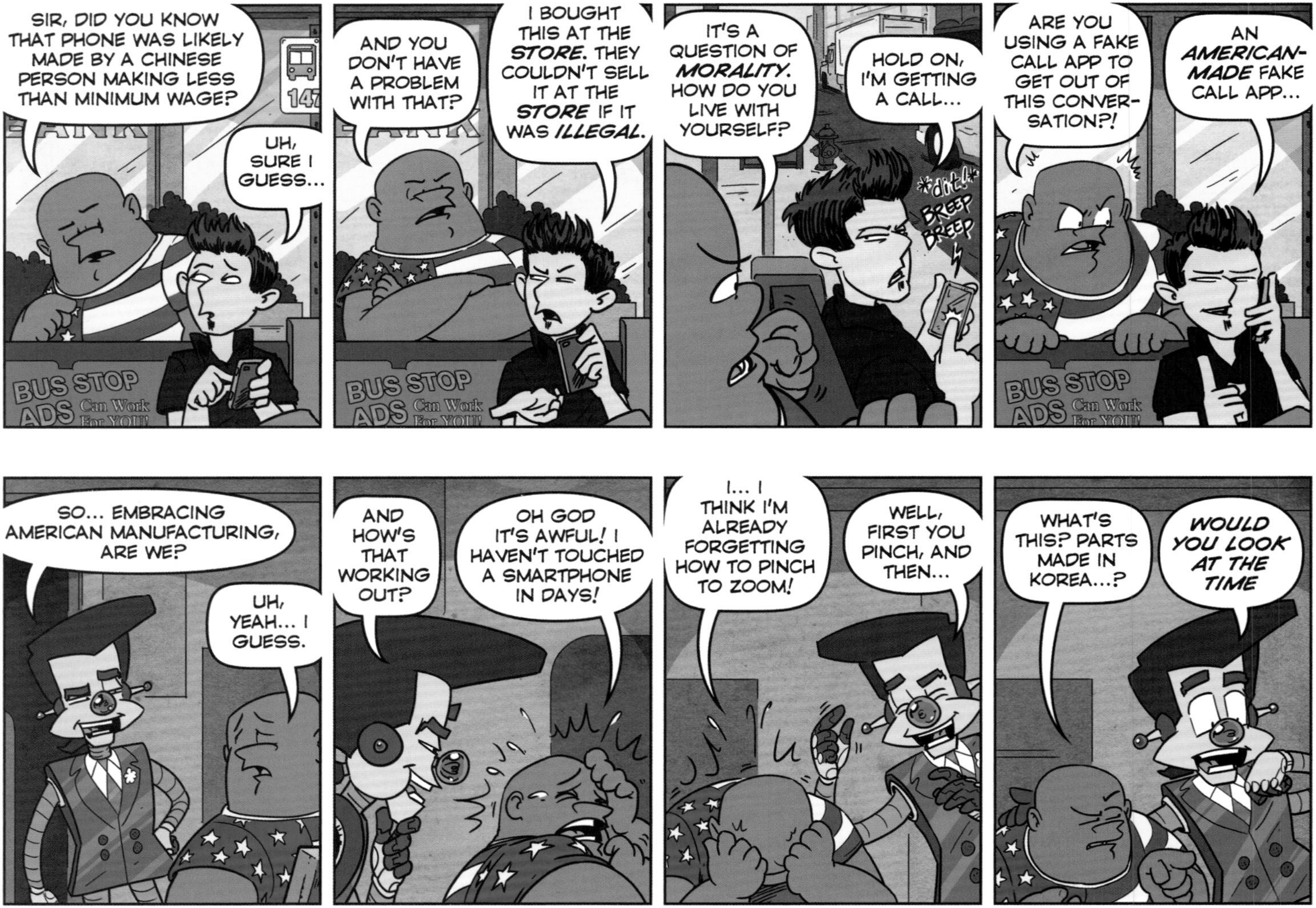
SIR, DID YOU KNOW THAT PHONE WAS LIKELY MADE BY A CHINESE PERSON MAKING LESS THAN MINIMUM WAGE?
UH, SURE I GUESS...
AND YOU DON'T HAVE A PROBLEM WITH THAT?
I BOUGHT THIS AT THE *STORE*. THEY COULDN'T SELL IT AT THE *STORE* IF IT WAS *ILLEGAL*.
IT'S A QUESTION OF *MORALITY*. HOW DO YOU LIVE WITH YOURSELF?
HOLD ON, I'M GETTING A CALL...
BREEP BREEP
ARE YOU USING A FAKE CALL APP TO GET OUT OF THIS CONVERSATION?!
AN *AMERICAN-MADE* FAKE CALL APP...
BUS STOP ADS Can Work For YOU!
SO... EMBRACING AMERICAN MANUFACTURING, ARE WE?
UH, YEAH... I GUESS.
AND HOW'S THAT WORKING OUT?
OH GOD IT'S AWFUL! I HAVEN'T TOUCHED A SMARTPHONE IN DAYS!
I... I THINK I'M ALREADY FORGETTING HOW TO PINCH TO ZOOM!
WELL, FIRST YOU PINCH, AND THEN...
WHAT'S THIS? PARTS MADE IN KOREA...?
WOULD YOU LOOK AT THE TIME

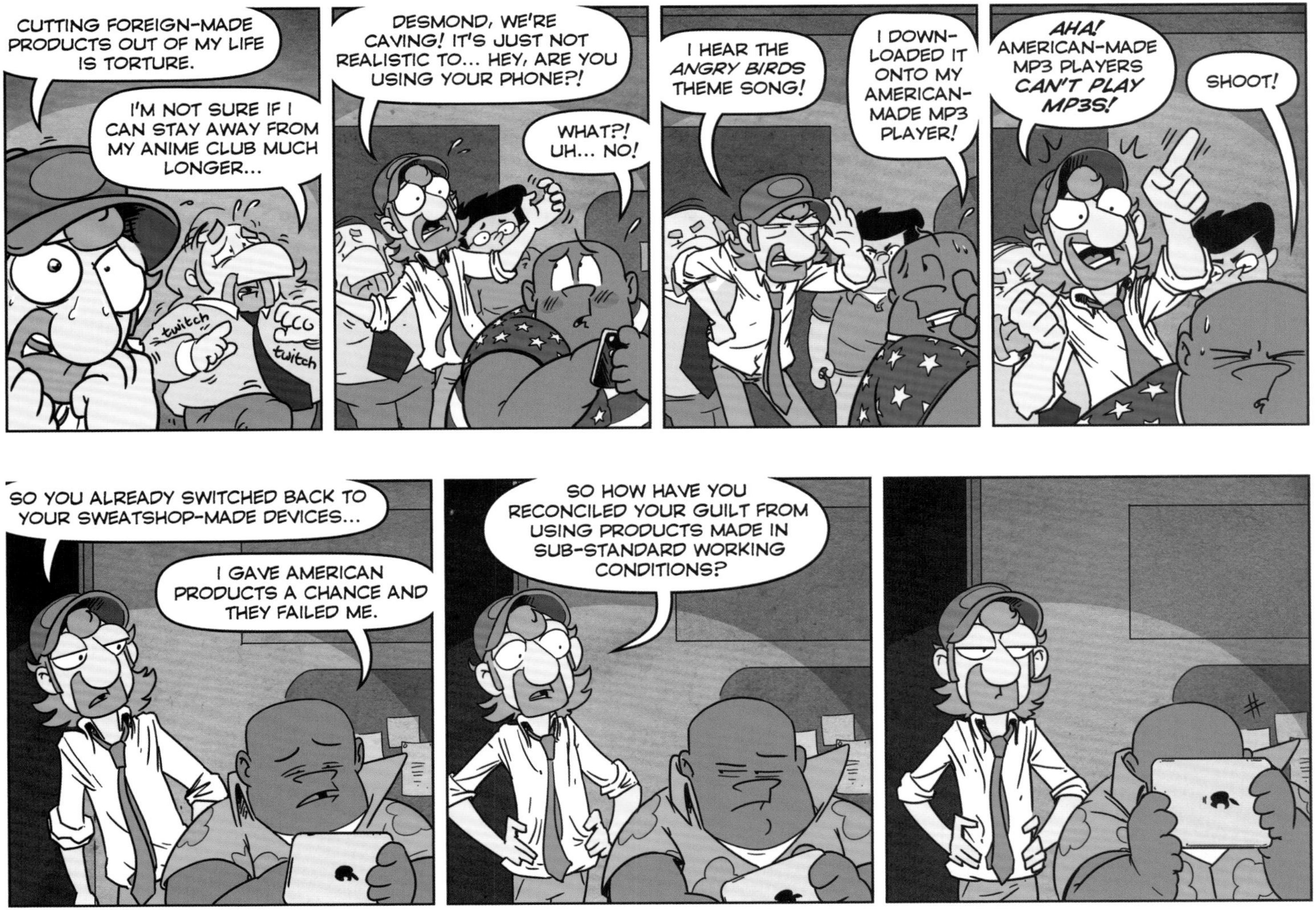
CUTTING FOREIGN-MADE PRODUCTS OUT OF MY LIFE IS TORTURE.
I'M NOT SURE IF I CAN STAY AWAY FROM MY ANIME CLUB MUCH LONGER...
twitch
twitch
DESMOND, WE'RE CAVING! IT'S JUST NOT REALISTIC TO... HEY, ARE YOU USING YOUR PHONE?!
WHAT?! UH... NO!
I HEAR THE ANGRY BIRDS THEME SONG!
I DOWN-LOADED IT ONTO MY AMERICAN-MADE MP3 PLAYER!
AHA! AMERICAN-MADE MP3 PLAYERS CAN'T PLAY MP3S!
SHOOT!
SO YOU ALREADY SWITCHED BACK TO YOUR SWEATSHOP-MADE DEVICES...
I GAVE AMERICAN PRODUCTS A CHANCE AND THEY FAILED ME.
SO HOW HAVE YOU RECONCILED YOUR GUILT FROM USING PRODUCTS MADE IN SUB-STANDARD WORKING CONDITIONS?

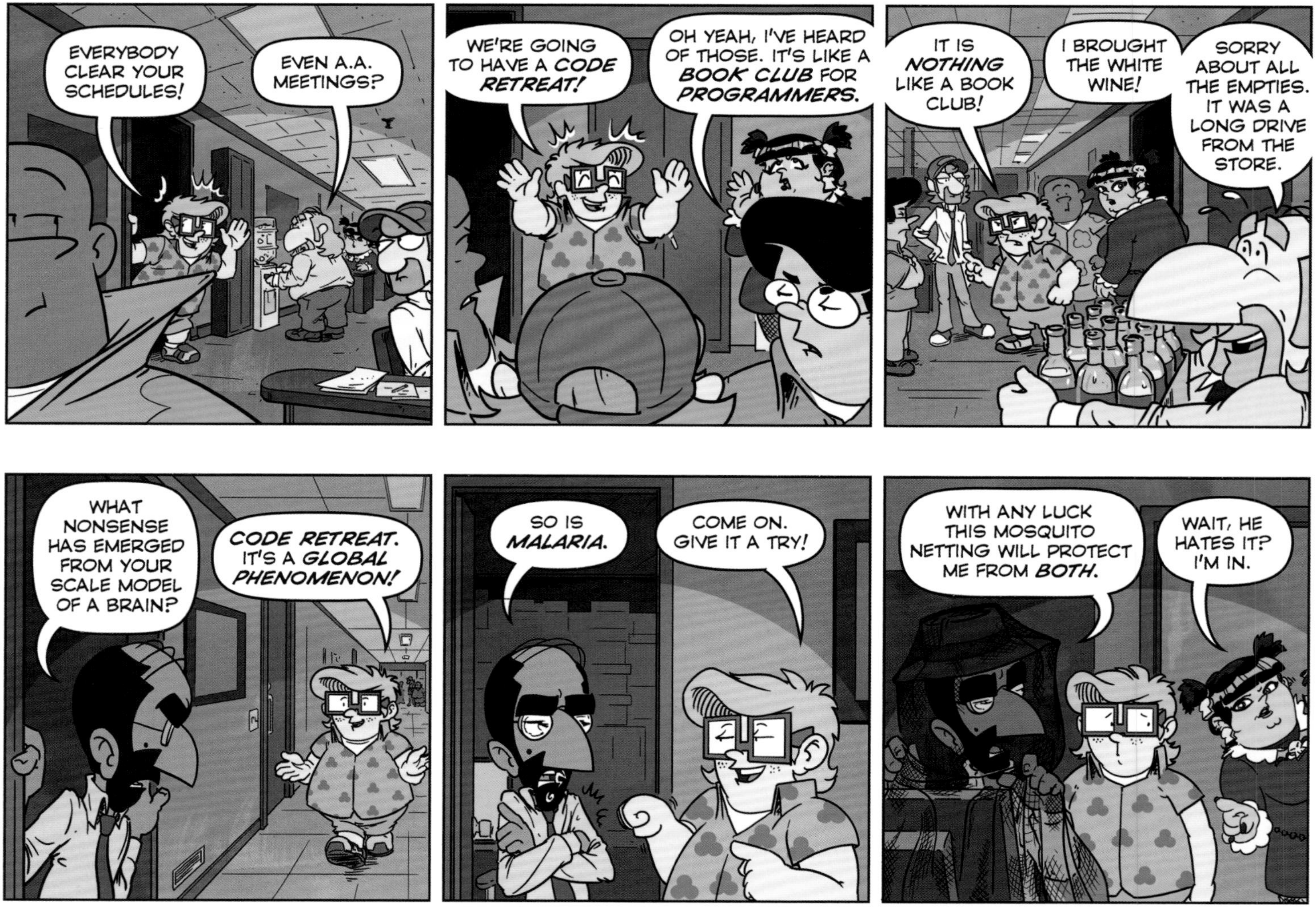
EVERYBODY CLEAR YOUR SCHEDULES!
EVEN A.A. MEETINGS?
WE'RE GOING TO HAVE A CODE RETREAT!
OH YEAH, I'VE HEARD OF THOSE. IT'S LIKE A BOOK CLUB FOR PROGRAMMERS.
IT IS NOTHING LIKE A BOOK CLUB!
I BROUGHT THE WHITE WINE!
SORRY ABOUT ALL THE EMPTIES. IT WAS A LONG DRIVE FROM THE STORE.
WHAT NONSENSE HAS EMERGED FROM YOUR SCALE MODEL OF A BRAIN?
CODE RETREAT. IT'S A GLOBAL PHENOMENON!
SO IS MALARIA.
COME ON. GIVE IT A TRY!
WITH ANY LUCK THIS MOSQUITO NETTING WILL PROTECT ME FROM BOTH.
WAIT, HE HATES IT? I'M IN.

FOR OUR FIRST *CODE RETREAT* EXERCISE WE'RE GOING TO WRITE *SETTLERS OF CATAN* IN *JAVASCRIPT!*

DONE. CAN I GET BACK TO WORK?

WAIT! FIRST YOU NEED TO FIND A PARTNER.

DONE. CAN I GET BACK TO WORK?

WAIT! FIRST YOU NEED TO WRITE TEST CASES.

CAN I --

NO YOU CANNOT GET BACK TO WORK YET.

I'M HONESTLY SURPRISED TO SEE YOU PARTICIPATING IN THIS CODE RETREAT THING, DESMOND. I ALWAYS THINK OF YOU AS BEING STUCK IN YOUR WAYS.

I'M JUST SUPPORTING GEORDI.

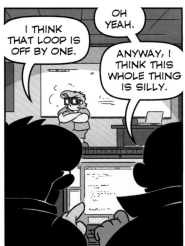

I THINK THAT LOOP IS OFF BY ONE.

OH YEAH.

ANYWAY, I THINK THIS WHOLE THING IS SILLY.

MAYBE BREAK THAT CODE INTO A SUBROUTINE?

GOOD IDEA.

YEAH, SO WHAT A WASTE OF TIME THIS IS, RIGHT?

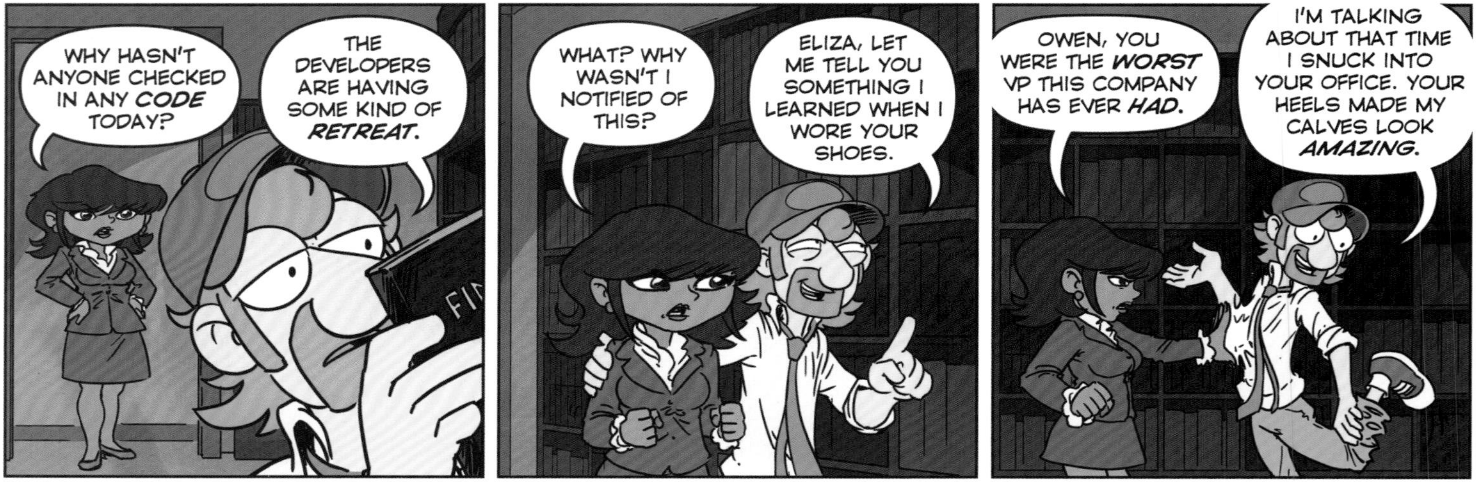
WHY HASN'T ANYONE CHECKED IN ANY CODE TODAY?
THE DEVELOPERS ARE HAVING SOME KIND OF RETREAT.
WHAT? WHY WASN'T I NOTIFIED OF THIS?
ELIZA, LET ME TELL YOU SOMETHING I LEARNED WHEN I WORE YOUR SHOES.
OWEN, YOU WERE THE WORST VP THIS COMPANY HAS EVER HAD.
I'M TALKING ABOUT THAT TIME I SNUCK INTO YOUR OFFICE. YOUR HEELS MADE MY CALVES LOOK AMAZING.

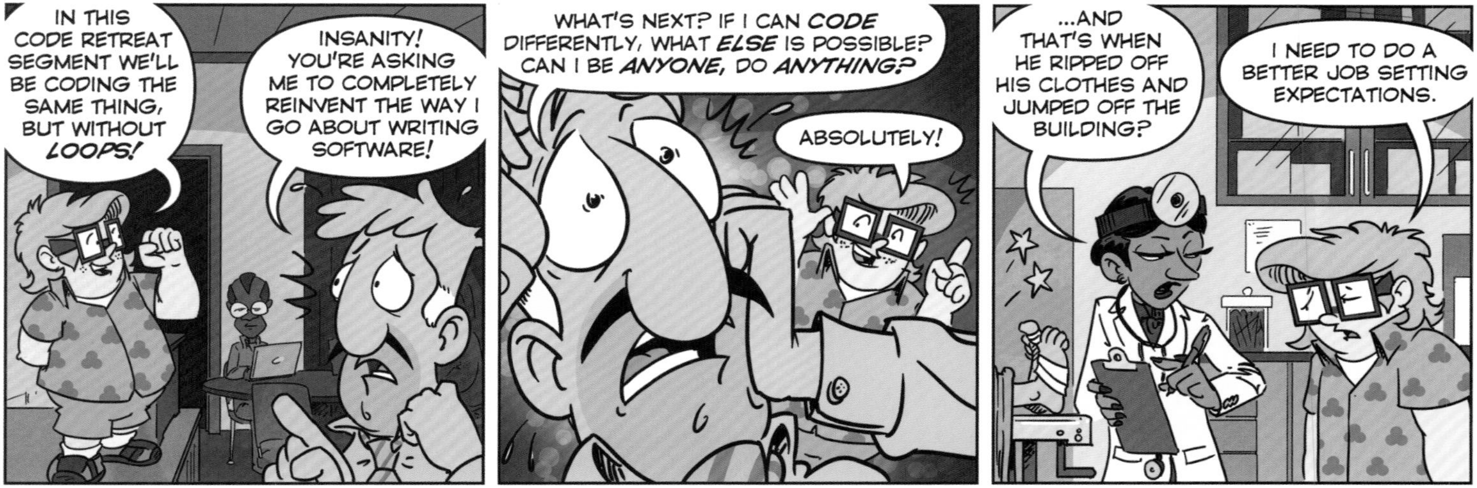
IN THIS CODE RETREAT SEGMENT WE'LL BE CODING THE SAME THING, BUT WITHOUT LOOPS!
INSANITY! YOU'RE ASKING ME TO COMPLETELY REINVENT THE WAY I GO ABOUT WRITING SOFTWARE!
WHAT'S NEXT? IF I CAN CODE DIFFERENTLY, WHAT ELSE IS POSSIBLE? CAN I BE ANYONE, DO ANYTHING?
ABSOLUTELY!
...AND THAT'S WHEN HE RIPPED OFF HIS CLOTHES AND JUMPED OFF THE BUILDING?
I NEED TO DO A BETTER JOB SETTING EXPECTATIONS.

UPGRADE PATH

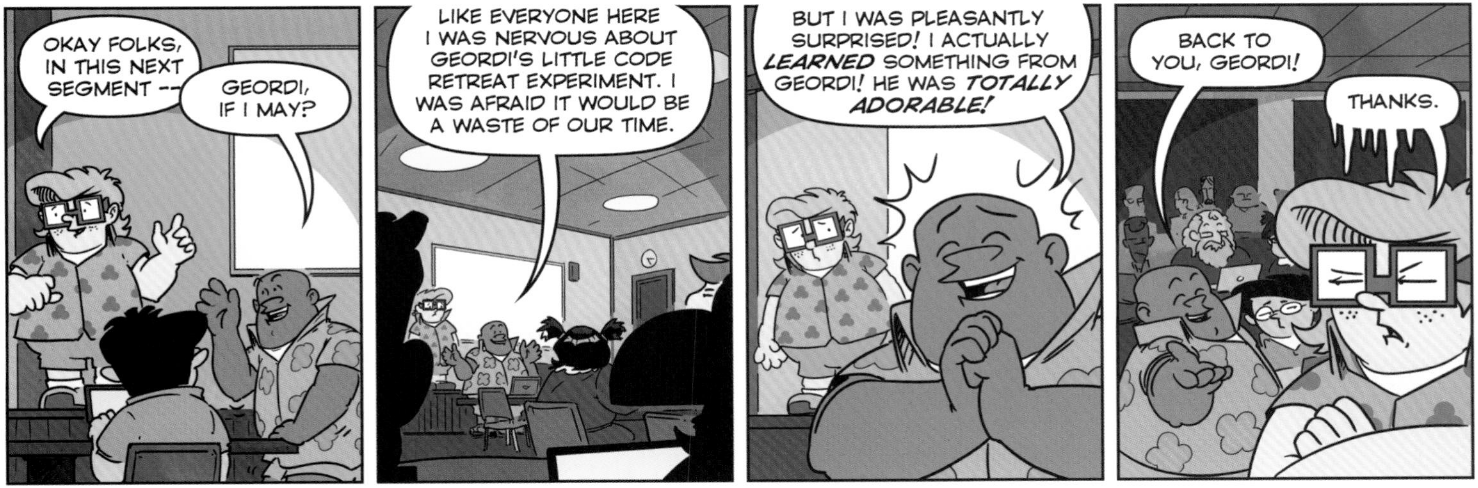
OKAY FOLKS, IN THIS NEXT SEGMENT --
GEORDI, IF I MAY?
LIKE EVERYONE HERE I WAS NERVOUS ABOUT GEORDI'S LITTLE CODE RETREAT EXPERIMENT. I WAS AFRAID IT WOULD BE A WASTE OF OUR TIME.
BUT I WAS PLEASANTLY SURPRISED! I ACTUALLY *LEARNED* SOMETHING FROM GEORDI! HE WAS *TOTALLY ADORABLE!*
BACK TO YOU, GEORDI!
THANKS.

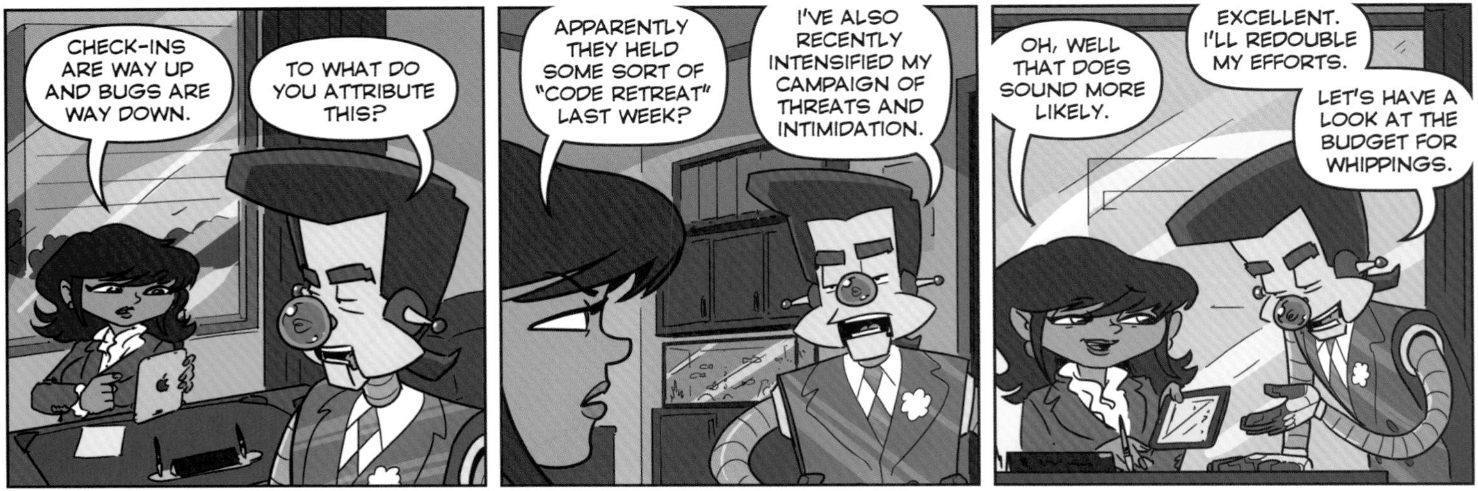
CHECK-INS ARE WAY UP AND BUGS ARE WAY DOWN.
TO WHAT DO YOU ATTRIBUTE THIS?
APPARENTLY THEY HELD SOME SORT OF "CODE RETREAT" LAST WEEK?
I'VE ALSO RECENTLY INTENSIFIED MY CAMPAIGN OF THREATS AND INTIMIDATION.
OH, WELL THAT DOES SOUND MORE LIKELY.
EXCELLENT. I'LL REDOUBLE MY EFFORTS.
LET'S HAVE A LOOK AT THE BUDGET FOR WHIPPINGS.

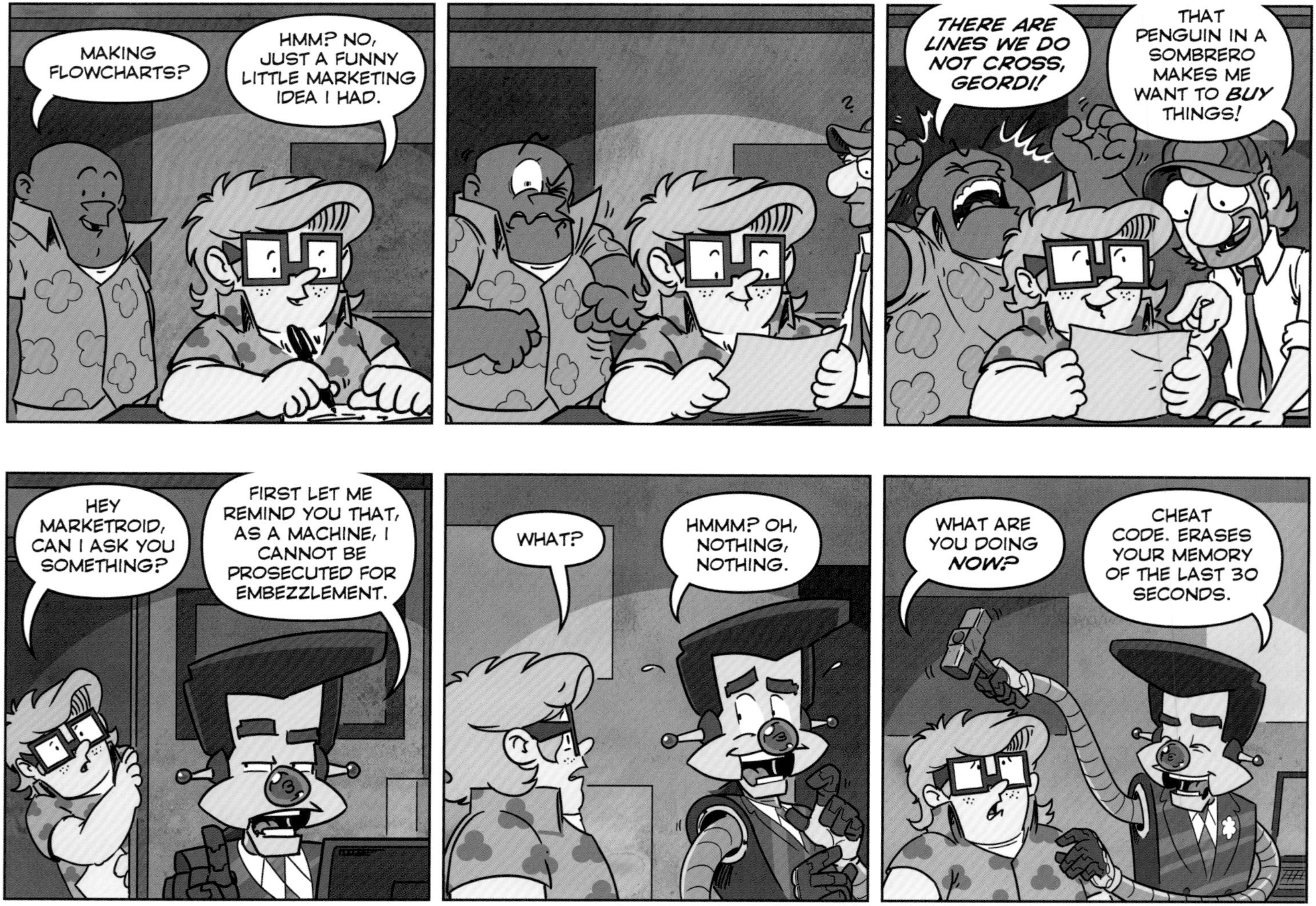
MAKING FLOWCHARTS?
HMM? NO, JUST A FUNNY LITTLE MARKETING IDEA I HAD.
THERE ARE LINES WE DO NOT CROSS, GEORDI!
THAT PENGUIN IN A SOMBRERO MAKES ME WANT TO BUY THINGS!
HEY MARKETROID, CAN I ASK YOU SOMETHING?
FIRST LET ME REMIND YOU THAT, AS A MACHINE, I CANNOT BE PROSECUTED FOR EMBEZZLEMENT.
WHAT?
HMMM? OH, NOTHING, NOTHING.
WHAT ARE YOU DOING NOW?
CHEAT CODE. ERASES YOUR MEMORY OF THE LAST 30 SECONDS.

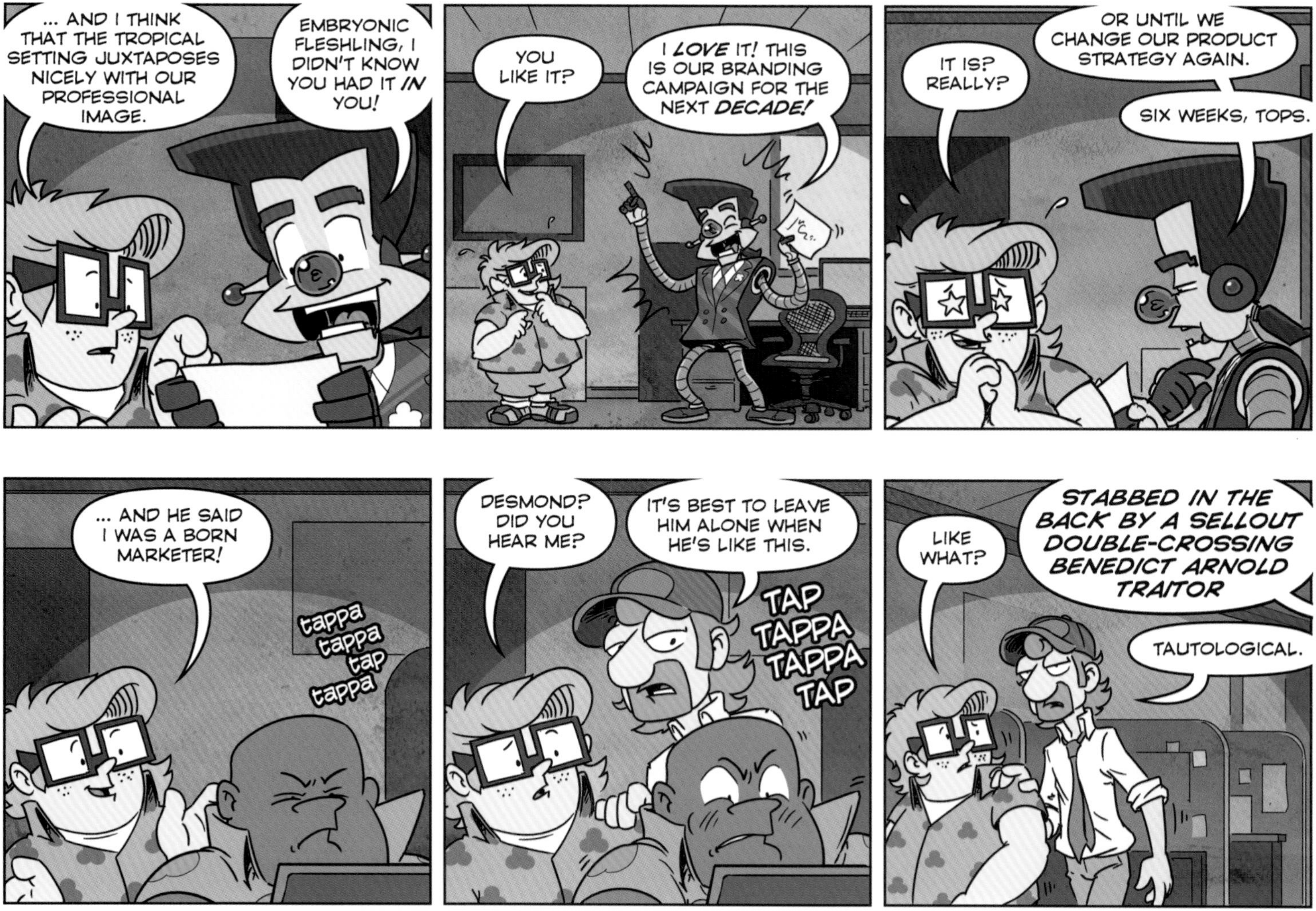
... AND I THINK THAT THE TROPICAL SETTING JUXTAPOSES NICELY WITH OUR PROFESSIONAL IMAGE.
EMBRYONIC FLESHLING, I DIDN'T KNOW YOU HAD IT *IN* YOU!
YOU LIKE IT?
I *LOVE* IT! THIS IS OUR BRANDING CAMPAIGN FOR THE NEXT *DECADE!*
IT IS? REALLY?
OR UNTIL WE CHANGE OUR PRODUCT STRATEGY AGAIN.
SIX WEEKS, TOPS.
... AND HE SAID I WAS A BORN MARKETER!
tappa tappa tap tappa
DESMOND? DID YOU HEAR ME?
IT'S BEST TO LEAVE HIM ALONE WHEN HE'S LIKE THIS.
TAP TAPPA TAPPA TAP
LIKE WHAT?
STABBED IN THE BACK BY A SELLOUT DOUBLE-CROSSING BENEDICT ARNOLD TRAITOR
TAUTOLOGICAL.

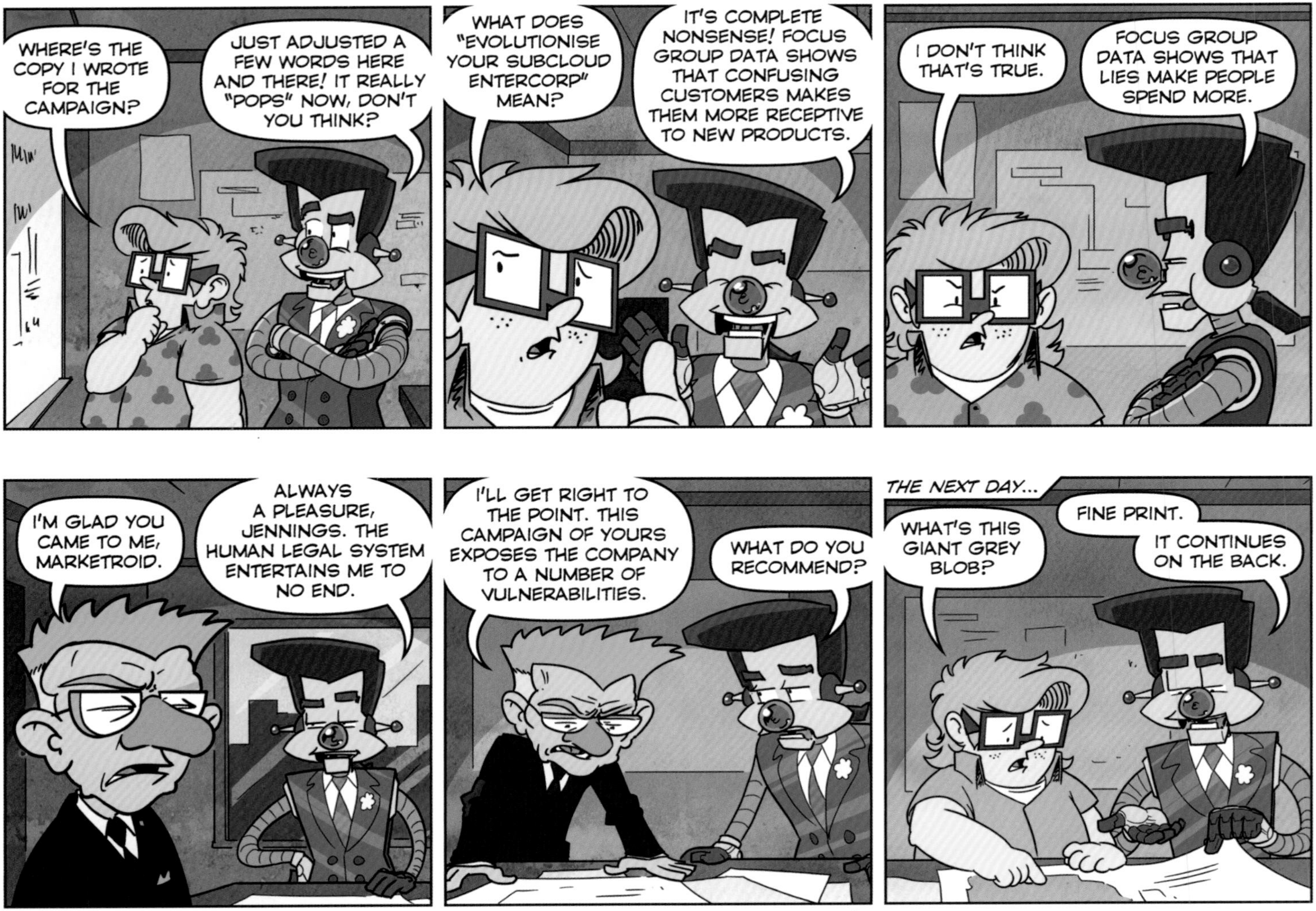
WHERE'S THE COPY I WROTE FOR THE CAMPAIGN?
JUST ADJUSTED A FEW WORDS HERE AND THERE! IT REALLY "POPS" NOW, DON'T YOU THINK?
WHAT DOES "EVOLUTIONISE YOUR SUBCLOUD ENTERCORP" MEAN?
IT'S COMPLETE NONSENSE! FOCUS GROUP DATA SHOWS THAT CONFUSING CUSTOMERS MAKES THEM MORE RECEPTIVE TO NEW PRODUCTS.
I DON'T THINK THAT'S TRUE.
FOCUS GROUP DATA SHOWS THAT LIES MAKE PEOPLE SPEND MORE.
I'M GLAD YOU CAME TO ME, MARKETROID.
ALWAYS A PLEASURE, JENNINGS. THE HUMAN LEGAL SYSTEM ENTERTAINS ME TO NO END.
I'LL GET RIGHT TO THE POINT. THIS CAMPAIGN OF YOURS EXPOSES THE COMPANY TO A NUMBER OF VULNERABILITIES.
WHAT DO YOU RECOMMEND?
THE NEXT DAY...
WHAT'S THIS GIANT GREY BLOB?
FINE PRINT.
IT CONTINUES ON THE BACK.

UPGRADE PATH

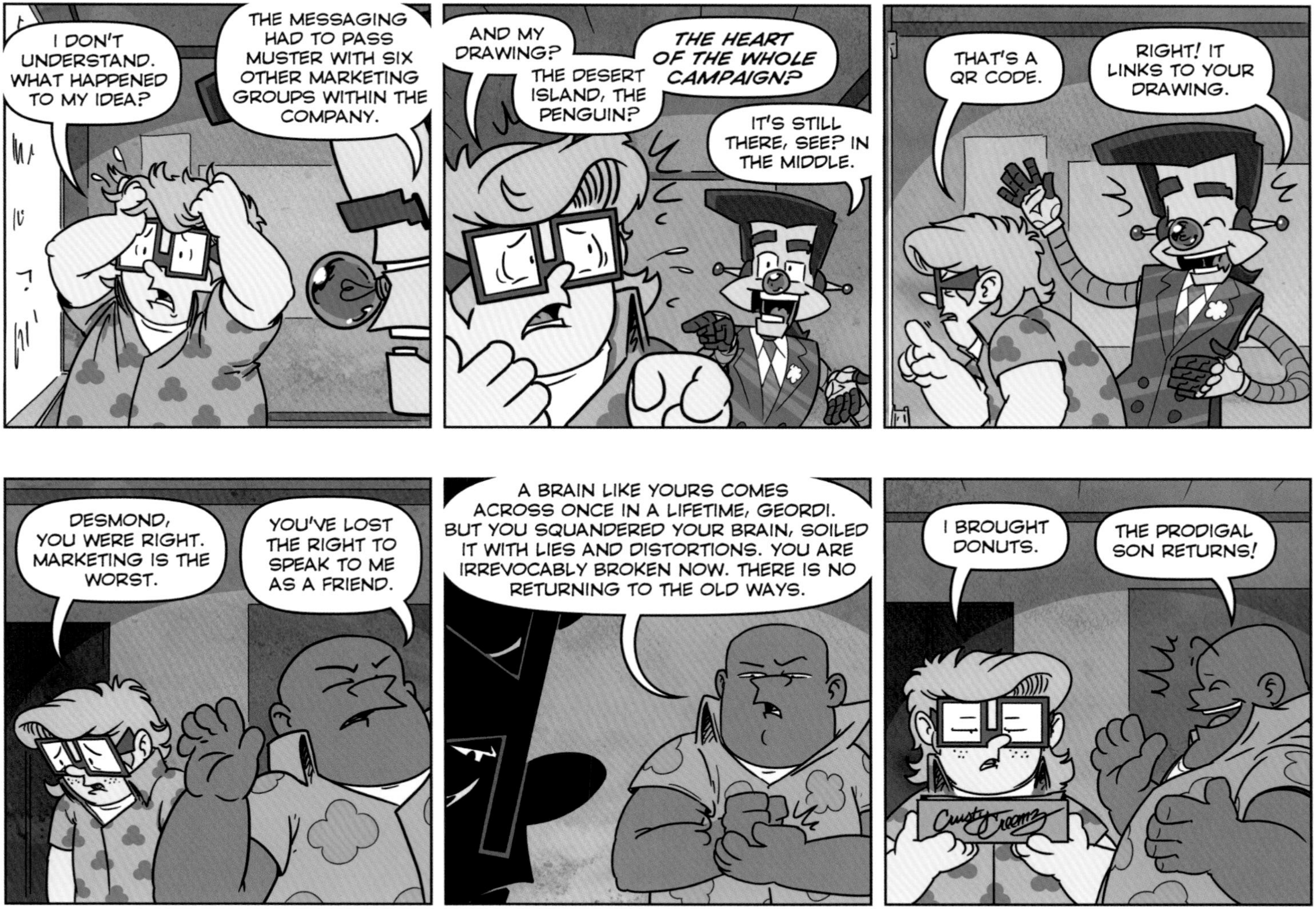
I DON'T UNDERSTAND. WHAT HAPPENED TO MY IDEA?
THE MESSAGING HAD TO PASS MUSTER WITH SIX OTHER MARKETING GROUPS WITHIN THE COMPANY.
AND MY DRAWING?
THE DESERT ISLAND, THE PENGUIN?
THE HEART OF THE WHOLE CAMPAIGN?
IT'S STILL THERE, SEE? IN THE MIDDLE.
THAT'S A QR CODE.
RIGHT! IT LINKS TO YOUR DRAWING.
DESMOND, YOU WERE RIGHT. MARKETING IS THE WORST.
YOU'VE LOST THE RIGHT TO SPEAK TO ME AS A FRIEND.
A BRAIN LIKE YOURS COMES ACROSS ONCE IN A LIFETIME, GEORDI. BUT YOU SQUANDERED YOUR BRAIN, SOILED IT WITH LIES AND DISTORTIONS. YOU ARE IRREVOCABLY BROKEN NOW. THERE IS NO RETURNING TO THE OLD WAYS.
I BROUGHT DONUTS.
THE PRODIGAL SON RETURNS!

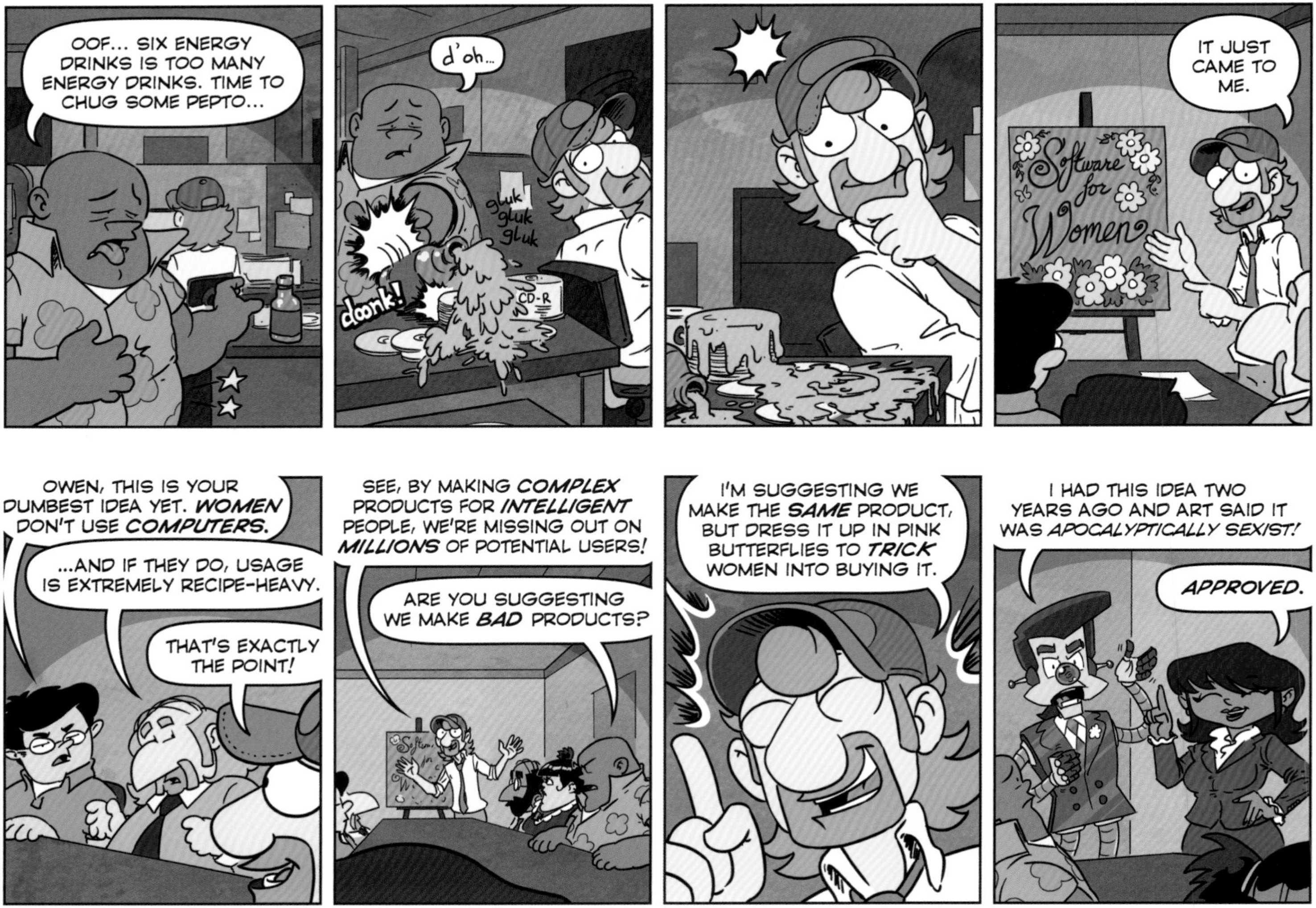
OOF... SIX ENERGY DRINKS IS TOO MANY ENERGY DRINKS. TIME TO CHUG SOME PEPTO...
d'oh...
gluk gluk gluk
doonk!
CD-R
IT JUST CAME TO ME.
Software for Women
OWEN, THIS IS YOUR DUMBEST IDEA YET. WOMEN DON'T USE COMPUTERS.
...AND IF THEY DO, USAGE IS EXTREMELY RECIPE-HEAVY.
THAT'S EXACTLY THE POINT!
SEE, BY MAKING COMPLEX PRODUCTS FOR INTELLIGENT PEOPLE, WE'RE MISSING OUT ON MILLIONS OF POTENTIAL USERS!
ARE YOU SUGGESTING WE MAKE BAD PRODUCTS?
I'M SUGGESTING WE MAKE THE SAME PRODUCT, BUT DRESS IT UP IN PINK BUTTERFLIES TO TRICK WOMEN INTO BUYING IT.
I HAD THIS IDEA TWO YEARS AGO AND ART SAID IT WAS APOCALYPTICALLY SEXIST!
APPROVED.

UPGRADE PATH

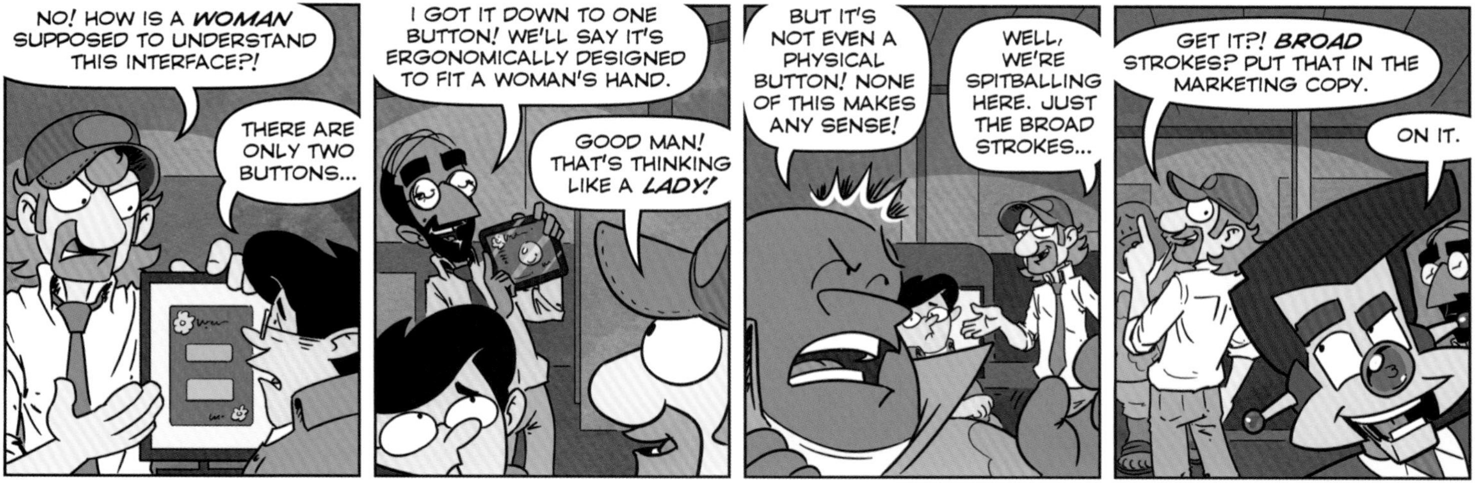
NO! HOW IS A *WOMAN* SUPPOSED TO UNDERSTAND THIS INTERFACE?!
THERE ARE ONLY TWO BUTTONS...
I GOT IT DOWN TO ONE BUTTON! WE'LL SAY IT'S ERGONOMICALLY DESIGNED TO FIT A WOMAN'S HAND.
GOOD MAN! THAT'S THINKING LIKE A *LADY!*
BUT IT'S NOT EVEN A PHYSICAL BUTTON! NONE OF THIS MAKES ANY SENSE!
WELL, WE'RE SPITBALLING HERE. JUST THE BROAD STROKES...
GET IT?! *BROAD* STROKES? PUT THAT IN THE MARKETING COPY.
ON IT.

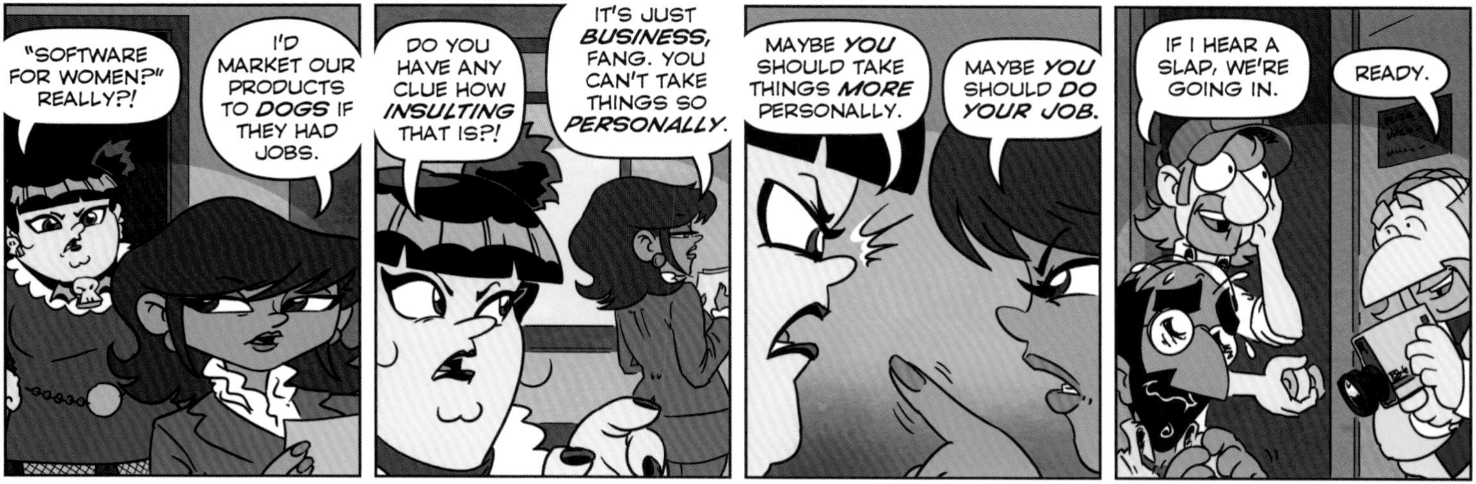
"SOFTWARE FOR WOMEN?" REALLY?!
I'D MARKET OUR PRODUCTS TO *DOGS* IF THEY HAD JOBS.
DO YOU HAVE ANY CLUE HOW *INSULTING* THAT IS?!
IT'S JUST *BUSINESS,* FANG. YOU CAN'T TAKE THINGS SO *PERSONALLY.*
MAYBE *YOU* SHOULD TAKE THINGS *MORE* PERSONALLY.
MAYBE *YOU* SHOULD *DO YOUR JOB.*
IF I HEAR A SLAP, WE'RE GOING IN.
READY.

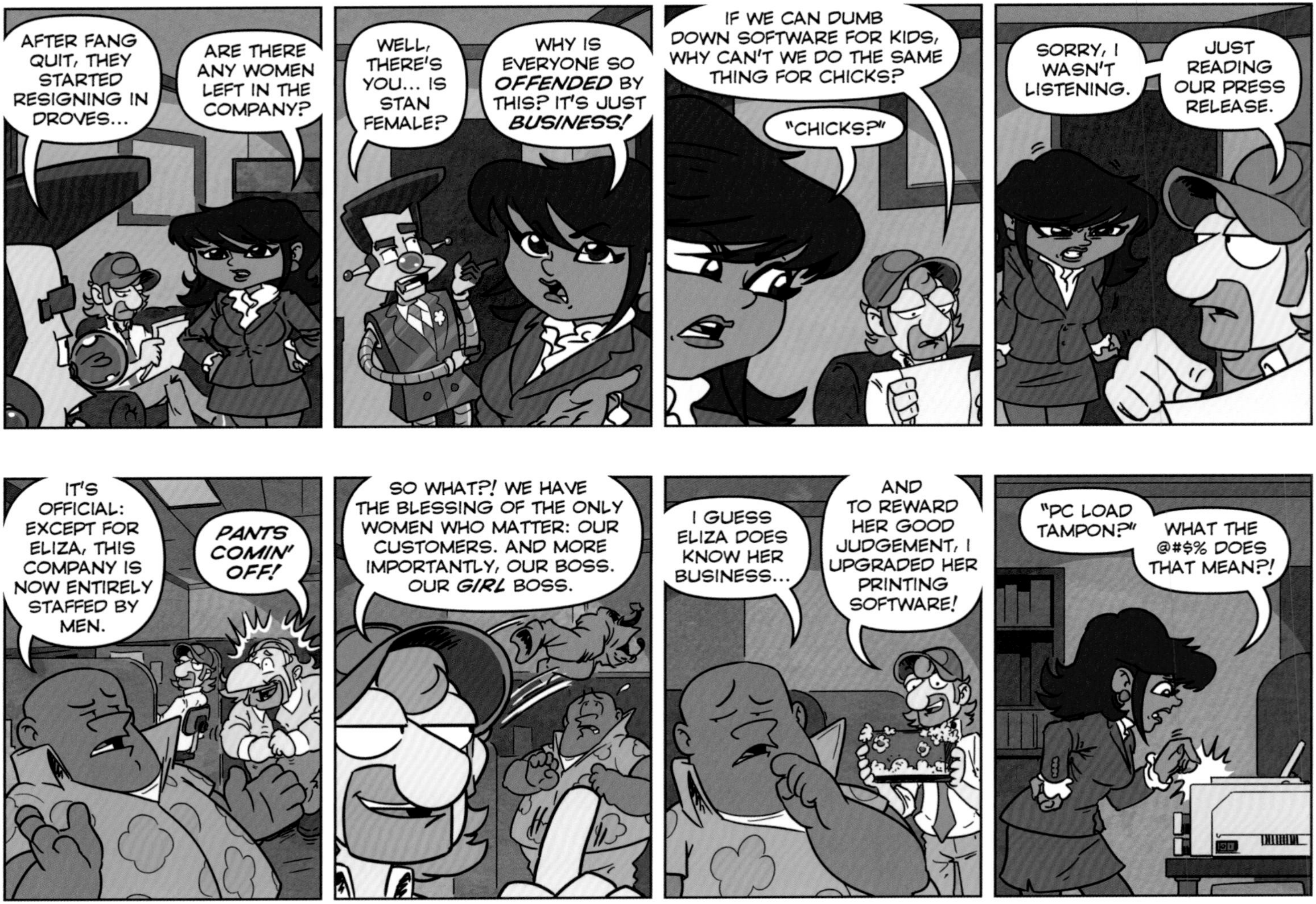
AFTER FANG QUIT, THEY STARTED RESIGNING IN DROVES...
ARE THERE ANY WOMEN LEFT IN THE COMPANY?
WELL, THERE'S YOU... IS STAN FEMALE?
WHY IS EVERYONE SO *OFFENDED* BY THIS? IT'S JUST *BUSINESS!*
IF WE CAN DUMB DOWN SOFTWARE FOR KIDS, WHY CAN'T WE DO THE SAME THING FOR CHICKS?
"CHICKS?"
SORRY, I WASN'T LISTENING.
JUST READING OUR PRESS RELEASE.
IT'S OFFICIAL: EXCEPT FOR ELIZA, THIS COMPANY IS NOW ENTIRELY STAFFED BY MEN.
PANTS COMIN' OFF!
SO WHAT?! WE HAVE THE BLESSING OF THE ONLY WOMEN WHO MATTER: OUR CUSTOMERS. AND MORE IMPORTANTLY, OUR BOSS. OUR *GIRL* BOSS.
I GUESS ELIZA DOES KNOW HER BUSINESS...
AND TO REWARD HER GOOD JUDGEMENT, I UPGRADED HER PRINTING SOFTWARE!
"PC LOAD TAMPON?"
WHAT THE @#$% DOES THAT MEAN?!

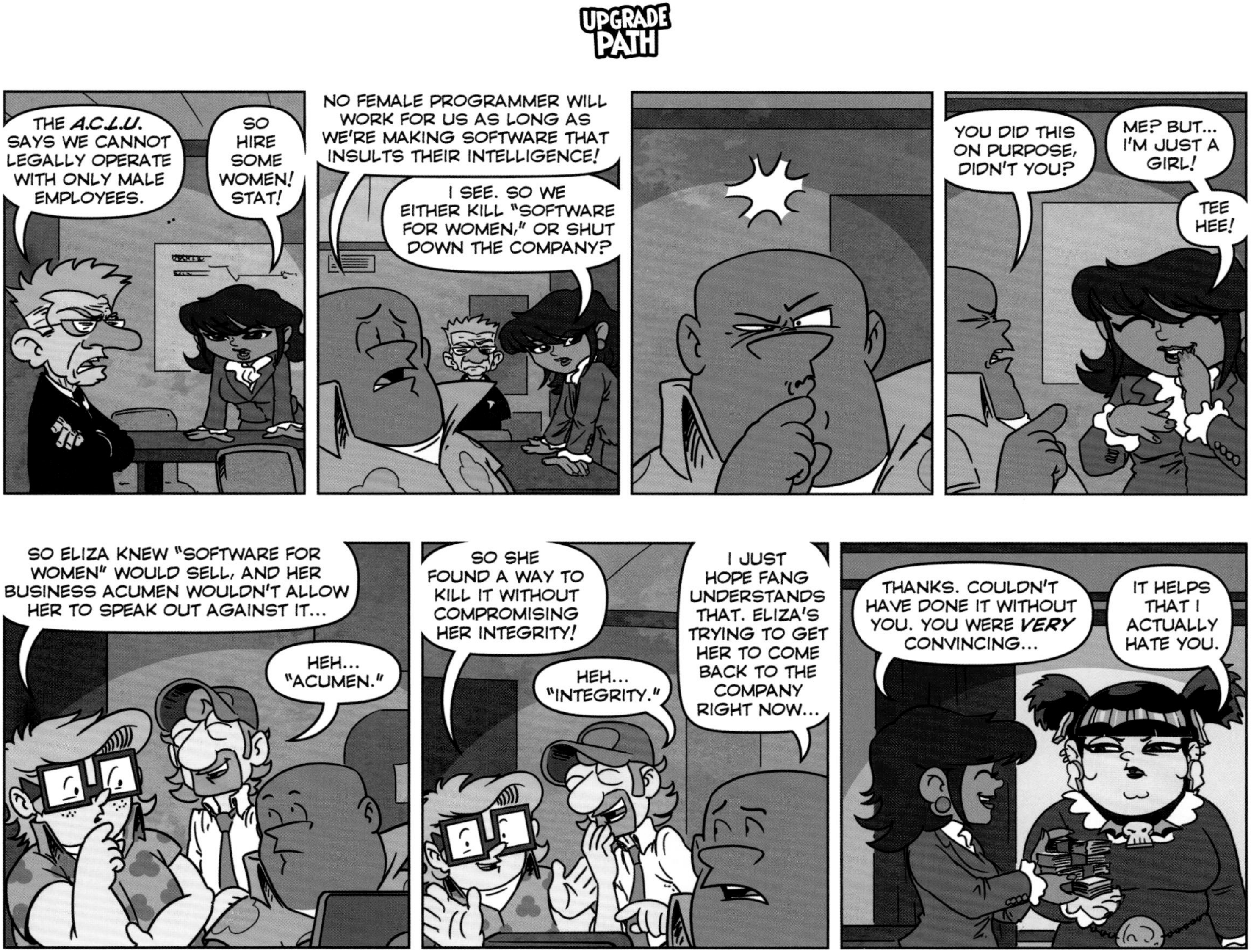
UPGRADE PATH
THE A.C.L.U. SAYS WE CANNOT LEGALLY OPERATE WITH ONLY MALE EMPLOYEES.
SO HIRE SOME WOMEN! STAT!
NO FEMALE PROGRAMMER WILL WORK FOR US AS LONG AS WE'RE MAKING SOFTWARE THAT INSULTS THEIR INTELLIGENCE!
I SEE. SO WE EITHER KILL "SOFTWARE FOR WOMEN," OR SHUT DOWN THE COMPANY?
YOU DID THIS ON PURPOSE, DIDN'T YOU?
ME? BUT... I'M JUST A GIRL!
TEE HEE!
SO ELIZA KNEW "SOFTWARE FOR WOMEN" WOULD SELL, AND HER BUSINESS ACUMEN WOULDN'T ALLOW HER TO SPEAK OUT AGAINST IT...
HEH... "ACUMEN."
SO SHE FOUND A WAY TO KILL IT WITHOUT COMPROMISING HER INTEGRITY!
HEH... "INTEGRITY."
I JUST HOPE FANG UNDERSTANDS THAT. ELIZA'S TRYING TO GET HER TO COME BACK TO THE COMPANY RIGHT NOW...
THANKS. COULDN'T HAVE DONE IT WITHOUT YOU. YOU WERE VERY CONVINCING...
IT HELPS THAT I ACTUALLY HATE YOU.

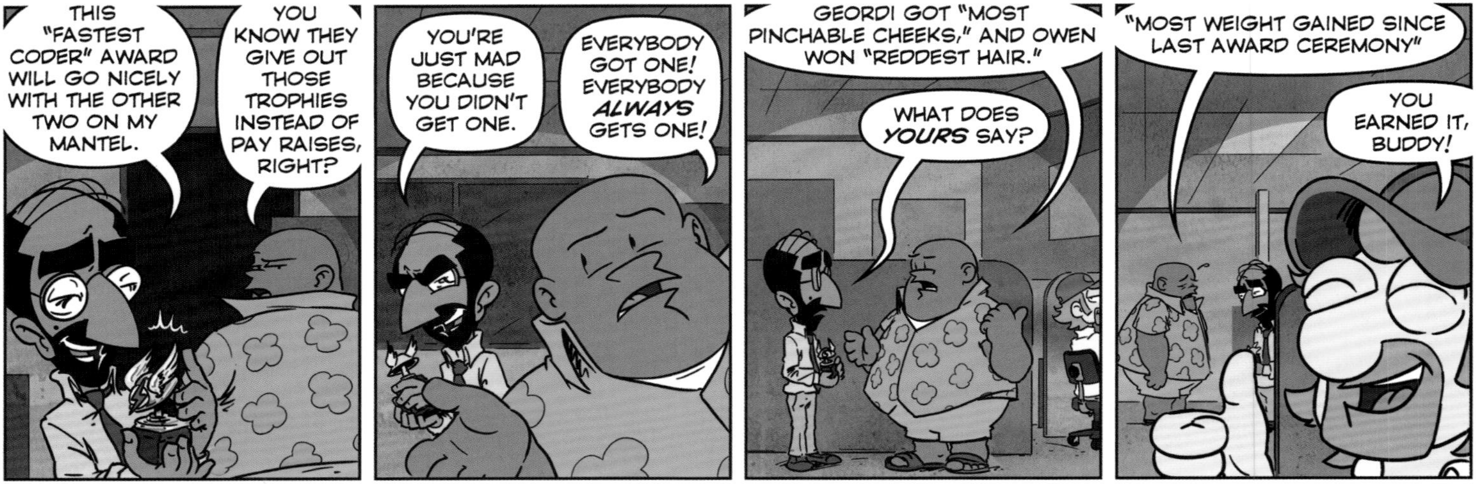
THIS "FASTEST CODER" AWARD WILL GO NICELY WITH THE OTHER TWO ON MY MANTEL.
YOU KNOW THEY GIVE OUT THOSE TROPHIES INSTEAD OF PAY RAISES, RIGHT?
YOU'RE JUST MAD BECAUSE YOU DIDN'T GET ONE.
EVERYBODY GOT ONE! EVERYBODY *ALWAYS* GETS ONE!
GEORDI GOT "MOST PINCHABLE CHEEKS," AND OWEN WON "REDDEST HAIR."
WHAT DOES *YOURS* SAY?
"MOST WEIGHT GAINED SINCE LAST AWARD CEREMONY"
YOU EARNED IT, BUDDY!

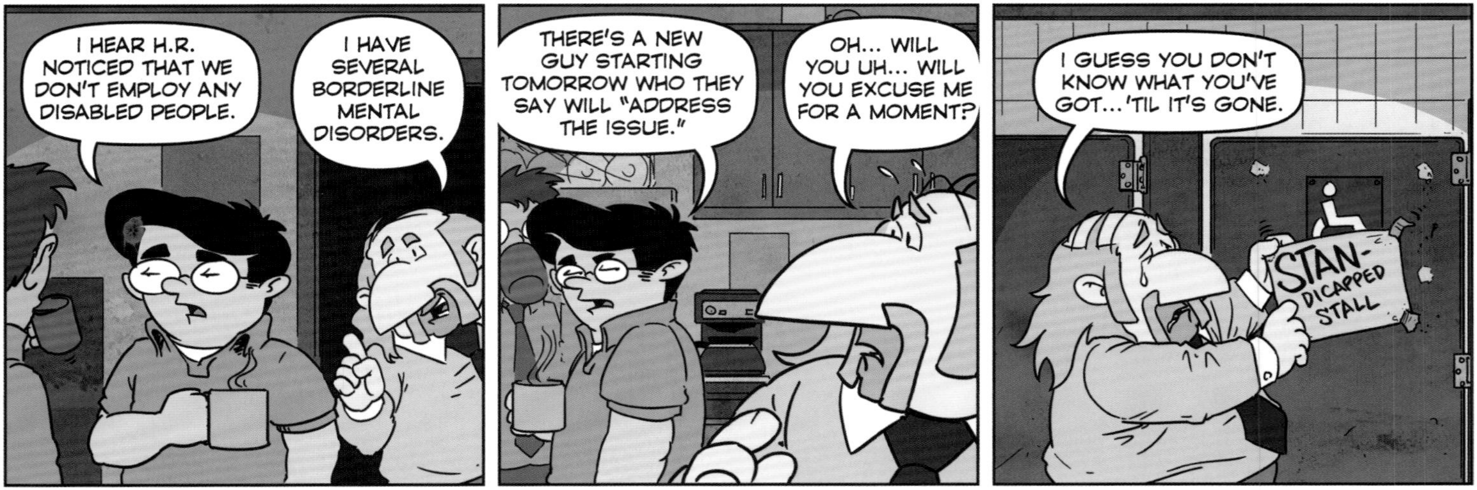
I HEAR H.R. NOTICED THAT WE DON'T EMPLOY ANY DISABLED PEOPLE.
I HAVE SEVERAL BORDERLINE MENTAL DISORDERS.
THERE'S A NEW GUY STARTING TOMORROW WHO THEY SAY WILL "ADDRESS THE ISSUE."
OH... WILL YOU UH... WILL YOU EXCUSE ME FOR A MOMENT?
I GUESS YOU DON'T KNOW WHAT YOU'VE GOT...'TIL IT'S GONE.
STAN-DICAPPED STALL

UPGRADE PATH

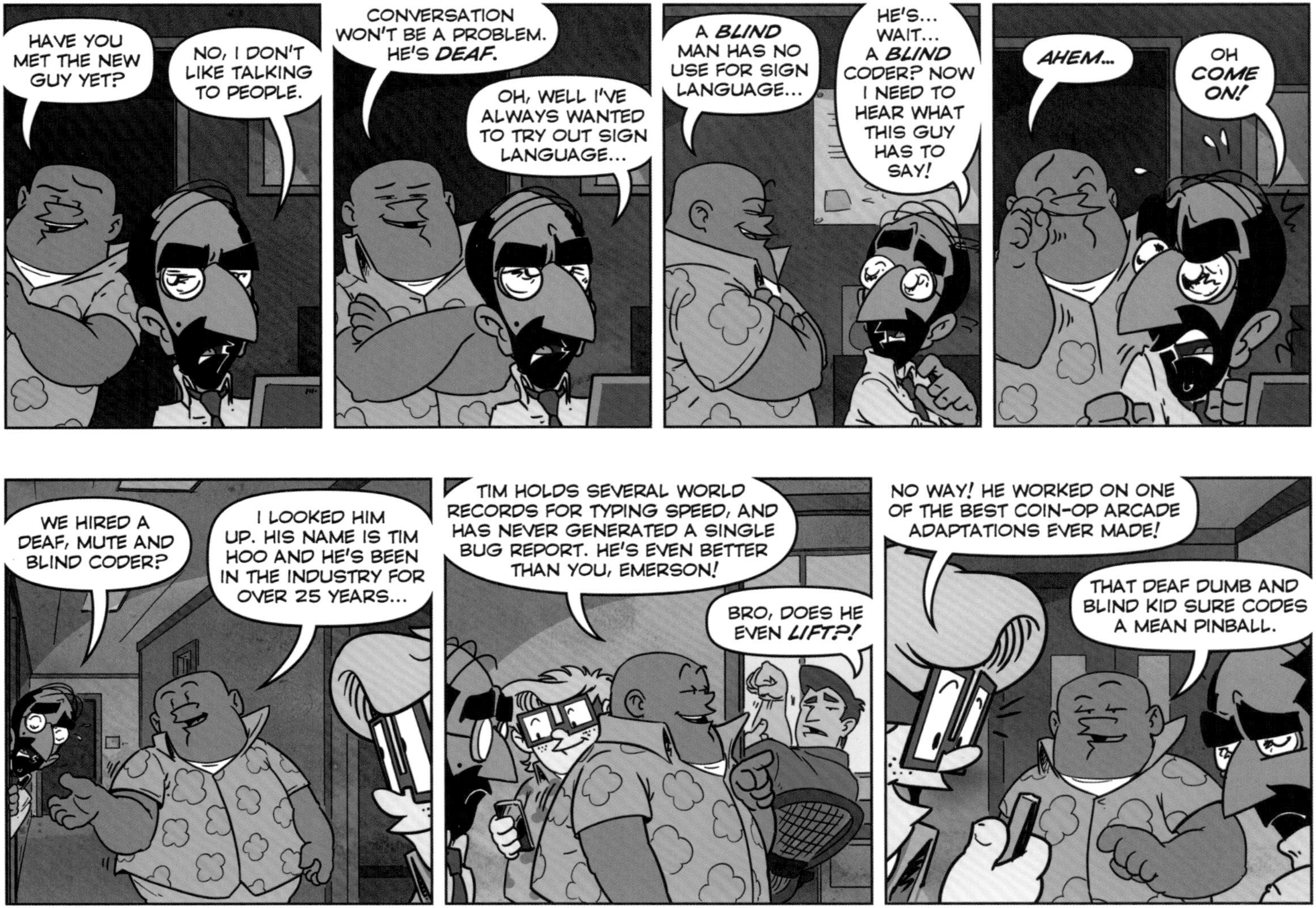
HAVE YOU MET THE NEW GUY YET?
NO, I DON'T LIKE TALKING TO PEOPLE.
CONVERSATION WON'T BE A PROBLEM. HE'S *DEAF*.
OH, WELL I'VE ALWAYS WANTED TO TRY OUT SIGN LANGUAGE...
A *BLIND* MAN HAS NO USE FOR SIGN LANGUAGE...
HE'S... WAIT... A *BLIND* CODER? NOW I NEED TO HEAR WHAT THIS GUY HAS TO SAY!
AHEM...
OH *COME ON!*
WE HIRED A DEAF, MUTE AND BLIND CODER?
I LOOKED HIM UP. HIS NAME IS TIM HOO AND HE'S BEEN IN THE INDUSTRY FOR OVER 25 YEARS...
TIM HOLDS SEVERAL WORLD RECORDS FOR TYPING SPEED, AND HAS NEVER GENERATED A SINGLE BUG REPORT. HE'S EVEN BETTER THAN YOU, EMERSON!
BRO, DOES HE EVEN *LIFT?!*
NO WAY! HE WORKED ON ONE OF THE BEST COIN-OP ARCADE ADAPTATIONS EVER MADE!
THAT DEAF DUMB AND BLIND KID SURE CODES A MEAN PINBALL.

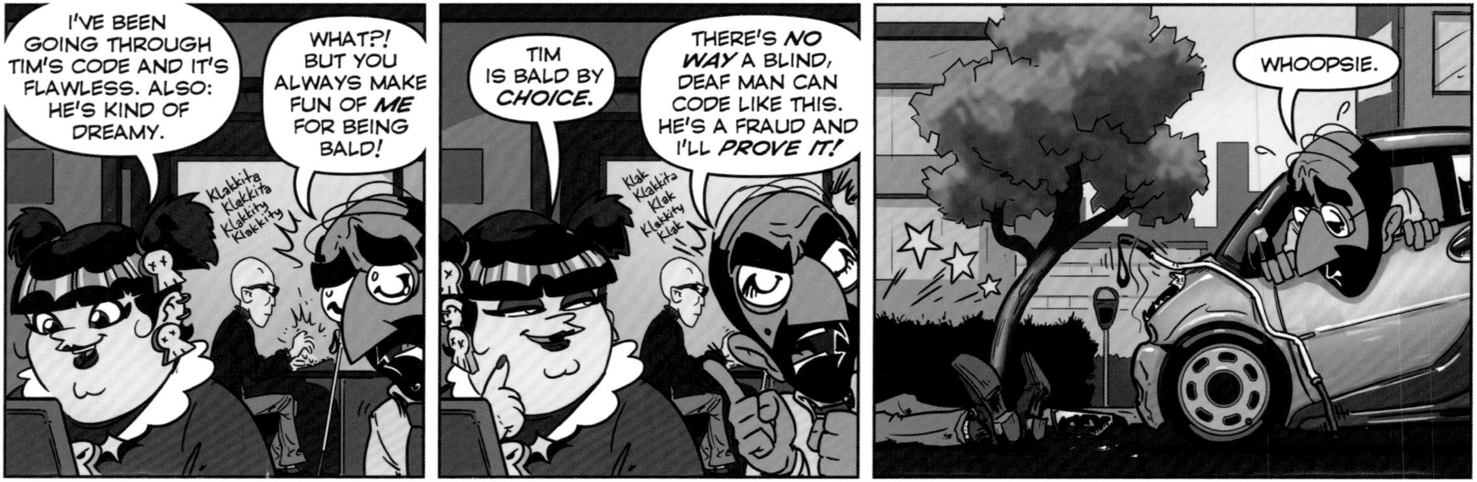
I'VE BEEN GOING THROUGH TIM'S CODE AND IT'S FLAWLESS. ALSO: HE'S KIND OF DREAMY.
WHAT?! BUT YOU ALWAYS MAKE FUN OF ME FOR BEING BALD!
Klakkita Klakkita Klakkity Klakkity
TIM IS BALD BY CHOICE.
THERE'S NO WAY A BLIND, DEAF MAN CAN CODE LIKE THIS. HE'S A FRAUD AND I'LL PROVE IT!
Klak Klakkita Klak Klakkity Klak
WHOOPSIE.

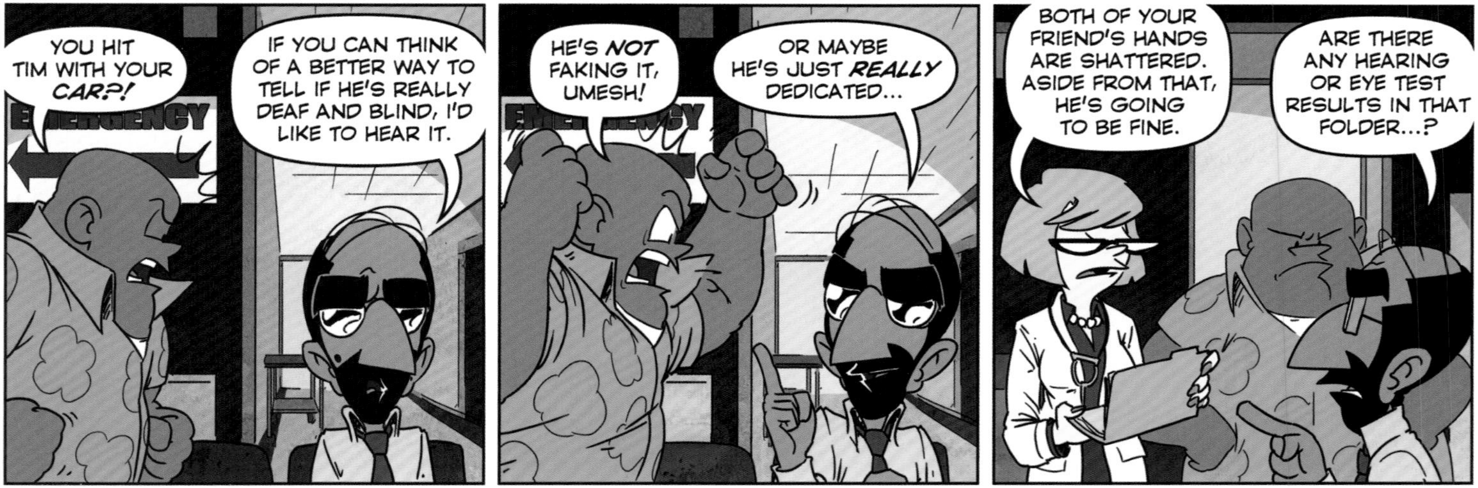
YOU HIT TIM WITH YOUR CAR?!
EMERGENCY
IF YOU CAN THINK OF A BETTER WAY TO TELL IF HE'S REALLY DEAF AND BLIND, I'D LIKE TO HEAR IT.
HE'S NOT FAKING IT, UMESH!
OR MAYBE HE'S JUST REALLY DEDICATED...
BOTH OF YOUR FRIEND'S HANDS ARE SHATTERED. ASIDE FROM THAT, HE'S GOING TO BE FINE.
ARE THERE ANY HEARING OR EYE TEST RESULTS IN THAT FOLDER...?

UPGRADE PATH

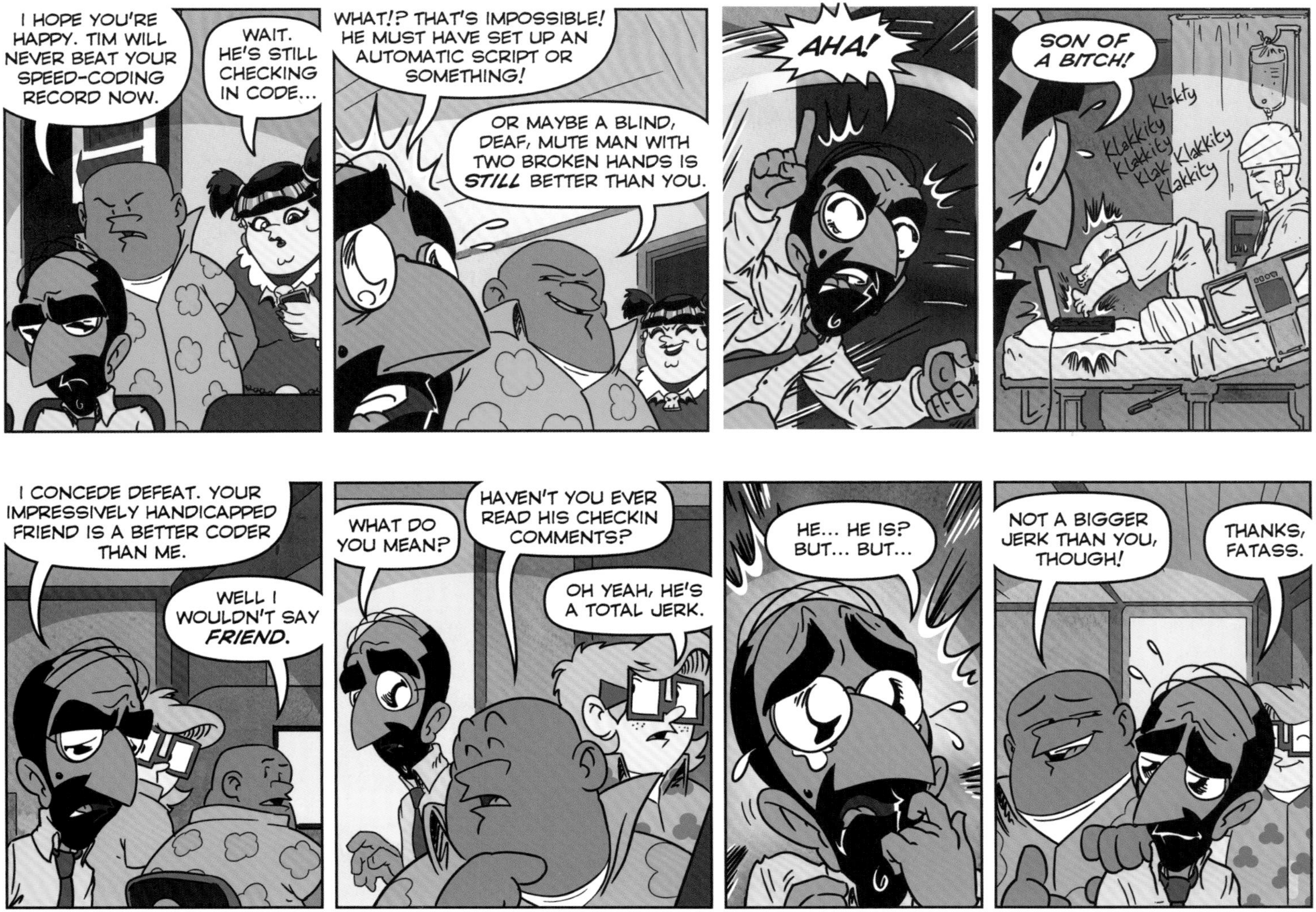
I HOPE YOU'RE HAPPY. TIM WILL NEVER BEAT YOUR SPEED-CODING RECORD NOW.
WAIT. HE'S STILL CHECKING IN CODE...
WHAT!? THAT'S IMPOSSIBLE! HE MUST HAVE SET UP AN AUTOMATIC SCRIPT OR SOMETHING!
OR MAYBE A BLIND, DEAF, MUTE MAN WITH TWO BROKEN HANDS IS STILL BETTER THAN YOU.
AHA!
SON OF A BITCH!
Klakty
Klakkity Klakkity Klak Klakkity Klakkity Klakkity
I CONCEDE DEFEAT. YOUR IMPRESSIVELY HANDICAPPED FRIEND IS A BETTER CODER THAN ME.
WELL I WOULDN'T SAY FRIEND.
WHAT DO YOU MEAN?
HAVEN'T YOU EVER READ HIS CHECKIN COMMENTS?
OH YEAH, HE'S A TOTAL JERK.
HE... HE IS? BUT... BUT...
NOT A BIGGER JERK THAN YOU, THOUGH!
THANKS, FATASS.

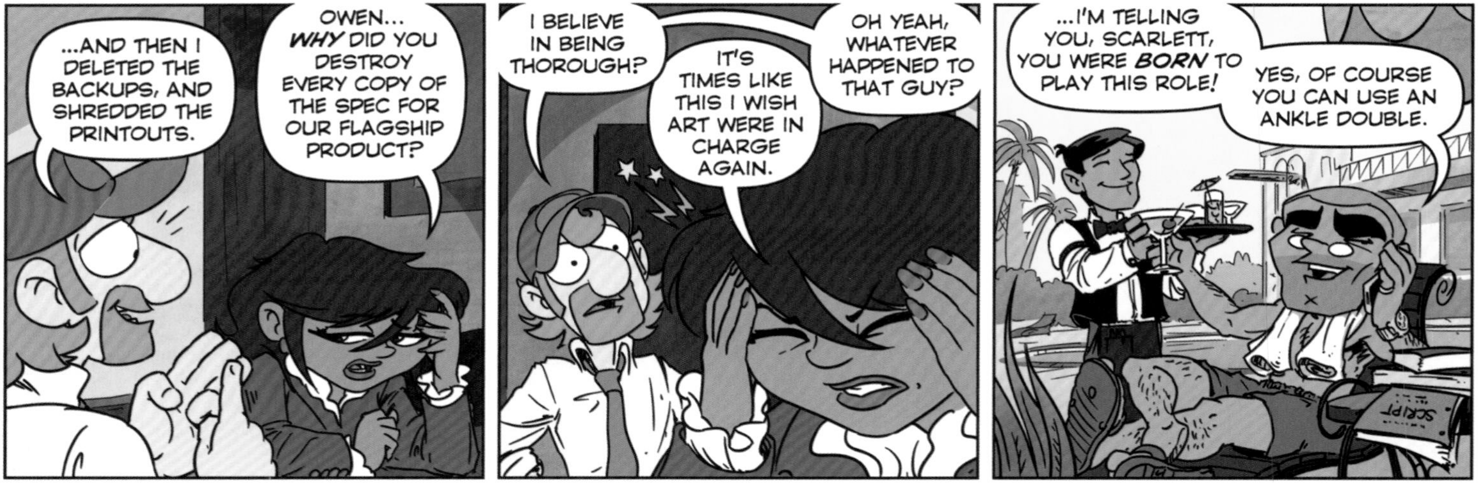
...AND THEN I DELETED THE BACKUPS, AND SHREDDED THE PRINTOUTS.
OWEN... *WHY* DID YOU DESTROY EVERY COPY OF THE SPEC FOR OUR FLAGSHIP PRODUCT?
I BELIEVE IN BEING THOROUGH?
IT'S TIMES LIKE THIS I WISH ART WERE IN CHARGE AGAIN.
OH YEAH, WHATEVER HAPPENED TO THAT GUY?
...I'M TELLING YOU, SCARLETT, YOU WERE *BORN* TO PLAY THIS ROLE!
YES, OF COURSE YOU CAN USE AN ANKLE DOUBLE.
SCRIPT

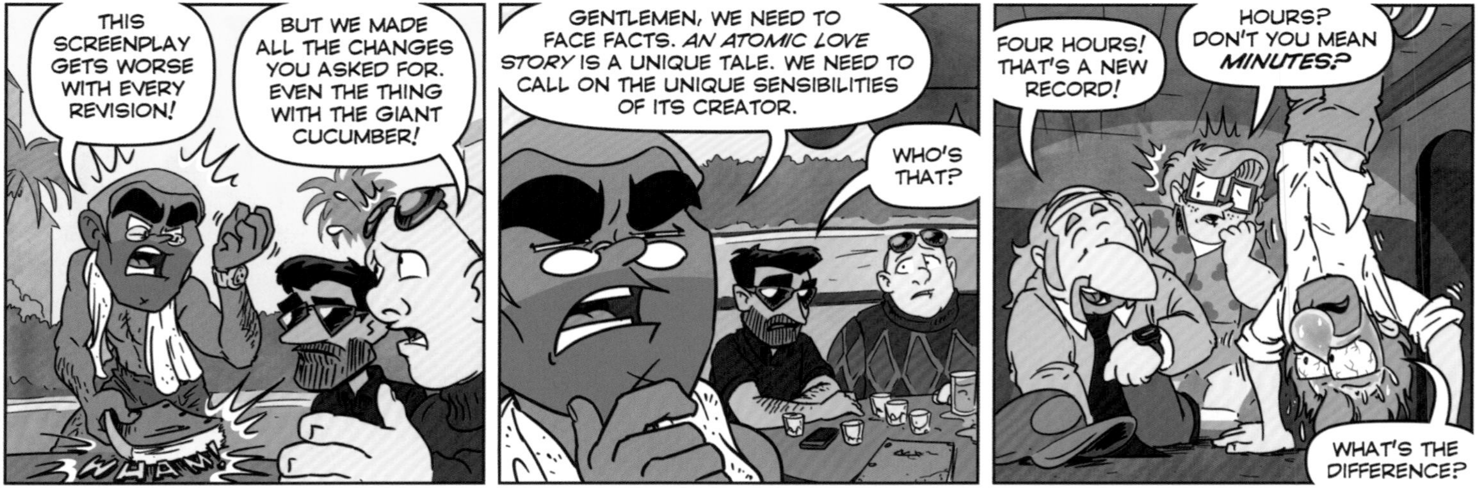
THIS SCREENPLAY GETS WORSE WITH EVERY REVISION!
BUT WE MADE ALL THE CHANGES YOU ASKED FOR. EVEN THE THING WITH THE GIANT CUCUMBER!
WHAM!
GENTLEMEN, WE NEED TO FACE FACTS. *AN ATOMIC LOVE STORY* IS A UNIQUE TALE. WE NEED TO CALL ON THE UNIQUE SENSIBILITIES OF ITS CREATOR.
WHO'S THAT?
FOUR HOURS! THAT'S A NEW RECORD!
HOURS? DON'T YOU MEAN *MINUTES?*
WHAT'S THE DIFFERENCE?

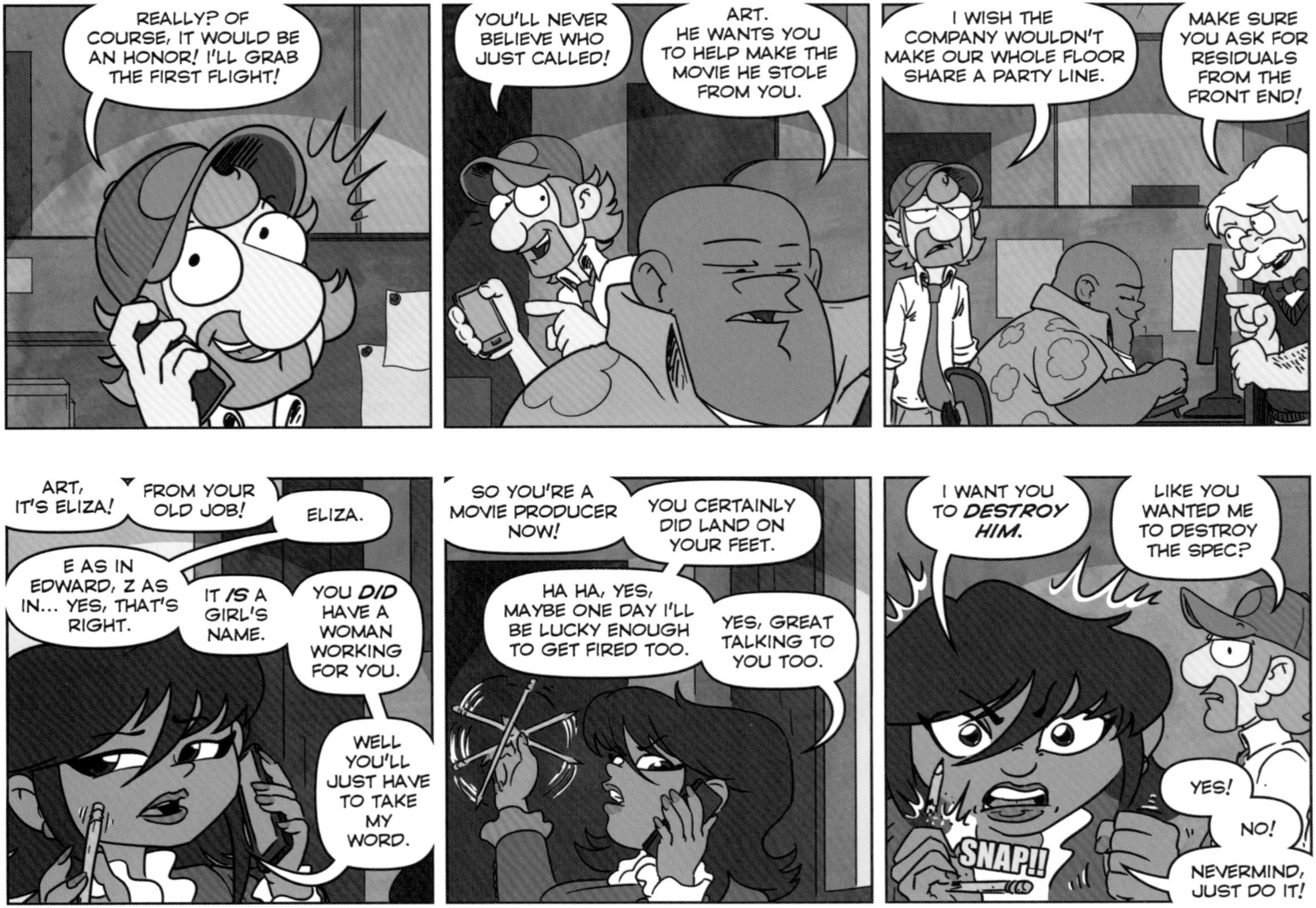
REALLY? OF COURSE, IT WOULD BE AN HONOR! I'LL GRAB THE FIRST FLIGHT!
YOU'LL NEVER BELIEVE WHO JUST CALLED!
ART. HE WANTS YOU TO HELP MAKE THE MOVIE HE STOLE FROM YOU.
I WISH THE COMPANY WOULDN'T MAKE OUR WHOLE FLOOR SHARE A PARTY LINE.
MAKE SURE YOU ASK FOR RESIDUALS FROM THE FRONT END!
ART, IT'S ELIZA!
FROM YOUR OLD JOB!
ELIZA.
E AS IN EDWARD, Z AS IN... YES, THAT'S RIGHT.
IT *IS* A GIRL'S NAME.
YOU *DID* HAVE A WOMAN WORKING FOR YOU.
WELL YOU'LL JUST HAVE TO TAKE MY WORD.
SO YOU'RE A MOVIE PRODUCER NOW!
YOU CERTAINLY DID LAND ON YOUR FEET.
HA HA, YES, MAYBE ONE DAY I'LL BE LUCKY ENOUGH TO GET FIRED TOO.
YES, GREAT TALKING TO YOU TOO.
I WANT YOU TO ***DESTROY HIM.***
LIKE YOU WANTED ME TO DESTROY THE SPEC?
SNAP!!
YES!
NO!
NEVERMIND, JUST DO IT!

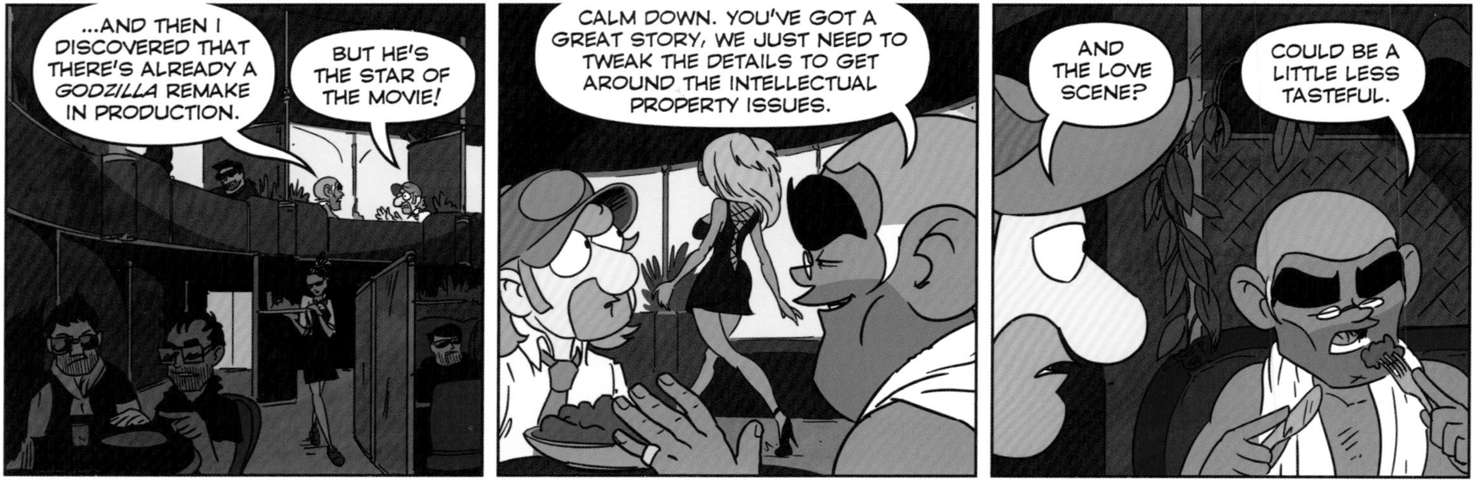
...AND THEN I DISCOVERED THAT THERE'S ALREADY A *GODZILLA* REMAKE IN PRODUCTION.
BUT HE'S THE STAR OF THE MOVIE!
CALM DOWN. YOU'VE GOT A GREAT STORY, WE JUST NEED TO TWEAK THE DETAILS TO GET AROUND THE INTELLECTUAL PROPERTY ISSUES.
AND THE LOVE SCENE?
COULD BE A LITTLE LESS TASTEFUL.

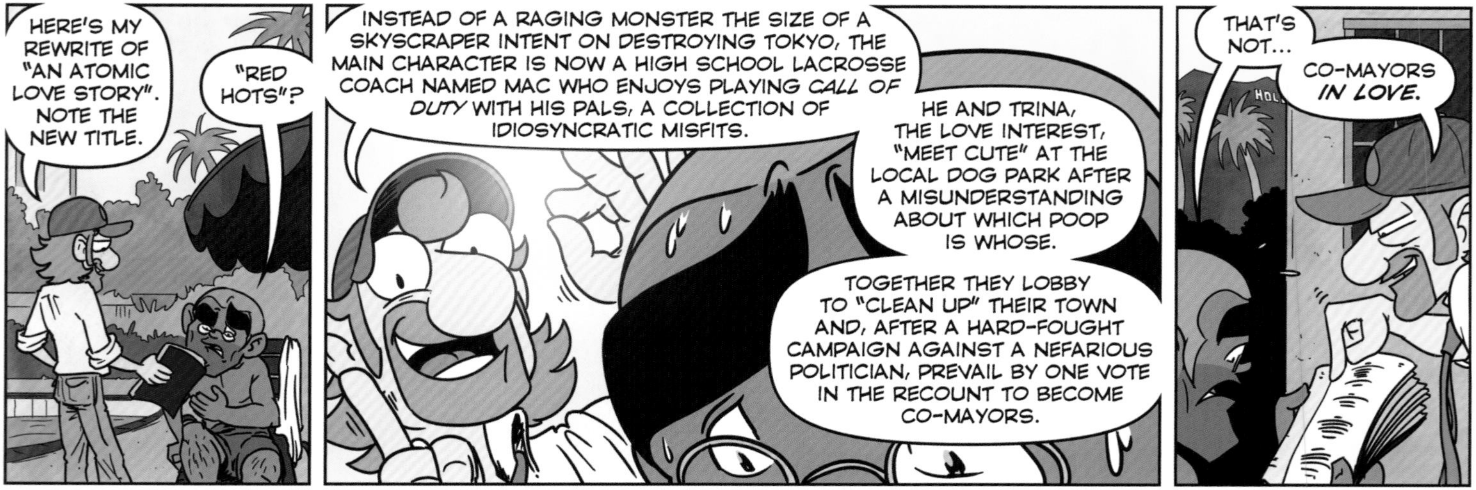
HERE'S MY REWRITE OF "AN ATOMIC LOVE STORY". NOTE THE NEW TITLE.
"RED HOTS"?
INSTEAD OF A RAGING MONSTER THE SIZE OF A SKYSCRAPER INTENT ON DESTROYING TOKYO, THE MAIN CHARACTER IS NOW A HIGH SCHOOL LACROSSE COACH NAMED MAC WHO ENJOYS PLAYING *CALL OF DUTY* WITH HIS PALS, A COLLECTION OF IDIOSYNCRATIC MISFITS.
HE AND TRINA, THE LOVE INTEREST, "MEET CUTE" AT THE LOCAL DOG PARK AFTER A MISUNDERSTANDING ABOUT WHICH POOP IS WHOSE.
TOGETHER THEY LOBBY TO "CLEAN UP" THEIR TOWN AND, AFTER A HARD-FOUGHT CAMPAIGN AGAINST A NEFARIOUS POLITICIAN, PREVAIL BY ONE VOTE IN THE RECOUNT TO BECOME CO-MAYORS.
THAT'S NOT...
CO-MAYORS ***IN LOVE.***

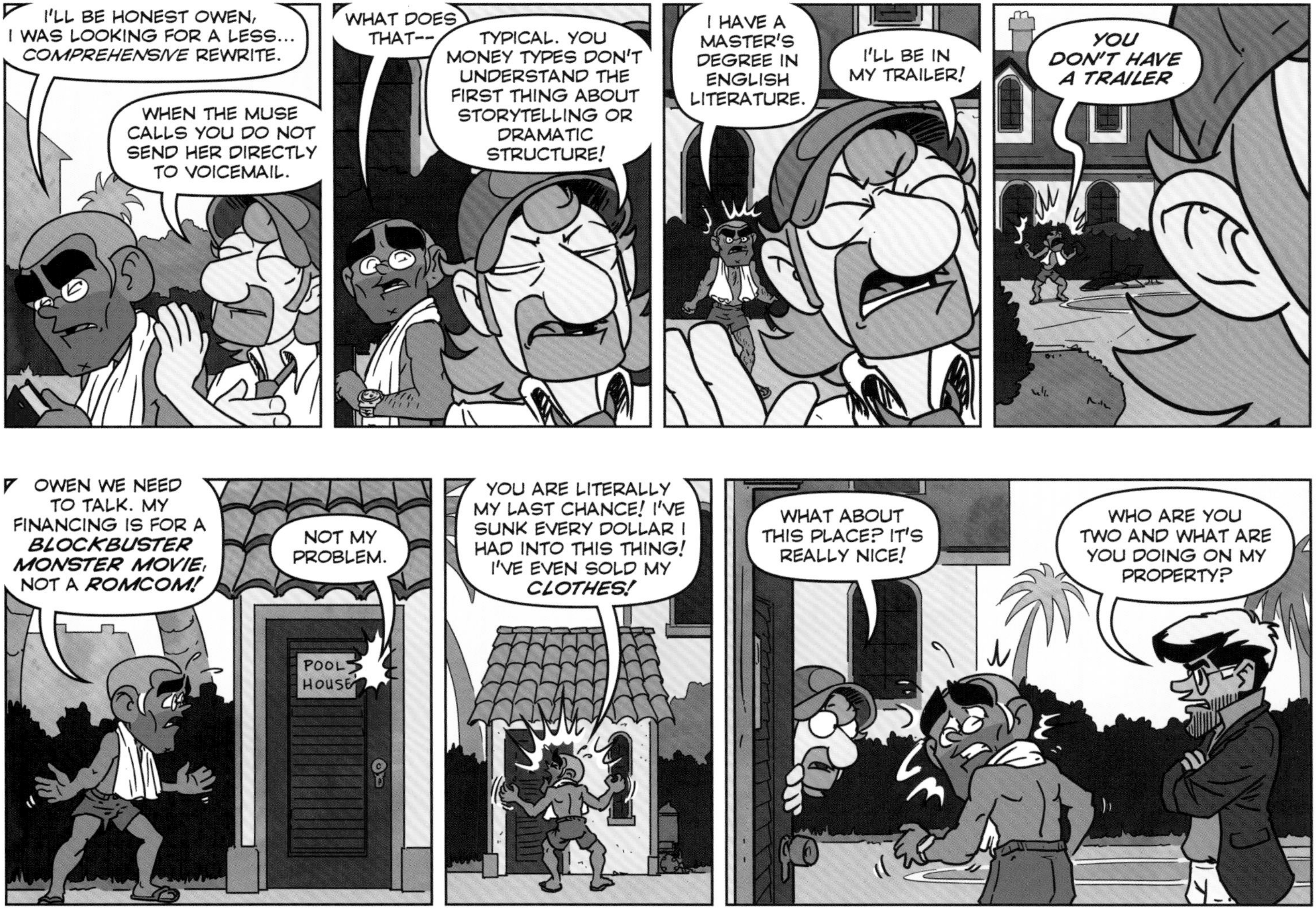
I'LL BE HONEST OWEN, I WAS LOOKING FOR A LESS... COMPREHENSIVE REWRITE.
WHEN THE MUSE CALLS YOU DO NOT SEND HER DIRECTLY TO VOICEMAIL.
WHAT DOES THAT--
TYPICAL. YOU MONEY TYPES DON'T UNDERSTAND THE FIRST THING ABOUT STORYTELLING OR DRAMATIC STRUCTURE!
I HAVE A MASTER'S DEGREE IN ENGLISH LITERATURE.
I'LL BE IN MY TRAILER!
YOU DON'T HAVE A TRAILER
OWEN WE NEED TO TALK. MY FINANCING IS FOR A BLOCKBUSTER MONSTER MOVIE, NOT A ROMCOM!
NOT MY PROBLEM.
POOL HOUSE
YOU ARE LITERALLY MY LAST CHANCE! I'VE SUNK EVERY DOLLAR I HAD INTO THIS THING! I'VE EVEN SOLD MY CLOTHES!
WHAT ABOUT THIS PLACE? IT'S REALLY NICE!
WHO ARE YOU TWO AND WHAT ARE YOU DOING ON MY PROPERTY?

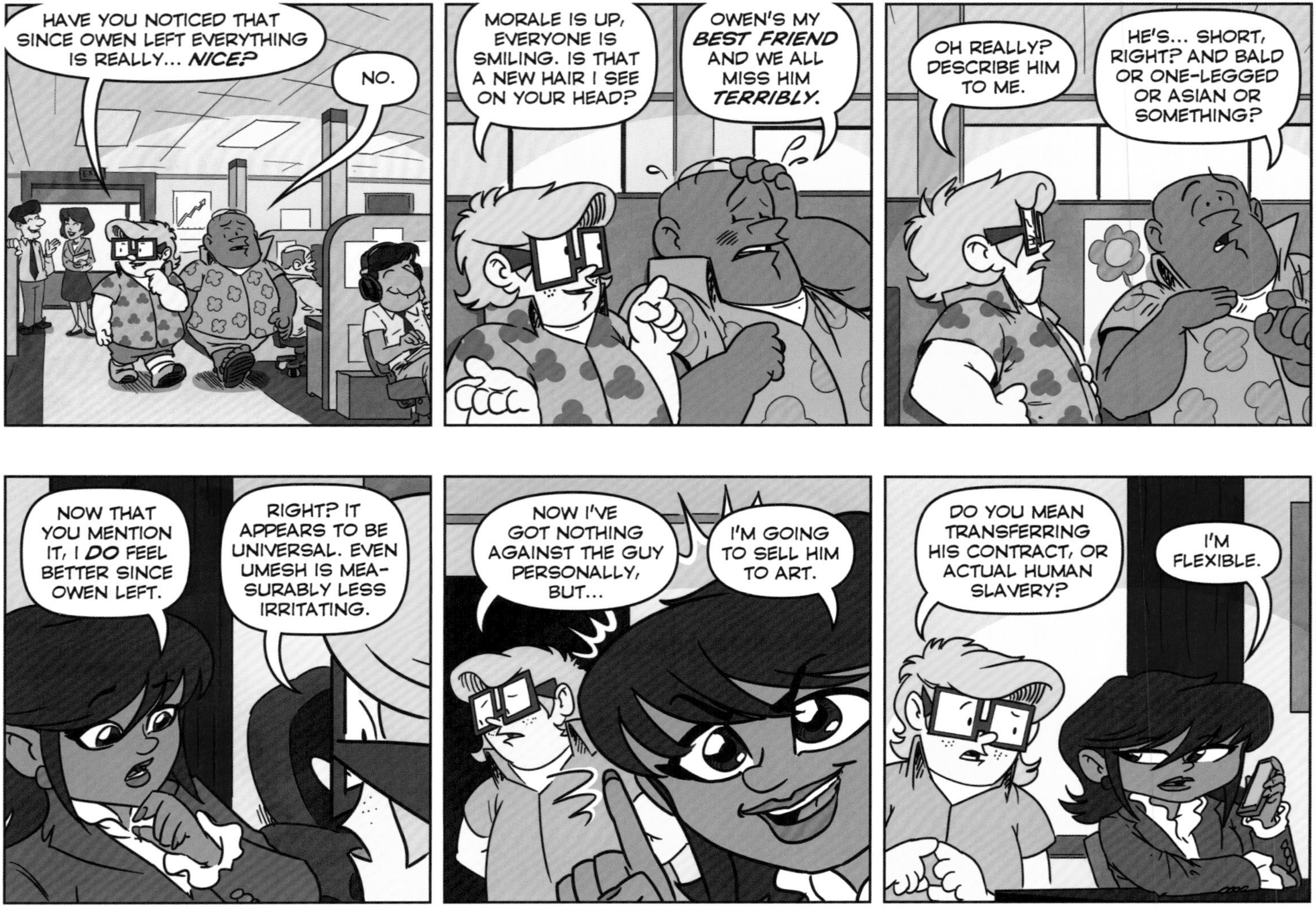
HAVE YOU NOTICED THAT SINCE OWEN LEFT EVERYTHING IS REALLY... *NICE?*
NO.
MORALE IS UP, EVERYONE IS SMILING. IS THAT A NEW HAIR I SEE ON YOUR HEAD?
OWEN'S MY *BEST FRIEND* AND WE ALL MISS HIM *TERRIBLY.*
OH REALLY? DESCRIBE HIM TO ME.
HE'S... SHORT, RIGHT? AND BALD OR ONE-LEGGED OR ASIAN OR SOMETHING?
NOW THAT YOU MENTION IT, I *DO* FEEL BETTER SINCE OWEN LEFT.
RIGHT? IT APPEARS TO BE UNIVERSAL. EVEN UMESH IS MEA-SURABLY LESS IRRITATING.
NOW I'VE GOT NOTHING AGAINST THE GUY PERSONALLY, BUT...
I'M GOING TO SELL HIM TO ART.
DO YOU MEAN TRANSFERRING HIS CONTRACT, OR ACTUAL HUMAN SLAVERY?
I'M FLEXIBLE.

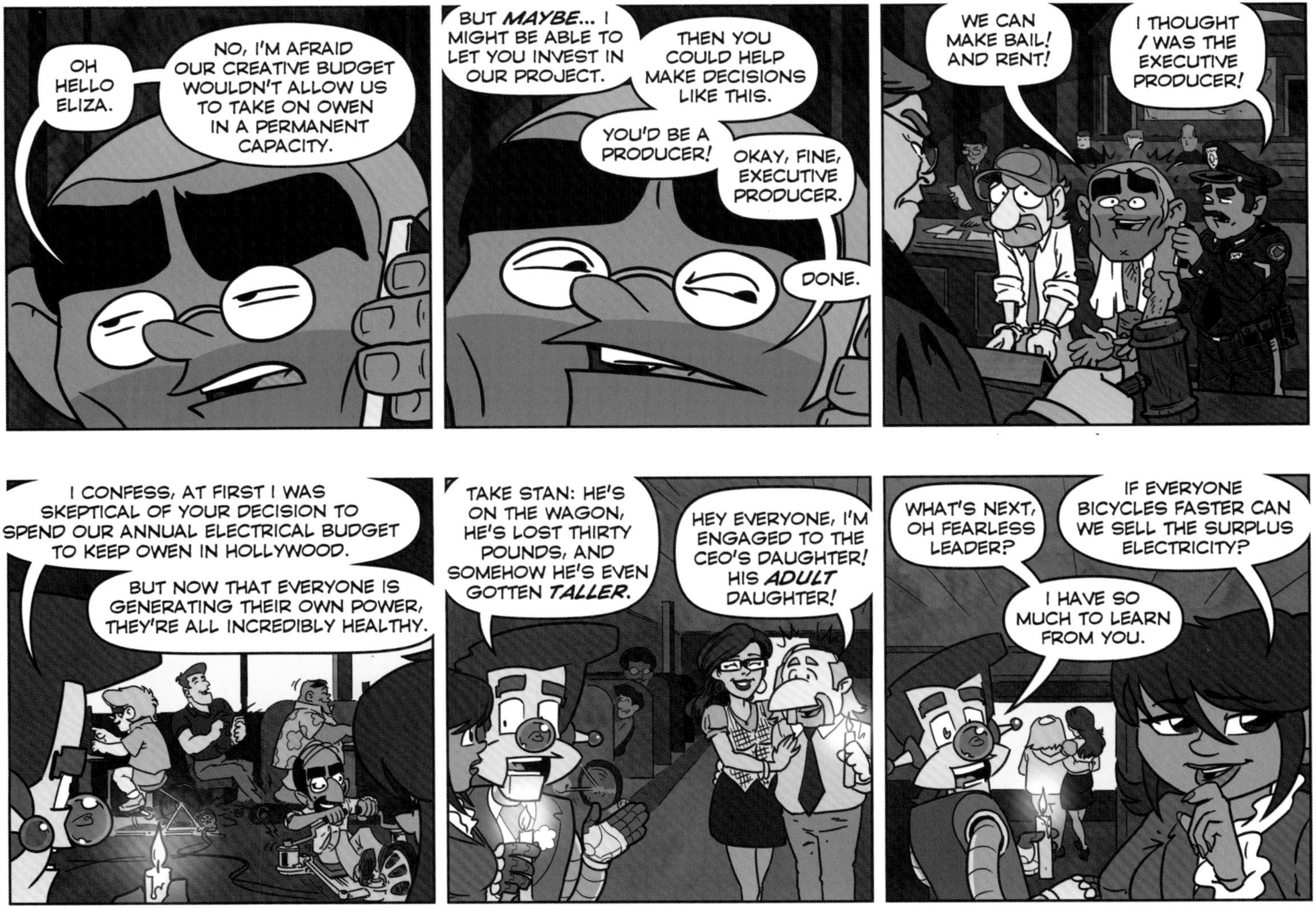
OH HELLO ELIZA.
NO, I'M AFRAID OUR CREATIVE BUDGET WOULDN'T ALLOW US TO TAKE ON OWEN IN A PERMANENT CAPACITY.
BUT *MAYBE*... I MIGHT BE ABLE TO LET YOU INVEST IN OUR PROJECT.
THEN YOU COULD HELP MAKE DECISIONS LIKE THIS.
YOU'D BE A PRODUCER!
OKAY, FINE, EXECUTIVE PRODUCER.
DONE.
WE CAN MAKE BAIL! AND RENT!
I THOUGHT *I* WAS THE EXECUTIVE PRODUCER!
I CONFESS, AT FIRST I WAS SKEPTICAL OF YOUR DECISION TO SPEND OUR ANNUAL ELECTRICAL BUDGET TO KEEP OWEN IN HOLLYWOOD.
BUT NOW THAT EVERYONE IS GENERATING THEIR OWN POWER, THEY'RE ALL INCREDIBLY HEALTHY.
TAKE STAN: HE'S ON THE WAGON, HE'S LOST THIRTY POUNDS, AND SOMEHOW HE'S EVEN GOTTEN *TALLER*.
HEY EVERYONE, I'M ENGAGED TO THE CEO'S DAUGHTER! HIS *ADULT* DAUGHTER!
WHAT'S NEXT, OH FEARLESS LEADER?
IF EVERYONE BICYCLES FASTER CAN WE SELL THE SURPLUS ELECTRICITY?
I HAVE SO MUCH TO LEARN FROM YOU.

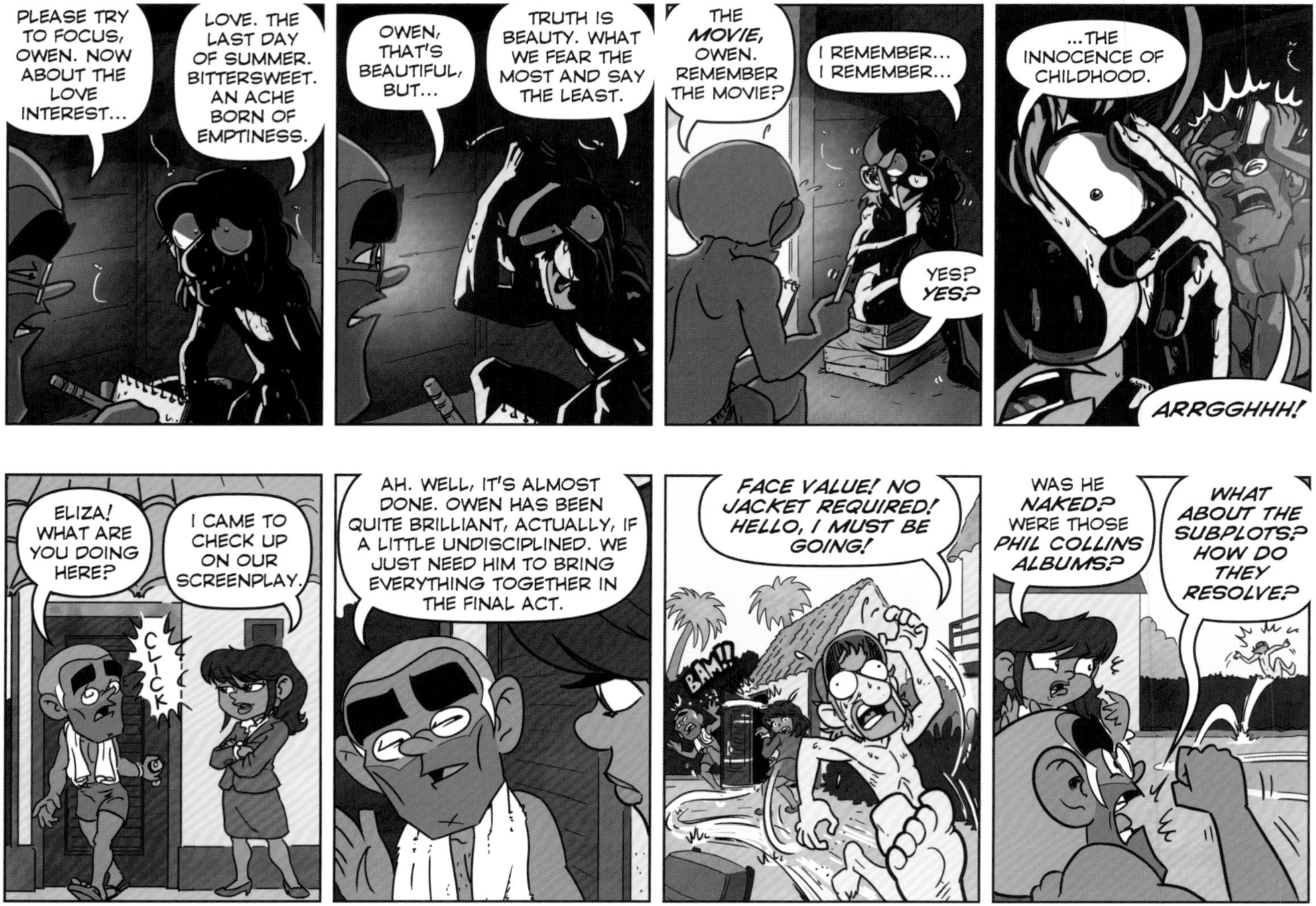
PLEASE TRY TO FOCUS, OWEN. NOW ABOUT THE LOVE INTEREST...
LOVE. THE LAST DAY OF SUMMER. BITTERSWEET. AN ACHE BORN OF EMPTINESS.
OWEN, THAT'S BEAUTIFUL, BUT...
TRUTH IS BEAUTY. WHAT WE FEAR THE MOST AND SAY THE LEAST.
THE *MOVIE,* OWEN. REMEMBER THE MOVIE?
I REMEMBER... I REMEMBER...
YES? *YES?*
...THE INNOCENCE OF CHILDHOOD.
ARRGGHHH!
ELIZA! WHAT ARE YOU DOING HERE?
CLICK
I CAME TO CHECK UP ON OUR SCREENPLAY.
AH. WELL, IT'S ALMOST DONE. OWEN HAS BEEN QUITE BRILLIANT, ACTUALLY, IF A LITTLE UNDISCIPLINED. WE JUST NEED HIM TO BRING EVERYTHING TOGETHER IN THE FINAL ACT.
FACE VALUE! NO JACKET REQUIRED! HELLO, I MUST BE GOING!
BAM!!
WAS HE *NAKED?* WERE THOSE *PHIL COLLINS ALBUMS?*
WHAT ABOUT THE SUBPLOTS? HOW DO THEY RESOLVE?

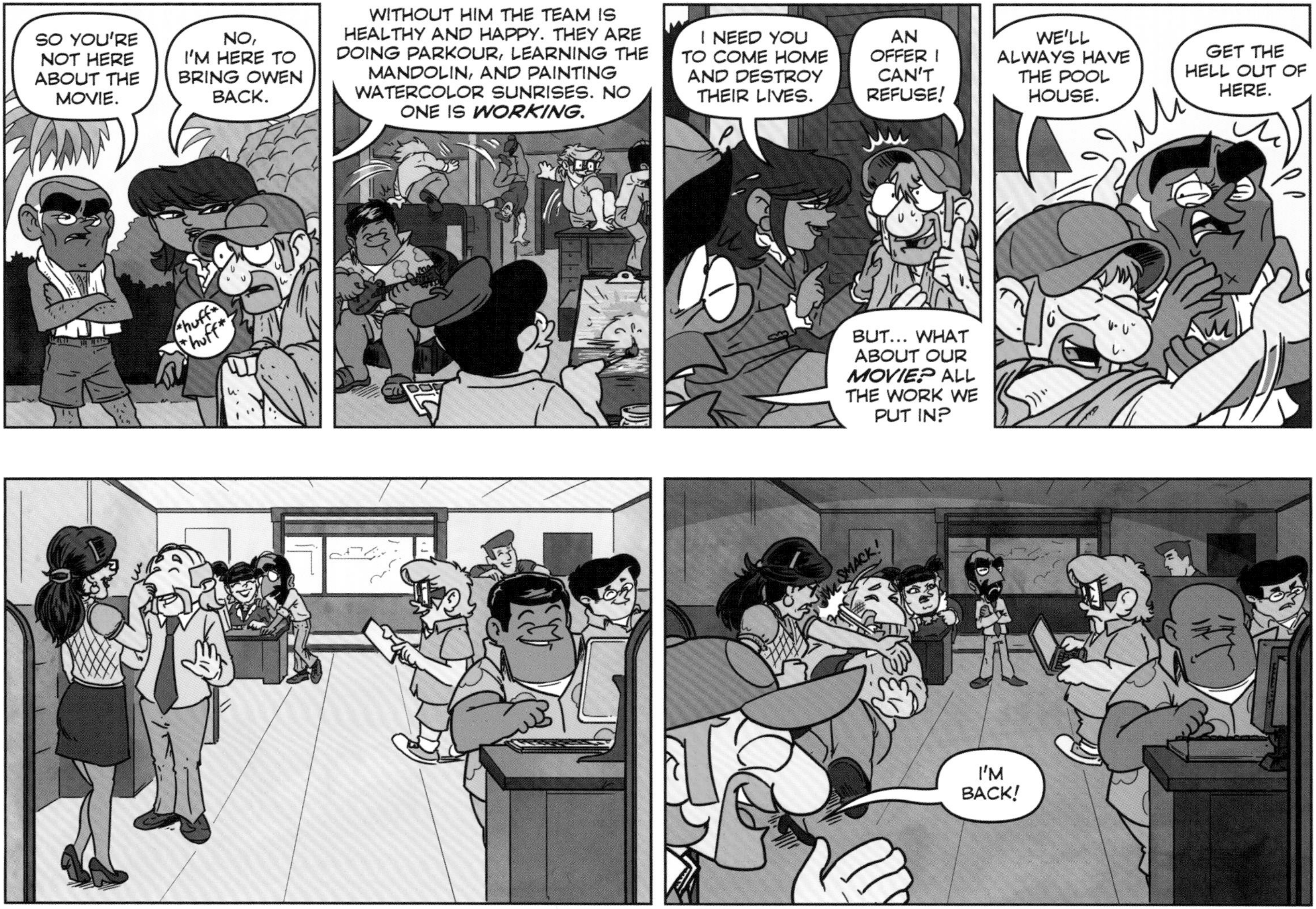
SO YOU'RE NOT HERE ABOUT THE MOVIE.
NO, I'M HERE TO BRING OWEN BACK.
huff *huff*
WITHOUT HIM THE TEAM IS HEALTHY AND HAPPY. THEY ARE DOING PARKOUR, LEARNING THE MANDOLIN, AND PAINTING WATERCOLOR SUNRISES. NO ONE IS WORKING.
I NEED YOU TO COME HOME AND DESTROY THEIR LIVES.
AN OFFER I CAN'T REFUSE!
BUT... WHAT ABOUT OUR MOVIE? ALL THE WORK WE PUT IN?
WE'LL ALWAYS HAVE THE POOL HOUSE.
GET THE HELL OUT OF HERE.
SMACK!
I'M BACK!

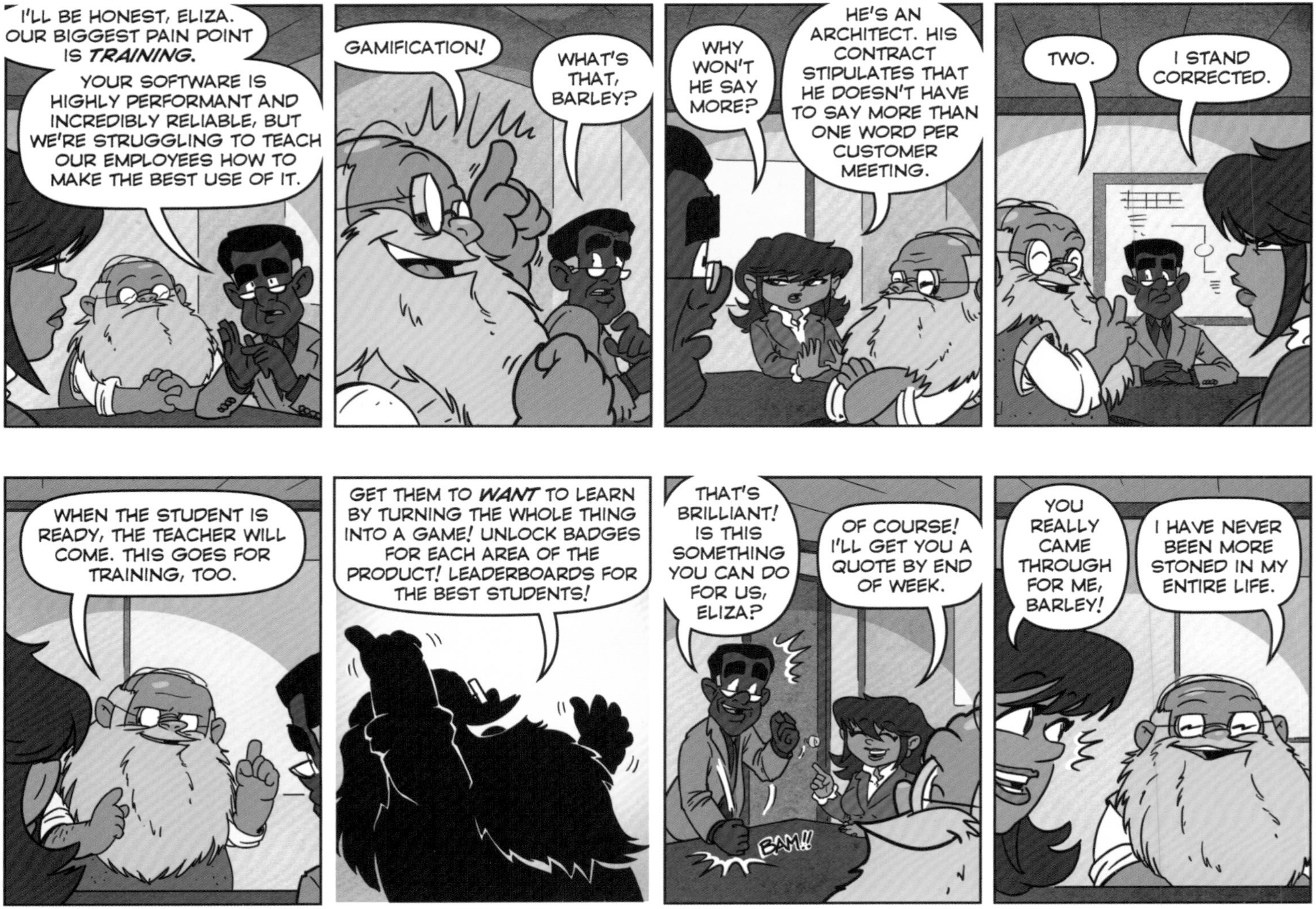
I'LL BE HONEST, ELIZA. OUR BIGGEST PAIN POINT IS *TRAINING*.
YOUR SOFTWARE IS HIGHLY PERFORMANT AND INCREDIBLY RELIABLE, BUT WE'RE STRUGGLING TO TEACH OUR EMPLOYEES HOW TO MAKE THE BEST USE OF IT.
GAMIFICATION!
WHAT'S THAT, BARLEY?
WHY WON'T HE SAY MORE?
HE'S AN ARCHITECT. HIS CONTRACT STIPULATES THAT HE DOESN'T HAVE TO SAY MORE THAN ONE WORD PER CUSTOMER MEETING.
TWO.
I STAND CORRECTED.
WHEN THE STUDENT IS READY, THE TEACHER WILL COME. THIS GOES FOR TRAINING, TOO.
GET THEM TO *WANT* TO LEARN BY TURNING THE WHOLE THING INTO A GAME! UNLOCK BADGES FOR EACH AREA OF THE PRODUCT! LEADERBOARDS FOR THE BEST STUDENTS!
THAT'S BRILLIANT! IS THIS SOMETHING YOU CAN DO FOR US, ELIZA?
OF COURSE! I'LL GET YOU A QUOTE BY END OF WEEK.
BAM!!
YOU REALLY CAME THROUGH FOR ME, BARLEY!
I HAVE NEVER BEEN MORE STONED IN MY ENTIRE LIFE.

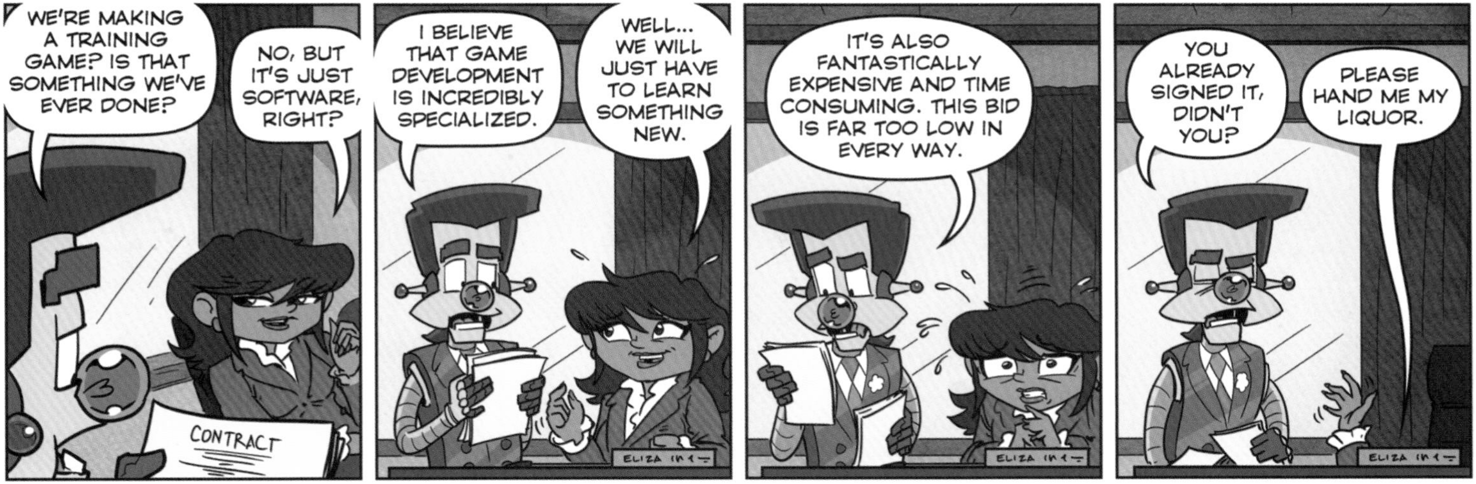
WE'RE MAKING A TRAINING GAME? IS THAT SOMETHING WE'VE EVER DONE?
NO, BUT IT'S JUST SOFTWARE, RIGHT?
CONTRACT
I BELIEVE THAT GAME DEVELOPMENT IS INCREDIBLY SPECIALIZED.
WELL... WE WILL JUST HAVE TO LEARN SOMETHING NEW.
IT'S ALSO FANTASTICALLY EXPENSIVE AND TIME CONSUMING. THIS BID IS FAR TOO LOW IN EVERY WAY.
YOU ALREADY SIGNED IT, DIDN'T YOU?
PLEASE HAND ME MY LIQUOR.

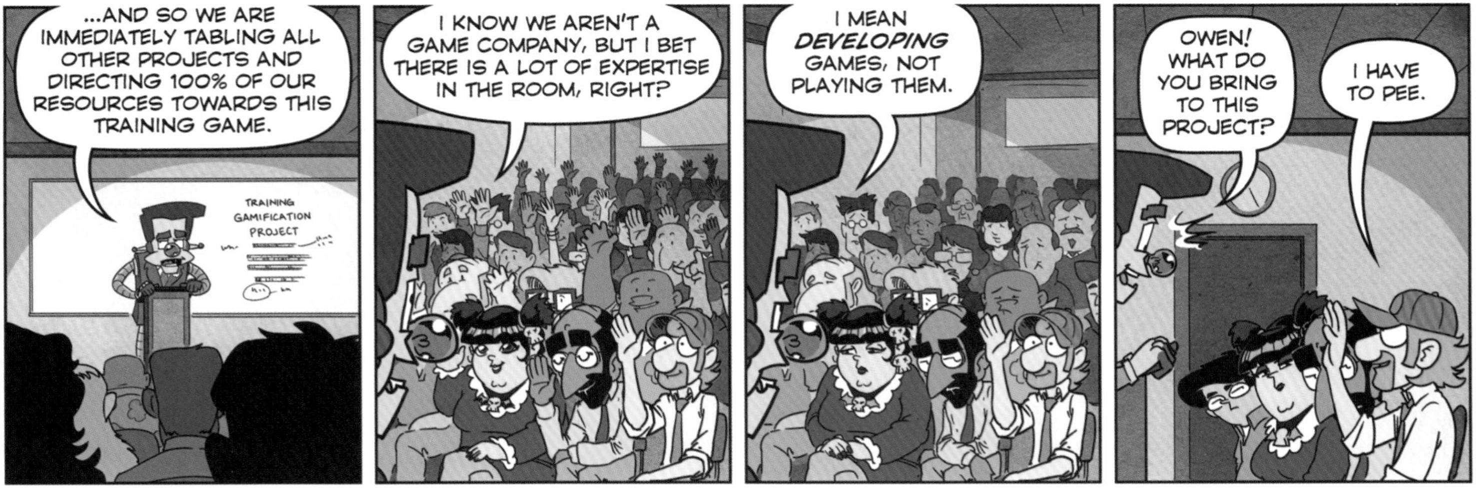
...AND SO WE ARE IMMEDIATELY TABLING ALL OTHER PROJECTS AND DIRECTING 100% OF OUR RESOURCES TOWARDS THIS TRAINING GAME.
TRAINING GAMIFICATION PROJECT
I KNOW WE AREN'T A GAME COMPANY, BUT I BET THERE IS A LOT OF EXPERTISE IN THE ROOM, RIGHT?
I MEAN *DEVELOPING* GAMES, NOT PLAYING THEM.
OWEN! WHAT DO YOU BRING TO THIS PROJECT?
I HAVE TO PEE.

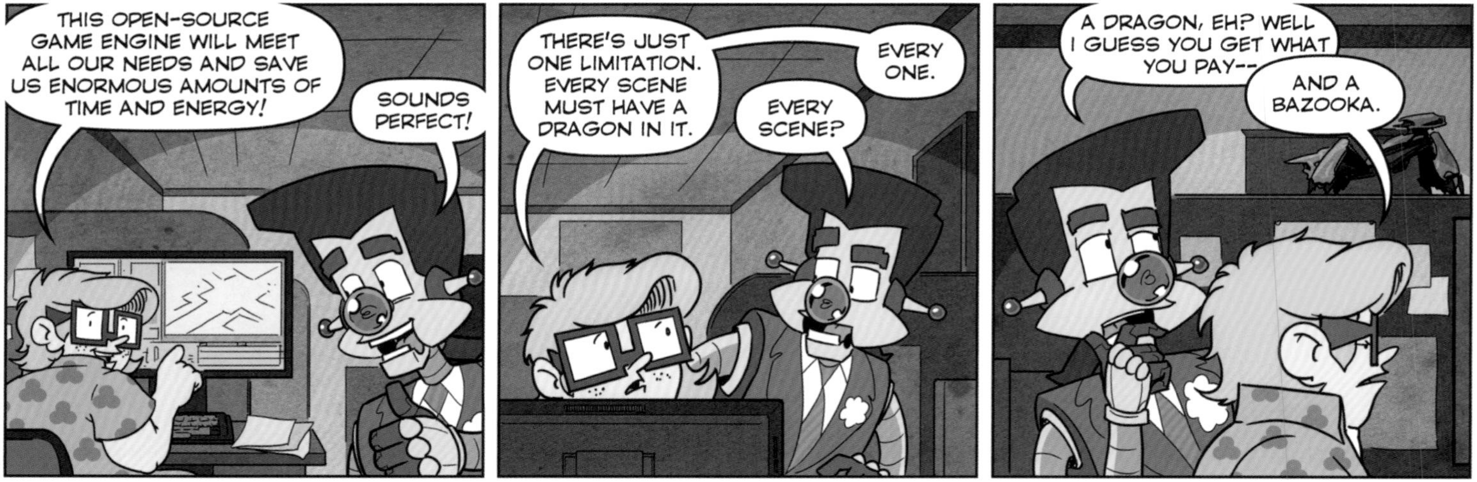
THIS OPEN-SOURCE GAME ENGINE WILL MEET ALL OUR NEEDS AND SAVE US ENORMOUS AMOUNTS OF TIME AND ENERGY!
SOUNDS PERFECT!
THERE'S JUST ONE LIMITATION. EVERY SCENE MUST HAVE A DRAGON IN IT.
EVERY SCENE?
EVERY ONE.
A DRAGON, EH? WELL I GUESS YOU GET WHAT YOU PAY--
AND A BAZOOKA.

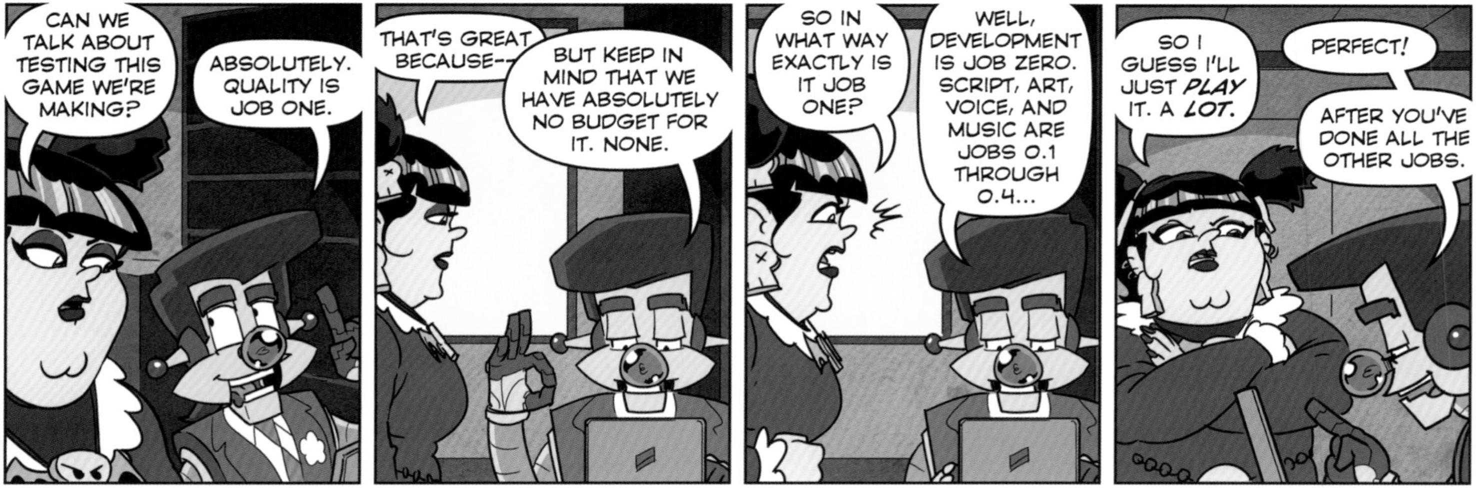
CAN WE TALK ABOUT TESTING THIS GAME WE'RE MAKING?
ABSOLUTELY. QUALITY IS JOB ONE.
THAT'S GREAT BECAUSE--
BUT KEEP IN MIND THAT WE HAVE ABSOLUTELY NO BUDGET FOR IT. NONE.
SO IN WHAT WAY EXACTLY IS IT JOB ONE?
WELL, DEVELOPMENT IS JOB ZERO. SCRIPT, ART, VOICE, AND MUSIC ARE JOBS 0.1 THROUGH 0.4...
SO I GUESS I'LL JUST PLAY IT. A LOT.
PERFECT!
AFTER YOU'VE DONE ALL THE OTHER JOBS.

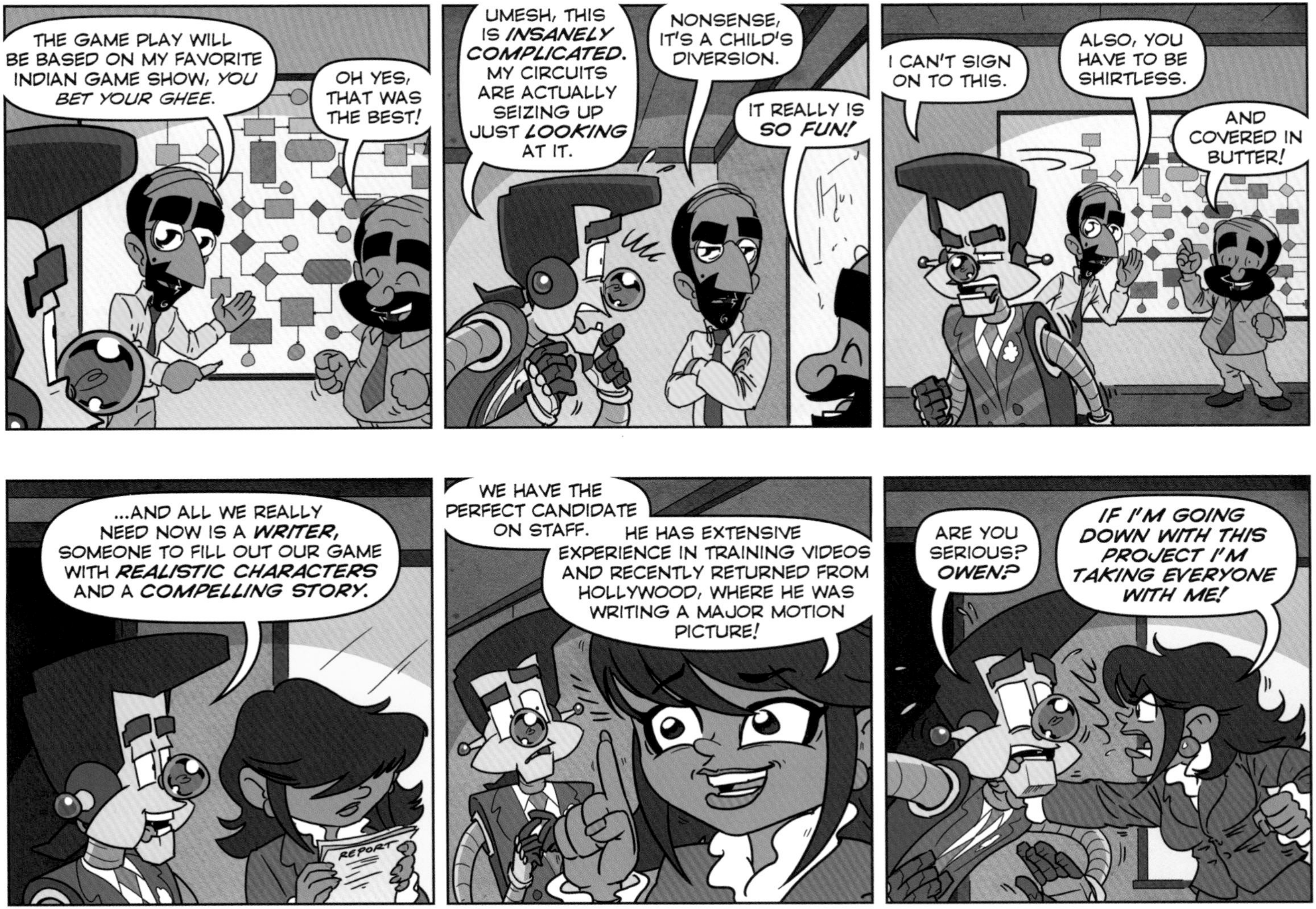
THE GAME PLAY WILL BE BASED ON MY FAVORITE INDIAN GAME SHOW, *YOU BET YOUR GHEE*.
OH YES, THAT WAS THE BEST!
UMESH, THIS IS *INSANELY COMPLICATED.* MY CIRCUITS ARE ACTUALLY SEIZING UP JUST *LOOKING* AT IT.
NONSENSE, IT'S A CHILD'S DIVERSION.
IT REALLY IS *SO FUN!*
I CAN'T SIGN ON TO THIS.
ALSO, YOU HAVE TO BE SHIRTLESS.
AND COVERED IN BUTTER!
...AND ALL WE REALLY NEED NOW IS A *WRITER,* SOMEONE TO FILL OUT OUR GAME WITH *REALISTIC CHARACTERS* AND A *COMPELLING STORY.*
REPORT
WE HAVE THE PERFECT CANDIDATE ON STAFF.
HE HAS EXTENSIVE EXPERIENCE IN TRAINING VIDEOS AND RECENTLY RETURNED FROM HOLLYWOOD, WHERE HE WAS WRITING A MAJOR MOTION PICTURE!
ARE YOU SERIOUS? *OWEN?*
IF I'M GOING DOWN WITH THIS PROJECT I'M TAKING EVERYONE WITH ME!

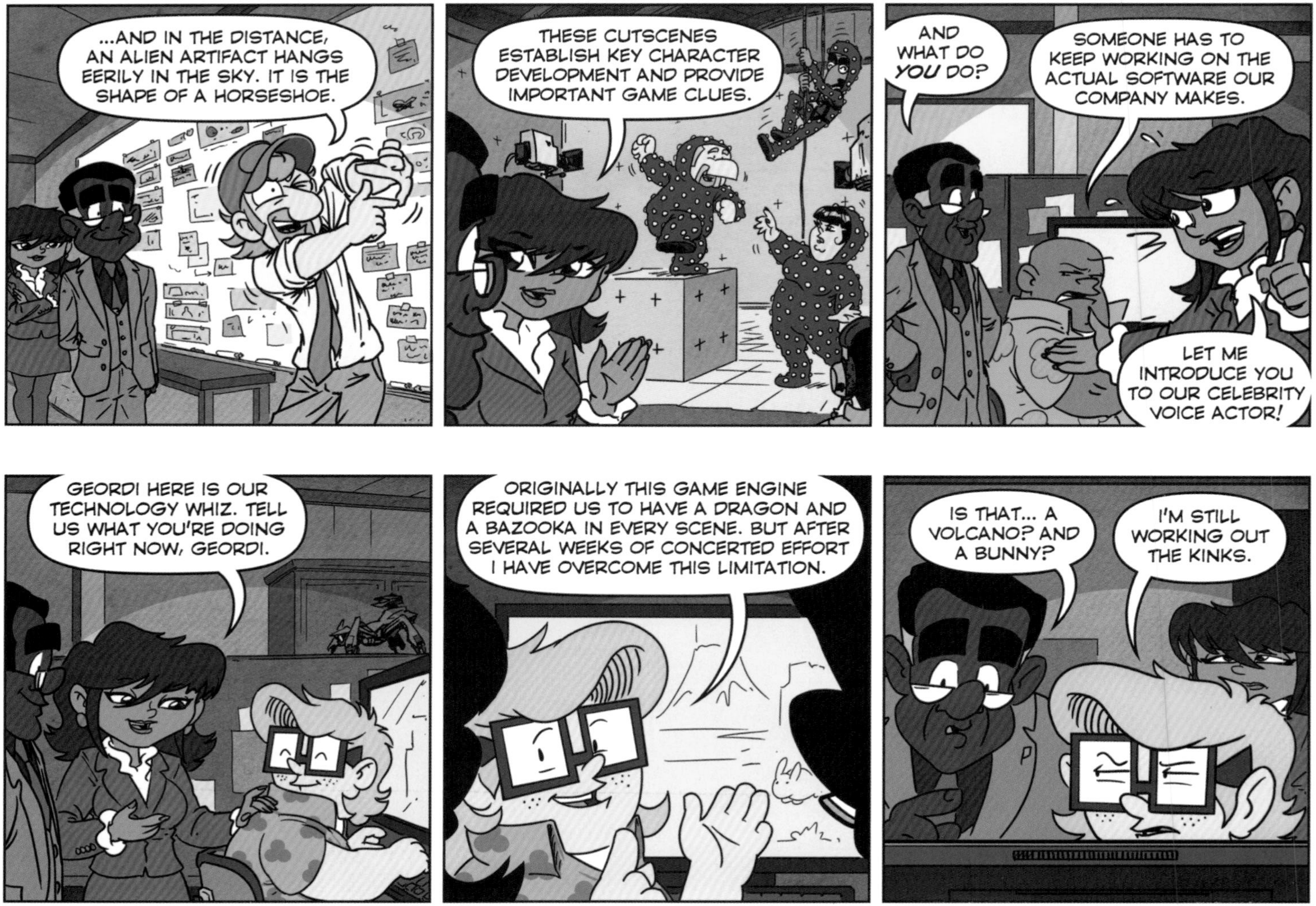

...AND IN THE DISTANCE, AN ALIEN ARTIFACT HANGS EERILY IN THE SKY. IT IS THE SHAPE OF A HORSESHOE.
THESE CUTSCENES ESTABLISH KEY CHARACTER DEVELOPMENT AND PROVIDE IMPORTANT GAME CLUES.
AND WHAT DO *YOU* DO?
SOMEONE HAS TO KEEP WORKING ON THE ACTUAL SOFTWARE OUR COMPANY MAKES.
LET ME INTRODUCE YOU TO OUR CELEBRITY VOICE ACTOR!
GEORDI HERE IS OUR TECHNOLOGY WHIZ. TELL US WHAT YOU'RE DOING RIGHT NOW, GEORDI.
ORIGINALLY THIS GAME ENGINE REQUIRED US TO HAVE A DRAGON AND A BAZOOKA IN EVERY SCENE. BUT AFTER SEVERAL WEEKS OF CONCERTED EFFORT I HAVE OVERCOME THIS LIMITATION.
IS THAT... A VOLCANO? AND A BUNNY?
I'M STILL WORKING OUT THE KINKS.

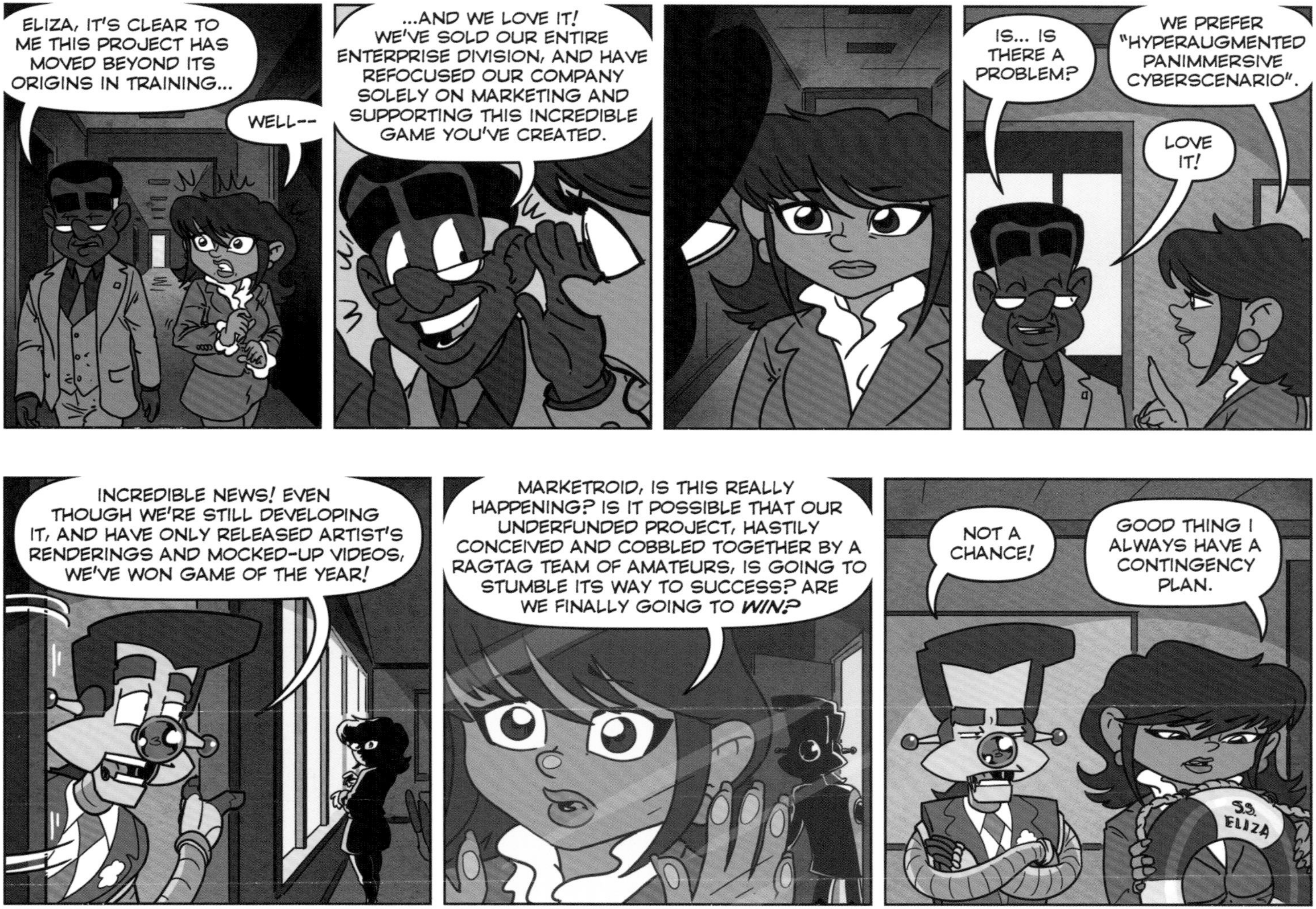
ELIZA, IT'S CLEAR TO ME THIS PROJECT HAS MOVED BEYOND ITS ORIGINS IN TRAINING...
WELL--
...AND WE LOVE IT! WE'VE SOLD OUR ENTIRE ENTERPRISE DIVISION, AND HAVE REFOCUSED OUR COMPANY SOLELY ON MARKETING AND SUPPORTING THIS INCREDIBLE GAME YOU'VE CREATED.
IS... IS THERE A PROBLEM?
WE PREFER "HYPERAUGMENTED PANIMMERSIVE CYBERSCENARIO".
LOVE IT!
INCREDIBLE NEWS! EVEN THOUGH WE'RE STILL DEVELOPING IT, AND HAVE ONLY RELEASED ARTIST'S RENDERINGS AND MOCKED-UP VIDEOS, WE'VE WON GAME OF THE YEAR!
MARKETROID, IS THIS REALLY HAPPENING? IS IT POSSIBLE THAT OUR UNDERFUNDED PROJECT, HASTILY CONCEIVED AND COBBLED TOGETHER BY A RAGTAG TEAM OF AMATEURS, IS GOING TO STUMBLE ITS WAY TO SUCCESS? ARE WE FINALLY GOING TO *WIN*?
NOT A CHANCE!
GOOD THING I ALWAYS HAVE A CONTINGENCY PLAN.
S.S. ELIZA

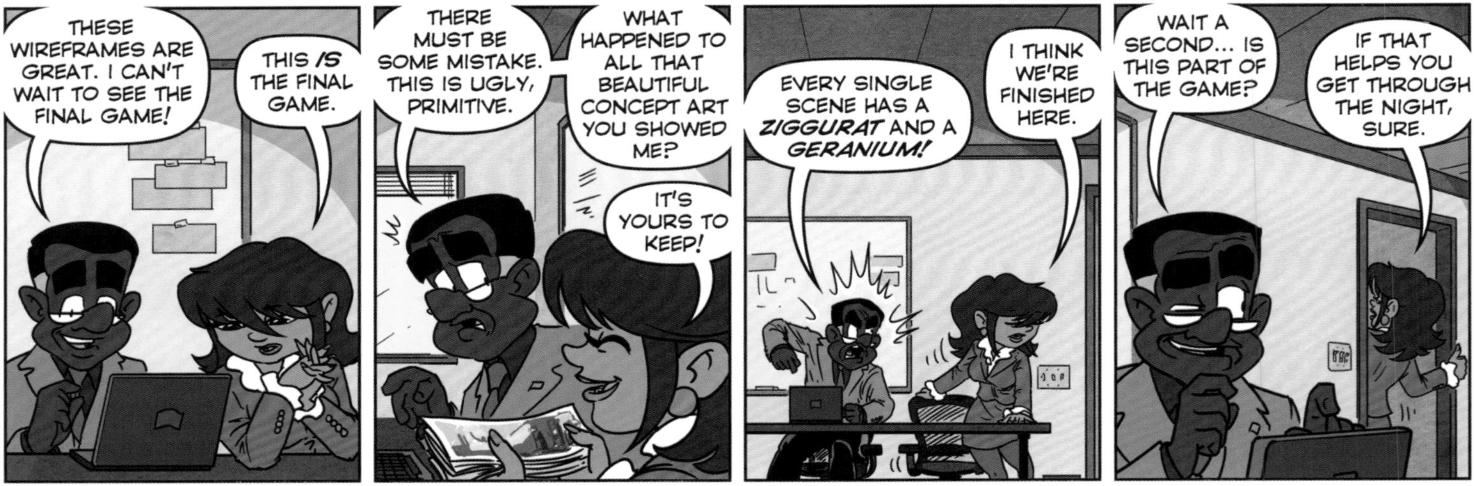
THESE WIREFRAMES ARE GREAT. I CAN'T WAIT TO SEE THE FINAL GAME!
THIS *IS* THE FINAL GAME.
THERE MUST BE SOME MISTAKE. THIS IS UGLY, PRIMITIVE.
WHAT HAPPENED TO ALL THAT BEAUTIFUL CONCEPT ART YOU SHOWED ME?
IT'S YOURS TO KEEP!
EVERY SINGLE SCENE HAS A *ZIGGURAT* AND A *GERANIUM!*
I THINK WE'RE FINISHED HERE.
WAIT A SECOND... IS THIS PART OF THE GAME?
IF THAT HELPS YOU GET THROUGH THE NIGHT, SURE.

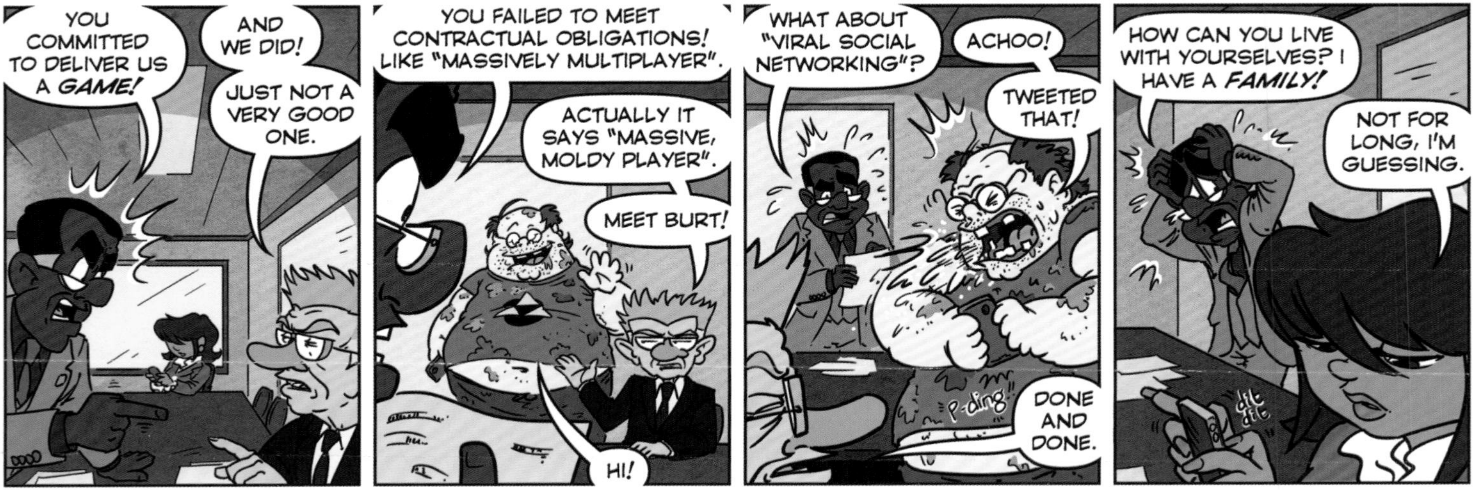
YOU COMMITTED TO DELIVER US A *GAME!*
AND WE DID!
JUST NOT A VERY GOOD ONE.
YOU FAILED TO MEET CONTRACTUAL OBLIGATIONS! LIKE "MASSIVELY MULTIPLAYER".
ACTUALLY IT SAYS "MASSIVE, MOLDY PLAYER".
MEET BURT!
HI!
WHAT ABOUT "VIRAL SOCIAL NETWORKING"?
ACHOO!
TWEETED THAT!
DONE AND DONE.
HOW CAN YOU LIVE WITH YOURSELVES? I HAVE A *FAMILY!*
NOT FOR LONG, I'M GUESSING.

UPGRADE PATH

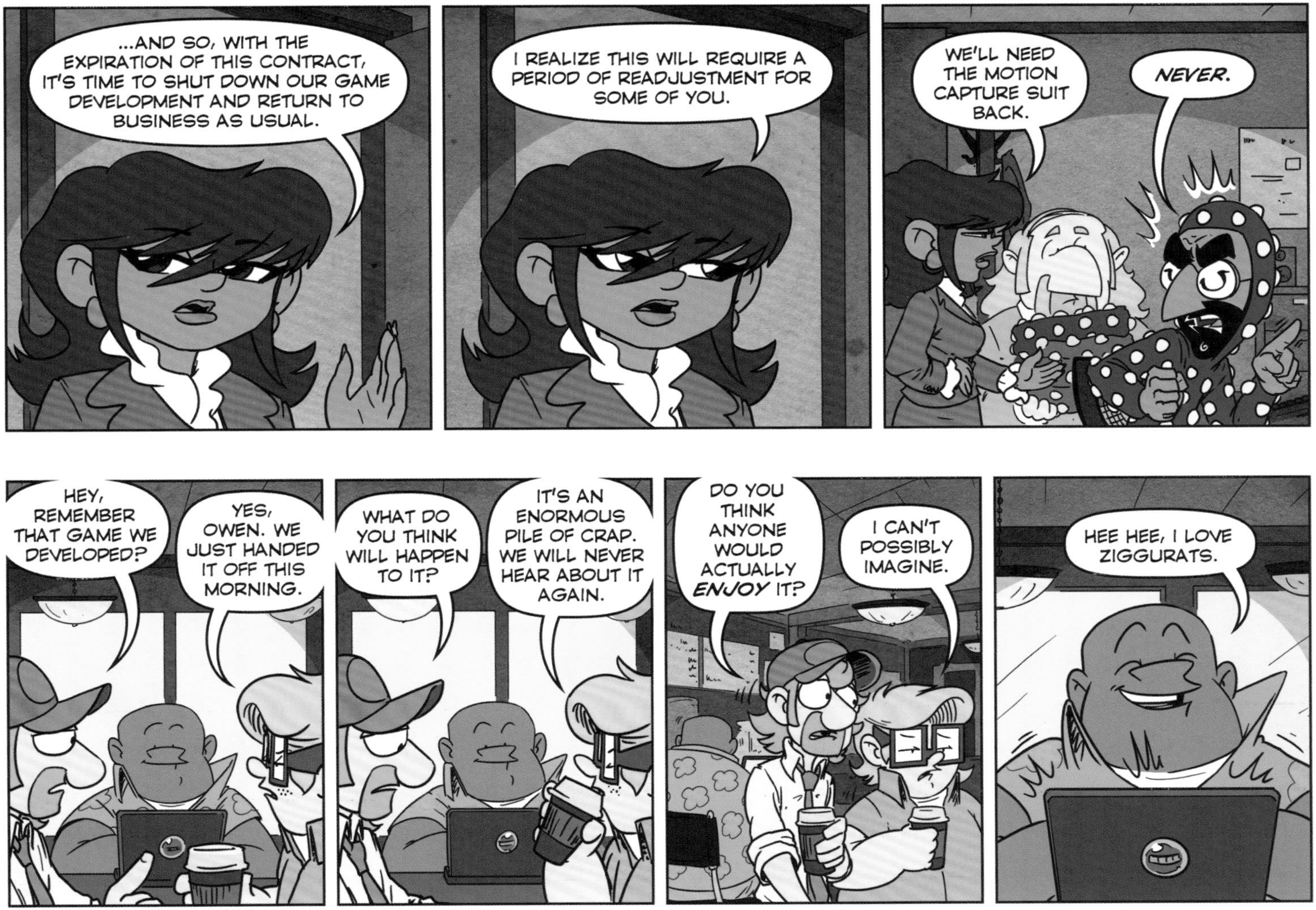
...AND SO, WITH THE EXPIRATION OF THIS CONTRACT, IT'S TIME TO SHUT DOWN OUR GAME DEVELOPMENT AND RETURN TO BUSINESS AS USUAL.
I REALIZE THIS WILL REQUIRE A PERIOD OF READJUSTMENT FOR SOME OF YOU.
WE'LL NEED THE MOTION CAPTURE SUIT BACK.
NEVER.
HEY, REMEMBER THAT GAME WE DEVELOPED?
YES, OWEN. WE JUST HANDED IT OFF THIS MORNING.
WHAT DO YOU THINK WILL HAPPEN TO IT?
IT'S AN ENORMOUS PILE OF CRAP. WE WILL NEVER HEAR ABOUT IT AGAIN.
DO YOU THINK ANYONE WOULD ACTUALLY *ENJOY* IT?
I CAN'T POSSIBLY IMAGINE.
HEE HEE, I LOVE ZIGGURATS.

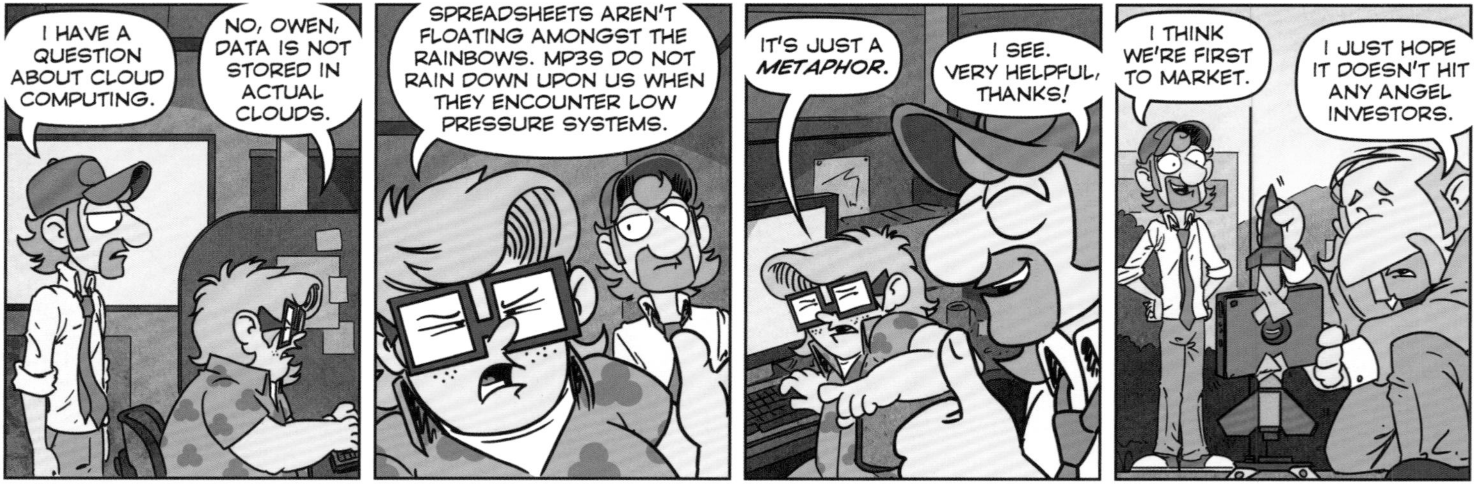
I HAVE A QUESTION ABOUT CLOUD COMPUTING.
NO, OWEN, DATA IS NOT STORED IN ACTUAL CLOUDS.
SPREADSHEETS AREN'T FLOATING AMONGST THE RAINBOWS. MP3S DO NOT RAIN DOWN UPON US WHEN THEY ENCOUNTER LOW PRESSURE SYSTEMS.
IT'S JUST A *METAPHOR*.
I SEE. VERY HELPFUL, THANKS!
I THINK WE'RE FIRST TO MARKET.
I JUST HOPE IT DOESN'T HIT ANY ANGEL INVESTORS.

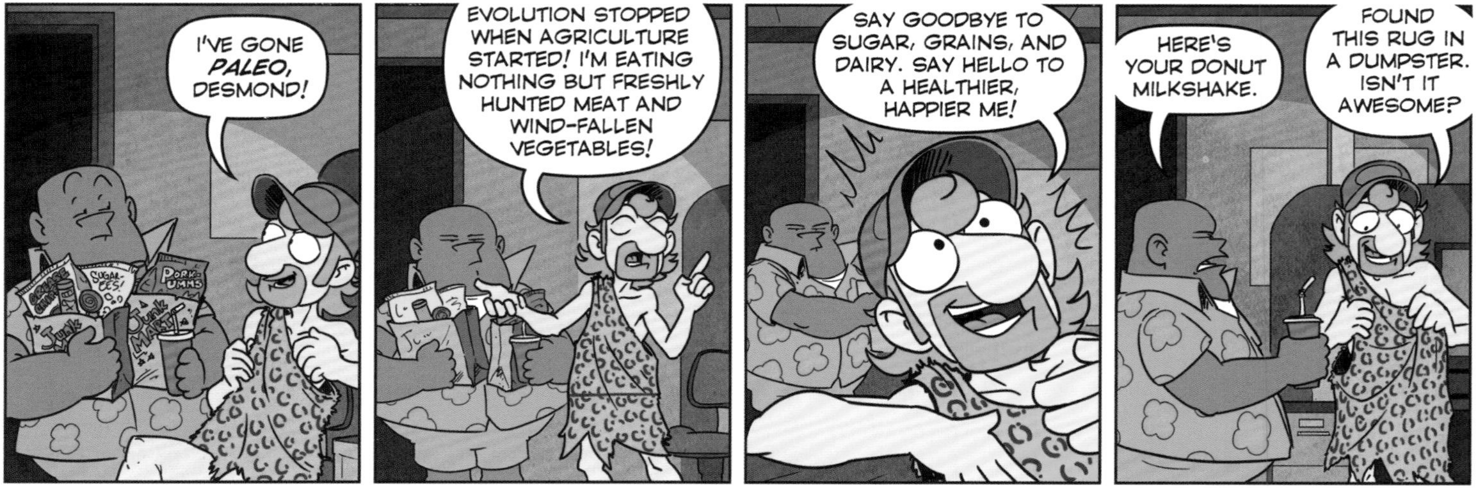
I'VE GONE *PALEO*, DESMOND!
EVOLUTION STOPPED WHEN AGRICULTURE STARTED! I'M EATING NOTHING BUT FRESHLY HUNTED MEAT AND WIND-FALLEN VEGETABLES!
SAY GOODBYE TO SUGAR, GRAINS, AND DAIRY. SAY HELLO TO A HEALTHIER, HAPPIER ME!
HERE'S YOUR DONUT MILKSHAKE.
FOUND THIS RUG IN A DUMPSTER. ISN'T IT AWESOME?

UPGRADE PATH

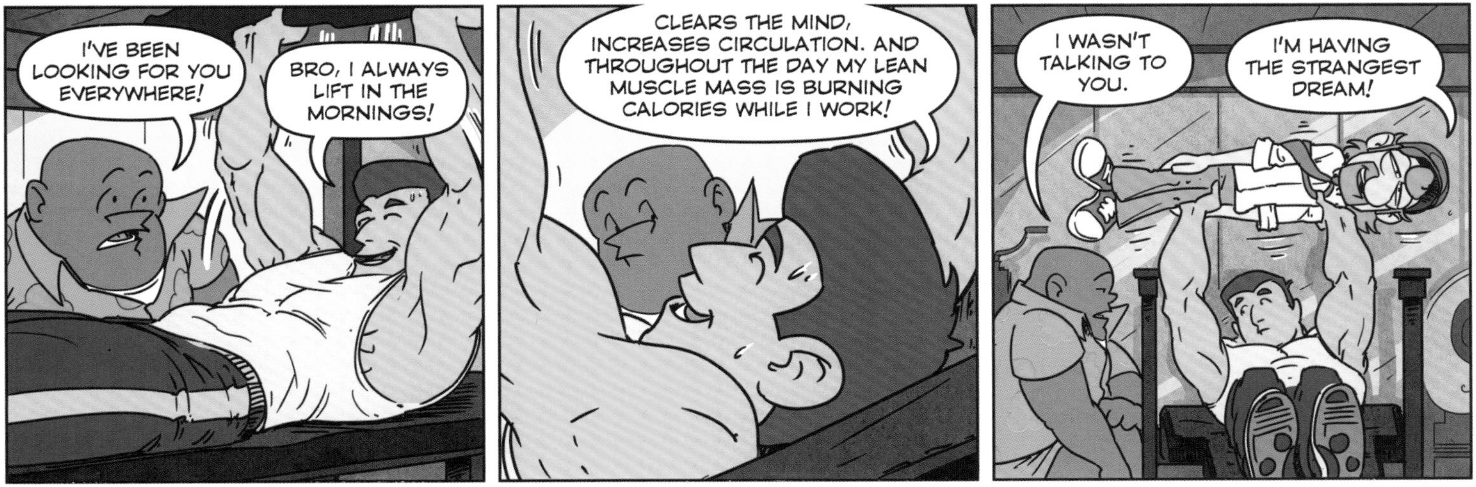
I'VE BEEN LOOKING FOR YOU EVERYWHERE!
BRO, I ALWAYS LIFT IN THE MORNINGS!
CLEARS THE MIND, INCREASES CIRCULATION. AND THROUGHOUT THE DAY MY LEAN MUSCLE MASS IS BURNING CALORIES WHILE I WORK!
I WASN'T TALKING TO YOU.
I'M HAVING THE STRANGEST DREAM!

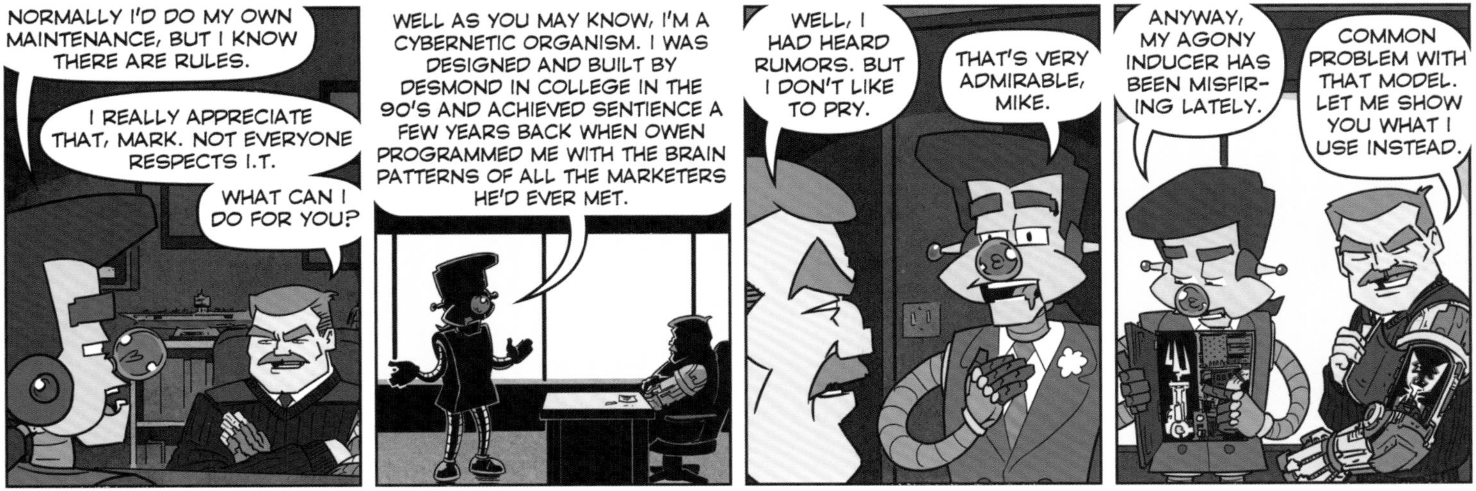
NORMALLY I'D DO MY OWN MAINTENANCE, BUT I KNOW THERE ARE RULES.
I REALLY APPRECIATE THAT, MARK. NOT EVERYONE RESPECTS I.T.
WHAT CAN I DO FOR YOU?
WELL AS YOU MAY KNOW, I'M A CYBERNETIC ORGANISM. I WAS DESIGNED AND BUILT BY DESMOND IN COLLEGE IN THE 90'S AND ACHIEVED SENTIENCE A FEW YEARS BACK WHEN OWEN PROGRAMMED ME WITH THE BRAIN PATTERNS OF ALL THE MARKETERS HE'D EVER MET.
WELL, I HAD HEARD RUMORS. BUT I DON'T LIKE TO PRY.
THAT'S VERY ADMIRABLE, MIKE.
ANYWAY, MY AGONY INDUCER HAS BEEN MISFIR-ING LATELY.
COMMON PROBLEM WITH THAT MODEL. LET ME SHOW YOU WHAT I USE INSTEAD.

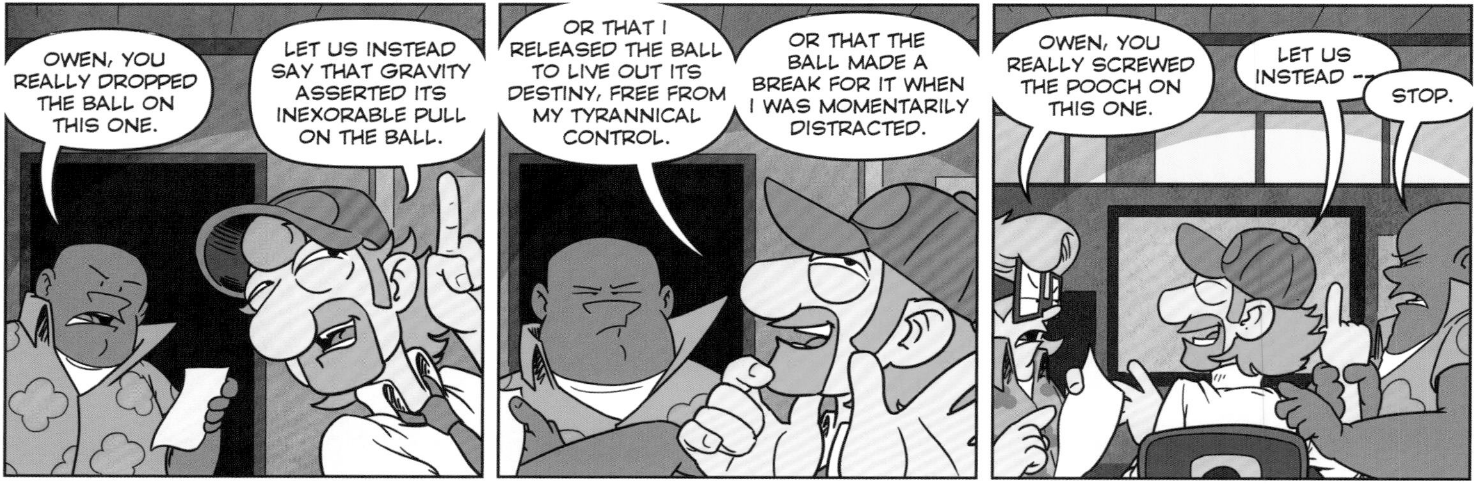
OWEN, YOU REALLY DROPPED THE BALL ON THIS ONE.
LET US INSTEAD SAY THAT GRAVITY ASSERTED ITS INEXORABLE PULL ON THE BALL.
OR THAT I RELEASED THE BALL TO LIVE OUT ITS DESTINY, FREE FROM MY TYRANNICAL CONTROL.
OR THAT THE BALL MADE A BREAK FOR IT WHEN I WAS MOMENTARILY DISTRACTED.
OWEN, YOU REALLY SCREWED THE POOCH ON THIS ONE.
LET US INSTEAD --
STOP.

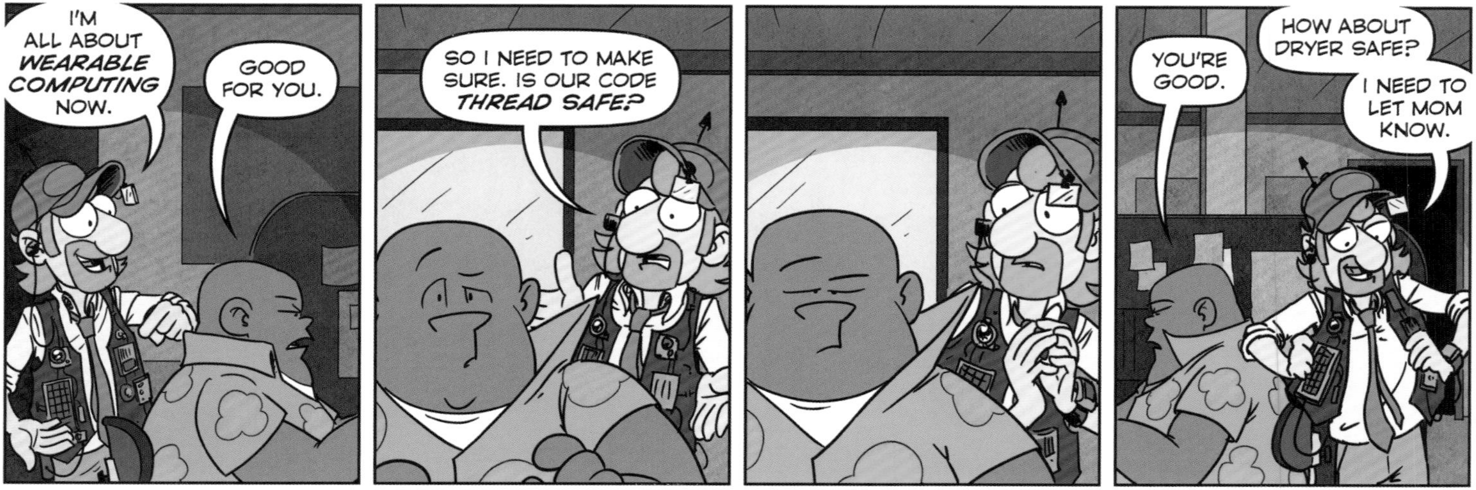
I'M ALL ABOUT *WEARABLE COMPUTING* NOW.
GOOD FOR YOU.
SO I NEED TO MAKE SURE. IS OUR CODE *THREAD SAFE?*
YOU'RE GOOD.
HOW ABOUT DRYER SAFE?
I NEED TO LET MOM KNOW.

UPGRADE PATH

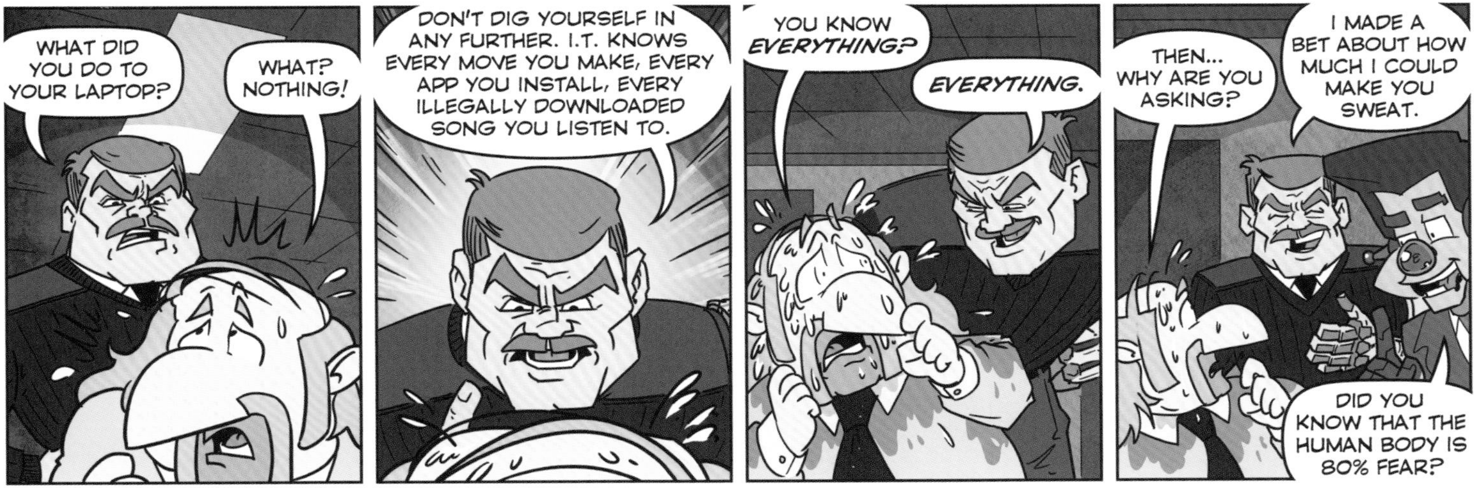
WHAT DID YOU DO TO YOUR LAPTOP?
WHAT? NOTHING!
DON'T DIG YOURSELF IN ANY FURTHER. I.T. KNOWS EVERY MOVE YOU MAKE, EVERY APP YOU INSTALL, EVERY ILLEGALLY DOWNLOADED SONG YOU LISTEN TO.
YOU KNOW *EVERYTHING?*
EVERYTHING.
THEN... WHY ARE YOU ASKING?
I MADE A BET ABOUT HOW MUCH I COULD MAKE YOU SWEAT.
DID YOU KNOW THAT THE HUMAN BODY IS 80% FEAR?

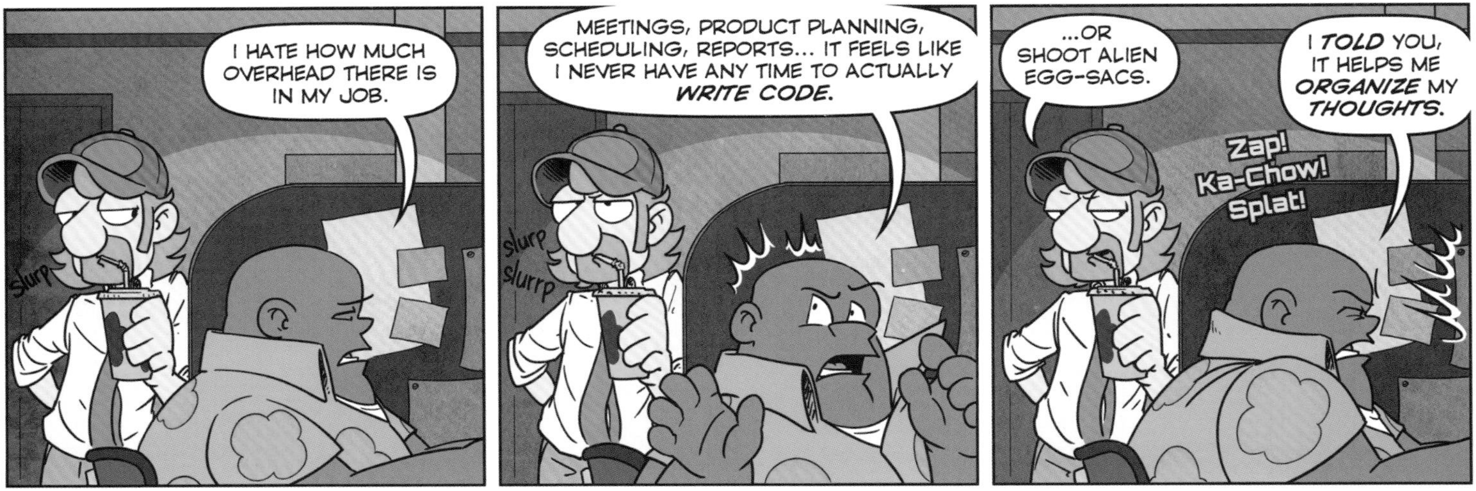
I HATE HOW MUCH OVERHEAD THERE IS IN MY JOB.
slurp
MEETINGS, PRODUCT PLANNING, SCHEDULING, REPORTS... IT FEELS LIKE I NEVER HAVE ANY TIME TO ACTUALLY *WRITE CODE.*
slurp
slurrp
...OR SHOOT ALIEN EGG-SACS.
Zap!
Ka-Chow!
Splat!
I *TOLD* YOU, IT HELPS ME *ORGANIZE* MY *THOUGHTS.*

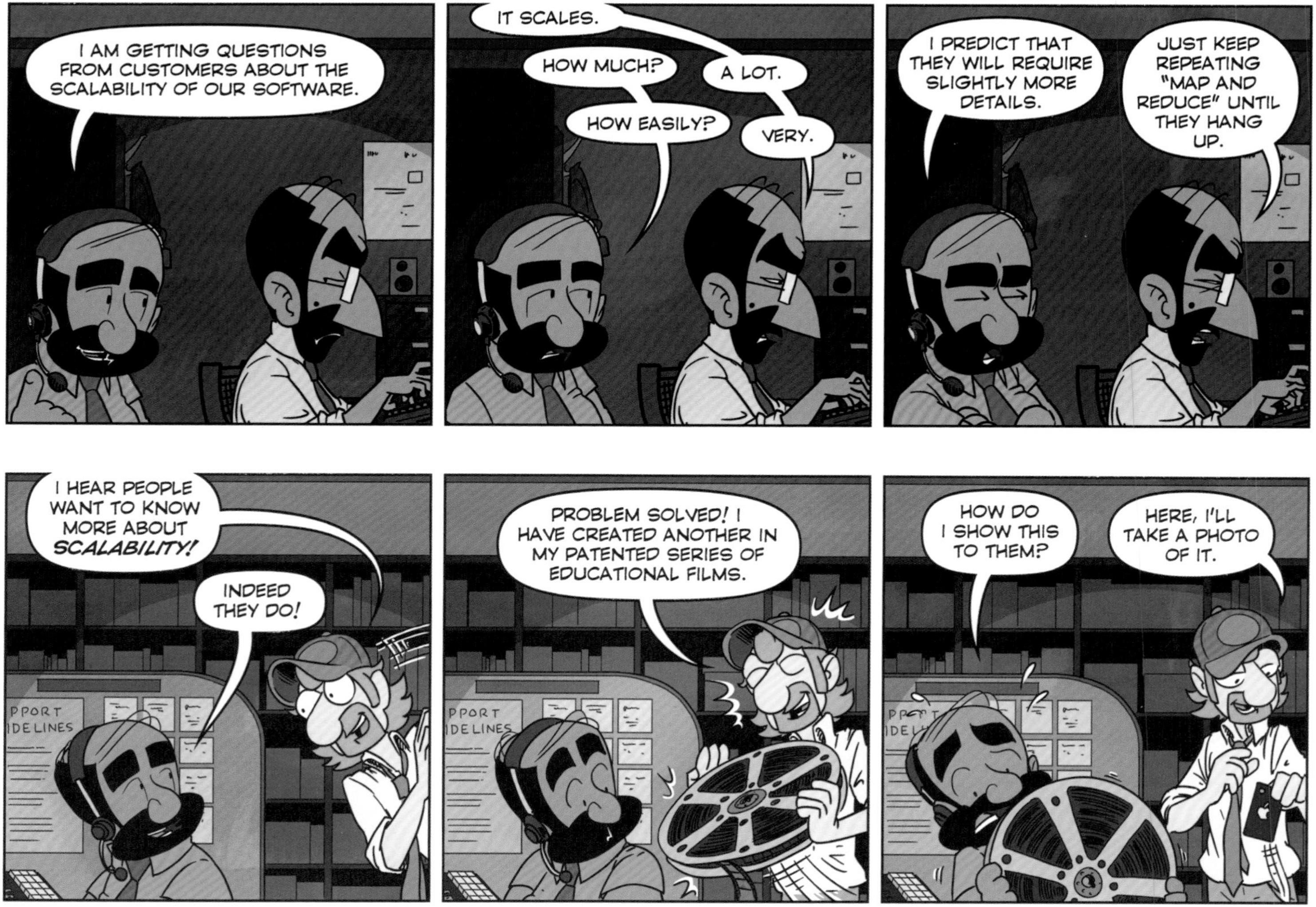
I AM GETTING QUESTIONS FROM CUSTOMERS ABOUT THE SCALABILITY OF OUR SOFTWARE.
IT SCALES.
HOW MUCH?
A LOT.
HOW EASILY?
VERY.
I PREDICT THAT THEY WILL REQUIRE SLIGHTLY MORE DETAILS.
JUST KEEP REPEATING "MAP AND REDUCE" UNTIL THEY HANG UP.
I HEAR PEOPLE WANT TO KNOW MORE ABOUT *SCALABILITY!*
INDEED THEY DO!
PROBLEM SOLVED! I HAVE CREATED ANOTHER IN MY PATENTED SERIES OF EDUCATIONAL FILMS.
HOW DO I SHOW THIS TO THEM?
HERE, I'LL TAKE A PHOTO OF IT.

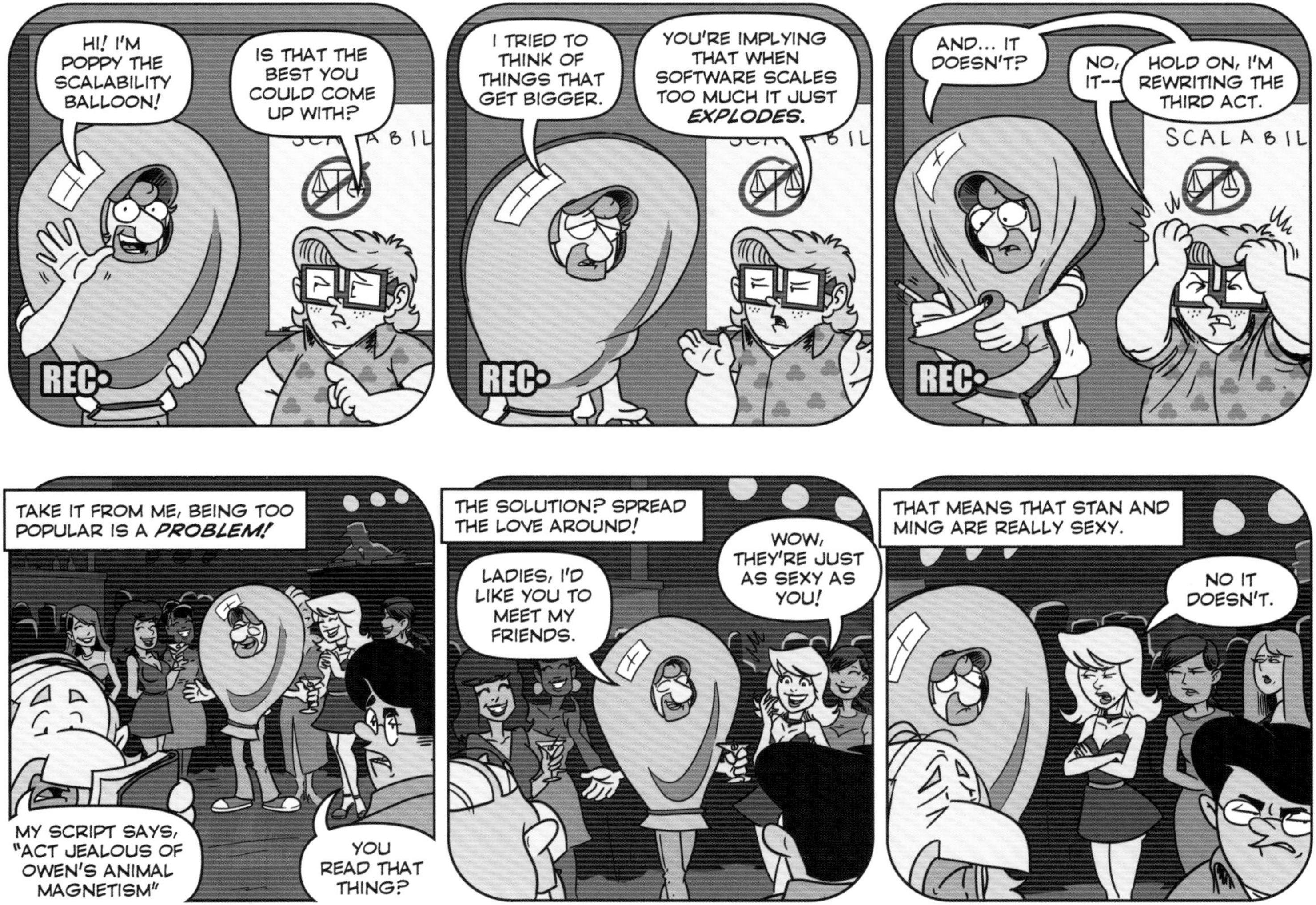
HI! I'M POPPY THE SCALABILITY BALLOON!
IS THAT THE BEST YOU COULD COME UP WITH?
REC
I TRIED TO THINK OF THINGS THAT GET BIGGER.
YOU'RE IMPLYING THAT WHEN SOFTWARE SCALES TOO MUCH IT JUST *EXPLODES.*
REC
AND... IT DOESN'T?
NO, IT--
HOLD ON, I'M REWRITING THE THIRD ACT.
SCALABIL
REC
TAKE IT FROM ME, BEING TOO POPULAR IS A *PROBLEM!*
MY SCRIPT SAYS, "ACT JEALOUS OF OWEN'S ANIMAL MAGNETISM"
YOU READ THAT THING?
THE SOLUTION? SPREAD THE LOVE AROUND!
LADIES, I'D LIKE YOU TO MEET MY FRIENDS.
WOW, THEY'RE JUST AS SEXY AS YOU!
THAT MEANS THAT STAN AND MING ARE REALLY SEXY.
NO IT DOESN'T.

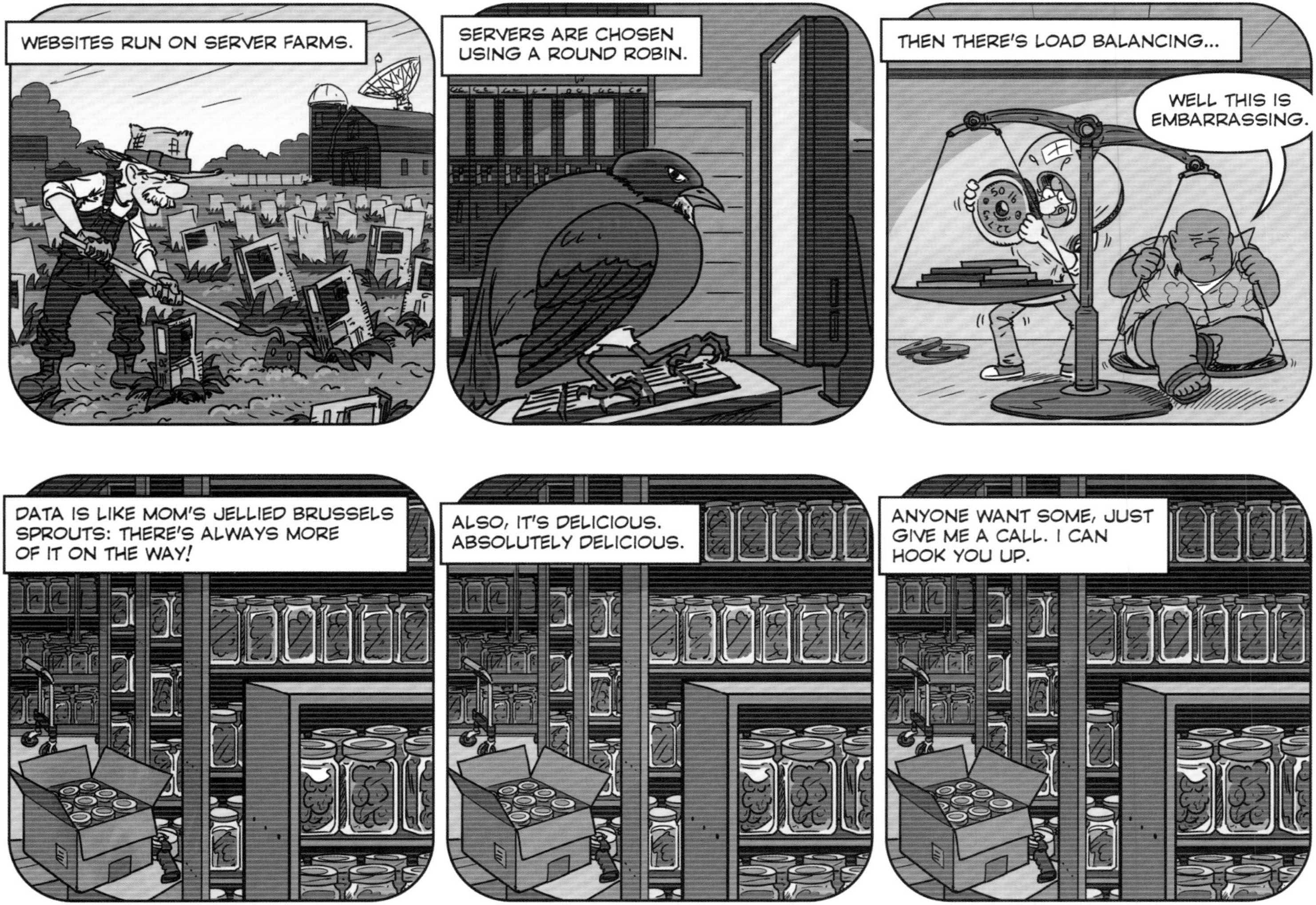
WEBSITES RUN ON SERVER FARMS.
SERVERS ARE CHOSEN USING A ROUND ROBIN.
THEN THERE'S LOAD BALANCING...
WELL THIS IS EMBARRASSING.
DATA IS LIKE MOM'S JELLIED BRUSSELS SPROUTS: THERE'S ALWAYS MORE OF IT ON THE WAY!
ALSO, IT'S DELICIOUS. ABSOLUTELY DELICIOUS.
ANYONE WANT SOME, JUST GIVE ME A CALL. I CAN HOOK YOU UP.

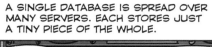

A SINGLE DATABASE IS SPREAD OVER MANY SERVERS. EACH STORES JUST A TINY PIECE OF THE WHOLE.

I'VE GOT YOUR NAME!

I'VE GOT YOUR ADDRESS!

I'VE GOT YOUR BROWSING HISTORY!

YOU'RE A BAD, BAD PERSON.

HOW TO KNOW WHAT'S STORED WHERE? A NICE LIBRARIAN NAMED MILDRED!

I'M LOOKING FOR MY MEDICAL RECORDS.

THEY'RE OVER THERE SOMEWHERE.

SHE'S *VERY* NICE!

I'M STILL NOT FORGIVING YOUR FINE, YOUNG MAN.

...AND THEN AN OVERLOADED SERVER DIVIDES INTO TWO SERVERS THROUGH A PROCESS KNOWN AS "MITOSIS"!

PLEASE EXCUSE ME, BUT I DON'T THINK ANY OF THIS IS ACCURATE.

KRISHNA, KRISHNA, KRISHNA. YOU CAN'T GET BOGGED DOWN IN *DETAILS*. WHAT MATTERS IS WHETHER IT'S *EMOTIONALLY* TRUE.

I BELIEVE THIS FILM WOULD MAKE OUR CUSTOMERS VERY VERY ANGRY.

MISSION ACCOMPLISHED!

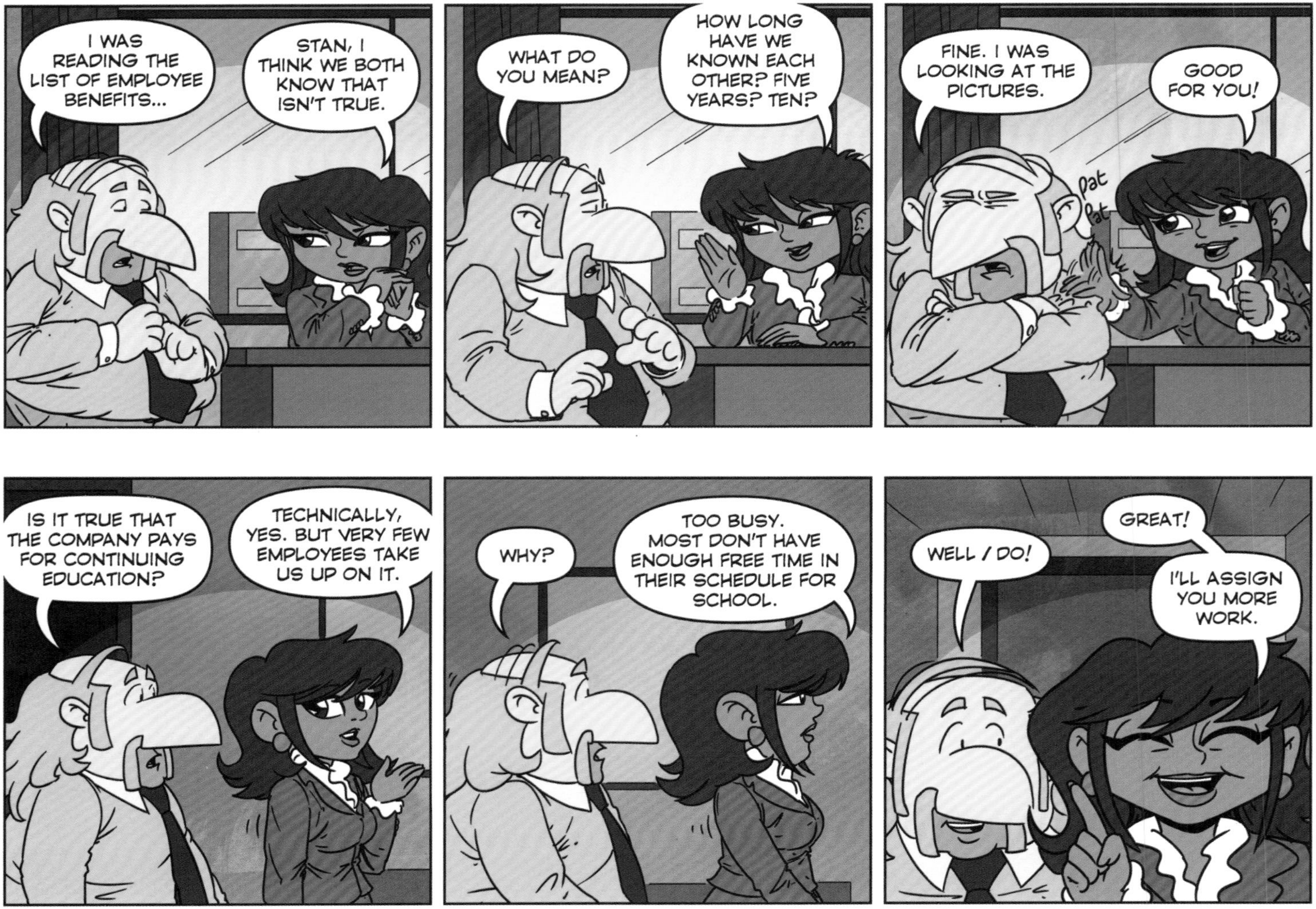
I WAS READING THE LIST OF EMPLOYEE BENEFITS...
STAN, I THINK WE BOTH KNOW THAT ISN'T TRUE.
WHAT DO YOU MEAN?
HOW LONG HAVE WE KNOWN EACH OTHER? FIVE YEARS? TEN?
FINE. I WAS LOOKING AT THE PICTURES.
GOOD FOR YOU!
Pat Pat
IS IT TRUE THAT THE COMPANY PAYS FOR CONTINUING EDUCATION?
TECHNICALLY, YES. BUT VERY FEW EMPLOYEES TAKE US UP ON IT.
WHY?
TOO BUSY. MOST DON'T HAVE ENOUGH FREE TIME IN THEIR SCHEDULE FOR SCHOOL.
WELL I DO!
GREAT!
I'LL ASSIGN YOU MORE WORK.

UPGRADE PATH

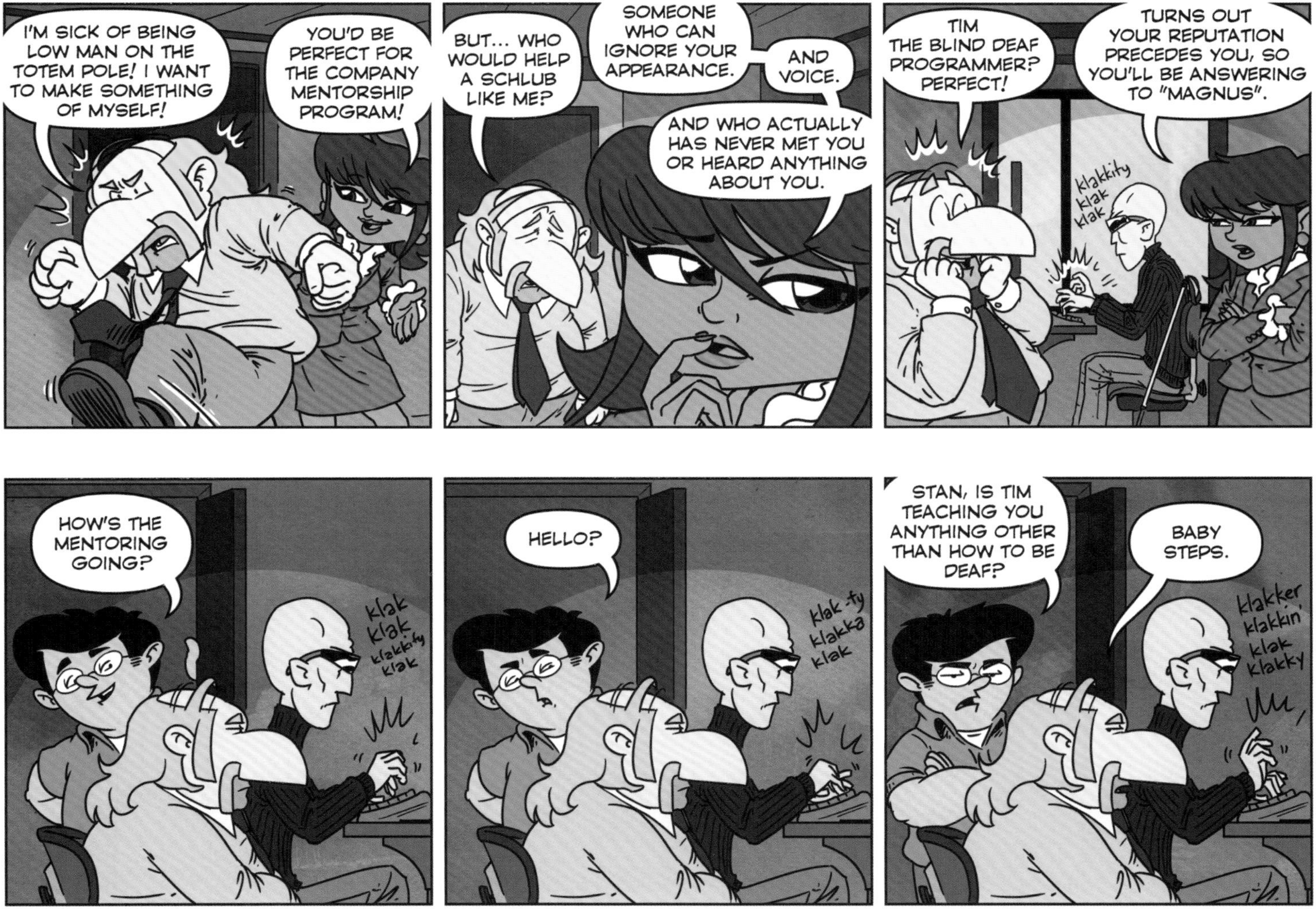
I'M SICK OF BEING LOW MAN ON THE TOTEM POLE! I WANT TO MAKE SOMETHING OF MYSELF!
YOU'D BE PERFECT FOR THE COMPANY MENTORSHIP PROGRAM!
BUT... WHO WOULD HELP A SCHLUB LIKE ME?
SOMEONE WHO CAN IGNORE YOUR APPEARANCE.
AND VOICE.
AND WHO ACTUALLY HAS NEVER MET YOU OR HEARD ANYTHING ABOUT YOU.
TIM THE BLIND DEAF PROGRAMMER? PERFECT!
TURNS OUT YOUR REPUTATION PRECEDES YOU, SO YOU'LL BE ANSWERING TO "MAGNUS".
klakkity klak klak
HOW'S THE MENTORING GOING?
klak klak klakkity klak
HELLO?
klak-ty klakka klak
STAN, IS TIM TEACHING YOU ANYTHING OTHER THAN HOW TO BE DEAF?
BABY STEPS.
klakker klakkin' klak klakky

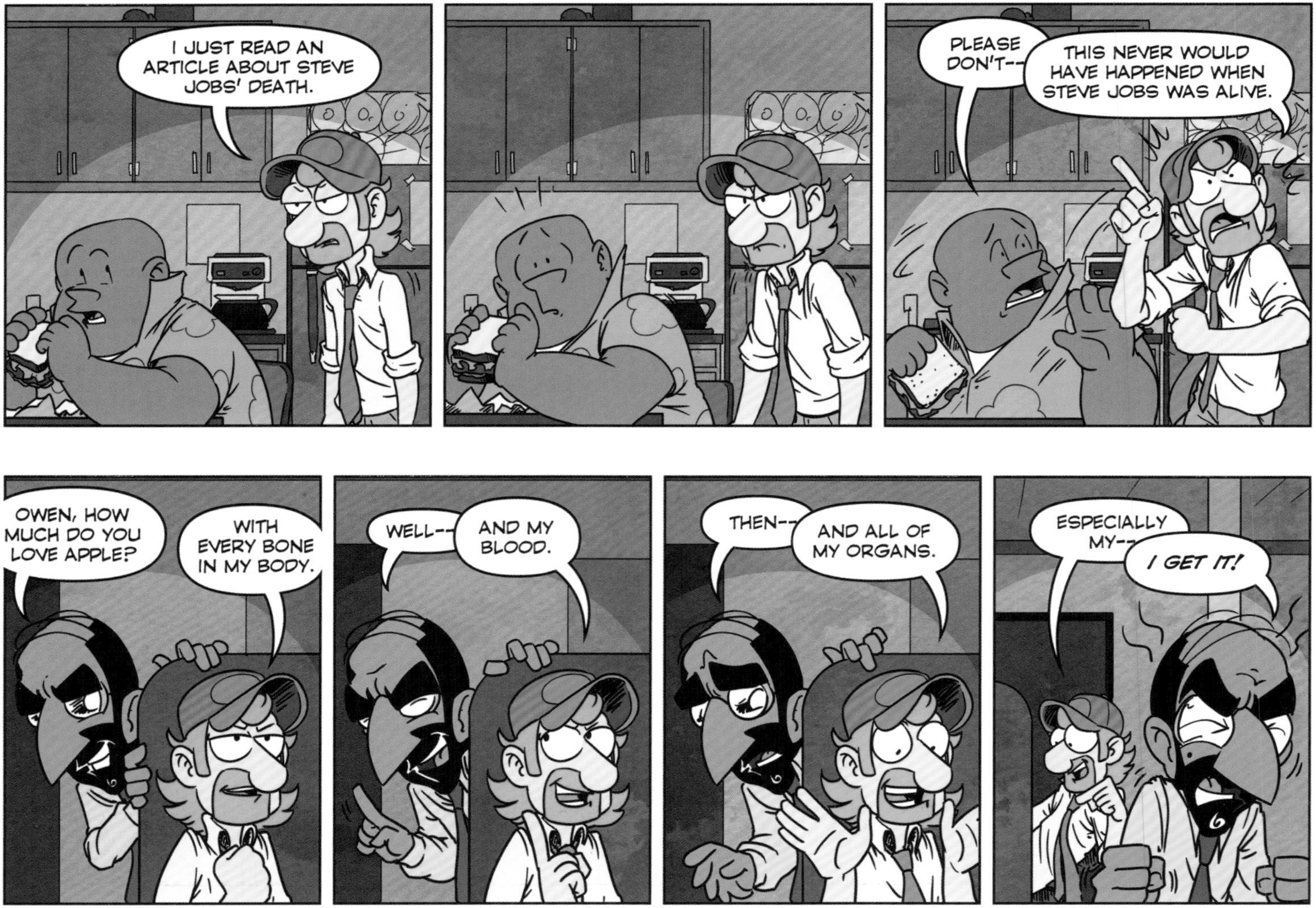
I JUST READ AN ARTICLE ABOUT STEVE JOBS' DEATH.
PLEASE DON'T--
THIS NEVER WOULD HAVE HAPPENED WHEN STEVE JOBS WAS ALIVE.
OWEN, HOW MUCH DO YOU LOVE APPLE?
WITH EVERY BONE IN MY BODY.
WELL--
AND MY BLOOD.
THEN--
AND ALL OF MY ORGANS.
ESPECIALLY MY--
I GET IT!

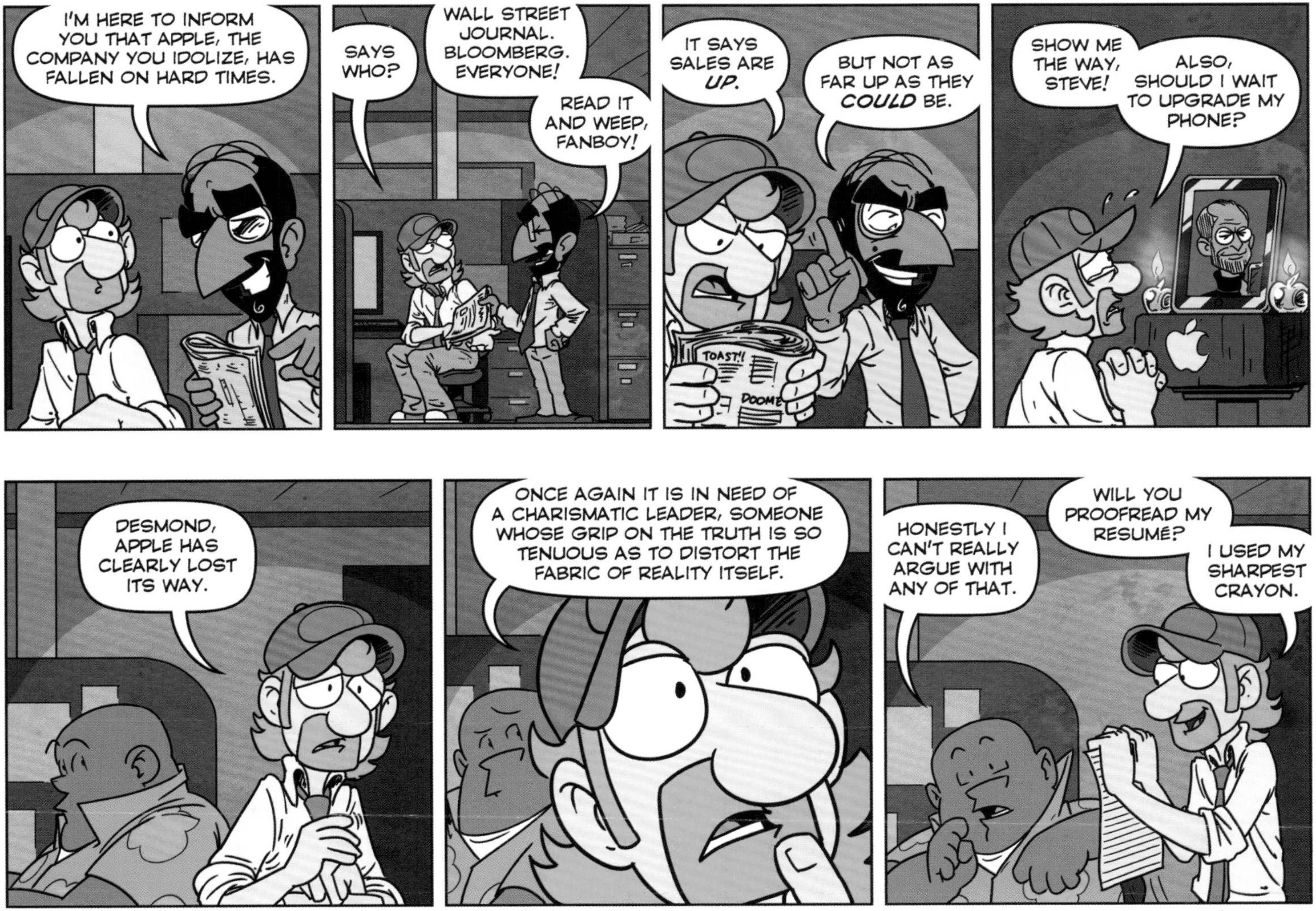
I'M HERE TO INFORM YOU THAT APPLE, THE COMPANY YOU IDOLIZE, HAS FALLEN ON HARD TIMES.
SAYS WHO?
WALL STREET JOURNAL. BLOOMBERG. EVERYONE!
READ IT AND WEEP, FANBOY!
IT SAYS SALES ARE *UP*.
TOAST!!
DOOM!
BUT NOT AS FAR UP AS THEY *COULD* BE.
SHOW ME THE WAY, STEVE!
ALSO, SHOULD I WAIT TO UPGRADE MY PHONE?
DESMOND, APPLE HAS CLEARLY LOST ITS WAY.
ONCE AGAIN IT IS IN NEED OF A CHARISMATIC LEADER, SOMEONE WHOSE GRIP ON THE TRUTH IS SO TENUOUS AS TO DISTORT THE FABRIC OF REALITY ITSELF.
HONESTLY I CAN'T REALLY ARGUE WITH ANY OF THAT.
WILL YOU PROOFREAD MY RESUMÉ?
I USED MY SHARPEST CRAYON.

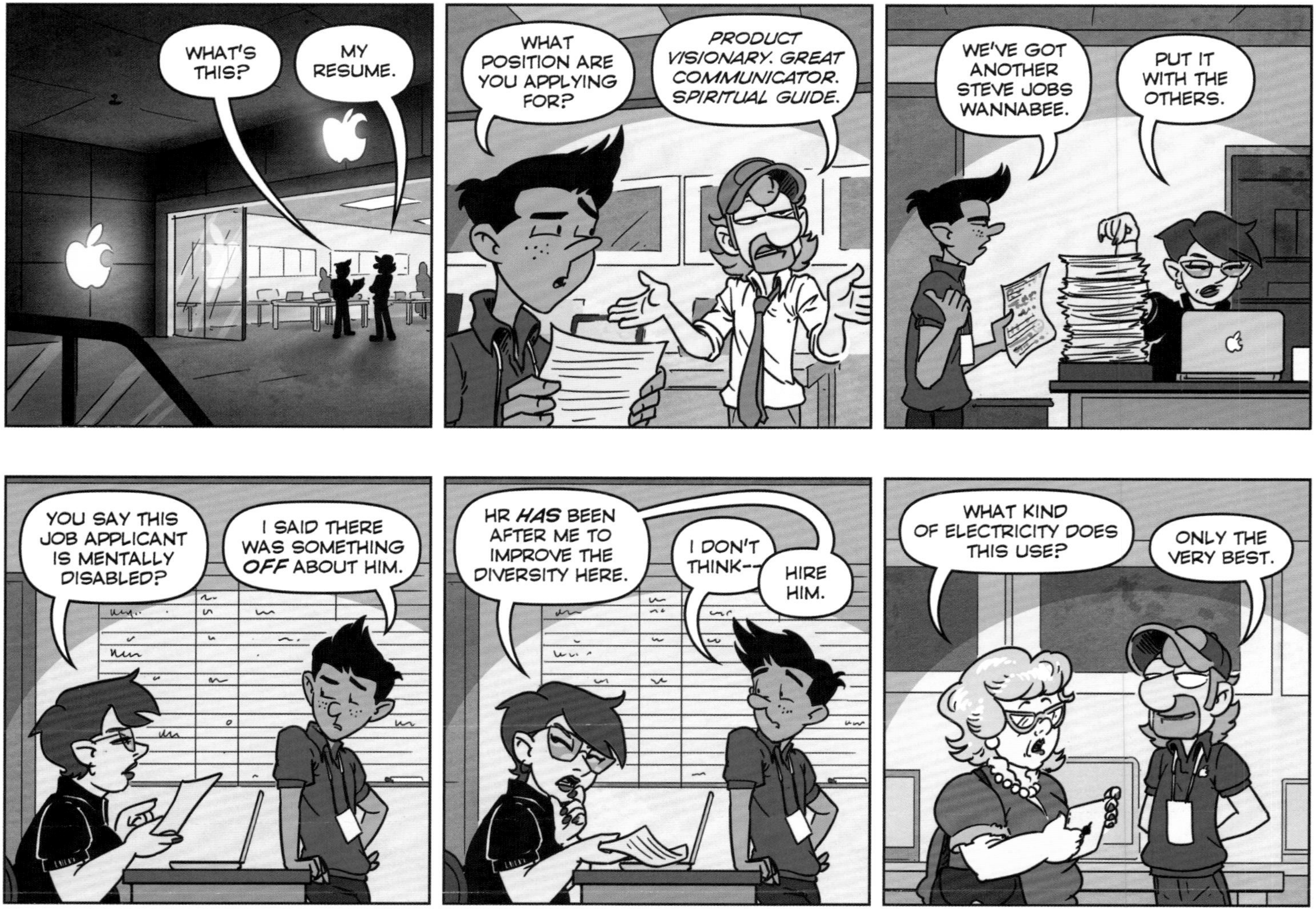
WHAT'S THIS?
MY RESUME.
WHAT POSITION ARE YOU APPLYING FOR?
PRODUCT VISIONARY. GREAT COMMUNICATOR. SPIRITUAL GUIDE.
WE'VE GOT ANOTHER STEVE JOBS WANNABEE.
PUT IT WITH THE OTHERS.
YOU SAY THIS JOB APPLICANT IS MENTALLY DISABLED?
I SAID THERE WAS SOMETHING OFF ABOUT HIM.
HR HAS BEEN AFTER ME TO IMPROVE THE DIVERSITY HERE.
I DON'T THINK--
HIRE HIM.
WHAT KIND OF ELECTRICITY DOES THIS USE?
ONLY THE VERY BEST.

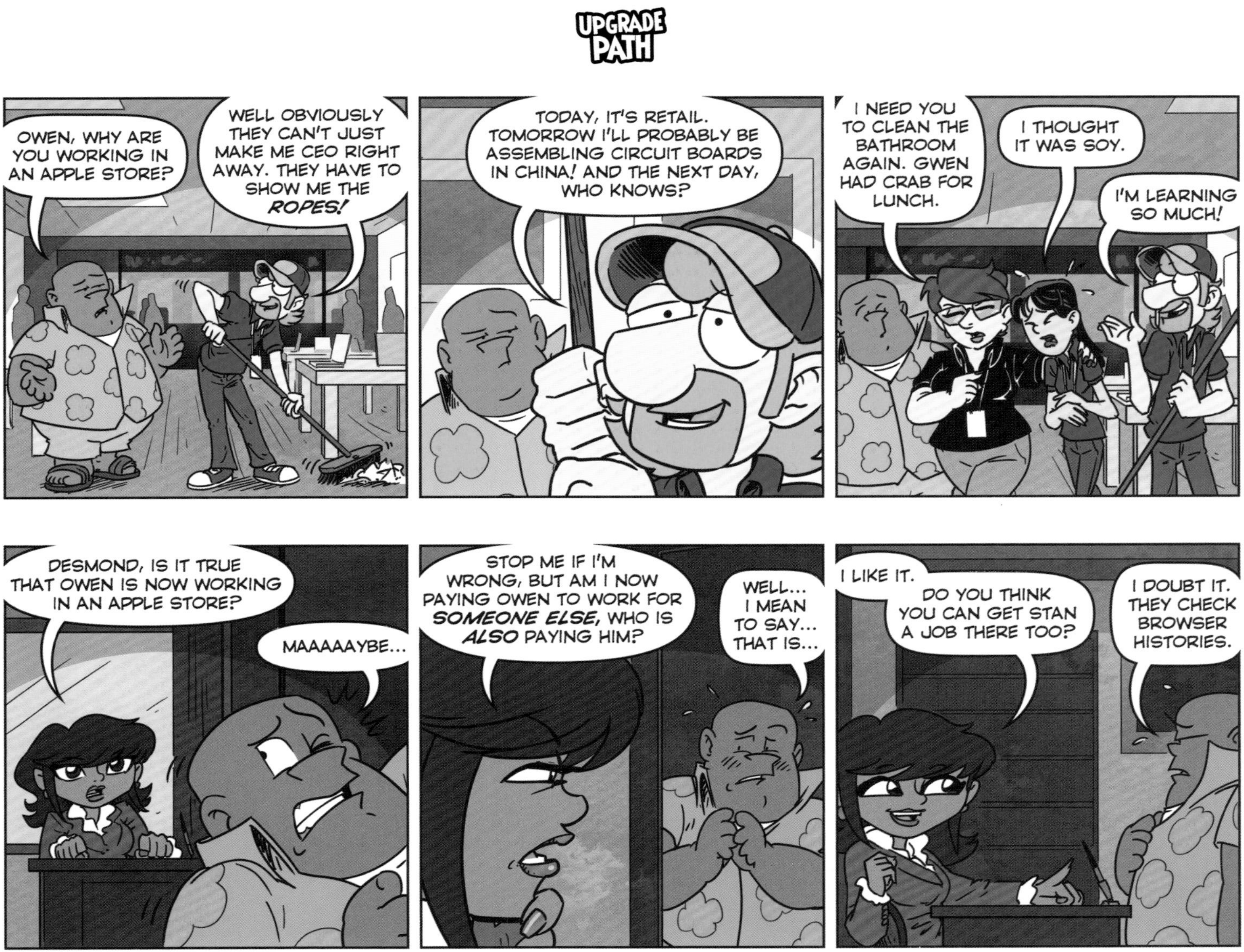
UPGRADE PATH
OWEN, WHY ARE YOU WORKING IN AN APPLE STORE?
WELL OBVIOUSLY THEY CAN'T JUST MAKE ME CEO RIGHT AWAY. THEY HAVE TO SHOW ME THE ROPES!
TODAY, IT'S RETAIL. TOMORROW I'LL PROBABLY BE ASSEMBLING CIRCUIT BOARDS IN CHINA! AND THE NEXT DAY, WHO KNOWS?
I NEED YOU TO CLEAN THE BATHROOM AGAIN. GWEN HAD CRAB FOR LUNCH.
I THOUGHT IT WAS SOY.
I'M LEARNING SO MUCH!
DESMOND, IS IT TRUE THAT OWEN IS NOW WORKING IN AN APPLE STORE?
MAAAAAYBE...
STOP ME IF I'M WRONG, BUT AM I NOW PAYING OWEN TO WORK FOR SOMEONE ELSE, WHO IS ALSO PAYING HIM?
WELL... I MEAN TO SAY... THAT IS...
I LIKE IT.
DO YOU THINK YOU CAN GET STAN A JOB THERE TOO?
I DOUBT IT. THEY CHECK BROWSER HISTORIES.

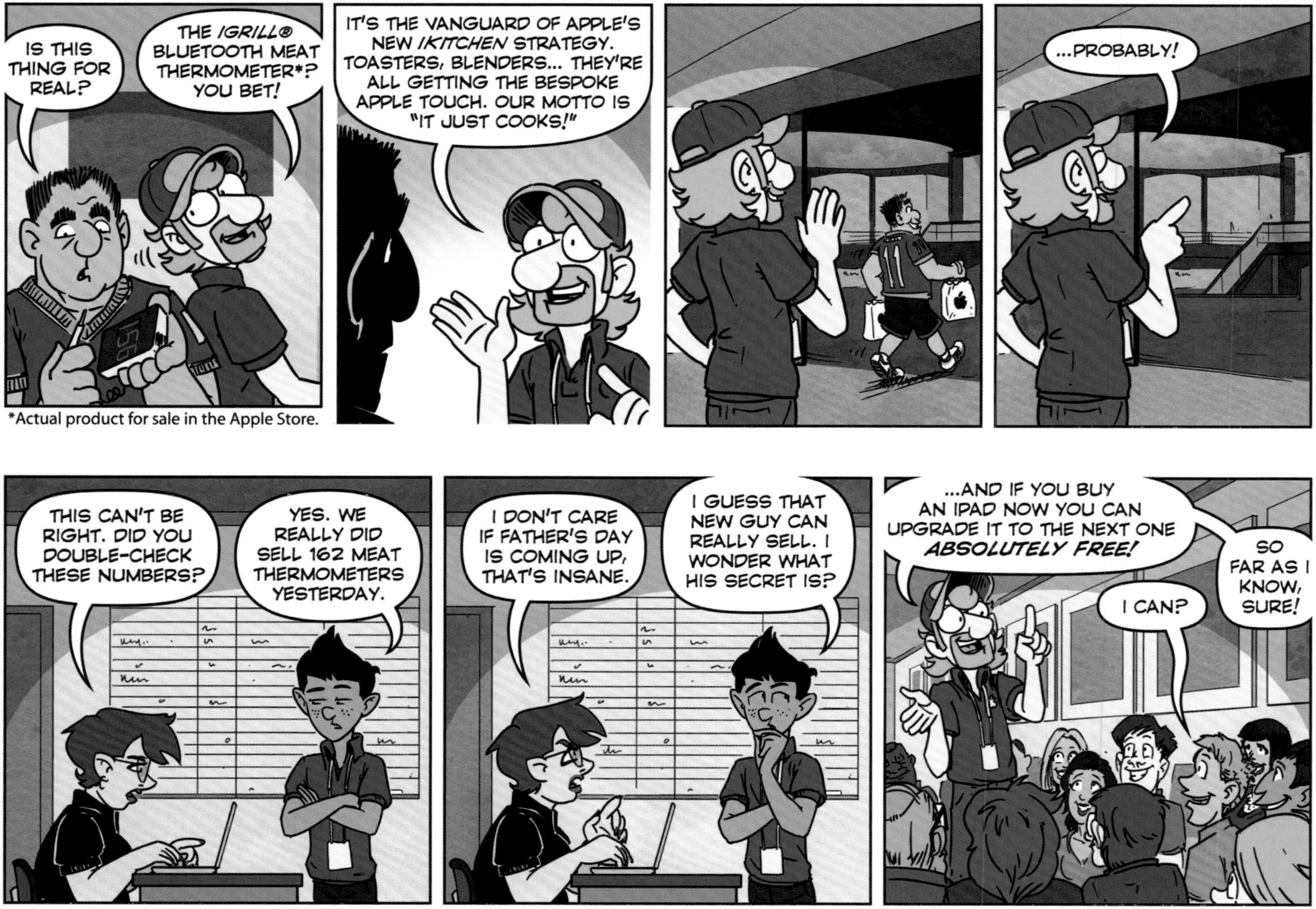
IS THIS THING FOR REAL?
THE IGRILL® BLUETOOTH MEAT THERMOMETER*? YOU BET!
*Actual product for sale in the Apple Store.
IT'S THE VANGUARD OF APPLE'S NEW IKITCHEN STRATEGY. TOASTERS, BLENDERS... THEY'RE ALL GETTING THE BESPOKE APPLE TOUCH. OUR MOTTO IS "IT JUST COOKS!"
...PROBABLY!
THIS CAN'T BE RIGHT. DID YOU DOUBLE-CHECK THESE NUMBERS?
YES. WE REALLY DID SELL 162 MEAT THERMOMETERS YESTERDAY.
I DON'T CARE IF FATHER'S DAY IS COMING UP, THAT'S INSANE.
I GUESS THAT NEW GUY CAN REALLY SELL. I WONDER WHAT HIS SECRET IS?
...AND IF YOU BUY AN IPAD NOW YOU CAN UPGRADE IT TO THE NEXT ONE ABSOLUTELY FREE!
I CAN?
SO FAR AS I KNOW, SURE!

UPGRADE PATH

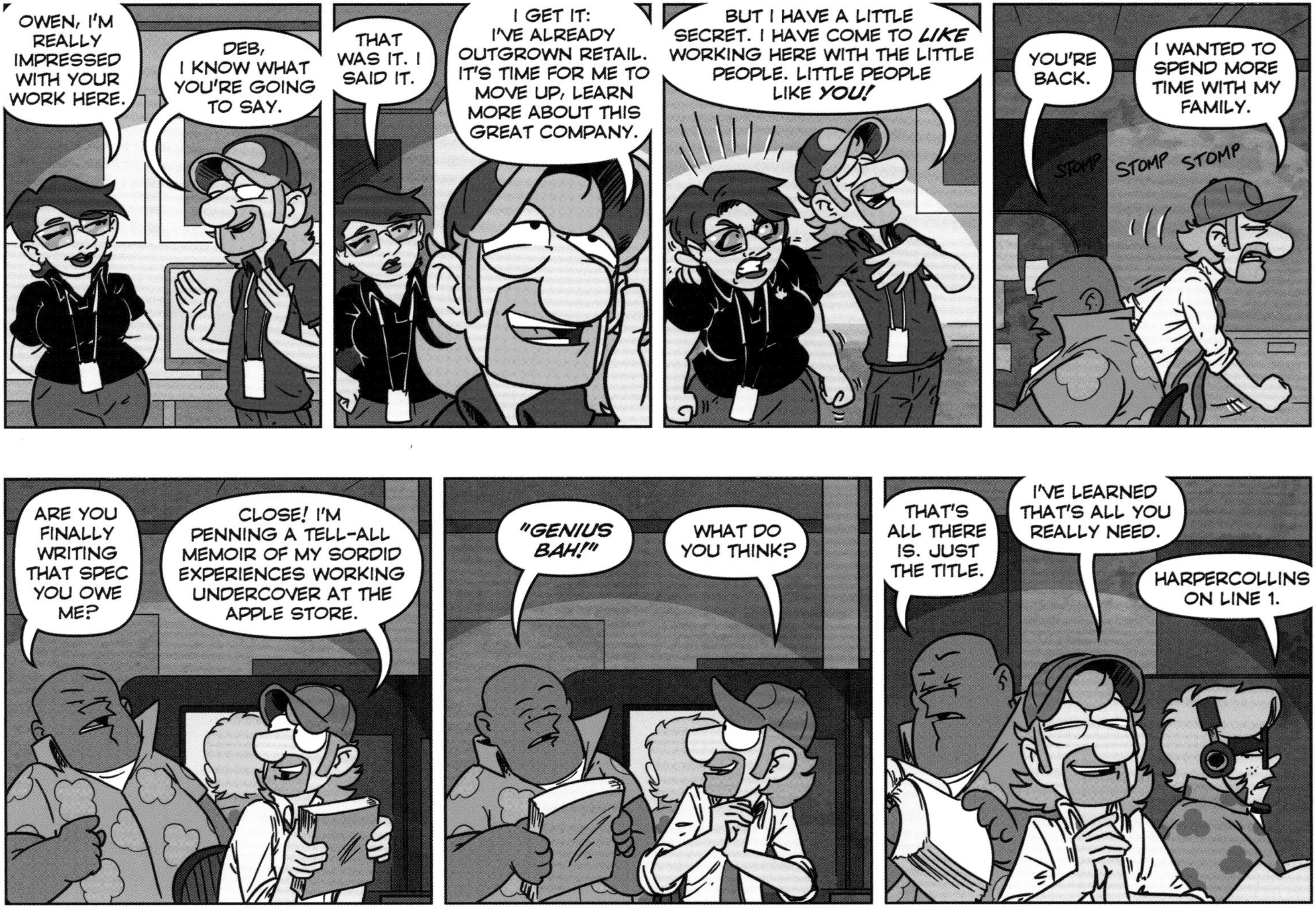
OWEN, I'M REALLY IMPRESSED WITH YOUR WORK HERE.
DEB, I KNOW WHAT YOU'RE GOING TO SAY.
THAT WAS IT. I SAID IT.
I GET IT: I'VE ALREADY OUTGROWN RETAIL. IT'S TIME FOR ME TO MOVE UP, LEARN MORE ABOUT THIS GREAT COMPANY.
BUT I HAVE A LITTLE SECRET. I HAVE COME TO *LIKE* WORKING HERE WITH THE LITTLE PEOPLE. LITTLE PEOPLE LIKE *YOU!*
YOU'RE BACK.
STOMP STOMP STOMP
I WANTED TO SPEND MORE TIME WITH MY FAMILY.
ARE YOU FINALLY WRITING THAT SPEC YOU OWE ME?
CLOSE! I'M PENNING A TELL-ALL MEMOIR OF MY SORDID EXPERIENCES WORKING UNDERCOVER AT THE APPLE STORE.
"GENIUS BAH!"
WHAT DO YOU THINK?
THAT'S ALL THERE IS. JUST THE TITLE.
I'VE LEARNED THAT'S ALL YOU REALLY NEED.
HARPERCOLLINS ON LINE 1.

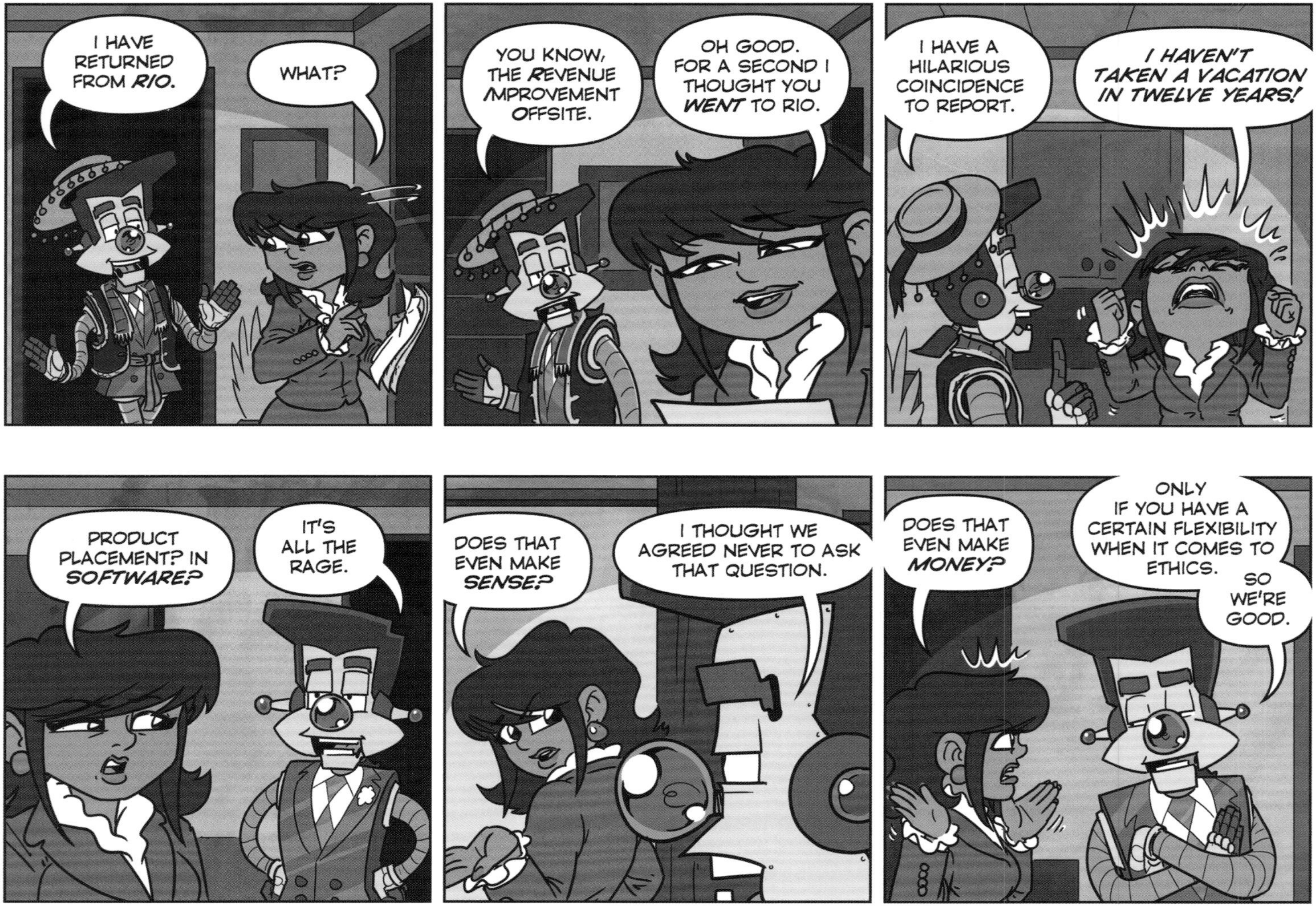
I HAVE RETURNED FROM *RIO.*
WHAT?
YOU KNOW, THE *R*EVENUE *I*MPROVEMENT *O*FFSITE.
OH GOOD. FOR A SECOND I THOUGHT YOU *WENT* TO RIO.
I HAVE A HILARIOUS COINCIDENCE TO REPORT.
I HAVEN'T TAKEN A VACATION IN TWELVE YEARS!
PRODUCT PLACEMENT? IN *SOFTWARE?*
IT'S ALL THE RAGE.
DOES THAT EVEN MAKE *SENSE?*
I THOUGHT WE AGREED NEVER TO ASK THAT QUESTION.
DOES THAT EVEN MAKE *MONEY?*
ONLY IF YOU HAVE A CERTAIN FLEXIBILITY WHEN IT COMES TO ETHICS.
SO WE'RE GOOD.

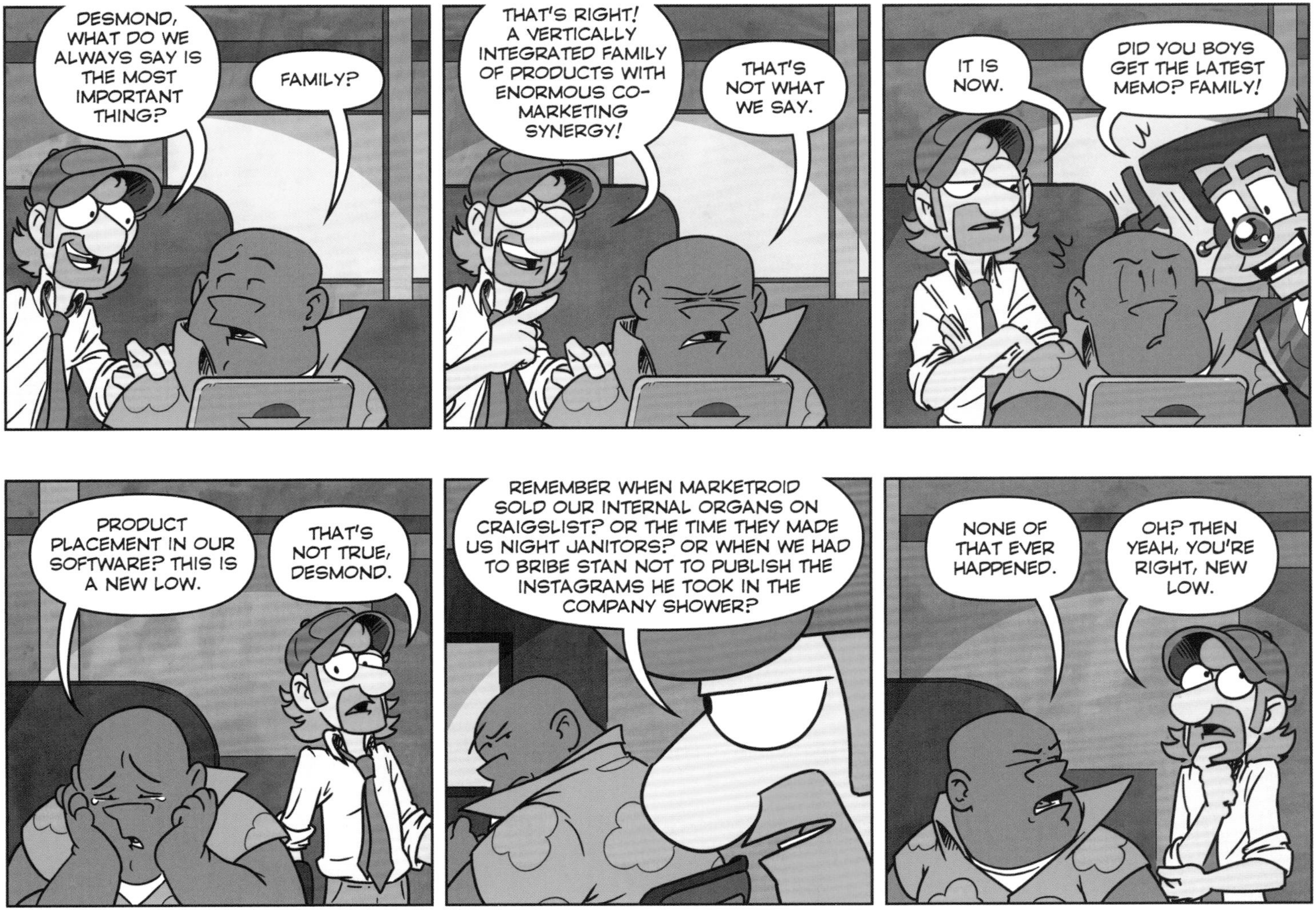
DESMOND, WHAT DO WE ALWAYS SAY IS THE MOST IMPORTANT THING?
FAMILY?
THAT'S RIGHT! A VERTICALLY INTEGRATED FAMILY OF PRODUCTS WITH ENORMOUS CO-MARKETING SYNERGY!
THAT'S NOT WHAT WE SAY.
IT IS NOW.
DID YOU BOYS GET THE LATEST MEMO? FAMILY!
PRODUCT PLACEMENT IN OUR SOFTWARE? THIS IS A NEW LOW.
THAT'S NOT TRUE, DESMOND.
REMEMBER WHEN MARKETROID SOLD OUR INTERNAL ORGANS ON CRAIGSLIST? OR THE TIME THEY MADE US NIGHT JANITORS? OR WHEN WE HAD TO BRIBE STAN NOT TO PUBLISH THE INSTAGRAMS HE TOOK IN THE COMPANY SHOWER?
NONE OF THAT EVER HAPPENED.
OH? THEN YEAH, YOU'RE RIGHT, NEW LOW.

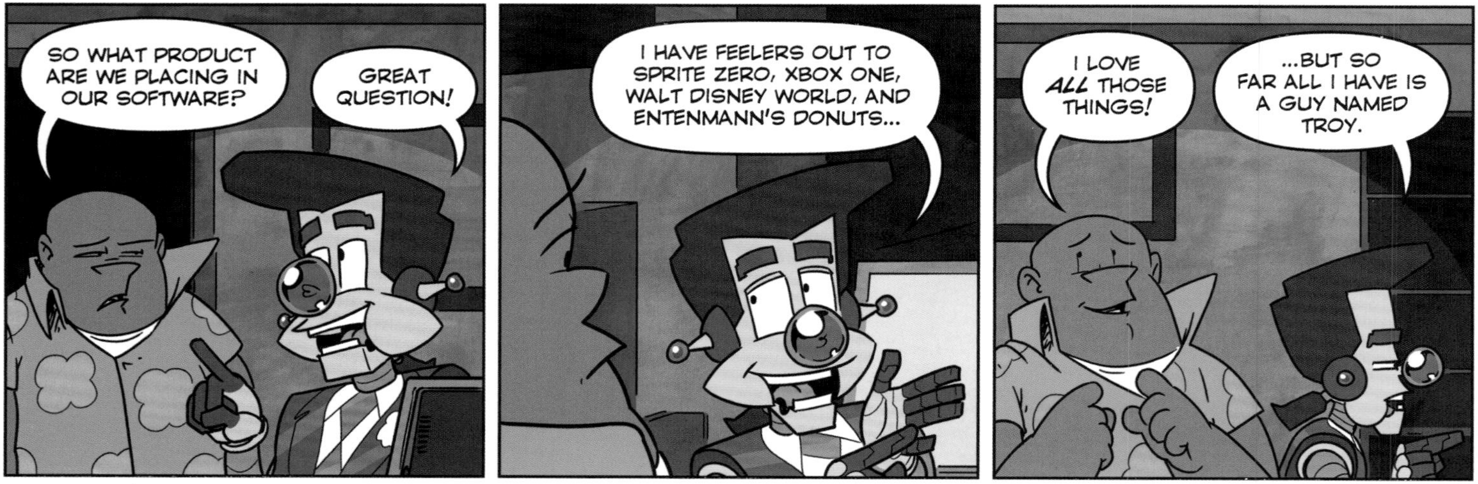
SO WHAT PRODUCT ARE WE PLACING IN OUR SOFTWARE?
GREAT QUESTION!
I HAVE FEELERS OUT TO SPRITE ZERO, XBOX ONE, WALT DISNEY WORLD, AND ENTENMANN'S DONUTS...
I LOVE ALL THOSE THINGS!
...BUT SO FAR ALL I HAVE IS A GUY NAMED TROY.

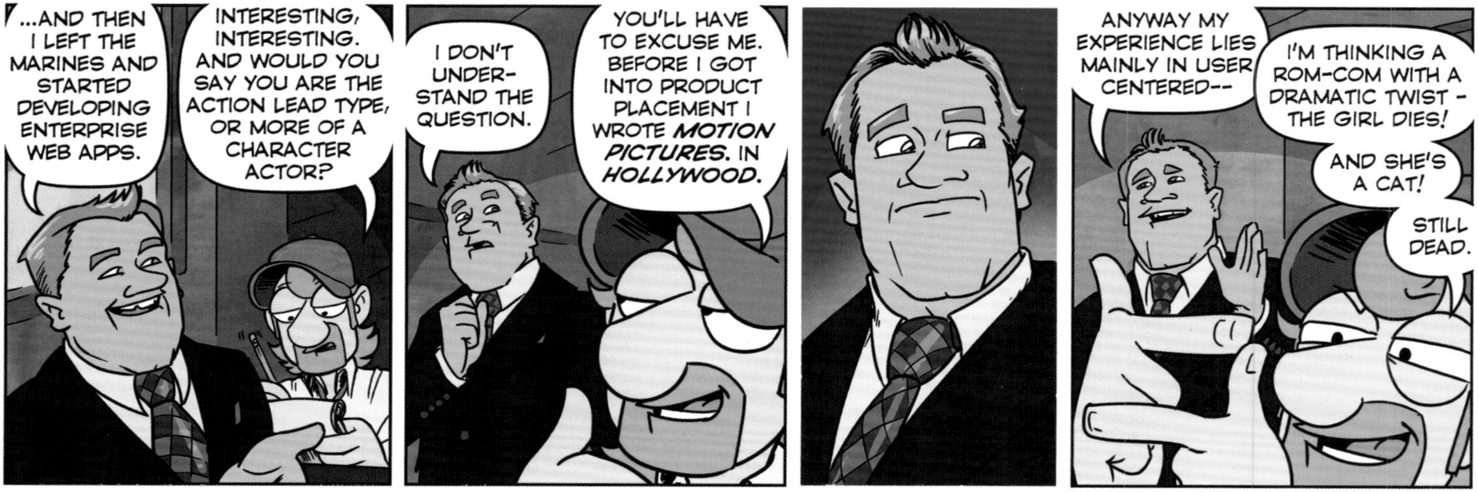
...AND THEN I LEFT THE MARINES AND STARTED DEVELOPING ENTERPRISE WEB APPS.
INTERESTING, INTERESTING. AND WOULD YOU SAY YOU ARE THE ACTION LEAD TYPE, OR MORE OF A CHARACTER ACTOR?
I DON'T UNDER-STAND THE QUESTION.
YOU'LL HAVE TO EXCUSE ME. BEFORE I GOT INTO PRODUCT PLACEMENT I WROTE MOTION PICTURES. IN HOLLYWOOD.
ANYWAY MY EXPERIENCE LIES MAINLY IN USER CENTERED--
I'M THINKING A ROM-COM WITH A DRAMATIC TWIST - THE GIRL DIES!
AND SHE'S A CAT!
STILL DEAD.

UPGRADE PATH

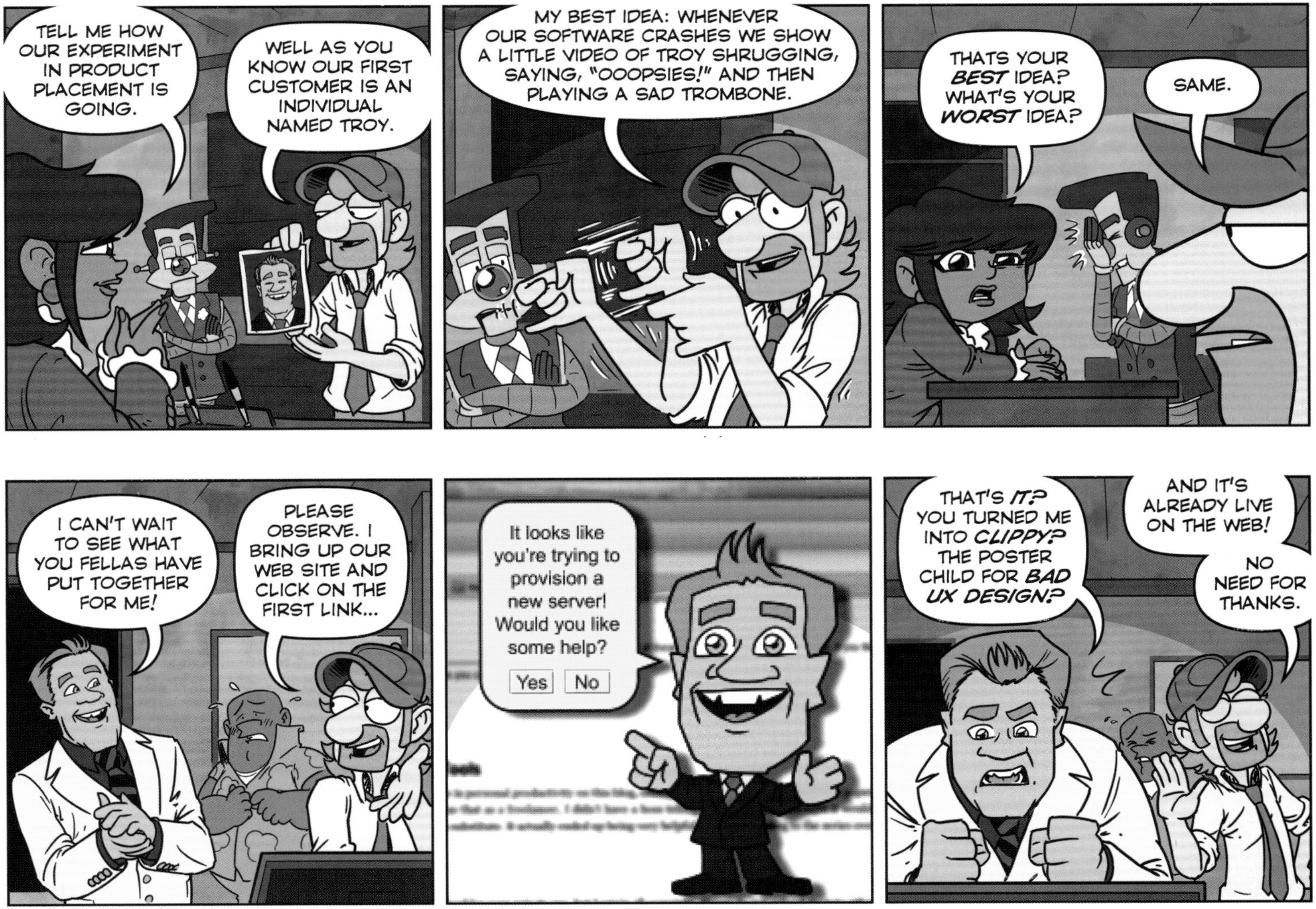
TELL ME HOW OUR EXPERIMENT IN PRODUCT PLACEMENT IS GOING.
WELL AS YOU KNOW OUR FIRST CUSTOMER IS AN INDIVIDUAL NAMED TROY.
MY BEST IDEA: WHENEVER OUR SOFTWARE CRASHES WE SHOW A LITTLE VIDEO OF TROY SHRUGGING, SAYING, "OOOPSIES!" AND THEN PLAYING A SAD TROMBONE.
THATS YOUR BEST IDEA? WHAT'S YOUR WORST IDEA?
SAME.
I CAN'T WAIT TO SEE WHAT YOU FELLAS HAVE PUT TOGETHER FOR ME!
PLEASE OBSERVE. I BRING UP OUR WEB SITE AND CLICK ON THE FIRST LINK...
It looks like you're trying to provision a new server! Would you like some help?
Yes
No
THAT'S IT? YOU TURNED ME INTO CLIPPY? THE POSTER CHILD FOR BAD UX DESIGN?
AND IT'S ALREADY LIVE ON THE WEB!
NO NEED FOR THANKS.

Bonus Strips

UPGRADE PATH

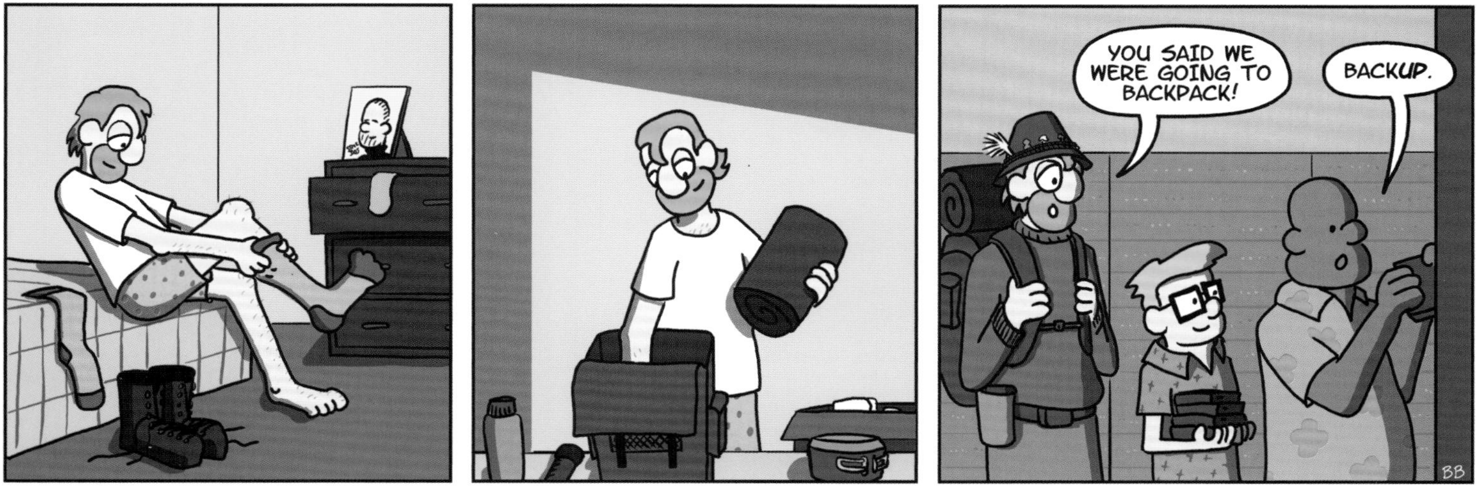
YOU SAID WE WERE GOING TO BACKPACK!
BACKUP.

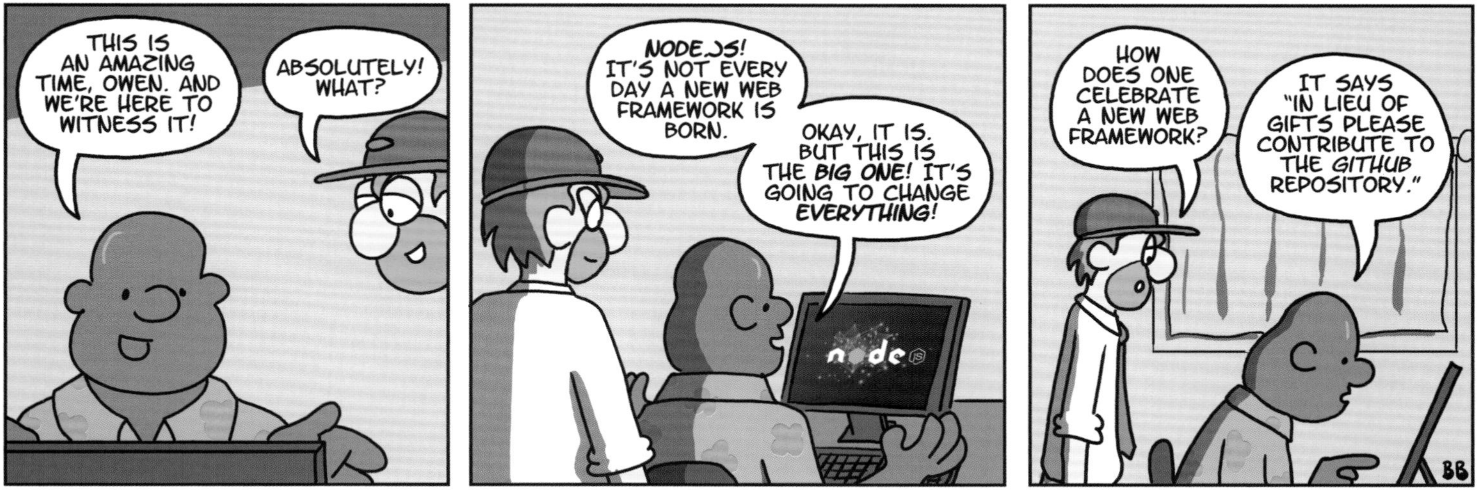
THIS IS AN AMAZING TIME, OWEN. AND WE'RE HERE TO WITNESS IT!
ABSOLUTELY! WHAT?
NODE.JS! IT'S NOT EVERY DAY A NEW WEB FRAMEWORK IS BORN.
OKAY, IT IS. BUT THIS IS THE BIG ONE! IT'S GOING TO CHANGE EVERYTHING!
HOW DOES ONE CELEBRATE A NEW WEB FRAMEWORK?
IT SAYS "IN LIEU OF GIFTS PLEASE CONTRIBUTE TO THE GITHUB REPOSITORY."

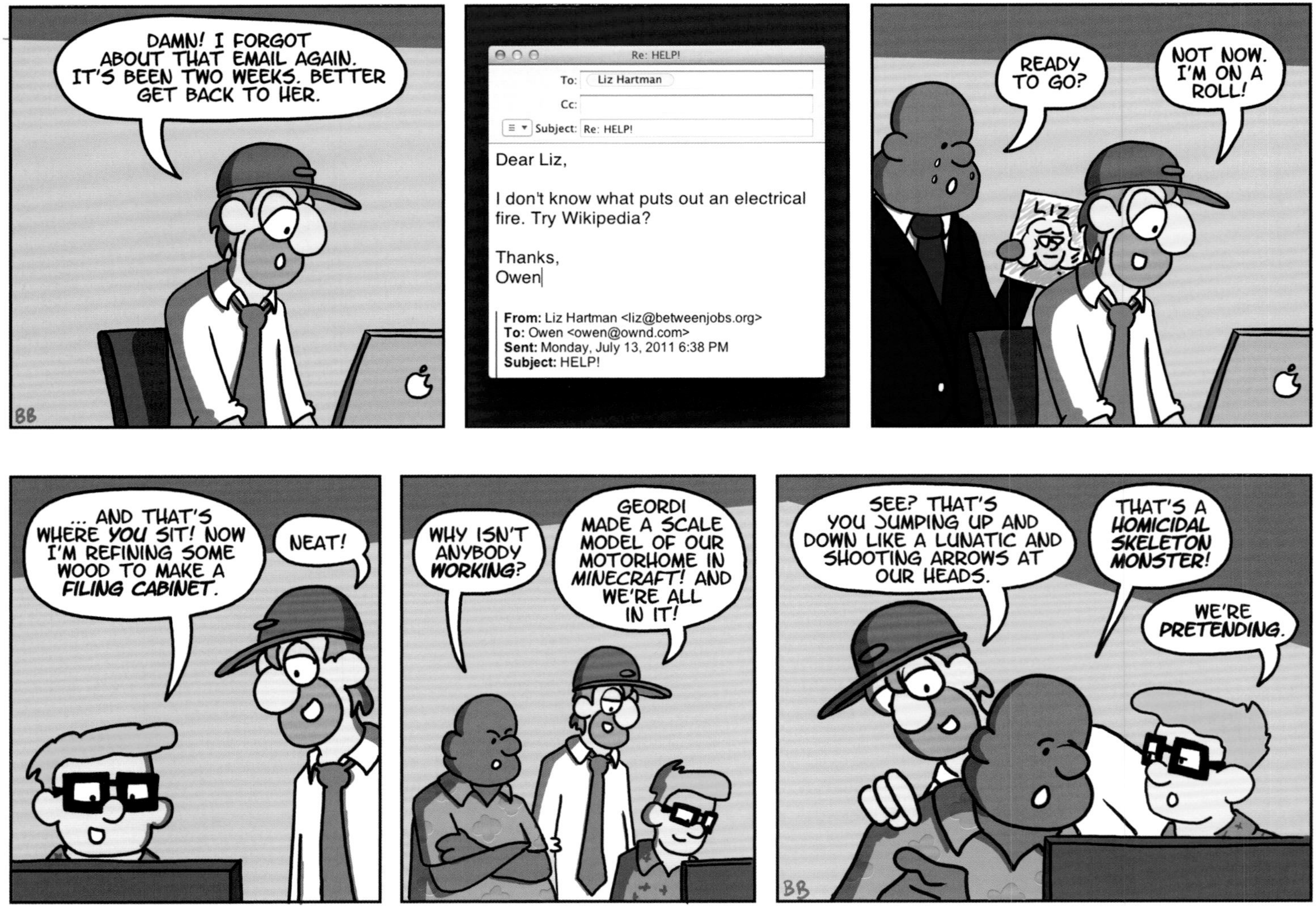
DAMN! I FORGOT ABOUT THAT EMAIL AGAIN. IT'S BEEN TWO WEEKS. BETTER GET BACK TO HER.
Re: HELP!
To: Liz Hartman
Cc:
Subject: Re: HELP!
Dear Liz,
I don't know what puts out an electrical fire. Try Wikipedia?
Thanks,
Owen
From: Liz Hartman <liz@betweenjobs.org>
To: Owen <owen@ownd.com>
Sent: Monday, July 13, 2011 6:38 PM
Subject: HELP!
READY TO GO?
NOT NOW. I'M ON A ROLL!
LIZ
... AND THAT'S WHERE *YOU* SIT! NOW I'M REFINING SOME WOOD TO MAKE A *FILING CABINET*.
NEAT!
WHY ISN'T ANYBODY *WORKING*?
GEORDI MADE A SCALE MODEL OF OUR MOTORHOME IN *MINECRAFT*! AND WE'RE ALL IN IT!
SEE? THAT'S YOU JUMPING UP AND DOWN LIKE A LUNATIC AND SHOOTING ARROWS AT OUR HEADS.
THAT'S A *HOMICIDAL SKELETON MONSTER*!
WE'RE *PRETENDING*.

UPGRADE PATH

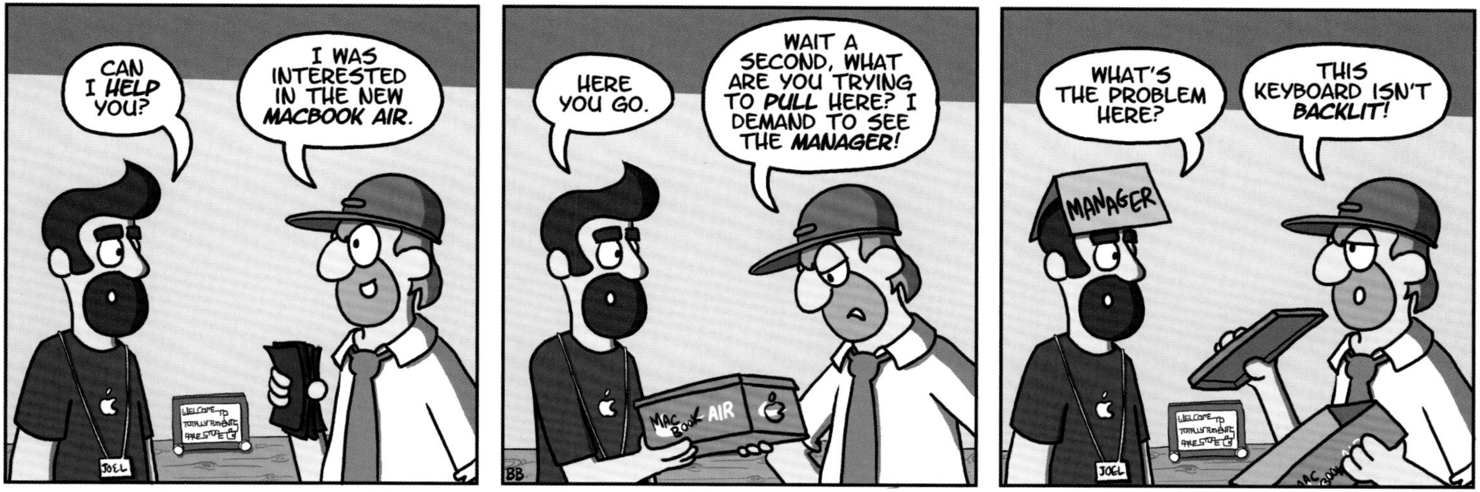
CAN I HELP YOU?
I WAS INTERESTED IN THE NEW MACBOOK AIR.
HERE YOU GO.
MAC BOOK AIR
WAIT A SECOND, WHAT ARE YOU TRYING TO PULL HERE? I DEMAND TO SEE THE MANAGER!
MANAGER
WHAT'S THE PROBLEM HERE?
THIS KEYBOARD ISN'T BACKLIT!

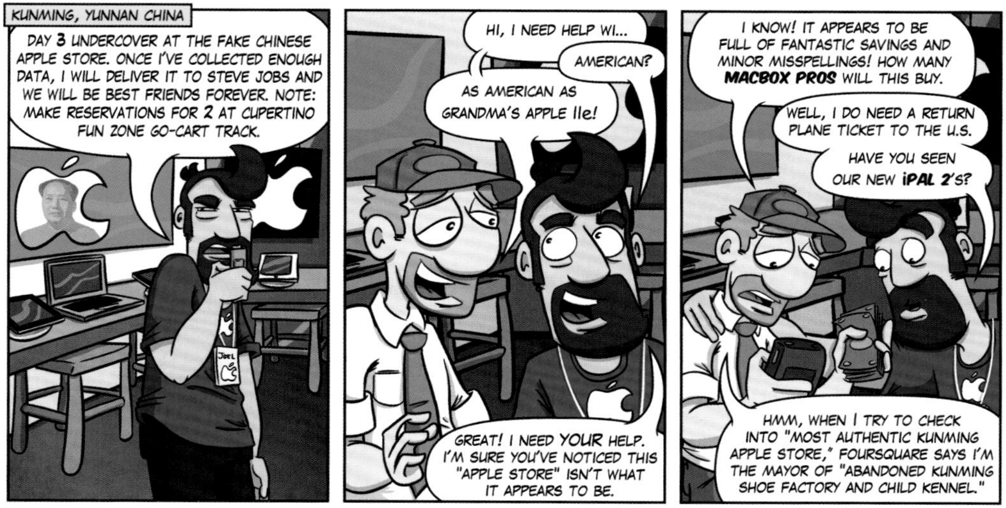
KUNMING, YUNNAN CHINA
DAY 3 UNDERCOVER AT THE FAKE CHINESE APPLE STORE. ONCE I'VE COLLECTED ENOUGH DATA, I WILL DELIVER IT TO STEVE JOBS AND WE WILL BE BEST FRIENDS FOREVER. NOTE: MAKE RESERVATIONS FOR 2 AT CUPERTINO FUN ZONE GO-CART TRACK.
HI, I NEED HELP WI...
AMERICAN?
AS AMERICAN AS GRANDMA'S APPLE IIe!
GREAT! I NEED YOUR HELP. I'M SURE YOU'VE NOTICED THIS "APPLE STORE" ISN'T WHAT IT APPEARS TO BE.
I KNOW! IT APPEARS TO BE FULL OF FANTASTIC SAVINGS AND MINOR MISSPELLINGS! HOW MANY MACBOX PROS WILL THIS BUY.
WELL, I DO NEED A RETURN PLANE TICKET TO THE U.S.
HAVE YOU SEEN OUR NEW iPAL 2'S?
HMM, WHEN I TRY TO CHECK INTO "MOST AUTHENTIC KUNMING APPLE STORE," FOURSQUARE SAYS I'M THE MAYOR OF "ABANDONED KUNMING SHOE FACTORY AND CHILD KENNEL."

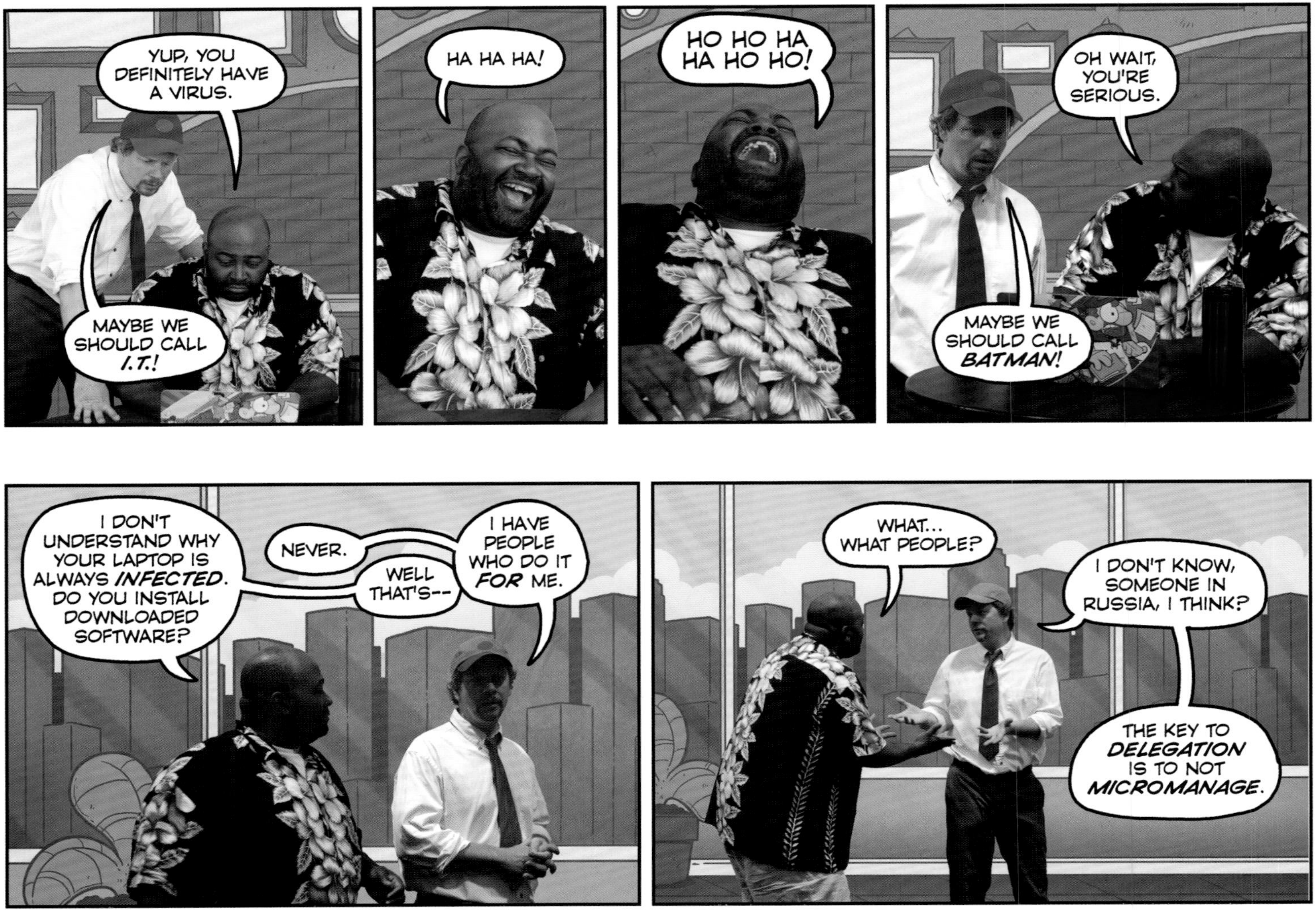
YUP, YOU DEFINITELY HAVE A VIRUS.
MAYBE WE SHOULD CALL *I.T.!*
HA HA HA!
HO HO HA HA HO HO!
OH WAIT, YOU'RE SERIOUS.
MAYBE WE SHOULD CALL *BATMAN!*
I DON'T UNDERSTAND WHY YOUR LAPTOP IS ALWAYS *INFECTED*. DO YOU INSTALL DOWNLOADED SOFTWARE?
NEVER.
WELL THAT'S--
I HAVE PEOPLE WHO DO IT *FOR* ME.
WHAT... WHAT PEOPLE?
I DON'T KNOW, SOMEONE IN RUSSIA, I THINK?
THE KEY TO *DELEGATION* IS TO NOT *MICROMANAGE*.

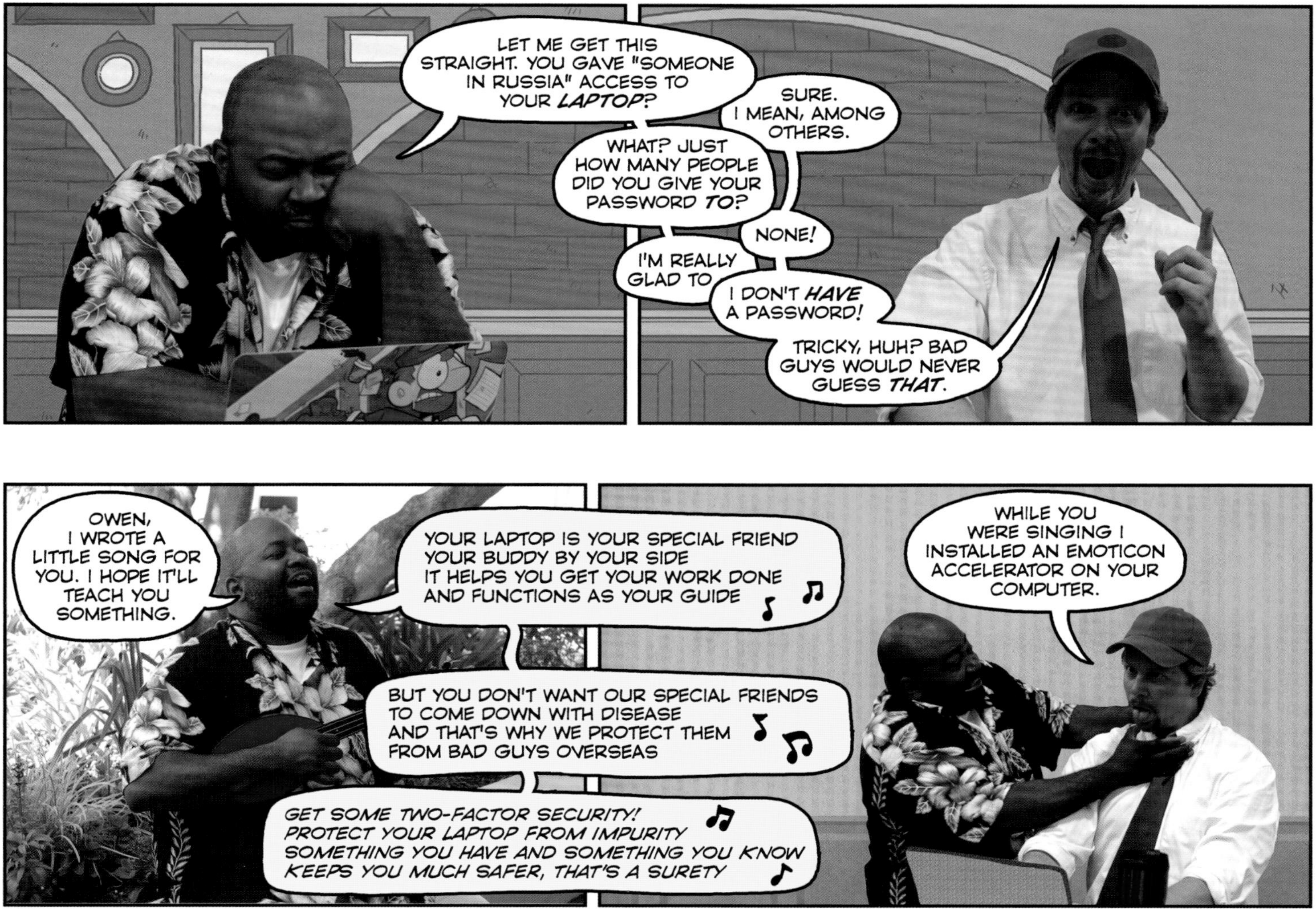
LET ME GET THIS STRAIGHT. YOU GAVE "SOMEONE IN RUSSIA" ACCESS TO YOUR *LAPTOP*?
SURE. I MEAN, AMONG OTHERS.
WHAT? JUST HOW MANY PEOPLE DID YOU GIVE YOUR PASSWORD *TO*?
NONE!
I'M REALLY GLAD TO
I DON'T *HAVE* A PASSWORD!
TRICKY, HUH? BAD GUYS WOULD NEVER GUESS *THAT*.
OWEN, I WROTE A LITTLE SONG FOR YOU. I HOPE IT'LL TEACH YOU SOMETHING.
YOUR LAPTOP IS YOUR SPECIAL FRIEND YOUR BUDDY BY YOUR SIDE IT HELPS YOU GET YOUR WORK DONE AND FUNCTIONS AS YOUR GUIDE
BUT YOU DON'T WANT OUR SPECIAL FRIENDS TO COME DOWN WITH DISEASE AND THAT'S WHY WE PROTECT THEM FROM BAD GUYS OVERSEAS
GET SOME TWO-FACTOR SECURITY! PROTECT YOUR LAPTOP FROM IMPURITY SOMETHING YOU HAVE AND SOMETHING YOU KNOW KEEPS YOU MUCH SAFER, THAT'S A SURETY
WHILE YOU WERE SINGING I INSTALLED AN EMOTICON ACCELERATOR ON YOUR COMPUTER.

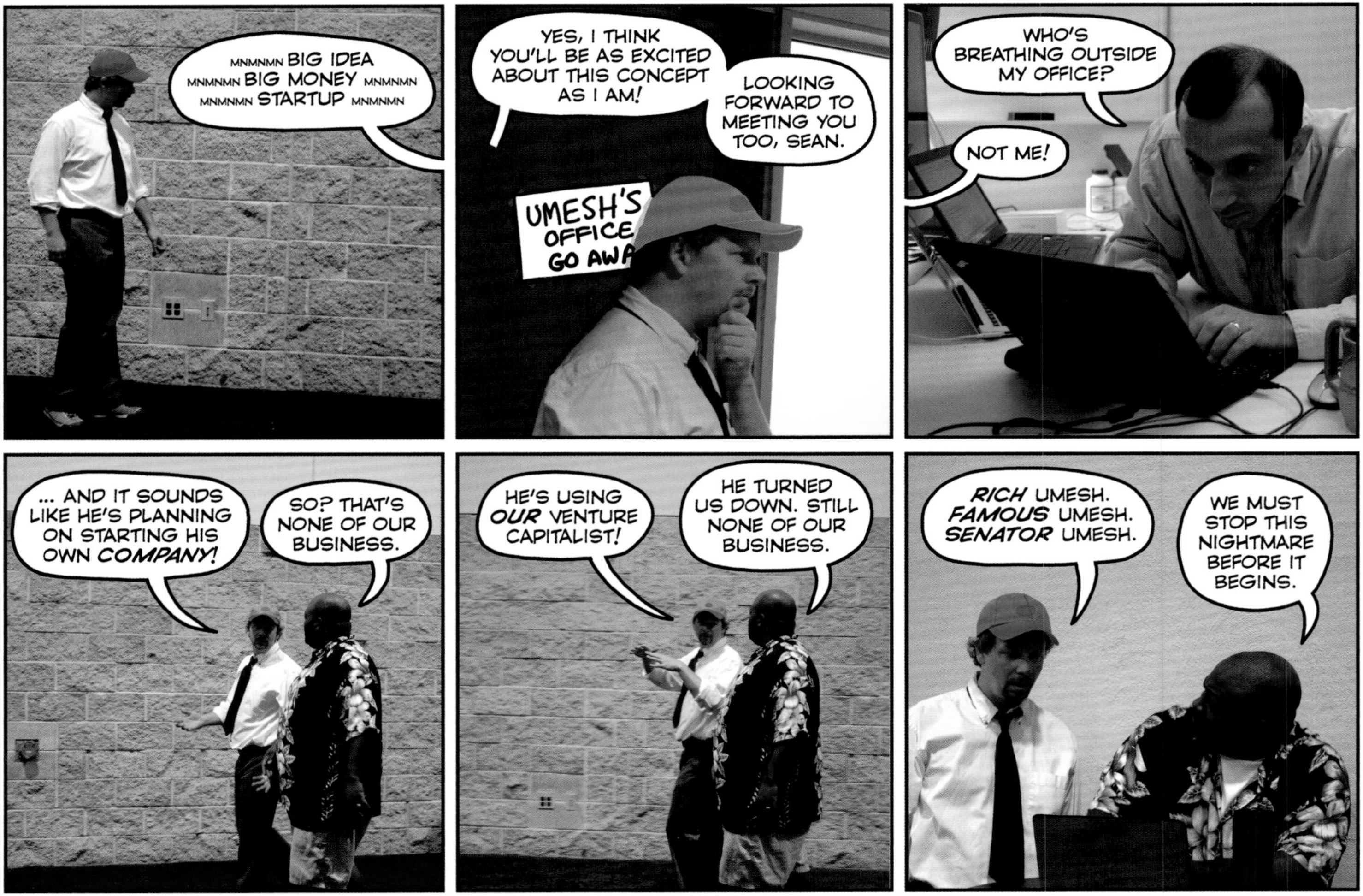
MNMNMN BIG IDEA
MNMNMN BIG MONEY MNMNMN
MNMNMN STARTUP MNMNMN
YES, I THINK YOU'LL BE AS EXCITED ABOUT THIS CONCEPT AS I AM!
LOOKING FORWARD TO MEETING YOU TOO, SEAN.
UMESH'S OFFICE GO AWA
WHO'S BREATHING OUTSIDE MY OFFICE?
NOT ME!
... AND IT SOUNDS LIKE HE'S PLANNING ON STARTING HIS OWN *COMPANY!*
SO? THAT'S NONE OF OUR BUSINESS.
HE'S USING *OUR* VENTURE CAPITALIST!
HE TURNED US DOWN. STILL NONE OF OUR BUSINESS.
RICH UMESH. *FAMOUS* UMESH. *SENATOR* UMESH.
WE MUST STOP THIS NIGHTMARE BEFORE IT BEGINS.

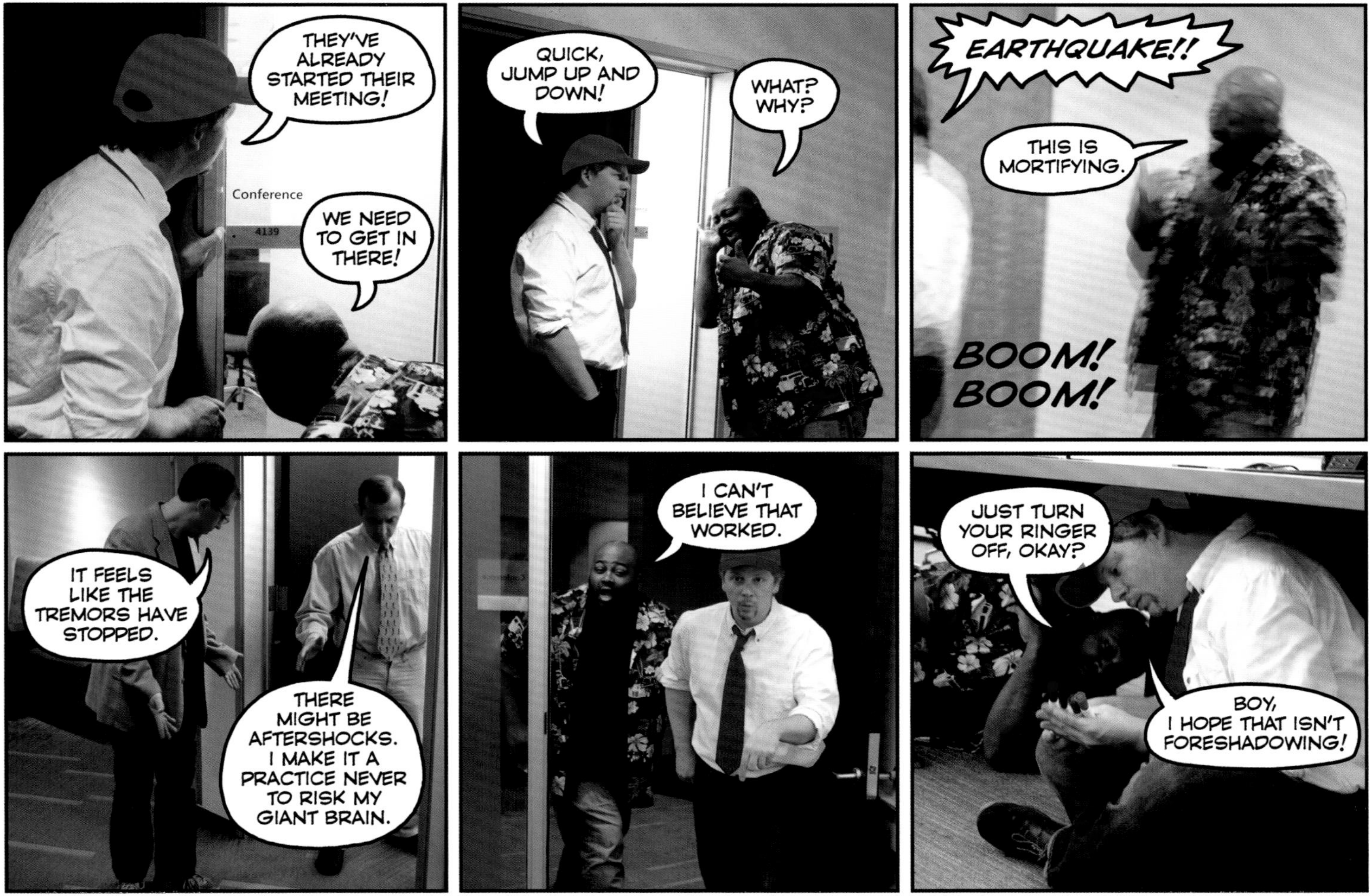
THEY'VE ALREADY STARTED THEIR MEETING!
Conference
4139
WE NEED TO GET IN THERE!
QUICK, JUMP UP AND DOWN!
WHAT? WHY?
EARTHQUAKE!!
THIS IS MORTIFYING.
BOOM! BOOM!
IT FEELS LIKE THE TREMORS HAVE STOPPED.
THERE MIGHT BE AFTERSHOCKS. I MAKE IT A PRACTICE NEVER TO RISK MY GIANT BRAIN.
I CAN'T BELIEVE THAT WORKED.
JUST TURN YOUR RINGER OFF, OKAY?
BOY, I HOPE THAT ISN'T FORESHADOWING!

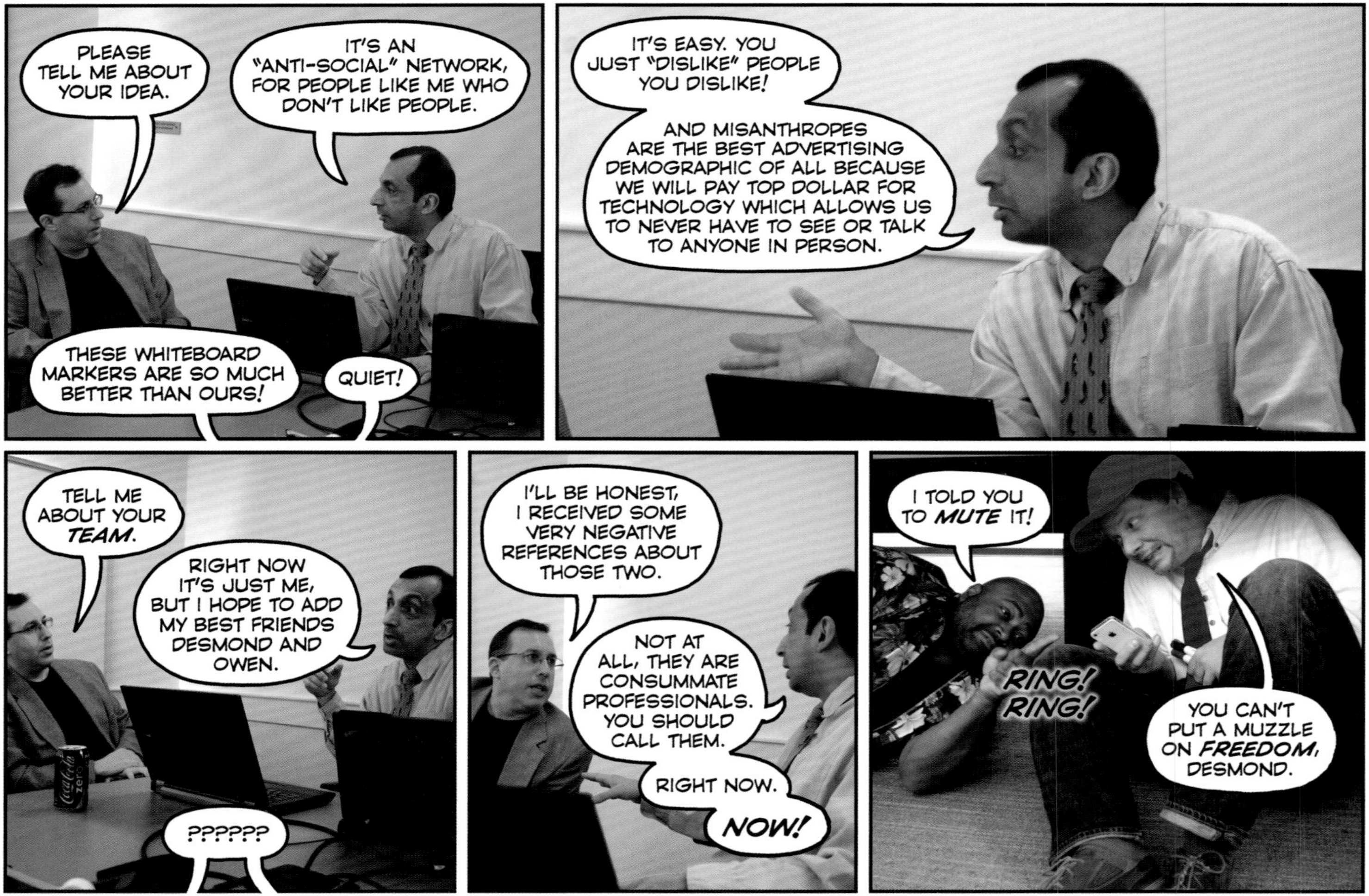
PLEASE TELL ME ABOUT YOUR IDEA.
IT'S AN "ANTI-SOCIAL" NETWORK, FOR PEOPLE LIKE ME WHO DON'T LIKE PEOPLE.
THESE WHITEBOARD MARKERS ARE SO MUCH BETTER THAN OURS!
QUIET!
IT'S EASY. YOU JUST "DISLIKE" PEOPLE YOU DISLIKE!
AND MISANTHROPES ARE THE BEST ADVERTISING DEMOGRAPHIC OF ALL BECAUSE WE WILL PAY TOP DOLLAR FOR TECHNOLOGY WHICH ALLOWS US TO NEVER HAVE TO SEE OR TALK TO ANYONE IN PERSON.
TELL ME ABOUT YOUR *TEAM*.
RIGHT NOW IT'S JUST ME, BUT I HOPE TO ADD MY BEST FRIENDS DESMOND AND OWEN.
??????
I'LL BE HONEST, I RECEIVED SOME VERY NEGATIVE REFERENCES ABOUT THOSE TWO.
NOT AT ALL, THEY ARE CONSUMMATE PROFESSIONALS. YOU SHOULD CALL THEM.
RIGHT NOW.
NOW!
I TOLD YOU TO *MUTE* IT!
RING! RING!
YOU CAN'T PUT A MUZZLE ON *FREEDOM*, DESMOND.

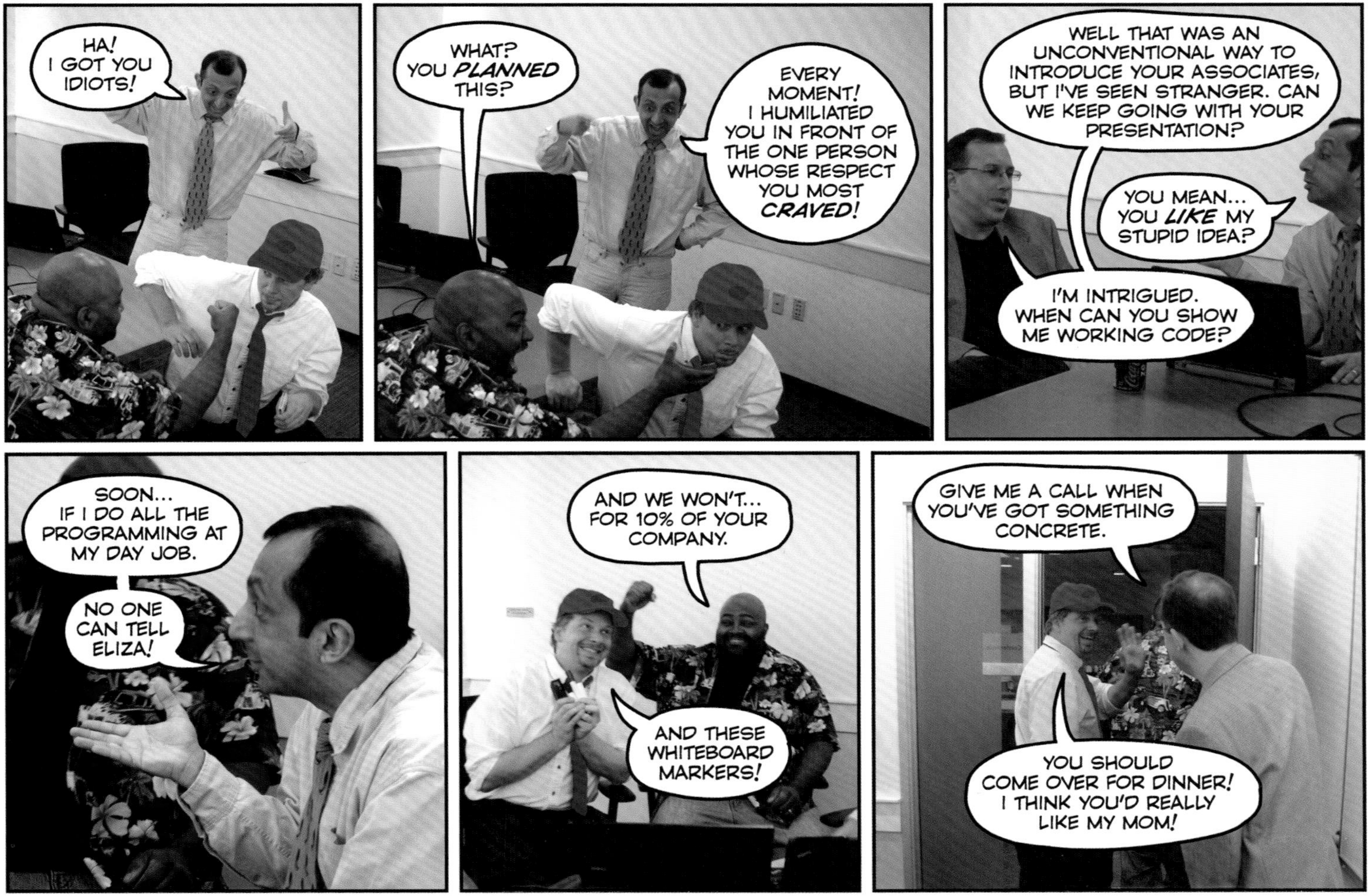
HA! I GOT YOU IDIOTS!
WHAT? YOU *PLANNED* THIS?
EVERY MOMENT! I HUMILIATED YOU IN FRONT OF THE ONE PERSON WHOSE RESPECT YOU MOST *CRAVED*!
WELL THAT WAS AN UNCONVENTIONAL WAY TO INTRODUCE YOUR ASSOCIATES, BUT I'VE SEEN STRANGER. CAN WE KEEP GOING WITH YOUR PRESENTATION?
YOU MEAN... YOU *LIKE* MY STUPID IDEA?
I'M INTRIGUED. WHEN CAN YOU SHOW ME WORKING CODE?
SOON... IF I DO ALL THE PROGRAMMING AT MY DAY JOB.
NO ONE CAN TELL ELIZA!
AND WE WON'T... FOR 10% OF YOUR COMPANY.
AND THESE WHITEBOARD MARKERS!
GIVE ME A CALL WHEN YOU'VE GOT SOMETHING CONCRETE.
YOU SHOULD COME OVER FOR DINNER! I THINK YOU'D REALLY LIKE MY MOM!

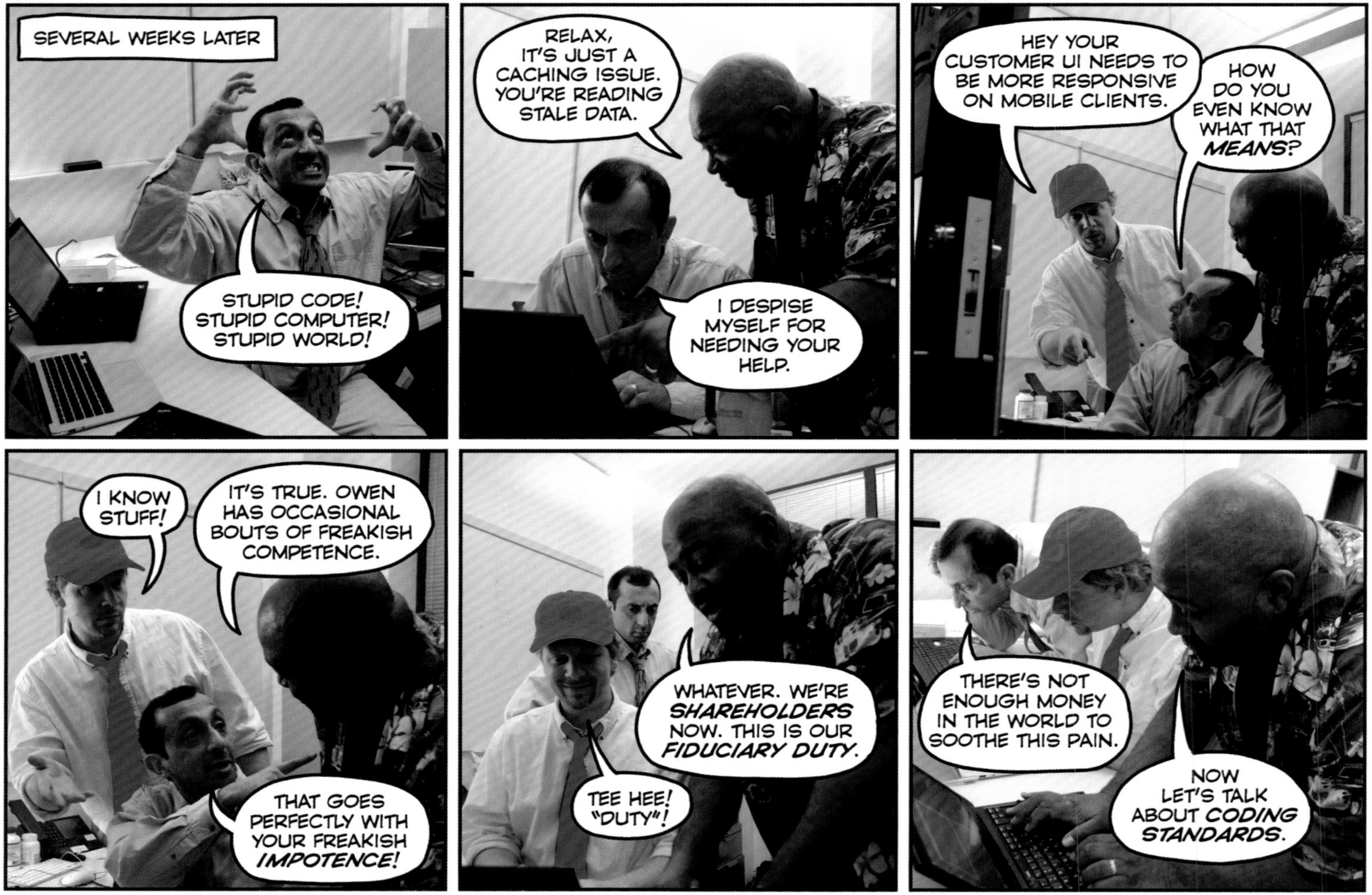
SEVERAL WEEKS LATER
STUPID CODE! STUPID COMPUTER! STUPID WORLD!
RELAX, IT'S JUST A CACHING ISSUE. YOU'RE READING STALE DATA.
I DESPISE MYSELF FOR NEEDING YOUR HELP.
HEY YOUR CUSTOMER UI NEEDS TO BE MORE RESPONSIVE ON MOBILE CLIENTS.
HOW DO YOU EVEN KNOW WHAT THAT *MEANS*?
I KNOW STUFF!
IT'S TRUE. OWEN HAS OCCASIONAL BOUTS OF FREAKISH COMPETENCE.
THAT GOES PERFECTLY WITH YOUR FREAKISH *IMPOTENCE*!
WHATEVER. WE'RE *SHAREHOLDERS* NOW. THIS IS OUR *FIDUCIARY DUTY*.
TEE HEE! "DUTY"!
THERE'S NOT ENOUGH MONEY IN THE WORLD TO SOOTHE THIS PAIN.
NOW LET'S TALK ABOUT *CODING STANDARDS*.

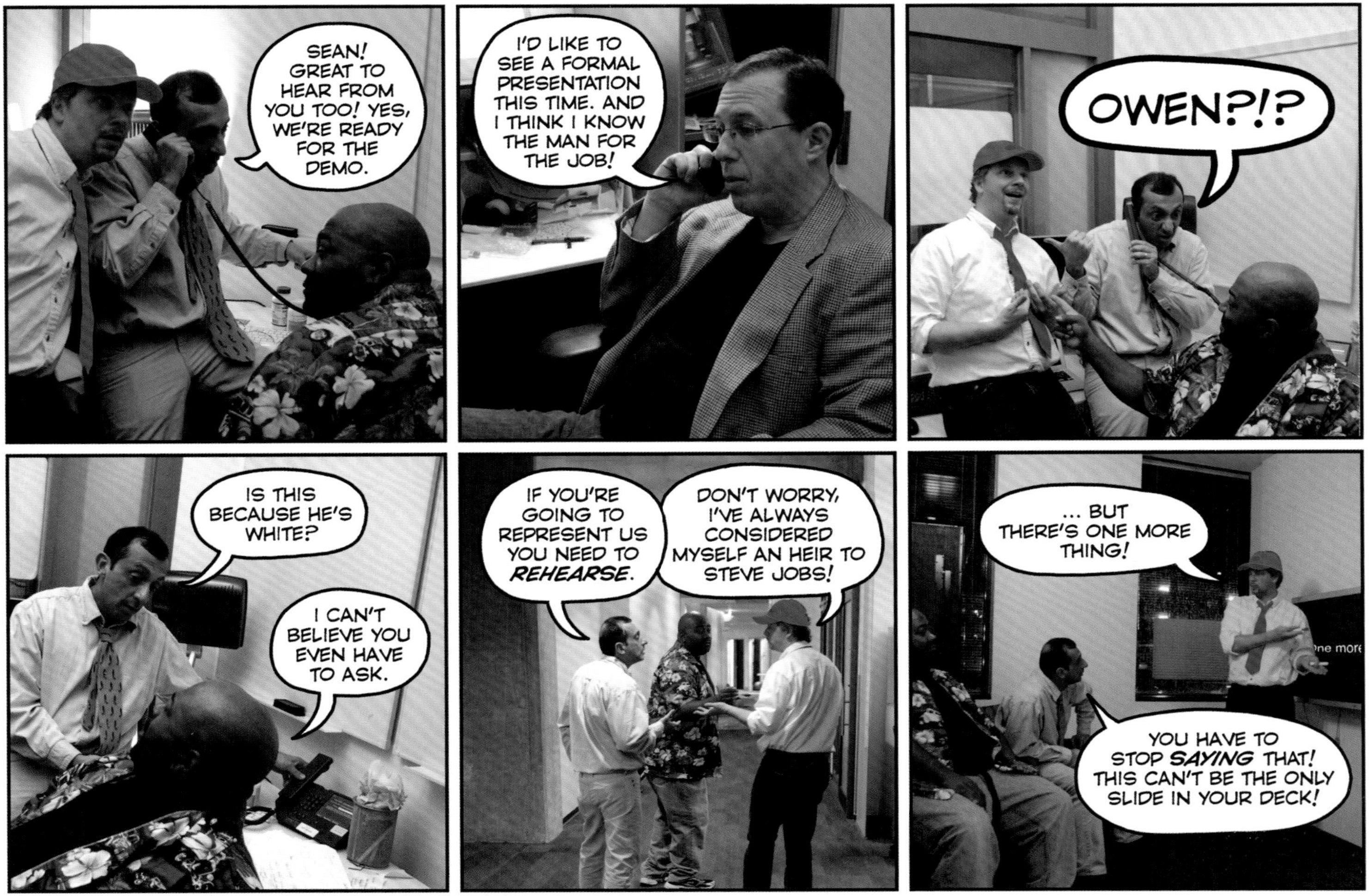
SEAN! GREAT TO HEAR FROM YOU TOO! YES, WE'RE READY FOR THE DEMO.
I'D LIKE TO SEE A FORMAL PRESENTATION THIS TIME. AND I THINK I KNOW THE MAN FOR THE JOB!
OWEN?!?
IS THIS BECAUSE HE'S WHITE?
I CAN'T BELIEVE YOU EVEN HAVE TO ASK.
IF YOU'RE GOING TO REPRESENT US YOU NEED TO ***REHEARSE***.
DON'T WORRY, I'VE ALWAYS CONSIDERED MYSELF AN HEIR TO STEVE JOBS!
... BUT THERE'S ONE MORE THING!
YOU HAVE TO STOP ***SAYING*** THAT! THIS CAN'T BE THE ONLY SLIDE IN YOUR DECK!

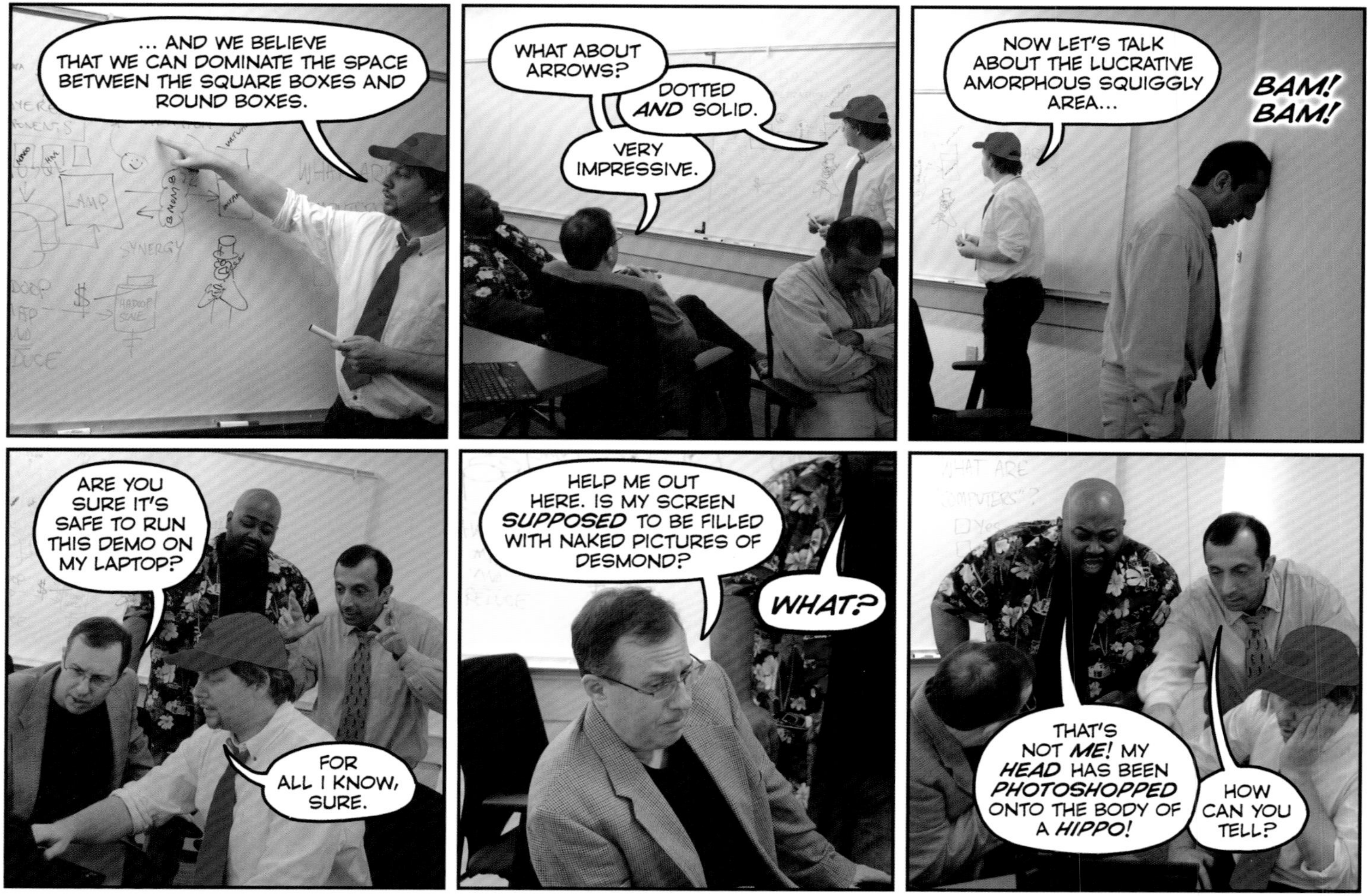
... AND WE BELIEVE THAT WE CAN DOMINATE THE SPACE BETWEEN THE SQUARE BOXES AND ROUND BOXES.
WHAT ABOUT ARROWS?
DOTTED AND SOLID.
VERY IMPRESSIVE.
NOW LET'S TALK ABOUT THE LUCRATIVE AMORPHOUS SQUIGGLY AREA...
BAM! BAM!
ARE YOU SURE IT'S SAFE TO RUN THIS DEMO ON MY LAPTOP?
FOR ALL I KNOW, SURE.
HELP ME OUT HERE. IS MY SCREEN SUPPOSED TO BE FILLED WITH NAKED PICTURES OF DESMOND?
WHAT?
THAT'S NOT ME! MY HEAD HAS BEEN PHOTOSHOPPED ONTO THE BODY OF A HIPPO!
HOW CAN YOU TELL?

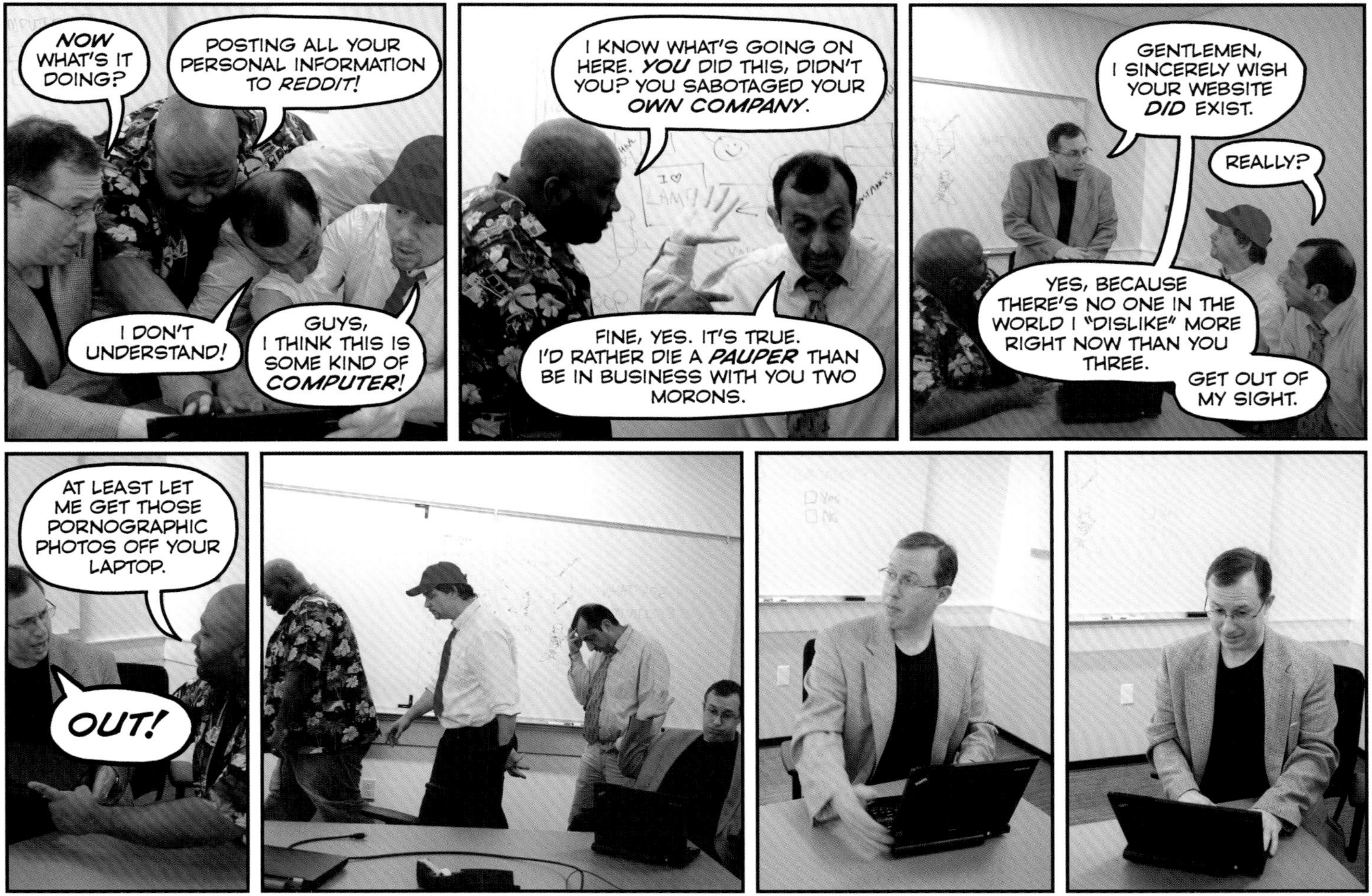
NOW WHAT'S IT DOING?
POSTING ALL YOUR PERSONAL INFORMATION TO REDDIT!
I DON'T UNDERSTAND!
GUYS, I THINK THIS IS SOME KIND OF COMPUTER!
I KNOW WHAT'S GOING ON HERE. YOU DID THIS, DIDN'T YOU? YOU SABOTAGED YOUR OWN COMPANY.
FINE, YES. IT'S TRUE. I'D RATHER DIE A PAUPER THAN BE IN BUSINESS WITH YOU TWO MORONS.
GENTLEMEN, I SINCERELY WISH YOUR WEBSITE DID EXIST.
REALLY?
YES, BECAUSE THERE'S NO ONE IN THE WORLD I "DISLIKE" MORE RIGHT NOW THAN YOU THREE.
GET OUT OF MY SIGHT.
AT LEAST LET ME GET THOSE PORNOGRAPHIC PHOTOS OFF YOUR LAPTOP.
OUT!

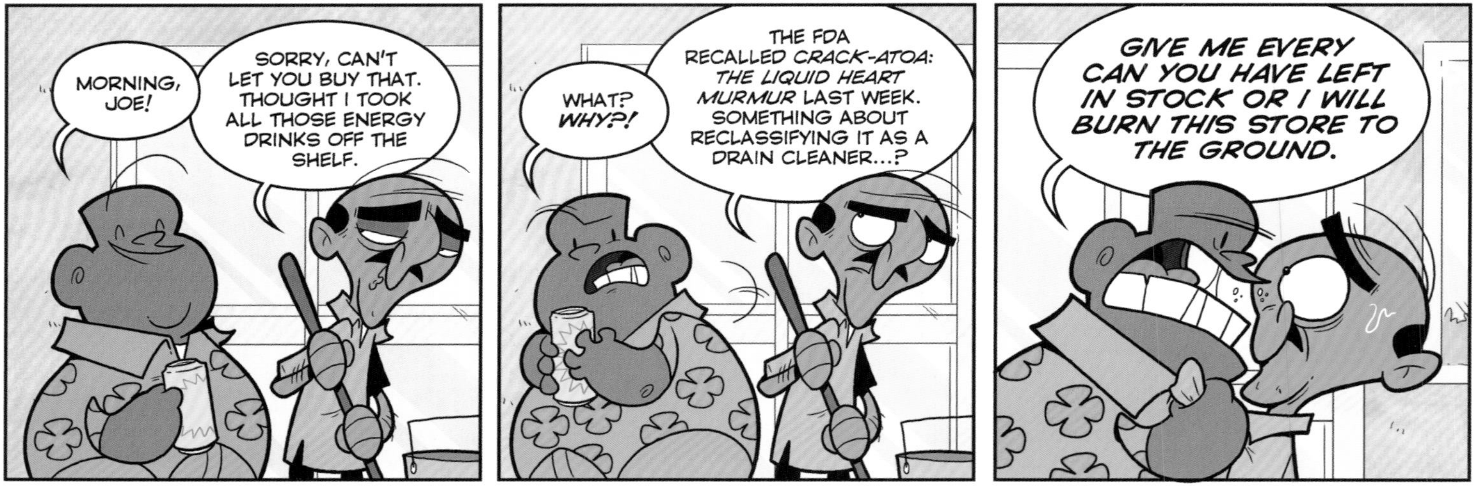
MORNING, JOE!
SORRY, CAN'T LET YOU BUY THAT. THOUGHT I TOOK ALL THOSE ENERGY DRINKS OFF THE SHELF.
WHAT? *WHY?!*
THE FDA RECALLED *CRACK-ATOA: THE LIQUID HEART MURMUR* LAST WEEK. SOMETHING ABOUT RECLASSIFYING IT AS A DRAIN CLEANER...?
GIVE ME EVERY CAN YOU HAVE LEFT IN STOCK OR I WILL BURN THIS STORE TO THE GROUND.

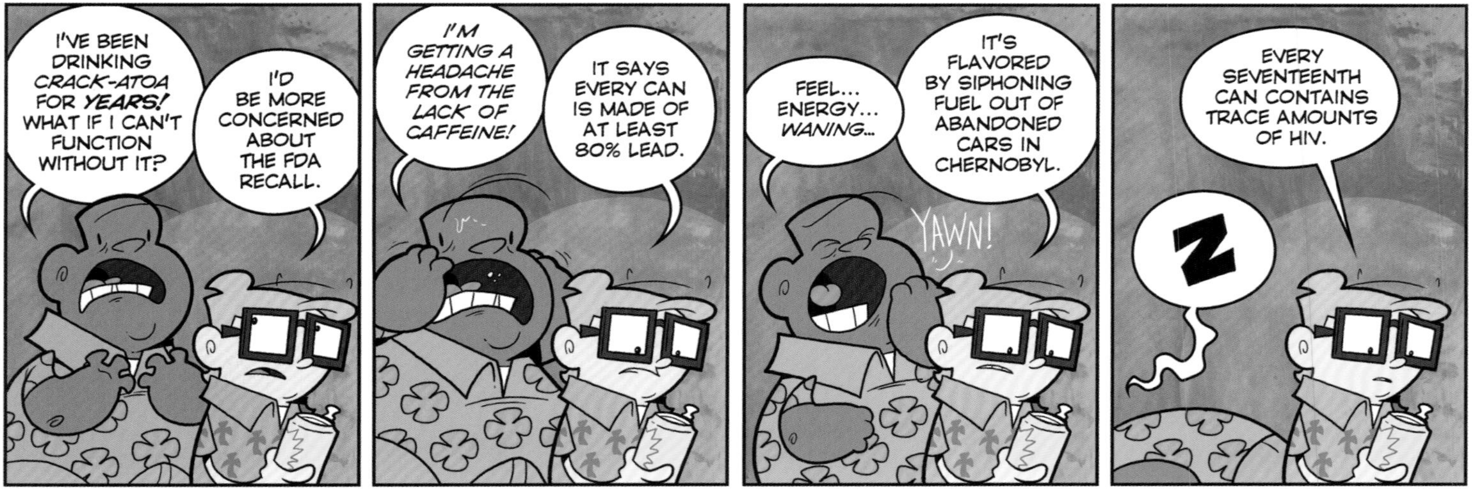
I'VE BEEN DRINKING *CRACK-ATOA* FOR ***YEARS!*** WHAT IF I CAN'T FUNCTION WITHOUT IT?
I'D BE MORE CONCERNED ABOUT THE FDA RECALL.
I'M GETTING A HEADACHE FROM THE LACK OF CAFFEINE!
IT SAYS EVERY CAN IS MADE OF AT LEAST 80% LEAD.
FEEL... ENERGY... *WANING...*
YAWN!
IT'S FLAVORED BY SIPHONING FUEL OUT OF ABANDONED CARS IN CHERNOBYL.
Z
EVERY SEVENTEENTH CAN CONTAINS TRACE AMOUNTS OF HIV.

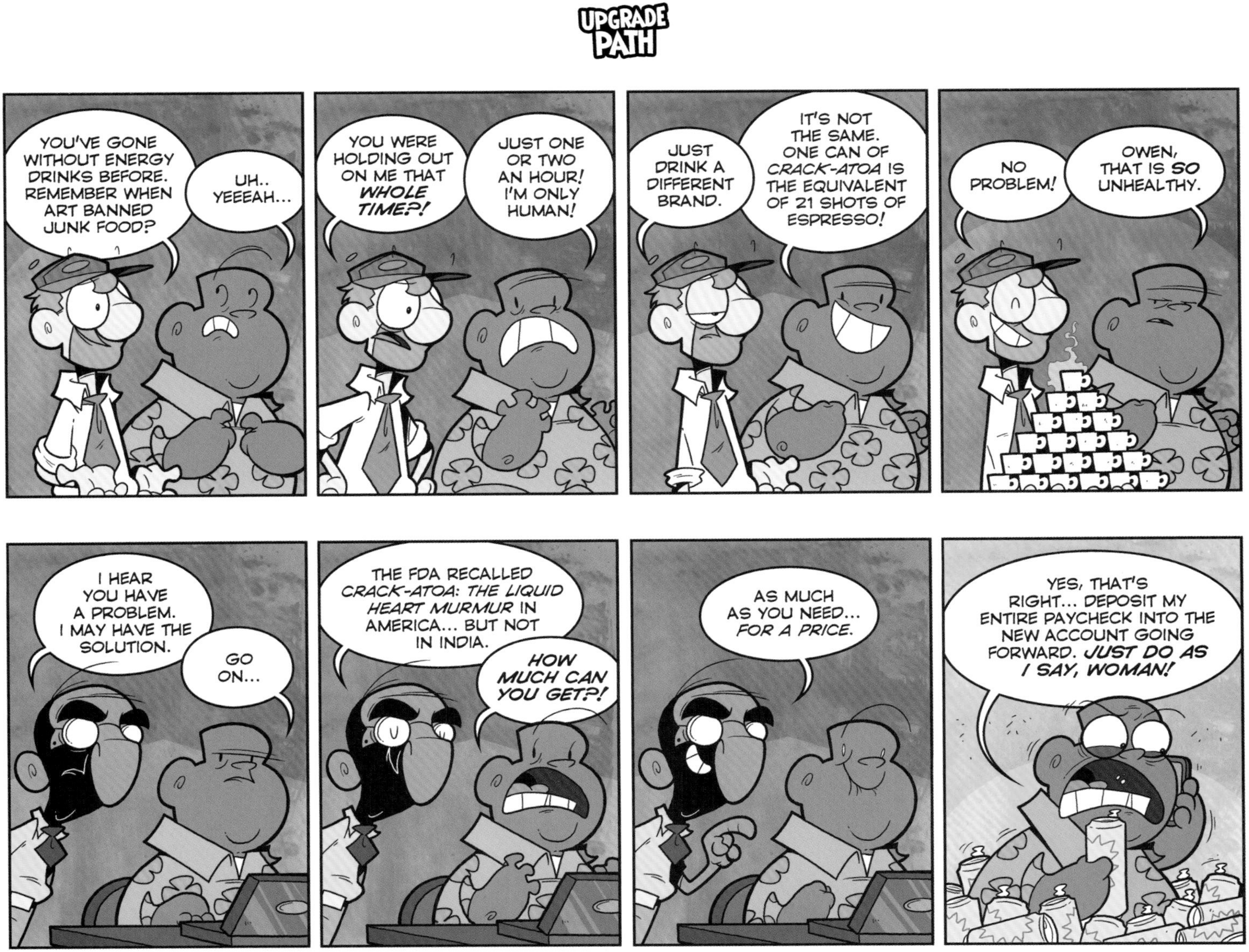

UPGRADE PATH
YOU'VE GONE WITHOUT ENERGY DRINKS BEFORE. REMEMBER WHEN ART BANNED JUNK FOOD?
UH.. YEEEAH...
YOU WERE HOLDING OUT ON ME THAT *WHOLE TIME?!*
JUST ONE OR TWO AN HOUR! I'M ONLY HUMAN!
JUST DRINK A DIFFERENT BRAND.
IT'S NOT THE SAME. ONE CAN OF *CRACK-ATOA* IS THE EQUIVALENT OF 21 SHOTS OF ESPRESSO!
NO PROBLEM!
OWEN, THAT IS **SO** UNHEALTHY.
I HEAR YOU HAVE A PROBLEM. I MAY HAVE THE SOLUTION.
GO ON...
THE FDA RECALLED *CRACK-ATOA: THE LIQUID HEART MURMUR* IN AMERICA... BUT NOT IN INDIA.
HOW MUCH CAN YOU GET?!
AS MUCH AS YOU NEED... *FOR A PRICE.*
YES, THAT'S RIGHT... DEPOSIT MY ENTIRE PAYCHECK INTO THE NEW ACCOUNT GOING FORWARD. ***JUST DO AS I SAY, WOMAN!***

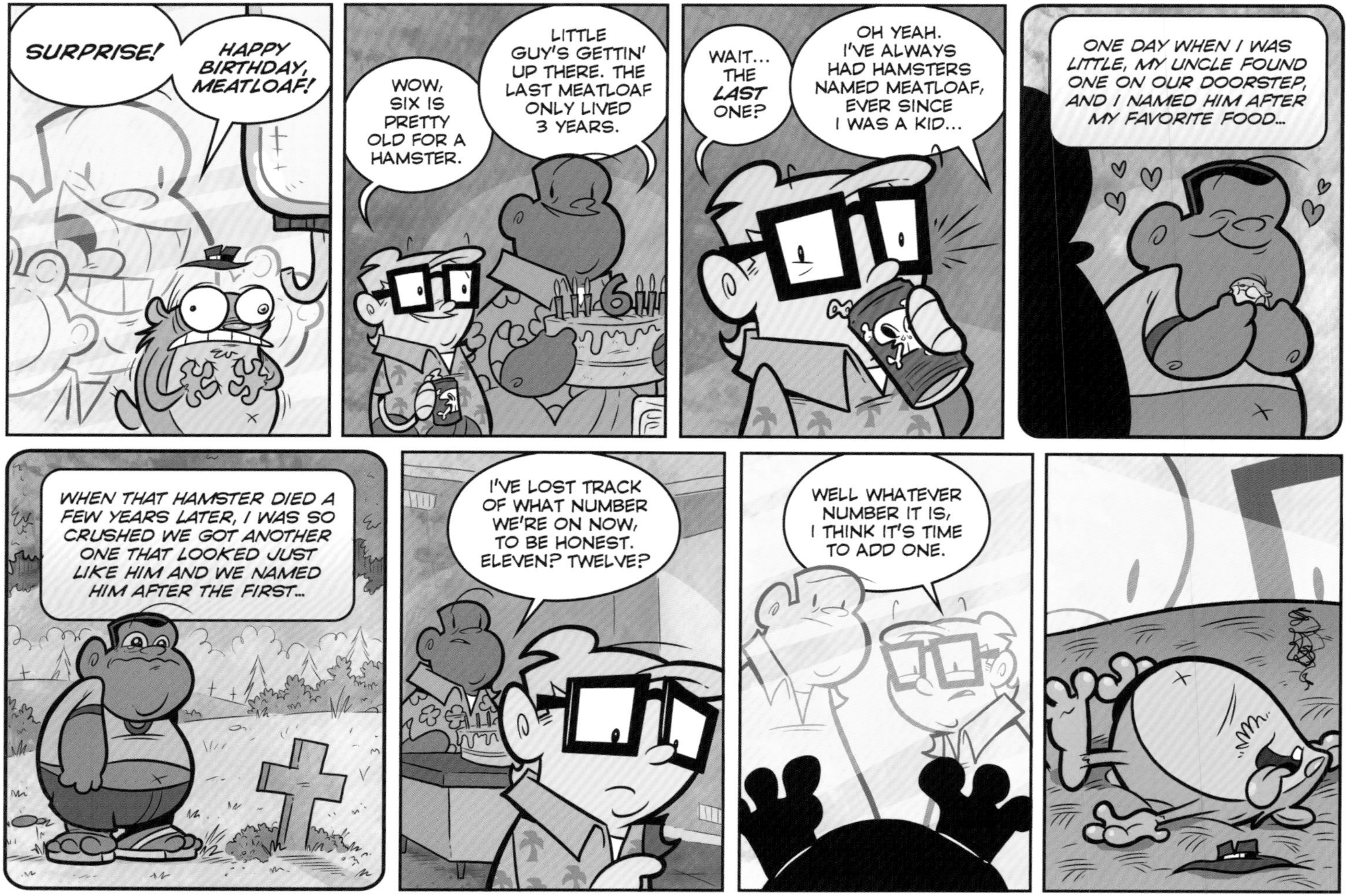
SURPRISE!
HAPPY BIRTHDAY, MEATLOAF!
WOW, SIX IS PRETTY OLD FOR A HAMSTER.
LITTLE GUY'S GETTIN' UP THERE. THE LAST MEATLOAF ONLY LIVED 3 YEARS.
WAIT... THE LAST ONE?
OH YEAH. I'VE ALWAYS HAD HAMSTERS NAMED MEATLOAF, EVER SINCE I WAS A KID...
ONE DAY WHEN I WAS LITTLE, MY UNCLE FOUND ONE ON OUR DOORSTEP, AND I NAMED HIM AFTER MY FAVORITE FOOD...
WHEN THAT HAMSTER DIED A FEW YEARS LATER, I WAS SO CRUSHED WE GOT ANOTHER ONE THAT LOOKED JUST LIKE HIM AND WE NAMED HIM AFTER THE FIRST...
I'VE LOST TRACK OF WHAT NUMBER WE'RE ON NOW, TO BE HONEST. ELEVEN? TWELVE?
WELL WHATEVER NUMBER IT IS, I THINK IT'S TIME TO ADD ONE.

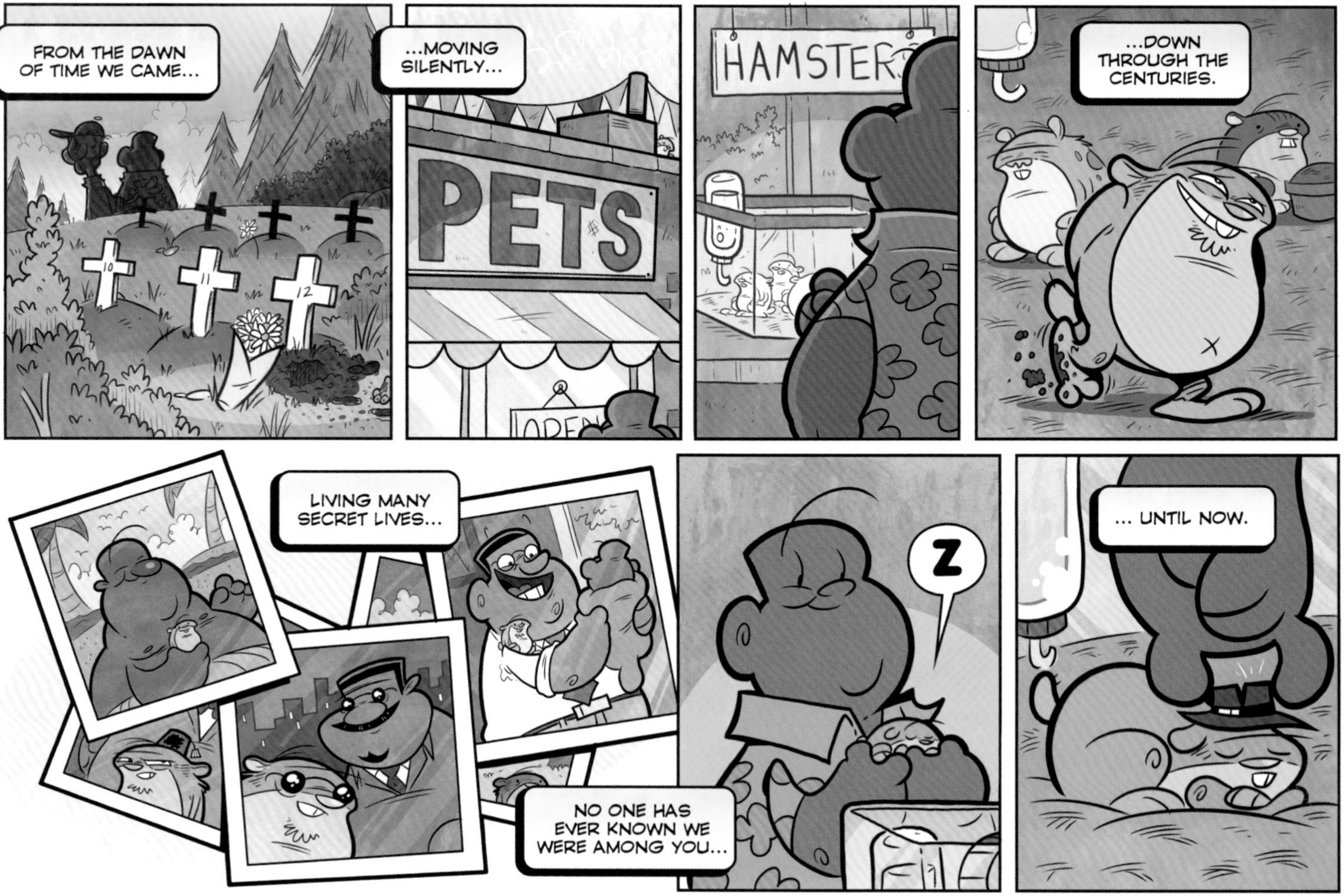
FROM THE DAWN OF TIME WE CAME...
10
11
12
...MOVING SILENTLY...
PETS
HAMSTER
...DOWN THROUGH THE CENTURIES.
LIVING MANY SECRET LIVES...
NO ONE HAS EVER KNOWN WE WERE AMONG YOU...
Z
... UNTIL NOW.

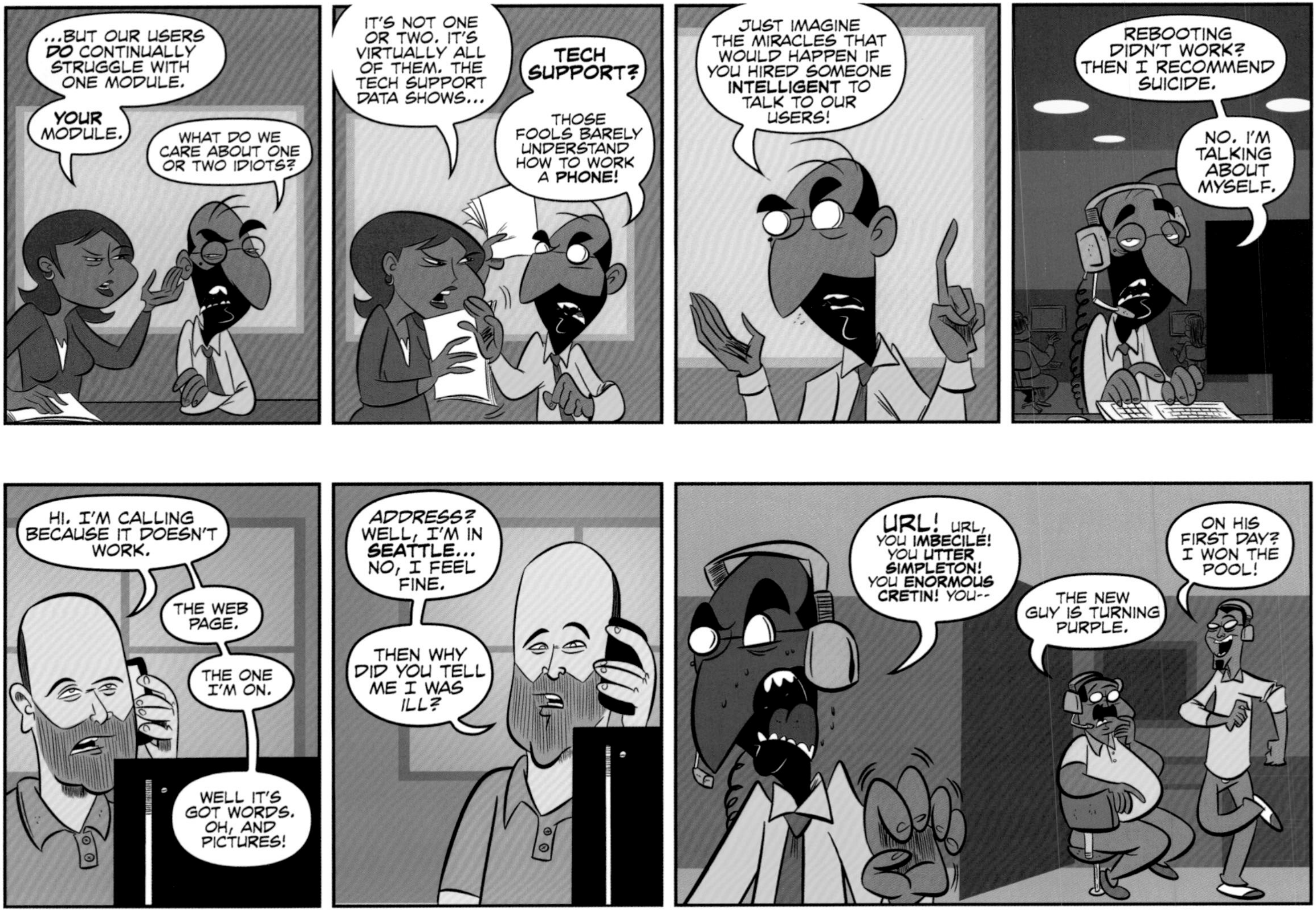
...BUT OUR USERS DO CONTINUALLY STRUGGLE WITH ONE MODULE.
YOUR MODULE.
WHAT DO WE CARE ABOUT ONE OR TWO IDIOTS?
IT'S NOT ONE OR TWO. IT'S VIRTUALLY ALL OF THEM. THE TECH SUPPORT DATA SHOWS...
TECH SUPPORT?
THOSE FOOLS BARELY UNDERSTAND HOW TO WORK A PHONE!
JUST IMAGINE THE MIRACLES THAT WOULD HAPPEN IF YOU HIRED SOMEONE INTELLIGENT TO TALK TO OUR USERS!
REBOOTING DIDN'T WORK? THEN I RECOMMEND SUICIDE.
NO, I'M TALKING ABOUT MYSELF.
HI. I'M CALLING BECAUSE IT DOESN'T WORK.
THE WEB PAGE.
THE ONE I'M ON.
WELL IT'S GOT WORDS. OH, AND PICTURES!
ADDRESS? WELL, I'M IN SEATTLE... NO, I FEEL FINE.
THEN WHY DID YOU TELL ME I WAS ILL?
URL! URL, YOU IMBECILE! YOU UTTER SIMPLETON! YOU ENORMOUS CRETIN! YOU--
THE NEW GUY IS TURNING PURPLE.
ON HIS FIRST DAY? I WON THE POOL!

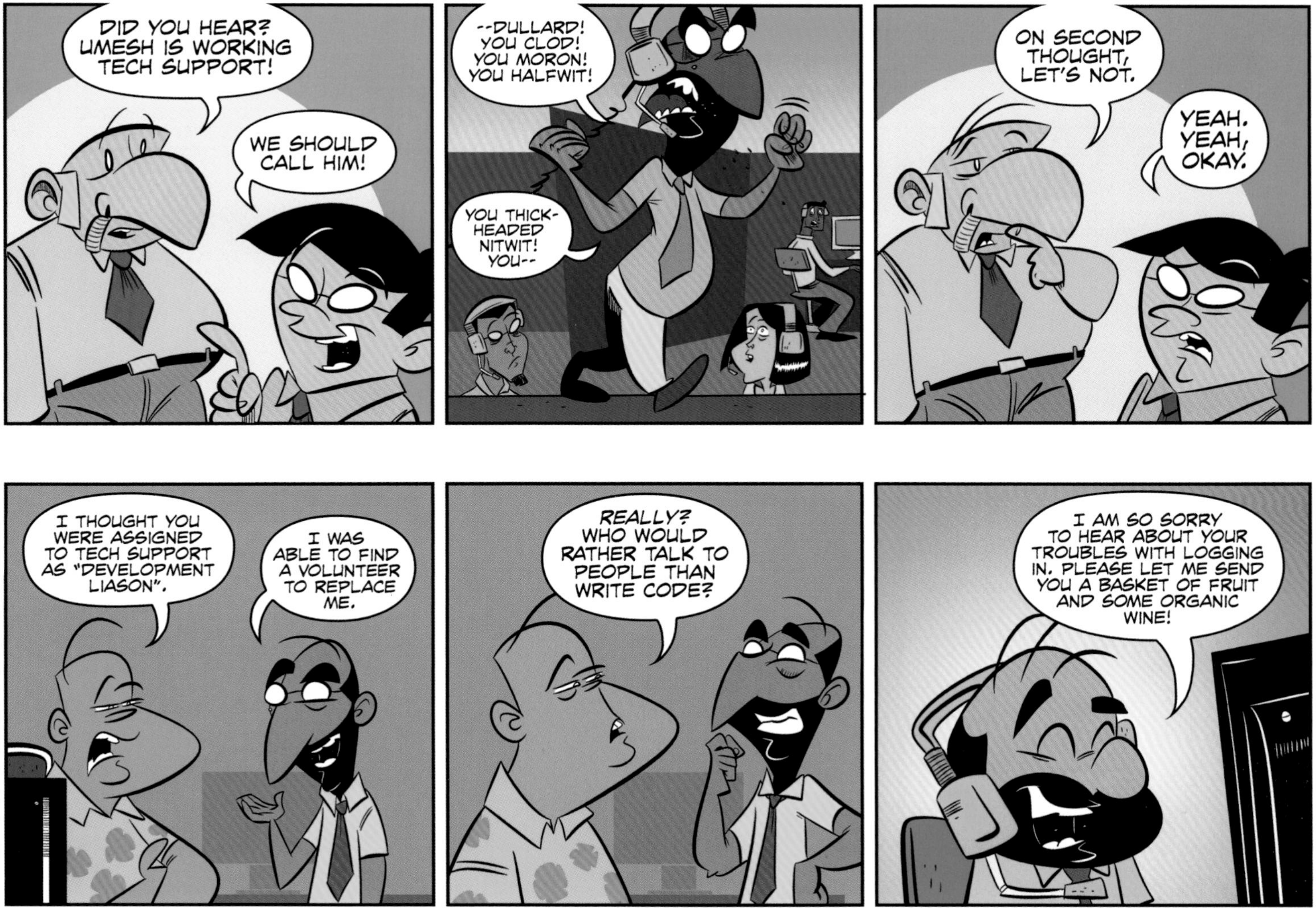
DID YOU HEAR? UMESH IS WORKING TECH SUPPORT!
WE SHOULD CALL HIM!
--DULLARD! YOU CLOD! YOU MORON! YOU HALFWIT!
YOU THICK-HEADED NITWIT! YOU--
ON SECOND THOUGHT, LET'S NOT.
YEAH. YEAH, OKAY.
I THOUGHT YOU WERE ASSIGNED TO TECH SUPPORT AS "DEVELOPMENT LIASON".
I WAS ABLE TO FIND A VOLUNTEER TO REPLACE ME.
REALLY? WHO WOULD RATHER TALK TO PEOPLE THAN WRITE CODE?
I AM SO SORRY TO HEAR ABOUT YOUR TROUBLES WITH LOGGING IN. PLEASE LET ME SEND YOU A BASKET OF FRUIT AND SOME ORGANIC WINE!

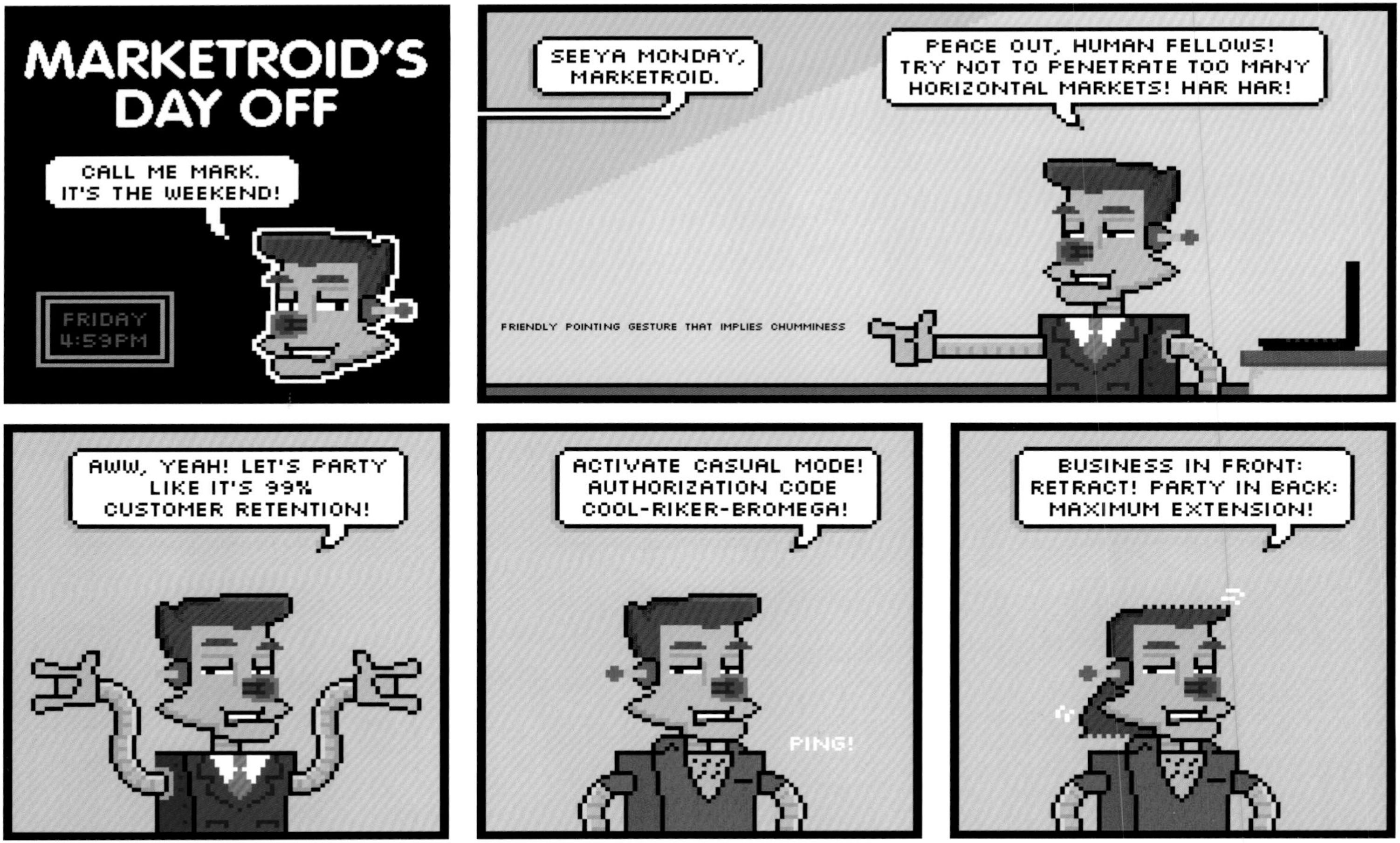
MARKETROID'S DAY OFF
CALL ME MARK. IT'S THE WEEKEND!
FRIDAY 4:59PM
SEEYA MONDAY, MARKETROID.
PEACE OUT, HUMAN FELLOWS! TRY NOT TO PENETRATE TOO MANY HORIZONTAL MARKETS! HAR HAR!
FRIENDLY POINTING GESTURE THAT IMPLIES CHUMMINESS
AWW, YEAH! LET'S PARTY LIKE IT'S 99% CUSTOMER RETENTION!
ACTIVATE CASUAL MODE! AUTHORIZATION CODE COOL-RIKER-BROMEGA!
PING!
BUSINESS IN FRONT: RETRACT! PARTY IN BACK: MAXIMUM EXTENSION!

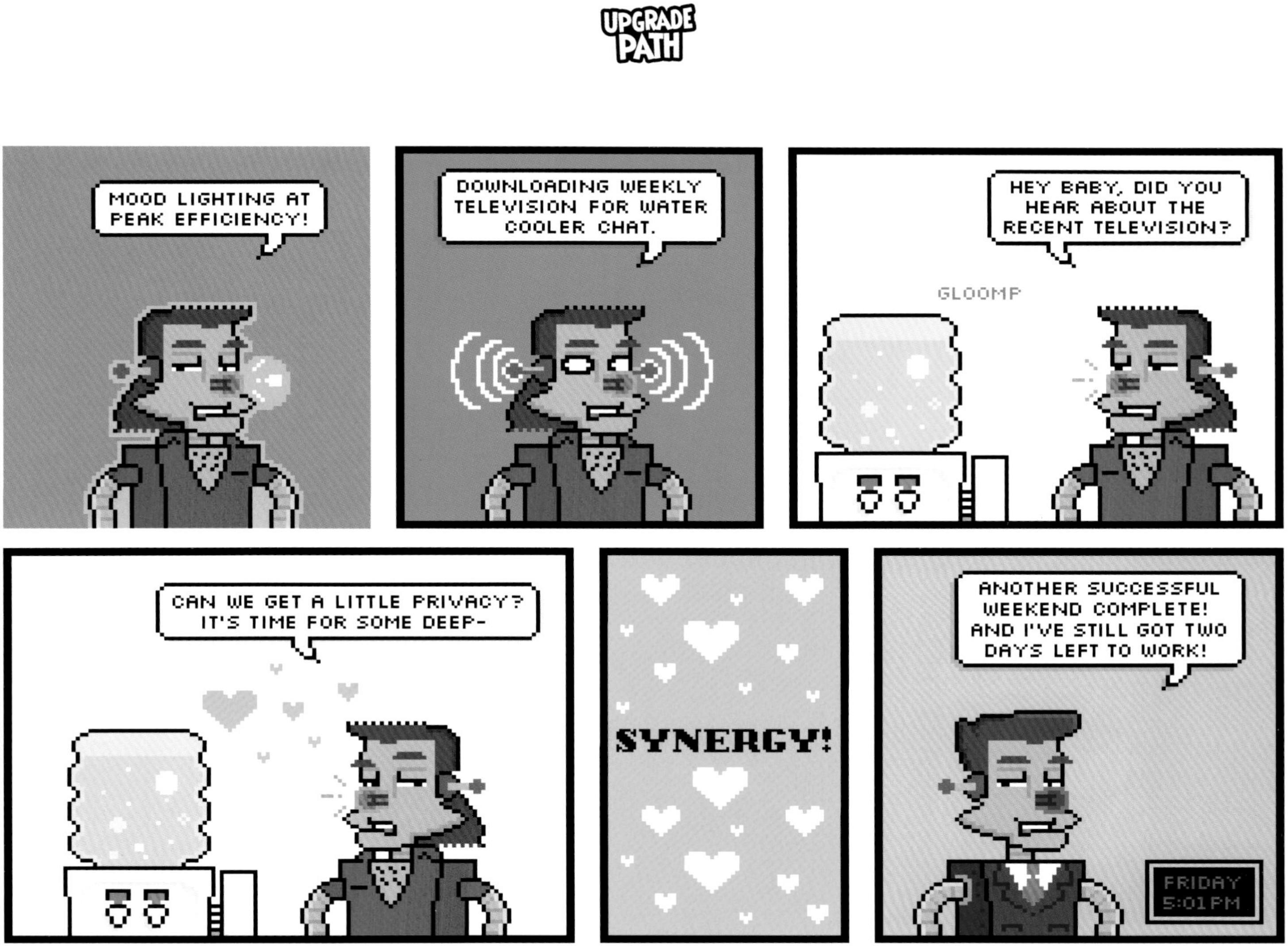
UPGRADE PATH
MOOD LIGHTING AT PEAK EFFICIENCY!
DOWNLOADING WEEKLY TELEVISION FOR WATER COOLER CHAT.
HEY BABY, DID YOU HEAR ABOUT THE RECENT TELEVISION?
GLOOMP
CAN WE GET A LITTLE PRIVACY? IT'S TIME FOR SOME DEEP-
SYNERGY!
ANOTHER SUCCESSFUL WEEKEND COMPLETE! AND I'VE STILL GOT TWO DAYS LEFT TO WORK!
FRIDAY 5:01PM

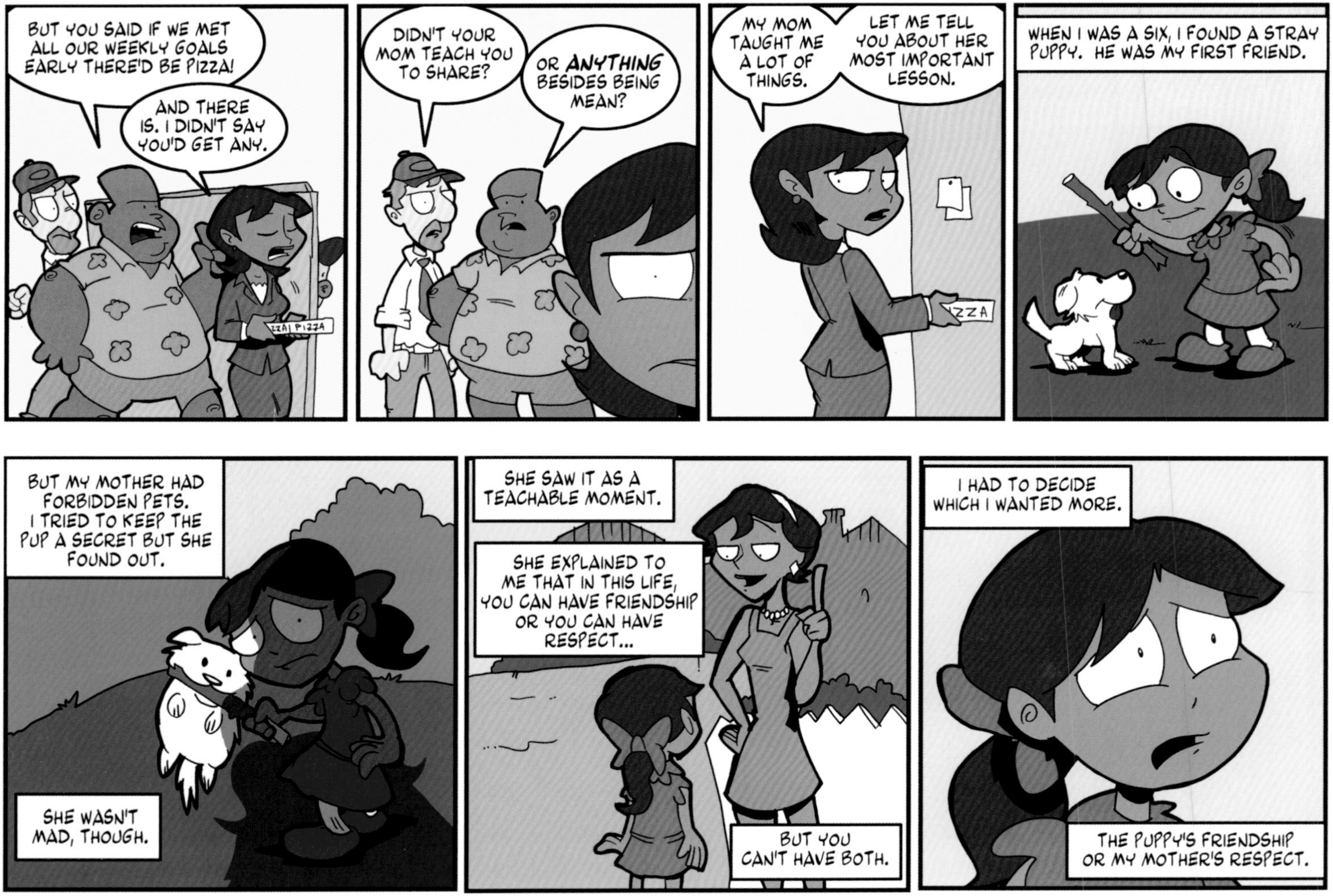

BUT YOU SAID IF WE MET ALL OUR WEEKLY GOALS EARLY THERE'D BE PIZZA!
AND THERE IS. I DIDN'T SAY YOU'D GET ANY.
PIZZA
DIDN'T YOUR MOM TEACH YOU TO SHARE?
OR ANYTHING BESIDES BEING MEAN?
MY MOM TAUGHT ME A LOT OF THINGS.
LET ME TELL YOU ABOUT HER MOST IMPORTANT LESSON.
ZZA
WHEN I WAS A SIX, I FOUND A STRAY PUPPY. HE WAS MY FIRST FRIEND.
BUT MY MOTHER HAD FORBIDDEN PETS. I TRIED TO KEEP THE PUP A SECRET BUT SHE FOUND OUT.
SHE WASN'T MAD, THOUGH.
SHE SAW IT AS A TEACHABLE MOMENT.
SHE EXPLAINED TO ME THAT IN THIS LIFE, YOU CAN HAVE FRIENDSHIP OR YOU CAN HAVE RESPECT...
BUT YOU CAN'T HAVE BOTH.
I HAD TO DECIDE WHICH I WANTED MORE.
THE PUPPY'S FRIENDSHIP OR MY MOTHER'S RESPECT.

THE PUPPY WAS SO NEW AND LOVED ME UNCONDITIONALLY.

BUT... SHE WAS MY MOM. AND I WANTED HER RESPECT. IT WAS ALL I EVER WANTED.

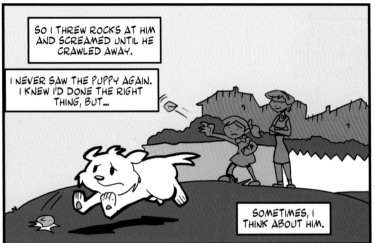

SO I THREW ROCKS AT HIM AND SCREAMED UNTIL HE CRAWLED AWAY.

I NEVER SAW THE PUPPY AGAIN. I KNEW I'D DONE THE RIGHT THING, BUT...

SOMETIMES, I THINK ABOUT HIM.

WOW... I DUNNO--

LET'S GIVE HER A MOMENT.

ELIZA, I'M SORRY.

ZA|PIZZA

I'M CONFUSED.

WHAT WAS THE LESSON YOUR MOTHER TAUGHT YOU?

IF YOU CAN SELL IDIOTS A BUNCH OF CRAP AND SLAP A FEW TEARS ON IT, YOU CAN PRETTY MUCH GET WHAT YOU WANT FOR A WHILE.

Epilogue

RING!
WHY YES, AS IT HAPPENS I AM CURRENTLY HOPEN TO NEW HOPPORTUNITIES. WHAT DO YOU HAVE IN MIND?
LET'S JUST SAY WE'RE LOOKING FOR SOMEONE WITH EXPERIENCE IN... ACQUISITIONS.